L

BPP COLLEGE LIBRARY AND
INFORMATION SERVICE

2 4 MAY 2012

G58 M

D1388733

Contemporary Management

European Edition

BPP College

067590

B

BPP COLLEGE LIBRARY AND
INFORMATION SERVICE

24 MAY 20??

Contemporary Management

European Edition

Edgar Meyer, Melanie Ashleigh,
Jennifer M. George and
Gareth R. Jones

 **McGraw-Hill
Higher Education**

London Boston   Burr Ridge, IL   Dubuque, IA   Madison, WI   New York   San Francisco
St. Louis Bangkok Bogotá Caracas Kuala Lumpur Lisbon Madrid Mexico City
Milan Montreal New Delhi Santiago Seoul Singapore Sydney Taipei Toronto

Contemporary Management, European Edition
Edgar Meyer, Melanie Ashleigh, Jennifer M. George and Gareth R. Jones
ISBN-13 978-0-07-711115-1
ISBN-10 0-07-711115-X

Published by McGraw-Hill Education
Shoppenhangers Road
Maidenhead
Berkshire
SL6 2QL
Telephone: 44 (0) 1628 502 500
Fax: 44 (0) 1628 770 224
Website: www.mcgraw-hill.co.uk

British Library Cataloguing in Publication Data
A catalogue record for this book is available from the British Library

Library of Congress Cataloging in Publication Data
The Library of Congress data for this book has been applied for from the Library of Congress

Acquisitions Editor: Rachel Gear
Development Editor: Hannah Cooper
Senior Marketing Manager: Alice Duijser
Senior Production Editor: Beverley Shields

Text Design by Hard Lines
Cover design by Fielding Design
Printed and bound in Spain by Mateu Cromo Artes Graficas

Published by McGraw-Hill Education (UK) Limited an imprint of The McGraw-Hill
Companies, Inc., 1221 Avenue of the Americas, New York, NY 10020. Copyright © 2007 by
McGraw-Hill Education (UK) Limited. All rights reserved. No part of this publication may be
reproduced or distributed in any form or by any means, or stored in a database or retrieval
system, without the prior written consent of The McGraw-Hill Companies, Inc., including, but
not limited to, in any network or other electronic storage or transmission, or broadcast for
distance learning.

ISBN-13 978-0-07-711115-1
ISBN-10 0-07-711115-X
© 2007. Exclusive rights by The McGraw-Hill Companies, Inc. for manufacture and export. This
book cannot be re-exported from the country to which it is sold by McGraw-Hill.

Brief Table of Contents

Detailed Table of Contents

Preface

Many changes have taken place in the world of business since this book was last revised in its original format. Even more changes need to be taken into account in this first European edition.

Globalisation, the proliferation of Information Technology (IT) and the socially responsible behaviour of companies have all been key issues in the modern business world. The sometimes unethical behaviour of companies and the changes in the business environment have left some companies bankrupt and others on the verge of insolvency. The Internet/dot-com boom and bust, the increase in service industries and the decline in manufacturing jobs in major European countries and the radical and rapid advances in IT have all resulted in tens of thousands of employees losing their jobs, small investors losing large sums of their savings and a generally more complex and volatile environment. As a consequence of these developments, many people have begun to take a closer look at the way organisations are managed and people are beginning to hold managers accountable for their actions.

The fast-changing environment, nationally and globally, also requires managers to respond in new and different ways in order to maintain and improve an organisation's performance. There are mounting pressures on managers to integrate not only emerging technology, but also the increasing diversity of the workforce. The latter has made it imperative for managers to understand how and why people differ, so that they can effectively manage and enjoy the benefits of diversity. The continuing need to innovate and improve the quality of products and services to allow an organisation to compete effectively in today's marketplace confronts managers on a daily basis. The European edition of *Contemporary Management* has been significantly revised to reflect and address these challenges to managers and the organisations of which they are part. Encouraged by the favourable reception and increasing support of the original George and Jones' book, and based on the reactions and suggestions of reviewers and users, we have added new case studies that highlight managerial issues within a European context, and adapted some of the global examples to illustrate that the business world of today is often without national borders.

Content Changes

In revising the book, we have kept at the forefront the fact that the users and reviewers are very supportive of the attempts to integrate contemporary management theories and issues into the analysis of management and organisations. As in previous editions, this first European edition aims to distil new and classical theorising and research into a contemporary framework that is compatible with the focus of management on planning, leading, organising and controlling without being constrained by traditional approaches.

Because users reported great appreciation of the way management is presented, we have kept the overall 'feel' of the book, which was very well received by reviewers. We have retained the presentation of the material so that it is relevant, even if exposure to a real-life management context is lacking: all the changes within this European edition are in keeping with this tradition.

The last revision of the original text included the addition of a number of updated topics and issues that have gained even more prominence in the last two years. We have built on these and aimed to situate emerging issues within a European context.

The major changes in this text include the introduction of cases that are rooted within Europe. Examples such as Virgin Atlantic, Innocent Drinks, H&M, Lego, B&Q or Carrefour provide insights into a wide range of large global organisations. Other examples of smaller organisations have been introduced to highlight the relevance of managerial issues to small, medium and large organisations, whether these operate within the public or the private sector.

One of the major new additions are the pedagogical features in the European edition. We have aimed to facilitate student learning to reiterate managerial ideas and allow readers to become independent learners.

Each chapter includes not only a range of exercises, but also sections on 'Reaction Time'. These allow students to review the content discussed and provide an opportunity to reflect on new learning. Each chapter also includes 'Tips for Practice'. This feature aims to aid students and young managers to retain some of the important lessons learned in each chapter – practical tips and considerations that will help students and young managers to apply new ideas about leading, planning, organising and controlling.

We have also included more work on personality and team roles that will further support your understanding of individual differences in behaviour and how this can influence managing within an organisational context. We have also extended the work on diversity and planning. Finally, we have combined the chapters on IT and Innovation. We feel that entrepreneurship, advances in IT and changes in product development are all interdependent: while some of the material has been shortened, the essence has remained in that the new chapter 18 now highlights the emerging themes of Contemporary Management.

Chapter Outline

The European edition of *Contemporary Management* has removed the division of chapters into parts. Management is a complex and interdependent concept which makes it difficult to divide it into exclusive areas. The contemporary approach addresses many issues and concepts that are not necessarily part of other textbooks. You will discover that chapters build upon each other to provide you with a rounded view of what it means to be a manager. The text further illustrates this by bringing the manager back into the subject matter of management: the book is written from the perspective of a current or future manager to demonstrate the problems and opportunities they face.

Chapter 1

This introduces *management* and *managing*, not just as a concept but as something that is practised by individuals on a daily basis. It outlines what is meant by managing and why it is an important activity. The chapter goes on to introduce some principles of management, what roles managers can adopt within an organisation and what responsibilities managers hold at different levels within it. Chapter 1 finally raises some key challenges that managers face in today's global business environment.

Chapter 2

This provides an introduction into the evolution of *managerial theory*. It highlights aspects of efficiency and effectiveness, how over time the role of a manager and associated behaviour has changed and how management theory can try to respond to the growing complexity of organisational environments.

Chapter 3

Based on the understanding of how managerial theory evolved, Chapter 3 discusses the manager as an *individual*, who has emotions, feelings and values. The chapter explores how personality and individual characteristics can influence management. This chapter also introduces organisational culture and shows how individuals, especially managers, can influence organisational culture.

Chapter 4

This introduces the pivotal concept of *ethics* and *social responsibility*. The chapter highlights, through various case studies, why ethics matter. The relationship between ethical and responsible behaviour and the law is discussed, as well as how organisations and managers can behave ethically and in a socially responsible manner.

Chapter 5

This continues the ethics and responsibility theme by looking at how managers and organisations need to be aware of the *diversity* that exists in today's world. The chapter introduces different aspects of diversity and how managers can play a pivotal role in managing the differences that exist. Besides providing an ethical argument for treating diversity as an important aspect of organisational life, the chapter also outlines the business case for diversity. This discussion is complemented by theorising and exemplifying how stereotypes and prejudices can be formed, and how they can be challenged.

Chapter 6

This puts your new understanding of diversity into the context of *organisational management*. The chapter discusses the challenge of globalisation, and its impact on organisations.

Chapter 7

This returns to focus on the manager and specific tasks he or she has to perform. The chapter explores how managers arrive at *decisions*, how decisions can be made more effectively, what biases can exist in decision making and how organisations can learn to improve effectiveness and efficiency in the decisions they make.

Chapter 8

This provides further detail on how managers use the decisions they have made. *Planning* and *strategising* are explored in order to highlight the responsibility of different organisational levels in the business processes, and how strategies and plans can be influential in securing long-term organisational success.

Chapter 9

This extends Chapter 8 by outlining some fundamental ideas on how to achieve superior quality and deliver products and services that customers want, and how different organisational arrangements (both physical and structural) can influence *competitive advantage*.

Chapter 10

This looks at the way an organisation is *structured*, how responsibilities and tasks are distributed and integrated and how different organisational structures suit different types of business. The chapter also explores what structures can be implemented outside an organisation to achieve and maintain a competitive advantage.

Chapter 11

This discusses one key managerial principle in more detail: *control*. The chapter describes the advantages and disadvantages of different types of control and how these can be executed. The chapter also explores the relationship between control and organisational change. The chapter will thus further your understanding of how different structures may influence the types of control used.

Chapter 12

This deals with the *human capital* of an organisation and what an organisation needs to consider when recruiting and selecting staff. To ensure a competitive advantage, staff need to be trained and developed, and to identify the level of training needed staff often undergo an appraisal process. The chapter also explores issues of rewards and pay.

Chapter 13

This extends the discussion by looking at *motivational* issues. The chapter deals with intrinsic and extrinsic rewards and how perceived inequity can undermine conducive work environments and a satisfied staff.

Chapter 14

This looks beyond general motivational issues and examines the management principle of *leadership*. The chapter identifies the evolution of leadership theory, what it means to be a leader, the relationship that exists between leaders and followers and the problems that can still exist about gender and formal leadership positions.

Chapter 15

This builds upon your understanding of leadership, motivation and an organisation's goal of being effective and efficient. This chapter provides details on *groups* and *teams* – what their impact is on organisational effectiveness, their role in shaping organisational culture and how teams and groups may differ in regard to their motivational and leadership needs.

Chapter 16

This defines how key organisational messages need to be *communicated*. The chapter introduces models of communication and the idea of communication networks, and emphasises the need of organisations to consider new technology when auditing or creating communication channels within an organisation.

Chapter 17

This raises the issue of conflict that is likely to occur when *people interact*. The chapter outlines what conflict is and how a manager can go about finding a solution. The chapter should also make you aware that organisations are political and that this requires negotiation skills in order to be as fair as possible to all stakeholders.

Chapter 18

The last chapter, Chapter 18, introduces some recent concepts that are important in contemporary management. The chapter discusses innovation and its importance in driving competitive advantage. It also introduces the notion of entrepreneurs and their role in today's business world.

Guided Tour

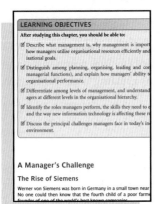

Learning Objectives

Each chapter opens with a set of learning objectives, summarising what readers should learn from each chapter.

Case Studies

The book includes case studies integrated within each chapter, as well as extended end of chapter cases entitled 'Application in Today's Business World'. These are designed to test how well you can apply the main techniques learned. Each case study has its own set of questions.

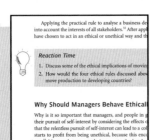

Reaction Time

These recaps are provided throughout each chapter, to give you an opportunity to consolidate your learning by reflecting on the material as you work through it.

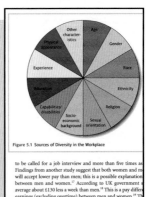

Figures and Tables

Each chapter provides a number of figures and tables to help you to visualise the various management models, and to illustrate and summarise important concepts.

Tips for Practice

These tips apply the theory of the chapter to real management situations, equipping you to deal with the challenges you will face as a potential manager.

Summary and Review

This briefly reviews and reinforces the main topics you will have covered in each chapter to ensure you have acquired a solid understanding of the key topics.

Topic for Action

This feature asks you to apply your learning in a practical sense by carrying out a management activity in your university or community.

Applied Independent Learning

This feature is the perfect way to practise the techniques you have been taught. There are a range of different exercises to suit individual and group study.

Technology to Enhance Learning and Teaching

Visit www.mcgraw-hill.co.uk/textbooks/meyerandashleigh today

Online Learning Centre (OLC)

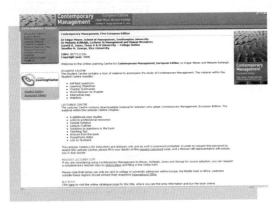

After completing each chapter, log on to the supporting Online Learning Centre website. Take advantage of the study tools offered to reinforce the material you have read in the text, and to develop your knowledge of management in a fun and effective way.

Resources for students include:

- Chapter outlines and summaries
- Weblinks
- Interactive map with tips on country-specific management practice
- Self-test questions
- Glossary

- Additional case studies
- Links to professional resources
- PowerPoint slides
- Lecture outlines
- Sample syllabus
- Solutions to questions in the book

Also available for lecturers:

EZTest

EZTest, a new computerised testbank format from McGraw-Hill, is available with this title. EZTest enables you to upload testbanks, modify questions and add your own questions, thus creating a testbank that's totally unique to your course! Find out more at: http://mcgraw-hill.co.uk/he/eztest/

Lecturers: Customise Content for your Courses using the McGraw-Hill Primis Content Centre

Now it's incredibly easy to create a flexible, customised solution for your course, using content from both US and European McGraw-Hill Education textbooks, content from our Professional list including Harvard Business Press titles, as well as a selection of over 9,000 cases from Harvard, Insead and Darden. In addition, we can incorporate your own material and course notes.

For more information, please contact your local rep who will discuss the right delivery options for your custom publication – including printed readers, e-Books and CD-ROMs. To see what McGraw-Hill content you can choose from, visit **www.primisonline.com**.

Study Skills

Open University Press publishes guides to study, research and exam skills to help undergraduate and postgraduate students through their university studies.

Visit www.openup.co.uk/ss to see the full selection of study skills titles, and get a **£2 discount** by entering the promotional code **study** when buying online!

Computing Skills

If you'd like to brush up on your computing skills, we have a range of titles covering MS Office applications such as Word, Excel, PowerPoint, Access and more.

Get a £2 discount off these titles by entering the promotional code **app** when ordering online at www.mcgraw-hill.co.uk/app.

Acknowledgements

Finding a way to integrate and present the rapidly growing literature on contemporary management and make it interesting and meaningful for students is not an easy task. This is especially true if one sets ambitious goals for content and pedagogy of the textbook. Our aim was to develop a textbook that is relevant to students and allows them to understand and use the theoretical underpinnings of management. We were also extremely conscious to integrate a pedagogy that facilitates independent learning.

In editing and revising this book for a European audience, we have been very fortunate to have the assistance of several contributors. First, we would like to thank Caroline Prodger and Rachel Gear, who approached us to undertake this work and who have shown great faith in our abilities. Secondly, we are very grateful to Hannah Cooper, our development editor, who has supported us throughout this project through her co-ordination of the overall process.

When undertaking a project like this, it is often impossible to remain objective. Thus, we would like to thank all the reviewers who gave such valuable and useful comments and feedback that aided us in tailoring this book and make it relevant for the intended market.

We would also like to thank the teams who have worked in the background to support this project, such as the production team, the design team and the copy editors: without any of them the book would not have been possible.

We are extremely grateful to **Jennifer M. George** and **Gareth R. Jones** for the excellent material they provided for us to work from. Without their detailed work and excellent structure this European edition would have been much more difficult to create.

Lastly, we would like to acknowledge all the academics who contributed to other editions of *Contemporary Management*. We hope that we have done justice to the original authors and all other reviewers and contributors.

The publisher's thanks go to the following reviewers for their comments at various stages in the text's development:

Dirk Akkermans, Gronigen University, Netherlands
James Cunningham, National University of Ireland, Galway
Nigel Holden, Nottingham Trent University
Josie Kinge, University of East Anglia
Gillian Mould, Stirling University
Ulrica Nylen, Umea School of Business, Sweden
Mike O'Connor, Loughborough University
Noel Pearse, Rhodes University, South Africa
Gerrie Roodt, University of Pretoria, South Africa
Andy Sharp, Glasgow Caledonian University
Ian Spurr, University of Hertfordshire
Jeanette Thomsen, Copenhagen Business School, Denmark
Siobhan Tiernan, University of Limerick, Ireland

Karen Verduyn, Vrije University, Netherlands
Richard West, Westminster Business School

Every effort has been made to trace and acknowledge ownership of copyright and to clear permission for material reproduced in this book. The publishers will be pleased to make suitable arrangements to clear permission with any copyright holders whom it has not been possible to contact.

Chapter 1

Managers and Managing

LEARNING OBJECTIVES

After studying this chapter, you should be able to:

☑ Describe what management is, why management is important, what managers do, and how managers utilise organisational resources efficiently and effectively to achieve organisational goals.

☑ Distinguish among planning, organising, leading and controlling (the four principal managerial functions), and explain how managers' ability to handle each one can affect organisational performance.

☑ Differentiate among levels of management, and understand the responsibilities of managers at different levels in the organisational hierarchy.

☑ Identify the roles managers perform, the skills they need to execute those roles effectively, and the way new information technology is affecting these roles and skills.

☑ Discuss the principal challenges managers face in today's increasingly competitive global environment.

A Manager's Challenge

The Rise of Siemens

Werner von Siemens was born in Germany in a small town near Hannover in December 1816. No one could then know that the fourth child of a poor farmer's family would become the founder of one of the world's best-known companies.

While showing ample potential in science and engineering, Werner was denied a university education due to the financial constraints of his family. He thus chose the security of the Army as a profession. It was quickly noticed that he was inventive and apt at engineering problems and this aptitude also translated into business acumen. During his time in the army, Werner and his brother registered their first patent and sold the rights to it – leaving them financially comfortable and allowing Werner to research further into his main interest – telegraphy. This field was at the time relatively underdeveloped, but Werner showed truly managerial foresight in predicting it to be the 'technology of the future'. Through developing a superior product, Werner finally opened his first business with a skilled mechanical engineer, Johann Georg Halske, in Berlin in 1847.

The success of this company was rapid and Werner soon had to dedicate his entire time to the business. Werner realised that the technology that Telegraphen-Bau-Anstalt Siemens & Halske was providing would predominantly be bought by governments and large corporations. Thus, in order to advance the company, Werner internationalised and opened the first two offices outside Prussia (then a distinct part of the German empire), showing entrepreneurial spirit ahead of his time. The first international office opened was in London in 1850 with a second office in St Petersburg in 1855 and a third in Austria three years later. To maintain close control over the foreign subsidiaries, Werner's brothers managed the branches in London and St Petersburg. Within 10 years of operating, Siemens had already become a truly global company due to Werner's instinct and managerial abilities to spot developing and new markets.

Werner continued his innovation and astute management of the business. His biggest success was the invention of the dynamo-machine, with which he coined the term 'electrical engineering'.

However, it was not just Werner's innovations or his entrepreneurial spirit that made the company what it is today. Werner was a manager who cared for his employees, noticing that 'the firm could only be made to develop satisfactorily if one could further its interest by ensuring that all employees work together in a cheerful and efficient manner'. Werner negotiated social benefits that were ahead of their time. Siemens & Halske had a company pension scheme by 1872, a 9-hour working day (the norm was 10–12 for labour) and a profit-sharing scheme called 'stocktaking bonus' which was launched in 1866.

After Werner's retirement the company re-formed as a stock corporation in 1897 and developed to be one of the largest international companies by 1914, with 10 foreign subsidiaries and branch offices in another 49 countries.

The astute management of the company was taken forward by Werner's descendents, who managed the firm through rising competition and two world wars. It was Werner's third son, Carl Friedrich, who continued in his father's tradition of being ahead of his time in business. Carl started to rebuild the company after the First World War by concentrating and focusing the company direction based on its expertise and withdrawing from non-traditional areas of business. Carl was also responsible for various strategic alliances, mergers and acquisitions during his time at the helm. Siemens was the first company that ever posted sales figures in excess of 1 billion Marks. In the 1930s and 1940s Siemens was the largest electrical company in the world despite the Great Depression.

Due to its strong family values Siemens managed to survive the devastating Second World War in which nearly 80 per cent of its assets were lost and through some decisive management and its belief in people the company turned into the largest employer in Germany in the 1960s and 1970s.

Today Siemens operates in 190 countries, has nearly half a million employees and still believes that employees and innovation are its strongest assets. The success speaks for the effective management of the company, which had sales exceeding €75 billion and profits exceeding €2 billion in 2005.

Overview

The history of Siemens' ups and downs through competition, political instabilities and industrial volatilities illustrates many of the challenges facing people who become managers. Managing a large company is a complex activity, and effective managers must possess many skills, knowledge and abilities. Management is an unpredictable process. Making the right decision is difficult; even effective managers often make mistakes, but the most effective managers are the ones who learn from their mistakes and continually strive to find ways to help their companies increase their competitive advantage, improve performance and essentially survive in the volatile business environment.

This chapter looks at what managers do, and what skills and abilities they must develop if they are to manage their organisations successfully over time. It also identifies the different kinds of managers that organisations need, and the skills and abilities they must develop if they are to be successful. Finally, some of the challenges that managers must address if their organisations are to grow and prosper are addressed.

What Is Management?

When you think of a 'manager', what kind of person comes to mind? Do you see someone who, like Werner von Siemens, can determine the future prosperity of a large for-profit company? Or do you see the administrator of a not-for-profit organisation, such as a school, library or charity, or the person in charge of your local supermarket or McDonald's restaurant, or the person *you* answer to if you have a part-time job? What do all these managers have in common?

First, they all work in organisations. **Organisations** are collections of people who work together and co-ordinate their actions to achieve a wide variety of *goals*, or desired future outcomes.[1] Second, as managers, they are the people responsible for supervising the use of an organisation's social capital and other, more tangible, resources to achieve its goals. This use of resources needs to be co-ordinated over time. **Management**, then, is the planning, organising, leading and controlling of social capital and other resources to achieve organisational goals efficiently and effectively. An organisation's *resources* include assets such as people and their skills, know-how and knowledge; machinery; raw materials; computers and IT; and financial capital.

Achieving High Performance: A Manager's Goal

One of the most important goals that organisations and their members try to achieve is to provide some kind of product or service that *customers desire*. The principal goal of any Chief Executive Officer (CEO) is to manage an organisation so that a new stream of products and services are created that customers are willing to buy. For Werner von Siemens, these were generators, and for Siemens now it is medical devices, for example. The principal goal of doctors, nurses and hospital administrators is to increase their hospital's ability to make sick people well. Likewise, the principal goal of each McDonald's restaurant manager is to produce burgers, fries and shakes that people want to pay for and eat. All these activities have to be undertaken within set standards, rules, regulations and codes of practice. The achievements of such organisational goals and functions is called **organisational performance**.

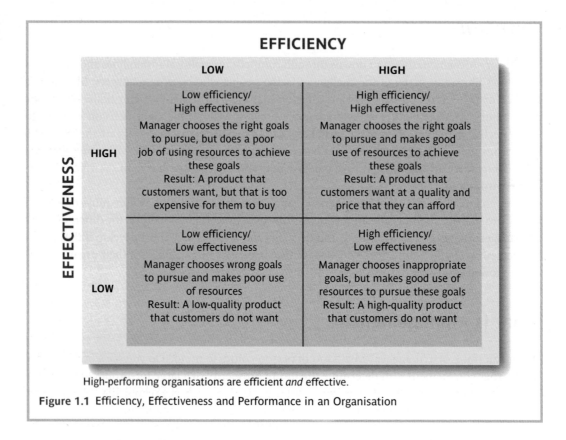

EFFICIENCY

	LOW	**HIGH**
HIGH	Low efficiency/ High effectiveness Manager chooses the right goals to pursue, but does a poor job of using resources to achieve these goals Result: A product that customers want, but that is too expensive for them to buy	High efficiency/ High effectiveness Manager chooses the right goals to pursue and makes good use of resources to achieve these goals Result: A product that customers want at a quality and price that they can afford
LOW	Low efficiency/ Low effectiveness Manager chooses wrong goals to pursue and makes poor use of resources Result: A low-quality product that customers do not want	High efficiency/ Low effectiveness Manager chooses inappropriate goals, but makes good use of resources to pursue these goals Result: A high-quality product that customers do not want

(left axis label: **EFFECTIVENESS**)

High-performing organisations are efficient *and* effective.

Figure 1.1 Efficiency, Effectiveness and Performance in an Organisation

Organisational performance is a measure of how efficiently and effectively managers use resources to *satisfy customers* and *achieve organisational goals*. Organisational performance increases in direct proportion to increases in **efficiency** and **effectiveness** (Fig. 1.1).

Efficiency is a measure of how well or how productively resources are used to *achieve a goal*.[2] Organisations are efficient when managers minimise the amount of input resources (such as labour, raw materials and component parts) or the amount of time needed to produce a given output of products or services. For example, McDonald's developed a more efficient deep fryer that not only reduced the amount of oil used in cooking by 30 per cent but also speeded up the cooking of French fries. Werner von Siemens invented the first dynamo that allowed the cheaper production of electricity. A manager's responsibility is to ensure that an organisation and its members perform as efficiently – i.e. with as few resources as possible – all the activities needed to provide goods and services to customers.

Effectiveness is a measure of the *appropriateness* of the goals that managers have selected for the organisation to pursue, and of the degree to which the organisation achieves those goals. Organisations are effective when managers choose appropriate goals and then achieve them. Some years ago, for example, managers at McDonald's decided on the goal of providing breakfast service to attract more customers. The choice of this goal has proved very smart, for sales of breakfast food now account for more than 30 per cent of McDonald's revenues. High-performing organisations, such as Siemens, McDonald's, ASDA, Intel, IKEA and Accenture, are simultaneously efficient and effective, as shown in Fig. 1.1. Effective managers are those who choose the right organisational goals to pursue, and have the skills to utilise resources efficiently.

Why Study Management?

Today, more and more students than ever before are enrolling for places in business courses. The number of people wishing to pursue Master of Business Administration (MBA) degrees – today's passport to an advanced management position – either on campus or from online universities, is at an all-time high. Student numbers are also increasing at an undergraduate level – including a growing demand for business courses. Why is the study of management currently so popular?[3]

First, *resources* in the twenty-first century are *valuable* and *scarce*, so the more efficient and effective use that organisations can make of them, the greater the benefit for all. In addition, the efficient and effective use of resources has a direct impact on the socio-economic situation and prosperity of people in society. Because managers are the people who decide how to use many of a society's resources – its skilled employees, raw materials like oil and land, computers and information systems and financial assets – their decisions directly impact the socio-economic situation of a society and the people in it. Understanding what managers do, and how they do it, is of central importance to understanding how a society works, and how it creates prosperity.

Second, although most people are not managers, and many may never intend to become managers, almost all of us encounter managers because most people have jobs and bosses. Moreover, many people today are working in groups and teams and have to deal with co-workers. Studying management helps people to understand how to deal with their bosses and their co-workers: it reveals how other people *behave* and *make decisions at work* that enable organisations to work in harmony and drive forward the achievement of organisational goals. Management also teaches people not yet in positions of authority how to lead co-workers, solve conflicts between them and increase team performance.

Third, in today's society people often feel that they are in competition for a well-paying job and an interesting and satisfying career in a volatile labour market. Understanding management is one important path towards obtaining such a position. Complexity and increasing responsibility often provide more stimulating and interesting jobs; any person who desires a motivating job that changes over time might therefore do well to develop management skills and become promotable. A person who has been working for several years and then returns to university for an MBA can usually, after earning the degree, significantly enhance their career prospects.

Indeed, once one reaches the top echelons within an organisation, rewards can be immense. The CEOs and other top executives or managers of companies, for example, receive millions in salary, bonuses and share options each year.[4] What is it that managers actually do to receive such rewards?[5]

Managerial Functions

The job of management is to help an organisation make the best use of its resources to achieve its goals. How do managers accomplish this objective? They do so by performing four essential managerial functions: **planning, organising, leading** and **controlling** (Fig. 1.2). The arrows linking these functions in Fig. 1.2 suggest the sequence in which managers typically perform these functions. The French manager Henri Fayol first outlined the nature of these managerial activities around the turn of the twentieth century in *General and Industrial Management*, a book that remains the classic statement of what managers must do to create a high-performing organisation.[6]

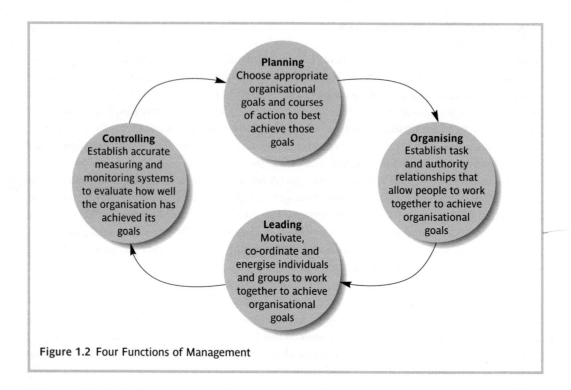

Figure 1.2 Four Functions of Management

Managers at all levels and in all departments – whether in small or large organisations, for-profit or not-for-profit organisations, or organisations that operate in one country or throughout the world – are responsible for performing these four functions, which we look at next. How well managers perform these functions determines how *efficient* and *effective* their organisations are.

Planning

Planning is a process that managers use to identify and select *appropriate goals and courses of action*. The three steps in the planning process are (1) deciding which goals the organisation will pursue, (2) deciding what actions to adopt to attain these goals and (3) deciding how to allocate organisational resources to accomplish them. The performance level is determined by how effective managers are at planning.[7]

As an example of planning in action, consider the situation confronting Michael Dell, CEO of Dell Computer, the very profitable PC maker.[8] In 1984, the 19-year-old Dell saw an opportunity to enter the PC market by assembling PCs and then selling them directly to customers. Dell began to plan how to put his idea into practice. First, he decided that his goal was to sell an inexpensive PC, to undercut the prices of companies such as Compaq. Second, he had to decide on a course of action to achieve this goal. He decided to sell directly to customers by telephone and to bypass expensive computer stores that sold Compaq or Apple PCs. He also had to decide how to obtain low-cost components and how to tell potential customers about his products. Third, he had to decide how to allocate his limited funds (he had only £2,750) to buy labour and other resources. He chose to hire three people and work with them around a table to assemble his PCs.

To put his vision of making and selling PCs into practice, Dell had to *plan*. Despite organisational growth or complexity (both of which Dell experienced), the process of planning remains a constant. This does not mean that plans themselves are not subject to change, as change is a part of any organisation. Dell and his managers continually plan how to maintain its position as the biggest and highest-performing PC maker that sells predominantly online and through the telephone. In 2003, Dell announced it would begin to sell printers and personal digital assistants (PDAs); this brought it into direct competition with Hewlett-Packard (HP), the leading printer maker, and Palm One, the maker of the Palm Pilot. In the same year, Dell also brought out its own Internet music player, the Digital Jukebox, to compete against Apple's iPod, and in 2004 it reduced the price of its player to compete more effectively against Apple. In April 2004, Dell's player was selling at a significantly lower price than Apple's, and analysts were wondering what effect this would have on iPod sales and Apple's future performance.

Such continuous and stringent planning results in a **strategy**: a cluster of decisions concerning what organisational goals to pursue, what actions to take and how to use resources to achieve goals. The decisions that were the outcome of Michael Dell's planning formed a *low-cost strategy*. A low-cost strategy is a way of obtaining customers' loyalty by making decisions that allow the organisation to make its products or services cheaper than its competitors so that prices can be kept low. Dell has constantly refined this strategy and explored new ways to reduce costs. Dell has become the most profitable PC maker as a result of its low-cost strategy, and it is hoping to repeat its success in the music player business. By contrast, Apple's strategy has been to deliver new, exciting and different computer and digital products, such as the iPod, to its customers – a strategy known as **differentiation**. The mini iPod was developed for people on the go, for example; it is as small as a (thick) credit card, has unique, easy-to-use controls and comes in a variety of bright contemporary colours.[9]

Planning is a difficult activity because normally the goals that an organisation should pursue and how best to pursue them – which strategies to adopt – are not immediately clear. Managers take risks when they commit organisational resources to pursue a particular strategy: both success or failure are possible outcomes of the planning process. Dell succeeded spectacularly, but many other PC makers either went out of business (such as Packard Bell and Digital) or lost huge sums of money (like IBM) trying to compete in this industry. In Chapter 8 we focus on the planning process and the strategies organisations can select, and also how these strategies can help organisations to respond to the opportunities or threats in an industry. The story of Rolf Eriksen (Case 1.1) highlights how planning and strategising can lead a company forward.

Case 1.1: New CEO brings change at H&M

One global company that required new and innovative thinking to take it forward was Swedish clothing retailer H&M. Hennes & Mauritz, as it was known when it was established in 1947 by Erling Persson, has moved from being a solely Nordic player to a global fashion retailer. This was achieved mainly through the appointment of the Dane Rolf Eriksen as CEO in 2000. Prior to this role, Eriksen had been responsible for the Danish and Swedish operation of H&M. Within his first year of being CEO he managed to increase net income by 49.5 per cent, to £211.3 million; sales rose by 29 per cent, to £2.61 billion. In the first quarter of 2002, earnings rose by 33 per cent. By 2005 it was argued that H&M had benefited from a constant growth of 21 per cent per ▶

▶ year over the previous decade, and it was expected that sales figures would exceed £4.4 billion in 2006. H&M has now 1,200 stores in more than 20 countries, and by 2007 Eriksen expects to manage another 100 stores worldwide.

Achieving such a successful growth was a result of Eriksen's management of the company: he has shown that he can respond to opportunities. H&M was the pioneer of affordable, fashionable clothing. The company's strength under Eriksen is to quickly translate current trends into products for the masses, aided by the CEO's realisation that 'The world is becoming smaller and smaller, especially for the young customers'. Eriksen has been able to slash costs, streamline distribution and broaden H&M's lines by assuming a similar taste in fashion around the world, whether be it New York, Paris, Stockholm or Berlin. With his vision, he has been able to position H&M as a growing rival of well-established brands such as GAP or Benetton. Eriksen has been successful in realigning H&M's target group to middle-class customers, away from a 'cheap and cheerful' image towards affordable clothing that can be changed according to trends in fashion.

One of Eriksen's most successful ventures in driving forward H&M as a leading fashion retailer was the commissioning of one-off clothing lines with Chanel designer Karl Lagerfeld in 2004. The collection sold out within three days of the launch and stores reported a 12 per cent increase in sales in that month. Such a special edition was repeated, with a one-off 40-piece line from Stella McCartney, a member of the Gucci fashion group. H&M is hoping to appeal to fashion-conscious people who cannot afford the signature line: a stroke of genius in exploiting the current climate for branded fashion.

Eriksen has the ability to see potential growth, such as Eastern European and Asian markets, or collaborations with upmarket designers – a vision that has made H&M the global company it is today. For Eriksen as CEO, planning and organising are vital functions that must be continuously worked on by managers at all levels of the company.

Organising

Organising is a process that managers use to establish a *structure of working relationships* that allow organisational members to interact and co-operate to achieve organisational goals. Organising involves grouping people into departments according to the kinds of job-specific tasks they perform. In organising, managers also lay out the *lines of authority* and *responsibility* between different individuals and groups, and decide how best to co-ordinate organisational resources, particularly human resources.

The outcome of organising is the creation of an **organisational structure**, a formal system of task and reporting relationships that co-ordinates and motivates members so that they work together to achieve organisational goals. Organisational structure determines how an organisation's resources can be best used to create products and services. As Siemens grew, for example, Werner von Siemens faced the issue of how to structure the organisation. Early on, Siemens was hiring new employees at a staggering rate, and deciding how to design the **managerial hierarchy** (the structure of the reporting relationships) to best motivate and co-ordinate managers' activities was important. As Siemens grew and internationalised, more complex kinds of organisational structures needed to be created to achieve its goals. The aspects that influence organisational structure and the process of organising this structure will be examined in more detail in Chapters 9–11.

Leading

The concept of **leadership** is both a complex and interdependent process involving leaders and followers in a *reciprocal relationship*. The various theoretical frameworks and concepts available to explain this phenomenon are examined in more detail in Chapter 14. However as leadership is one of the four principal functions of management, it is briefly described here within the context of performing these functions. A key facet of leadership is to articulate a *clear vision* for organisational members to follow. This should enable organisational members to understand the role they play in achieving organisational goals. Leadership can depend on the use of power, influence, vision, persuasion and communication skills to co-ordinate the behaviours of individuals and groups so that their activities and efforts are in harmony. The ideal outcome of good leadership is a high level of motivation and commitment among organisational members. Employees at Dell Computer, for examples, responded well to Michael Dell's 'hands-on' leadership style, which resulted in a hardworking, committed workforce.

Controlling

In controlling, managers evaluate how well an organisation is *achieving* its goals, and take action to maintain or improve performance. Managers monitor the performance of individuals, departments and the organisation as a whole, for example, to see whether they are meeting desired performance standards. If standards are not being met, managers must take action to improve performance.

The outcome of the control process is the ability to measure performance accurately and regulate organisational efficiency and effectiveness. To exercise control, managers must decide *which goals to measure* – perhaps goals pertaining to productivity, quality, or responsiveness to customers – and then they must design *information and control systems* that will provide the data they need to assess performance. The controlling function also allows managers to evaluate how well they themselves are performing the other three functions of management – planning, organising and leading – and to take corrective action where necessary. This relies on organisational **feedback mechanisms**.

Michael Dell had difficulty establishing effective control systems because his company was growing so rapidly and he lacked experienced managers. In 1988 Dell's costs soared because no controls were in place to monitor inventory, which had built up rapidly. In 1993 financial problems arose because of ill-advised foreign currency transactions. In 1994 Dell's new line of laptop computers crashed because poor quality control resulted in defective products, some of which caught fire. To solve these and other control problems, Dell hired experienced managers to put the correct control systems in place. As a result, by 1998 Dell was able to make computers for about 10 per cent less than its competitors, creating a major source of competitive advantage. By 2001 Dell had become so efficient it was driving its competitors out of the market because it had realised a 15–20 per cent cost advantage over them.[10] By 2003 it was the biggest PC maker in the world. Controlling, like the other managerial functions, is an ongoing, dynamic, ever-changing process that demands constant attention and action. Because controlling is a function essential to organisational survival, the influence and impact of this function on all aspects of organisational behaviour will be revisited throughout the text.

The four managerial functions – planning, organising, leading and controlling – are all essential to a manager's job. At all levels in a managerial hierarchy, and across all departments in an organisation, effective management means making decisions and managing these four activities successfully.

Types of Managers

To perform efficiently and effectively, organisations employ different types of managers – for example, **first-line managers**, **middle managers** and **senior managers**, who are arranged in a hierarchy (Fig. 1.3). Typically, first-line managers report to middle managers and middle managers report to senior managers. Managers at each level have different but related responsibilities for utilising organisational resources to increase efficiency and effectiveness. Within each department, various levels of management may exist that reflect this particular categorisation and organisational hierarchy. A **department**, such as manufacturing, accounting or engineering, is a group of people who work together and may possess similar skills or use the same kind of knowledge, tools or techniques to perform one function that helps to achieve the overall organisational goal. The chapter next examines the reasons why organisations use a hierarchy of managers and group them into departments. We then examine some recent changes taking place in managerial hierarchies.

Levels of Management

As just discussed, organisations normally have various levels of management. Figure 1.3 is one possible example.

First-line managers

At the base of the managerial hierarchy are first-line managers, often called *supervisors*. They are responsible for the *daily supervision* of the non-managerial employees who perform many of the

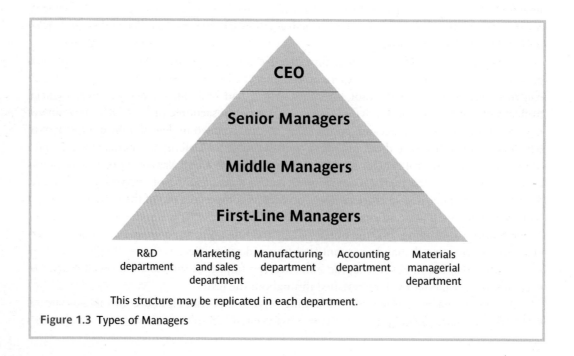

This structure may be replicated in each department.

Figure 1.3 Types of Managers

specific (primary) activities necessary to produce goods and services. First-line managers work in all departments or functions of an organisation.

Examples of first-line managers include the supervisor of a work team in the manufacturing department of a car plant, the ward sister in an obstetrics ward of a hospital, or the foreman overseeing a crew of labourers on a construction site. At Dell Computer, first-line managers include the supervisors responsible for controlling the quality of Dell computers or the level of customer service provided by Dell's telephone salespeople. When Michael Dell started his company, he personally controlled the computer assembly process and thus performed as a first-line manager or supervisor.

Middle managers

Middle managers are responsible for finding the best way to *organise human and other resources* to achieve organisational goals. To increase efficiency, middle managers find ways to help subordinates better to utilise resources to reduce manufacturing costs or improve customer service. To increase effectiveness, middle managers evaluate whether the goals that the organisation is pursuing are appropriate and suggest to senior managers ways in which goals should be changed. Very often, the suggestions that middle managers make to senior managers can dramatically increase organisational performance. A major part of the middle manager's job is developing and fine-tuning *skills* and *know-how*, such as manufacturing or marketing expertise, that allow the organisation to be efficient and effective. Middle managers make thousands of specific decisions about the production of goods and services. Some of the decisions a middle-manager may face are:

- Which supervisor should be chosen for a particular project?

- Where can we find the highest-quality resources?

- How should employees be organised to allow them to make the best use of resources?

Behind any successful and committed team, department or individual employee, there will usually be a first-class middle manager, who is able to motivate, lead and reward staff to find ways to obtain the resources they need to do outstanding and innovative jobs in the workplace.

Senior managers

In contrast to middle managers, senior managers are responsible for the performance of *all* departments:[11] they have *cross-departmental responsibility*. Senior managers establish organisational goals, such as which products and services the company should produce; they decide how the different departments should interact; and they monitor how well middle managers in each department utilise resources to achieve goals.[12] Senior managers are ultimately responsible for the success or failure of an organisation, and their performance (like Werner von Siemens or Rolf Eriksen of H&M) is continually scrutinised by people inside and outside the organisation, such as other employees and investors.[13]

The *CEO* is a company's most senior manager, the one to whom all other senior managers report. Together, the CEO and the **chief operating officer (COO)** – also called **Managing Director (MD)** – are responsible for developing good working relationships among the senior managers of various departments (for example, manufacturing and marketing). A central concern of the CEO is the creation of a smoothly functioning **senior-management team**, a group composed of the CEO, the COO/MD and the department heads of an organisation to help to achieve organisational goals.[14]

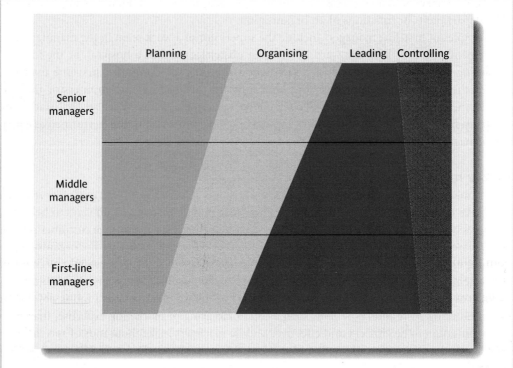

Figure 1.4 Relative Amount of Time That Managers Spend on the Four Managerial Functions

The relative importance of planning, organising, leading and controlling – the four managerial functions – to any particular manager depends on their position in the managerial hierarchy.[15] The amount of time that managers spend planning and organising the resources to maintain and improve organisational performance increases as they ascend the hierarchy (Fig. 1.4).[16] Senior managers usually devote most of their time to planning and organising, the functions so crucial to determining an organisation's long-term performance. The lower that managers' positions are in the hierarchy, the more time the managers tend to spend leading and controlling first-line managers or non-managerial employees.

The Managerial Hierarchy

Because so much of a manager's responsibility is to acquire and develop critical resources, managers are typically members of specific departments.[17] Managers inside a department possess job-specific skills and are known, for example, as marketing managers or manufacturing managers. As Fig. 1.3 indicates, first-line, middle and senior managers, who differ from one another by virtue of their job-specific responsibilities, are found in each of an organisation's major departments. Inside each department, a *managerial hierarchy* thus emerges.

At Dell Computer, for example, Michael Dell hired experts to take charge of the marketing, sales and manufacturing departments and to develop work procedures to help first-line managers control the company's explosive sales growth. The head of manufacturing quickly found that he had no time to supervise computer assembly, so he recruited manufacturing middle managers from other companies to assume this responsibility.

Reaction Time

1. Describe the difference between efficiency and effectiveness, and identify any real organisations that you think are, or are not, efficient and effective.

2. Identify an organisation that you believe is high-performing and one that you believe is low-performing. Give five reasons why you think the performance levels of the two organisations differ so much.

3. Try to identify the managerial hierarchy of your university department.

Recent Changes in Managerial Hierarchies

The tasks and responsibilities of managers at different levels have been changing dramatically in recent years. Three major factors that have led to these changes are global competition and advances in new IT and in **e-commerce**. Intense competition for resources from organisations, both nationally and internationally, has put increased pressure on all managers to improve efficiency, effectiveness and organisational performance. Increasingly, senior managers are encouraging lower-level managers to look beyond the goals of their own departments and take a *cross-departmental view* to find new opportunities to improve organisational performance. New ITs give managers at all levels access to more and better information and improve their ability to plan, organise, lead and control; this has also revolutionised the way the managerial hierarchy works.[18]

Restructuring and Outsourcing

To take advantage of IT and e-commerce and their ability to reduce operating costs, CEOs and senior management teams have been restructuring organisations and outsourcing specific organisational activities to reduce the number of employees on the payroll.

Restructuring

Restructuring involves the use of IT to *downsize* an organisation or *shrink its operations* by eliminating the jobs of large numbers of top, middle or first-line managers and non-managerial employees. In some industries, for example car manufacturing, IT allows fewer employees to perform a given task because it increases each person's ability to process information and make decisions more quickly and accurately. UK overall investment into information and communication technology (ICT) has increased by 133 per cent since 1992, to £25.7 billion in 2001.[19] In the US, companies are spending over £27.3 billion a year on advanced IT, and it is likely that a large part of this investment has been made to improve efficiency and effectiveness. Some of the effects of IT on management are discussed in Chapter 18.

Restructuring, however, can produce some powerful *negative outcomes*. IT can reduce the morale of the remaining employees, who are worried about their own job security, and senior managers of many downsized organisations can come to realise that they have downsized too far, because employees complain they are overworked and because more customers complain about poor-quality service.[20] Some more recent restructuring initiatives – for example in the National Health Service (NHS) in the UK – are about creating more effective and efficient job descriptions to streamline the delivery of a service. The Department of Health (DoH) in England has created new levels of qualifications, such as associate practitioner roles, to restructure its service delivery.[21]

Outsourcing

Outsourcing involves contracting with another company, usually in a low-cost country abroad, so that it can perform an activity – such as manufacturing or marketing – the organisation previously performed itself. Outsourcing promotes efficiency by reducing costs and by allowing an organisation to make better use of its remaining resources. The need to respond to low-cost global competition has speeded up outsourcing dramatically since 2000: 3 million US jobs in the manufacturing sector have been lost as companies moved their operations to countries such as China, Taiwan and Malaysia. Tens of thousands of high-paying jobs in IT have moved to countries such as India and Russia, where programmers work for one-third the salary of those in the US. In the UK, an ongoing decline in manufacturing industry has seen a decrease in manufacturing jobs of nearly 4 per cent per annum since 2000, which is more than double the **EU–25** average. This means that manufacturing jobs now account for approximately 14.9 per cent of employment in the UK:[22] in 2004 approximately 3.5 million people were employed in manufacturing compared to over 7 million in the late 1970s.[23] While some of this decline may be due to natural wastage, the majority can be assigned to the move away from expensive western European labour to workers in cheaper countries.

Large for-profit organisations today typically employ 10–20 per cent fewer employees than they did 10 years ago because of restructuring and outsourcing. Siemens, IBM, HP, Dell and Du Pont are among the thousands of organisations that have streamlined their operations to increase efficiency and effectiveness. The argument is that the managers and employees who have lost their jobs will find employment in new and growing organisations where their skills and experience will be better utilised. The millions of manufacturing jobs that have been lost overseas are expected to be replaced by higher-paying jobs in the service sector that are made possible because of the growth in global trade. However, the downside of outsourcing and reengineering is an *overreliance on technology*. This can prove to be detrimental to organisational performance, especially in light of the emerging discipline of **knowledge management** (KM) where loss of staff may also mean *loss of expertise* and *performance-enhancing knowledge*. The issues surrounding the retaining of knowledge and information will be further examined in Chapter 18.

Empowerment and Self-managed Teams

Another major change in management has taken place at the level of first-line managers, who typically supervise the employees engaged in producing goods and services. Many companies have taken two key steps to reduce costs and improve quality. One is the **empowerment** of their workforces to expand employees' knowledge, tasks and responsibilities. The other is the creation of **self-managed teams** – groups of employees given responsibility for supervising their own activities and for monitoring the quality of the goods and services they provide.[24] Members of self-managed teams assume many of the responsibilities and duties previously performed by first-line managers.[25]

What is the role of the first-line manager in this new work context? First-line managers act as *coaches* or *mentors* whose job is not to tell employees what to do but to provide advice and guidance and help teams find new ways to perform their tasks more efficiently.[26] Both self-managed teams and empowerment are concepts that will be discussed as part of the leadership debate and effective team working in Chapters 14 and 15.

TIPS FOR PRACTICE

1. Think about how customers perceive the products and services that your organisation offers, if these adequately meet their needs and how they might be improved.

2. Explore whether your organisation can be better at obtaining or using resources to increase efficiency and effectiveness.

3. Think about how the skills and know-how of departments is helping your organisation to achieve its competitive advantage. Take steps to improve these skills whenever possible.

IT and Managerial Roles and Skills

A **managerial role** is a set of specific tasks that a manager is expected to perform because of the position he or she holds in an organisation. One well-known model of managerial roles was developed by Henry Mintzberg, who detailed 10 specific roles that effective managers undertake. Although Mintzberg's roles overlap with Fayol's model (p. 41) they are useful because they focus on what managers do in a typical hour, day or week in an organisation as they go about the job of managing.[27] We now discuss these roles and the skills managers need to develop to perform effectively.

Managerial Roles Identified by Mintzberg

Henry Mintzberg developed a model of managerial behaviours that reduces the thousands of specific tasks that managers need to perform as they plan, organise, lead and control organisational resources to 10 roles.[28] Managers assume each of these roles to influence the behaviour of individuals and groups inside and outside the organisation. The people who are directly or indirectly affected by what the organisation does are called *organisational stakeholders*, and they can be identified as internal or external. People inside the organisation (internal stakeholders) include other managers and employees. People outside the organisation (external stakeholders) can include shareholders, customers, suppliers, the local community in which an organisation is located and any local or government agency that has an interest in the organisation and what it does.[29] Mintzberg grouped the 10 roles into three broad categories: *decisional*, *informational* and *interpersonal*, as described in Table 1.1. Managers often perform many of these roles from minute to minute while engaged in the more general functions of planning, organising, leading and controlling.

Decisional roles

Decisional roles are closely associated with the methods managers use to *plan strategy and utilise resources*. The role of the **entrepreneur** is to provide more and better information to use in deciding which projects or programmes to initiate and resources to invest to increase organisational performance. As a *disturbance handler*, a manager has to move quickly to manage the unexpected event or crisis that may threaten the organisation and to implement solutions quickly. As a *resource allocator*, a manager has to decide how best to use people and other resources to increase organisational performance. While engaged in that role, the manager must also be a *negotiator*, reaching agreements with other managers or groups or with the organisation and

Table 1.1 Managerial roles identified by Mintzberg

Type of role	Specific role	Examples of role activities
Decisional	Entrepreneur	Commit organisational resources to develop innovative goods and services; decide to expand internationally to obtain new customers for the organisation's products
	Disturbance handler	Move quickly to take corrective action to deal with unexpected problems facing the organisation from the external environment (such as a crisis like an oil spill), or from the internal environment (such as producing faulty goods or services)
	Resource allocator	Allocate organisational resources among different functions and departments of the organisation; set budgets and salaries of middle and first-level managers
	Negotiator	Work with suppliers, distributors and labour unions to reach agreements about the quality and price of input, technical and human resources; work with other organisations to establish agreements to pool resources to work on joint projects
Informational	Monitor	Evaluate the performance of managers in different functions and take corrective action to improve their performance; watch for changes occurring in the external and internal environments that may affect the organisation in the future
	Disseminator	Inform employees about changes taking place in the external and internal environments that will affect them and the organisation; communicate the organisation's vision and purpose to employees
	Spokesperson	Launch a national advertising campaign to promote new goods and services; give a speech to inform the local community about the organisation's future intentions
Interpersonal	Figurehead	Outline future organisational goals to employees at company meetings; open a new corporate headquarters; state the organisational ethical guidelines and the principles of behaviour that employees should follow in their dealings with customers and suppliers
	Leader	Provide an example for employees to follow; give direct commands and orders to subordinates; make decisions concerning the use of human resource and technical resources; mobilise employee support for specific organisational goals
	Liaison	Co-ordinate the work of managers in different departments; establish alliances between different organisations to share resources to produce new goods and services

outside groups such as suppliers or customers. The advancement of IT may enable managers to perform these roles more efficiently and effectively.

Informational roles

Informational roles are closely associated with the tasks necessary to *obtain and seek information*, which is the **monitor** role. Acting as a *disseminator*, a manager should be able to transmit information to employees to influence their work attitudes and behaviour. As a *spokesperson* a manager should be able to promote the organisation so that people inside and outside it respond positively. While these roles may be influenced by IT, the function of those roles more specifically relates to the brokering of internal and external knowledge sources, and developments in IT may facilitate this process.

Interpersonal roles

Managers assume interpersonal roles to provide *direction and supervision* for both employees and the organisation as a whole. The role of a **figurehead** is to inform employees and other interested parties, such as shareholders, about what the organisation's mission is, and what it is seeking to achieve. At all levels managers can act as figureheads and role models who establish appropriate ways to behave in the organisation. In order to perform better as **leaders**, managers should focus on training, counselling and mentoring subordinates to help them reach their full potential. Finally, as a *liaison*, a manager should be able to show his or her ability to link and co-ordinate the activities of people and groups both inside and outside the organisation. As with the other roles, IT may prove to be a useful tool in facilitating these functions.

Being a Manager

Our discussion of managerial roles may seem to suggest that a manager's job is highly orchestrated and that management is a logical, orderly process in which managers rationally calculate the best way to use resources to achieve organisational goals. In reality, being a manager often involves acting emotionally and relying on intuition and instinct. Quick, immediate reactions to situations, rather than deliberate thought and reflection, are an important aspect of managerial action.[30] Managers are often overloaded with responsibilities and do not have time to spend on analysing every nuance of a situation. Managers therefore make decisions in uncertain conditions and often without all the necessary and appropriate information, leaving the outcome ambiguous.[31] For senior managers, in particular, the situation is constantly changing, and a decision that seems right today may prove to be wrong tomorrow. In addition, the job of a manager involves constant interaction with other individuals; Chapter 5 will discuss the diversity of human beings and will show that people are not predictable and thus may cause managers at times to act in a non-rational and subjective manner.

Managers have to face a range of problems (*high variety*). Managers frequently must deal with many problems simultaneously (*fragmentation*), often must make snap decisions (*brevity*) and must frequently rely on experience gained throughout their careers to do their jobs to the best of their abilities.[32] It is no small wonder that many managers claim that they are performing their jobs well if they are right just half of the time, and it is understandable why experienced managers should accept failure by their subordinates as a normal part of the learning experience. Managers and their subordinates learn from both their successes and their failures.

Managerial Skills

Both education and experience enable managers to recognise and develop the personal skills they need to put organisational resources to their best use. Michael Dell realised from the start that he lacked sufficient experience and technical expertise in marketing, finance and planning to guide his company alone. He recruited experienced managers from other IT companies, such as IBM and HP, to help him build his company. Research has shown that education and experience help managers acquire three principal types of skills: **conceptual**, **human**, and

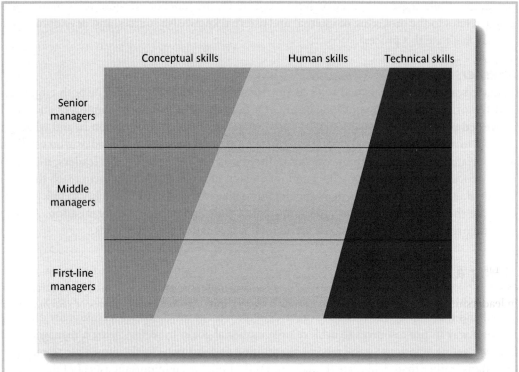

Figure 1.5 Conceptual, Human and Technical Skills Needed by the Three Levels of Management

technical.[33] As you might expect, the level of these skills that managers need depends on their level in the managerial hierarchy. Typically planning and organising require higher levels of conceptual skills, while leading and controlling require more human and technical skills (Fig. 1.5).

Conceptual skills

Conceptual skills are demonstrated in the ability to *analyse* and *diagnose* a situation and to distinguish between cause and effect. Senior managers require the best conceptual skills because their primary responsibilities are planning and organising.[34] By all accounts, Werner von Siemens' success came from his ability to identify new opportunities and mobilise resources to take advantage of them.

Formal education and training can be very important in helping managers develop conceptual skills, by introducing the variety of **conceptual tools** (theories and techniques in marketing, finance and other areas) that managers need to perform their roles effectively. The study of management helps to develop the skills that allow managers to understand the bigger picture confronting an organisation. The ability to focus *holistically* on the organisational context enables managers to see beyond the situation immediately at hand and consider choices, while keeping in mind the organisation's long-term goals.

Continuing management education and training, including training in advanced IT, is now an integral step in building managerial skills, because new theories and techniques, such as **business-to-business (B2B)** networks, are constantly being developed to improve organisational effectiveness. A quick scan through a magazine such as *The Economist* or *Management Today* reveals a host of seminars on topics such as advanced marketing, finance, leadership and **human resources management** (HRM) that are offered to managers at many levels in the organisation, from the most senior corporate executives to middle managers. Within the private sector many companies – Shell, British Airways or Motorola, and many other organisations, for example – designate a budget for attending management development programmes. The public sector also invests large amounts of money in developing the managerial capabilities of their staff.

In addition, many non-managerial employees who are performing at a high level (because they have studied management) are often sent to intensive management training programmes to develop their management skills and to prepare them for promotion to higher management positions.

Human skills

Human skills include the ability to understand, alter, lead and control the behaviour of other individuals and groups. The ability to communicate, to co-ordinate, to motivate people and to mould individuals into cohesive teams, distinguishes effective from ineffective managers.

Like conceptual skills, human skills can be learned through education and training, as well as be developed through experience.[35] Organisations increasingly utilise advanced programmes in leadership skills and team training as they seek to capitalise on the advantages of *self-managed teams*.[36] To manage personal interactions effectively, each person in an organisation needs to learn how to empathise with other people – to understand their viewpoints and the problems they face. One way to help managers understand their personal strengths and weaknesses is to have their superiors, peers and subordinates provide **feedback** about their performance. Thorough and direct feedback allows managers to develop their human skills: in some contexts, such feedback is known as a '360 degree approach', in which superiors, subordinates and peers comment on an individual's behaviour. There are a variety of tools available to assess an individual's skill set, but providing the feedback generated by such tools needs to be carefully managed for it to be constructive.

Technical skills

Technical skills are the *job-specific knowledge and techniques* required to perform an organisational role. Examples include a manager's specific manufacturing, accounting, marketing – and, increasingly, IT – skills. Managers need a range of technical skills to be effective. The array of technical skills managers need depends on their position in their organisation. The manager of a restaurant, for example, may need accounting and bookkeeping skills to keep track of receipts and costs and to administer the payroll, and aesthetic skills to keep the restaurant looking attractive for customers.

Effective managers need all three kinds of skills – conceptual, human and technical. The absence of even one of these can lead to failure. One of the biggest problems that people who start small businesses confront is their lack of appropriate conceptual and human skills. Someone who has the technical skills to start a new business does not necessarily know how to manage the venture successfully. Similarly, one of the biggest problems that scientists or engineers who switch careers from research to management confront is their lack of effective human skills. Management skills, roles and functions are closely related, and wise managers or prospective managers are constantly in search of the latest educational contributions to help them develop the conceptual, human and technical skills they need to function in today's changing and increasingly competitive global environment.

Today, the term **competencies** is often used to refer to a specific set of skills, abilities and experiences that gives one manager the ability to perform at a higher level than in a particular organisational setting. Developing such competencies through education and training has become a major priority for both aspiring managers and the organisations they work for. As we discussed earlier, many people are enrolling in advanced management courses, but companies such as IBM have established their own colleges to train and develop their employees and managers at all levels. Every year, for example, General Electric (GE) puts thousands of its employees through management programmes designed to identify the employees whom the company believes have superior competencies and whom it can develop to become its future senior managers. In many organisations promotion is closely tied to a manager's ability to acquire the competencies that a particular company believes are important.[37] At 3M, the company that developed the Post-it note, for example, the ability to successfully lead a new product development team is viewed as a vital requirement for promotion; at IBM, the ability to attract and retain clients is viewed as a vital competency its consultants must possess. We discuss specific kinds of managerial competencies throughout this book.

TIPS FOR PRACTICE

1. Think about how much time managers spend performing each of the four tasks of planning, organising, leading and controlling. Decide if managers are spending the appropriate amount of time on each.

2. To compare how well managers perform their different roles, you may want to use Mintzberg's model and compare a manager against it to assess his or her behaviour.

3. Find out whether managers possess the right levels of conceptual, technical and human skills to perform their jobs effectively.

Challenges for Management in a Global Environment

Because the world has been changing more rapidly than ever before, managers and other employees throughout an organisation need to perform at higher and higher levels.[38] In the last 20 years, competition between organisations nationally and internationally has increased dramatically. The rise of **global organisations** – organisations that operate and compete in more than one country – has put severe pressure on many organisations to improve their performance and to identify better ways to use their resources. The successes of the German chemical companies Schering and Hoechst, Italian furniture manufacturer Natuzzi, Korean electronics companies Samsung and LG, Brazilian plane maker Embraer and Europe's Airbus Industries are putting pressure on organisations in other countries to raise their level of performance to compete successfully.

Even in the not-for-profit sector, global competition is driving change. Schools, universities, police forces and government agencies are re-examining their operations. Some English universities now have a campus in other countries, for example. European and Asian hospital systems have learned much from the very effective US model.

Managers who make no attempt to learn and adapt to changes in the global environment will find themselves *reacting* rather than innovating, and their organisations often become uncompetitive and fail.[39] Four major challenges stand out for managers in today's world:

- Building a competitive advantage
- Maintaining ethical standards
- Managing a diverse workforce
- Utilising new information systems and technologies.

All of these topics will be discussed in more detail in later chapters and all these factors play an important role in understanding both modern management and its practices.

Building Competitive Advantage

What are the most important lessons for managers and organisations to learn if they are to reach, and remain at, the top of the competitive business environment? The answer relates to the use of organisational resources to build a **competitive advantage**. Competitive advantage is the ability of one organisation to outperform others because it produces desired products or services more efficiently and effectively than its competitors. One model of competitive advantage is the 'four building blocks' that advocates superior *efficiency*; *quality*; *speed*, *flexibility* and *innovation*; and *responsiveness to customers* (Fig. 1.6).

Increasing efficiency

Organisations increase their efficiency when they reduce the quantity of resources (such as people and raw materials) they use to produce goods or services. In today's competitive environment, organisations constantly are seeking new ways of using their resources to improve efficiency.

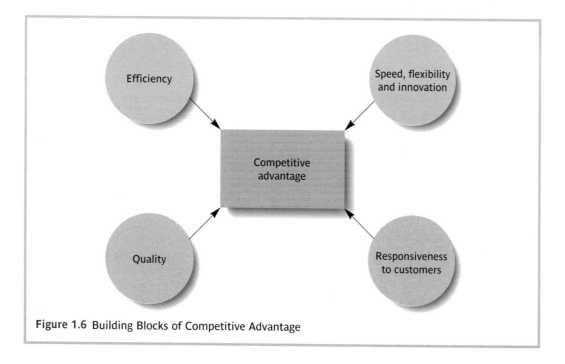

Figure 1.6 Building Blocks of Competitive Advantage

Many organisations are training their workforces in the new skills and techniques that are needed to operate within today's sophisticated technologically advanced working environment. Similarly, *cross-training* gives employees the range of multi-tasking skills and organising employees in new ways (such as in self-managed teams, see p. 14) allows them to make good use of their skills. These are all key steps in the effort to improve productivity. Japanese and German companies invest far more in training employees than do American or Italian companies. In the UK in 2002, 90 per cent of employers provided some form of training to their staff, with 62 per cent providing off-the-job training.[40]

Managers must improve efficiency if their organisations are to compete successfully with companies operating in India, Malaysia, China and other countries where employees are paid comparatively low wages. New methods must be devised either to increase efficiency or to gain some other competitive advantage – higher-quality products, for example – if outsourcing and the loss of jobs to low-cost countries are to be prevented.

Increasing quality

The challenge from global organisations such as Korean electronics manufacturers, Mexican agricultural producers and European marketing and financial firms has also increased pressure on companies to improve the skills and abilities of their workforce in order to improve the quality of their products and services. One major way to improve quality has been to introduce different techniques to ensure tighter quality controls. One of these quality-enhancing techniques is known as **total quality management** (TQM). Employees involved in TQM are often organised into *quality control teams* responsible for continually finding new and better ways to perform their jobs; they also must monitor and evaluate the quality of the products they produce at all stages of the development and production cycle. TQM is based on a significant new philosophy of managing behaviour in organisations; a detailed discussion of this approach, and ways of managing TQM successfully, can be found in Chapter 9.

Increasing speed, flexibility and innovation

Today, companies can win or lose the competitive race depending on their *speed* – how fast they can bring new products to market – or their *flexibility* – how easily they can change or alter the way they perform their activities to respond to the actions of their competitors. Companies that have speed and flexibility are *agile competitors*: their managers have superior planning and organising abilities; they can think ahead, decide what to do and then speedily mobilise their resources to respond to a changing environment. We examine how managers can build speed and flexibility in their organisations in Chapters 7 and 8.

Innovation – the process of creating new or improved products and services that customers want or developing better ways to produce or provide goods and services – poses a particular challenge. Managers must create an organisational setting in which people are encouraged to be innovative. Typically, innovation takes place in small groups or teams. Management decentralises control of work activities to team members and creates an organisational culture that rewards risk taking. Understanding and managing innovation and creating such a work setting are among the most difficult of managerial tasks. Chapter 18 discusses innovation in more detail.

Increasing responsiveness to customers

Organisations compete for customers with their products and services, so training employees to be responsive to customers' needs is vital for all organisations, and particularly for service organisations. Retail stores, banks and hospitals, for example, depend entirely on their employees to provide high-quality service at a reasonable cost.[41] As many countries (like the UK) move toward a more service-based economy (in part because of the loss of manufacturing jobs to China, Malaysia and other countries with low labour costs), managing behaviour in service organisations is becoming increasingly important. Many organisations are empowering their customer service employees and giving them the authority to take the lead in providing high-quality customer service. As noted previously, the empowering of non-managerial employees changes the role of first-line managers, and often leads to the more efficient use of organisational resources.

Maintaining Ethical and Socially Responsible Standards

Managers at all levels are under considerable pressure to increase the level at which their organisations perform.[42] For example, senior managers receive pressure from shareholders to increase the performance of the entire organisation to boost the stock price, improve profits, or raise dividends. In turn, senior managers may then pressure middle managers to find new ways to use organisational resources to increase efficiency or quality, and thus attract new customers and earn more revenues.

Pressure to increase performance can be healthy for an organisation because it causes managers to question the way the organisation is working and it encourages them to find new and better ways to plan, organise, lead and control. However, too much pressure to perform can be harmful.[43] It may induce managers to behave unethically in dealings with stakeholders both inside and outside the organisation.[44] For example, a purchasing manager for a large retail chain might buy inferior clothing as a cost-cutting measure; or to secure a large foreign contract, a sales manager in a large defence company might offer bribes to foreign officials. The issue of **corporate social responsibility** concerns the obligations that a company should have toward all stakeholders within the communities in which they operate. An example of companies that act in a socially irresponsible and unethical way is now described (Case 1.2).

Case 1.2: **Death through painkillers**

On 30 September 2004 the painkiller Vioxx, manufactured by Merck, one of the largest German pharmaceutical companies, was banned after it had been claimed that more than 60,000 people had died from the drug worldwide. This case caused a series of investigations in Britain, where 103 deaths had been officially linked to the use of Vioxx, although it was believed that the actual figure of Vioxx-related deaths is close to 2,000.

The drug had been sold since 1999 and it was believed that worldwide it had been prescribed to nearly 20 million patients. In the UK the drug had been prescribed to 400,000 patients as it was believed to be a 'miracle drug' treating everything from severe arthritis pain to minor injuries – but without the nasty side-effects of stomach ulcers commonly associated with other painkillers. However, as it turned out, this was not the case: many people died of heart attacks, strokes, or related illnesses.

In their attempts to obtain and maintain market share in an increasingly competitive industry, Merck behaved in an unethical and socially irresponsible way. Investigations uncovered evidence that the cardiovascular problems associated with the drug had been identified by the   ▶

▶ head of research, Edward Scolnick, in 2000. Merck was accused of deliberately withholding information about fatal side-effects in both the US and the UK. A review of confidential material and consent forms for a trial of the drug in the UK showed that many patients had not been told about the risks and concerns related to the use of the drug.

While the UK Legal Service Commission has decided not to fund law suits against Merck, many British relatives of people who died from Vioxx-related side-effects are now considering joining US proceedings against the company, supported by a landmark ruling in Texas where Merck was found negligent and the widow of a Vioxx patient was awarded £141 million.

Unethical behaviour of pharmaceutical companies has already been costly to the industry; Eli Lilly – a research-based pharmaceutical company also operating in the UK – had to pay settlements of more than £380 million when one of its drugs was found to increase the risk of diabetes. However, the company earned more than £2.4 billion from the drug in 2004. Do companies – for profit reasons – take such dangers to patients to be a calculated risk worth taking?!

Managing a Diverse Workforce

Another challenge for managers is to recognise the need to treat human resources in a fair and equitable manner. Today, the age, gender, race, ethnicity, religion, sexual preference and socio-economic makeup of the workforce present new challenges. Managers must establish employment procedures and practices that are legal and fair and do not discriminate against any organisational members.[45]

In the past, white male employees dominated the ranks of management. Today increasing numbers of organisations are realising that to motivate effectively and take advantage of the talents of a diverse workforce, they must make promotion opportunities available to all employees, including women and minorities.[46] Managers must also recognise the performance-enhancing possibilities in the ability to take advantage of the skills and experiences of different kinds of people.[47]

Managers who value their diverse employees not only invest in developing these employees' skills and capabilities but also link rewards to their performance. They are the managers who succeed in promoting performance in the long term.[48] Today, more and more organisations are realising that people are their most important resource and that developing and protecting human resources is an important challenge for management in a competitive global environment. We discuss the complex issues surrounding the management of a diverse workforce in Chapter 5.

Utilising IT and E-Commerce

As has already been discussed, another important challenge for managers is the efficiency of new IT and e-commerce.[49] New technologies such as computer-controlled manufacturing and information systems that link and enable employees in new ways are continually being developed. In a setting that uses self-managed teams, for example, sophisticated computer information systems link the activities of team members so that each member knows what the others are doing. This co-ordination helps to improve quality and increase the pace of innovation. Microsoft, Hitachi, IBM and other companies make extensive use of information systems such as email, the Internet and videoconferencing, accessible by means of PCs, to build a competitive advantage. The importance of IT is discussed in detail in Chapters 16 and 18.

Reaction Time

1. What are the building blocks of competitive advantage? Why is obtaining a competitive advantage important to managers?

2. In what ways do you think managers' jobs have changed the most over the last 10 years? Why have these changes occurred?

Summary and Review

What is management? A manager is a person responsible for supervising the use of an organisation's resources to meet its goals. An organisation is a collection of people who work together and co-ordinate their actions to achieve a wide variety of goals. Management is the process of using organisational resources to achieve organisational goals effectively and efficiently through planning, organising, leading and controlling. An efficient organisation makes the most productive use of its resources. An effective organisation pursues appropriate goals and achieves them by using its resources to create the goods or services that customers want.

Managerial functions The four principal managerial functions are planning, organising, leading and controlling. Managers at all levels of the organisation and in all departments perform these functions. Effective management means managing these activities successfully.

Types of managers Organisations typically have three levels of management. First-line managers are responsible for the day-to-day supervision of non-managerial employees. Middle managers are responsible for developing and utilising organisational resources efficiently and effectively. Senior managers have cross-departmental responsibility. The senior manager's job is to establish appropriate goals for the entire organisation and to verify that department managers are utilising resources to achieve those goals. To increase efficiency and effectiveness, some organisations have altered their managerial hierarchies by restructuring, empowering their workforces, utilising self-managed teams and utilising new IT.

IT and managerial roles and skills According to Mintzberg, managers play 10 different roles: figurehead, leader, liaison, monitor, disseminator, spokesperson, entrepreneur, disturbance handler, resource allocator and negotiator. Three types of skills help managers perform these roles effectively: conceptual, human and technical skills. IT is changing both the way managers perform their roles and the skills they need to perform these roles because it provides richer and more meaningful information.

Challenges for management in a global environment Today's competitive global environment presents many interesting challenges to managers. One of the main challenges is building a competitive advantage by increasing efficiency; quality; speed, flexibility and innovation; and customer responsiveness. Others are behaving ethically toward people inside and outside the organisation; managing a diverse workforce; and utilising new information systems and technologies.

Topic for Action

- Choose an organisation such as a school or a bank; visit it; then list the different organisational resources it uses.

- Visit an organisation, and talk to first-line, middle and senior managers about their respective management roles in the organisation and what they do to help the organisation be efficient and effective.

- Ask a middle or senior manager, perhaps someone you already know, to give examples of how he or she performs the managerial functions of planning, organising, leading and controlling. How much time does he or she spend in performing each function?

- Like Mintzberg, try to find a co-operative manager who will allow you to follow him or her around for a day. List the roles the manager plays, and indicate how much time he or she spends performing them.

Applied Independent Learning

Building Management Skills

Thinking About Managers and Management

Think of an organisation that has provided you with work experience and of the manager to whom you reported (or talk to someone who has had extensive work experience); then answer these questions.

1. Think of your direct supervisor. Of what department is he or she a member, and at what level of management is this person?

2. How do you characterise your supervisor's approach to management? For example, which particular management functions and roles does this person perform most often? What kinds of management skills does this manager have?

3. Do you think the functions, roles and skills of your supervisor are appropriate for the particular job he or she performs? How could this manager improve his or her task performance? How can IT affect this?

4. How did your supervisor's approach to management affect your attitudes and behaviour? For example, how well did you perform as a subordinate, and how motivated were you?

5. Think of the organisation and its resources. Do its managers utilise organisational resources effectively? Which resources contribute most to the organisation's performance?

6. Describe the way the organisation treats its human resources. How does this treatment affect the attitudes and behaviours of the workforce?

7. If you could give your manager one piece of advice or change one management practice in the organisation, what would it be?

8. How attuned are the managers in the organisation to the need to increase efficiency, quality, innovation or responsiveness to customers? How well do you think the organisation performs its prime goals of providing the goods or services that customers want or need the most?

Managing Ethically

Think about an example of unethical behaviour that you observed in the past. The incident could be something you experienced as an employee or a customer or something you observed informally.

1. Either by yourself or in a group, give three reasons why you think the behaviour was unethical. For example, what rules or norms were broken? Who benefited or was harmed by what took place? What was the outcome for the people involved?
2. What steps might you take to prevent such unethical behaviour in the future and encourage people to behave in an ethical way?

Small Group Breakout Exercise

Opening a New Restaurant

Form groups of three or four people, and appoint one group member as the spokesperson who will communicate your findings to the entire class when called on by the instructor. Then discuss the following scenario.

You and your partners have decided to open a large, full service restaurant in your local community; it will be open from 7 a.m. to 10 p.m. to serve breakfast, lunch and dinner. Each of you is investing £50,000 in the venture, and together you have secured a bank loan for an additional £300,000 to begin operations. You and your partners have little experience in managing a restaurant beyond serving meals or eating in restaurants, and you now face the task of deciding how you will manage the restaurant and what your respective roles will be.

1. Decide what each partner's managerial role in the restaurant will be. For example, who will be responsible for the necessary departments and specific activities? Describe your managerial hierarchy.
2. Which building blocks of competitive advantage do you need to establish to help your restaurant succeed? What criteria will you use to evaluate how successfully you are managing the restaurant?
3. Discuss the most important decisions that must be made about (a) planning, (b) organising, (c) leading and (d) controlling, to allow you and your partners to utilise organisational resources effectively and build a competitive advantage.
4. For each managerial function, list the issue that will contribute the most to your restaurant's success.

Exploring the World Wide Web

Use the Internet to find a company or a manager and discover how he or she deals with the four principles of management. Online resources you may want to consider are *The Economist*, *BusinessWeek*, the *Financial Times*, *Management Today* or other current periodicals, newspaper business sections, or professional magazines.

Application in Today's Business World

Can A US-Style Boss Rev Up Siemens?

CEO-designate Kleinfeld cut his teeth in America, but he may meet resistance from labour and polls at home

It's safe to say Klaus Kleinfeld didn't have much trouble adjusting to life in America after Siemens (**SI**) made him chief operating officer of its US units in 2001. Kleinfeld soon won invitations to join the boards of a dozen prestigious organisations including the Metropolitan Opera and Alcoa, Inc. (**AA**) He ran two New York marathons and frequented the city's jazz clubs. Under Kleinfeld, who was promoted to CEO of Siemens' US unit in 2002, the company played a big role in building Houston's Reliant Stadium, scene in February of that most American of events, the Super Bowl.

Now, Kleinfeld, 46, is set to become the latest German manager to parlay US experience and attitude into a top job at a German corporate icon. On 7 July, Siemens announced that, effective in January, Kleinfeld would succeed Heinrich von Pierer as CEO of the $89 billion Munich conglomerate, which makes everything from light bulbs and power plants to trains and mobile phones. The question is whether the energetic Kleinfeld will fare better than some other German bosses who tried to import US-style management techniques, with their emphasis on speed and profit. 'Kleinfeld stands for the modern approach in German industry, of trying to cope with globalisation and move out of the old, well-trodden path,' says Jens van Scherpenberg, head of the Americas Research Unit at the German Institute for International & Security Affairs, a Berlin think tank.

The Right Stuff?

Trouble is, others who fit that description haven't always fared so well. Remember Thomas Middelhoff, the self-styled 'American with a German passport'? He was ousted as CEO of media giant Bertelsmann in 2002 after disagreeing with the controlling family over plans to go public. Then there was Ulrich Schumacher, CEO of chipmaker Infineon Technologies (**IFX**), who led a successful initial public offering on Wall Street but lost his job in March. Schumacher alienated board members and labour representatives with his inclination to act without consulting others – a no-no in consensus-driven Germany.

Kleinfeld, a member of Siemens' corporate executive committee, seems to be a different breed. By choosing Kleinfeld as his successor, von Pierer clearly hopes his young protégé will be more in the mould of Deutsche Telekom (**DT**): CEO Kai-Uwe Ricke, 42, has led a turnaround at the telecom giant. Kleinfeld isn't talking to the press, waiting at least until 28 July, when the Siemens supervisory board is expected to ratify his appointment. But those who know Kleinfeld, who joined Siemens in 1987, say he combines an ability to push change with an antenna for human nature. 'He's young, and he belongs to another generation, but he's also a Siemens guy who knows Siemens culture,' says Roland Berger, chairman of Munich-based Roland Berger Strategy Consultants.

The CEO-designate has already begun to make changes. His fingerprints were on Siemens' decision, also announced on 7 July, to merge the mobile phone division with the land-line telecom unit. In the US, Kleinfeld managed to get Siemens' disparate fiefdoms to co-operate more on marketing. One result was the contract to provide everything from telecom equipment to computer networks for Houston's $750 million Reliant Park convention and sporting complex.

In fact, Kleinfeld probably won the top job because he showed he could get Siemens divisions to work together to win big orders. The company has struggled for years to prove that synergies among branches justify the inherent unwieldiness of a far-flung conglomerate. He also got Siemens' legions of proud engineers to see things more from their customers' point of view. After a $553 million loss in 2001, Siemens reported an $810 million profit for its US units in 2002 and a $561 million profit in 2003, after which he returned to Germany. 'He was instrumental in getting it working,' says Gerhard Schulmeyer, Kleinfeld's predecessor as CEO of Siemens in the US.

Back home, Kleinfeld will have to spend a lot of time smoothing out relations with politicians and unions. In the US, where Siemens had sales of $16.6 billion in 2003, the company cut staff by 15,000 to 65,000, by selling or closing unprofitable units but also by shifting work to lower-wage countries such as India. Von Pierer has reduced the German workforce by more than 50,000 (to 167,000) since becoming CEO in 1992.

Investor Pressure

But by imposing cuts gradually, the diplomatic von Pierer managed to avoid serious confrontation with Germany's powerful labour unions and their allies in Parliament. That is becoming more difficult. Labour leaders are sore that they were forced recently to give in to demands that workers at a mobile phone factory put in extra hours without extra pay: Siemens threatened to shift the work to Hungary. 'Siemens has damaged its image with that kind of action,' says Wolfgang Müller, a worker on the supervisory board.

Siemens' shareholders are another restive constituency. The company's shares have fallen 8.9 per cent this year, vs. a 6.9 per cent gain for their rival the General Electric Co. (**GE**). While Siemens is profitable, earning $1.45 billion on sales of $21 billion in the last quarter, there are problem areas. The telecommunications equipment businesses have wobbly margins, and the transportation unit is in the midst of a costly recall of defective streetcars. Kleinfeld will face pressure from investors to slim down the company. Some analysts also say it would make sense for Siemens to put its mobile-handset business into a **joint venture (JV)** with another manufacturer such as Samsung Electronics Co.

Kleinfeld will have to do a lot of creative thinking. But people who have worked with him say he's good at that. 'He was exceptionally exact but not narrow-minded; on the contrary, very independent and creative,' says Peter Fassheber, a retired professor at Georg-August University in Göttingen who supervised Kleinfeld's research in the early 1980s. Kleinfeld focused on the intersection of psychology and economics. If Kleinfeld can reconcile human nature with economic reality at Siemens, he might just succeed.

Questions

1. How would you describe Klaus Kleinfeld's approach to managing?

2. What skills and abilities helped him rise to become Siemen's CEO?

Source: Jack Ewing, 'Can a US-Style Boss Rev Up Siemens?', adapted and reprinted from *BusinessWeek*, July 26, 2004 by special permission. Copyright © 2004 by the McGraw-Hill Companies, Inc.

Notes and References

1 G. R. Jones, *Organizational Theory, Design, and Change* (Upper Saddle River, NJ: Pearson, 2003).

2 J. P. Campbell, 'On the Nature of Organizational Effectiveness', in P. S. Goodman, J. M. Pennings *et al.*, *New Perspectives on Organizational Effectiveness* (San Francisco: Jossey-Bass, 1977).

3 M. J. Provitera, 'What Management Is: How It Works and Why It's Everyone's Business', *Academy of Management Executive* 17 (August 2003), 152–54.

4 J. McGuire and E. Matta, 'CEO Stock Options: The Silent Dimension of Ownership', *Academy of Management Journal* 46 (April 2003), 255–66.

5 J. G. Combs and M. S. Skill, 'Managerialist and Human Capital Explanations for Key Executive Pay Premium: A Contingency Perspective', *Academy of Management Journal* 46 (February 2003), 63–74.

6 H. Fayol, *General and Industrial Management* (New York: IEEE Press, 1984). Fayol actually identified five different managerial functions, but most scholars today believe that these four capture the essence of his ideas.

7 P. F. Drucker, *Management Tasks, Responsibilities, and Practices* (New York: Harper & Row, 1974).

8 D. McGraw, 'The Kid Bytes Back', *U.S. News & World Report*, December 12, 1994, 70–71.

9 www.apple.com, press release, 2003.

10 G. McWilliams, 'Lean Machine – How Dell Fine-Tunes Its PC Pricing to Gain Edge in a Slow Market', *The Wall Street Journal*, June 8, 2001, A1.

11 J. Kotter, *The General Managers* (New York: Free Press, 1992).

12 C. P. Hales, 'What Do Managers Do? A Critical Review of the Evidence', *Journal of Management Studies*, January 1986, 88–115; A. I. Kraul, P. R. Pedigo, D. D. McKenna and M. D. Dunnette, 'The Role of the Manager: What's Really Important in Different Management Jobs', *Academy of Management Executive*, November 1989, 286–93.

13 A. K. Gupta, 'Contingency Perspectives on Strategic Leadership', in D. C. Hambrick, ed., *The Executive Effect: Concepts and Methods for Studying Top Managers* (Greenwich, CT: JAI Press, 1988), 147–78.

14 D. G. Ancona, 'Top Management Teams: Preparing for the Revolution', in J. S. Carroll, ed., *Applied Social Psychology and Organizational Settings* (Hillsdale, NJ: Erlbaum, 1990); D. C. Hambrick and P. A. Mason, 'Upper Echelons: The Organization as a Reflection of Its Top Managers', *Academy of Management Journal* 9 (1984), 193–206.

15 T. A. Mahony, T. H. Jerdee and S. J. Carroll, 'The Jobs of Management', *Industrial Relations* 4 (1965), 97–110; L. Gomez-Mejia, J. McCann and R. C. Page, 'The Structure of Managerial Behaviors and Rewards', *Industrial Relations* 24 (1985), 147–54.

16 W. R. Nord and M. J. Waller, 'The Human Organization of Time: Temporal Realities and Experiences', *Academy of Management Review* 29 (January 2004), 137–40.

17 R. Stewart, 'Middle Managers: Their Jobs and Behaviors', in J. W. Lorsch, ed., *Handbook of Organizational Behavior* (Englewood Cliffs, NJ: Prentice Hall, 1987), 385–91.

18 K. Labich, 'Making over Middle Managers', *Fortune*, May 8, 1989, 58–64.

19 Office for National Statistics, Information, Communications, and Technology, Economic Trends 603, February 2004.

20 B. Wysocki, 'Some Companies Cut Costs Too Far, Suffer from Corporate Anorexia', *The Wall Street Journal*, July 5, 1995, A1.

21 Department of Health, *Agenda for Change*, 2004.

22 Statistics in Focus, Science, and Technology, 'European Employment Increasing in Services and Especially in Knowledge-Intensive Services', EUROSTAT, 10/2004.

23 National Office for Statistics, Time Series Data.

24 V. U. Druskat and J. V. Wheeler, 'Managing from the Boundary: The Effective Leadership of Self-Managing Work Teams', *Academy of Management Journal* 46 (August 2003), 435–58.

25 S. R. Parker, T. D. Wall and P. R. Jackson, 'That's Not My Job: Developing Flexible Work Orientations', *Academy of Management Journal* 40 (1997), 899–929.

26 B. Dumaine, 'The New Non-Manager', *Fortune*, February 22, 1993, 80–84.

27 H. Mintzberg, 'The Manager's Job: Folklore and Fact', *Harvard Business Review*, July–August 1975, 56–62.

28 H. Mintzberg, *The Nature of Managerial Work* (New York: Harper & Row, 1973).

29 *Ibid.*

30 R. H. Guest, 'Of Time and the Foreman', *Personnel* 32 (1955), 478–86.

31 L. Hill, *Becoming a Manager: Mastery of a New Identity* (Boston: Harvard Business School Press, 1992).

32 *Ibid.*

33 R. L. Katz, 'Skills of an Effective Administrator', *Harvard Business Review*, September–October 1974, 90–102.

34 *Ibid.*

35 P. Tharenou, 'Going Up? Do Traits and Informal Social Processes Predict Advancing in Management?', *Academy of Management Journal* 44 (October 2001), 1005–18.

36 C. J. Collins and K. D. Clark, 'Strategic Human Resource Practices, Top Management Team Social Networks, and Firm Performance: The Role of Human Resource Practices in Creating Organizational Competitive Advantage', *Academy of Management Journal* 46 (December 2003), 740–52.

37 S. C. de Janasz, S. E. Sullivan and V. Whiting, 'Mentor Networks and Career Success: Lessons for Turbulent Times', *Academy of Management Executive*, 17 (November 2003), 78–92.

38 H. G. Baum, A. C. Joel and E. A. Mannix, 'Management Challenges in a New Time', *Academy of Management Journal* 45 (October 2002), 916–31.

39 A. Shama, 'Management Under Fire: The Transformation of Management in the Soviet Union and Eastern Europe', *Academy of Management Executive* 10 (1993), 22–35.

40 National Statistics First Release, SFR 02/2003.

41 K. Seiders and L. L. Berry, 'Service Fairness: What It Is and Why It Matters', *Academy of Management Executive* 12 (1998), 8–20.

42 T. Donaldson, 'Editor's Comments: Taking Ethics Seriously – A Mission Now More Possible', *Academy of Management Review* 28 (July 2003), 363–67.

43 C. Anderson, 'Values-Based Management', *Academy of Management Executive* 11 (1997), 25–46.

44 W. H. Shaw and V. Barry, *Moral Issues in Business*, 6th ed. (Belmont, CA: Wadsworth, 1995); T. Donaldson, *Corporations and Morality* (Englewood Cliffs, NJ: Prentice Hall, 1982).

45 S. Jackson *et al.*, *Diversity in the Workplace: Human Resource Initiatives* (New York: Guilford Press, 1992).

46 G. Robinson and C. S. Daus, 'Building a Case for Diversity', *Academy of Management Executive* 3 (1997), 21–31; S. J. Bunderson and K. M. Sutcliffe, 'Comparing Alternative Conceptualizations of Functional Diversity in Management Teams: Process and Performance Effects', *Academy of Management Journal* 45 (October 2002), 875–94.

47 D. Jamieson and J. O'Mara, *Managing Workforce 2000: Gaining a Diversity Advantage* (San Francisco: Jossey-Bass, 1991).

48 T. H. Cox and S. Blake, 'Managing Cultural Diversity: Implications for Organizational Competitiveness', *Academy of Management Executive*, August 1991, 49–52.

49 D. R. Tobin, *The Knowledge Enabled Organization* (New York: AMACOM, 1998).

Chapter

2

The Evolution of Management Thought

LEARNING OBJECTIVES

After studying this chapter, you should be able to:

☑ Describe how the need to increase organisational efficiency and effectiveness has guided the evolution of management theory.

☑ Explain the principle of job specialisation and division of labour, and say why the study of person–task relationships is central to the pursuit of increased efficiency.

☑ Identify the principles of administration and organisation that underlie effective organisations.

☑ Trace the changes in theories about how managers should behave to motivate and control employees.

☑ Explain the contributions of management science to the efficient use of organisational resources.

☑ Explain why the study of the external environment and its impact on an organisation has become a central issue in management thought.

A Manager's Challenge

Finding Better Ways to Make Cars

What is the best way to use people's skills?

Car production has changed dramatically over the years as managers have applied different principles of management to organise and control work activities. Prior to 1900, small groups of skilled workers co-operated to hand-build cars with parts that often had to be altered and modified to fit together. This system, a type of **small-batch production**, was very expensive; assembling just one car took considerable time and effort and skilled workers could produce only a few cars in a day. Although these cars were of high quality, they were too expensive; managers needed better techniques to increase efficiency, reduce costs and sell more cars.

Henry Ford revolutionised the car industry. In 1913, Ford opened the Highland Park car plant in Detroit to produce the Model T Ford, and his team of manufacturing managers pioneered the development of **mass-production manufacturing**, a system that made the small-batch system almost obsolete overnight. In mass production, moving conveyor belts bring the cars to the workers. Each worker performs a single assigned task along a production line and the speed of the conveyor belt is the primary means of controlling workers' activities. Ford experimented to discover the most efficient way for each worker to perform an assigned task. The result was that each worker performed one narrow, specialised task, such as bolting on the door or attaching the door handle, and jobs in the Ford car plant became very repetitive, requiring little use of a worker's skills.[1] Ford's management approach increased efficiency and reduced costs by so much that by 1920 he was able to reduce the price of a car by two-thirds and to sell more than 2 million cars a year.[2] Ford became the leading car company in the world, and competitors rushed to adopt the new mass-production techniques.

Lean manufacturing

The next change in management thinking about car assembly occurred in Japan when Ohno Taiichi, a Toyota production engineer, pioneered the development of **lean manufacturing** in the 1960s after touring the US plants of the 'Big Three' car companies. The management philosophy behind lean manufacturing is to continuously find methods to improve the efficiency of the production process in order to reduce costs, increase quality and reduce car assembly time. Lean production is based on the idea that if workers have input and can participate continually in the decision-making process, their skills and knowledge can be used to increase efficiency.

In lean manufacturing, workers work on a moving production line, but they are organised into small teams, each of which is responsible for a particular phase of car assembly, such as installing the car's transmission or electrical wiring system. Each team member is expected to learn the tasks of all the members of that team, and each work group is responsible not only for assembling cars but also for continuously finding ways to increase quality and reduce costs. By 1970, Japanese managers had applied the new lean production system so efficiently that they were producing higher-quality cars at lower prices than their US counterparts. By 1980 Japanese companies dominated the global car market.

To compete with the Japanese, managers of US car makers visited Japan to learn the new management principles of lean production. As a result, companies such as General Motors (GM) established the Saturn plant to experiment with this new way of involving workers; GM also established a joint venture with Toyota called New United Motor Manufacturing Inc. (NUMMI), to learn how to achieve the benefits of lean production. Meanwhile, Ford and Chrysler began to change their work processes to take advantage of employees' skills and knowledge.

The balance between people, computers and IT

In the 1990s global car companies increased the number of robots used on the production line and began to use advanced IT to build and track the quality of cars being produced. Indeed, for a time it seemed that robots rather than employees would be building cars in the future. However, Toyota discovered something interesting at its fully roboticised car plant. When only robots build cars, efficiency does not continually increase because, unlike people, robots cannot provide input to improve the work process. The crucial thing is to find the right balance between using people, computers and IT.

In the 2000s, global car companies are continuing to compete fiercely to improve and perfect better ways of making cars. Toyota is constantly pioneering new ways to manage its assembly lines to increase efficiency; however, other Japanese car makers such as Nissan are catching up fast. US car makers are catching up, too: Ford, which made major advances in the 1990s, has now been surpassed by both Chrysler and GM. Both announced in 2004 that their productivity was fast approaching that of Japanese companies and that they expected to match the leaders, Toyota and Nissan, within the next 10 years.

Overview

As this sketch of the evolution of management thinking in global car manufacturing suggests, changes in management practices occur as managers, theorists, researchers and consultants seek new ways to increase organisational efficiency and effectiveness. The driving force behind the evolution of management theory is the search for *better ways to utilise organisational resources.* Advances in management thought typically occur as managers and researchers find better ways to perform the principal management tasks: planning, organising, leading and controlling human and other organisational resources.

This chapter examines how management thought has evolved in modern times and the central concerns that have guided ongoing advances in management theory. First, the so-called 'classical management theories' that emerged around the turn of the twentieth century are examined. These include **scientific management**, which focuses on matching people and tasks to maximise efficiency, and **administrative management**, which focuses on identifying the principles that will lead to the creation of the most efficient system of organisation and management. Next, the chapter considers **behavioural management** theories developed both before and after the Second World War; these focus on how managers should lead and control their workforces to increase performance. A discussion of **management science theory**, which developed during

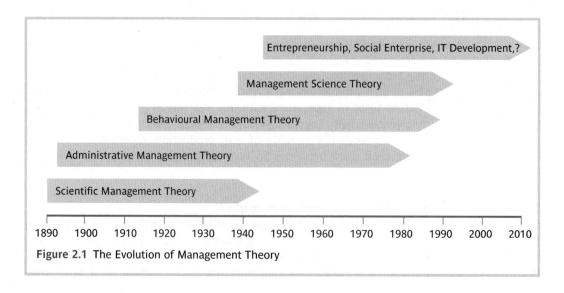

Figure 2.1 The Evolution of Management Theory

the Second World War and has become increasingly important as researchers have developed rigorous analytical and **quantitative techniques** to help managers measure and control organisational performance, follows. Finally, the chapter discusses business in the 1960s and 1970s and focuses on the theories developed to help explain how the external environment can affect the way organisations and managers operate (Fig. 2.1).

Scientific Management Theory

The evolution of modern management began in the closing decades of the nineteenth century, after the industrial revolution had swept through Europe and America. In the new economic climate, managers of all types of organisations – political, educational and economic – were increasingly trying to find better ways to satisfy customers' needs. Many major economic, technical and cultural changes were taking place at this time. The introduction of steam power and the development of sophisticated machinery and equipment changed the way goods were produced, particularly in the weaving and clothing industries. Small workshops run by skilled workers who produced hand-manufactured products (a system called *crafts production*) were being replaced by large factories in which sophisticated machines were controlled by thousands of unskilled or semi-skilled workers who made the products. For example, raw cotton and wool, which in the past had been spun into yarn by families or whole communities, were instead now shipped to factories where workers operated machines that spun and wove large quantities of yarn into cloth.

Owners and managers of the new factories found themselves unprepared for the challenges accompanying the change from small-scale crafts production to large-scale mechanically supported manufacturing. Moreover, many of the managers and supervisors in these workshops and factories were engineers who had the technical skills to support the machinery, but often lacked the craft-specific expertise. Other problems that emerged through this new organisation of production were the social problems that occurred when people worked together in large groups in a factory or shop system. Managers began to search for new techniques to manage their organisations' resources, and soon they began to focus on ways to increase the efficiency of the worker–task mix.

Job Specialisation and the Division of Labour

Initially, management theorists were interested in the subject of why the new machine shops and factory system were more efficient and produced greater quantities of goods and services than older, crafts-style production operations. In the mid-eighteenth century, Adam Smith had been one of the first writers to investigate the advantages associated with producing goods and services in factories. A famous economist, Smith journeyed around England studying the effects of the industrial revolution.[3] In a study of factories that produced various pins or nails, Smith identified two different manufacturing methods. The first was similar to crafts-style production, in which each worker was responsible for all of the 18 tasks involved in producing a pin. The other had each worker performing only one or a few of the 18 tasks that went into making a complete pin.

When he compared the relative performance of these different ways of organising production, Smith found that the performance of the factories in which workers specialised in only one or a few tasks was much greater than the performance of the factory in which each worker performed all 18 pin making tasks. In fact, Smith found that 10 workers specialising in a particular task could make 48,000 pins a day, whereas those workers who performed all the tasks could make only a few thousand at most.[4] Smith reasoned that this difference in performance was due to the fact that the workers who specialised became much more skilled at their specific tasks. Groups were thus able to produce a product faster than groups of individual workers who each performed many tasks. Smith concluded that increasing the level of **job specialisation** increased efficiency and led to higher organisational performance.[5]

Armed with the insights gained from Adam Smith's observations, other managers and researchers began to investigate how to improve job specialisation to increase performance. Management practitioners and theorists focused on how managers should *organise* and *control* the work process to maximise the advantages of job specialisation and the division of labour.

F. W. Taylor and Scientific Management

Frederick W. Taylor (1856–1915) is best known for defining a set of principles known as *scientific management*. This is a systematic study of the relationships between people and tasks for the purpose of redesigning the work process in order to increase efficiency. Taylor was a manufacturing manager who eventually became a consultant and taught other managers how to apply his techniques. Taylor believed that if the amount of time and effort to produce a unit of output could be reduced by increasing job specialisation the production process would become more efficient. According to Taylor, the way to create the most efficient division of labour could best be determined by scientific management techniques. His approach was informed by the natural sciences. He used the scientific method (a systematic approach to test and retest hypotheses) rather than intuitive or informal rule-of-thumb knowledge to identify an *optimal performance level*. Based on his experiments and observations as a manufacturing manager in a variety of settings, he developed four principles to increase efficiency in the workplace:

- **Principle 1**: *Study the way workers perform their tasks, gather all the informal job knowledge that workers possess, and experiment with ways of improving how tasks are performed*

  To discover the most efficient method of performing specific tasks, Taylor studied in great detail and measured the ways different workers went about performing their tasks. One of the main tools he used was a *time-and-motion study*, which involves the careful timing and recording of the actions taken to perform a particular task. Once Taylor understood the existing method of performing a task, he then experimented to increase specialisation. He tried different methods of dividing and co-ordinating the various tasks necessary to produce a finished product: this meant simplifying jobs and having each worker perform fewer, more routine tasks, as at the pin factory or on Ford's car assembly line. Taylor also sought to find ways to improve each worker's ability to perform a particular task, by reducing the number of motions workers made to complete the task, by changing the layout of the work area or the type of tools workers used, or by experimenting with tools of different sizes.

- **Principle 2**: *Codify the new methods of performing tasks into written rules and standard operating procedures*

  Once the best method of performing a particular task was determined, Taylor specified that it should be *recorded* so that this procedure could be taught to all workers performing the same task. These new methods further standardised and simplified jobs by routinising jobs even further, the aim being to increase efficiency throughout an organisation.

■ **Principle 3**: *Carefully select workers who possess skills and abilities that match the needs of the task, and train them to perform the task according to the established rules and procedures*

To increase specialisation, Taylor believed that workers had to understand the tasks that were required of them. They needed to be thoroughly trained to perform the tasks at the optimal level. Workers who could not be trained to this level were to be transferred to a job where they were able to reach the minimum required level of proficiency.[6]

■ **Principle 4**: *Establish a fair or acceptable level of performance for a task, and then develop a pay system that provides a reward for performance above the acceptable level*

To encourage workers to perform at a high level of efficiency, Taylor advocated that workers would benefit from any gains in performance. He provided them with an incentive to reveal the most efficient techniques for performing a task. They should be paid a bonus and receive some percentage of the performance gains achieved through the more efficient work process.[7]

By 1910 Taylor's system of scientific management had become nationally known and in many instances was faithfully and fully practised.[8] However, managers in many organisations chose to implement the new principles of scientific management selectively. This decision ultimately resulted in problems. For example, some managers using scientific management obtained increases in performance, but rather than sharing performance gains with workers through bonuses, as Taylor had advocated, they simply increased the amount of work that each worker was expected to do. Many workers within such a work system found that as their performance increased, they were required to do more work for the same pay. Workers also learned that increases in performance often meant fewer jobs and a greater threat of job loss because fewer workers were needed. In addition, the specialised, simplified jobs were often monotonous and repetitive, and many workers became dissatisfied with their work.

Scientific management brought many workers more hardship than gain, and a distrust of managers who did not seem to care about their well-being.[9] These dissatisfied workers resisted attempts to use the new scientific management techniques and at times even withheld their job knowledge from managers to protect their jobs and pay. It is not difficult for workers to conceal the true potential of a work system to protect their interests: experienced machine operators, for example, can slow their machines in undetectable ways by manipulating this machinery to delay the work process. Workers sometimes even develop informal work rules that discourage high performance and encourage shirking as work groups attempt to identify an acceptable or fair performance level.

Unable to inspire workers to accept the new scientific management techniques for performing tasks, some organisations increased the *mechanisation* of the work process. For example, one reason why Henry Ford introduced moving conveyor belts in his factory was the realisation that when a conveyor belt controls the pace of work (instead of workers setting their own pace), workers can be pushed to perform at higher levels – levels that they might have thought were beyond their reach. Henry Ford also used the principles of scientific management to identify the tasks that each worker should perform on the production line and thus to determine the most effective way to create job specialisation to suit the needs of a mechanised production system.

From a performance perspective, the combination of the two management practices – (1) achieving the right mix of worker–task specialisation and (2) linking people and tasks by the speed of the production line – makes sense. It produces the huge savings in cost and greater increases in output that can occur in large, organised work settings. For example, in 1908 managers at the Franklin Motor Company, using scientific management principles, redesigned the work process. The result was that the output of cars increased from 100 cars a *month* to 45 cars a *day*; workers' wages, however, increased by only 90 per cent.[10] From other perspectives, however, scientific management practices raise many concerns. The definition of workers' rights, not by the workers themselves but by the owners or managers as a result of the introduction of the new management practices, raised an ethical issue, which is examined in Case 2.1.

Case 2.1: Fordism in practice

From 1908 to 1914, through trial and error, Henry Ford's talented team of production managers pioneered the development of the moving conveyor belt and thus changed manufacturing practices forever. Although the technical aspects of the move to mass production were a dramatic financial success for Ford and for the millions of Americans who could now afford cars, for the workers who actually produced the cars many human and social problems resulted.

With simplification of the work process, workers grew to hate the monotony of the moving conveyor belt. By 1914 Ford's car plants were experiencing huge *employee turnover* – often reaching levels as high as 300 or 400 per cent per year as workers left because they could not handle the work-induced stress.[11] Henry Ford recognised these problems and made an announcement: from that point on, to motivate his workforce, he would reduce the length of the workday from 9 hours to 8 hours, and the company would *double* the basic wage from £2.50 to £5.00 per day. This was a dramatic increase, similar to an announcement today of an overnight doubling of the minimum wage. Ford became an internationally famous figure, and the word **Fordism** was coined for his new approach.[12]

Ford's apparent generosity, however, was matched by an intense effort to control the resources – both human and material – with which his empire was built. He employed hundreds of inspectors to check up on employees, both inside and outside his factories. In the factory, supervision was close and confining. Employees were not allowed to leave their places at the production line, and they were not permitted to talk to one another: their job was to concentrate fully on the task at hand. Few employees could adapt to this system, and they developed ways of talking out of the sides of their mouths, like ventriloquists, and invented a form of speech that became known as the 'Ford Lisp'.[13] Ford's obsession with control brought him into greater and greater conflict with managers, who often were fired when they disagreed with him. As a result, many talented people left Ford to join a growing number of rival car companies.

Outside the workplace, Ford went so far as to establish what he called the 'Sociological Department' to check up on how his employees lived and the ways they spent their time. Inspectors from this department visited the homes of employees and investigated their habits and problems. Employees who exhibited behaviours contrary to Ford's standards (for instance, if they drank too much or were always in debt) were likely to be fired. Clearly, Ford's efforts to control his employees led both him and his managers to behave in ways that today would be considered unacceptable and unethical and in the long run would impair an organisation's ability to prosper.

Despite the problems of worker turnover, absenteeism and discontent, managers of the other car companies watched Ford become more efficient through the application of the new management principles. They believed that their companies would have to imitate Ford if they were to survive. They followed Taylor and used many of his followers as consultants to teach them how to adopt the techniques of scientific management. In addition, Taylor elaborated his principles in several books, including *Shop Management* (1903) and *The Principles of Scientific Management* (1911), which explain in detail how to apply the principles of scientific management to reorganise the work system.[14]

Taylor's work has had an enduring effect on the management of production systems. Managers in every organisation, whether it produces goods or services, now carefully analyse the basic tasks that must be performed and try to devise the *work systems* that allow their organisations to operate most efficiently.

Two prominent followers of Taylor were Frank Gilbreth (1868–1924) and Lillian Gilbreth (1878–1972), who refined Taylor's analysis of work movements and made many contributions to time-and-motion study.[15] Their aims were to break down work tasks into individual actions and optimise them so that those actions were performed more efficiently. The aim was to become even more efficient and use less time and effort.

Another aspect of the Gilbreths' research was the study of *worker fatigue*. They identified and tried to manipulate various environmental factors – for example, lighting, heating and design of tools or machines – in order to reduce workers' stress levels. Their pioneering studies paved the way for new advances in management theory.[16]

The Influence of Bureaucracy on Management Theory

Alongside scientific management other research focused on *administrative management*, the study of how to create an *organisational structure* that leads to high efficiency and effectiveness. Organisational structure is used to control the way that employees use resources to achieve the organisation's goals through a system of *task* and *reporting relationships*. Two of the most influential views regarding the creation of efficient systems of organisational administration were developed in Europe: Max Weber, a German professor of sociology, developed the theory of **bureaucracy** and Henri Fayol, a French manager, was the first person to introduce a model of management outlining managerial activities.

The Theory of Bureaucracy

Max Weber (1864–1920) wrote at the turn of the twentieth century when Germany was undergoing its industrial revolution.[17] To help Germany manage its growing industrial enterprises, at a time when it was striving to become a world power, Weber developed the principles of bureaucracy. This is a formal system of organisation and administration designed to ensure efficiency and effectiveness. Bureaucracy is based on the five principles summarised in Fig. 2.2.

- **Principle 1:** *In a bureaucracy, a manager's formal* **authority** *derives from the position he or she holds in the organisation*

  Authority is the power to hold people accountable for their actions and to make decisions concerning the use of organisational resources. Authority gives managers the right to direct and control their subordinates' behaviour to achieve organisational goals. In a bureaucracy,

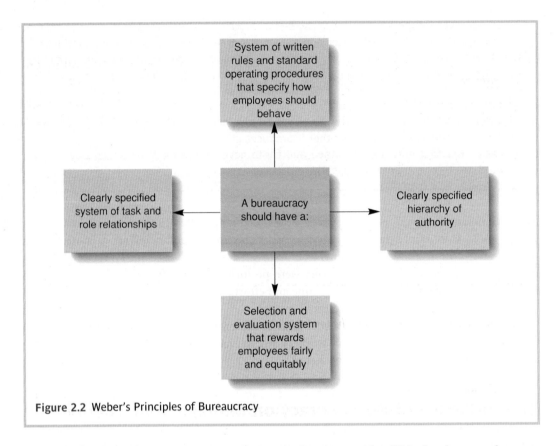

Figure 2.2 Weber's Principles of Bureaucracy

compliance is owed to a manager, not because of any personal qualities but because the manager occupies a position that is associated with a certain level of status and responsibility.[18] Authority is not to be confused with *leadership*, where the relationship is based on the leader's personal qualities.

- **Principle 2:** *In a bureaucracy, people should occupy positions because of their performance, not because of their social standing or personal contacts*

  This principle was not always followed in Weber's time, and is often ignored today. Some organisations and industries are still affected by social networks in which personal contacts and relations, not job-related skills, influence hiring and promotional decisions.

- **Principle 3:** *The extent of each position's formal authority and task responsibilities, and its relationship to other positions in an organisation, should be clearly specified*

  When tasks and authority are clearly specified, managers and workers know what is expected of them, and what to expect from each other. Moreover, an organisation can hold all the employees strictly *accountable* for their actions as their exact responsibilities are known

- **Principle 4:** *Authority can be exercised effectively in an organisation when positions are arranged hierarchically, so employees know whom to report to and who reports to them*[19]

  Managers must create an **organisational hierarchy** of authority that makes it clear who reports to whom, and to whom managers and workers should go if conflicts or problems arise. This principle is especially important in organisations that deal with sensitive issues involving possible major repercussions (e.g. military, government, or intelligence services).

It is vital that managers at the top of the hierarchy are able to hold subordinates accountable for their actions.

- **Principle 5**: *Managers must create a well-defined system of* **rules, standard operating procedures** *and* **norms** *so that they can effectively control behaviour within an organisation*

  Rules are formal, written instructions that specify actions to be taken in different circumstances in order to achieve specific goals. (If a fire alarm is activated, calmly leave the building and assemble at a fire point.)

  Standard operating procedures (SOPs) are specified sets of written instructions about how to perform a certain aspect of a task. A rule might state that at the end of the workday employees are to leave their machines in good order, and a set of SOPs would specify exactly how they should do so, itemising which machine parts should be oiled or replaced.

  Norms are unwritten, informal codes of conduct that prescribe how people should behave in particular situations. Norms usually originate within a community (e.g. a society, a club, a religious group, etc.) and sometimes can become rules. For example, attending lectures at university is an expected code of conduct (a norm). However this could become a rule by making it a formal requirement: non-attendance will result in loss of marks.

Rules, SOPs and norms provide *behavioural guidelines* that increase the performance of a bureaucratic system because they specify the best ways to accomplish organisational tasks. Companies such as McDonald's and Asda have developed extensive rules and procedures to specify the behaviours required of their employees, such as 'Always greet the customer with a smile'.

Weber believed that organisations that implemented all five principles would establish a bureaucratic system improving organisational performance. The specification of positions and the use of rules and SOPs to regulate how tasks are performed made it easier for managers to organise and control the work of subordinates. The behaviour of organisational members was also guided by tacit codes of conduct or norms that were specific to that organisation. Rules, SOPs and norms also informed selection and promotion systems within a bureaucracy. These must be fair and equitable in order to encourage organisational members to act ethically and further promote the interests of the organisation.[20]

If bureaucracies are not managed well, problems can occur. Sometimes managers allow rules and SOPs to take over so that decision making is slow and inefficient and organisations are unable to change. When managers rely too much on rules to solve problems, and not enough on their own skills and judgement, their behaviour becomes inflexible. A key challenge for managers is to use bureaucratic principles to benefit, rather than harm, an organisation.

Fayol's Principles of Management

Henri Fayol (1841–1925), was the CEO of Comambault Mining. Working at the same time as, Weber, Fayol identified 14 principles of management (summarised in Table 2.1) that he believed essential to increase the efficiency of the management process.[21] These principles are discussed in detail here because, although they were developed at the turn of the twentieth century, they remain the foundation on which much of recent management theory and research is based.

Division of labour

Fayol was a champion of job specialisation and the associated idea of the **division of labour**. He nevertheless was also among the first to point out the downside of too much specialisation,

Table 2.1 Fayol's 14 principles of management

- **Division of labour** Job specialisation and the division of labour should increase efficiency, especially if managers take steps to lessen workers' boredom

- **Authority and responsibility** Managers have the right to give orders and the power to exhort subordinates to obey them

- **Unity of command** An employee should receive orders from only one superior

- **Line of authority** The length of the chain of command that extends from the top to the bottom of an organisation should be limited

- **Centralisation** Authority should not be concentrated at the top of the chain of command

- **Unity of direction** The organisation should have a single plan of action to guide managers and workers

- **Equity** All organisational members are entitled to be treated with justice and respect

- **Order** The arrangement of organisational positions should maximise organisational efficiency and provide employees with satisfying career opportunities

- **Initiative** Managers should allow employees to be innovative and creative

- **Discipline** Managers need to create a workforce that strives to achieve organisational goals

- **Remuneration of personnel** The system that managers use to reward employees should be equitable for both employees and the organisation

- **Stability of tenure of personnel** Long-term employees develop skills that can improve organisational efficiency

- **Subordination of individual interests to the common interest** Employees should understand how their performance affects the performance of the whole organisation

- **Esprit de corps** Managers should encourage the development of shared feelings of comradeship, enthusiasm or devotion to a common cause

namely boredom, which may result in a reduction of product quality, worker initiative and flexibility. As a result, Fayol advocated that workers should be given more duties to perform or be encouraged to assume more responsibility for work outcomes, a principle increasingly applied today in organisations that empower their workers.

Authority and responsibility

Like Weber, Fayol emphasised the importance of authority and responsibility. In contrast to Weber, Fayol recognised **informal authority** that derives from personal expertise, technical knowledge, moral worth and the ability to lead and to generate commitment from subordinates. (The study of authority is the subject of recent research into leadership, discussed in Chapter 14.)

Unity of command

The principle of **unity of command** specifies that an employee should receive orders from, and report to, only one superior. Fayol believed that *dual command* – the reporting relationship that exists when two supervisors give orders to the same subordinate – should be avoided. Dual command confuses subordinates, undermines order and discipline and creates difficulties within the formal hierarchy of authority. Not knowing the extent of authority and responsibility held by a manager makes following orders and reporting back a complex task.

Line of authority

The **line of authority** is the chain of command extending from the top to the bottom of an organisation. Fayol was one of the first management theorists to point out the importance of *limiting the length of the chain of command* by controlling the number of levels in the managerial hierarchy. The greater the number of levels in the hierarchy, the more complex and slow communication between managers becomes. Careful consideration of the number of hierarchical levels to lessen these communication problems enables an organisation to act quickly and flexibly; this is one of the reasons for the recent arguments in establishing *flatter* hierarchies (with fewer levels of management).

Fayol also pointed out that when organisations are split into different departments or functions, each with its own hierarchy, it is important to allow middle and first-line managers in each department to interact with managers at similar levels in other departments. This interaction helps to speed decision making because managers know each other and know whom to go to when problems arise. For *cross-departmental integration* to work, Fayol noted how important it was to keep one's superiors informed about what was taking place so that lower-level decisions did not harm activities taking place in other parts of the organisation. One alternative to cross-departmental integration is to create **cross-functional teams**.

Centralisation

Fayol also was one of the first management writers to focus on **centralisation**, the concentration of authority at the senior of the managerial hierarchy. Fayol, as we have seen, believed that authority should not be concentrated at the top of the chain of command. One of the most significant issues that senior managers face is how much authority to centralise at the top of the organisation and what authority to *decentralise* to managers and workers at lower hierarchical levels. This is an important issue, because it affects the behaviour of people at all levels in the organisation.

If authority is centralised, only managers at the top make important decisions, and subordinates simply follow orders. This arrangement gives senior managers control over organisational activities and helps ensure that the organisation is pursuing its strategy, but it makes it difficult for the people who are closest to problems and issues to respond to them in a timely manner. It also can lower the motivation of middle and first-line managers and make them less flexible and adaptable because they become reluctant to make decisions on their own, even when doing so is necessary. They get used to being *reactive* to decisions being made at the top of the hierarchy. A recent trend is toward decentralisation, as organisations seek to empower middle managers and create self-managed teams that monitor and control their own activities to increase organisational flexibility by being able to respond to problems as and when they occur. This enables a reduction in operating costs and increases efficiency.

Unity of direction

Just as there is a need for unity of command, there is also a need for **unity of direction**, one single purpose that makes possible the creation of a single plan of action to guide managers and workers as they use organisational resources. An organisation without a single guiding plan becomes inefficient and ineffective; its activities become unfocused, and individuals and groups work towards different goals. Successful planning starts with senior managers working as a team to craft the organisation's strategy, which they communicate to middle managers, who decide how to use organisational resources to implement it.

Equity

As Fayol wrote, 'For personnel to be encouraged to carry out their duties with all the devotion and loyalty of which they are capable, they must be treated with respect for their own sense of integrity, and equity results from the combination of respect and justice'.[22] **Equity** – the justice, impartiality and fairness to which all organisational members are entitled – is receiving much attention today: the desire to treat employees fairly should be a primary concern for all managers.

Order

Fayol was also interested in analysing jobs, positions and individuals to ensure that the organisation was using its resources as efficiently as possible. To Fayol, **order** meant the methodical arrangement of positions to provide the organisation with the greatest benefit and to provide employees with career opportunities that satisfied their needs. Fayol recommended the use of *organisational charts* to show the position and duties of each employee and to indicate which positions an employee might move to or be promoted into in the future. He also advocated that managers engage in extensive *career planning* to help ensure orderly career paths. Career planning is of primary interest today as organisations increase the resources they are willing to devote to training and developing their workforces.

Initiative

Although order and equity are important means of fostering commitment and loyalty among employees, Fayol believed that managers must also encourage employees to exercise **initiative**, the ability to act and react on their own, without direction from a superior. Used properly, encouraging initiative can be a major source of strength for an organisation because it leads to *creativity* and *innovation*. Managers need skill and tact to achieve the difficult balance between the organisation's need for order and the employees' desire for initiative: Fayol believed that the ability to strike this balance was a key indicator of a superior manager.

Discipline

In focusing on the importance of **discipline** – obedience, energy, application and other outward marks of respect for a superior's authority – Fayol was addressing the concern of many early managers: how could they create a workforce that was reliable and hardworking and would strive to achieve organisational goals? According to Fayol, discipline results in respectful relations between organisational members and reflects the quality of an organisation's leadership and a manager's ability to act fairly and equitably.

Remuneration of personnel

Fayol proposed **reward systems**, including bonuses and profit-sharing plans, which are increasingly utilised today as organisations seek to improve ways to motivate employees. Convinced by his own experience that an organisation's payment system has important implications for organisational success, Fayol believed that effective reward systems should be equitable for both employees and the organisation, encourage productivity by rewarding well-directed effort, not be subject to abuse and be uniformly applied to employees.

Stability of tenure of personnel

Fayol also recognised the importance of *long-term employment*, an idea that has been discussed extensively within contemporary management. Even though stability of tenure was positively advocated within the twentieth century, its achievement in the twenty-first century has become more complex. One of the advantages when employees stay with an organisation for extended periods of time is that they develop skills that improve the organisation's overall ability to utilise its resources.[23]

Subordination of individual interests to the common interest

The interests of the organisation as a whole must take precedence over the interests of any one individual or group if the organisation is to survive (this is known as 'utilitarianism'). Equitable agreements must be established between the organisation and its members to ensure that employees are treated fairly and rewarded for their performance, and to maintain the disciplined organisational relationships vital to an efficient system of administration.

Esprit de corps

As this discussion of Fayol's ideas suggests, the appropriate design of an organisation's hierarchy of authority and the right mix of order and discipline foster co-operation and commitment. Likewise, a key element in a successful organisation is the development of **esprit de corps**, a French expression that refers to shared feelings of comradeship, enthusiasm or devotion to a common cause among members of a group – not unlike a norm (Case 2.2). *Esprit de corps* can result when managers encourage personal, verbal contact between managers and workers and encourage communication to solve problems and implement solutions. (Today, the term **organisational culture** is used to refer to these shared feelings; this concept is discussed at length in Chapter 3.)

Case 2.2: Peters and Waterman's excellent companies[24]

In the early 1980s, Tom Peters and Robert Waterman identified 62 organisations that they considered to be the best-performing US organisations. They asked the question: Why do these companies perform better than their rivals? They discovered that successful organisations have managers who manage according to three sets of related principles, which have a great deal in common with Fayol's principles that we have just discussed.

First, Peters and Waterman argued, senior managers of successful companies create principles and guidelines that emphasise managerial autonomy and entrepreneurship and encourage risk taking and *initiative*. For example, they allow middle managers to develop new products, even though there is no assurance that these products will be winners. In high-performing organisations, senior managers are closely involved in the day-to-day operations of the company, provide *unity of command* and *unity of direction*, and do not simply make decisions in an isolated ivory tower. Senior managers *decentralise authority* to lower-level managers and non-managerial employees, and give them the freedom to get involved and the motivation to get things done.

The second approach that managers of excellent organisations use to increase performance is to create one central plan that puts **organisational goals** at centre stage. In high-performing organisations, managers focus attention on *what the organisation does best*, and the emphasis is on continuously improving the goods and services the organisation provides to its customers. Managers of top-performing companies resist the temptation to get sidetracked into pursuing ventures outside their area of expertise just because they seem to promise a quick return. These managers also focus on customers and establish close relationships with them to learn their needs for, as we have seen, responsiveness to customers increases competitive advantage. ▶

▶
> The third set of management principles pertains to organising and controlling the organisation. Excellent companies establish a *division of labour* and a *division of authority and responsibility* that will motivate employees to subordinate their individual interests to the common interest (remember Fayol). Inherent in this approach is the belief that high performance derives from individual skills and abilities and that *equity, order, initiative* and other indications of respect for the individual create the *esprit de corps* that fosters productive behaviour. An emphasis on entrepreneurship and respect for every employee leads the best managers to create a structure that gives employees room to exercise initiative and motivates them to succeed. Because a simple, streamlined managerial hierarchy is best suited to achieve this outcome, senior managers keep the line of authority as short as possible. They also decentralise authority to permit employee participation, but they keep enough control to maintain *unity of direction*.

As this insight into contemporary management suggests, the basic concerns that motivated Fayol continue to motivate management theorists today.[25] The principles that Fayol and Weber set out have in the past provided a clear and appropriate set of guidelines that managers can use to create a work setting that makes efficient and effective use of organisational resources. These principles remain a foundation of modern management theory and more recent researchers have refined or developed them to suit modern conditions. For example, Weber's and Fayol's concerns for equity and for establishing appropriate links between performance and reward are central themes in contemporary theories of motivation and leadership. However, today's organisational internal and external environments have become more complex. General managerial principles are not always implementable or appropriate across different contexts. Some authors argue that these 'practices do not match advanced sustainability principles' in modern organisations.[26]

Behavioural Management Theory

Behavioural management theory emanates from American management theorists who began where Taylor and his followers reached their height. Although their writings were all very different, these theorists all espoused a theme that focused on *behavioural management* – the study of how managers should personally behave to motivate employees and encourage them to perform at high levels and be committed to achieving organisational goals.

Mary Parker Follett (1868–1933) was one such theorist who focused her work on the way managers should behave toward workers. She criticised Taylor's scientific approach because it took little account of individual differences and ignored the human side of the organisation. She pointed out that management often overlooks the multitude of ways in which employees can contribute to the organisation when managers allow them to participate and exercise initiative in their everyday work lives.[27]

Whereas Taylor used time-and-motion experts to analyse workers' jobs for them, Follett thought the workers themselves should be involved in the job analysis process. Follett argued that as the workers knew most about their own jobs, they should be allowed to participate in the work development process. Follett proposed that 'authority should go with knowledge . . . whether it is up the line or down'.[28] In other words, if workers have the relevant knowledge, then workers, rather than managers, should be in control of the work process itself, and managers should behave as *coaches* and *facilitators* – not as monitors and supervisors. Follett thus anticipated the current interest in self-managed teams and empowerment. She also recognised the importance of managers being able to directly communicate with each other across different departments in order to optimise decision making. She advocated what she called 'cross-functioning': members of different departments working together in cross-departmental teams to accomplish projects – an approach that is increasingly utilised today.[29]

Fayol saw expertise and knowledge as important sources of managers' authority, but Follett went further. Whereas Fayol argued that leaders emerged from managers' formal authority derived from their position in the hierarchy, Follett proposed that knowledge and expertise should decide who would lead at any particular moment. She believed, as do many management theorists today, that *power is fluid* and should flow to the person who can best help the organisation achieve its goals. In contrast to Fayol's hierarchical bureaucratic approach, Follett took a *horizontal* view of power and authority, and believed that effective management came from the way people interacted and reinforced each other – an approach that was very radical for its time.

The Hawthorne Studies and the Human Relations Movement

Follett's work began to focus on the 'human' which until quite recently was unappreciated by both managers and researchers. Most continued to follow in the footsteps of Taylor to increase efficiency and studied ways to improve various characteristics of the work setting, such as job specialisation or the kinds of tools workers used. One series of studies was conducted from 1924 to 1932 at the Hawthorne Works of the Western Electric Company.[30] This research, now known as the *Hawthorne studies*, began as an attempt to investigate how characteristics of the work setting – specifically, the level of lighting or illumination – affected worker fatigue and performance. The researchers conducted an experiment in which they systematically measured worker productivity at various levels of illumination.

The experiment produced some unexpected results. The researchers found that regardless of whether they raised or lowered the level of illumination, productivity increased. In fact, productivity began to fall only when the level of illumination dropped so low that, presumably, workers could no longer see well enough to do their work efficiently.

The researchers found these results puzzling and invited a noted Harvard psychologist, Elton Mayo, to help them. Mayo proposed another series of experiments known as the *relay assembly test experiments*. These were designed to investigate the effects of other aspects of the work context on job performance, such as the effect of the number and length of rest periods and hours of work on fatigue and monotony.[31] The goal was to raise productivity.

During a two-year study of a small group of female workers, the researchers again observed that productivity increased over time, but that the increases could not be solely attributed to the effects of changes in the work setting. Gradually, the researchers discovered that, to some degree, the results they were obtaining were influenced by the fact that the researchers themselves had become part of the experiment. In other words, the presence of the researchers was affecting the results because the workers enjoyed receiving attention and being the subject of study, and were willing to co-operate with the researchers to produce the results that they believed the researchers desired.

Subsequently, it was found that many other factors also influenced worker behaviour, and it was not clear what actually was influencing the Hawthorne workers' behaviour. However, this particular effect – which became known as the **Hawthorne effect** – seemed to suggest that workers' attitudes toward their managers affected the level of workers' performance. In particular, the significant finding was that each manager's personal behaviour or leadership approach can affect performance. This finding led many researchers to turn their attention to managerial behaviour and leadership. If supervisors could be trained to behave in ways that would elicit co-operative behaviour from their subordinates, then productivity could be increased. From this view emerged the **human relations movement**, which advocated that supervisors should be behaviourally trained to manage subordinates in ways that elicited their co-operation and increased their productivity.

The importance of behavioural or human relations training became even clearer to its supporters after another series of experiments – the *bank wiring room experiments*. In a study of workers making telephone switching equipment, researchers Elton Mayo and F. J. Roethlisberger discovered that the workers, as a group, had deliberately adopted a norm of output restriction to protect their jobs. Workers who violated this informal production norm were subjected to sanctions by other group members. Those who violated group performance norms and performed above the norm were called 'rate-busters'; those who performed below the norm were called 'chiselers'.

The experimenters concluded that both types of workers threatened the group as a whole. Rate-busters threatened group members because they revealed to managers how fast the work could be done. Chiselers were looked down on because they were not doing their share of the work. Work-group members disciplined both rate-busters and chiselers to create a pace of work that the workers (not the managers) thought was fair. A work group's influence over output can thus be as great as the supervisors' influence. Since the work group can influence the behaviour of its members, some management theorists argue that supervisors should be trained to behave in ways that gain the goodwill and co-operation of workers so that supervisors, not workers, control the level of work-group performance.

One of the main implications of the Hawthorne studies was that the behaviour of managers and workers in the work setting is as important in explaining the level of performance as the technical aspects of the task. Managers must understand the workings of the **informal organisation** – the system of behavioural rules and norms that emerges in a group when they try to manage or change behaviour in an organisation. Many studies have found that, as time passes, groups often develop elaborate procedures and norms that bond members together, allowing unified action either to co-operate with management to raise performance or to restrict output and thwart the attainment of organisational goals.[32] The Hawthorne studies demonstrated the importance of understanding how the feelings, thoughts and behaviour of work-group members and managers affect performance. It was becoming increasingly clear to researchers that understanding behaviour in organisations was a complex process that was critical to increasing performance.[33] Indeed, the increasing interest in the area of management known as **organisational behaviour** – the study of the factors that have an impact on how individuals and groups respond to and act in organisations – dates from these early studies.

Theory X and Theory Y

Several studies after the Second World War revealed how assumptions about workers' attitudes and behaviour affected managers' behaviour. One influential approach was developed by Douglas McGregor. He proposed two sets of assumptions about how work attitudes and behaviours not only dominate the way managers think but also affect how they behave in organisations. McGregor named these two contrasting sets of assumptions **Theory X** and **Theory Y** (Fig. 2.3).[34]

THEORY X	THEORY Y
The average employee is lazy, dislikes work and will try to do as little as possible	Employees are not inherently lazy: given the chance, employees will do what is good for the organisation
To ensure that employees work hard, managers should closely supervise employees	To allow employees to work in the organisation's interest, managers must create a work setting that provides opportunities for workers to exercise initiative and self-direction
Managers should create strict work rules and implement a well-defined system of rewards and punishments to control employees	Managers should decentralise authority to employees and make sure employees have the resources necessary to achieve organisational goals

Figure 2.3 Theory X versus Theory Y

Source: Adapted from D. McGregor, *The Human Side of Enterprise* (New York: McGraw-Hill, 1960), reproduced with permission of the McGraw-Hill Companies, Inc.

Theory X

Theory X rests on an essentially *negative* view of people. It assumes that the average worker is lazy, dislikes work and will try to do as little as possible. Moreover, workers have little ambition and wish to avoid responsibility. The manager's task is thus to counteract workers' natural tendencies to avoid work. To keep workers' performance at a high level, the manager must supervise workers closely and control their behaviour by means of 'the carrot and stick' – rewards and punishments.

Managers who accept the assumptions of Theory X design and shape the work setting to maximise their control over workers' behaviours and minimise workers' control over the pace of work. These managers believe that workers must be made to do what is necessary for the success of the organisation, and they focus on developing rules, SOPs and a well-defined system of rewards and punishments to control behaviour. They see little point in giving workers autonomy to solve their own problems because they think that the workforce neither expects nor desires co-operation. Theory X managers see their role as closely monitoring workers to ensure that they contribute to the production process and do not threaten product quality. Henry Ford, who closely supervised and managed his workforce, fits McGregor's description of a manager who holds Theory X assumptions.

Theory Y

In contrast, Theory Y rests on a *positive* view of people and assumes that workers are not inherently lazy, do not naturally dislike work and, if given the opportunity, will do what is good for the organisation. According to Theory Y, the characteristics of the work setting determine whether workers consider work to be a source of satisfaction or punishment, and managers do not need to closely control workers' behaviour to make them perform at a high level because workers exercise self-control when they are committed to organisational goals. The implication of Theory Y, according to McGregor, is that 'the limits of collaboration in the organisational setting are not limits of human nature but of management's ingenuity in discovering how to realise the potential represented by its human resources'.[35] It is the manager's task to create a work setting that encourages commitment to organisational goals and provides opportunities for workers to be imaginative and to exercise initiative and self-direction.

When managers design the organisational setting to reflect the assumptions about attitudes and behaviour suggested by Theory Y, the characteristics of the organisation are quite different from those of an organisational setting based on Theory X. Managers who believe that workers are motivated to help the organisation reach its goals can decentralise authority and give more control over the job to workers, both as individuals and in groups. In this setting, individuals and groups are still accountable for their activities, but the manager's role is not to control employees but to provide support and advice, to make sure employees have the resources they need to perform their jobs, and to evaluate them on their ability to help the organisation meet its goals. Henri Fayol's approach to administration more closely reflects the assumptions of Theory Y rather than Theory X. One company that has always operated with the type of management philosophy inherent in Theory Y is Hewlett-Packard, the subject of Case 2.3.

Case 2.3: **The Hewlett-Packard way**

Managers at the electronics company Hewlett-Packard (HP) consistently put into practice principles derived from Theory Y. (Go to the company's website at www.hp.com for additional information.) Founders William Hewlett and David Packard – Bill and Dave, as they are still known throughout the organisation – established a philosophy of management known as the 'HP Way' that is people-oriented, stresses the importance of treating every person with consideration and respect and offers recognition for achievements.[36]

HP's philosophy rests on a few guiding principles. One is a policy of long-term employment. HP goes to great lengths not to lay off workers. At times when fewer people were needed, rather than lay off workers management cut pay and shortened the workday until demand for HP products picked up. This policy strengthened employees' loyalty to the organisation.

The HP Way is based on several golden rules about how to treat members of the organisation so that they feel free to be innovative and creative. HP managers believe that every employee of the company is a member of the HP team. They emphasise the need to increase the level of communication among employees, believing that horizontal communication between peers, not just vertical communication up and down the hierarchy, is essential for creating a positive climate for innovation.

To promote communication and co-operation between employees at different levels of the hierarchy, HP encourages informality. Managers and workers are on a first-name basis with each other and with the founders, Bill and Dave. In addition, Bill and Dave pioneered the technique known as 'managing by wandering around'. People are expected to wander around learning what others are doing so that they can tap into opportunities to develop new products or find new avenues for co-operation. Bill and Dave also pioneered the principle that employees should spend 15 per cent of their time working on projects of their own choosing, and they encouraged employees to take equipment and supplies home to experiment with them in their own time. HP's product design engineers leave their current work out in the open on their desks so that anybody can see what they are doing, can learn from it or can suggest ways to improve it. Managers are selected and promoted because of their ability to engender excitement and enthusiasm for innovation in their subordinates. HP's offices have low walls and shared laboratories to facilitate communication and co-operation between managers and workers. In all these ways, HP managers seek to promote each employee's desire to be innovative and also to create a team and family atmosphere based on co-operation.[37]

The results of HP's practices helped it become one of the leading electronics companies in the world. In 2001, however, HP, like most other high-tech companies, was experiencing major problems because of the collapse of the telecommunications industry, and the company announced that it was searching for ways to reduce costs. At first, its current CEO, Carly Fiorino, in keeping with the management philosophy and values of the company's founders, announced that HP would not lay off employees but asked them to accept lower salaries and unpaid leave to help the company through this rough spot. It soon became clear, however, that HP's very survival was at stake as it battled with efficient global competitors such as Dell and Canon. To fight back, HP merged with Compaq, but by 2004 it had been forced to lay off over 40 per cent of its employees and outsource thousands of jobs abroad in order to remain competitive. Fiorino still believes, however, that HP's values will survive its crisis and help it become the global leader in the next decade.[38]

Reaction Time

Describe the division of labour and job specialisation that your university adopts to produce its service to students, and consider how this might be improved.

The Systems View

An important milestone in the history of management development occurred when researchers went beyond the study of how managers could influence behaviour within organisations to consider how managers control the organisation's relationship with its *external environment*, or organisational environment. This is the set of forces and conditions that operate beyond an organisation's boundaries but affect a manager's ability to acquire and utilise resources. Resources in the organisational environment include the raw materials and skilled people that an organisation requires to produce goods and services, as well as the support of groups including customers who buy these goods and services and provide the organisation with financial resources. One way of determining the relative success of an organisation is to consider how effective its managers are at obtaining scarce and valuable resources.[39] The importance of studying the environment became clear after the development of open-systems theory and contingency theory during the 1960s.

One of the most influential views of how an organisation is affected by its external environment was developed by Daniel Katz, Robert Kahn and James Thompson in the 1960s.[40] These theorists viewed the organisation as an open system – a system that takes in resources from its external environment and converts or transforms them into products and services that are sent back to that environment, where they are bought by customers (Fig. 2.4).

At the *input stage* an organisation acquires resources such as raw materials, money and skilled workers to produce goods and services. Once the organisation has gathered the necessary

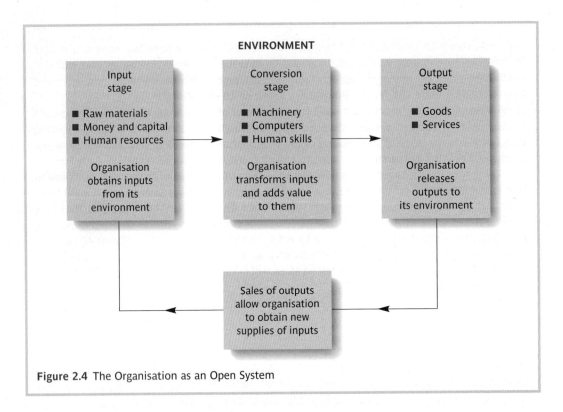

Figure 2.4 The Organisation as an Open System

resources, transformation begins. At the *transformation stage* the organisation's workforce, using appropriate tools, techniques and machinery, transforms the inputs into outputs of finished products and services such as cars, hamburgers or flights to Europe. At the *output stage* the organisation releases finished products and services to its external environment, where customers purchase and use them to satisfy their needs. The money the organisation obtains from the sales of its outputs allows the organisation to acquire more resources so that the cycle can begin again.

The system just described is said to be 'open' because the organisation draws from, and interacts with, the external environment in order to survive: in other words, the organisation is open to its environment. A **closed system**, in contrast, is a self-contained system that is not affected by changes in its external environment. Organisations that operate as closed systems – that ignore the external environment and fail to acquire inputs – are likely to experience **entropy** – the tendency of a closed system to lose its ability to control itself and thus to dissolve and disintegrate. However, closed systems are unlikely to exist in either the natural world or the world of management. No organisation can exist in a vacuum as they all have to interact with customers, suppliers, the workforce and other factors within the external environment.

Management theorists can model the activities of most organisations by using the open-systems view. Manufacturing companies such as Ford and Siemens, for example, buy inputs such as component parts, skilled and semi-skilled labour, and robots and computer-controlled manufacturing equipment; at the transformation stage they use their manufacturing skills to assemble inputs into outputs of cars and appliances.

Researchers using the systems view are also interested in how the various parts of a system work together to promote efficiency and effectiveness. Systems theorists like to argue that the whole is greater than the sum of its parts; they mean that an organisation performs at a higher level when its departments work together rather than separately. **Synergy** – the performance gains that result from the *combined* actions of individuals and departments – is possible only in an organised system. The recent interest in using teams combined or composed of people from different departments reflects systems theorists' interest in designing organisational systems to create synergy, and thus increase efficiency and effectiveness. While each individual or department can exist as a viable unit, the increase in efficiency and effectiveness results from the ability to perform a task that neither of the individual units can perform alone. This is known as an **emergent property**.

Management Science Theory

Management science theory is a contemporary approach to management that adopts a systems view. It focuses on the use of rigorous quantitative techniques to help managers to maximise the use of organisational resources to produce goods and services. In essence, management science theory is a contemporary extension of scientific management, which also took a quantitative approach to measuring the worker–task mix to raise efficiency. What scientific management did not achieve was to account for the external factors that influence an organisation.

Essentially, within the social sciences there are two polarising views of the world that have evolved from philosophy. A *quantitative* approach such as scientific management, or management science, is also referred to as an objective approach or 'positivism' – the proposition being that the world reflects an objective reality that can be represented unambiguously in management models. In contrast, a world view based on the assumption that society is socially constructed is known as a *qualitative* approach. Here the proposition is that we make sense of the world through our own thought processes and social interactions with others. Such an approach reflects our subjective experience of the world and is also called a 'phenomenological' approach.[41] An example of this view is behavioural management theory.

There are many branches of management science and each uses different approaches in order to develop tools and techniques and best management practices. Each branch of management science deals with a specific set of concerns:

- **Quantitative management** utilises mathematical techniques – such as linear and non-linear programming, modelling, simulation, queuing theory and chaos theory – to help managers decide, for example, how much inventory to hold at different times of the year, where to locate a new factory and how best to invest an organisation's financial capital. As this represents a systems view, new IT offers managers new and improved ways of handling information so that they can make more accurate assessments of the situation and better decisions.

- **Operations management** provides managers with a set of techniques that they can use to analyse any aspect of an organisation's production system to increase efficiency. *TQM*, for example, focuses on analysing an organisation's input, transformation and output activities to increase product quality.[42] TQM represents the most sophisticated systems view of quality management; however, it is part of a wider set of approaches to quality management.

- **Management information systems (MIS)** help managers design systems that provide information about events occurring inside the organisation as well as in its external environment – information that is vital for effective decision making. IT gives managers access to more and better information and allows more managers at all levels to participate in the decision-making process.

■ **Soft systems approaches** to management adopt a system view to help managers deal with the human aspect of organisations. Their prime concern is the modelling of the subjective experiences of the people within the organisation to solve performance-related problems.[43]

All these subfields of management science provide tools and techniques that managers can use to help improve the quality of their decision making and problem solving to increase efficiency and effectiveness. Many important developments in management science theory informed other aspects of management such as managing information systems and technologies, and operations management.

Contingency Theory

Another milestone in management theory was the development of *contingency theory* in the 1960s by Tom Burns and G. M. Stalker in Britain and Paul Lawrence and Jay Lorsch in the United States.[44] The crucial message of contingency theory is that *there is no one best way to organise*: the organisational structures and the control systems that managers choose depend on – are *contingent* on – characteristics of the external environment in which the organisation operates. According to contingency theory, the characteristics of the environment affect an organisation's ability to obtain resources. In order to maximise the likelihood of gaining access to resources, managers must allow individual departments to organise and control their own activities in ways most likely to allow them to obtain resources. Each environment poses different challenges to organisations. In other words, how managers design the organisational hierarchy, choose a control system and lead and motivate their employees is contingent on the characteristics of the organisational environment (Fig. 2.5).

An important characteristic of the external environment that affects an organisation's ability to obtain resources is the degree to which the environment is *changing*. Changes in the organisational environment can include changes in technology, which can lead to the creation of new

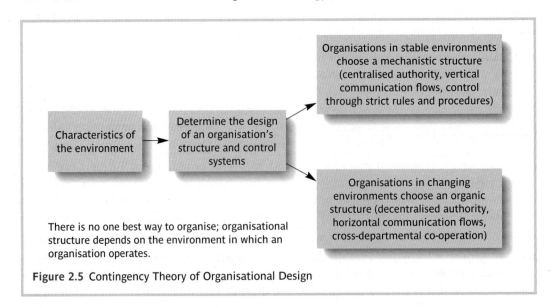

Organisations in stable environments choose a mechanistic structure (centralised authority, vertical communication flows, control through strict rules and procedures)

Characteristics of the environment

Determine the design of an organisation's structure and control systems

Organisations in changing environments choose an organic structure (decentralised authority, horizontal communication flows, cross-departmental co-operation)

There is no one best way to organise; organisational structure depends on the environment in which an organisation operates.

Figure 2.5 Contingency Theory of Organisational Design

products (such as compact discs) and result in the obsolescence of existing products (eight-track tapes); the entry of new competitors (such as foreign organisations that compete for available resources); and unstable economic conditions. In general, the more rapidly the organisational environment changes the greater are the problems associated with gaining access to resources. Therefore, managers need to find different ways to co-ordinate the activities of people in different departments to respond to the environment quickly and effectively.

Mechanistic and organic structures

Drawing on Weber's and Fayol's principles of organisation and management, Burns and Stalker proposed two basic ways in which managers can organise and control an organisation's activities to respond to characteristics of its external environment: They can use a **mechanistic structure** or an **organic structure**.[45] As you will see, a mechanistic structure typically rests on *Theory X* assumptions and an organic structure typically rests on *Theory Y* assumptions.

When the environment surrounding an organisation is stable, managers tend to choose a mechanistic structure to organise and control activities and make employee behaviour predictable. In a mechanistic structure, authority is centralised at the senior of the managerial hierarchy and the vertical hierarchy of authority is the main means to control subordinates' behaviour. Tasks and roles are clearly specified, subordinates are closely supervised and the emphasis is on strict discipline and order. Everyone knows his or her place, and there is a place for everyone. A mechanistic structure provides the most efficient way to operate in a stable environment because it may allow managers to obtain inputs at the lowest cost, giving an organisation the most control over its transformation processes and enabling the most efficient production of goods and services with the smallest expenditure of resources (job specialisation). McDonald's restaurants operate within a mechanistic structure: supervisors make all the important decisions, employees are closely supervised and follow well-defined rules and standard operating procedures.

In contrast, when the environment is changing rapidly, it is difficult to obtain access to resources, and managers need to organise their activities in a way that allows them to co-operate. In addition managers need to act quickly to acquire resources (such as new types of inputs to produce new kinds of products), and to respond effectively to the unexpected. In an organic structure, authority is decentralised to middle and first-line managers to encourage them to take responsibility and pursue scarce resources. Departments are encouraged to take a cross-departmental or functional perspective and, as in Mary Parker Follett's model, authority rests with the individuals and departments best positioned to control the current problems the organisation is facing. In an organic structure, control is much looser than in a mechanistic structure, and reliance on shared norms to guide organisational activities is greater. Managers in an organic structure can react more quickly to a changing environment than can managers in a mechanistic structure. However, an organic structure is generally more expensive to operate because it requires that more managerial time, money and effort be spent on co-ordination. So it is used only when needed – when the organisational environment is unstable and rapidly changing.

Management Theory in the Twenty-first Century

Theories used in the past may have relevance only for an understanding of how organisations evolved into what we observe in the twenty-first century. As complex as the problems are in today's organisations, authors argue that no one management model can be applied for every organisational challenge in every type of organisation.[46]

It is important to understand the evolution of management because human and management problems remain basically unchanged over time. While our value systems and perspective may have changed, experts have gained a better understanding of what motivates workers. Peter Drucker, a management guru, observed that at various times in history (usually in times of economic depression) there has been hostility towards business. For this reason management across the public sector today was 'renamed' public administration and treated as a separate discipline with its own university departments. Obviously the basic principles of management are applicable to all types of organisations – however, the difference is not in the principles, but how those principles are applied. So whether you are managing a community welfare agency, a software company, a retail firm or a library, the differences, says Drucker, 'amount to only about 10 per cent of your work'.[47]

Drucker believed that management had to do with empowering one's workers and believed in the social dimension of management. He saw employees as resources, rather than simply costs. He disagreed with the assembly-line mentality of manufacturing as it failed to allow workers any individual creativity. In the 1990s Drucker argued that the world was moving from an *economy of goods* to an *economy of knowledge* and became one of America's leading critics of exorbitantly paid executives. Drucker believes that management has to move away from a 'Taylorism' mentality – treating people as cogs in a huge inhuman machine – and begin to treat them as if they had a brain. He therefore considered that knowledge, and hence education, was the single most important resource for any advanced society.[48]

Although Drucker was an advocate of the human relations movement, he was also objective in his approach: he invented one of the key rational ideas in management – **management by objectives (MBO)**.[49]

Reaction Time

1. In what ways are Weber's and Fayol's ideas about bureaucracy and administration similar? In what ways do they differ?
2. What is contingency theory? What kinds of organisations familiar to you have been successful or unsuccessful in dealing with contingencies from the external environment?

TIPS FOR PRACTICE

1. Think about whether your organisation's division of labour is meeting its current needs. Consider ways to change the level of job specialisation to improve performance.
2. Find out how your organisation works with reference to Weber's and Fayol's principles. Decide if the distribution of authority in the hierarchy best meets the organisation's needs. Similarly, decide if the right system to discipline or remunerate employees is being used.
3. Explore your organisational policies to see if managers are consistently behaving in an equitable manner and whether these policies are leading to ethical employee behaviour.

Summary and Review

In this chapter we examined the evolution of management theory and research over the last century. Much of the material in the rest of this book stems from developments and refinements of this work.

Scientific management theory The search for efficiency started with the study of how managers could improve person–task relationships to increase efficiency. The concept of job specialisation and division of labour remains the basis for the design of work settings in modern organisations. New developments such as lean production and TQM are often viewed as advances on the early scientific management principles developed by Taylor.

The influence of bureacracy on management theory Max Weber and Henri Fayol outlined principles of bureaucracy and administration that are as relevant to managers today as they were when developed at the turn of the twentieth century. Much of modern management research refines these principles to suit contemporary conditions. For example, the increasing interest in the use of cross-functional teams and the empowerment of workers are issues that managers also faced a century ago.

Behavioural management theory Researchers have described many different approaches to managerial behaviour, including Theories X and Y. Often the managerial behaviour that researchers suggest reflects the context of their own historical era and culture. Mary Parker Follett advocated managerial behaviours that did not reflect accepted modes of managerial behaviour at the time, and her work was largely ignored until conditions changed.

The systems view The importance of studying the organisation's external environment became clear after the development of open-systems theory and contingency theory during the 1960s. A main focus of contemporary management research is to find methods to help managers improve the ways they utilise organisational resources and compete successfully in the global environment. Strategic management and TQM are two important approaches intended to help managers make better use of organisational resources.

Management science theory The various branches of management science theory provide rigorous quantitative techniques that give managers more control over each organisation's use of resources to produce goods and services.

Topic for Action

- Question a manager about his or her views of the relative importance of Fayol's 14 principles of management.
- Visit at least two organisations in your community, and identify those that seem to operate with a Theory X or a Theory Y approach to management.

Applied Independent Learning

Building Management Skills

Managing Your Own Business

Now that you understand the concerns addressed by management thinkers over the twentieth century, use this exercise to apply your knowledge to developing your management skills.

Imagine that you are the founding entrepreneur of a software company that specialises in developing games for home computers. Customer demand for your games has increased so much that over the last year your company has grown from a busy one-person operation to one with 16 employees. In addition to yourself, you employ six software developers to produce the software, three graphic artists, two computer technicians, two marketing and sales personnel and two secretaries. In the next year you expect to hire 30 new employees, and you are wondering how best to manage your growing company.

1. Use the principles of Weber and Fayol to decide on the system of organisation and management that you think will be most effective for your growing organisation. How many levels will the managerial hierarchy of your organisation have? How much authority will you decentralise to your subordinates? How will you establish the division of labour between subordinates? Will your subordinates work alone and report to you or work in teams?

2. Which management approach (for example, Theory X or Y) do you propose to use to run your organisation? In 50 words or fewer write a statement describing the management approach you believe will motivate and co-ordinate your subordinates, and say why you think this style will be best.

Managing Ethically

Mr Edens Profits from Watching His Workers' Every Move

Read the case below, 'Mr Edens Profits from Watching His Workers' Every Move', and think about the following issues.

Control is one of Ron Edens' favourite words. 'This is a controlled environment,' he says of the blank brick building that houses his company, Electronic Banking System, Inc. (EBS).

Inside, long lines of women sit at spartan desks, slitting envelopes, sorting contents and filling out 'control cards' that record how many letters they have opened and how long it has taken them. Workers here, in 'the cage', must process three envelopes a minute. Nearby, other women tap keyboards, keeping pace with a quota that demands 8,500 strokes an hour.

The room is silent. Talking is forbidden. The windows are covered. Coffee mugs, religious pictures and other adornments are barred from workers' desks.

In his office upstairs, Mr Edens sits before a TV monitor that flashes images from eight cameras posted through the plant. 'There's a little bit of Sneaky Pete to it,' he says, using a remote control to zoom in on a document on a worker's desk. 'I can basically read that and figure out how someone's day is going.'

This day, like most others, is going smoothly, and Mr Edens's business has boomed as a result. 'We maintain a lot of control,' he says. 'Order and control are everything in this business.'

Mr Edens' business belongs to a small but expanding financial service known as 'lockbox processing'. Many companies and charities that once did their paperwork in-house now 'outsource' clerical tasks to firms like EBS, which processes donations to groups such as Mothers Against Drunk Driving, the Doris Day Animal League, Greenpeace and the National Organisation for Women.

More broadly, EBS reflects the explosive growth of jobs in which workers perform low-wage and limited tasks in white-collar settings. This has transformed towns like Hagerstown – a blue-collar community hit hard by industrial layoffs in the 1970s – into sites for thousands of jobs in factory-sized offices.

Many of these jobs, though, are part time and most pay far less than the manufacturing occupations they replaced. Some workers at EBS start at the minimum wage of $4.25 an hour and most earn about $6 an hour. The growth of such jobs – which often cluster outside major cities – also completes a curious historic circle. During the Industrial Revolution, farmers' daughters went to work in textile towns like Lowell, Mass. In post-industrial America, many women of modest means and skills are entering clerical mills where they process paper instead of cloth (coincidentally, EBS occupies a former garment factory).

'The office of the future can look a lot like the factory of the past,' says Barbara Garson, author of *The Electronic Sweatshop* and other books on the modern workplace. 'Modern tools are being used to bring 19th-century working conditions into the white-collar world.'

The time-and-motion philosophies of Frederick Taylor, for instance, have found a 1990s correlate in the phone, computer and camera, which can be used to monitor workers more closely than a foreman with a stopwatch ever could. Also, the nature of the work often justifies a vigilant eye. In EBS workers handle thousands of dollars in checks and cash, and Mr Edens says cameras help deter would-be thieves. Tight security also reassures visiting clients. 'If you're disorderly, they'll think we're out of control and that things could get lost,' says Mr Edens, who worked as a financial controller for the National Rifle Association before founding EBS in 1983.

But tight observation also helps EBS monitor productivity and weed out workers who don't keep up. 'There's multiple uses,' Mr Edens says of surveillance. His desk is covered with computer printouts recording the precise toll of keystrokes tapped by each data-entry worker. He also keeps a day-to-day tally of errors. The work floor itself resembles an enormous classroom in the throes of exam period. Desks point toward the front, where a manager keeps watch from a raised platform that workers call 'the pedestal' or 'the birdhouse'. Other supervisors are positioned toward the back of the room. 'If you want to watch someone,' Mr Edens explains, 'it's easier from behind because they don't know you're watching.' There also is a black globe hanging from the ceiling, in which cameras are positioned.

Mr Edens sees nothing Orwellian about this omniscience. 'It's not a Big Brother attitude,' he says. 'It's more of a calming attitude.'

But studies of workplace monitoring suggest otherwise. Experts say that surveillance can create a hostile environment in which workers feel pressured, paranoid and prone to

▶ stress-related illness. Surveillance also can be used punitively, to intimidate workers or to justify their firing.

Following a failed union drive at EBS, the National Labor Relations Board filed a series of complaints against the company, including charges that EBS threatened, interrogated and spied on workers. As part of an out-of-court settlement, EBS reinstated a fired worker and posted a notice that it would refrain from illegal practices during a second union vote, which also failed.

'It's all noise,' Mr Edens says of the unfair labor charges. As to the pressure that surveillance creates, Mr Edens sees that simply as 'the nature of the beast'. He adds: 'It's got to add stress when everyone knows their production is being monitored. I don't apologise for that.'

Mr Edens also is unapologetic about the Draconian work rules he maintains, including one that forbids all talk unrelated to the completion of each task. 'I'm not paying people to chat. I'm paying them to open envelopes,' he says. Of the blocked windows, Mr Edens adds: 'I don't want them looking out – it's distracting. They'll make mistakes.'

This total focus boosts productivity but it makes many workers feel lonely and trapped. Some try to circumvent the silence rule, like kids in a school library. 'If you don't turn your head and sort of mumble out of the side of your mouth, supervisors won't hear you most of the time,' Cindy Kesselring explains during her lunch break. Even so, she feels isolated and often longs for her former job as a waitress. 'Work is your social life, particularly if you've got kids,' says the 27-year-old mother. 'Here it's hard to get to know people because you can't talk.'

During lunch, workers crowd in the parking lot outside, chatting non-stop. 'Some of us don't eat much because the more you chew the less you can talk,' Ms Kesselring says. There aren't other breaks and workers aren't allowed to sip coffee or eat at their desks during the long stretches before and after lunch. Hard candy is the only permitted desk snack.

New technology, and the breaking down of labour into discrete, repetitive tasks, also have effectively stripped jobs such as those at EBS of whatever variety and skills clerical work once possessed. Workers in the cage (an antiquated banking term for a money-handling area) only open envelopes and sort contents; those in the audit department compute figures; and data-entry clerks punch in the information that the others have collected. If they make a mistake, the computer buzzes and a message such as 'check digit error' flashes on the screen.

'We don't ask these people to think – the machines think for them,' Mr Edens says. 'They don't have to make any decisions.' This makes the work simpler but also deepens its monotony. In the cage, Carol Smith says she looks forward to envelopes that contain anything out of the ordinary, such as letters reporting that the donor is deceased. Or she plays mental games. 'I think to myself, A goes in this pile, B goes here and C goes there – sort of like Bingo.' She says she sometimes feels 'like a machine', particularly when she fills out the 'control card' on which she lists 'time in' and 'time out' for each tray of envelopes. In a slot marked 'cage operator' Ms Smith writes her code number, 3173. 'That's me,' she says.

Barbara Ann Wiles, a keyboard operator, also plays mind games to break up the boredom. Tapping in the names and addresses of new donors, she tries to imagine the faces behind the names, particularly the odd ones. 'Like this one, Mrs Fittizzi,' she chuckles. 'I can picture her as a very stout lady with a strong accent, hollering on a street corner.' She picks out another: 'Doris Angelroth – she's very sophisticated, a monocle maybe, drinking tea on an overstuffed mohair couch.'

It is a world remote from the one Ms Wiles inhabits. Like most EBS employees, she must juggle her low-paying job with child care. On this Friday, for instance, Ms Wiles will finish her eight-hour shift at about 4 p.m., go home for a few hours, then return for a second shift from midnight to 8 a.m. Otherwise, she would have to come in on Saturday to finish the week's work.

'This way I can be home on the weekend to look after my kids,' she says.

Others find the work harder to leave behind at the end of the day. In the cage, Ms Smith says her husband used to complain because she often woke him in the middle of the night. 'I'd be shuffling my hands in my sleep,' she says, mimicking the motion of opening envelopes.

Her cage colleague, Ms Kesselring, says her fiancé has a different gripe. 'He dodges me for a couple of hours after work because I don't shut up – I need to talk, talk, talk,' she says. And there is one household task she can no longer abide.

'I won't pay bills because I can't stand to open another envelope,' she says. 'I'll leave letters sitting in the mailbox for days.'

Questions

1. Which of the management theories described in the chapter does Ron Edens make most use of?

2. What do you think are the effects of this approach on (a) workers and (b) supervisors?

3. Do you regard Ron Eden's approach to management as ethical and acceptable or unethical and unacceptable in the 2000s? Why?

Source: Adapted from Tony Horwitz, 'Mr Edens Profits from Watching His Workers' Every Move', *The Wall Street Journal*, December 1, 1994.

Small Group Breakout Exercise

Modelling an Open System

Form groups of three–five people, and appoint one group member as the spokesperson who will communicate your findings to the class when called on by the instructor. Then discuss the following scenario.

Think of an organisation with which you are all familiar, such as a local restaurant, store or bank. After choosing an organisation, model it from an open-systems perspective. Identify its input, conversion and output processes and identify forces in the external environment that can help or hurt the organisation's ability to obtain resources and dispose of its goods or services.

Exploring the World Wide Web

Explore the World Wide Web and see if you can identify companies that still apply Fordist ideas. How successful do you think these companies are?

Application in Today's Business World

What You Don't Know About Dell

Dell is the master at selling direct, bypassing middlemen to deliver PCs cheaper than any of its rivals. And few would quarrel that it's the model of efficiency, with a far-flung supply chain knitted together so tightly that it's like one electrical wire, humming 24/7. Yet all this has been true for more than a decade. And although the entire computer industry has tried to replicate Dell's tactics, none can hold a candle to the company's results.

As it turns out, it's how Michael Dell manages the company that has elevated it far above its sell-direct business model. What's Dell's secret? At its heart is his belief that the status quo is never good enough, even if it means painful changes for the man with his name on the door. When success is achieved, it's greeted with 5 seconds of praise followed by 5 hours of *post mortem* on what could have been done better. Says Michael Dell: 'Celebrate for a nanosecond. Then move on.' After the outfit opened its first Asian factory, in Malaysia, the CEO sent the manager heading the job one of his old running shoes to congratulate him. The message: This is only the first step in a marathon.

Just as crucial is Michael Dell's belief that once a problem is uncovered, it should be dealt with quickly and directly, without excuses. 'There's no "The dog ate my homework" here,' says Dell. No, indeed. After Randall D. Groves, then head of the server business, delivered 16 per cent higher sales last year, he was demoted. Never mind that none of its rivals came close to that. It could have been better, say two former Dell executives. Groves referred calls to a Dell spokesman, who says Groves' job change was part of a broader reorganisation.

Above all, Michael Dell expects everyone to watch each dime – and turn it into at least a quarter. Unlike most tech bosses, Dell believes every product should be profitable from Day One. To ensure that, he expects his managers to be walking databases, able to cough up information on everything from top-line growth to the average number of times a part has to be replaced in the first 30 days after a computer is sold.

But there's one number he cares about most: operating margin. To Dell, it's not enough to rack up profits or grow fast. Execs must do both to maximize long-term profitability. That means products need to be priced low enough to induce shoppers to buy, but not so low that they cut unnecessarily into profits. When Dell's senior managers in Europe lost out on profits in 1999 because they hadn't cut costs far enough, they were replaced. 'There are some organisations where people think they're a hero if they invent a new thing,' says Rollins. 'Being a hero at Dell means saving money.'

It's this combination – reaching for the heights of perfection while burrowing down into every last data point – that no rival has been able to imitate. 'It's like watching Michael Jordan stuff the basketball,' says Merrill Lynch & Co. technology strategist Steven Milunovich. 'I see it. I understand it. But I can't do it.'

How did Mike come by his management philosophy? It started 19 years ago, when he was ditching classes to sell homemade PCs out of his University of Texas dorm room. Dell was the scrappy underdog, fighting for his company's life against the likes of IBM and Compaq Computer Corp. with a direct sales model that people thought was plain nuts. Now, Michael Dell is worth £9.4 billion, while his 40,000-employee company is about to top £22 billion in sales. Yet he continues to manage Dell with the urgency and determination of a college kid with his back to the wall. 'I still think of us as a challenger,' he says. 'I still think of us attacking.'

All this has kept Dell on track as rivals have gone off the rails. Since 2000, the company has been adding market share at a faster pace than at any time in its history – nearly 3 percentage points in 2002. A renewed effort to control costs sliced overhead expenses to just 9.6 per cent of revenue in the most recent quarter and boosted productivity to nearly £550,000 in revenue per employee. That's three times the revenue per employee at IBM and almost twice Hewlett-Packard Co.'s rate.

Still, for the restless Michael Dell, that's not nearly enough. He wants to make sure the company he has spent half his life building can endure after he's gone. So he and Rollins have sketched out an ambitious financial target: £33 billion in revenues by 2006. That's twice what the company did in 2001 and enough to put it in league with the largest, most powerful companies in the world. Getting there will require the same kind of success that the company achieved in PCs – but in altogether new markets. Already, Michael Dell is moving the company into printers, networking, hand-held computers and tech services. His latest foray: Dell is entering the cut-throat £52.3 billion consumer electronics market with a portable digital music player, an online music store and a flat-panel television set slated to go on sale in October 2004.

Dell also faces an innovation dilemma. Its penny-pinching ways leave little room for investments in product development and future technologies, especially compared with rivals. Even in the midst of the recession, IBM spent £2.62 billion or 5.9 per cent of its revenues, on research and development (R&D) in 2002, while HP ponied up £1.8 billion, or 4.8 per cent of revenues. And Dell? Just a paltry £250.5 million, or 1.3 per cent. Rivals say that handicaps Dell's ability to move much beyond PCs, particularly in such promising markets as digital imaging and utility computing. 'Dell is a great company, but they are a one-trick pony,' says HP CEO Carleton S. Fiorina. What's more, Dell has shown little patience for the costs of entering new markets, killing off products – like its high-end server – when they didn't produce quick profits, rather than staying committed to a long-term investment. 'They're the best in the world at what they do,' says IBM server chief William M. Zeitler. 'The question is, will they be best at the Next Big Thing?'

Dell's track record suggests that the CEO will meet his $60 billion revenue goal by 2006. Already, Dell has grabbed large chunks of the markets for inexpensive servers and data storage gear. After just two quarters, its first hand-held computer has captured 37 per cent of the US market for such devices. And Rollins says that initial sales of Dell printers are double its internal targets. With the potential growth in PCs and new markets, few analysts doubt that Dell can generate the 15 per cent annual growth needed to reach the mark.

Questions

1. What are the main principles behind Michael Dell's approach to managing?
2. List these principles then compare them to those developed by Henry Fayol. In what ways are they similar or different?

Source: Andrew Park and Peter Burrows, 'What You Don't Know About Dell', adapted and reprinted from BusinessWeek Online, November 3, 2003 by special permission. Copyright © 2003 by the McGraw-Hill Companies, Inc.

Notes and References

1   H. Ford, 'Progressive Manufacture', *Encyclopaedia Britannica*, 13th ed. (New York: Encyclopaedia Britannica, 1926).
2   R. Edwards, *Contested Terrain: The Transformation of the Workplace in the Twentieth Century* (New York: Basic Books, 1979).
3   A. Smith, *The Wealth of Nations* (London: Penguin, 1982).

4 *Ibid.*, 110.

5 J. G. March and H. A. Simon, *Organisations* (New York: Wiley, 1958).

6 L. W. Fry, 'The Maligned F. W. Taylor: A Reply to His Many Critics', *Academy of Management Review* 1 (1976), 124–29.

7 F. W. Taylor, *Shop Management* (New York: Harper, 1903); F. W. Taylor, *The Principles of Scientific Management* (New York: Harper, 1911).

8 J. A. Litterer, *The Emergence of Systematic Management as Shown by the Literature from 1870–1900* (New York: Garland, 1986).

9 H. R. Pollard, *Developments in Management Thought* (New York: Crane, 1974).

10 D. Wren, *The Evolution of Management Thought* (New York: Wiley, 1994), 134.

11 Edwards, *Contested Terrain*.

12 J. M. Staudenmaier, Jr., 'Henry Ford's Big Flaw', *Invention and Technology* 10 (1994), 34–44.

13 H. Beynon, *Working for Ford* (London: Penguin, 1975).

14 Taylor, *Scientific Management*.

15 F. B. Gilbreth, *Primer of Scientific Management* (New York: Van Nostrand Reinhold, 1912).

16 F. B. Gilbreth, Jr. and E. G. Gilbreth, *Cheaper by the Dozen* (New York: Crowell, 1948).

17 M. Weber, *From Max Weber: Essays in Sociology*, ed. H. H. Gerth and C. W. Mills (New York: Oxford University Press, 1946); M. Weber, *Economy and Society*, ed. G. Roth and C. Wittich (Berkeley: University of California Press, 1978).

18 C. Perrow, *Complex Organisations*, 2nd ed. (Glenview, IL: Scott, Foresman, 1979).

19 Weber, *From Max Weber*, 331.

20 See C. Perrow, *Complex Organisations*, Chapter 1, for a detailed discussion of these issues.

21 H. Fayol, *General and Industrial Management* (New York: IEEE Press, 1984).

22 *Ibid.*, 79.

23 M. Paoli and A. Prencipe, 'Memory of the Organisation and Memory within the Organisation', *Journal of Management and Governance* 7 (2), 2003, 145–62.

24 T. J. Peters and R. H. Waterman, Jr., *In Search of Excellence: Lessons from America's Best-Run Companies* (New York: Harper & Row, 1982).

25 R. E. Eccles and N. Nohira, *Beyond the Hype: Rediscovering the Essence of Management* (Boston: Harvard Business School Press, 1992).

26 M. van Marrewijk and J. Timmers, 'Human Capital Management: New Possibilities in People Management', *Journal of Business Ethics* 44 (2–3), 2003, 171–84.

27 P. Graham, *M. P. Follett – Prophet of Management: A Celebration of Writings from the 1920s* (Boston: Harvard Business School Press, 1995).

28 *Ibid.*

29 M. P. Follett, *Creative Experience* (London: Longmans, 1924).

30 E. Mayo, *The Human Problems of Industrial Civilization* (New York: Macmillan, 1933); F. J. Roethlisberger and W. J. Dickson, *Management and the Worker* (Cambridge, MA: Harvard University Press, 1947).

31 D. W. Organ, 'Review of *Management and the Worker*, by F. J. Roethlisberger and W. J. Dickson', *Academy of Management Review* 13 (1986), 460–64.

32 D. Roy, 'Banana Time: Job Satisfaction and Informal Interaction', *Human Organisation* 18 (1960), 158–61.

33 For an analysis of the problems in determining cause from effect in the Hawthorne studies and in social settings in general, see A. Carey, 'The Hawthorne Studies: A Radical Criticism', *American Sociological Review* 33 (1967), 403–16.

34 D. McGregor, *The Human Side of Enterprise* (New York: McGraw-Hill, 1960).

35 *Ibid.*, 48.

36 Peters and Waterman, *In Search of Excellence*.

37   J. Pitta, 'It Had to Be Done and We Did It', *Forbes*, April 26, 1993, 148–52.

38   www.hp.com, press release, June 2001.

39   J. D. Thompson, *Organisations in Action* (New York: McGraw-Hill, 1967).

40   D. Katz and R. L. Kahn, *The Social Psychology of Organisations* (New York: Wiley, 1966); Thompson, *Organisations in Action.*

41   M. Easterby-Smith, R. Thorpe and A. Lowe, *Management Research: An Introduction*, 2nd ed. (London: Sage, 2002).

42   W. E. Deming, *Out of the Crisis* (Cambridge, MA: MIT Press, 1986).

43   For a discussion of various approaches, see R. L. Flood and M. C. Jackson, *Creative Problem Solving: Total Systems Intervention* (Chichester: John Wiley, 1991).

44   T. Burns and G. M. Stalker, *The Management of Innovation* (London: Tavistock, 1961); P. R. Lawrence and J. R. Lorsch, *Organization and Environment* (Boston: Graduate School of Business Administration, Harvard University, 1967).

45   Burns and Stalker, *The Management of Innovation.*

46   Robert E. Quinn, S. R. Faerman, M. P. Thompson and Michael R. McGrath, *Becoming a Master Manager: A Competency Framework*, 3rd ed. (New York: John Wiley, 2002).

47   Drucker, Peter F., *Management: Tasks, Responsibilities, Practices* (New York: Harper & Row, 1973).

48   Drucker, Peter F., *Managing the Non-Profit Organization: Principles and Practices* (New York: Harper & Row, 1990).

49   Drucker, Peter F., *Concept of the Corporation* (Somerset, NJ: Transaction Publishers, 1993).

The Manager as a Person: Values, Attitudes, Emotions and Culture

LEARNING OBJECTIVES

After studying this chapter, you should be able to:

☑ Describe the various personality traits that affect how managers think, feel and behave.

☑ Explain what values and attitudes are and describe their impact on managerial action.

☑ Appreciate how moods and emotions influence all members of an organisation.

☑ Describe the nature of emotional intelligence and its role in management.

☑ Define organisational culture and explain how managers both create and are influenced by organisational culture.

A Manager's Challenge

Employees and Innovation Come First at Virgin plc

How an individual's values and characteristics can inform a successful organisational culture

Virgin is one of the first truly global brands in the twenty-first century. It is widely respected and has created over 200 companies in 30 countries worldwide, employing over 25,000 staff around the world. Its revenue exceeded £4 billion in 2002.

It all began in 1968 when Richard Branson, the founder and chairman of Virgin Group plc, published *Student* magazine. Within 15 years, by 1983, he had created music labels, record stores and other ventures amounting to annual turnovers of £50 million. After launching some of the ventures on the London Stock Exchange (LSE) in 1986, Virgin Group plc reached a turnover of £279 million in 1987. But it didn't stop there. The 1990s saw an ever-increasing portfolio of business ventures including rail companies, cinemas and airlines.

One of the reasons that Virgin has gone from strength to strength in an increasingly difficult business environment is its charismatic and innovative founder and chairman. Richard Branson created a culture that reflects his spirit – that of 'value for money, quality, innovation, fun and a sense of competitive challenge'. Its employees are encouraged to take this spirit on board to provide excellent and outstanding customer service. The brand specifically looks to supplement their teams with people that think differently and are innovative, in order to create lasting customer experiences and create new business ventures. But it is not all about the customer.[1]

Virgin's success can also be attributed to the way that the company treats its staff. Richard Branson and Virgin believe that when a company takes good care of its employees, the staff will take good care of their customers. Open communication is encouraged and staff receive deserved recognition for their achievements. Virgin prides itself on being a family – in which 'bosses' are mentors and allow people to hold far more accountability and responsibility at an earlier age – rather than a hierarchical organisation. One of the ways in which Richard Branson promotes these values is by helping staff to attain a well-balanced work–life ratio. He created a Paradise Island just off the Sunshine Coast in Queensland, Australia for his staff to 'spend time together and get to know each other outside the work environment'.[2]

Richard Branson remains a chairman who is accessible to his staff and nurtures a culture of co-operation. Many of the new business ventures are supported by current staff and while Virgin comprises many independent small businesses, they help each other out when necessary. Virgin also fosters a culture of communication and has recently developed an ICT strategy for Virgin Atlantic that allows each member of staff to communicate across the company electronically.

New suggestions from employees are not only encouraged, but are expected. Virgin recognises that front-line staff are often in the best position to make suggestions for improvements. Richard Branson's and Virgin's values, and the culture these create, emphasise putting employees and innovation first; this employee- and innovation-centred approach makes good business sense. Employees at Virgin really want the company to continue to grow and succeed; they are highly motivated and committed to providing the best service they can to their customers.

Overview

Like people everywhere, managers have their own distinctive personalities, values, ways of viewing things and personal challenges and disappointments. In this chapter, the focus is on the manager as a feeling, thinking human being. This chapter begins by describing enduring characteristics that influence how managers 'manage', as well as how they view other people, their organisations and the world around them. It also discusses how managers' values, attitudes and moods can affect an organisation, shaping its organisational culture. By the end of this chapter, you will have a good appreciation of how the personal characteristics of managers can influence the process of management in general and organisational culture in particular.

Enduring Characteristics: Personality, Traits and Types

All people, including managers, have certain enduring characteristics that influence how they think, feel and behave. These characteristics are **personality traits**, particular tendencies to feel, think and act in certain ways that can be used to describe the personality of every individual. It is important to understand the personalities of managers, because their personalities influence their behaviour and their approach to managing people and resources.

Some managers are demanding, difficult to get along with and highly critical of other people.[3] Others, like Richard Branson, CEO of the Virgin Group, may be as concerned about effectiveness and efficiency as highly critical managers but are easier to get along with, are likeable and frequently praise the people around them. Both styles of management may produce excellent results, but their effect on employees is quite different. Do managers deliberately decide to adopt one or the other of these approaches to management, or is their behaviour determined by their innate personality?

Research suggests that the way people react to different conditions depends, in part, on their personalities.[4] Studying personality is a complex phenomenon. There are several psychological theories that try to explain whether personality is innate or develops from socialisation, but in fact our personality usually develops from both – some innate characteristics as well as how we develop through parenting and education, etc. There is a distinction within the literature between the *traits* people hold and the *type* of personality they fit into. Type approaches fit people into categories possessing the same behaviour patterns – e.g. extrovert or neurotic – so people can *belong to a type*. Alternatively, a trait is a predisposition towards an enduring behaviour that occurs at different times and *traits belong to people*.

The most influential type theory emanates from Carl Jung's psychoanalytical approach during the 1950s.[5] The Myers–Briggs Type Indicator (MBTI) was developed from this approach after the Second World War and then adapted several times during the later 1940s and 1950s by the mother and daughter team Katherine Briggs and Isabel Myers.[6] According to Myers–Briggs Theory, while types and traits are both inborn to a degree, traits can be improved in a similar way to skills, whereas types, if supported by a healthy environment, naturally differ over a lifetime. The MBTI attempts to capture individual preferences and cluster them into types.

The MBTI categorises people's types via dichotomous characteristics, based on people's preferences. These are:

- Extroversion/introversion
- Sensing/intuition
- Thinking/feeling
- Judging/perceiving.

Participants are given one of 16 four-letter acronyms, such as ESTJ or INFP, indicating what their preferences are. For example, for someone whose preferences categorised into an ENFP you would have a type of preferring your energies to be outward-looking when dealing with people and information. You would have a preference towards receiving data from the unconscious, or seeing relationships via insights rather than from your senses. If you have a feeling function, you tend to make judgements based on 'more or less' evaluations when making decisions and prefer not to use such logical 'what if' scenarios as thinking people would. Finally on the preference of judging and perceiving, 'P' types are more likely to have the attitude of leaving things open, unlike 'J' types, who would prefer to be rule-based. The MBTI is used widely across organisations in all kinds of contexts including training, personal development, selection and recruitment.

The 'Big Five' Personality Traits

From this perspective we can think of an individual's personality as being composed of five general traits or characteristics:

- Extraversion
- Negative affectivity
- Agreeableness
- Conscientiousness
- Openness to experience.[7]

Researchers often consider these the 'Big Five' personality traits.[8] Each of them can be viewed as a continuum along which every individual falls (Fig. 3.1).

Some managers may be at the 'high end' of one trait continuum, others at the 'low end' and still others somewhere in between. An easy way to understand how these traits can affect a person's approach to management is to describe what people are like at the high and low ends

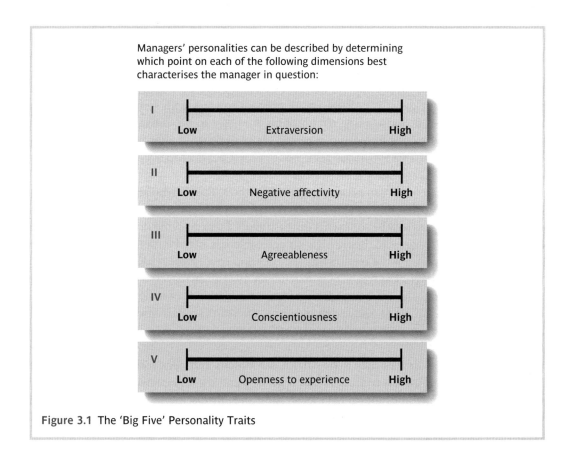

Figure 3.1 The 'Big Five' Personality Traits

of each trait continuum. As will become evident in each trait, no single trait is 'right' or 'wrong' for being an effective manager. Rather, effectiveness is determined by a complex interaction between the characteristics of managers (including personality traits) and the nature of the job and organisation in which they are working. Moreover, personality traits that enhance managerial effectiveness in one situation may actually impair it in another, making *context* a crucial component.

Extraversion

Extraversion is the tendency to experience positive emotions and moods and feel good about oneself and the rest of the world. People who are high on extraversion (often called *extraverts*) tend to be sociable, affectionate, outgoing and friendly. Those who are low on extraversion (often called *introverts*) tend to be less inclined toward social interactions and have a less positive outlook on life. Being high on extraversion may be an asset for managers whose jobs entail especially high levels of social interaction. Individuals who are low on extraversion may nevertheless be highly effective and efficient, especially when their jobs do not require excessive social interaction. Their more 'quiet' approach may enable them to accomplish large amounts of work in limited time. (See Fig. 3.2 for an example of a scale that can be used to measure a person's level of extraversion.)

Negative affectivity

Negative affectivity is the tendency to experience negative emotions and moods, feel distressed and be critical of oneself and others. People high on this trait may often feel angry and dissatisfied and complain about their own and others' lack of progress. Individuals who are low on negative affectivity do not tend to experience many negative emotions and moods and are less pessimistic and critical of themselves and others. On the plus side, the critical approach of a person high on negative affectivity may sometimes be effective if it spurs them on to improve their performance. Nevertheless, it is probably more pleasant to work with someone who is low on negative affectivity, as better working relationships are likely to be cultivated. Figure 3.3 is an example of a scale developed to measure a person's level of negative affectivity.

Agreeableness

Agreeableness is the tendency to get along well with others. People who are high on the agreeableness continuum are likeable, tend to be affectionate and care about other people. Those who are low on agreeableness may be somewhat distrustful of others, unsympathetic, unco-operative and even at times antagonistic. Being high on agreeableness may be especially important for managers whose responsibilities require that they develop good, close relationships with others. Nevertheless, a low level of agreeableness may be an asset in managerial jobs where they are required to be antagonistic – such as drill sergeants and other kinds of senior military personnel. (See Fig. 3.2 for an example of a scale that measures a person's level of agreeableness.)

Conscientiousness

Conscientiousness is the tendency to be careful, scrupulous and persevering.[9] People who are high on the conscientiousness continuum are organised and self-disciplined; those who are low on this trait might sometimes appear to lack direction and self-discipline. Conscientiousness has been found to be a good predictor of performance in many kinds of jobs, including managerial jobs in a variety of organisations.[10] CEOs of major companies, such as Carly Fiorino of Hewlett-

Listed below are phrases describing people's behaviours. Please use the rating scale below to describe how accurately each statement describes *you*. Describe yourself as you generally are now, not as you wish to be in the future. Describe yourself as you honestly see yourself, in relation to other people you know of the same sex as you are and roughly your same age.

1	2	3	4	5
Very inaccurate	Moderately inaccurate	Neither inaccurate nor accurate	Moderately accurate	Very accurate

_____ 1. Am interested in people

_____ 2. Have a rich vocabulary

_____ 3. Am always prepared

_____ 4. Am not really interested in others*

_____ 5. Leave my belongings around*

_____ 6. Am the life of the party

_____ 7. Have difficulty understanding abstract ideas*

_____ 8. Sympathise with others' feelings.

_____ 9. Don't talk a lot*

_____ 10. Pay attention to details

_____ 11. Have a vivid imagination

_____ 12. Insult people*

_____ 13. Make a mess of things*

_____ 14. Feel comfortable around people

_____ 15. Am not interested in abstract ideas*

_____ 16. Have a soft heart

_____ 17. Get chores done right away

_____ 18. Keep in the background*

_____ 19. Have excellent ideas

_____ 20. Start conversations

_____ 21. Am not interested in other people's problems*

_____ 22. Often forget to put things back in their proper place*

_____ 23. Have little to say*

_____ 24. Do not have a good imagination*

_____ 25. Take time out for others

_____ 26. Like order

_____ 27. Talk to a lot of different people at parties

_____ 28. Am quick to understand things

_____ 29. Feel little concern for others*

_____ 30. Shirk my duties*

_____ 31. Don't like to draw attention to myself*

_____ 32. Use difficult words

_____ 33. Feel others' emotions

_____ 34. Follow a schedule

_____ 35. Spend time reflecting on things

_____ 36. Don't mind being the centre of attention

_____ 37. Make people feel at ease

_____ 38. Am exacting in my work

_____ 39. Am quiet around strangers*

_____ 40. Am full of ideas

* Item is reverse-scored: 1 = 5, 2 = 4, 4 = 2, 5 = 1
Scoring: Sum responses to items for an overall scale.

      Extraversion = sum of items 6, 9, 14, 18, 20, 23, 27, 31, 36, 39

      Agreeableness = sum of items 1, 4, 8, 12, 16, 21, 25, 29, 33, 37

      Conscientiousness = sum of items 3, 5, 10, 13, 17, 22, 26, 30, 34, 38

      Openness to experience = sum of items 2, 7, 11, 15, 19, 24, 28, 32, 35, 40

Figure 3.2 Measures of Extraversion, Agreeableness, Conscientiousness and Openness to Experience

Source: Adapted from Lewis R. Goldberg, Oregon Research Institute, http://ipip.ori.org/ipip/.

Instructions: Listed below are a series of statements a person might use to describe her/his attitudes, opinions, interests and other characteristics. If a statement is true or largely true, put a 'T' in the space next to the item. Or if the statement is false or largely false, mark an 'F' in the space.

Please answer every statement, even if you are not completely sure of the answer. Read each statement carefully, but don't spend too much time deciding on the answer.

_____ 1. I often find myself worrying about something

_____ 2. My feelings are hurt rather easily

_____ 3. Often I get irritated at little annoyances

_____ 4. I suffer from nervousness

_____ 5. My mood often goes up and down

_____ 6. I sometimes feel 'just miserable' for no good reason

_____ 7. Often I experience strong emotions – anxiety, anger – without really knowing what causes them

_____ 8. I am easily startled by things that happen unexpectedly

_____ 9. I sometimes get myself into a state of tension and turmoil as I think of the day's events

_____ 10. Minor setbacks sometimes irritate me too much

_____ 11. I often lose sleep over my worries

_____ 12. There are days when I'm 'on edge' all of the time

_____ 13. I am too sensitive for my own good

_____ 14. I sometimes change from happy to sad, or vice versa, without good reason

Scoring: Level of negative affectivity is equal to the number of items answered 'True'.

Figure 3.3 A Measure of Negative Affectivity

Source: Adapted from Auke Tellegen, _Brief Manual for the Differential Personality Questionnaire_. Copyright © 1982. Reproduced by permission.

Packard and or Rolf Eriksen of IKEA often show signs of being high on conscientiousness – the long hours they work, their attention to detail and their ability to handle their multiple responsibilities in an organised manner. Figure 3.2 provides an example of a scale that measures conscientiousness.

Openness to experience

Openness to experience is the tendency to be original, have broad interests, be open to a wide range of stimuli, be daring and take risks.[11] People who are high on this trait continuum may be especially likely to take risks and be innovative in their planning and decision making. Entrepreneurs who start their own businesses – like Bill Gates of Microsoft, Richard Branson of Virgin Group and Anita Roddick of The Body Shop – are, in all likelihood, high on openness to experience, which has contributed to their success as entrepreneurs and managers. People who are low on openness to experience may be less prone to take risks and more conservative in their planning and decision making. In certain organisations and positions, this tendency may be an asset. The manager of the fiscal office in a university, for example, must ensure that all university departments and units follow the rules and regulations pertaining to budgets, spending accounts and reimbursements of expenses. Figure 3.2 provides an example of a measure of openness to experience.

Managers who initiate major changes in their organisations often are high on openness to experience, as is true of IBM CEO and chairman Samuel Palmisano, profiled in the Case 3.1.

Case 3.1: Sam Palmisano reinvents IBM

Samuel Palmisano started his career at IBM in the 1970s as a sales representative. He went on to head many of IBM's major divisions before becoming CEO in 2002 and chairman of the board in 2004.[12] Palmisano is leading a major redirection of IBM that will change the company's focus and activities in fundamental ways. Essentially, he is transforming IBM from being a hardware and software provider to being a business solution provider to corporate customers.[13] IBM is now focusing on developing close, long-term relationships with customers that will enable it to help them with their urgent business problems, ranging from purchasing and marketing to production and customer service. In becoming close to its customers and helping them meet their business needs, IBM will also be providing them with its long-standing hardware and software. But the latter is part of a bigger package oriented around being a total-solution provider to meet customers' business needs.[14]

To accomplish this aim, Palmisano has taken many bold steps. For example, IBM acquired PricewaterhouseCoopers' consulting business and Rational Software in 2002 at a cost of over £3 billion. These acquisitions will help IBM provide more high-level, all-encompassing consulting-type services to its customers. Realising that these changes will require changes in the mindsets and skills of employees, Palmisano spent £425 million on employee education in 2004.[15]

Palmisano is encouraging IBM managers to go out and talk to customers, learn about their business needs and develop comprehensive solutions to meet them. The solutions should be the kind that address fundamental problems that organisations in a particular industry face and, thus, can be sold to other companies in that industry. As Palmisano puts it: 'If they got out there and actually solved the problem with the client . . . they would understand what they needed to do.' For example, while IBM has sold hardware and data centre services to FinnAir for years, it has now begun using mathematical modelling to help FinnAir improve customer loyalty while reducing marketing costs – a major concern for FinnAir today.[16]

Interestingly enough, Palmisano's personality and management style are very different from those of his highly successful predecessor, former CEO Lou Gerstner. While Gerstner was formal and direct, Palmisano is more relaxed and understated. Industry watchers suggest that Palmisano's bold changes are right on track with where the hardware and software industry needs to be headed, and competitors like Hewlett-Packard and Microsoft seem to be copying some of his initiatives. While time will tell if Palmisano's vision for the new IBM will deliver on its promises, his openness to experience contributes to his confidence that 'we are on the verge of the next great opportunity for our company, and for the entire information technology industry'.[17]

By now, it should be clear that successful managers like Palmisano and Gerstner occupy a variety of positions on the 'Big Five' personality-trait continua. One highly effective manager may be high on extraversion and negative affectivity, another equally effective manager may be low on both these traits and still another may be somewhere in between. Members of an organisation must understand these differences among managers because they can shed light on how managers behave and on their approach to planning, leading, organising or controlling. If subordinates realise, for example, that their manager is low on extraversion, they will not feel upset when he or she seems to be aloof because they will realise that by nature they are simply not outgoing.

Managers themselves also need to be aware of their own personality traits and the traits of others, including their subordinates and fellow managers. A manager who knows that s/he has a tendency to be highly critical of other people may try to tone down their negative approach. Similarly, a manager who realises chronically complaining subordinates are negative because of their personality may appreciate that these complaints may not be as bad as they seem.

In order for all members of an organisation to work well together and with people outside the organisation, such as customers and suppliers, they must *understand each other*. Such understanding comes, in part, from an appreciation of some of the fundamental ways in which people differ from one another – that is, an appreciation of personality traits.

Other Characteristics That Affect Managerial Behaviour

Many other specific traits in addition to the 'Big Five' describe people's personalities. This section looks at traits that are particularly important for understanding managerial effectiveness:

- Locus of control
- Self-esteem
- The need for achievement, affiliation and power.

Locus of control

People differ in their views about how much control they have over what happens to and around them. The locus-of-control trait captures these beliefs.[18] People with an **internal locus of control** believe that they are responsible for their own fate. They see their own actions and behaviours as being decisive determinants of important outcomes such as attaining levels of job performance, being promoted or being turned down for a choice job assignment. Some managers with an internal locus of control see the success of a whole organisation resting on their shoulders. An internal locus of control also helps to ensure ethical behaviour and decision making in an organisation because people feel accountable and responsible for their own actions. Managers with an internal locus may also feel obligated to expose wrongdoing in an organisation, even if they are personally not responsible for it (Case 3.2).

Case 3.2: Taking responsibility for exposing wrongdoing

Does an employee have the responsibility to disclose misconduct[19] – his own or that of colleagues? A court case in 2004 decided 'yes'.

Mr Fassihi, sales and marketing director of Item Software, a UK company supplying reliability software, was judged guilty of breach of duty.[20] The company also traded products of a different company called Isograph. Mr Fassihi approached Isograph with the intention of diverting their products to his own company and selling them for his own benefit and profit. Isograph, after failing to come to an agreement with Mr Fassihi, ended their contract with Item Software. Item Software became aware of Fassihi's misconduct, terminated his contract and brought a legal action against him as he had been in breach of duty to disclose the misconduct to his employers.

The courts agreed with Item Software's claim and argued that 'one route by which it might be concluded that Fassihi had a duty to disclose his own wrongdoing is that no logical distinction can be drawn between a rule that an employee must disclose his own wrongdoing and a rule that he should disclose the wrongdoing of fellow employees even if that involves disclosing his own wrongdoing too'.[21]

This decision was strengthened by another court case in 2004 involving Tesco (one of the UK's biggest supermarkets), in which it was found that not only directors, but also senior managers, had the responsibility to disclose misconduct and wrongdoing in the workplace.[22] Reporting misconduct today is everyone's responsibility.

People with an **external locus of control** believe that outside forces are responsible for what happens to and around them; they do not think that their own actions make much of a difference. As such, they tend not to intervene to try to change a situation or solve a problem, leaving it to someone else.

Managers need to have an internal locus of control because they are responsible for what happens in organisations: they need to believe that they can and do make a difference. Moreover, managers are responsible for ensuring that organisations and their members behave ethically, and for this they need to have an internal locus of control: they need to know and feel that they can make a difference.

Self-esteem

Self-esteem is the degree to which individuals feel good about themselves and their capabilities. People with high self-esteem believe that they are competent, deserving and capable of handling most situations. People with low self-esteem have poor opinions of themselves, are unsure about their capabilities and question their ability to succeed at different endeavours.[23] Research suggests that people tend to choose activities and goals consistent with their levels of self-esteem. High self-esteem is desirable for managers because it facilitates their setting and keeping high standards for themselves, pushes them ahead on difficult projects and gives them the confidence they need to make and carry out important decisions.

Need for achievement, affiliation and power

Psychologist David McClelland has extensively researched the needs for achievement, affiliation and power.[24] The **need for achievement** is the extent to which an individual has a strong desire to perform challenging tasks well and to meet personal standards for excellence. People with a high need for achievement often set clear goals for themselves and like to receive performance feedback. The **need for affiliation** is the extent to which an individual is concerned about establishing and maintaining good interpersonal relations, being liked and having the people around them get along with one another. The **need for power** is the extent to which an individual desires to control or influence others.[25]

Research suggests that high needs for achievement and for power are assets for first-line and middle managers, and that a high need for power is especially important for upper-level managers.[26]

One study found that US presidents with a relatively high need for power tended to be especially effective during their terms of office.[27] A high need for affiliation may not always be desirable in managers because it may lead them to try too hard to be liked by others (including subordinates) rather than doing all they can to ensure that performance is as high as it can and should be. Although most research on these needs has been done in the US, some studies suggest that these findings may also be applicable to people in other countries such as India and New Zealand.[28]

Taken together, these characteristics for managers – an internal locus of control, high self-esteem and high need for achievement and power – suggest that managers need to be assertive people who not only believe that their own actions are decisive in determining their own and their organisation's fates but also believe in their own capabilities. Such managers have a personal desire for accomplishment and influence over others.

Reaction Time

Discuss the influence of personality traits and characteristics on a manager's effectiveness.

Values and Attitudes and Moods and Emotions

What are managers striving to achieve? How do they think they should behave? What do they think about their jobs and organisations, and how do they actually feel at work? Some answers to these questions can be found by exploring **values**, **attitudes** and **moods**.

Values and attitudes and moods and **emotions** capture how managers – and other employees – experience their jobs as individuals. Values and attitudes and moods and emotions differ in their *stability*. Values tend to be deeply routed in individual's socialisation and learning, whereas attitudes emerge through personal development and social interaction. Attitudes are less stable and therefore easier to change than values. Moods and emotions on the other hand are the least stable characteristic as they can change quickly. *Values* describe what managers are trying to achieve through work, and how they think they should behave. *Attitudes* capture their thoughts and feelings about their specific jobs and organisations. *Moods and emotions* encompass how managers actually feel when they are managing. Although these three aspects of managers' work experience are highly personal, they also have important implications for understanding how managers behave, how they treat and respond to others and how, through their efforts, they help contribute to organisational effectiveness through planning, leading, organising and controlling.

Values: Terminal and Instrumental

The two kinds of personal values are *terminal* and *instrumental*. A **terminal value** is a personal conviction about lifelong goals or objectives; an **instrumental value** is a personal conviction about desired modes of conduct or ways of behaving.[29] Terminal values often lead to the formation of *norms* for behaviours considered important by most members of a group or organisation, such as behaving honestly or courteously.

Milton Rokeach, one of the leading researchers in the area of human values, identified 18 terminal values and 18 instrumental values that describe each person's value system (Fig. 3.4).[30]

Terminal Values	Instrumental Values
A comfortable life (a prosperous life) An exciting life (a stimulating, active life) A sense of accomplishment (lasting contribution) A world at peace (free of war and conflict) A world of beauty (beauty of nature and the arts) Equality (brotherhood, equal opportunity for all) Family security (taking care of loved ones) Freedom (independence, free choice) Happiness (contentedness) Inner harmony (freedom from inner conflict) Mature love (sexual and spiritual intimacy) National security (protection from attack) Pleasure (an enjoyable, leisurely life) Salvation (saved, eternal life) Self-respect (self-esteem) Social recognition (respect, admiration) True friendship (close companionship) Wisdom (a mature understanding of life)	Ambitious (hard-working, aspiring) Broad-minded (open-minded) Capable (competent, effective) Cheerful (lighthearted, joyful) Clean (neat, tidy) Courageous (standing up for your beliefs) Forgiving (willing to pardon others) Helpful (working for the welfare of others) Honest (sincere, truthful) Imaginative (daring, creative) Independent (self-reliant, self-sufficient) Intellectual (intelligent, reflective) Logical (consistent, rational) Loving (affectionate, tender) Obedient (dutiful, respectful) Polite (courteous, well-mannered) Responsible (dependable, reliable) Self-controlled (restrained, self-disciplined)

Figure 3.4 Terminal and Instrumental Values

Source: Reprinted with permission of The Free Press, a Division of Simon & Schuster Adult Publishing Group, from Milton Rokeach, *The Nature of Human Values*. Copyright © 1973 by The Free Press. All rights reserved.

By rank ordering the terminal values from 1 (most important as a guiding principle in one's life) to 18 (least important as a guiding principle in one's life) and then ranking the instrumental values from 1 to 18, people can illustrate their **value systems** – what they are striving to achieve in life and how they want to behave.[31] (You can gain a good understanding of your own values by ranking first the terminal values and then the instrumental values listed in Fig. 3.4).

Several of the terminal values listed in Fig. 3.4 seem to be especially important for managers – *a sense of accomplishment (lasting contribution), equality (brotherhood, equal opportunity for all)* and *self-respect (self-esteem)*. A manager who thinks a sense of accomplishment is of paramount importance might focus on making a lasting contribution to an organisation by developing a new product that can save or prolong lives (as might be true for Siemens' medical device division), or by opening a new foreign subsidiary. A manager who places equality at the top of their list of terminal values may be at the forefront of an organisation's efforts to support, provide equal opportunities to and capitalise on the many talents of an increasingly diverse workforce.

Other values are likely to be considered important by many managers, such as *a comfortable life (a prosperous life), an exciting life (a stimulating, active life), freedom (independence, free choice)* and *social recognition (respect, admiration)*. The relative importance that managers place on each terminal value helps to explain what they are striving to achieve in their organisations, and on what they will focus their efforts.

Several of the instrumental values listed in Fig. 3.4 seem to be important modes of conduct for managers, such as being *ambitious (hardworking, aspiring), broad-minded (open-minded), capable (competent, effective), responsible (dependable, reliable)* and *self-controlled (restrained, self-disciplined)*. Moreover, the relative importance a manager places on these and other instrumental values may be a significant determinant of actual behaviours on the job. A manager who considers being *imaginative (daring, creative)* to be highly important, for example, is more likely to be innovative and take risks than is a manager who considers this to be less important (all else being equal). A manager who considers being *honest (sincere, truthful)* to be of paramount importance may be a driving force for taking steps to ensure that all members of a unit or organisation behave ethically (Case 3.3).

Case 3.3: **The courage to be honest**

Fraudulent behaviour is on the rise in the UK. Statistics show that there was an increase of 80 per cent in the value of fraudulent acts from 2004 to 2005. The reported amount of fraud is currently £1 billion.

One example is the case of a council officer from Havering, UK, who awarded contracts to relatives. Because of this deal, the local council spent a considerable amount of money over the odds. 'Awarding contracts to businesses secretly owned by family or friends is a very common method used by fraudsters,' said Andrew Durrant, head of fraud at BDO Stoy Hayward, a UK-based accounting and audit firm. It takes managers and employees to report such incidences in order to bring the fraudsters to justice. 90 per cent of participants in a survey said that they would report any knowledge of serious fraud.[32] Some, however, are discouraged by the lenient sentences some of the fraudsters receive. May one argue that society has built up a tolerance towards fraud?

Such incidences are not isolated. Allegations of 'insider trading' of shares were voiced when South African-based insurer Old Mutual bid for Skandia, a Swedish savings and investment company, in order to enter the Nordic market and boost Old Mutual's UK revenues.[33]

In 2003, two years after the merger of AOL and Time Warner, various executives, including the chairman and the vice-president of the media giant, were sued for allegedly overstating earnings to accelerate the merger and cash in on their share options.[34] These things would not surface unless there were individuals prepared to stand up for what they believe in order to uphold their values.

Value systems signify what an individual is trying to accomplish and become in their personal lives and at work. Thus, managers' value systems are fundamental guides to their behaviour and efforts at planning, leading, organising and controlling.

Attitudes

An *attitude* is, as we have seen, a collection of feelings and beliefs. Like everyone else, managers have attitudes about their jobs and organisations, and these attitudes affect how they approach their jobs. Two of the most important attitudes in this context are **job satisfaction** and **organisational commitment**.

Job satisfaction

Job satisfaction is the collection of feelings and beliefs that managers have about their current jobs.[35] Managers who have high levels of job satisfaction generally like their jobs, feel that they are being fairly treated and believe that their jobs have many desirable features or characteristics (such as interesting work, good pay and job security, autonomy or nice co-workers). Figure 3.5 shows sample items from two scales that managers can use to measure job satisfaction. Levels of job satisfaction tend to increase as one progresses up the hierarchy in an organisation: senior managers, in general, tend to be more satisfied with their jobs than entry-level employees.

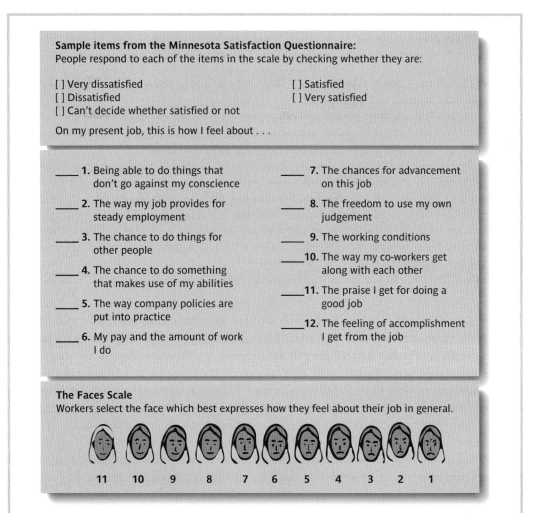

Sample items from the Minnesota Satisfaction Questionnaire:
People respond to each of the items in the scale by checking whether they are:

[ ] Very dissatisfied   [ ] Satisfied
[ ] Dissatisfied   [ ] Very satisfied
[ ] Can't decide whether satisfied or not

On my present job, this is how I feel about . . .

_____ 1. Being able to do things that don't go against my conscience

_____ 2. The way my job provides for steady employment

_____ 3. The chance to do things for other people

_____ 4. The chance to do something that makes use of my abilities

_____ 5. The way company policies are put into practice

_____ 6. My pay and the amount of work I do

_____ 7. The chances for advancement on this job

_____ 8. The freedom to use my own judgement

_____ 9. The working conditions

_____ 10. The way my co-workers get along with each other

_____ 11. The praise I get for doing a good job

_____ 12. The feeling of accomplishment I get from the job

The Faces Scale
Workers select the face which best expresses how they feel about their job in general.

11 10 9 8 7 6 5 4 3 2 1

Figure 3.5 Sample Items from Two Measures of Job Satisfaction

Source: Copyright © 1975 by the American Psychological Association. Reprinted with permission. Adapted and reprinted by permission of Randall B. Dunham and J. B. Brett.

Case 3.4: Values of the overseas Chinese

Over 55 million Chinese people work outside China, manage much of the trade and investment in all East Asia (except for North Korea and Japan) and are now expanding beyond Asia to Europe and the US. Often referred to as the 'Overseas Chinese', they are prominent in business such as property and investment in countries such as Singapore and Malaysia.[36] They tend to be successful at what they do; so successful that some of them are now running multi-billion-pound companies. At the census date in 2001 there were more than 250,000 Chinese in Britain. Of all the minorities, they are likely to be the most successful and highest earning groups.[37]

Hong Kong-born Dr Johnny Hon is an example of a highly successful 'Overseas Chinese'. He has, after receiving a PhD in Psychiatry, worked as a private banker in Hong Kong, but is now chairman of Global Group (Europe) plc – a venture capital (VC) firm based in the UK – that includes a wide portfolio of interests including banking, property development, finance and leisure.[38] His combined turnover for 2005 was expected to reach well beyond £1 billion.

One distinguishing characteristic of some Overseas Chinese – whether managing a bank in Hong Kong or a truly global organisation – is their values. Above all else, they value hard work, ambition, strong family ties, family security, responsibility, self-control and competence. Given these values, you might think that the Overseas Chinese are somewhat risk-averse, but they are not. They also consider being daring and being creative to be important guiding principles, as evidenced by their multi-million-pound investment around the world.

Respect, admiration and social recognition also are important for these entrepreneurial managers. Many of the business deals between organisation owned and managed by Overseas Chinese are conducted through networks of managers who have developed close relationships of mutual trust and respect over decades. Personal relationships and connections built on respect and admiration are called *guanxi* and are the *modus operandi* for many Overseas Chinese. Similarly, *xinyong*, having a good reputation and a good credit rating, is a highly valued asset for many Overseas Chinese managers.[39]

In general, it is desirable for managers to be satisfied with their jobs, for at least two reasons. First, satisfied managers may be more likely to 'go the extra mile' for their organisation or perform **organisational citizenship behaviours (OCBs)**. These are behaviours that are not required of organisational members but that contribute to and are necessary for organisational efficiency, effectiveness and gaining a competitive advantage.[40] Managers who are satisfied with their jobs are more likely to perform these 'above and beyond the call of duty' behaviours, ranging from working extra-long hours when needed to overcome obstacles or to help a co-worker, subordinate, or superior (even when doing so entails considerable personal sacrifice).[41]

A second reason why it is desirable for managers to be satisfied with their jobs is that satisfied managers may be less likely to resign.[42] A manager who is highly satisfied may never even think about looking for another position; a dissatisfied manager may always be on the lookout for new opportunities. Staff turnover can seriously undermine an organisation because it results in the loss of the experience and knowledge that managers have gained about the company, its industry and its business environment.

A growing source of dissatisfaction for many lower- and middle-level managers, as well as for non-managerial employees, is the threat of unemployment and increased workloads from organisational downsizings. A study of 4,300 workers conducted by Wyatt Co. in the mid-1990s found that 76 per cent of the employees of expanding companies were satisfied with their jobs but only 57 per cent of the employees of companies that had downsized were satisfied.[43] Organisations that try to improve their efficiency through restructuring often eliminate a size-able number of first-line and middle-management positions. This decision obviously affects the managers who are laid off, and it also can reduce the job satisfaction levels of managers who remain as they may also fear being made redundant. The workloads of remaining managers are often also dramatically increased as a result of restructuring, and this also can contribute to dissatisfaction.

Organisational commitment

Organisational commitment is the collection of feelings and beliefs that managers have about their organisation as a whole. Managers who are committed to their organisation believe in what their organisation is doing, are proud of what the organisation stands for and feel a high degree of loyalty toward their organisation. Similar to job satisfaction, managers who are committed to the company are more likely to go above and beyond the call of duty and are less likely to leave.[44] Organisational commitment can be especially strong when employees and managers truly believe in organisational values; it can also lead to a strong organisational culture, as found in Virgin (see p. 66).

Organisational commitment is likely to help managers perform some of managerial roles as identified by Mintzberg, namely the roles of figurehead and spokesperson (Chapter 1). It is much easier for a manager to persuade others both inside and outside the organisation of the merits of what the organisation has done and is seeking to accomplish if the manager truly believes in and is committed to the organisation. Figure 3.6 is an example of a scale that managers can use to measure a person's level of organisational commitment.

Do managers in different countries have similar or different attitudes? Differences in the levels of job satisfaction and organisational commitment among managers in different countries are likely due to *cultural differences*. For example, such managers may have different kinds of opportunities and rewards and they also face different economic, political or socio-cultural forces in their organisations' general environment. In countries with relatively high unemployment rates, such as France and Germany, levels of job satisfaction may be higher among employed managers because they may be happy simply to have a job at all. Conversely, this may also have a negative effect due to the increased competition for managerial positions, which entail performance pressures on managers.

Levels of organisational commitment may also depend on the extent to which countries have legislation affecting redundancies and layoffs, and the extent to which citizens of a country are geographically mobile. In both France and Germany legislation protects workers (including managers) from being made redundant or laid off without appropriate reasons. US workers, in contrast, have very little protection. In addition, US managers are more willing to relocate than managers in France and Germany. In France citizens have relatively strong family and community ties and in Germany housing is expensive and difficult to find, especially in areas of economic prosperity. For those reasons, citizens in both countries tend to be less geographically mobile than Americans.[45] Managers who know that their jobs are secure and who are reluctant to relocate (such as those in Germany and France) may be more committed to their organisations than managers who know that their organisations could lay them off any day and who would not mind geographic relocation. However, there are indications that the attitudes of managers in Germany are changing due to the increased threat of unemployment.

People respond to each of the items in the scale by checking whether they:
[ ] Strongly disagree   [ ] Slightly agree
[ ] Moderately disagree   [ ] Moderately agree
[ ] Slightly disagree   [ ] Strongly agree
[ ] Neither disagree nor agree

_____ 1. I am willing to put in a great deal of effort beyond that normally expected in order to help this organisation be successful

_____ 2. I talk up this organisation to my friends as a great organisation to work for

_____ 3. I feel very little loyalty to this organisation*

_____ 4. I would accept almost any type of job assignment in order to keep working for this organisation

_____ 5. I find that my values and the organisation's values are very similar

_____ 6. I am proud to tell others that I am part of this organisation

_____ 7. I could just as well be working for a different organisation as long as the type of work was similar*

_____ 8. This organisation really inspires the very best in me in the way of job performance

_____ 9. It would take very little change in my present circumstances to cause me to leave this organisation*

_____10. I am extremely glad that I chose this organisation to work for over others I was considering at the time I joined

_____11. There's not too much to be gained by sticking with this organisation indefinitely*

_____12. Often, I find it difficult to agree with this organisation's policies on important matters relating to its employees*

_____13. I really care about the fate of this organisation

_____14. For me this is the best of all possible organisations for which to work

_____15. Deciding to work for this organisation was a definite mistake on my part*

Scoring: Responses to items 1, 2, 4, 5, 6, 8, 10, 13 and 14 are scored such that 1 = strongly disagree; 2 = moderately disagree; 3 = slightly disagree; 4 = neither disagree nor agree; 5 = slightly agree; 6 = moderately agree; and 7 = strongly agree. Responses to items 3, 7, 9, 11, 12 and 15 are scored 7 = strongly disagree; 6 = moderately disagree; 5 = slightly disagree; 4 = neither disagree nor agree; 3 = slightly agree; 2 = moderately agree; and 1 = strongly agree. Responses to the 15 items are averaged for an overall score from 1 to 7; the higher the score, the higher the level of organisational commitment.

Figure 3.6 A Measure of Organisational Commitment

Source: Adapted from L.W. Porter and F. J. Smith, 'Organisational Commitment Questionnaire', in J. D. Cook, S. J. Hepworth, T. D. Wall and P. B. Warr, eds., *The Experience of Work: A Compendium and Review of 249 Measures and Their Use* (New York: Academic Press, 1981), 84–86.

Moods and Emotions

A *mood* as we have seen, is a feeling or state of mind. When people are in a positive mood, they feel excited, enthusiastic, active or elated.[46] When people are in a negative mood, they feel distressed, fearful, scornful, hostile, jittery or nervous.[47] People who score high on extraversion are especially likely to experience positive moods; people who score high on negative affectivity are especially likely to experience negative moods. People's situations or circumstances also determine their moods; however, receiving a pay rise is likely to put most people in a good mood regardless of their personality traits. People who are high on negative affectivity are not always in a bad mood, and people who are low on extraversion still experience positive moods.[48]

Emotions as we have seen, are more intense feelings than moods, are often directly linked to whatever caused the emotion and are more short-lived. However, once whatever has triggered the emotion has been dealt with, the feelings may linger in the form of a less intense mood.[49] For example, a manager who gets very angry when one of his subordinates has engaged in an unethical behaviour may find his anger decreasing in intensity once he has decided how to address the problem. Yet he continues to be in a bad mood the rest of the day, even though he is not directly thinking about the incident.[50]

Research suggests that the subordinates of managers who experience positive moods at work may perform at somewhat higher levels and be less likely to resign and leave the organisation than the subordinates of managers who do not tend to be in a positive mood at work.[51]

Other research suggests that under certain conditions creativity may be enhanced by positive moods, whereas under other conditions negative moods may push people to work harder to come up with creative ideas.[52] Additional research suggests that moods and emotions (which are more intense and short-lived feelings that are triggered by something specific) may play an important role in ethical decision making. For example, researchers at Princeton University found that when people are trying to solve difficult personal moral dilemmas, the parts of their brains that are responsible for emotions and moods are especially active.[53]

Recognising the benefits of positive moods, the Northbrook, US accounting firm of Lipschultz, Levin & Gray has gone to great lengths to promote positive feelings among its employees. Chief executive Steven Siegel claims that positive feelings promote relaxation and alleviate stress, increase revenues and attract clients and reduce turnover. Positive moods are promoted in a variety of ways at Lipschultz, Levin & Gray. Siegel has been known to put on a gorilla mask at especially busy times; clerks sometimes don chicken costumes; a foghorn announces the signing of a new client; employees can take a break and play miniature golf in the office, play darts or exercise with a hulahoop. A casual dress code also lightens things up at the firm. By all accounts, positive moods seem to be paying off for this group of accountants, whose good feelings seem to be attracting new clients.

Patrick Corboy, president and chief executive of Austin Chemical, switched his account from a bigger firm to Lipschultz, Levin & Gray because he found the people at the bigger firm to be 'too stuffy and dour for us'. Of the accountant William Finestone, who now manages the Austin Chemical account, Corboy says the following: '[He] is a barrel of laughs . . . Bill not only solves our problems more quickly but he puts us at ease, too.'[54]

Nevertheless, negative moods can sometimes have their advantages. Some studies suggest that critical thinking and 'devil's advocacy' may be promoted by a negative mood, and sometimes especially accurate judgements may be made by managers in such a mood.[55]

Managers and other members of an organisation need to realise that how they feel affects how they treat others, and how others respond to them, including their subordinates. For example, a subordinate may be more likely to approach a manager with a somewhat far-out but potentially useful idea if the subordinate thinks the manager is in a good mood. Likewise, when managers are in very bad moods, their subordinates may try to avoid them at all costs. Figure 3.7 is an example of a scale that managers can use to measure the extent to which a person experiences positive and negative moods at work.

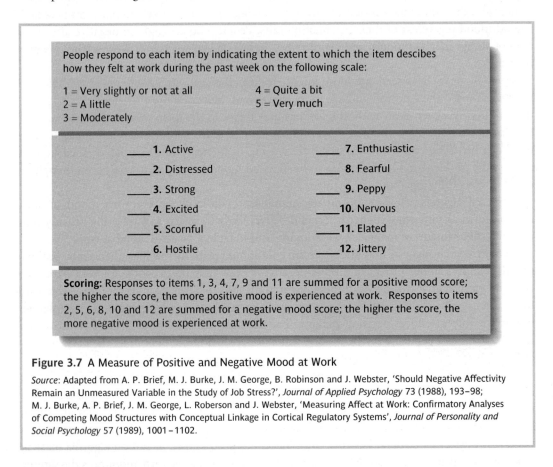

Figure 3.7 A Measure of Positive and Negative Mood at Work

Source: Adapted from A. P. Brief, M. J. Burke, J. M. George, B. Robinson and J. Webster, 'Should Negative Affectivity Remain an Unmeasured Variable in the Study of Job Stress?', *Journal of Applied Psychology* 73 (1988), 193–98; M. J. Burke, A. P. Brief, J. M. George, L. Roberson and J. Webster, 'Measuring Affect at Work: Confirmatory Analyses of Competing Mood Structures with Conceptual Linkage in Cortical Regulatory Systems', *Journal of Personality and Social Psychology* 57 (1989), 1001–1102.

Emotional Intelligence

In understanding the effects of managers' and all employees' moods and emotions, it is important to take into account their levels of **emotional intelligence**. Emotional intelligence is the ability to understand and manage one's own moods and emotions, and the moods and emotions of other people.[56] Managers with a high level of emotional intelligence are more likely to understand how they are feeling and why, and they are more able to effectively manage their feelings. When managers are experiencing stressful feelings and emotions such as fear or anxiety, emotional intelligence enables them to understand why and manage these feelings so that they do not get in the way of effective decision making.[57]

Emotional intelligence also can help managers perform their important roles such as their *interpersonal* roles (figurehead, leader and liaison).[58] Understanding how your subordinates feel, why they feel that way and how to manage these feelings is central to developing strong inter-personal bonds with them.[59] Moreover, emotional intelligence has the potential to contribute to effective leadership in multiple ways[60] and can help managers make lasting contributions to society.

Case 3.5: Bernie Goldhirsh's legacy

Bernard (Bernie) Goldhirsh founded *INC.* magazine in 1979, when entrepreneurs received more notoriety than respect if they were any paid attention to at all.[61] Goldhirsh was an entrepreneur himself at the time, with his own publishing company. He recognised the vast contributions entrepreneurs could make to society, creating something out of nothing, and also realised first-hand what challenges entrepreneurs faced.[62] His emotional intelligence helped him to understand the challenges and frustrations that entrepreneurs like himself faced and their need for support.

When Goldhirsh founded *INC.*, entrepreneurs had little they could turn to for advice, guidance and solutions to management problems. *INC.* was born to fill this gap and provide entrepreneurs with information and support by profiling successful and unsuccessful entrepreneurial ventures, highlighting management techniques that work and providing readers with first-hand accounts of how successful entrepreneurs developed and managed their businesses.[63]

Goldhirsh had an inquisitive mind and liked to go where his thoughts and conversations took him. Although he founded *INC.* magazine and inspired his staff, he let his writers and editors have free rein with the magazine's content. They were the experts he chose to write and edit the magazine, and he realised it was not his place to interfere with editorial matters. What he did do, and do very well, was inspire his staff to be enthusiastic about the mission of *INC.* and the role of the entrepreneur as a self-reliant explorer, going off into the unknown. As Goldhirsh put it, entrepreneurs create new businesses 'from nothing, just blank canvas. . . . It's amazing. Somebody goes into a garage, has nothing but an idea, and out of the garage comes a company, a living company. It's so special what they do. They are a treasure'.[64]

Goldhirsh's emotional intelligence helped him recognise the many barriers entrepreneurs face and the emotional roller-coaster of staking all one has on an idea that may or may not work. Goldhirsh believed that helping society understand the entrepreneurial process through *INC.* magazine not only helped entrepreneurs but also enlightened bankers, law makers and the public at large about the role these visionaries play, the challenges they face and the support on which their ventures depend.[65]

When Goldhirsh was diagnosed with brain cancer at age 60, he sold *INC.* magazine at the urging of his doctors. From the proceeds of the sale, he distributed £11 million to *INC.*'s employees, and dedicated £27.3 million to a foundation supporting brain cancer research. Goldhirsh inspired *INC.*'s employees to recognise that the magazine had only just started and had an important and growing future ahead, and this has certainly been the case.[66] It was a sad day at *INC.* when Goldhirsh died, but also an opportunity to reflect on the contributions of a man who saw the ultimate good in entrepreneurship and whose efforts to support it live on today through the magazine he founded.[67]

Emotional intelligence helps managers understand and relate well to other people.[68] It also helps them to maintain their enthusiasm and confidence and energise subordinates to help the organisation attain its goals.[69] Recent theorising and research suggest that emotional intelligence may be especially important in awakening employee creativity,[70] and managers themselves are increasingly recognising the importance of emotional intelligence. As Andrea Jung, CEO of

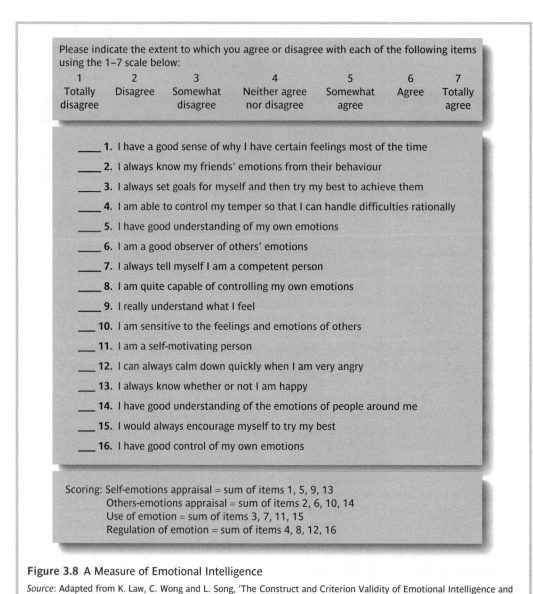

Figure 3.8 A Measure of Emotional Intelligence

Source: Adapted from K. Law, C. Wong and L. Song, 'The Construct and Criterion Validity of Emotional Intelligence and Its Potential Utility for Management Studies', *Journal of Applied Psychology* 89 (3) (2004), 496; C. S. Wong and K. S. Law, 'The Effects of Leader and Follower Emotional Intelligence on Performance and Attitude: An Exploratory Study', *Leadership Quarterly* 13 (2002), 243–74.

Avon Products, says: 'Emotional intelligence is in our DNA here at Avon because relationships are critical at every stage of our business.'[71] An example of a scale that measures emotional intelligence is provided in Fig. 3.8.

Reaction Time

1. Why might managers be disadvantaged by low levels of emotional intelligence?

Organisational Culture

Personality is a way of understanding why all managers and employees, as individuals, characteristically think and behave in different ways. However, when people belong to the same organisation, they often tend to share certain beliefs and values that lead them to act in similar ways.[72] *Organisational culture*, as we have seen, comprises the shared set of beliefs, expectations, values, norms and work routines that influence how members of an organisation relate to one another and work together to achieve organisational goals. In essence, organisational culture reflects the distinctive ways in which organisational members go about performing their jobs and relating to others inside and outside the organisation. It may, for example, be a distinctive way in which customers in a particular hotel chain are treated from the time they are greeted at check-in until their stay is completed; or it may be the shared work routines that research teams use to guide new product development. When organisational members share an intense commitment to cultural values, beliefs and routines and use them to achieve their goals, a *strong* organisational culture exists. When organisational members are not strongly committed to a shared system of values, beliefs and routines, organisational culture is *weak*.

The stronger the culture of an organisation, the more one can think about it as being the 'personality' of an organisation because it influences the way its members behave.[73] Organisations that possess strong cultures may differ on a wide variety of dimensions that determine how their members behave toward one another and perform their jobs. For example, organisations differ in terms of how members relate to each other (e.g. formally or informally), how important decisions are made (e.g. top-down or bottom-up), willingness to change (e.g. flexible or unyielding), innovation (e.g. creative or predictable) and playfulness (e.g. serious or serendipitous). In an innovative design firm like IDEO Product Development, employees are encouraged to adopt a 'playful' attitude to their work, look outside the organisation to find inspiration and adopt a flexible approach toward product design that uses multiple perspectives.[74] IDEO's culture is vastly different from that of companies such as Lloyds TSB and British Petroleum (BP), in which employees treat each other in a more formal or deferential way, employees are expected to adopt a serious approach to their work, and decision making is constrained by the hierarchy of authority.

These differences can also be explained by looking at organisations and determining whether they have a strong or a weak culture. Weak cultures tend to have little alignment between individuals' goals and values and organisational goals and values. On the other end of the continuum are strong cultures. These encourage responsive, proactive staff that are able to respond to new stimuli, as employees' values are close to those of the organisation.

Managers and Organisational Culture

While all members of an organisation can contribute to the development and maintenance of organisational culture, managers play a particularly important part in influencing it,[75] given their multiple and important roles (see Chapter 1). How managers create culture is most clearly evident in start-ups of new companies. Entrepreneurs who start their own companies are typically also the start-ups' senior managers until the companies grow and/or become profitable. Often referred to as the firms' founders, these managers literally create their organisation's culture.

Often, the founder's personal characteristics play an important role in the creation of organisational culture. Benjamin Schneider, a well-known management researcher, developed a model that helps to explain the role that founders' personal characteristics play in determining organisational culture.[76] His model, called the **attraction–selection–attrition (ASA) frame-work**, posits that when founders hire employees for their new ventures, they tend to be attracted to and choose employees whose personalities are similar to their own.[77] These employees are more likely to stay with the organisation. While employees who are dissimilar in personality may be hired, they are more likely to leave the organisation over time.[78] As a result of these attraction, selection and attrition processes, people in the organisation tend to have similar personalities, and the typical or dominant personality profile of organisational members determines and shapes the organisational culture.[79]

Managers who are satisfied with their jobs, are committed to their organisations and experience positive moods and emotions may also encourage these attitudes and feelings in others. The result will be an organisational culture emphasising positive attitudes and feelings. Research suggests that attitudes like job satisfaction and organisational commitment can be affected by the influence of others. Managers are in a particularly strong position to engage in social influence, given their multiple roles. Research also suggests that moods and emotions can be 'contagious' and that spending time with people who are excited and enthusiastic can increase one's own levels of excitement and enthusiasm.

The Role of Values and Norms in Organisational Culture

Shared terminal and instrumental values can play a particularly important role in organisational culture. *Terminal values* signify what an organisation and its employees are trying to accomplish, and *instrumental values* guide the ways in which the organisation and its members achieve organisational goals. In addition to values, *shared norms* also are a key aspect of organisational culture. Remember that norms are unwritten, informal rules or guidelines that prescribe appropriate behaviour in particular situations. Norms at IDEO, for example, include not being critical of others' ideas, coming up with multiple ideas before settling on one, and developing prototypes of new products.[80]

Managers determine and shape organisational culture through the kinds of values and norms they promote in an organisation. Some managers, like David Kelley of IDEO, cultivate values and norms that encourage risk taking, creative responses to problems and opportunities, experimentation, tolerance of failure in order to succeed and autonomy.[81] Senior managers at organisations such as Intel, Microsoft and Sun Microsystems encourage employees to adopt such values to support their commitment to innovation as a source of competitive advantage.

Other managers, however, may cultivate values and norms that indicate to employees that they should always be conservative and cautious in their dealings with others and should try to consult with their superiors before making important decisions or any changes to the status quo. Accountability for actions and decisions is stressed, and detailed records are kept to ensure that policies and procedures are followed. In settings where caution is needed – nuclear power stations, large oil refineries, chemical plants, financial institutions or insurance companies – a conservative, cautious approach to making decisions might be highly appropriate.[82] In a nuclear power plant, for example, the catastrophic consequences of a mistake make a high level of supervision vital. Similarly, in a bank or mutual fund company, the risk of losing investors' money makes a cautious approach to investing highly appropriate.

Managers of different kinds of organisations deliberately cultivate and develop the organisational values and norms that are best suited to their task and general environment, strategy or technology. Organisational culture is maintained and transmitted to organisational members

Figure 3.9 Factors That Maintain and Transmit Organisational Culture

through the values of the founder, the process of socialisation, ceremonies and rites and stories and language (Fig. 3.9).

Values of the founder

From the ASA model discussed above it is clear that the founders of an organisation can have profound and long-lasting effects on organisational culture. The founders' values inspire them to start their own companies and, in turn, drive the nature of these new companies and their defining characteristics. Thus, an organisation's founder and their terminal and instrumental values have a substantial influence on the values, norms and standards of behaviour that develop over time within the organisation.[83] Founders set the scene for the way cultural values and norms develop because their own values guide the building of the company, and they hire other managers and employees who they believe will share these values and help the organisation to attain them. New managers quickly learn from the founder what values and norms are appropriate in the organisation, and thus what is desired of them. Subordinates imitate the style of the founder and, in turn, transmit their values and norms to their subordinates. Gradually, over time, the founder's values and norms permeate the whole organisation.[84]

A founder who requires a great display of respect from subordinates and insists on proprieties such as formal job titles and formal modes of dress encourages subordinates to act in this way toward their subordinates. Often, a founder's personal values affect an organisation's competitive advantage. For example, Werner von Siemens or Richard Branson cultivated particular cultural and organisational values – Siemens was one of the first founders who cared about the welfare of its employees, for example.

Socialisation

Over time, organisational members learn from each other which values are important in an organisation and the norms that specify appropriate and inappropriate behaviours. Eventually, organisational members behave in accordance with the organisation's values and norms – often without realising they are doing so. **Organisational socialisation** is the process by which newcomers learn an organisation's values and norms and acquire the work behaviours necessary to perform jobs effectively.[85] As a result of their socialisation experiences, organisational members *internalise* an organisation's values and norms and behave in accordance with them not only because they think they have to but because they think that these values and norms describe the right and proper way to behave.[86]

Most organisations have some kind of socialisation programme to help new employees 'learn the ropes' – the values, norms and culture of the organisation. The military, for example, is well known for the rigorous socialisation process it uses to turn raw recruits into trained soldiers. Organisations such as the Walt Disney Co. also put new recruits through a rigorous training programme to provide them with the knowledge they need not only to perform well in their jobs but also to ensure that each employee plays their part in helping visitors to Disneyland have fun. New recruits at Disney are called 'cast members' and attend Disney University to learn the Disney culture and their own part in it. Disney's culture emphasises the values of safety, courtesy, entertainment and efficiency, and these values are brought to life for newcomers at Disney University. Newcomers also learn about the attraction area they will be joining (e.g. Adventureland or Fantasyland) at Disney University and then receive on-the-job socialisation in the area itself from experienced cast members.[87] Through organisational socialisation, the founders and managers of an organisation transmit to employees the cultural values and norms that shape the behaviour of organisational members. The values and norms of founder Walt Disney thus live on today at Disneyland as newcomers are socialised into the 'Disney way'.

Ceremonies and rites

Another way in which managers can create or influence organisational culture is by developing organisational *ceremonies and rites* – formal events that recognise incidents of importance to the organisation as a whole and to specific employees.[88] The most common rites that organisations use to transmit cultural norms and values to their members are rites of passage, of integration and of enhancement (Table 3.1).[89]

Rites of passage determine how individuals enter, advance within or leave the organisation. The socialisation programmes developed by military organisations (such as the Army) or by large accountancy and law firms are rites of passage. Likewise, the ways in which an organisation prepares people for promotion or retirement are rites of passage.

Rites of integration, such as shared announcements of organisational successes, office parties and company BBQs, build and reinforce common bonds among organisational members. IDEO, an innovation company designing services and products, uses many rites of integration to make its employees feel connected to one another and special. In addition to having wild 'end-of-year' celebratory bashes, groups of IDEO employees periodically take time off to go to a sporting event, movie or meal or, sometimes, on a long bike ride or sail. These kinds of shared activities not only reinforce IDEO's culture but also can be a source of inspiration on the job (e.g. IDEO has been involved in the making of movies such as *The Abyss* and *Free Willy*). One 35-member design studio at IDEO led by Dennis Boyle has bi-monthly lunch fests with no set agenda –

Table 3.1 Organisational rites

Type of rite	Example of rite	Purpose of rite
Rite of passage	Induction and basic training	Learn and internalise norms and values
Rite of integration	Office Christmas party	Build common norms and values
Rite of enhancement	Presentation of annual award	Motivate commitment to norms and values

anything goes. While enjoying great food, jokes and camaraderie, studio members often end up sharing ideas for their latest great products, and the freely flowing conversation that results often leads to creative insights.[90]

A company's annual meeting also may be used as a ritual of integration, offering an opportunity to communicate organisational values to managers, other employees and shareholders. ASDA, for example, makes its annual stockholders' meeting an extravagant ceremony that celebrates the company's success. ASDA believes that rewarding its supporters with entertainment reinforces the company's high-performance values and culture. The proceedings are shown live over closed-circuit television in all ASDA stores so that all employees can join in the rites celebrating the company's achievements.[91]

Rites of enhancement, such as awards dinners, newspaper releases and employee promotions, let organisations publicly recognise and reward employees' contributions and thus strengthen their commitment to organisational values. By bonding members within the organisation, rites of enhancement reinforce an organisation's values and norms.

Stories and language also communicate organisational culture. Stories (whether fact or fiction) about organisational heroes and villains and their actions provide important clues about values and norms. Such stories can reveal the kinds of behaviours that are valued by the organisation and the kinds of practices that are frowned on.[92] At the heart of McDonald's rich culture are hundreds of stories that organisational members tell about founder Ray Kroc. Most of these stories focus on how Kroc established the strict operating values and norms that are at the heart of McDonald's culture. Kroc was dedicated to achieving perfection in McDonald's quality, service, cleanliness and value for money (QSC&V), and these four central values permeate McDonald's culture. For example, an often retold story describes what happened when Kroc and a group of managers were touring various restaurants. One of the restaurants was having a bad day operationally. Kroc was incensed about the long lines of customers, and he was furious when he realised that the quality of product customers were receiving that day was not up to his high standards. To address the problem, he jumped up and stood on the front counter and got the attention of all customers and employees. He introduced himself, apologised for the long wait and cold food, and told the customers that they could have freshly cooked food or their money back – whichever they wanted. As a result, the customers left happy, and when Kroc checked on the restaurant later, he found that his message had gotten through to its managers and crew – performance had improved. Other stories describe Kroc scrubbing dirty toilets and picking up litter inside or outside a restaurant. These and similar stories are spread around the organisation by McDonald's employees. They are the stories that have helped establish Kroc as McDonald's 'hero'.

Because spoken language is a principal medium of communication in organisations, the characteristic slang or **jargon** – that is, organisation-specific words or phrases – that people use to frame and describe events can provide important clues about norms and values. 'McLanguage', for example, is prevalent at all levels of McDonald's. A McDonald's employee described as having 'ketchup in his (or her) blood' is someone who is truly dedicated to the McDonald's way – someone who has been completely socialised to its culture. McDonald's has an extensive training programme that teaches new employees 'McDonald's speak', and new employees are welcomed into the family with a formal orientation that illustrates Kroc's dedication to QSC&V.

The concept of organisational language encompasses not only spoken language but how people dress, the offices they occupy, the cars they drive and the degree of formality they use when they address one another. Casual dress reflects and reinforces Microsoft's entrepreneurial culture and values. Formal business attire supports the conservative culture found in many banks, which emphasise the importance of conforming to organisational norms such as respect for authority and staying within one's prescribed role. Traders in the Chicago futures and options trading pits frequently wear garish and flamboyant ties and jackets to make their presence known in a sea of faces. The demand for magenta, lime green and silver lamé jackets featuring bold images such as the Power Rangers – anything that helps the traders stand out and attract customers – is enormous.[93] When employees speak and understand the language of their organisation's culture, they know how to behave in the organisation, and what is expected of them.

Culture and Managerial Action

While founders and managers play a critical role in the development, maintenance and communication of organisational culture, this same culture shapes and controls the behaviour of all employees, including managers themselves. For example, culture influences the way managers perform their four main functions: planning, organising, leading and controlling. As we consider these functions, we continue to distinguish between senior managers who create organisational values and norms that encourage creative, innovative behaviour and senior managers who encourage a conservative, cautious approach by their subordinates. We saw earlier that both kinds of values and norms can be appropriate, depending upon the situation and type of organisation.

Planning

Senior managers in an organisation with an innovative culture are likely to encourage lower-level managers to participate in the planning process and develop a flexible approach to planning. They are likely to be willing to listen to new ideas and to take risks involving the development of new products. In contrast, senior managers in an organisation with conservative values are likely to emphasise formal 'top-down' planning. Suggestions from lower-level managers are likely to be subjected to a formal review process, which can significantly slow decision making. Although this deliberate approach may improve the quality of decision making in a nuclear power plant, it can have unintended consequences. In the past, at conservative IBM, the planning process became so formalised that managers spent most of their time assembling complex slide shows and overheads to defend their current positions rather than thinking about what they should be doing to keep IBM abreast of the changes taking place in the computer industry. When former CEO Lou Gerstner took over, he used every means at his disposal to abolish this culture, even building a brand-new campus-style headquarters to change managers' mind-sets. IBM's culture is now undergoing further changes initiated by its new CEO, Samuel Palmisano (see Chapter 3).

Organising

What kinds of organising will managers in innovative and in conservative cultures encourage? Valuing creativity, managers in innovative cultures are likely to try to create an *organic structure* – one that is flat, with few levels in the hierarchy, and one in which authority is decentralised so that employees are encouraged to work together to find solutions to ongoing problems. A product team structure may be very suitable for an organisation with an innovative culture. In contrast, managers in a conservative culture are likely to create a *well-defined hierarchy of authority* and establish *clear reporting relationships* so that employees know exactly whom to report to and how to react to any problems that arise.

Leading

In an innovative culture, managers are likely to lead by example, encouraging employees to take risks and experiment. They are supportive regardless of whether employees succeed or fail. In contrast, managers in a conservative culture are likely to use MBO and to constantly monitor subordinates' progress toward goals, overseeing their every move. Leadership is examined in detail in Chapter 14 where the style of leadership that managers can adopt to influence and shape employee behaviour is considered.

Controlling

The ways in which managers evaluate, and take actions to improve, performance differ depending upon whether the organisational culture emphasises formality and caution or innovation and change. Managers who want to encourage risk taking, creativity and innovation recognise that there are multiple potential paths to success and that failure must be accepted in order for creativity to thrive. They are thus less concerned about employees performing their jobs in a specific, predetermined manner and in strict adherence to preset goals and more concerned about employees being flexible and taking the initiative to come up with ideas for improving performance. Managers in innovative cultures are also more concerned about long-run performance than short-term targets because they recognise that real innovation entails the type of uncertainty that necessitates flexibility. In contrast, managers in cultures that emphasise caution and maintenance of the status quo often set specific, difficult goals for employees, frequently monitor progress toward these goals and develop a clear set of rules to which employees are expected to adhere.

The values and norms of an organisation's culture strongly affect the way managers perform their management functions. The extent to which managers buy into the values and norms of their organisation shapes their view of the world and their actions and decisions in particular circumstances.[94] In turn, the actions that managers take can have an impact on the performance of the organisation. Organisational culture, managerial action and organisational performance are thus all interlinked.

This linkage is apparent at Hewlett-Packard (HP), a leader in the electronic instrumentation and computer industries. Established in the 1940s, HP developed a culture that is an outgrowth of the strong personal beliefs of the company's founders, William Hewlett and David Packard. Bill and Dave, as they are known within the company, formalised HP's culture in 1957 in a statement of corporate objectives known as the 'HP Way'. The basic values informing the HP Way stress serving everyone who has a stake in the company with integrity and fairness, including customers, suppliers, employees, stockholders and society in general. Bill and Dave helped build this culture within HP by hiring like-minded people and by letting the HP Way guide their own actions as managers.

Although the Hewlett-Packard example illustrates how organisational culture can give rise to managerial actions that ultimately benefit the organisation, this is not always the case. The cultures of some organisations become *dysfunctional*, encouraging managerial actions that harm the organisation and discouraging actions that might lead to an improvement in performance.[95] Corporate scandals at large companies like Enron and WorldCom show how damaging a dysfunctional culture can be to an organisation and its members. For example, Enron's arrogant, 'success-at-all-costs' culture led to fraudulent behaviour on the part of its senior managers.[96] Unfortunately, hundreds of Enron employees have paid a heavy price for the unethical behaviour of these senior managers and the dysfunctional organisational culture. Not only have these employees lost their jobs, but many also have lost their life savings in Enron stock and pension funds, which became worth just a fraction of their former value when the wrongdoing at Enron came to light. The issue of ethics and ethical cultures is discussed in depth in Chapter 4.

Reaction Time

1. If you were the newly appointed manager of a company whose employees constantly complained and absenteeism and turnover were high, discuss what changes you would make, and explain why.

TIP FOR PRACTICE

1. Think about the differences that may exist in people and in different cultures. Before making a rush decision, consider why people may act in a particular way.

Summary and Review

Enduring characteristics: personality traits and types Personality is about the enduring traits that we possess or the type of preferences we have that influence the way we feel, think and act. The MBTI are made up of 16 different types. The 'Big Five' traits are extraversion, negative affectivity, agreeableness, conscientiousness and openness to experience. Other characteristics that affect managerial behaviour are locus of control, self-esteem and the need for achievement, affiliation and power.

Values and attitudes and moods and emotions A terminal value is a personal conviction about lifelong goals or objectives; an instrumental value is a personal conviction about modes of conduct. Terminal and instrumental values have an impact on what managers try to achieve in their organisations and the kinds of behaviours they engage in. An attitude is a collection of feelings and beliefs. Two attitudes important for understanding managerial behaviours include job satisfaction (the collection of feelings and beliefs that managers have about their jobs) and organisational commitment (the collection of feelings and beliefs that managers have about their organisations). A mood is a feeling or state of mind; emotions are intense feelings that are short-lived and directly linked to their causes. Managers' moods and emotions, or how they feel at work on a day-to-day basis, have the potential to impact not only their own behaviour and effectiveness but also those of their subordinates. Emotional intelligence is the ability to understand and manage one's own and other people's moods and emotions.

Organisational culture Organisational culture is the shared set of beliefs, expectations, values, norms and work routines that influences how members of an organisation relate to one another and work together to achieve organisational goals. Founders of new organisations and managers play an important role in creating and maintaining organisational culture. Organisational socialisation is the process by which newcomers learn an organisation's values and norms and acquire the work behaviours necessary to perform jobs effectively.

Topic for Action

- Interview a manager in a local organisation. Ask the manager to describe situations in which he or she is especially likely to act in accordance with his or her values. Ask the manager to describe situations in which he or she is less likely to act in accordance with his or her values.

- Watch a popular television show and, as you watch it, try to determine the emotional intelligence levels of the characters the actors in the show portray. Rank the characters from highest to lowest in terms of emotional intelligence. As you watched the show, what factors influenced your assessments of emotional intelligence levels?

- Go to an upmarket clothing store in your neighbourhood, and go to a clothing store that is definitely not upmarket. Observe the behaviour of employees in each store as well as the store's environment. In what ways are the organisational cultures in each store similar? In what ways are they different?

Applied Independent Learning

Building Management Skills

Diagnosing Culture

Think about the culture of the last organisation you worked for, your current university, or another organisation or club to which you belong. Then answer the following questions:

1. What values are emphasised in this culture?
2. What norms do members of this organisation follow?
3. Who seems to have played an important role in creating the culture?
4. In what ways is the organisational culture communicated to organisational members?

Managing Ethically

Some organisations rely on personality and interest inventories to screen potential employees. Other organisations attempt to screen employees by using paper-and-pencil honesty tests.

Questions

1. Either individually or in a group, think about the ethical implications of using personality and interest inventories to screen potential employees. How might this practice be unfair to potential applicants? How might organisational members who are in charge of hiring misuse it?

2. Because of measurement error and validity problems, some relatively trustworthy people may 'fail' an honesty test given by an employer. What are the ethical implications of trustworthy people 'failing' honesty tests, and what obligations do you think employers should have when relying on honesty tests for screening purposes?

▶

► ## Small Group Breakout Exercise

Making Difficult Decisions in Hard Times

Form groups of three or four people, and appoint one member as the spokesperson who will communicate your findings to the whole class when called on by the instructor. Then discuss the following scenario.

You are on the senior management team of a medium-size company that manufactures cardboard boxes, containers and other cardboard packaging materials. Your company is facing increasing levels of competition for major corporate customer accounts, and profits have declined significantly. You have tried everything you can to cut costs and remain competitive, with the exception of laying off employees. Your company has had a 'no-layoff' policy for the past 20 years, and you believe it is an important part of the organisation's culture. However, you are experiencing mounting pressure to increase your firm's performance, and your 'no-layoff' policy has been questioned by shareholders. Even though you haven't decided whether to lay off employees and thus break with a 20-year tradition for your company, rumours are rampant in your organisation that something is afoot, and employees are worried. You are meeting today to address this problem.

1. Develop a list of options and potential courses of action to address the heightened competition and decline in profitability that your company has been experiencing.

2. Choose your preferred course of action, and justify why you will take this route.

3. Describe how you will communicate your decision to employees.

4. If your preferred option involves a layoff, justify why. If it doesn't involve layoff, explain why.

Exploring the World Wide Web

Identify a company website of your choice and explore the site. What can you tell about the culture of this organisation? Who do you think would work for your chosen organisation? Where do you think the organisational values are coming from?

Application in Today's Business World

I'm a Bad Boss? Blame My Dad

For Peter Tilton, the office revelation came last February. He was sitting in a conference room at company headquarters, meeting with the group he managed, when an 'incompetent' colleague began needling him about his own progress on a project. Tilton felt the trip wire go off, the raw rush that made him feel as if he were slipping into a state of adolescent siege.

Within seconds, he was banging his fist on the whiteboard and 'yelling his face off'. Even at a place like Microsoft Corp., where Tilton says co-workers routinely blast each other's ideas as 'stupid', this wasn't exactly behaviour becoming a director-level executive. The emotional outburst, Tilton now realises, was eerily similar to one he had back in seventh grade, when his parents – 'chronic misunderstanders' – forbade him to wear his jeans with the holey knees to school. It was 1967, and he was deeply into his hippie protest phase. 'And they wanted me to wear slacks,' Tilton says.

For Bert Whitehead, CEO of Cambridge Connection, a financial planning company in Franklin Village, Mich., the epiphany came when, after announcing he would be away on a business trip, he noticed a stealthy rejoicing rippling through his offices. Today, he knows why. 'Nobody was ever quite good enough,' says Whitehead, who refers to himself as a moody stress generator. 'I had a mother I could never get approval from, and I had unknowingly really adopted that into my management style.'

That these highly rational, utterly left-brained executives are delving into their past illustrates a new strain of organisational therapy coursing through the inner sanctums of corporate power. The basic concept is that people tend to recreate their family dynamics at the office. The idea is being fanned by organisational experts, who say that corporate strivers can at times behave a bit like thumb-suckers in knee pants, yearning for pats on the back from boss 'daddies and mommies' and wishing those scenestealing co-worker 'siblings' would, well, die. Boardroom arguments can parallel spats at the family dinner table. Office politics can take on the dimensions of Icarus blowing off his Dad – or Hamlet offing Uncle Claudius.

Buttressed by new research in workplace dynamics, more high-profile coaches and consultants are applying family-systems therapy to business organisations, to grapple with what has come to be seen as a new frontier in productivity: emotional inefficiency, which includes all that bickering, back-stabbing and ridiculous playing for approval that are a mark of the modern workplace. A two-year study by Seattle psychologist Brian DesRoches found that such dramas routinely waste 20–50 per cent of workers' time. The theory is also gaining more resonance as corporations become ever-more cognizant that talented employees quit bosses, not companies, and that CEOs often get hired for their skills – and fired for their personalities.

Looking backward to move forward makes sense, say group dynamic researchers, considering that the first organisation people ever belong to is their families, with parents the first bosses and siblings the first colleagues. 'Our original notions of an institution, of an authority structure, of power and influence are all forged in the family,' says Warren Bennis, management guru and Professor of Business at the University of Southern California. Dr Scott C. Stacy, clinical programme director of the Professional Renewal Centre in Lawrence, Kan, adds: 'This is a huge piece of understanding how businesses everywhere work.'

Hero, Scapegoat, Martyr

This may seem like so much ESTera drivel, but by performing psychological X-rays on clients' pasts, coaches have helped executives at companies as diverse as *The Los Angeles Times*, State Farm Insurance and American Express understand their own and others' dysfunctional behaviour. They learn how to recognise the shadowy emotional subtext that drives many encounters, deconstructing how they may be subconsciously sabotaging themselves, shying from authority figures, or engaging in hypercritical judgements of subordinates. Or why they may unwittingly play the role of the hero, scapegoat or martyr. 'I'm not suggesting that our employees are our kids,' says Kenneth Sole, a consulting social psychologist who has worked with Apple Computer, Inc. and the UN. 'But the psychology is parallel.'

Indeed, brain research over the past decade has shown that during stress – when people's need to feel included, competent and liked is thwarted – their minds are hardwired to default to defensive family scripts. 'We project onto others the conflicts we experienced growing up,'

▶

▶ says Robert Pasick, President of LeadersConnect in Ann Arbor, Mich. He teaches a course at the University of Michigan Business School on how family dynamics affect teams.

Such corporate head-shrinking is gaining more ground in part because of how much interdependence companies face on the global stage. In the manual economy, work was a regimented, militaristic affair in which it was easier to subsume personality differences. Today, success hinges on teams performing as seamlessly as the flawless machinery in a showcase Six Sigma plant. And corporations hire workers whose families are more likely to resemble The Osbournes than Ozzie and Harriet. Personalities, emotions, behavioural tics – all have started to take on a bigger dimension in an era in which businesses increasingly sell the ideas that come from employees' heads, not just the products from their machines.

Moreover, as scandals have heightened the need for transparency, disclosure and ethics, many execs have begun to see the importance of matching the corporate culture with employees' personal cultures, given that most people get their ethical foundations from their families. That's why a number of financial, utility and manufacturing clients are lobbing interview questions about families at job candidates in the hope of yielding unvarnished responses, says Neil Lebovits, president of Ajilon Finance in Saddle Brook, NJ. Anything to avoid hiring the next Jeffrey K. Skilling.

Of course, plenty of leaders and their consultants object to therapy invading the office. 'The workplace is not the place to explore psychological foibles,' says Richard A. Chaifetz, CEO of ComPsych Corp., a Chicago employee-assistance firm. 'It can open up a can of worms.' Chaifetz approves of this kind of inquiry only if it's done offsite, one-on-one, and with a trained professional. And many work dynamics can't be analysed solely through a family filter. More likely, say critics, work teams carry traits that are characteristic of all group dynamics. Pairing off, for example, usually happens any time people gather. So does complaining.

Historic Hysterics

Still, someone's familial past can certainly seep into the office scene. It's most recognisable, say experts, when a co-worker or supervisor has highly emotional, intense reactions: When it's hysterical, it's historical. Other symptoms are an inability to maintain a reflective distance, repeated outbursts of anger and having the same battles with the same people over and over.

In Tilton's case, the Microsoft exec had disdained therapy 'ever since my parents tried to send me to a pipe-smoking guy in seventh grade'. But in the months he has been working with an executive coach, he only wishes he could have cracked through his denial sooner. Like many, he realises that being analytically savvy isn't enough. Being emotionally competent is now part of the job, too.

Questions

1. In what ways do people's personalities and experiences as they were growing up affect them in later life in the workplace?

2. Why might personality be becoming a more important factor in understanding managerial effectiveness?

3. Why aren't technical and analytical skills alone sufficient for being an effective manager?

4. What roles does emotional intelligence play in managerial effectiveness?

Source: Adapted and reprinted from *BusinessWeek*, May 10, 2004 by special permission. Copyright © 2004 by the McGraw-Hill Companies, Inc.

52   George and Brief, 'Feeling Good–Doing Good'; J. M. George and J. Zhou, 'Understanding When Bad Moods Foster Creativity and Good Ones Don't: The Role of Context and Clarity of Feelings', Paper presented at the Academy of Management Annual Meeting, 2001; A. M. Isen and R. A. Baron, 'Positive Affect as a Factor in Organizational Behavior', in B. M. Staw and L. L. Cummings, eds, *Research in Organizational Behavior*, 13 (Greenwich, CT: JAI Press, 1991), 1–53.

53   J. D. Greene, R. B. Sommerville, L. E. Nystrom, J. M. Darley and J. D. Cohen, 'An FMRI Investigation of Emotional Engagement in Moral Judgment', *Science*, September 14, 2001, 2105–08; L. Neergaard, 'Brain Scans Show Emotions Key to Resolving Ethical Dilemmas', *Houston Chronicle*, September 14, 2001, 13A.

54   L. Berton, 'It's Audit Time! Send in the Clowns', *The Wall Street Journal*, January 18, 1995, B1, B6.

55   R. C. Sinclair, 'Mood, Categorization Breadth, and Performance Appraisal: The Effects of Order of Information Acquisition and Affective State on Halo, Accuracy, Informational Retrieval, and Evaluations', *Organizational Behavior and Human Decision Processes* 42 (1988), 22–46.

56   D. Goleman, *Emotional Intelligence* (New York: Bantam Books, 1994); J. D. Mayer and P. Salovey, 'The Intelligence of Emotional Intelligence', *Intelligence* 17 (1993), 433–42; J. D. Mayer and P. Salovey, 'What Is Emotional Intelligence?', in P. Salovey and D. Sluyter, eds, *Emotional Development and Emotional Intelligence: Implications for Education* (New York: Basic Books. 1997); P. Salovey and J. D. Mayer, 'Emotional Intelligence', *Imagination, Cognition, and Personality* 9 (1989–90), 185–211.

57   S. Epstein, *Constructive Thinking* (Westport, CT: Praeger, 1998).

58   'Leading by Feel', *Inside the Mind of the Leader* (January 2004), 27–37.

59   P. C. Early and R. S. Peterson, 'The Elusive Cultural Chameleon: Cultural Intelligence as a New Approach to Intercultural Training for the Global Manager', *Academy of Management Learning and Education* 3(1) (2004), 100–15.

60   George, 'Emotions and Leadership'; S. Begley, 'The Boss Feels Your Pain', *NewsWeek*, October 12, 1998, 74; D. Goleman, *Working With Emotional Intelligence* (New York: Bantam Books, 1998).

61   J. Bercovici, 'Remembering Bernie Goldhirsh', www.medialifemagazine.com/news2003/jun03/jun30/4_thurs/news1thursday.html, April 15, 2004.

62   B. Burlingham, 'Legacy: The Creative Spirit', *INC.*, September, 2003, 11–12.

63   *Ibid.*

64   *Ibid.*

65   *Ibid.*

66   *Ibid.*

67   Adapted from 'Bernard Goldhirsh, Magazine Founder and MIT Alumnus, Dies at 63', web.mit.edu/newsoffice/nr/2003/goldhirsh.html, July 1, 2003.

68   'Leading by Feel', *Inside the Mind of the Leader*, January, 2004, 27–37.

69   George, 'Emotions and Leadership'.

70   J. Zhou and J. M. George, 'Awakening Employee Creativity: The Role of Leader Emotional Intelligence', *Leadership Quarterly* 14 (2003), 545–68

71   A. Jung, 'Leading by Feel: Seek Frank Feedback', *Inside the Mind of the Leader*, January 2004, 31.

72   H. M. Trice and J. M. Beyer, *The Cultures of Work Organizations* (Englewood Cliffs, NJ: Prentice Hall, 1993).

73   B. Schneider and D. B. Smith, eds, *Personality and Organizations*, (Mahway, NJ: Lawrence Erlbaum, 2004), 347–69; J. E. Slaughter, M. J. Zickar, S. Highhouse and D. C. Mohr, 'Personality Trait Inferences About Organizations: Development of a Measure and Assessment of Construct Validity', *Journal of Applied Psychology* 89(1) (2004), 85–103.

74   T. Kelley, *The Art of Innovation: Lessons in Creativity from IDEO, America's Leading Design Firm* (New York: Random House, 2001).

75   Schneider and Smith, 'Personality and Organizations'.

76   B. Schneider, 'The People Make the Place', *Personnel Psychology* 40 (1987), 437–53.

77   Schneider and Smith, 'Personality and Organizations'.

78 *Ibid.*

79 B. Schneider, H. B. Goldstein and D. B. Smith, 'The ASA Framework: An Update', *Personnel Psychology* 48 (1995), 747–73; J. Schaubroeck, D. C. Ganster and J. R. Jones, 'Organizational and Occupational Influences in the Attraction–Selection–Attrition Process', *Journal of Applied Psychology* 83 (1998), 869–91.

80 Kelley, *The Art of Innovation.*

81 *Ibid.*

82 D. C. Feldman, 'The Development and Enforcement of Group Norms', *Academy of Management Review* 9 (1984), 47–53.

83 G. R. Jones, *Organizational Theory, Design, and Change* (Englewood Cliffs, NJ: Prentice Hall, 2003).

84 H. Schein, 'The Role of the Founder in Creating Organizational Culture', *Organizational Dynamics* 12 (1983), 13–28.

85 J. M. George, 'Personality, Affect, and Behavior in Groups', *Journal of Applied Psychology* 75 (1990), 107–16.

86 J. Van Maanen, 'Police Socialization: A Longitudinal Examination of Job Attitudes in an Urban Police Department', *Administrative Science Quarterly* 20 (1975), 207–28.

87 www.intercotwest.com/Disney; M. N. Martinez, 'Disney Training Works Magic', *HRMagazine*, May 1992, 53–57.

88 P. L. Berger and T. Luckman, *The Social Construction of Reality* (Garden City, NY: Anchor Books, 1967).

89 H. M. Trice and J. M. Beyer, 'Studying Organizational Culture Through Rites and Ceremonials', *Academy of Management Review* 9 (1984), 653–69.

90 Kelley, *The Art of Innovation.*

91 H. M. Trice and J. M. Beyer, *The Cultures of Work Organizations* (Englewood Cliffs, NJ: Prentice Hall, 1993).

92 B. Ortega, 'Wal-Mart's Meeting Is a Reason to Party', *The Wall Street Journal*, June 3, 1994, A1.

93 Trice and Beyer, 'Studying Organizational Culture'.

94 S. McGee, 'Garish Jackets Add to Clamor of Chicago Pits', *The Wall Street Journal*, July 31, 1995, C1.

95 K. E. Weick, *The Social Psychology of Organization* (Reading, MA: Addison-Wesley, 1979).

96 B. McLean and P. Elkind, *The Smartest Guys in the Room: The Amazing Rise and Scandalous Fall of Enron* (New York: Penguin Books, 2003); R. Smith and J. R. Emshwiller, *24 Days: How Two* Wall Street Journal *Reporters Uncovered the Lies That Destroyed Faith in Corporate America* (New York: HarperCollins, 2003); M. Swartz and S. Watkins, *Power Failure: The Inside Story of the Collapse of ENRON* (New York: Doubleday, 2003).

Chapter 4

Ethics and Social Responsibility

LEARNING OBJECTIVES

After studying this chapter, you should be able to:

☑ Understand the relationship between ethics and the law.

☑ Appreciate why it is important to behave ethically.

☑ Differentiate between the claims of the different stakeholder groups that are affected by managers and their companies' actions.

☑ Describe four rules that can be used to help companies and their managers to act in ethical ways.

☑ Identify the four main sources of managerial ethics.

☑ Distinguish between the four main approaches toward social responsibility that a company can take.

A Manager's Challenge

Sparkle, Ethics and the Swan[1]

What is the right or ethical thing to do?

Swarovski is one of the best known crystal producers in the world. Operating globally and having factories in 15 countries, Swarovski has worked with some of the most famous fashion brands (Versace, Chanel, Cavalli, Dior) to promote itself to a £1.1bn company in 2005. It has come a long way since its inception in Austria by engineer Daniel Swarovski in 1892. Having started out with producing crystal figurines, the company has now branched out into every product that can be covered by crystal. P. Diddy owns a Swarovski crystal-encrusted mobile phone and the Duchess of Cornwall, Camilla Parker-Bowles, was wearing Swarovski in her wedding hat.

Swarovski has discovered a new market – one that cannot get enough of its sparkle. In India the demand for clothing that is embroided with Swarovski crystals is on the rise. Everyone wants to own a sari with them. Price is usually not a problem and no decent Indian middle-class wedding can now go without a Swarovski-embroidered sari. But it is not only for the Indian market that producers in India are using the crystals. The UK, France and the US are grateful customers for the beautiful gowns that come from India.

Surely it cannot be an easy job to put all those sequins on cloth? And this is where the problem starts. The *Observer*[2] investigated the production of the beautiful clothes that have Swarovski written all over. It found that only small fingers can put the sequins on the saris and this means children. The conditions in which these children have to work and live are less than humane. Dirty, small rooms with inappropriate lighting and no provision of proper seating or working space are the environment for these kids. Some sweatshop owners say that the kids are free to leave at any time and are fed three times a day.

The Austrian company maintains that it is not responsible for this, as it is not running those sweatshops. True – but should they sell to people who do? The problem does not end there. The efficient marketing of the crystal caused a number of fake crystals entering the Indian market. These counterfeits are now causing more child labour in order to produce cheaper reproductions of Swarovski-type outfits.[3] Swarovski's answer is that it is a general problem that needs attacking from all members of the clothing industry and is not their sole responsibility, maintaining that they do not 'authorise or condone'[4] such practices and they are not knowingly working with partners who do.

Overview

As the story of Swarovski suggests, an important *ethical dimension* is present in most kinds of decision making. In business, every party seeks to profit from the exchange of products, services and money, but it is no easy matter to determine what is a fair or equitable division of profit in a particular business activity or relationship. Clothing and accessory companies have no desire to see their revenues fall because potential customers are 'profiting' from illegal production processes. Companies have a responsibility to make profits so that they can reward their shareholders and pay their employees salaries. Of course, they also have a responsibility toward customers – they should charge only a fair price for their product.

This chapter examines the nature of the obligations and responsibilities of managers and the companies they work for toward the people and society that are affected by their actions. First, the nature of ethics and the sources of ethical problems are examined. Second, the chapter discusses the major groups of people, called *stakeholders*, who are affected by the way companies operate. Third, four rules or guidelines that managers can use to decide whether a specific business decision is ethical or unethical are explored. Finally, a consideration of the sources of managerial ethics, and the reasons why it is important for a company to behave in a socially responsible manner, are examined. By the end of this chapter you will understand the central role that ethics can play in shaping the practice of business and the life of a people, a society and a nation.

The Nature of Ethics

Suppose you see a person being mugged in the street. How will you behave? Will you act in some way to help, even though you risk being hurt? Will you walk away? Perhaps you might adopt a 'middle way' and not intervene but call the police? Does the way you act depend on whether the person being mugged is a fit male, an elderly person or even a homeless person? Does it depend on whether there are other people around, so you can tell yourself, 'Oh well, someone else will help or call the police, I don't need to'?

Ethical Dilemmas

The situation described above is an example of an **ethical dilemma**, the quandary people find themselves in when they have to decide if they should act in a way that might help another person or group, and is the 'right' thing to do, even though doing so might go against their own self-interest.[5] A dilemma may also arise when a person has to decide between two different courses of action, knowing that whichever course he or she chooses will result in harm to one person or group even while it may benefit another. The ethical dilemma here is to decide which course of action is the 'lesser of two evils'.

People often know they are confronting an ethical dilemma when their moral scruples come into play and cause them to hesitate, debate and reflect upon the 'rightness' or 'goodness' of a course of action. Moral scruples are thoughts and feelings that tell a person what is right or wrong; they are a part of a person's ethics. **Ethics** are the inner-guiding moral principles, values and beliefs that people use to analyse or interpret a situation and then decide what is the 'right' or appropriate way to behave. At the same time, ethics also indicate what inappropriate behaviour is, and how a person should behave to avoid doing harm to another person.

The essential problem in dealing with ethical issues, and thus solving moral dilemmas, is that there are no absolute or indisputable rules or principles that can be developed to decide if an action is ethical or unethical. Put simply, different people or groups may dispute which actions are ethical or unethical depending on their own personal self-interest and specific attitudes, beliefs and values – concepts that were discussed in Chapter 3. How, therefore, are we and companies and their managers and employees to decide what is 'ethical' and so act appropriately toward other people and groups?

Ethics and the Law

The first answer to this question is that society as a whole, using the political and legal process, can lobby for and pass laws that specify what people can and cannot do. Many different kinds of laws exist to govern business – for example, laws against fraud and deception and laws governing how companies can treat their employees and customers. Laws also specify what sanctions or punishments will follow if those laws are broken. Different groups in society lobby for which laws should be passed based on their own personal interests and beliefs with regard to what is right or wrong. The group that can summon most support is able to pass the laws that most closely align with its interests and beliefs. Once a law is passed, a decision about what the appropriate behaviour is with regard to a person or situation is taken from the personally determined ethical realm to the societal determined legal realm. If you do not conform to the law, you can be prosecuted; and if you are found guilty of breaking the law, you can be punished. You have little say in the matter; your fate is in the hands of the court and its lawyers.

In studying the relationship between ethics and law, it is important to understand that *neither laws nor ethics are fixed principles*; they are not cast in stone, but are likely to change over time. Ethical beliefs alter and change as time passes, and as they do laws change to reflect the changing ethical beliefs of a society. It was seen as ethical, and it was legal, for example, to acquire and possess slaves in ancient Rome and Greece and in the US until the nineteenth century. Ethical views regarding whether slavery was morally right or appropriate changed over time. Slavery was made illegal in most countries across the world when those in power decided that slavery degraded the very meaning of being human. Slavery is a statement about the value or worth of human beings and about their right to life, liberty and the pursuit of happiness. And if I deny these rights to other people, how then can I claim to have any natural or 'god-given' rights to these things oneself?

Moreover, what is to stop any person or group that becomes powerful enough to take control of the political and legal process from enslaving me and denying me the right to be free and to own property – something seen in many countries that operate under dictatorships? In denying freedom to others, one risks losing it oneself, just as stealing from others opens the door for them to steal from me in return. 'Do unto others as you would have them do unto you' is a commonly used ethical or moral rule that people apply in such situations to decide what the right thing to do is, and it is discussed in detail below.

Changes in Ethics over Time

There are many types of behaviour – such as murder, theft, slavery, rape or driving while intoxicated – that most, if not all, people currently believe are totally unacceptable and unethical and should therefore be illegal. There are also, however, many other kinds of actions and behaviours whose ethical nature is open to debate. Some people might believe that a particular behaviour – for example, smoking tobacco or possessing guns – is unethical and so should be made illegal. Others might argue that it is up to the individual or a group to decide if such behaviours are ethical or not and thus whether a particular behaviour should remain legal. While driving intoxicated is illegal, the amounts of toxins that you are allowed to consume are different across different European countries and could be seen as a reflection on their attitudes and ethics towards drink driving. In the UK, the limit is 0.4 mg of alcohol per 1 litre of blood. In Germany the limit is 0.25 mg/l and in Norway it is even lower with 0.1 mg/l.[6] Ethical beliefs are thus relative to the context in which they have been created.

As ethical beliefs change over time, some people may begin to question whether existing laws that make specific behaviours illegal are still appropriate today. They might argue that although a specific behaviour is deemed illegal, this does not make it unethical and thus the law should be changed. In the UK, for example, it is illegal to possess or use marijuana (cannabis). To justify this law, it is commonly argued that smoking marijuana leads people to try more dangerous drugs. Once the habit of taking drugs has been acquired, people can get addicted to them. More powerful drugs such as heroin are addictive, and most people cannot stop using them without help from others. Thus, the use of marijuana, because it might lead to further harm, is an unethical practice.

It has been documented medically, however, that the use of marijuana has many medical benefits for people with certain illnesses.[7] For example, for cancer sufferers who are undergoing chemotherapy and for those with AIDS who are on potent medications, marijuana offers relief from many of the treatment's side-effects, such as nausea and lack of appetite. People with severe arthritis and multiple sclerosis (MS) have argued that the use of marijuana relieves pain and increases their mobility. Yet, it is illegal for doctors to prescribe marijuana for these patients, so their suffering goes on. Since 1996, however, 35 states in the US have made it legal to prescribe marijuana for medical purposes; nevertheless, the federal government has sought to stop such state legislation. People in many states are currently lobbying for a relaxation of the law against the use of marijuana for medical purposes, and in June 2004 the US Supreme Court agreed to hear a case on the medical use of the drug.[8] In Canada there has been a widespread movement to decriminalise marijuana; while not making the drug legal, decriminalisation removes the threat of prosecution even for uses that are not medically related. Similar movements of decriminalisation have taken place in Germany and the UK. The Netherlands has legalised the sale and smoking of marijuana. The results show that there was no increase in uptake of more serious drugs,[9] but a major ethical debate is currently raging over this issue in many countries.

The important point to note is that while ethical beliefs lead to the development of laws and regulations to prevent certain behaviours or encourage others, laws themselves can and do change or even disappear as ethical beliefs change. In Britain in 1830 there were over 350 different crimes for which a person could be executed, including sheep stealing. Today there are none; capital punishment and the death penalty are no longer legal. Thus, both ethical and legal rules are relative: no absolute or unvarying standards exist to determine how we should behave, and people are caught up in moral dilemmas all the time. Because of this, we have to make ethical choices. Ethics and laws do not only change over time, but are also influenced by the local context. While slavery was still legal in the US in the nineteenth century, it was illegal and seen as morally wrong in other parts of this world.

The discussion above highlights an important issue in understanding the relationship between ethics, law and business. Some recent scandals in the UK have highlighted this even further. When the Labour Party announced their nominations for peerage, it became clear that some of the proposed peers were wealthy citizens who loaned money to the Labour Party – money that is needed by the party to fund its operations. While it is not illegal to take private loans from wealthy backers, it raised some serious questions about the transparency of party finances. At the moment, only donations larger than £5,000 need to be declared. In the process of the investigation, various parties had to admit to large sums being loaned to them by private financiers, including the Conservatives and the Liberal Democrats.[10] The question raised is if it is ethical to receive such loans and then nominate the lenders for peerage. Is it ethical, or does it mean one can buy a peerage? Is it the first step to buy influence or a seat in the House of Lords? This also raises questions how senior civil servants – who are in fact senior managers – should handle the party finance system to ensure equity and democratic principles. While legislation is in place to uphold democratic and ethical principles, this row seems to confirm that the law and the ethical standpoint is not strong enough, and suggestions to change the law have already been voiced.

Stakeholders and Ethics

Just as people have to work out the right and wrong ways to act, so do companies. When the law does not specify how companies should behave, their managers must decide what is the right or ethical way to behave toward the people and groups affected by their actions. Who are the people or groups that are affected by a company's business decisions? If a company behaves in an ethical way how does this benefit people and society? Conversely, how are people harmed by a company's unethical actions?

The people and groups affected by the way a company behaves are called its *stakeholders*. Stakeholders are people, or groups of people, who can affect or are directly affected by a company.

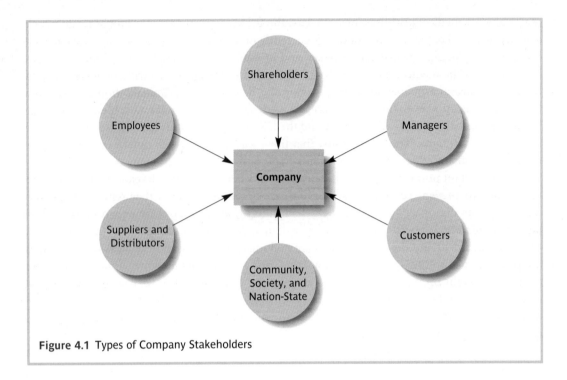

Figure 4.1 Types of Company Stakeholders

Because of this relationship, these people supply a company with its productive resources; as a result, they have a claim on and stake in the company.[11] Since stakeholders can directly benefit or be harmed by its actions, the ethics of a company and its managers are important to them. Who are a company's major stakeholders? What do they contribute to a company, and what do they claim in return? Below we examine the claims of some of these stakeholders – shareholders, managers, employees, suppliers and distributors, customers, and community, society and the state (Fig. 4.1).

Shareholders

Shareholders, also called stockholders, have a claim on a company because when purchasing its stock or shares they become its owners. Whenever the founder of a company decides to publicly list the business to raise capital, shares of the stock of that company are issued. These shares grant its buyers ownership of a certain percentage of the company and the right to receive any future stock dividends. For example, Philip Green, the owner of the Arcadia fashion group located in the UK that houses retail outlets such as Topshop and Miss Selfridge, paid himself a dividend of £1.17 billion.[12] The ethical dilemma that this payout causes involves the fact that the money is paid to his wife, who is resident in Monaco and thus is not liable to pay UK taxes on the income.

Shareholders are interested in the way a company operates because they want to maximise the return on their investment. They watch the company and its managers closely to ensure that management is working diligently to increase the company's profitability.[13] Shareholders also want to ensure that managers are behaving ethically and not risking investors' capital by engaging in actions that could hurt the company's reputation. The fall of Enron from being one of the biggest and most profitable companies in the US to declaring itself bankrupt took less than one year after the illegal and unethical actions of its senior managers came to light. The Enron tragedy was brought about by a handful of greedy senior managers who abused their positions of trust. It has been estimated that Enron's collapse, by precipitating the crash of the stock market, caused the average US household to lose over £35,900 of its hard-earned savings as trillions of pounds were wiped off the value of the shares of publicly listed US companies.

Managers

Managers are a vital stakeholder group because they are responsible for using a company's financial and human resources to increase its performance, and thus its share price.[14] Managers have a claim on an organisation because they bring to it their skills, expertise and experience. They have the right to expect a good return or reward by investing their human capital to improve a company's performance. Such rewards include good salaries and benefits, the prospect of promotion and a career – and at times share options and bonuses tied to company performance.

Managers are the stakeholder group with the responsibility of deciding which goals an organisation should pursue to most benefit the other stakeholders and how to make the most efficient use of resources to achieve such goals. In making such decisions, managers are frequently in the position of having to juggle the interests of different stakeholders, including themselves.[15] These decisions are sometimes very difficult and challenge managers to uphold ethical values because in some cases decisions that benefit some stakeholder groups (for instance managers and shareholders) harm other groups (for instance individual workers and local communities). In economic downturns or when a company experiences performance shortfalls, redundancies may help to cut costs (thus benefiting shareholders) at the expense of the employees laid off, for example. Many managers of big companies, such as Siemens or Abbey, have recently been faced with this decision. Redundancy decisions are always difficult, as they not only take a heavy toll on workers, their families and local communities but also mean the loss of the contributions of valued employees to an organisation. Whenever decisions such as these are made – benefiting some groups at the expense of others – ethics come into play.

As was discussed in Chapter 1, managers must be motivated and given incentives to work hard in the interests of shareholders. Their behaviour must also be scrutinised to ensure they do not behave illegally or unethically, pursuing goals that threaten shareholders' and the company's interests, but also other stakeholders'.[16] Unfortunately, we have seen in the 2000s how easy it is for senior managers to find ways to ruthlessly pursue their self-interest at the expense of shareholders and employees because laws and regulations were not strong enough to force them to behave ethically.

The problem has been that in many companies corrupt managers focus not on building the company's capital and stockholders' wealth but on maximising their own personal capital and wealth. In an effort to prevent future scandals governments began to rework the rules governing a company's relationship with its auditors, as well as the regulations concerning share options, and to increase the power of outside directors to scrutinise executive directors. Provisions have been made to identify *non-executive directors* as vital instruments of an organisation's governance.[17] The goal is to turn many acts that were only unethical behaviour into illegal behaviour in the near future. Managers can then be prosecuted if they engage in these acts.

Many experts also argue that the rewards given to senior managers, particularly the CEO and COO, grew out of control in the 1990s. Senior managers are the new 'aristocrats' today: through their ability to influence the board of directors and raise their own pay, they have amassed personal fortunes worth hundreds of millions of pounds. For example, while in 1982 a typical CEO earned about 18 times as much as the average worker, by 2002 that number had risen to 2,600 times as much – a staggering increase. Michael Eisner, CEO of Disney, has received over £434 million in Disney share options. These salary packages are less common in the UK; it has been suggested that UK CEOs earn 10 times less than their American counterparts,[18] earning on average £600k per year.[19] However, that does not mean that there are no unusual salary packages in the UK. Tesco's board of directors, for example, is paid handsomely, with salaries ranging from £1.9 million to £8.6 million.[20]

Is it ethical for senior managers to receive such vast amounts of money from their companies? Do they really earn it? Remember, this money could have gone to shareholders in the form of dividends. It could also have gone to reduce the huge salary gap between those at the top and those at the bottom of the hierarchy. Many people argue that the growing disparity between the rewards given to CEOs and to other employees is unethical and should be regulated. CEO pay has become too high because CEOs are the people who set and control the going rate for salaries and bonuses: they sit on the boards of other companies, as outside directors, and thus can control the salaries and share options paid to other CEOs.

Others argue that because senior managers play an important role in building a company's capital and wealth, they deserve a significant share of its profits. But is this worth such a huge reward? A debate is currently raging over how much money CEOs and other senior managers should be paid. Some changes at Walt Disney illustrate many of these issues, as discussed in Case 4.1.

Case 4.1: **Walt Disney's new board of directors**

In the last few years, the performance of the Walt Disney Company has fallen off. In 2004 many analysts were wondering if Michael Eisner, who had been its CEO for the last 18 years, was still the right person to run the company. Eisner had always had a 'hands-on' approach to running the business: he wanted to be involved in every major business decision, and he kept a tight rein on his managers. In recent years he was criticised because, although over 60 and due to retire in less than five years, he had not laid out a succession plan indicating which managers would assume the top roles in Disney after he stepped down. Such a plan is important because many companies flounder if a new CEO has not been groomed to take over the top job.

In addition, Eisner was criticised for creating a weak, or 'captive', board of directors that was unable or unwilling to scrutinise and question his business decisions, some of which seem to have been major errors. Over the years, Eisner created a 16-member board of directors in the company, at least eight of whom had personal ties to him. This weak board allowed him to make all the important decisions, and it did not serve Disney's shareholders well because his decisions did not increase company performance but sometimes actually reduced it. For example, Eisner pushed through the merger of Disney with Capital/ABC. Since then the ABC television network has been a poor performer, dragging down Disney's share price. In the meantime, Eisner received more than £434 million in share options from the company and enjoyed all the lavish incentives, such as corporate jets, penthouse suites and all-expenses-paid business trips, that most CEOs of large companies receive today.

With its performance falling, Eisner came under increasing criticism for his autocratic management style. His lack of a succession plan for the company, his creation of a weak board of directors, as well as the fact that he was still paid vast sums of money despite his company's poor performance led to further disapproval. In 2003 the company began to reorganise its board of directors. Two new special outside directors were appointed, one of whom would chair two board meetings a year that Eisner – who normally chairs these meetings – would not be permitted to attend. The board would have more freedom to assess Eisner's performance. Under pressure from the board, Eisner also chose his successor.

Some analysts say these changes are not enough. Eisner still has the backing of the majority of the board, who are loyal to him. He is still in control of all Disney's important committees. The question is what the board of directors will do if Disney's performance continues to deteriorate. Will it continue to let Eisner make all the important decisions, or will it demand fresh leadership at the top and force Eisner to step down as CEO? Only time will tell, but Eisner is still in the driver's seat and, like most CEOs, will do all he can to retain his privileged position.

Employees

A company's employees are the hundreds of thousands of people who work in its various departments and functions, such as research, sales and manufacturing. Employees expect that they will receive rewards consistent with their performance. One way that a company can act ethically toward employees and meet their expectations is by creating an occupational structure that fairly and equitably rewards employees for their contributions. Companies, for example, need to develop **recruitment, training, performance appraisal** and reward systems that do not discriminate between employees, and that employees believe are fair.

Suppliers and Distributors

No company operates alone. Every company is in a network of relationships with other companies that supply it with the inputs (e.g. raw materials, component parts, contract labour and clients) that it needs to operate. It also depends on intermediaries such as wholesalers and retailers to distribute its products to the final customer. Suppliers expect to be paid fairly and promptly for their inputs; distributors expect to receive quality products at agreed-upon prices.

Once again, many ethical issues arise in the way companies contract and interact with their suppliers and distributors. Important issues concerning how and when payments are to be made or product quality specifications are governed by the terms of the legal contracts a company signs with its suppliers and distributors. Many other issues are dependent on business ethics. For example, numerous products sold in stores worldwide have been outsourced to countries that do not have the regulations and laws most developed countries have in place to protect the workers who make these products. Philip Green's Arcadia group, for example, is under increased pressure to change its production and product sourcing practices in some developing countries as the current practices seem to exploit workers by paying them extremely low wages.[21] Umbro, the British-born sports apparel company that sponsors the English football team, has also been under increased pressure to abandon child labour and excessive working hours in its foreign factories.[22] All companies must take an ethical position on the way they obtain and make the products they sell. This stance is commonly published on the company's website. Table 4.1 presents Umbro's 2005 statement on its approach to global ethics.[23]

Table 4.1 Supplier's code of conduct

Working conditions

1. Employers will provide safe working conditions for all employees and will not subject them to dangerous working practices. Where local industry standards are higher than the legal requirements then these should apply.

2. Employers shall not employ forced, bonded or prison labour in their operations.

   Workers are not required to lodge 'deposits' or their identity papers with their employer and are free to leave their employer after reasonable notice.

3. Employers should recruit, train and promote employees on equal terms on the basis of their ability to do their job.

4. Accommodation, where provided, shall be clean, safe and meet the basic needs of the workers.

5. There is no discrimination in hiring, compensation, access to training, promotion, termination or retirement based on race, caste, national origin, religion, age, disability, gender, marital status, sexual orientation, union membership or political affiliation.

6. Physical abuse or discipline, the threat of physical abuse, sexual or other harassment and verbal abuse or other forms of intimidation shall be prohibited.

7. Employers will respect the right of employees to join and organise associations of their own choosing. Employers adopt an open attitude towards the activities of trade unions and their organisational activities.

   Workers representatives are not discriminated against and have access to carry out their representative functions in the workplace.

8. Employees will be paid at least the minimum legal wage or a wage that is consistent with local industry standards, whichever is the greater. In any event wages should always be enough to meet basic needs and to provide some discretionary income.

9. Wages will be paid directly to the employee. Information relating to wages will be available in an understandable form.

   Deductions from wages as a disciplinary measure shall not be permitted nor shall any deductions from wages not provided for by national law be permitted without the expressed permission of the worker concerned. All disciplinary measures should be recorded.

10. Working hours comply with national laws and benchmark industry standards, whichever affords greater protection.

    In any event, workers shall not on a regular basis be required to work in excess of 48 hours per week and shall be provided with at least one day off for every 7 day period on average.

    Overtime shall be voluntary, shall not exceed 12 hours per week, shall not be demanded on a regular basis and shall always be compensated at a premium rate.

11. Children below the age of 15 (or 14 in countries with insufficiently developed economies and education facilities) will not be employed.

12. Children and young persons under 18 shall not be employed at night or in hazardous conditions.

13. There shall be no new recruitment of child labour (a person younger than 15).

    Employers shall develop or participate in and contribute to policies and programmes which provide for the transition of any child found to be performing child labour to enable her or him to attend and remain in quality education until no longer a child; 'child' and 'child labour' being defined in Appendix A.

14. Lighting, heating and ventilation systems should be adequate in the working environment, and clean sanitary facilities should be available at all times.

15. Obligations to employees under labour or social security laws and regulations arising from the regular employment relationship shall not be avoided through the use of labour-only contracting, sub-contracting, or home-working arrangements, or through apprenticeship schemes where there is no real intent to impart skills or provide regular employment, nor shall any such obligations be avoided through the excessive use of fixed-term contracts of employment.

Many websites are now available that help consumers to become aware of serious infringements of companies and which companies are trying to behave ethically.

Customers

Customers are often regarded as the most critical stakeholder group. If a company cannot attract them to buy its products, it cannot stay in business. Thus, managers and employees must work to increase efficiency and effectiveness in order to create loyal customers and attract new ones. They do so by selling customers quality products at a fair price and providing good after-sales service. They can also strive to improve their products over time.

Many laws exist that protect customers from companies that attempt to provide dangerous or inferior products. Laws exist that allow customers to sue a company whose product causes them injury or harm, such as a defective tyre or vehicle. Other laws force companies to clearly disclose the interest rates they charge on purchases, for example through store cards – an important hidden cost that customers frequently do not factor into their purchase decisions. Every year thousands of companies are prosecuted for breaking these laws, so 'buyers beware' is an important rule customers must follow when buying goods and services.

Community, Society and Nation

The effects of the decisions made by companies and their managers permeate all aspects of the communities, societies and nations in which they operate. **Community** refers to physical locations such as towns or cities or to social milieux such as ethnic neighbourhoods in which companies are located. A community provides a company with the physical and social infrastructure that allows it to operate; its utilities and labour force; the homes in which its managers and employees live; the schools, colleges and hospitals that service their needs, and so on.

Through the salaries, wages and taxes it pays, a company contributes to the economy of the town or region and often determines whether the community prospers or declines. A recent example of the large influence of companies on its communities is the car manufacturer Rover. When the company went into administration, not only did more than 5,000 people lose their jobs, numerous suppliers – such as Stadco – were also faced with closure,[24] thus resulting in more job losses. This is likely to have a detrimental affect on the community in and around Birmingham, UK. Similarly, a company can affect the prosperity of a society and a nation and, to the degree that a company is involved in global trade, all the countries it operates in and thus the prosperity of the global economy as a whole. We have already discussed many of the issues surrounding *global outsourcing* and the loss of jobs in home countries, for example.

For instance, although the individual effects of the way each McDonald's restaurant operates might be small, the combined effects of the way all McDonald's and other fast-food companies do business are enormous. Large numbers of people work in the fast-food industry, and many thousands of suppliers like farmers, paper cup manufacturers, builders and so on, depend on it for their livelihood. No wonder, then, that the ethics of the fast-food business are scrutinised closely. The industry is the major lobbyer against attempts to raise the UK national minimum wage, which is £4.25 for 18–21-year-olds and £5.05 for people aged 22 or over, because a higher minimum wage would substantially increase its operating costs. (These rates are £4.45 and £5.35, respectively, from 1 October 2006.) However, responding to protests about chickens raised in cages where they cannot move their wings, McDonald's issued new ethical guidelines concerning cage size and related matters that its egg suppliers must abide by if they are to retain its business. What ethical rules does McDonald's use to decide its stance toward minimum pay or minimum cage size?

Business ethics are also important because the failure of companies can have catastrophic effects on a community: a general decline in business activity can affect a whole nation. The decision of a large company to pull out of a community, for example, can seriously threaten the community's future. Some companies may attempt to improve their profits by engaging in actions that, although not illegal, can hurt communities and nations. One of these actions is pollution. For example, the Czech Republic has suffered from a large amount of 'waste tourism' that has resulted in a number of illegal dumps. While it is not illegal to transport waste within the European Economic Area (EEA), dumping it on illegal sites raises problems about safeguarding the environment that will be affected by unsuitable storage of waste at these illegal or unofficial waste dumps.[25]

Rules for Ethical Decision Making

When a stakeholder perspective is taken, questions on company ethics proliferate.[26] What is the appropriate way to manage the claims of all stakeholders? Company decisions that favour one group of stakeholders, for example, are likely to harm the interests of others.[27] High prices to customers may lead to high returns to shareholders and high salaries for managers in the short run. If in the long run customers turn to companies that offer lower-cost products, however, the result may be declining sales, laid-off employees and the decline of the communities that support the high-price company's business activity.

When companies act ethically, their stakeholders support them. For example, banks are willing to supply them with new capital, they attract highly qualified job applicants and new customers are drawn to their products. Thus ethical companies grow and expand over time, and all their stakeholders benefit. The result of unethical behaviour is the loss of reputation and resources, shareholders who sell their shares, skilled managers and employees who leave the company and customers who turn to the products of more reputable companies.

When making business decisions, managers must take the claims of all stakeholders into consideration.[28] To help themselves and employees make ethical decisions and behave in ways that benefit their stakeholders, managers can use four ethical rules or principles to analyse the effects of their business decisions on stakeholders: the **utilitarian**, **moral rights**, **justice** and **practical** rules (Fig. 4.2).[29] These rules are useful guidelines that help managers decide on the appropriate way to behave in situations where it is necessary to balance a company's self-interest against the interests of its stakeholders. Remember, the right choices will lead resources to be used where they can create the most value. If all companies make the right choices, all stakeholders will benefit in the long run.[30]

Utilitarian rule

The *utilitarian rule* is that an ethical decision is a decision that produces the greatest good for the greatest number of people. To decide which is the most ethical course of business action, managers should first consider how different possible courses of business action would benefit or harm different stakeholders. They should then choose the course of action that provides the most benefits – or, conversely, the one that does the least harm – to stakeholders.[31]

The ethical dilemma for managers is: how do you measure the benefits and harms that will be done to each stakeholder group? Moreover, how do you evaluate the rights of different

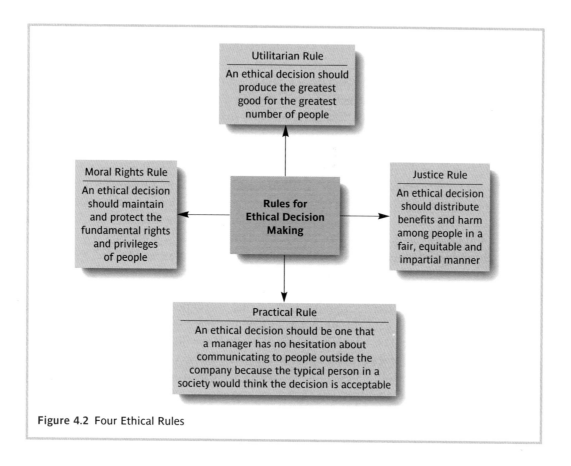

Figure 4.2 Four Ethical Rules

stakeholder groups, and the relative importance of each group, in coming to a decision? Since shareholders are the owners of the company, shouldn't their claims be held above those of employees? For example, managers might be faced with a choice of using global outsourcing to reduce costs and lower prices to customers or continuing with high-cost production at home. A decision to use global outsourcing benefits shareholders and customers, but will result in major redundancies that will harm employees and the communities in which they live. Typically, in a capitalist society, such as the UK or Germany, the interests of shareholders are put above those of employees, so production will move abroad. This is commonly regarded as being an ethical choice because in the long run the alternative (home production) might cause the business to collapse and go bankrupt, in which case greater harm will be done to all stakeholders. However, one of the trade-offs that may result in moving production to developing countries may be a loss of quality. This may affect the trust customers place in a product, and so could also greatly affect the performance of the company.

Moral rights rule

Under the *moral rights rule*, an ethical decision is a decision that best maintains and protects the fundamental or unchallengeable rights and privileges of the people affected by it. For example, ethical decisions protect people's rights to freedom, life and safety, property, privacy, free speech and freedom of conscience. The adage 'Do unto others as you would have them do unto you', is a moral rights principle that managers should use to decide which rights to uphold. The Swarovski case (p. 103) suggests that this is not always upheld.

From a moral rights perspective, managers should compare and contrast different courses of business action on the basis of how each course will affect the rights of the company's different stakeholders. Managers should then choose the course of action that best protects and upholds the rights of *all* the stakeholders. For example, decisions that might result in significant harm to the safety or health of employees or customers would clearly be unethical choices.

The ethical dilemma for managers is that decisions that will protect the rights of some stakeholders often will hurt the rights of others. How should they choose which group to protect? In deciding whether it is ethical to secretly monitor employees, or search them when they leave work to prevent theft, does an employee's right to privacy outweigh an organisation's right to protect its property? Suppose a co-worker is having personal problems and is coming in late and leaving early, placing you in the position of being forced to pick up the person's workload. Do you tell your boss even though you know this will probably get that person fired?

Justice rule

The *justice rule* is that an ethical decision is a decision that distributes benefits and harms among people and groups in a fair, equitable or impartial way. Managers should compare and contrast alternative courses of action based on the degree to which they will result in a fair or equitable distribution of outcomes for stakeholders. For example, employees who are similar in their level of skill, performance or responsibility should receive the same kind of pay. The allocation of outcomes should not be based on differences such as gender, race or religion.

The ethical dilemma for managers is to determine the fair rules and procedures for *distributing outcomes* to stakeholders. For example, managers must not reward people they like more generously than they those they do not like; or bend the rules to help their favourites. On the other hand, if employees want managers to act fairly toward them, then employees need to act fairly toward their companies and work hard and be loyal. Similarly, customers need to act fairly toward a company if they expect it to be fair to them – something people who illegally copy digital media should consider.

Practical rule

Each of the above rules offers a different and complementary way of determining whether a decision or behaviour is ethical, and all three rules should be used to decide on the ethics of a particular course of action. Ethical issues, as just discussed, are seldom clear-cut, because the rights, interests, goals and incentives of different stakeholders often conflict. For this reason many experts on ethics add a fourth rule to determine whether a business decision is ethical: The *practical rule* is that an ethical decision is one that a manager has no hesitation or reluctance about communicating to people outside the company because the typical person in a society would think it is acceptable. A business decision is probably acceptable on ethical grounds if a manager can answer yes to each of these questions:

1. Does my decision fall within the accepted *values* or *standards* that typically apply in business activity today?

2. Am I willing to see the decision *communicated* to all people and groups *affected* by it – for example, by having it reported in newspapers or on television?

3. Would the people with whom I have a *significant* personal relationship – such as family members, friends or even managers in other organisations – *approve* of the decision?

Applying the practical rule to analyse a business decision ensures that managers are taking into account the interests of all stakeholders.[32] After applying this rule managers can judge if they have chosen to act in an ethical or unethical way and they must abide by the consequences.

Reaction Time

1. Discuss some of the ethical implications of moving production to developing countries.

2. How would the four ethical rules discussed above differ in informing the decision to move production to developing countries?

Why Should Managers Behave Ethically?

Why is it so important that managers, and people in general, should act ethically and temper their pursuit of self-interest by considering the effects of their actions on others? The answer is that the relentless pursuit of self-interest can lead to a collective disaster when one or more people starts to profit from being unethical, because this encourages other people to act in the same way.[33] More and more people jump onto the bandwagon, and soon everybody is trying to manipulate the situation in the way that best serves their personal ends with no regard for the effects of the action on others.

Suppose that in an agricultural community there is common land that everybody has an equal right to use. Pursuing self-interest, each farmer acts to make the maximum use of the free resource by grazing their own cattle and sheep. Collectively, all the farmers over-graze the land, which quickly becomes worn out. Then a strong wind blows away the exposed topsoil, so the common land is destroyed. The pursuit of individual self-interest with no consideration for societal interests has led to disaster for each individual and for the whole society because scarce resources have been destroyed.[34] In the case of digital entertainment piracy (such as websites, Napster or the copying of movies) the tragedy that would result if all people were to steal digital media could be the disappearance of music, movie and book companies as creative people decided there was no point in their working hard to produce original songs, stories and so on.

We can look at the effects of unethical behaviour on business commerce and activity in another way. Suppose that companies and their managers operate in an unethical society, meaning one in which stakeholders routinely try to cheat and defraud one another. If stakeholders expect each other to cheat, how long will it take them to negotiate the purchase and shipment of products? When they do not trust each other, stakeholders will probably spend hours bargaining over fair prices, and this is a largely unproductive activity that reduces efficiency and effectiveness.[35] All the time and effort that could be spent improving product quality or customer service is being lost because it is spent on negotiating and bargaining. Unethical behaviour thus ruins business commerce, and society has a lower standard of living because fewer goods and services are produced, as Fig. 4.3 shows.

On the other hand, suppose that companies and their managers operate in an ethical society, meaning that stakeholders believe they are dealing with others who are basically moral and honest. In this society stakeholders have a greater reason to **trust** others, which means they have more confidence and faith in the other person's goodwill. When trust exists, stakeholders are more likely to signal their good intentions by co-operating and providing information that makes it easier to trade and price products and services. When one party does so, this encourages

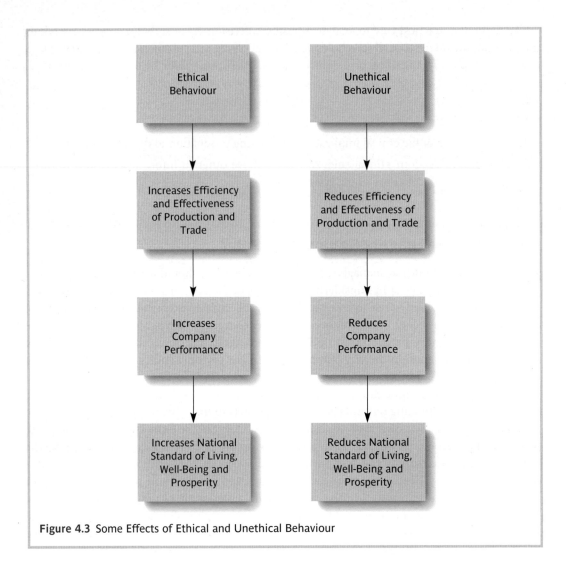

Figure 4.3 Some Effects of Ethical and Unethical Behaviour

others to act in the same way. Over time, greater trust between stakeholders allows them to work together more efficiently and effectively, and this raises company performance (Fig. 4.3). As people see the positive results of acting in an honest way, ethical behaviour becomes a valued social norm and society in general becomes increasingly ethical.

As noted in Chapter 1, one of the major tasks of managers is to protect and nurture the resources under their control. Any organisational stakeholders – managers, workers, shareholders, suppliers – who advance their own interests by behaving unethically toward other stakeholders, either by taking resources or by denying resources to others, *waste collective resources*. If other individuals or groups copy the behaviour of the unethical stakeholder ('If he can do it, we can do it, too'), the rate at which collective resources are misused increases, and eventually there are few resources for producing goods and services. Unethical behaviour that goes unpunished creates incentives for people to put their unbridled self-interests above the rights of others.[36] When this happens, the benefits that people reap from joining together in organisations disappear very quickly.

An important safeguard against unethical behaviour is the potential for loss of **reputation**.[37] *Reputation* – the esteem or high repute that individuals or organisations gain when they behave ethically – is an important asset. Shell and Nike had to invest large amounts of resources into rebuilding their reputations after engaging in unethical behaviour. Stakeholders have valuable reputations that they must protect because their ability to earn a living and obtain resources in the long run depends on the way they behave on a continuing basis.

If a manager misuses resources and other parties regard that behaviour as being at odds with acceptable standards, the manager's reputation will suffer. Behaving unethically in the short run can have serious long-term consequences. A manager who has a poor reputation will have difficulty finding employment with other companies. Shareholders who see managers behaving unethically may refuse to invest in their companies, and this will decrease the share price, undermine the companies' reputations, and ultimately put the managers' jobs at risk.[38]

All stakeholders have reputations to lose. Suppliers who provide inferior inputs find that organisations learn over time not to deal with them, and eventually they go out of business. Powerful customers who demand ridiculously low prices find that their suppliers become less willing to deal with them, and resources ultimately become harder for them to obtain. Workers who avoid responsibilities on the job find it hard to get new jobs when they are made redundant. In general, if a manager or company is known for being unethical, other stakeholders are likely to view that individual or organisation with suspicion and hostility, and the reputation of each will be poor. On the other hand, if a manager or company is known for ethical business practices, each will develop a good reputation.[39]

In summary, in a complex, diverse society, stakeholders, and people in general, need to recognise they are all part of a larger social group. The way in which they make decisions and act not only affects them personally but also affects the lives of many other people. The problem is that for some people their daily struggle to survive and succeed or their total disregard for the rights of others can lead them to lose any appreciation of other people. We can see our relationships towards our families and friends, to our school, church and so on, but we always need to keep in mind the effects of our actions on other people – people who will be judging our actions and whom we might harm by acting unethically.

Ethics and Corporate Social Responsibility

Some companies, like Johnson & Johnson, Prudential Insurance and Peugeot, are well known for their ethical business practices. Other companies, such as Arthur Andersen and Enron (which are now out of business) or phone company WorldCom, repeatedly engaged in unethical and illegal business activities. What explains such differences between the ethics of these companies and their managers?

There are four main determinants of differences in ethics between people, employees, companies and countries: **societal ethics, occupational ethics, individual ethics** and **organisational ethics**, especially the ethics of a company's senior managers[40] (Fig. 4.4).

Societal Ethics

Societal ethics are standards that govern how members of a society should deal with one another in matters involving issues such as fairness, justice, poverty and the rights of the individual.

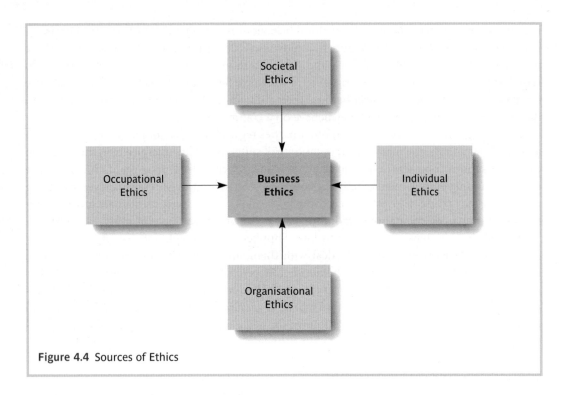

Figure 4.4 Sources of Ethics

Societal ethics emanate from a society's laws, customs and practices, and from the unwritten values and norms that influence how people interact with each other. People in a particular country may automatically behave ethically because they have *internalised* (i.e. made a part of their morals) certain values, beliefs and norms that specify how they should behave when confronted with an ethical dilemma.

Societal ethics can vary among societies. Countries like Germany, Japan, Sweden and Switzerland are well known as being some of the most ethical countries in the world, with strong values about social order and the need to create a society that protects the welfare of all groups of their citizens. In other countries, the situation is very different. In many economically poor countries bribery is standard practice to get things done – such as having a telephone installed or a contract awarded. In the UK and other economically advanced countries, bribery is considered unethical and has been made illegal.

BAE Systems, formerly known as British Aerospace, faced allegations in 2002 after it was discovered that large amounts of money had been paid to the Royal family of Qatar by various European and US arms manufacturers. BAE Systems was believed to have contributed £7 million in order to win a contract worth more than £500 million as part of a consortium to supply Qatar with weapons.

The payment of bribes violates the UK Anti-Terrorism, Crime and Security Act 2001, which forbids payment of bribes by UK nationals to secure contracts abroad, makes companies liable for the actions of their foreign managers and allows companies found in violation to be prosecuted in the UK.

Countries also differ widely in their beliefs about the appropriate treatment of their employees. In general, the poorer a country is, the more likely employees are to be treated with little regard. One issue of particular concern on a global level is whether it is ethical to use child labour, as discussed in Case 4.2.

Case 4.2: Is it right to use child labour?

In recent years, the number of companies that buy their products from low-cost foreign suppliers has been growing, and concern about the ethics associated with employing young children in factories has been increasing. In Pakistan, children as young as six work long hours in deplorable conditions to make rugs and carpets for export to Western countries. Children in poor countries throughout Africa, Asia and South America work in similar conditions. Is it ethical to employ children in factories, and should companies buy and sell products made by these children?

Opinions about the ethics of child labour vary widely. Robert Reich, an economist and secretary of labour in the first Clinton Administration, believes that the practice is totally reprehensible and should be outlawed on a global level. Another view, championed by *The Economist* magazine, is that, while nobody wants to see children employed in factories, citizens of rich countries need to recognise that in poor countries children are often a family's only bread-winners. Denying children employment would cause whole families to suffer, and one wrong (child labour) might produce a greater wrong (poverty). Instead, *The Economist* favours regulating the conditions under which children are employed in the hope that, over time, as poor countries become richer, the need for child employment will disappear.

Many retailers typically buy their clothing from low-cost foreign suppliers, and managers in these companies have had to take their own ethical stance on child labour. Managers in ASDA and Umbro (Table 4.1) have followed Western standards and rules and have policies dictating that their foreign suppliers should not employ child labour. They also agreed to sever ties with any foreign supplier found to be in violation of this standard.

However, retailers differ widely in the way they choose to enforce such policies. It has been estimated that more than 300,000 children under the age of 14 are being employed in garment factories in Guatemala, a popular low-cost location for clothing manufacturers. These children frequently work more than 60 hours a week and often are paid less than £1.60 a day, close to the minimum wage. Many retailers do not check up on their foreign suppliers: clearly, if retailers are to be true to their ethical stance on this issue, they cannot ignore the fact that they are buying clothing made by children and they must do more to regulate the conditions under which these children work.

Occupational Ethics

Occupational ethics are standards that govern how members of a profession, trade or craft should conduct themselves when performing work-related activities.[41] For example, medical ethics govern the way doctors and nurses should treat their patients. Doctors are expected to perform only necessary medical procedures and to act in the patient's interest (the Hippocratic Oath). The ethics of scientific research require that scientists conduct their experiments and present their findings in ways that ensure the validity of their conclusions. One example that highlights the fact that these occupational ethics are not always adhered to is the case of the South Korean researcher, Hwang Woo Suk, who falsified the data of his research for publication.

Like society at large, most professional groups can impose punishments for violations of ethical standards.[42] Doctors and lawyers can be prevented from practising their professions if they disregard professional ethics and put their own interests first.

Within an organisation, occupational rules and norms often govern how employees such as lawyers, researchers and accountants should make decisions to further stakeholder interests. Employees internalise the rules and norms of their occupational group (just as they do those of society) and often follow them automatically when deciding how to behave. Because most people tend to follow established rules of behaviour, people often take ethics for granted. However, when occupational ethics are violated – such as when scientists fabricate data in order to get published – ethical issues come to the fore.

Individual Ethics

Individual ethics are personal standards and values that determine how people view their responsibilities to other people and groups and thus how they should act in situations when their own self-interests are at stake.[43] Sources of individual ethics include the influence of one's family and peers and socialisation in general. The experiences gained over a lifetime – through membership in social institutions such as schools and religions – also contribute to the development of personal standards and values. These are applied to decide what is right or wrong and whether to perform certain actions or make certain decisions.

Many decisions or behaviours that one person finds unethical – such as using animals for cosmetics testing – may be acceptable to another person. If decisions or behaviours are not illegal, individuals may agree to disagree about their ethical beliefs, or they may try to impose their own beliefs on other people and make those beliefs the law. In all cases, however, people should develop and follow the ethical criteria described earlier to balance their self-interests against those of others when determining how they should behave in a particular situation.

Organisational Ethics

Organisational ethics are the guiding practices and beliefs through which a particular company and its managers view their responsibility toward their stakeholders. The individual ethics of a company's founders and senior managers are especially important in shaping the organisation's code of ethics. Organisations whose founders had a vital role in creating a highly ethical code of organisational behaviour include Merck, Hewlett-Packard, Johnson & Johnson and the Prudential Insurance Company. Johnson & Johnson's code of ethics – its credo – reflects a well-developed concern for its stakeholders (Table 4.2). Company credos, such as that of Johnson & Johnson, are meant to deter self-interested, unethical behaviour. They demonstrate to managers and employees that a company will not tolerate people who, because of their own poor ethics, put their personal interests above the interests of other organisational stakeholders and ignore the harm that they may inflict on others. They also demonstrate that those who act unethically will be punished.

Managers or workers may behave unethically if they feel pressured to do so by the situation they are in and by unethical senior managers. Once again, if a company's senior managers consistently endorse the ethical principles in its corporate credo, they can prevent this perception from occurring. Employees are much more likely to act unethically when a credo does not exist, or is disregarded. Arthur Andersen, for example, did not follow its credo at all; its

Table 4.2 Forms of socially responsible behaviour

Managers are being socially responsible and showing their support for their stakeholders when they:
■ Provide severance payments to help laid-off workers make ends meet until they can find another job
■ Provide workers with opportunities to enhance their skills and acquire additional education so that they can remain productive and do not become obsolete because of changes in technology
■ Allow employees to take time off when they need to and provide health care and pension benefits
■ Contribute to charities or support various civic-minded activities in the cities or towns in which they are located
■ Decide to keep open a factory whose closure would devastate the local community
■ Decide to spend money to improve a new factory so that it will not pollute the environment
■ Decline to invest in countries that have poor human rights records
■ Choose to help poor countries develop an economic base to improve living standards

unscrupulous partners ordered middle managers to shred records that showed evidence of their wrongdoing. Although middle managers knew this was wrong, they followed orders because they responded to the personal power and status of the partners and not the company's code of ethics. They were afraid they would lose their jobs if they did not behave unethically, but their actions still cost them their jobs.

Senior managers play a crucial role in determining a company's ethics. It is clearly important, then, that when making appointment decisions the board of directors should scrutinise the reputations and ethical records of senior managers. It is the responsibility of the board to decide if a prospective CEO has the maturity, experience and integrity needed to head a company and be entrusted with the capital and wealth of the organisation, on which the fate of all its stakeholders depends.

A track record of success is not enough to decide this issue, for a manager may have achieved this success through unethical or illegal means. It is important to investigate prospective senior managers and examine their credentials. In the early 2000s it was disclosed that the senior managers of several major companies did not have the kinds of degrees or experience they had claimed on their CVs and that they had acted unethically to get their current jobs! Often, the best predictor of future behaviour is past behaviour, but the board of directors needs to be on guard against people who use unethical means to rise to the top of the organisational hierarchy.

Approaches to Corporate Social Responsibility

A company's ethics are the result of differences in societal, organisational, occupational and individual ethics. In turn, a company's ethics determine its stance or position on *corporate social responsibility*. A company's stance on corporate social responsibility is the way its managers and employees view their duty or obligation to make decisions that protect, enhance and promote the welfare and well-being of stakeholders and society as a whole.[44] As previously mentioned, when no laws exist that specify how a company should act towards its stakeholders, managers must decide what the right, ethical and socially responsible thing is to do. Differences in business ethics can lead companies to take very different positions or views on what their responsibility is towards their stakeholders.

Many kinds of actions demonstrate a company's beliefs about its obligations to make socially responsible business decisions. The decision to spend money on training and educating employees is one such decision; so is the decision to minimise or avoid redundancies whenever possible. The decision to act promptly and warn customers when a batch of defective merchandise has been accidentally sold is another. Companies that try to hide such problems show little regard for corporate social responsibility. In the 1990s, both Fiat and Ford tried to hide the fact that several of their vehicles had defects that rendered them dangerous to drive; the companies were penalised with hundreds of millions of pounds in damages for their unethical behaviour. On the other hand, in 2002, when Campbell Soup discovered that thousands of cans of soup labelled as cream of mushroom actually contained clam chowder, it quickly announced the problem. Since the mislabelling could cause severe problems to customers with allergies to shellfish, informing the public was the right thing to do.[45] The way a company announces business problems or admits its mistakes provides strong clues about its stance on corporate social responsibility.

Four Different Approaches

The strength of companies' commitment to corporate social responsibility can range from low to high (Fig. 4.5). At the low end of the range is an **obstructionist approach**, in which companies and their managers choose *not* to behave in a socially responsible way. Instead, they behave unethically and illegally and do all they can to prevent knowledge of their behaviour from reaching other organisational stakeholders and society at large. Managers at tobacco companies – for example, British American Tobacco (BAT) – took this approach when they sought to hide evidence that cigarette smoking could cause lung cancer.

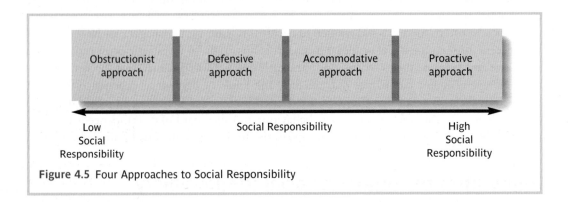

Figure 4.5 Four Approaches to Social Responsibility

Senior managers at Enron also acted in an obstructionist way when they prevented employees from selling Enron shares in their pension funds even before employees knew the company was in trouble. At the same time, senior managers sold hundreds of millions of pounds' worth of their own Enron stock. Senior partners at the accountants Arthur Andersen, who instructed their subordinates to shred files, chose, like the managers of all these organisations, an obstructionist approach. The result was not only a loss of reputation but devastation for the organisation and for all stakeholders involved. All these companies are no longer in business. Case 4.3 is another example.

Case 4.3: Watery meat

Food production in the Western world has its share of scandals every year, including the detection in 2002 of dangerous hormones in food as a result of using contaminated animal feed, a scandal that affected 15 countries in the EU[46], or the BSE crisis. The scandal of water-injected meat was a heavy blow to food production in the UK. It was discovered that raw meat had been sold next to meat that had been injected with water. The adding of water to meat is not a new phenomenon, but had not previously affected raw meat. Consumer lobbyists were outraged and afraid that it would further undermine the confidence in food production among British consumers. Spokespeople for large supermarket chains such as Tesco admitted that water had been added to improve the succulence and quality of meat, not to increase its weight or mislead the consumer. However, can we trust them, considering that in some meat the actual meat content is only 87 per cent? How can the consumer know which meat is genuine and which meat has been injected with water? Supermarkets argue that their products are clearly labelled, but is this really the case? Many meat products that have been injected with water are labelled as 'extra succulent' or the water added is referred to in small print, not easily identifiable. The Trading Standards Institute argues for clearer labelling that shows added water in the same size of label as the meat description itself. If supermarkets do not intend to mislead consumers this should not be a contentious issue, especially since many of the meats that have been injected with water are sold at a premium price for their succulence. The consumer should be made fully aware of what they are buying.[47]

A **defensive approach** indicates at least a commitment to ethical behaviour.[48] Defensive companies and managers stay within the law and abide strictly by legal requirements but make no attempt to exercise corporate social responsibility beyond what the law dictates. Thus they can, and often do, act unethically. These are the kinds of companies, like Computer Associates and WorldCom, that give their managers large share options and bonuses even when company performance is declining. The managers are the kind who sell their shares in advance of other shareholders because they know that their company's performance is about to fall. Although acting on 'inside information' is illegal, it is often very hard to prove since senior managers have the right to sell their shares whenever they choose. The founders of most dot-com companies took advantage of this legal loophole to sell hundreds of millions of pounds of their shares before their share price collapsed. When making ethical decisions, such managers put their own interests first and commonly harm other stakeholders.

An **accommodative approach** is an acknowledgement of the need to support corporate social responsibility. Accommodative companies and managers agree that organisational members ought to behave legally and ethically, and they try to balance the interests of different stakeholders against one another so that the claims of shareholders are seen in relation to the claims of other stakeholders. Managers adopting this approach want to make choices that are reasonable in the eyes of society, and want to do the right thing when called on to do so.

This approach is the one taken by the typical large company which has the most to lose from unethical or illegal behaviour. Generally, the older and more reputable a company, the more likely are its managers to curb attempts by their subordinates to act unethically. Large companies like BP, Intel, Du Pont and Shell seek every way to build their companies' competitive advantages. Nevertheless, they control attempts by their managers to behave unethically or illegally, knowing the grave consequences that such behaviour can have on future profitability.

Companies and managers taking a **proactive approach** actively embrace the need to behave in socially responsible ways. They go out of their way to learn about the needs of different stakeholder groups and are willing to utilise organisational resources to promote the interests not only of shareholders but also of other stakeholders. Such companies are at the forefront of campaigns for causes such as a pollution-free environment, recycling and conservation of resources, the minimisation or elimination of the use of animals in drug and cosmetics testing and the reduction of crime, illiteracy and poverty. Companies like McDonald's, The Body Shop and Innocent Drinks all have a reputation for being proactive in the support of stakeholders such as their suppliers or the community in which they operate.

Why Be Socially Responsible?

Several advantages result when companies and their managers behave in a socially responsible manner. First, demonstrating its corporate social responsibility helps a company build a good *reputation*. Reputation, as we have seen, is the trust, goodwill and confidence others have in a company that leads them to want to do business with it. The reward for a good company reputation is increased trade and improved ability to obtain resources from stakeholders. Reputation thus can enhance profitability and build shareholder wealth. Behaving socially responsibly is therefore the economically right thing to do, because companies that do so benefit from increasing business and rising profits.

A second major reason for companies to act socially responsibly toward employees, customers and society is that in a capitalist system companies, as well as the government, have to bear the costs of protecting their stakeholders, providing health care and income, paying taxes and so on. So if all companies in a society act socially responsibly, the quality of life as a whole increases.

Moreover, the way companies behave toward their employees determines many of a society's values and norms and the ethics of its citizens, as noted above. It has been suggested that if all organisations adopted a caring approach and agreed that their responsibility was to promote the interests of their employees, a climate of caring would pervade the wider society. Experts point to Japan, Sweden, Germany, the Netherlands and Switzerland as countries where organisations are highly socially responsible and where, as a result, crime, poverty and unemployment rates are relatively low, literacy rates are relatively high and socio-cultural values promote harmony between different groups of people. Business activity affects all aspects of people's lives, so the way businesses behave toward stakeholders affects how stakeholders will behave toward business. You 'reap what you sow', as the adage goes.

The Role of Organisational Culture

While an organisation's code of ethics guides decision making when ethical questions arise, managers can go one step further by ensuring that important ethical values and norms are key features of an organisation's culture. Richard Branson and Virgin Atlantic's culture, for example, values employee well-being; this translates into norms dictating that redundancies should be avoided.[49] When ethical values and norms such as these are part of an organisation's culture, they help organisational members resist self-interested action and recognise that they are part of something bigger than themselves.[50]

Managers' roles in developing ethical values and standards in other employees are very important. Employees naturally look to those in authority to provide leadership, and managers become ethical role models whose behaviour is scrutinised by their subordinates. If senior managers are not ethical, their subordinates are not likely to behave in an ethical manner either. Employees may think that if it's all right for a senior manager to engage in dubious behaviour, than it's all right for them. The actions of senior managers such as CEOs and Heads of State are scrutinised so closely for ethical improprieties because their actions represent the values of their organisations – and, in the case of presidents, the values of a nation.

Managers can also provide a visible means of support to develop an ethical culture. Increasingly, organisations are creating the role of ethics officer, or **ethics ombudsman**, to monitor their ethical practices and procedures. The ethics ombudsman is responsible for communicating ethical standards to all employees, for designing systems to monitor employees' conformity to those standards and for teaching managers and employees at all levels of the organisation how to respond appropriately to ethical dilemmas.[51] Because the ethics ombudsman has organisationwide authority, organisational members in any department can communicate instances of unethical behaviour by their managers or co-workers without fear of retribution. This arrangement makes it easier for everyone to behave ethically. In addition, an ethics ombudsman can provide guidance when organisational members are uncertain about whether or not an action is ethical. Some organisations have an organisationwide *ethics committee* to provide guidance on ethical issues and help write and update the company's code of ethics.

Ethical organisational cultures encourage organisational members to behave in a socially responsible manner. As discussed in Case 4.4, Unilever aims to enhance its local community by encouraging its staff to make a difference.

Case 4.4: **Unilever does it locally!**

Unilever is one of the world's most successful consumer product companies that originated in nineteenth-century England. Unilever produces foods and home and personal care products under a variety of brand names. In the UK it is responsible for products such as Domestos, CIF, Lipton, Vaseline and Flora.

Unilever has built its strong ethical values on its founder's mission to balance profits with responsible corporate behaviour. Unilever argues that it is still committed to 'the highest standards of corporate behaviour towards our employees, consumers and the societies and world in which we live'.[52] Unilever is engaged in a multitude of projects that aim at reflecting those values.

In order to preserve the environment, Unilever works closely with the World Wildlife Fund (WWF) in its efforts to use palm oil – a major ingredient in some personal care products – in a sustainable manner without having to resort to expanding into rainforest or using fire to clear fields for further cultivation. Unilever also works closely with farmers across Europe to reduce the use of pesticides and develop sustainable farming methods.

Unilever also excels in making a difference in the local community. In 2005 Unilever won the prestigious European Engagement Excellence Award for the 'Give a Little' campaign that was rolled out across Europe. The initiative aimed at getting employees involved in local communities. Overall 3,500 employees across Europe took part and 5,000 disadvantaged people and more than 65 charities benefited from the scheme. Each employee in Europe was given time off work to participate in a project that had direct benefit to the local communities. The employee had to be part of the planning process of the initiative and the initiative had to respond to key local needs such as homelessness, people with disabilities, or the environment. In Finland, for example, employees recorded books for visually impaired children.[53]

The Unilever example shows that strong values held by an organisation can make a real impact in the communities in which it is situated.

TIPS FOR PRACTICE

1. Do your personal values match your organisation's ethical standards? If there are discrepancies, what can you do?
2. Why do you have a personal responsibility for behaving ethically?

Reaction Time

1. Choose any company that faces ethical dilemmas and discuss what approach to corporate social responsibility they adopt.
2. Can you think of any ethical issues that relate to university life?

Summary and Review

The nature of ethics Ethical issues are central to the way companies and their managers make decisions, and they affect not only the efficiency and effectiveness of the way companies operate but also the prosperity of a nation. The result of ethical behaviour is a general increase in company performance and in a nation's standard of living, well-being and wealth.

An ethical dilemma is the quandary people find themselves in when they have to decide if they should act in a way that might help another person or group, and is the 'right' thing to do, even though it might go against their own self-interest. Ethics are the inner-guiding moral principles, values and beliefs that people use to analyse or interpret a situation and then decide what is the 'right' or appropriate way to behave.

Ethical beliefs alter and change as time passes, and as they do so laws change to reflect the changing ethical beliefs of a society.

Stakeholders and ethics Stakeholders are people and groups who have a claim on, and a stake in, a company. The main stakeholder groups are shareholders, managers, employees, suppliers and distributors, customers and a community, society and nation. Companies and their managers need to make ethical business decisions that promote the well-being of their stakeholders and avoid doing them harm.

To determine if a business decision is ethical, managers can use four ethical rules to analyse it: the utilitarian, moral rights, justice and practical rules. Managers should behave ethically because this avoids the escalation of unethical behaviour and results in a general increase in efficiency, effectiveness and company performance. The main determinants of differences in a manager's, a company's and country's business ethics are societal, occupational, individual and organisational.

Ethics and corporate social responsibility A company's stance on corporate social responsibility is the way its managers and employees view their duty or obligation to make decisions that protect, enhance and promote the welfare and well-being of stakeholders and society as a whole.

Approaches to corporate social responsibility There are four main approaches to corporate social responsibility: obstructionist, defensive, accommodative and proactive. The rewards from behaving in a socially responsible way are a good reputation, the support of all organisational stakeholders and thus superior company performance.

Topic for Action

- Find a manager and ask about the most important ethical rules that he or she uses to make the right decisions.
- Find an example of (a) a company that has an obstructionist approach to social responsibility and (b) one that has an accommodative approach.

Applied Independent Learning

Building Management Skills

Dealing with Ethical Dilemmas

Use the chapter material to decide how you, as a manager, should respond to each of the following ethical dilemmas:

1. You are planning to leave your job to go and work for a competitor; your boss invites you to an important meeting where you will learn about new products your company will be bringing out next year. Do you go to the meeting?

2. You are the manager of sales in an expensive sports-car dealership. A young executive who has just received a promotion comes in and wants to buy a car that you know is out of his or her price range. Do you encourage the executive to buy it so that you can receive a big commission on the sale?

3. You sign a contract to manage a young rock band, and that group agrees to let you produce their next seven records, for which they will receive royalties of 5 per cent. Their first record is a smash hit and sells millions. Do you increase their royalty rate on their future records?

Managing Ethically

As the chapter has discussed, Arthur Andersen's culture had become so strong that some of the company's partners and their subordinates acted unethically and pursued their own interests at the expense of other stakeholders. Many employees knew they were doing wrong but were afraid to refuse to follow orders.

▶

▶ ## Questions

1. Why is it that an organisation's values and norms can become too strong and lead to unethical behaviour?

2. What steps can a company take to prevent this problem – to stop its values and norms from becoming so inwardly focused that managers and employees lose sight of their responsibility to their stakeholders?

Small Group Breakout Exercise

Is Chewing Gum the 'Right' Thing to Do?

Read the paragraph below. Then break up into groups of three or four people and answer the discussion questions.

We take the right to chew gum for granted. Although it is often against the rules to chew gum in the school classroom, church and so on, it is legal to do so on the street. If you possess or chew gum on a street in Singapore, you can be arrested. Chewing gum has been made illegal in Singapore because those in power believe that it creates a disgusting mess on pavements and feel that people cannot be trusted to dispose of their gum properly and thus should have no right to use it.

1. What makes chewing gum acceptable in your country and unacceptable in Singapore?

2. Why can you chew gum on the street but not in a church?

3. How can you use ethical principles to decide when gum-chewing is ethical or unethical and if and when it should be made illegal?

Exploring the World Wide Web

Go to an international company's website and read the information there about the company's stance on the ethics of global outsourcing and the treatment of workers in countries abroad. Then search the Web for some recent stories about global purchasing practices and reports on the enforcement of its code of conduct.

Application in Today's Business World

Can Boeing Get Out of Its 'Ethical Cloud'?

The unexpected resignation of Boeing chairman and CEO Philip M. Condit on 1 December 2003 followed a year of turbulence at the world's largest aerospace company. The final straw for Condit, 62, may have been the previous week's ousting of two senior Boeing officials for an alleged ethics lapse.

Condit's resignation created several daunting challenges for his immediate successor – Harry C. Stonecipher, former Boeing president and chief operating officer. Stonecipher, 67, who retired in 2002 and remained as a board member, immediately assumed the post of CEO and president of a company that had more than $54 billion in annual revenues.

In his first press conference as top gun, Stonecipher seemed to say all the right things by pledging to answer any and all questions, including those swirling around a highly criticized air-tanker deal with the federal government. The blunt-talking, no-nonsense leader would have to be true to his word and get Boeing soaring again.

Clearly, Stonecipher has his work cut out. Condit's resignation is tied to Boeing's persistent reluctance to disclose all the particulars of a controversial plan to lease Boeing 767 tankers to the US Air Force. The plan was blasted for the secrecy in which the contract was negotiated and for the fact that leasing would be much more expensive for the federal government than an outright purchase.

Condit's departure came a week after Boeing Chief Finance Officer (CFO) Michael Sears resigned. The company cited unethical conduct, saying that he had negotiated the hiring of an Air Force missile defense expert while she was still working for the Pentagon and had direct influence over Boeing's bid to secure the tanker contract. Sears denied any wrongdoing.

'It's very surprising for a company such as Boeing to have not one but two apparent ethical breaches in less than six months,' said Steven Ryan, a Washington (DC) attorney who represented contractors seeking work with the federal government. In July 2003 the Pentagon had punished Boeing for stealing trade secrets from rival Lockheed Martin to help win rocket-launch contracts. The punishment added up to $1 billion in lost business, and the Pentagon had indefinitely banned Boeing from bidding on military satellite-launching contracts.

'Condit's resignation is a reflection of the seriousness of the problem,' said Ryan. And the situation suggested that something wasn't right inside Boeing's culture – something that Stonecipher had helped change when he was president and was now responsible and accountable for coming clean.

'Everything the former leadership at Boeing did was surrounded by an ethical cloud of controversy and needed to be reviewed to ensure that it was in the best interest of the taxpayer and war-fighter,' said Steve Ellis, Vice President for Taxpayers for Common Sense. With Condit out, the board apparently chose the tough-talking Stonecipher because he was well regarded on Wall Street and because he knew the ways of the Pentagon. With the mandatory retirement set at 65 for Boeing execs, Stonecipher received a special exemption to return.

How Boeing got itself and its top execs in such a mess has yet to be fully explained. The stock, at just over $38, barely moved on the news of Condit's departure. And it had moved mostly higher in 2002 from an all-time low of just over $24 hit back in March 2003. Still, analysts say, the stock should have been much higher, and Stonecipher had a long way to go to regain the trust of angry and sceptical investors, public-interest groups and the US government.

Questions

1. In what kinds of unethical actions did Boeing's managers engage?

2. What effect did this have on the company and how could its CEO prevent future unethical behaviour?

Source: Stanley Holmes, 'Can Boeing Get Out of Its "Ethical Cloud"?', adapted and reprinted from *BusinessWeek Online*, December 1, 2003 by special permission. Copyright © 2003 by the McGraw-Hill Companies, Inc.

Notes and References

1   Dan McDougall, 'The price of sparkle is slavery', *The Observer*, 30 April 2006, 34.

2   *Ibid.*

3   *Ibid.*

4   *Ibid.*, 35.

5   A. E. Tenbrunsel, 'Misrepresentation and Expectations of Misrepresentation in an Ethical Dilemma: The Role of Incentives and Temptation', *Academy of Management Journal* 41 (June 1998), 330–40.

6   http://www.driving-abroad.info/alcohol.php.

7   R. W. Gorter, M. Butorac, E. P. Cobian and W. van der Sluis, 'Medical Use of Cannabis in the Netherlands', *Neurology* 64 (8 March 2005), 971–79.

8   D. Kravets, 'Supreme Court to Hear Case on Medical Pot', www.yahoo.com, 29 June 2004.

9   J. C. van Ours, 'Is cannabis a stepping-stone for cocaine?', *Journal of Health Economics* 22 (July 2003), 539–54.

10 www.bbc.co.uk/news 13th April 2006, 'Q&A: cash for peerages row'.

11 R. E. Freeman, *Strategic Management: A Stakeholder Approach* (Marshfield, MA: Pitman, 1984).

12 *Guardian*, 'Philip Green pays himself a record £1.2 bn', 21 October 2005.

13 J. A. Pearce, 'The Company Mission as a Strategic Tool', *Sloan Management Review*, Spring 1982, 15–24.

14 C. I. Barnard, *The Functions of the Executive* (Cambridge, MA: Harvard University Press, 1948).

15 Freeman, *Strategic Management: A Stakeholder Approach*.

16 P. S. Adler, 'Corporate Scandals: It's Time for Reflection in Business Schools', *Academy of Management Executive* 16 (August 2002), 148–50.

17 N. O'Sullivan, 'Managers as Monitors: An Analysis of the Non-Executive Role of Senior Executives in UK Companies', *British Journal of Management* 11 (1) (March 2000), 17–29.

18 http://www.res.org.uk.

19 J. Finch and J. Treanor, *Boardroom Bonanza goes on*, The Guardian Online, 2004.

20 *Ibid.*

21 http://www.labourbehindthelabel.org/content/view/17/53/ November 2005.

22 http://www.cleanclothes.org/companies/nike.htm.

23 (www.umbroplc.com).

24 http://news.bbc.co.uk/1/hi/business/4439283.stm.

25 'Kritik an illegalen Mülltransporten nach Tschechien beweist steigende Sensibilität der Bürger', 26 February 2006, http://www.radio.cz/.

26 T. L. Beauchamp and N. E. Bowie, eds, *Ethical Theory and Business* (Englewood Cliffs, NJ: Prentice Hall, 1979); A. MacIntyre, *After Virtue* (South Bend, IN: University of Notre Dame Press, 1981).

27 R. E. Goodin, 'How to Determine Who Should Get What', *Ethics*, July 1975, 310–21.

28 E. P. Kelly, 'A Better Way to Think About Business' (book review), *Academy of Management Executive* 14 (May 2000), 127–29.

29 T. M. Jones, 'Ethical Decision Making by Individuals in Organizations: An Issue Contingent Model', *Academy of Management Journal* 16 (1991), 366–95; G. F. Cavanaugh, D. J. Moberg and M. Velasquez, 'The Ethics of Organizational Politics', *Academy of Management Review* 6 (1981), 363–74.

30 L. K. Trevino, 'Ethical Decision Making in Organizations: A Person–Situation Interactionist Model', *Academy of Management Review* 11 (1986), 601–17; W. H. Shaw and V. Barry, *Moral Issues in Business*, 6th ed. (Belmont, CA: Wadsworth, 1995).

31 T. M. Jones, 'Instrumental Stakeholder Theory: A Synthesis of Ethics and Economics', *Academy of Management Review* 20 (1995), 404–37.

32 B. Victor and J. B. Cullen, 'The Organizational Bases of Ethical Work Climates', *Administrative Science Quarterly* 33 (1988), 101–25.

33 D. Collins, 'Organizational Harm, Legal Consequences and Stakeholder Retaliation', *Journal of Business Ethics* 8 (1988), 1–13.

34 R. C. Soloman, *Ethics and Excellence* (New York: Oxford University Press, 1992).

35 T. E. Becker, 'Integrity in Organizations: Beyond Honesty and Conscientiousness', *Academy of Management Review* 23 (January 1998), 154–62.

36 S. W. Gellerman, 'Why Good Managers Make Bad Decisions', in K. R. Andrews, ed., *Ethics in Practice: Managing the Moral Corporation* (Boston: Harvard Business School Press, 1989).

37 J. Dobson, 'Corporate Reputation: A Free Market Solution to Unethical Behavior', *Business and Society* 28 (1989), 1–5.

38 M. S. Baucus and J. P. Near, 'Can Illegal Corporate Behavior Be Predicted? An Event History Analysis', *Academy of Management Journal* 34 (1991), 9–36.

39 Trevino, 'Ethical Decision Making in Organizations'.

40 A. S. Waterman, 'On the Uses of Psychological Theory and Research in the Process of Ethical Inquiry', *Psychological Bulletin* 103 (3) (1988), 283–98.

41 M. S. Frankel, 'Professional Codes: Why, How, and with What Impact?' *Ethics* 8 (1989), 109–15.

42 J. Van Maanen and S. R. Barley, 'Occupational Communities: Culture and Control in Organizations', in B. Staw and L. Cummings, eds, *Research in Organizational Behavior*, 6 (Greenwich, CT: JAI Press, 1984), 287–365.

43 Jones, 'Ethical Decision Making by Individuals in Organizations'.

44 E. Gatewood and A. B. Carroll, 'The Anatomy of Corporate Social Response', *Business Horizons*, September–October 1981, 9–16.

45 *Ibid.*

46 http://www.newscientist.com/article.ns?id=dn2551.

47 http://foodqualitynews.com/news/ng.asp?id=53590&n=wh30&c=nbbgbvsktuxtxwj.

48 M. Friedman, 'A Friedman Doctrine: The Social Responsibility of Business Is to Increase Its Profits', *New York Times Magazine*, 13 September 1970, 33.

49 http://news.bbc.co.uk/2/hi/business/3035205.stm.

50 G. R. Jones, *Organizational Theory: Text and Cases* (Englewood Cliffs, NJ: Prentice Hall, 2003).

51 P. E. Murphy, 'Creating Ethical Corporate Structure', *Sloan Management Review*, Winter 1989, 81–87.

52 http://www.unilever.com/ourcompany/aboutunilever/history/default.asp.

53 http://www.unilever.com/ourvalues.

Chapter 5

Managing Diverse Employees in a Multicultural Environment

LEARNING OBJECTIVES

After studying this chapter, you should be able to:

☑ Appreciate the increasing diversity of the workforce and of the organisational environment.

☑ Recognise the central role that managers play in the effective management of diversity.

☑ Understand why the effective management of diversity is both an ethical and a business imperative.

☑ Appreciate how perception and the use of schemas can result in unfair treatment.

☑ Appreciate the steps managers can take to effectively manage diversity.

☑ Understand the two major forms of sexual harassment and how they can be eliminated.

A Manager's Challenge

Diversity in Organisations

How can managers diversify non-traditional work groups and organisations?
For demographic groups such as women, Asians and African-Caribbeans, non-traditional work groups and organisations are work settings in which they are much under-represented. For

example, given that women make up about half of the population, a non-traditional organisation for women is one in which fewer than 25 per cent of employees are women. Recognising that diversity on multiple dimensions makes good business sense, managers are increasingly seeking to diversify jobs and work groups that traditionally have comprised very few women or minorities. In the US and other countries such as Norway and Sweden, efforts to diversify non-traditional work settings are occurring at every organisational level.[1] The need for diversification at the very top of organisations is reflected in the composition of boards of directors. Research shows that only 4 per cent of executive directors of FTSE 100 companies are women;[2] however, only 2.3 per cent of FTSE 100 directorships are held by a member from an ethnic minority, whereby only 1.5 per cent are executive directors.[3]

The Royal Mail, UK, has been awarded an award for their efforts in trying to reflect the population's diversity mix within their organisation. One of the reasons for such attempts is in order to fully harness 'the talents of all our people . . . ensuring Royal Mail is competitive in a market where customers are diverse and expect to be served by people with whom they can identify'.[4] This statement by the Royal Mail's Director for Diversity and Inclusion, Satya Kartara, supports the assumption that a broad representation of experiences, backgrounds and perspectives can help an organisation appeal to diverse markets for its goods and services. However, the Royal Mail is by no means complacent about its achievements and is well aware that there is more to be done. One area which still needs further improvement is the recruitment of women. Their *Corporate Social Responsibility Review* of 2004 highlighted that only 19 per cent of their workforce was made up of women and out of 13 directors only two were women.[5] At lower levels in organisations, managers and employees alike are beginning to question why certain jobs, such as those in construction, tend to be dominated by men. Within the UK, only 1 per cent of women work in construction and in 2004 only 22 girls applied for apprenticeships in plumbing in England.[6] Often, in certain non-traditional jobs, people think that women are under-represented because of size and strength issues. However, petite women have successful careers as plumbers or within construction, as is represented by the Women in Plumbing Group, part of the Institute of Plumbing and Heat Engineering in the UK.[7] And for many positions, such as a painter or an electrician, physical differences between men and women really don't enter the picture even though many people assume they do.

In the health care arena, new guidelines regarding ethnic minorities have been introduced, as it is believed[8] that the effective management of diversity is important in all aspects of health care research and delivery and that a proactive approach to managing diversity is a necessity.[9] Whether it is scientific research, disease detection, participation in drug trials, laboratory testing or marketing to patients, diversity enters into the equation. And in all of these venues, good communication is a necessity, as is mutual understanding and the ability to converse in the same language.[10]

What about law enforcement? Women currently make up 16 per cent of the police forces in the UK.[11] Traditionally, even if a woman became a law enforcement officer, it was very unlikely that she would ever rise to the top and assume a leadership position. Often, the reasoning revolved around issues of physical strength. However, this situation is changing as women are currently assuming high-level leadership positions in law enforcement. For example, Della Cannings, Chief Constable of the Yorkshire Police, or Sue Fish, Assistant Chief Constable of Nottinghamshire Police[12], were chosen based on their credentials, and the decision had little to do with gender. As decision makers increasingly recognise that leaders in law enforcement need many of the same leadership qualities that are important in other kinds of organisations – intelligence, interpersonal skills, education, experience and the ability and desire to make difficult decisions – excluding women from serious consideration for such positions for irrelevant reasons will hopefully decline.

Overview

The effective management of **diversity** means much more than hiring diverse employees. It means learning to appreciate and respond appropriately to the needs, attitudes, beliefs and values that diverse people bring to an organisation. It also means correcting misconceptions about why and how different kinds of employee groups are different from one another and finding the most effective way to utilise the skills and talents of diverse employees.

In this chapter, the focus is on the effective management of diversity in an environment that is becoming increasingly diverse in all respects. Not only is the diversity of the global workforce increasing, but suppliers and customers are also becoming increasingly diverse. Managers need to proactively manage diversity to be able to attract and retain the best employees and compete effectively in a diverse global environment. For example, managers at the audit and consulting firm Deloitte & Touche have instituted a programme to encourage minority suppliers to compete for its business, and the firm sponsors schools and colleges that supply a stream of well-trained recruits.[13]

Sometimes well-intentioned managers inadvertently treat one group of employees differently from another, even though there are no performance-based differences between them. As illustrated at the beginning of the chapter, women were traditionally excluded from senior management positions in law enforcement for reasons that were irrelevant to performance in leadership roles. This chapter explores why differential treatment occurs, and the steps managers and organisations can take to ensure that diversity, in all its aspects, is effectively managed for the good of all organisational stakeholders.

The Increasing Diversity of the Workforce and the Environment

One of the most important management issues to emerge over the last 30 years has been the increasing diversity of the workforce. *Diversity* is dissimilarities – differences – among people due to age, gender, race, ethnicity, religion, sexual orientation, socio-economic background, education, experience, physical appearance, capabilities/disabilities and any other characteristic that is used to distinguish between people (Fig. 5.1).

Diversity raises important ethical issues and social responsibility issues (see Chapter 4). It is also a critical issue for organisations – one that if not handled well can bring an organisation to its knees, especially in our increasingly global environment. There are several reasons why diversity is such a pivotal concern and issue in both the popular press and for managers and organisations:

- There is a strong ethical imperative in many societies that diverse people receive equal opportunities and be treated fairly and justly. Unfair treatment is often illegal.
- Effectively managing diversity can improve organisational effectiveness.[14] When managers effectively manage diversity, they not only encourage other managers to treat diverse members of an organisation fairly and justly but also realise that diversity is an important organisational resource that can help an organisation gain a competitive advantage.
- There is substantial evidence that diverse individuals continue to experience unfair treatment in the workplace as a result of biases, stereotypes and overt discrimination.[15] In one study, résumés of equally qualified men and women were sent to leading restaurants (where potential earnings are high). Though equally qualified, men were more than twice as likely as women

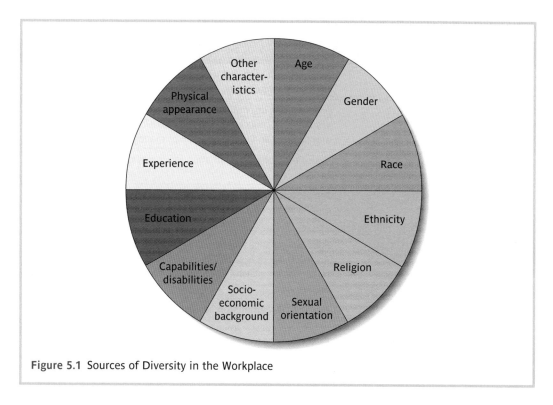

Figure 5.1 Sources of Diversity in the Workplace

to be called for a job interview and more than five times as likely to receive a job offer.[16] Findings from another study suggest that both women and men tend to believe that women will accept lower pay than men; this is a possible explanation for the continuing *gap in pay* between men and women.[17] According to UK government statistics, women still earn on average about £130 less a week than men.[18] This is a pay differential of 28 per cent on annual earnings (excluding overtime) between men and women.[19] The pay gap actually widened by 0.4 per cent from April 2001 to April 2002.[20]

Other kinds of diverse employees may face even greater barriers. For example, the federal Glass Ceiling Commission Report in the US indicated that African-Americans have the hardest time being promoted and climbing the corporate ladder, that Asians are often stereotyped into technical jobs and that Hispanics are assumed to be less well educated than other minority groups.[21] The picture in Europe is not that different. It is astounding how persistent the **glass ceiling** remains, 20 years after it was first identified as a problem[22] (the term 'glass ceiling' alludes to the invisible barriers that prevent minorities and women from being promoted to top corporate positions[23]).

Before we can discuss the multitude of issues surrounding the effective management of diversity, we must document just how diverse the workforce is becoming. The overview of diversity in the UK provides an example of how it has become a major part of organisational life. Other European countries face similar issues surrounding diversity, although the focus may differ from country to country – for example, gender issues may be dominant in one country, ethnic minorities may present more challenges in another. A summary of the major equal employment opportunity legislation that prohibits discrimination among diverse groups in the UK is summarised in Table 5.1.

Table 5.1 Major equal employment opportunity laws affecting HRM

Year	Law	Description
1975	Equal Pay Act (EPA)	Requires that men and women be paid equally if they are performing equal work
1975	Sex Discrimination Act	Prohibits sex discrimination against individuals in the areas of employment, education and the provision of goods, facilities and services and in the disposal or management of premises
		It also prohibits discrimination in employment against married people
1976	Race Relations Act	Prohibits discrimination on racial grounds in the areas of employment, education and the provision of goods, facilities and services and premises
		Following changes made by the Race Relations (Amendment) Act 2000, there is also now a positive duty on public authorities to eliminate unlawful discrimination and promote equality of opportunity
1989	Employment Act	Prohibits discrimination against women in employment decisions
1995	Disability Discrimination Act	Prohibits discrimination against disabled individuals in employment decisions and requires that employers make accommodations for disabled workers to enable them to perform their jobs
1996	Employment Rights Act	The right not to be unfairly dismissed
		A dismissal is automatically unfair if it is for a reason related to pregnancy, childbirth, maternity leave, parental leave or time off for dependants
		Also includes provision that employers have to accommodate for the changing circumstances of the workforce and the provision that employers need to offer alternative work
1997	Protection from Harassment Act	Creates a criminal offence of harassment
		It also creates a new type of civil claim, allowing individuals who are harassed to claim damages and/or seek a court order to stop the harasser from continuing the harassment
1998	National Minimum Wage Act	Provides that workers shall not be paid less than a designated minimum rate per hour
2002	Employment Act (Flexible Working Regulations)	Employees are allowed to request flexible working time
2003	The Employment Equality (Sexual Orientation) Regulations	Prohibit discrimination on the grounds of sexual orientation in the employment field
2003	The Employment Equality (Religion & Belief) Regulations	Prohibit discrimination on the grounds of religion in the employment field

Countries that are members of the European Union (EU) are often under an obligation to implement particular EU regulations and legislation. In 2000, Spain, for example, was on the way to integrate EU legislation on racism and discrimination. While it had made substantial progress, it had not yet fulfilled all the necessary requirements.[24]

Age

According to the latest data from the UK Office for National Statistics (ONS), the mean age of a person in the UK labour market has risen to 39.0 years.[25] By 2020, it is projected that 32 per cent of the working-age population will be between 50 and 65. In 2005 56.9 per cent of all people aged between 50–65 have been in employment; this is above the European average of 42.5 per cent. The median age of the population rose from 34.1 in 1971 to 38.4 in 2003.[26] The ageing of the population suggests that managers need to be vigilant that older employees are not discriminated against; managers also need to ensure that the policies and procedures they have in place treat all workers fairly, regardless of their age.

Gender

Women and men are almost equally represented in the UK workforce (approximately 54 per cent of the workforce is male and 46 per cent female),[27] yet women's average weekly earnings are estimated to be £420 compared to £557 for men.[28] Thus, the gender pay gap appears to be as alive and well as the glass ceiling. According to the non-profit organisation Catalyst, which studies women in business, while women comprise about 50.5 per cent of the employees in managerial and professional positions, only around 15.7 per cent of corporate officers in the *Fortune 500* are women, only 5.2 per cent of the top earners are women, only 7.9 per cent of those with the highest-ranking titles in corporate America (e.g. CEO or executive vice president) are women, and only eight *Fortune 500* companies have women as CEOs.[29] A report from the accounting firm Deloitte in 2004 showed this disparity even more severely, by suggesting that only 3 per cent of executive and 8 per cent of non-executive directorships were held by women.[30] However, as Sheila Wellington, president of Catalyst, indicates: 'Women either control or influence nearly all consumer purchases, so it's important to have their perspective represented on boards.'[31] Within the UK, in 2004 42 per cent of professionals were women. However, within the occupational group of Managers & Senior Officials, only 33 per cent were female.[32]

Research conducted by consulting firms suggests that female executives outperform their male colleagues on skills such as motivating others, promoting good communication, turning out high-quality work and being a good listener.[33] The Hagberg Group performed in-depth evaluations of 425 top executives in a variety of industries, with each executive rated by approximately 25 people. Of the 52 skills assessed, women received higher ratings than men on 42 skills, although at times the differences were small.[34] Results of a study conducted by Catalyst found that organisations with higher proportions of women in senior management positions had significantly better financial performance than organisations with lower proportions of female senior managers.[35] Studies such as these make one wonder why the glass ceiling continues to hamper the progress of women in business (a topic we address later in the chapter).

Race and Ethnicity

For official categorisation, the UK typically distinguishes between the following ethnic groups:[36] White (British, Irish, Other White Backgrounds), Mixed (White and Black Caribbean, White and Black African, White and Asian, Other Mixed Background), Asian or Asian British (Indian, Bangladeshi, Pakistani, Other Asian Backgrounds), Black or Black British (Caribbean, African, Other Black Background) and Chinese (these categories are likely to be slightly different in other European countries).

Ethnicity refers to a societal category of people who share cultural heritage or origin that may manifest itself through language, religion, family patterns or other cultural signifiers. The term 'race' often is used interchangeably with ethnicity. However, race is a *social category* that denotes difference through physical appearance. There have been substantial arguments from the natural and social sciences that race is a faulty and often misleading denominator for ethnic difference. Genetically, too, little difference exists between black people, Asian people and Caucasians.

The ethnic diversity of the UK population is increasing at an exponential rate, as is the composition of the workforce. According to the *National Census* of 2001, the minority ethnic population in Great Britain grew by 53 per cent between 1991 and 2001, from 3.0 million in 1991 to 4.6 million in 2001. Half of the total minority ethnic population were Asians of Indian, Pakistani, Bangladeshi or other Asian origin; 92.1 per cent of the population was white, 1.2 per cent mixed, 4 per cent Asian or Asian British, 2 per cent Black or Black British and 0.8 per cent Chinese and other. One reason is the rise is migration. In the UK, migration is expected to stay constant over the coming decades,[37] whereby others argue that this is a conservative estimate considering the general rise in net migration all over the world and based on data that suggest a steady influx of non-British migrants over the decade 1995–2005.[38]

The increasing ethnic diversity of the workforce and the population as a whole underscores the importance of effectively managing diversity. Statistics compiled by the UK government suggest that much needs to be done in terms of ensuring that diverse employees are provided with equal opportunities. While, for example, the Chinese and Indian minorities in the UK do well, other ethnic groups experience significantly higher unemployment rates and lower pay compared to White workers, especially people from a Caribbean, Pakistani or Bangladeshi background.[39] The average earnings of the most disadvantaged minority, Bangladeshi, were nearly 52 per cent below the average weekly earnings for Whites in 2000. Indians, the least disadvantaged ethnic group, earned around 8 per cent less than their White counterparts.[40] An American study showed that out of 10,092 corporate officers in *Fortune 500* companies, only 106 were African-American women.[41] In a study of the FTSE100 companies in the UK in 2000, it was found that only 5.4 per cent of the employees came from minority backgrounds (data from 26 companies)[42] versus a minority population of nearly 8 per cent of the entire UK population. This number decreased significantly in the higher echelons of these organisations – only 3.2 per cent of junior and middle managers and 1 per cent of senior managers were from an ethnic minority background. The difference amongst the different ethnic minorities is significant, with Indians being the most consistently represented minority.

In the remainder of this chapter, we focus on the fair treatment of diverse employees, explore why this is such an important challenge and consider what managers can do to meet it. We begin by taking a broader perspective and examining how increasing racial and ethnic diversity in an organisation's environment (e.g. customers and suppliers) affects decision making and organisational effectiveness.

Pressure is mounting on the media to increase diversity and fair representations of ethnic minorities. It has been suggested that the UK is slowly adapting to representing the needs and concerns of these minorities, such as appointing news readers from ethnic minorities and showing television programmes that represent ethnic minorities in an appropriate light. Within the retail sector home and automobile buyers, for instance, are increasingly diverse, reflecting the increasing diversity of the population as a whole.[43] Managers have also to be especially sensitive to avoid stereotyping different groups when they communicate with potential customers. Toyota

Motor Sales USA made a public apology to the Reverend Jesse Jackson and his Rainbow Coalition for using a print advertisement depicting an African-American man with a Toyota RAV4 sport utility image embossed on his gold front tooth, for example.[44]

Religion

The Race Relations Act 1976 prohibits discrimination based on religion (as well as based on race/ethnicity, country of origin and sex, see Table 5.1). In addition the Racial and Religious Hatred Act 2006 protects multi-ethnic faith groups from racial abuse. This legislation in regard to incitement and religious hatred is filling a loop-hole that thus far has protected only mono-ethnic faith groups.[45]

A key issue for managers when it comes to religious diversity is recognising and being aware of different religions and their beliefs, with particular attention being paid to when religious holidays fall. Critical meetings should not be scheduled during a holy day for members of a certain faith, and managers should be flexible in allowing people to have time off for religious observance. According to Lobna Ismail, director of a diversity training company, when managers acknowledge, respect and make even small accommodations for religious diversity, employee loyalty is often enhanced. Allowing employees to leave work early on certain days instead of taking a lunch break or posting holidays for different religions on the company calendar can go a long way toward making individuals of diverse religions feel respected and valued, as well as enabling them to practise their faith.[46]

Capabilities/Disabilities

The Disability Discrimination Act 1995 prohibits discrimination against persons with disabilities and also requires that employers make reasonable accommodation to enable these people to effectively perform their jobs. Such legislation may not be uncontroversial: on the surface, few would argue with its intent. However, as managers attempt to implement policies and procedures to comply with the Act, they face a number of challenges concerning interpretation and fairness.

On the one hand, some people with real disabilities warranting workplace accommodation are hesitant to reveal their disabilities to their employers and claim the accommodation they deserve.[47] On the other hand, some employees may abuse the Act by seeking unnecessary accommodation for disabilities that may or may not exist.[48] With regard to the impact on employment, within the period from 1998 to 2001 the employment rate of disabled people rose by 2.7 per cent, to 48 per cent of the disabled population. Compared to the non-disabled population (81 per cent in employment) this is significantly lower, and may raise questions regarding the commitment in implementing the legislation.[49] The employment statistic for disabled people in the public sector is significantly better, with an increase of 8.3 per cent from 1998 to 2004.[50] A key challenge for managers is to promote an environment in which employees needing accommodations feel comfortable disclosing their need and, at the same time, to ensure that the accommodations not only enable those with disabilities to effectively perform their jobs but also are perceived to be fair by those not disabled.[51] In addressing this challenge, managers must often educate both themselves and their employees about the disabilities, as well as the very real capabilities, of those who are disabled. For example, during Disability Awareness Week 2004 administrators at the University of Notre Dame sought to increase the public's knowledge of disabilities while also heightening awareness of the abilities of persons who are disabled.[52] The University of Houston conducted a similar programme called 'Think Ability'.[53] According to Cheryl Amoruso, director of the University of Houston's Centre for Students with Disabilities, many people are unaware of the prevalence of disabilities as well as misinformed about their consequences. She suggests, for example, that although students may not be able to see, they can still excel in their course-work and have very successful careers.[54] Accommodations enabling such students to perform up to their capabilities are covered under the Disability Act.

The Act also protects employees with acquired immune deficiency syndrome (AIDS) from being discriminated against in the workplace. Further amendments to strengthen this were made in 2005 to include MS, cancer and mental illnesses.[55] AIDS is caused by the human immunodeficiency virus (HIV) and is transmitted through sexual contact, infected needles and contaminated blood products. HIV is not spread through casual, non-sexual contact. Yet, out of ignorance, fear or prejudice, some people wish to avoid all contact with anyone infected with HIV. Infected individuals may not necessarily develop AIDS, and some individuals with HIV are able to remain effective performers of their jobs while not putting others at risk.[56]

AIDS awareness training can help people overcome their fears and also provide managers with a tool to prevent illegal discrimination against HIV-infected employees. Such training focuses on educating employees about HIV and AIDS, dispelling myths, communicating relev-ant organisational policies and emphasising the rights of HIV-positive employees to privacy and an environment that allows them to be productive.[57] The need for AIDS awareness training is underscored by some of the problems HIV-positive employees experience once others in their workplace become aware of their condition.[58] Organisations are also required to make reason-able accommodation to enable people with AIDS to effectively perform their jobs. Companies that have successfully implemented HIV awareness programmes are, among others, Barclays Bank, Heineken NV, HSBC, Renault, Royal Dutch Shell, Siemens and Virgin.[59]

Managers can thus be seen to have a moral obligation to educate employees about HIV and AIDS, dispel myths and the stigma of AIDS and ensure that HIV-related discrimination is not occurring in the workplace. Advances in medication and treatment mean that more infected individuals will be able to continue working or able to return to work after their condition improves.[60] Managers need to ensure that these employees are fairly treated by all members of their organisations. Managers and organisations that do not treat HIV-positive employees in a fair manner, as well as provide reasonable accommodation (e.g. allowing time off for doctor visits or to take medicine), risk costly lawsuits.

Socio-Economic Background

The term **socio-economic background** typically refers to a combination of social class and income-related factors. From a management perspective, *socio-economic diversity* (and, in par-ticular, diversity in income levels) requires that managers be sensitive and responsive to the needs and concerns of individuals who might not earn as much as others. Since the late 1990s the government has made efforts to decrease the rate of families living in low-income house-holds. These policies have increased employment amongst lone-parent families to just over 60 per cent. The number of families living in low-income families also shrank to 17 per cent of the population in 2000.[61] However, the economic downturn in the early 2000s resulted in national and international repercussions. In a very strong economy, it is much easier for poor people with few skills to find jobs; in a weak economy, when companies lay off employees, people who need their incomes the most are unfortunately often the first to lose their jobs – examples are manual labour positions in the automotive or mining industries.

Other factors that contribute to social inequalities are, for example, the increasing numbers of families that are facing the challenge of finding suitable child care arrangements that enable the adults to work long hours and/or through the night to maintain an adequate income level. New IT has led to more and more businesses operating 24 hours a day, creating real challenges for workers on the night shift, especially those with children.[62] Hundreds of thousands of parents across the country are scrambling to find someone to care for their children while they are working the night shift, commuting several hours a day, working weekends and holidays, or putting in long hours on one or more jobs. In the US this has led to the opening of day care facilities that operate around the clock, as well as to managers seeking ways to provide care for children of their employees. The Children's Choice Learning Center in Las Vegas, Nevada, for example, operates around the clock to accommodate employees working nights in neighbouring casinos as cashiers and dealers, as well as nurses, hospital workers and call-centre operators on the night shift. Randy Donahue, a security guard who works until midnight, picks his children up from the centre when he gets off work; his wife is a nurse on the night shift. There currently are five Children's Choice Learning Centers in the US operating 24 hours a day, and plans are under way to add seven more.

In the UK such facilities are not yet available, but great improvements have been made in regard to access to child care and thus the ability for parents, especially lone parents, to re-enter employment.[63]

In 1993, Ford Motor Company built an around-the-clock child care facility for 175 children of employees in Livonia, Michigan. However, a survey of child care needs indicates that many employees in other locations, such as Detroit and Kansas City, require such a facility. Some parents and psychologists feel uneasy having children separated from their families for so much time, and particularly at night. Most agree that unfortunately for many families this is not a choice but a necessity.[64]

Socio-economic diversity suggests that managers need to be sensitive and responsive to the needs and concerns of workers who may be less fortunate than themselves in terms of income and financial resources, child care and elder care options, housing opportunities and existence of sources of social and family support. Moreover – and equally important – managers should try to provide such individuals with opportunities to learn, advance and make meaningful contributions to their organisations while improving their economic well-being.

Sexual Orientation

Approximately 4–7 per cent of the UK population is gay or lesbian.[65] New legislation was introduced in 2003, namely The Employment Equality (Sexual Orientation) Regulations, that prohibits discrimination in the workplace against gay and lesbian employees. Until recently, one of the few areas in which gay and lesbian employers could be discriminated against was in regard to benefits that were given to married couples. However, with the introduction of the Civil Partnership Act 2004, all benefits that extend to married couples have to be extended to same-sex-registered couples. Similar legislation has been passed in Spain, Germany, Canada and the Netherlands. A number of organisations recognise the minority status of gay and lesbian employees, affirm their rights to fair and equal treatment and provide benefits to same-sex partners of gay and lesbian employees. For example, 95 per cent of *Fortune 500* companies prohibit discrimination based on sexual orientation, and 70 per cent of *Fortune 500* companies provide domestic-partner benefits.[66] A major gay and lesbian lobbying group within the UK has published a list of employers that joined their diversity champion programme that highlights organisations that are on the cutting edge of diversity management. Members include American Express, British Airways, HM Prison Service and the Metropolitan Police Service.[67] As indicated in Case 5.1, there are many steps that managers can take to ensure that sexual orientation is not used to discriminate unfairly among employees.

Case 5.1: **Gays and lesbians in the workplace**

While gays and lesbians have made great strides in terms of attaining fair treatment in the workplace, much more needs to be done. In a study conducted by Harris Interactive, Inc. (a research firm) and Witeck Communications, Inc. (a marketing firm), over 40 per cent of gay and lesbian employees indicated that they had been unfairly treated, denied a promotion or pushed to quit their jobs because of their sexual orientation.[68] Given continued harassment and discrimination despite the progress that has been made,[69] many gay and lesbian employees fear disclosing their sexual orientation in the workplace and thus live a life of secrecy. While there are a few openly gay senior managers, such as David Geffen (cofounder of DreamWorks SKG) and Allan Gilmour (Vice Chairman of Ford), many others choose not to disclose or discuss their personal lives, including their long-term partners.[70]

It is not surprising that many managers are therefore taking active steps to educate and train their employees in regard to issues of sexual orientation. S. C. Johnson & Sons, Inc. provides mandatory training to its plant managers to overturn stereotypes, as does Eastman Kodak. Other organisations, such as Lucent Technologies and Microsoft, IBM, Eastman Kodak and Lockheed Martin provide assistance to their gay and lesbian employees through gay and lesbian support groups.[71] As outlined above, in the UK a large number of companies have joined lobby groups to show their support against discrimination in the workplace.

More generally, the presence of a lesbian, gay, bisexual and transgender (LGBT) rights movement in the workplace is steadily increasing. From an individual employee perspective, these rights often boil down to receiving the same kind of treatment as one's heterosexual co-workers. Recent law suits have highlighted the necessity for the anti-discrimination laws that were put in place in December 2003, as people still seem to be being dismissed on the basis of their sexuality: in February 2005 Rob Whitfield won his case for unfair dismissal from his managerial position at Cleanaway UK, a waste management operator.[72]

Clearly, many highly qualified potential and current employees may happen to be gay or lesbian. An organisation that does not welcome and support such employees not only is unfairly discriminating against this group but also is losing the contributions of valued potential employees. An organisation that discriminates against this group also risks alienating customers. Research has shown that the gay and lesbian community holds a large amount of disposable income, with salary levels significantly higher than that of the national average.

Other Kinds of Diversity

There are other kinds of diversity that are important in organisations, which are critical for managers to deal with effectively and also potential sources of unfair treatment. For example, organisations and teams need members with diverse backgrounds and experiences. This is clearly illustrated by the prevalence of *cross-functional teams* in organisations whose members may come from various departments such as marketing, production, finance and sales (teams are discussed in more detail in Chapter 15). A team responsible for developing and introducing a new product, for example, often will need the expertise of employees not only from R&D and engineering but also from marketing, sales, production and finance.

Other types of diversity can also affect how employees are treated in the workplace. Employees differ from each other, for example, in how attractive they are (based on the standards of the culture(s) in which an organisation operates) and in terms of body weight. Whether individuals are attractive, or thin, or unattractive, or overweight has in most cases no bearing on their job performance unless they have jobs in which physical appearance plays a role, such as modelling. Yet sometimes these physical sources of diversity end up influencing advancement rates and salaries. A study published in the *American Journal of Public Health* found that highly educated obese women earned approximately 30 per cent less per year than women who were not obese and men (regardless of whether or not the men were obese).[73] Clearly, managers need to ensure that all employees are treated fairly, regardless of their physical appearance.

It needs to be noted that every country deals differently with these discriminatory issues. Legislation within Central and Western Europe seems to be moving in the right direction, but each country is influenced by its own history and ethical development and thus will have different viewpoints on progress towards genuine equality. While international migration is likely to show similar demographic changes in other, developed, European countries,[74] most examples in this chapter are based on the UK.

Reaction Time

1. Think about examples in which you have been confronted with discrimination – against yourself, against friends, families or acquaintance. Why did the discrimination occur?
2. Why do you think that workers who test positive for HIV sometimes get discriminated against, but not people who are diagnosed with other terminal illnesses?

Managers and the Effective Management of Diversity

The increasing diversity of the environment – which, in turn, increases the diversity of an organisation's workforce – increases the challenges managers face in effectively managing diversity. Each of the eight kinds of diversity discussed in the chapter presents managers with a particular set of issues they need to appreciate before they can respond to them effectively. Understanding these issues is not always a simple matter, as many informed managers have discovered. Research on how different groups are currently treated, and the unconscious biases that may adversely affect them, is critical. It helps managers become aware of the many subtle and unobtrusive ways in which diverse employee groups can come to be treated unfairly over time. There are many steps that managers can take to become sensitive to the ongoing effects of diversity in their organisations, take advantage of all the contributions diverse employees can make and prevent diverse employees from being unfairly treated.

Critical Managerial Roles

In each managerial role a manager adopts, he or she can either promote the effective management of diversity or derail such efforts; they are thus critical to this process. For example, in their interpersonal roles, managers can convey that the effective management of diversity is a valued goal and objective (figurehead role), can serve as a role model and institute policies and procedures to ensure that diverse organisational members are treated fairly (leader role). The manager can also enable diverse individuals and groups to co-ordinate their efforts and co-operate with each other both inside the organisation and at the organisation's boundaries (liaison role). In Table 5.2 we summarise some of the ways in which managers can ensure that diversity is effectively managed as they perform their different roles.

Table 5.2 Managerial roles and the effective management of diversity

Type of Role	Specific Role	Example
Interpersonal	Figurehead	Convey that the effective management of diversity is a valued goal and objective
	Leader	Serve as a role model and institute policies and procedures to ensure that diverse members are treated fairly
	Liaison	Enable diverse individuals to co-ordinate their efforts and co-operate with one another
Informational	Monitor	Evaluate the extent to which diverse employees are being treated fairly
	Disseminator	Inform employees about diversity policies and initiatives and the intolerance of discrimination
	Spokesperson	Support diversity initiatives in the wider community and speak to diverse groups to interest them in career opportunities
Decisional	Entrepreneur	Commit resources to develop new ways to effectively manage diversity and eliminate biases and discrimination
	Disturbance handler	Take rapid action to correct inequalities and curtail discriminatory behaviour
	Resource allocator	Allocate resources to support and encourage the effective management of diversity
	Negotiator	Work with organisations (e.g. suppliers) and groups (e.g. trades unions) to support and encourage the effective management of diversity

Given the formal authority that managers have in organisations, they typically have more influence than other employees. When managers commit to supporting diversity, as was true of the superiors who placed female officers in roles of authority at the start of the chapter, their authority and positions of power and status influence other members of an organisation to make a similar commitment.[75] Research on social influence supports such a link, as people are more likely to be influenced and persuaded by others who have high status.[76]

When managers commit to diversity, their commitment legitimises the diversity management efforts of others.[77] Resources are then devoted to such efforts and all members of an organisation believe that their diversity-related efforts are supported and valued. Consistent with this reasoning, senior management commitment and rewards for the support of diversity are often cited as critical ingredients for the success of diversity management initiatives.[78] Seeing managers express confidence in the abilities and talents of diverse employees causes other organisational members to be similarly confident and helps to reduce any misgivings they may have as a result of ignorance or stereotyping.[79]

Another important reason that managers are so central to the effective management of diversity hinges on two factors. The first factor is that women, Asians and other minorities often start out at a slight disadvantage due to the ways in which they are perceived by others in organisations, particularly in work settings where they are a numerical minority. As Virginia Valian, a psychologist who studies gender, indicates: 'In most organisations women begin at a slight disadvantage. A woman does not walk into the room with the same status as an equivalent man, because she is less likely than a man to be viewed as a serious professional.'[80]

The second factor is that research suggests that slight differences in treatment can cumulate and result in major disparities over time. Even small differences – such as a very slight favourable bias toward men for promotions – can lead over time to major differences in the number of male and female managers.[81] Thus, while women and other minorities are sometimes advised not to misinterpret the situation when they perceive that they have been unfairly treated, research conducted by Valian and others suggests that slight differences in treatment based on irrelevant distinctions such as race, gender or ethnicity can turn into conflict over time (i.e. major disparities in important outcomes such as promotions).[82] Once again, managers play a crucial role in ensuring that disparities in neither treatment nor outcomes due to irrelevant distinctions such as race or ethnicity occur in their organisations. Managers have the obligation, from both an ethical and a business perspective, to ensure that such disparities do not occur, and are not tolerated in their organisations.

The Ethical Imperative to Manage Diversity Effectively

Effectively managing diversity not only makes good business sense but also should be an ethical imperative in any society. Two moral principles can provide managers with guidance in their efforts to meet this imperative: **distributive justice** and **procedural justice**.

Distributive Justice

The principle of *distributive justice* dictates – in the context of managerial action – that the distribution of pay rises, promotions, job titles, interesting job assignments, office space and other organisational resources among members of an organisation should be fair. The distribution of these outcomes should be based on the meaningful contributions that individuals have made to the organisation (such as time, effort, education, skills, abilities and performance levels) and not on irrelevant personal characteristics over which individuals have no control (such as gender, race or age).[83] Managers have an obligation to ensure that distributive justice exists in their organisations. This does not mean that all members of an organisation receive identical or similar outcomes; rather, it means that members who receive more outcomes than others make substantially higher or more significant contributions to the organisation.

Is distributive justice common in organisations in the corporate world? Probably the best way to answer this question is by saying that things are getting better. In the 1960s, overt discrimination against women and minorities was not uncommon; today, organisations are inching closer toward the ideal of distributive justice. Statistics comparing the treatment of women and minorities with the treatment of other employees suggest that most managers need to take a proactive approach to achieving distributive justice in their organisations.[84] As we have seen,

Table 5.3 Weekly salaries, by gender and family type, 2003–04

Family Type	Women			Men		
	Total	Net	Disposable	Total	Net	Disposable
Single no children	252	205	160	292	231	182
Single pensioner	180	167	148	230	208	186
Single with children	268	245	203	429	347	284
Couple no children	270	214	171	480	368	316
Couple pensioner	130	117	101	311	267	250
Couple with children	242	203	144	566	424	362
Total	**227**	**191**	**152**	**408**	**319**	**272**

across occupations women consistently earn less than men according to data collected by the ONS[85] (Table 5.3). Even in occupations dominated by women, such as teacher assistants and primary and secondary school teachers, men tend to earn more.[86]

In many countries, managers not only have an ethical obligation to strive to achieve distributive justice in their organisations, but also a legal obligation to treat all employees fairly. They risk being sued by employees who believe that they are not being fairly treated. A sex-discrimination lawsuit was brought against Merrill Lynch & Co in London, in which a senior manager claimed that she had received unequal pay and had been overlooked for promotions based on her gender.[87]

Procedural Justice

The principle of *procedural justice* requires that managers use fair procedures to determine how to distribute outcomes to organisational members.[88] This principle applies to typical procedures such as appraising subordinates' performance, deciding who should receive a rise or a promotion and deciding whom to lay off when an organisation is forced to downsize. Procedural justice exists, for example, when managers (1) carefully appraise a subordinate's performance, (2) take into account any environmental obstacles to high performance beyond the subordinate's control – such as lack of supplies, machine breakdowns or dwindling customer demand for a product – and (3) ignore irrelevant personal characteristics such as the subordinate's age or ethnicity. Like distributive justice, procedural justice is necessary not only to ensure ethical conduct but also to avoid costly lawsuits.

Reaction Time

1. Discuss why violations of the principles of distributive and procedural justice continue to occur in modern organisations. What can managers do to uphold these principles in their organisations?

2. Why do you think some employees resent the accommodations made for employees with disabilities that are dictated by the Disabilities Act?

Effectively Managing Diversity Makes Good Business Sense

The diversity of organisational members can be a source of competitive advantage, helping an organisation to provide customers with better goods and services.[89] The variety of perspectives and approaches to problems and opportunities that diverse employees provide can improve managerial decision making. Suppose the Budget Gourmet frozen-food company is trying to come up with some creative ideas for new frozen meals that will appeal to health-conscious, time-conscious customers tired of the same old frozen-food fare. Which group do you think is likely to come up with the most creative ideas: a group of white women with master's degrees in marketing who grew up in upper-middle-class families in suburban London or a racially mixed group of men and women who grew up in families with varying income levels in different parts of the country and attended a mix of business schools? Most people would agree that the diverse group is likely to come up with a wider range of creative ideas. Although this example is simplistic, it highlights one way in which diversity can lead to a competitive advantage (see Case 5.2).

Just as the workforce is becoming increasingly diverse so, too, has the customer base for an organisation's products or services. In an attempt to address diversity, supermarkets, such as

---

Case 5.2: **Creating a business through sheer determination**

Approximately 7 per cent of all small to medium-sized businesses (SMEs) within the UK are owned by individuals from an ethnic minority background,[90] and are estimated to contribute around £30 million each year to the UK economy.[91]

One such example is the story of Patak's – a producer of jarred and pre-packed Indian food products. The business began as a small venture selling samosas and pickles from their home kitchen in North London. With the rise of popularity of Indian restaurants in the 1970s and 1980s Patak's developed a name for themselves by producing authentic pastes and sauces which inexperienced Bangladeshi and Indian chefs used to create authentic dishes.

The owners recognised that discrimination was still a problem and that the Asian population and its aspiring business flair to some extent frightened the City. However, they overcame a variety of obstacles, and now, nearly 40 years later, Patak's has grown into a business worth £50 million a year.[92]

Similar success stories can be found in nearly all the minority groups of the UK. Having diverse members within the business community or within an organisation is likely to attune the organisation to what products and services different segments of the markets require and desire.

Effectively managing diversity makes good business sense for another reason. More and more, managers and organisations concerned about diversity are insisting that their suppliers also support it. Managers of American Airlines, for example, recently announced that all the law firms they hire must submit quarterly reports indicating the extent to which diverse employees worked on the airline accounts. Similarly, DaimlerChrysler and General Motors also consider information about the extent to which law firms support diversity when they are deciding which firms will represent them.

By now, it should be clear that effectively managing diversity is a necessity on both ethical and business grounds. This brings us to the question of why diversity presents managers and all of us with so many challenges – a question we address in the next section.

ASDA, Tesco and Sainsbury's, are putting a lot of effort in providing not only a wide range of products, such as Halal meat for Muslim customers, but also to improve access for customers. Tesco, for example, has been recognised for its online shopping site that explicitly addresses the needs of customers with dyslexia or visual impairment.[93] Supermarkets also offer a variety of resources for physically disabled customers by providing assigned parking and electrical wheelchairs to ease shopping.

TIPS FOR PRACTICE

1. Be aware of local legislation concerning the treatment of diversity in the workplace.
2. How can you influence the effective management of diversity?
3. Why is it important for your business to manage diversity effectively?

Perception

Most people tend to think that the decisions that managers make and the actions they take are the result of some objective determination of the issues involved and the surrounding situation. However, each manager's interpretation of a situation or even of another person is precisely that – an *interpretation*. Nowhere are the effects of perception more likely to lead to different interpretations than in the area of diversity, because each person's interpretation of a situation – and their subsequent response to it – is affected by their own age, race, gender, religion, socio-economic status, capabilities and sexual orientation. For example, different managers may see the same 21-year-old, black, male, gay, gifted and talented subordinate in different ways: one may see a creative maverick with a great future in the organisation, while another may see a potential troublemaker who needs to be watched closely.

Perception is the process through which people select, organise and interpret sensory input – what they see, hear, touch, smell and taste – to give meaning and order to the world around them.[94] All decisions and actions that managers take are based on their subjective perceptions. When these perceptions are relatively accurate – close to the true nature of what is actually being perceived – good decisions are likely to be made and appropriate actions taken. Managers of fast-food restaurant chains such as McDonald's, Pizza Hut and Wendy's accurately perceived that their customers are becoming more health-conscious and added salad bars and low-fat items to their menus; current pressures, especially in the UK, to combat child obesity and malnutrition added to these changes. Managers at Kentucky Fried Chicken and Burger King took much longer to perceive this change.

One reason why McDonald's is so successful is that its managers go to great lengths to make sure that their perceptions of what customers want are accurate. McDonald's has 550 restaurants in Britain (1,070 in Japan, 694 in Canada, 535 in Germany, 411 in Australia, 314 in France, 23 in China and 3 in Russia) that generate approximately £1.9 billion in annual revenues. Key to McDonald's success in these diverse markets are managers' efforts to perceive accurately a country's culture and taste in food and then to act on these perceptions: McDonald's serves veggie burgers in Holland and blackcurrant shakes in Poland.[95]

When managers' perceptions are relatively inaccurate, managers are likely to make bad decisions and take inappropriate actions which can hurt organisational effectiveness. Bad decisions concerning diversity for reasons of age, ethnicity or sexual orientation include (1) not hiring qualified people, (2) failing to promote top-performing subordinates who subsequently decide to take their skills to competing organisations and (3) promoting poorly performing managers because they have the same 'diversity profile' as the manager or managers making the decision.

Factors That Influence Managerial Perception

Several managers' perceptions of the same person, event or situation are likely to differ because managers differ in personality, values, attitudes and moods. Each of these factors can influence the way someone perceives a person or situation. An older middle manager who is high on openness to experience is likely to perceive the recruitment of able young managers as a positive learning opportunity; a similar middle manager who is low on openness to experience may perceive able younger subordinates as a threat. A manager who has high levels of job satisfaction and organisational commitment may perceive a job transfer to another department or geographic location that has very different employees (age, ethnicity and so on) as an opportunity to learn and develop new skills. A dissatisfied, uncommitted manager may perceive the same transfer as a demotion.

Managers' and all organisational members' perceptions about one another are also affected by their past experience and acquired knowledge about people, events and situations – information that is organised into pre-existing schemas. **Schemas** are abstract knowledge structures stored in the memory that allow people to organise and interpret information about a person, an event or a situation.[96] Once a person develops a schema for a kind of person or event, any newly encountered person or situation that is related to the schema activates it and information is processed in ways consistent with the information stored in the schema. People thus tend to perceive others by using the expectations or preconceived notions contained in their schemas.[97] Once again, these expectations are derived from past experience and knowledge.

People tend to pay attention to information that is consistent with their schemas and ignore or discount inconsistent information. Schemas thus tend to be reinforced and strengthened over time because the information attended to is seen as confirming them. This also results in schemas being resistant to change.[98] This does not mean that schemas never change: if that were the case, people could never adapt to changing conditions and learn from their mistakes. Rather, it suggests that schemas are slow to change and that a considerable amount of contradictory information needs to be encountered for people to change them.

Schemas, when they are relatively accurate depictions of the true nature of a person or situation, are functional because they help people make sense of the world around them. People are typically confronted with so much information that it is not possible to make sense of it without relying on schemas. Schemas are dysfunctional when they are inaccurate because they cause managers and all members of an organisation to perceive people and situations inaccurately and assume certain things that are not necessarily true. Recall from the beginning of the chapter how some managers in law enforcement were guided by inaccurate schemas that led them to believe that women should not be promoted to senior management positions because of physical strength differences between men and women.

Psychologist Virginia Valian refers to such inaccurate preconceived notions of men and women as **gender schemas**. Gender schemas are a person's preconceived notions about the nature of men and women, their traits, attitudes, behaviours and preferences. Research suggests that gender schemas (or *gender stereotypes*) are continuously reinforced through the media – such as the portrayal of men as competitive, assertive, independent and task-focused. Women, on the other hand, are predominantly judged on values associated with postwar Britain, with gender schemas that show them as nurturing, caring, emotionally expressive and compliant. These gender schemas are also expected behaviour in organisational contexts.[99] Any schemas such as these – which assume that a single visible characteristic such as one's sex causes a person to possess specific traits and tendencies – are bound to be inaccurate. For example, not all women are alike and not all men are alike, and there are many women who are more independent and task-focused than men. Gender schemas can be learned in childhood and reinforced in a number of ways in society. For instance, while young girls may be encouraged by their parents to play with toy trucks and tools (stereotypically masculine toys), boys generally are not encouraged, and sometimes are actively discouraged, from playing with dolls (stereotypically feminine toys).[100] As children grow up, they learn that occupations dominated by men have higher status than occupations dominated by women.

Perception as a Determinant of Unfair Treatment

Even though most people would agree that distributive justice and procedural justice are desirable goals, diverse organisational members are sometimes treated unfairly, as previous examples illustrate. Why does this problem occur? One important overarching reason is *inaccurate perceptions*. To the extent that managers and other members of an organisation rely on inaccurate schemas such as gender schemas to guide their perceptions of each other, unfair treatment is likely to occur.

Gender schemas are a kind of **stereotype**, simplistic and often inaccurate beliefs about the typical characteristics of particular groups of people. Stereotypes are usually based on a highly visible characteristic such as a person's age, gender or race.[101] Managers who allow stereotypes to influence their perceptions assume erroneously that a person possesses a whole host of characteristics simply because the person happens to be an Asian woman, a white man or a lesbian, for example. African-American men are often stereotyped as good athletes, Asian women as subservient.[102] Obviously, there is no reason to assume that every African-American man is a good athlete or that every Asian woman is subservient – think of in the UK TV reality show 'The Apprentice', in which a female Asian contestant did not conform to these stereotypes, but was aggressive, dominant and loud. Stereotypes, however, lead people to make such erroneous assumptions. A manager who accepts stereotypes might, for example, decide not to promote a highly capable Asian woman into a management position because the manager is certain that she will not be assertive enough to supervise others.

Inaccurate perceptions leading to unfair treatment of diverse members of an organisation also can be due to **bias**. Bias is a systematic tendency to use information about others in ways that result in inaccurate perceptions. Because of the way bias operates, people often are unaware that their perceptions of others are inaccurate. There are three common types of bias.

The *similar-to-me effect* is the tendency to perceive others who are similar to ourselves more positively than we perceive people who are different.[103] The similar-to-me effect is summed up by the saying: 'Birds of a feather flock together'. It can lead to unfair treatment of diverse employees simply because they are different from the managers who judge and evaluate them. Decisions made on such a basis can affect an employee's future in the organisation.

Managers (particularly senior managers) are likely to be white men. Although these managers may endorse the principles of distributive and procedural justice, they may unintentionally fall into the trap of perceiving other white men more positively than they perceive women and minorities. This is the similar-to-me effect. Being aware of this bias as well as using objective information about employees' capabilities and performance as much as possible in decision making about job assignments, pay rises, promotions and other outcomes can help managers avoid the trap.

Social status, a person's real or perceived position in a society or an organisation, can be the source of another bias. The *social status effect* is the tendency to perceive individuals with high social status more positively than those with low social status. A high-status person may be perceived as smarter and more believable, capable, knowledgeable and responsible than a low-status person, even in the absence of objective information about either person.

Imagine being introduced to two people at a company Christmas party. Both are white men in their late 30s, and you learn that one is a member of the company's senior management team and the other is a supervisor in the mailroom. From this information alone you are likely to assume that the senior manager is smarter, more capable, more responsible and even more interesting than the mailroom supervisor. Because women and minorities have traditionally had lower social status than white men, the social status effect may lead some people to perceive women and minorities less positively than they perceive white men.

Have you ever stood out in a crowd? Maybe you were the only man in a group of women; or maybe you were dressed formally for a social gathering, and everyone else was in jeans. Salience (i.e. conspicuousness) is another source of bias. The *salience effect* is the tendency to focus attention on individuals who are conspicuously different from us. When people are salient, they often feel as though all eyes are watching them, and this perception is not too far off the mark. Salient individuals are more often the object of attention than are other members of a work group, for example. A manager who has six white subordinates and one Asian subordinate reporting to her may inadvertently pay more attention to the Asian in group meetings because of the salience effect.

Individuals who are salient are often perceived to be primarily responsible for outcomes and operations and are evaluated more extremely, in either a positive or a negative direction.[104] Thus, when the Asian subordinate does a good job on a project, she receives excessive praise and when she misses a deadline, she is excessively chastised.

Overt Discrimination

Inaccurate schemas and perceptual biases can lead well-meaning managers and organisational members to unintentionally discriminate against others due to their inaccurate perceptions. On the other hand, **overt discrimination**, or knowingly and willingly denying diverse individuals access to opportunities and outcomes in an organisation, is intentional and deliberate. Overt discrimination is not only unethical but also illegal: unfortunately, just as some managers steal from their organisations, others engage in overt discrimination.

Overt discrimination is a clear violation of the principles of distributive and procedural justice. Moreover, when managers are charged with overt discrimination, costly lawsuits can ensue, as indicated in Case 5.3.

Case 5.3: Gender discrimination

In June 2001, six Wal-Mart employees filed a class-action lawsuit against the retailer alleging widespread discrimination against women. In September 2002, additional female employees of Wal-Mart were added as plaintiffs in the case.[105] Potentially the largest discrimination lawsuit targeting a private employer, the suit claimed that women were assigned to the lowest-level positions in Wal-Mart and had little chance of advancement.[106] In April 2004, the case advanced when the California Supreme Court denied a requested reconsideration of the class-action status of the case filed by an Alameda county judge.[107] The number of employees represented in the California case could be over 200,000. A case currently pending could potentially involve over 1 million former and current female Wal-Mart employees alleging sex discrimination in promotions and rises.[108]

While 72 per cent of Wal-Mart employees are women, only about 33 per cent of the managers at Wal-Mart are women. Kim Miller, a Wal-Mart sales associate and a party to the lawsuit, indicates that her performance was appraised positively; she received compliments from customers and was honoured with the Employee of the Year Award. Yet she repeatedly was passed over for promotions during a nine-year period, and sometimes less qualified men received the promotions. Miller's complaints to managers fell on deaf ears, and she believes she was even retaliated against for complaining in the first place.[109] However, if you think sexual harassment and discrimination lawsuits are a US phenomenon – think again! An example is the Merrill Lynch & Co. employer in London,[110] just one example of 14,284 claims filed at Britain's Employment Tribunals Service in 2004. Unfortunately, usually only cases that involve large financial or law firms make it into the media in the UK, such as the case of two senior female lawyers at a London-based law firm, Sinclair Roche & Temperley, who won just under £1 million for being discriminated against. But there are less fortunate women who also experience discrimination. British Airways flight attendants have filed claims that they are being penalised for working part-time after they have had children.

Even though those cases are serious, the UK is well on its way to establishing a more equal working environment. The rest of Europe has yet to learn. In France and Germany in particular, sex discrimination is more common and women are less protected and safeguarded against it. In Germany only few cases make it to court and usually the rulings are less than favourable for the women. For example, a woman who was inappropriately groped by her boss in front of a witness received only £345 in compensation. A French female regional manager of Onyx waste management was frustrated to learn that her salary was significantly lower than that of her male counterparts. Because sex discrimination is taken less seriously in France she took her case to a British Tribunal which ruled in her favour.

One can hope that the EU legislation that defines sexual harassment as discrimination and took effect from October 2005 will make a difference, especially in continental Europe.[111] However, discrimination is not just based on gender. A case of race discrimination resulted in the Ministry of Defence having to pay compensation of £171,000 to a soldier who was a victim of a systematic campaign of discrimination based on his skin colour.[112]

How to Manage Diversity Effectively

Various kinds of barriers arise to managing diversity effectively in organisations. Some barriers have their origins in the person doing the perceiving; some in the information and schemas that

Table 5.4 Promoting the effective management of diversity

- Secure senior management commitment
- Increase the accuracy of perceptions
- Increase diversity awareness
- Increase diversity skills
- Encourage flexibility
- Pay close attention to how employees are evaluated
- Consider the numbers
- Empower employees to challenge discriminatory behaviours, actions and remarks
- Reward employees for effectively managing diversity
- Provide training utilising a multi-pronged, ongoing approach
- Encourage mentoring of diverse employees

have built up over time concerning the person being perceived. To overcome these barriers and effectively manage diversity, managers (and other organisational members) must possess or develop certain attitudes, values and skills in order to change other people's attitudes and values.

Steps in Managing Diversity Effectively

Managers can take a number of steps to change attitudes and values and promote the effective management of diversity. Here, we describe these steps, some of which we have referred to previously (Table 5.4).

Secure senior management commitment

As we mentioned earlier in the chapter, senior management's *commitment to diversity* is crucial for the success of any diversity-related initiatives. Senior managers need to develop the correct ethical values and performance or business-oriented attitudes that allow them to make appropriate use of their human resources.

Increase the accuracy of perceptions

One aspect of developing the appropriate values and attitudes is to take steps to increase the accuracy of perceptions. Managers should consciously attempt to be open to other points of view and perspectives, seek them out and encourage their subordinates to do the same.[113] Organisational members who are open to other perspectives put their own beliefs and knowledge to an important reality test and will be more inclined to modify or change them when necessary. Managers should not be afraid to change their views about a person, issue or event; moreover, they should encourage their subordinates to be open to changing their views in the light of disconfirming evidence. Additionally, managers and all members of an organisation should strive to avoid making *instant judgements* about people – judgements should be made only when sufficient and relevant information has been gathered.[114]

Increase diversity awareness

It is natural for managers and other members of an organisation to view other people from *their own perspective*, because their own feelings, thoughts, attitudes and experiences guide their perceptions and interactions. The ability to appreciate diversity, however, requires that people become aware of different perspectives and the various attitudes and experiences of others. Many diversity awareness programmes in organisations strive to increase managers' and workers' awareness of (1) their own attitudes, biases and stereotypes and (2) the differing perspectives of diverse managers, subordinates, co-workers and customers. Diversity awareness programmes often have six main goals:[115]

- Providing organisational members with accurate information about diversity
- Uncovering personal biases and stereotypes
- Assessing personal beliefs, attitudes and values and learning about other points of view
- Overturning inaccurate stereotypes and beliefs about different groups
- Developing an atmosphere in which people feel free to share their differing perspectives and points of view
- Improving understanding of others who are different from oneself.

Sometimes, simply taking the time to interact with someone who is different on some dimension can help to increase awareness. When employees and managers are at social functions or just having lunch with a co-worker, often the people they interact with are those they feel most comfortable with. If all members of an organisation make an effort to interact with people they ordinarily would not meet, mutual understanding is likely to be enhanced.[116]

Increase diversity skills

Efforts to increase diversity skills focus on improving the way managers and their subordinates interact with each other and on improving their ability to work with different kinds of people.[117] An important issue here is being able to *communicate* with diverse employees. Diverse organisational members may have different styles of communication, may differ in their language fluency, may use words differently, may differ in the non-verbal signals they send through facial expression and body language and may differ in the way they perceive and interpret information. Managers and their subordinates must learn to communicate effectively with one another if an organisation is to take advantage of the skills and abilities of its diverse workforce. Educating organisational members about differences in ways of communicating is often a good starting point.

Organisational members should also feel comfortable enough to 'clear the air' and solve communication difficulties and misunderstandings as they occur rather than letting problems grow and fester without acknowledgement. Diversity education can help managers and subordinates gain a better understanding of how people may interpret certain kinds of comments. Diversity education also can help employees learn how to resolve any misunderstanding.

Encourage flexibility

Managers and their subordinates must learn how to be *open* to different approaches and ways of doing things. This does not mean that organisational members have to suppress their personal styles. Rather, it means that they must be open to, and not feel threatened by, different approaches and perspectives and must have the patience and flexibility needed to understand and appreciate diverse perspectives.[118]

Where it is possible, managers should also be flexible enough to incorporate the differing needs of diverse employees. We mentioned earlier that religious diversity suggests that people of certain religions may need time off for holidays that are traditionally workdays in western countries such as the UK or Sweden; managers need to anticipate and respond to such needs with flexibility (e.g. letting people skip the lunch hour so that they can leave work early). Flexible work hours, having the option to work from home and 'cafeteria-style' benefit plans (see Chapter 13) are just a few of the many ways in which managers can be responsive to the differing needs of diverse employees while enabling those employees to be effective contributors to an organisation.

Pay close attention to how employees are evaluated

Whenever feasible, it is desirable to rely on *objective performance indicators* (see Chapter 13), as they are less subject to bias. When objective indicators are not available or are inappropriate, managers should ensure that adequate time and attention is focused on the evaluation of employees' performance and that evaluators are held accountable for their evaluations.[119] Vague performance standards should be avoided.[120]

Consider the numbers

Looking at the numbers of members of different minority groups and women in various positions, at various levels in the hierarchy, in locations that differ in their desirability and in any other relevant categorisations in an organisation, can provide managers with important information about potential problems and ways to rectify them, as it has done for many organisations such as Deloitte & Touche.[121] If members of certain groups are very under-represented in particular kinds of jobs or units, managers need to understand why this is the case, and resolve any problems that they might uncover. Legislation has been introduced in various countries addressing the *quota* of minority employment. In Germany, for example, firms with more than 20 employees have to fill at least 5 per cent of positions with disabled people. If organisations ignore this, the employer is liable to pay a compensatory tax.[122]

Empower employees to challenge discriminatory behaviours, actions and remarks

When managers or employees witness another organisational member being unfairly treated, they should be encouraged to speak up and rectify the situation. Senior managers can make this happen by creating an organisational culture that has a *zero tolerance policy* towards discrimination. As part of such a culture, organisational members should feel empowered to challenge discriminatory behaviour, whether the behaviour is directed at them or they witness it being directed at another employee.[123]

Reward employees for effectively managing diversity

If the effective management of diversity is a valued organisational objective, then employees should be *rewarded* for their contributions. For example, after settling a major race discrimination lawsuit, the Coca-Cola Company now ties managers' pay to their achievement of diversity goals. Other examples of organisations that link executive pay to achievement of diversity goals include American Express and the Bayer Corporation.[124]

Provide training utilising a multi-pronged, ongoing approach

Many managers use a *multi-tiered approach* to increase diversity awareness and skills in their organisations; they use films and printed materials supplemented by experiential exercises to uncover hidden biases and stereotypes. Sometimes simply providing a forum for people to learn about and discuss their differing attitudes, values and experiences can be a powerful means for increasing awareness. *Role-plays* that enact problems resulting from lack of awareness and indicate the increased understanding that comes from appreciating others' viewpoints are also useful. Accurate information and training experiences can debunk stereotypes: group exercises, role-plays and diversity-related experiences can help organisational members develop the skills they need to work effectively with a variety of people. Many organisations hire outside consultants to provide diversity training, in addition to utilising their own in-house diversity experts.[125]

United Parcel Service (UPS), a package delivery company, developed an innovative community internship programme to increase the diversity awareness and skills of its managers and, at the same time, benefit the wider community. Upper and middle managers participating in the programme take one month off the job to be community interns. They work in community organisations helping people who in many instances are very different from themselves – such organisations include a detention centre in McAllen, Texas, for Mexican immigrants; homeless shelters; AIDS centres; Head Start programmes; migrant farm worker assistance groups; and groups aiming to halt the spread of drug abuse in inner cities. Approximately 40 managers a year are community interns at an annual cost to UPS of £226,000. Since the programme began in 1968, 800 managers have been community interns. Interacting with and helping diverse people enhances awareness of diversity because they experience it first-hand. Bill Cox, a UPS division manager who spent a month in the McAllen detention centre, summed up his experience of diversity: 'You've got these [thousands of] migrant workers down in McAllen . . . and they don't want what you have. All they want is an opportunity to earn what you have. That's a fundamental change in understanding that only comes from spending time with these people.'[126]

Many managers who complete the UPS community internship programme develop superior diversity skills as a result of their experiences. During their internships, they learn about different cultures and approaches to work and life; they learn to interact effectively with people with whom they ordinarily do not come into contact; and they are forced to learn flexibility because of the dramatic difference they find between their role at the internship sites and their role as managers at UPS.

Encourage mentoring of diverse employees

Asians and other minorities continue to be less likely to attain high-level positions in their organisations and for those who do, the climb up the corporate ladder typically takes longer than it does for white men. David Thomas, a professor at the Harvard Business School, has studied the careers of minorities in corporate America. One of his major conclusions is that **mentoring** is very important for minorities, most of whom have reached high levels in their organisations by having a solid network of mentors and contacts.[127] Mentoring is a process by which an experienced member of an organisation (the *mentor*) provides advice and guidance to a less experienced member (the *protégé* or *mentee*) and helps the less experienced member learn how to advance in the organisation and in their career.

According to Thomas, effective mentoring is more than providing instruction, offering advice, helping build skills and sharing technical expertise. Of course, these aspects of mentoring are important and necessary. However, equally important is developing a high-quality, close and supportive relationship with the protégé. Emotional bonds between a mentor and a protégé can enable a protégé, for example, to express fears and concerns, and sometimes even reluctance to follow a mentor's advice. The mentor can then help the protégé build his or her confidence and feel comfortable engaging in unfamiliar work behaviours.[128]

Pat Carmichael, a senior vice president at JP Morgan Chase who happens to be an African-American woman, has mentored hundreds of protégés throughout her career and exemplifies effective mentoring.[129] She encourages her protégés to seek out difficult assignments and feedback from their supervisors. She also helps her protégés build networks of contacts and has a very extensive network herself. She serves as both a coach and a counsellor to her protégés and encourages them to seek out opportunities to address their weaknesses and broaden their horizons.[130]

TIPS FOR PRACTICE

1. Consider how perceptions of your colleagues may be unintentionally biased or inaccurate.
2. Think of ways in which you can enhance the knowledge about diversity awareness of your colleagues.
3. Think about ways in which you can address needs of diverse employees.
4. Live zero tolerance as an example to promote diversity actively.

Sexual Harassment

Sexual harassment seriously damages both the people who are harassed and the reputation of the organisation in which it occurs. It also can cost organisations large amounts of money, as has already been shown. Sixty per cent of the 607 women surveyed by the National Association for Female Executives indicated that they had experienced some form of sexual harassment.[131] Sexual harassment victims can be women or men, and their harassers do not necessarily have to be of the opposite sex.[132] However, women are the most frequent victims of sexual harassment, particularly those in male-dominated occupations or those who occupy positions stereotypically associated with certain gender relationships, such as a female secretary reporting to a male boss. Though it occurs less frequently, men can also be victims of sexual harassment. Several male employees at Jenny Craig, a weight loss programme in the US, for instance, filed a lawsuit claiming that they had been subject to lewd and inappropriate comments from female co-workers and managers. Sexual harassment is not only unethical; it is also illegal. Managers have an ethical obligation to ensure that they, their co-workers and their subordinates never engage in sexual harassment, even unintentionally.

Forms of Sexual Harassment

There are two basic forms of sexual harassment: *quid pro quo* **sexual harassment** and **hostile work environment sexual harassment.** *Quid pro quo* sexual harassment occurs when a harasser asks or forces an employee to perform sexual favours to keep a job, receive a promotion, receive a rise, obtain some other work-related opportunity or avoid receiving negative consequences such as demotion or dismissal.[133] This 'Sleep with me, honey, or you're fired' form of harassment is the more extreme type, and leaves no doubt in anyone's mind that sexual harassment has taken place.[134]

Hostile work environment sexual harassment is more subtle. It occurs when organisational members are faced with an intimidating, hostile or offensive work environment because of their sex.[135] Lewd jokes, sexually oriented comments or innuendos, vulgar language, displays of pornography, displays or distribution of sexually oriented objects and sexually oriented remarks about one's physical appearance are examples of hostile work environment sexual harassment.[136] A hostile work environment interferes with organisational members' ability to perform their jobs effectively and has been deemed illegal by the courts. Managers who engage in hostile work environment harassment, or allow others to do so, risk costly lawsuits for their organisations.

Steps Managers Can Take to Eradicate Sexual Harassment

Managers have an ethical obligation to eradicate sexual harassment in their organisations. There are many ways to accomplish this objective, and there are four key initial steps that managers can take:[137]

- *Develop and clearly communicate a sexual harassment policy endorsed by senior management* This policy should include prohibitions against both *quid pro quo* and hostile work environment sexual harassment. It should contain (1) examples of types of behaviour that are unacceptable, (2) a procedure for employees to use to report instances of harassment, (3) a discussion of the disciplinary actions that will be taken when harassment has taken place and (4) a commitment to educate and train organisational members about sexual harassment.

- *Use a fair complaints procedure to investigate charges of sexual harassment* Such a procedure should (1) be managed by a neutral third party, (2) ensure that complaints are dealt with promptly and thoroughly, (3) protect and fairly treat victims and (4) ensure that alleged harassers are fairly treated.

- *When it has been determined that sexual harassment has taken place, take corrective action as soon as possible* Action can vary depending on the severity of the harassment. When harassment is extensive, prolonged over a period of time, of a *quid pro quo* nature or severely objectionable in some other manner, corrective action may include firing the harasser.

- *Provide sexual harassment education and training to all organisational members, including managers* The majority of *Fortune 500* firms currently provide this education and training for their employees. Managers at Du Pont, for example, developed 'A Matter of Respect' programme to help educate employees about sexual harassment and eliminate its occurrence. The programme includes a four-hour workshop in which participants are given information that defines sexual harassment, sets out the company's policy against it and explains how to report complaints and access a 24-hour hotline. Participants watch video clips showing actual instances of harassment. One clip shows a saleswoman having dinner with a male client who, after much negotiating, seems about to give her company his business when he suddenly suggests that they continue their conversation in his hotel room. The saleswoman is confused about what to do. Will she be reprimanded if she says no and the deal is lost? After watching a video, participants discuss what they have seen, why the behaviour is inappropriate, and what organisations can do to alleviate the problem.[138] Throughout the programme, managers stress to employees that they do not have to tolerate sexual harassment or get involved in situations in which harassment is likely to occur.

Barry S. Roberts and Richard A. Mann, experts on business law and authors of several books on the topic, suggest a number of additional factors that managers and all members of an organisation need to keep in mind about sexual harassment:[139]

- Every sexual harassment charge should be taken very seriously.

- Employees who go along with unwanted sexual attention in the workplace can be sexual harassment victims.

- Employees sometimes wait before they file complaints of sexual harassment.

- An organisation's sexual harassment policy should be communicated to each new employee, and reviewed with current employees on a periodic basis.

- Suppliers and customers need to be familiar with an organisation's sexual harassment policy.

- Managers should provide employees with alternative ways to report incidents of sexual harassment.

- Employees who report sexual harassment must have their rights protected; this includes being protected from any potential retaliation.

- Allegations of sexual harassment should be kept confidential; those accused of harassment should have their rights protected.

- Investigations of harassment charges and any resultant disciplinary actions need to proceed in a very timely manner.

- Managers must protect employees from sexual harassment from any third-party employees they may interact with in the course of performing their jobs, such as suppliers or customers.

Reaction Time

1. Discuss the ways in which schemas can be functional and dysfunctional.

2. Discuss an occasion when you may have been treated unfairly because of stereotypical thinking. What stereotypes were applied to you? How did they result in your being treated unfairly?

3. Why is mentoring particularly important for minorities?

4. Why is it important to consider the numbers of different groups of employees at various levels in an organisation's hierarchy?

Summary and Review

The increasing diversity of the workforce and the environment Diversity is dissimilarity or difference among people. Diversity is a pressing concern for managers and organisations for business and ethical reasons. There are multiple forms of diversity, such as age, gender, race and ethnicity, religion, capabilities/disabilities, socio-economic background, sexual orientation and physical appearance.

▶

▶ **Managers and the effective management of diversity** Both the workforce and the organisational environment are increasingly diverse, and effectively managing this diversity is an essential component of management. In each of their managerial roles, managers can encourage the effective management of diversity, which is both an ethical and a business imperative.

Perception Perception is the process through which people select, organise and interpret sensory input to give meaning and order to the world around them. It is inherently subjective. Schemas guide perception; when schemas are based on a single visible characteristic such as race or gender, they are stereotypes and highly inaccurate, leading to unfair treatment. Unfair treatment also can result from bias and overt discrimination.

How to manage diversity effectively There are a number of steps that managers can take to effectively manage diversity. The effective management of diversity is an ongoing process that requires frequent monitoring.

Sexual harassment Two forms of sexual harassment are *quid pro quo* sexual harassment and hostile work environment sexual harassment. Steps that managers can take to eradicate sexual harassment include development and communication of a sexual harassment policy endorsed by senior management, use of fair complaints procedures, prompt corrective action when harassment occurs and sexual harassment training and education.

Topic for Action

- Choose a *Fortune 500* company not mentioned in the chapter. Conduct research to determine what steps this organisation has taken to effectively manage diversity and eliminate sexual harassment.

- Choose a country different to the UK and investigate differences in demographic changes or in legislation pertaining to discrimination.

Applied Independent Learning

Building Management Skills
Solving Diversity-Related Problems

Think about the last time that you (1) were treated unfairly because you differed from a decision maker on a particular dimension of diversity or (2) observed someone else being treated unfairly because that person differed from a decision maker on a particular dimension of diversity. Then answer these questions:

1. Why do you think the decision maker acted unfairly in this situation?

2. In what ways, if any, were biases, stereotypes or overt discrimination involved in this situation?

3. Was the decision maker aware that he or she was acting unfairly?

4. What could you or the person who was treated unfairly have done to improve matters and rectify the injustice on the spot?

5. Was any sexual harassment involved in this situation? If so, what kind was it?

6. If you had authority over the decision maker (e.g. if you were his or her manager or supervisor), what steps would you take to ensure that the decision maker no longer treated diverse individuals unfairly?

Managing Ethically

Some companies require that their employees work very long hours and travel extensively. Employees with young children, employees taking care of elderly relatives and employees who have interests outside the workplace sometimes find that their careers are jeopardised if they try to work more reasonable hours or limit their work-related travel. Some of these employees feel that it is unethical for their manager to expect so much of them in the workplace and not understand their needs as parents and care givers.

Questions

1. Either individually or in a group, think about the ethical implications of requiring long hours and extensive amounts of travel for some jobs.

2. What obligations do you think managers and companies have to enable employees to have a balanced life and meet non-work needs and demands?

Small Group Breakout Exercise
Determining if a Problem Exists

Form groups of three or four people, and appoint one member as the spokesperson who will communicate your findings to the whole class when called on. Then discuss the following scenario.

You and your partners own and manage a local chain of restaurants, with moderate to expensive prices, that are open for lunch and dinner during the week and for dinner on weekends. Your staff is diverse, and you believe that you are effectively managing diversity. Yet on visits to the different restaurants you have noticed that your Black Afro-Caribbean employees tend to congregate together and communicate mainly with each other. The same is true for your Asian employees and your white employees. You are meeting with your partners today to discuss this observation.

1. Discuss why the patterns of communication that you observed might be occurring in your restaurants.

2. Discuss whether your observation reflects an underlying problem. If so, why? If not, why not?

3. Discuss whether you should address this issue with your staff and in your restaurants. If so, how and why? If not, why not?

Application in Today's Business World

Shifting Work Offshore? Outsourcer Beware

Like a lot of companies, Intentia International, a $430 million business-software maker with operations in Stockholm and Palo Alto, CA, was looking for ways to cut costs. So two years ago it farmed out a software-programming project to a small outfit in India, expecting to cut expenses by 40 per cent. But the savings never materialised. The main reason: the code the Indians delivered was riddled with errors. Intentia's own engineers had to redo it from scratch. 'Indian companies are very aggressive,' says Linus Parker, president of US subsidiary Intentia America Inc. However, leaders of this Indian company, which he would not name, 'overstated their technical skills'.

These days, it's all the rage among corporations to shift a wide array of computer-programming and customer-service operations to low-cost countries. They expect to cut their labour costs by 25–75 per cent by using workers in India, China and the Philippines. But, as Intentia's experience shows, these shifts overseas carry risks that need to be considered along with the potential rewards. Shoddy quality, security glitches and poor customer service often wipe out any benefits.

Until recently, the downside of 'offshoring' wasn't clear. Studies by Forrester Research, Inc. and Gartner, Inc. however, suggest that the practice should not be undertaken lightly. Gartner said that, based on a survey of 219 clients who outsourced projects offshore and domestically, it expected half of such projects undertaken in 2003 to fail to deliver anticipated savings. The main cause of problems, according to analysis, is poor project management by the companies shipping work overseas. 'It's all about how you monitor,' says Dale L. Fuller, CEO of Borland Software Corp. in Scotts Valley, CA.

There are still plenty of good reasons to shift some tasks offshore. In addition to low labour costs, companies can tap into a skilled workforce that in many cases is just as effective, if not more so, than in-house staff. Indian programming, for instance, is fast reaching US levels. A survey of 104 software projects by the Center for eBusiness at Massachusetts Institute of Technology (MIT) in June 2003 found that the median Indian project had just 10 per cent more bugs than comparable US projects. So it's not a matter of whether to send work offshore, but rather under what circumstances and how to minimize risks.

Choose Carefully

Figuring out what tasks to move overseas is a critical first step. Jobs that involve repetition and are predictable work best. Any job that requires strong English-language skills, deep knowledge of US accounting rules or law, or think-on-your-feet decision-making, probably won't fly. Nemo Azamian, senior vice-president for customer service at Gateway, Inc., says that Gateway does not send business customers to its Indian call centre because they require a more nuanced level of communication than many offshore companies may be able to provide. 'No matter how hard you try to Americanize a non-American, it's just not the same as talking to someone in Salt Lake City,' he says.

Once you've decided to send work offshore, picking a reliable partner is the next key step. Most analysts say the largest providers, such as India's Infosys Technologies Ltd., generally do quality work. But smaller companies that have jumped into the business recently may be riskier. Sunil Mehta, Vice President of NASSCOM, the leading Indian technology trade group, concedes there are differences in the quality of Indian tech shops. 'You have to do due diligence on the vendor,' he says. That means checking the company's customer's references, financial health and software-certification levels.

Companies that have done extensive offshoring say it's best to start with a small project. That cautious approach saved Brookfield, CT, Web-hosting company Web.com when it ran into trouble after farming out some of its customer service to 24/7 Customer, based in Bangalore, India. Hundreds of customers began leaving, complaining that service reps didn't understand the technology. It could have been worse. Web.com had handed over only night and weekend service calls. When Web.com pulled the plug last summer, it took just eight weeks to hire and train US staff. 24/7 Customer blames Web.com for the problems. 'It's a very small company,' says CEO P. V. Kannan, 'they did not have well-defined processes.'

Security is also a thorny issue: it's simply harder to safeguard projects handled by other companies thousands of miles away. One reason is differing legal systems and values. India, for instance, has the world's sixteenth-highest piracy rate. Outright theft can also be a problem. Last year, after SolidWorks Corp., a software maker in Concord, MA, outsourced programming to India-based Geometric Software Solutions Co., a Geometric employee allegedly stole Solid-Works' intellectual property (IP) and tried to sell it to the company's rivals. The FBI helped the Indian authorities make an arrest, and the programmer is awaiting trial.

Despite the theft, Solidworks continues to send work offshore. It even stuck with Geometric, which beefed up security and says it wants to make amends. 'The efficiencies are so compelling that we're not willing to give [offshoring] up,' says SolidWorks counsel Holly Stratford. For SolidWorks and other American companies under pressure to cut costs, the trick is learning to manage the shift overseas closely. If they don't, they'd better brace themselves for some nasty – and costly – surprises.

Questions

1. What are the advantages and disadvantages of outsourcing work offshore?

2. What kinds of tasks might be appropriate to outsource offshore? What kinds of tasks might be inappropriate to outsource? Why?

3. When considering outsourcing, what factors do managers need to take into account?

4. Do you think outsourcing work offshore will increase in popularity or decrease? Why?

Source: S. E. Ante, 'Shifting Work Offshore? Outsourcer Beware', adapted and reprinted from *BusinessWeek*, January 12, 2004 by special permission. Copyright © 2004 by the McGraw-Hill Companies, Inc.

Notes and References

1   C. Hymowitz, 'In the US What Will it Take to Create Diverse Boardrooms?', *The Wall Street Journal*, July 8, 2003.
2   *Financial Times*, 12 May 2005.
3   *The Female FTSE Report 2004*, Cranfield University School of Management.
4   'Royal Mail wins BITC Diversity Award' Press Release, 6 July 2005.
5   *Corporate Social Responsibility Report*, September 2004.
6   *Tackling Gender Barriers to Better Jobs, Final Report England*, Equal Opportunities Commission, March 2005.
7   http://www.iphe.org.uk/.
8   DoH, July 2005, 2005/0272.
9   L. M. Sixel, 'Making Diversity Work a Full-Time Job for this Doctor', *Houston Chronicle*, April 16, 2004.

10   *Ibid.*

11   *The Gender Agenda*, British Association of Women in Policing, 2001.

12   www.BAWP.org.

13   D. McCracken, 'Winning the Talent War for Women' *Harvard Business Review*, November–December 2000, 159–67.

14   W. B. Swan, J. T. Polzer, D. C. Seyle and S. J. Ko, 'Finding Value in Diversity: Verification of Personal and Social Self-Views in Diverse Groups', *Academy of Management Review*, 29(1) (2004), 9–27.

15   'Usual Weekly Earnings Summary', *News: Bureau of Labor Statistics*, April 16, 2004. www.bls.gov/news.release/whyeng.nr0.htm; 'Facts on Affirmative Action in Employment and Contracting', *Americans for a Fair Chance*, January 28, 2004 (fairchance.civilrights.org/research_center/details.cf m?id =18076); 'Household Data Annual Averages', www.bls.gov, April 28, 2004.

16   'Prejudice: Still on the Menu', *BusinessWeek*, April 3, 1995, 42.

17   'She's a Woman, Offer Her Less', *BusinessWeek*, May 7, 2001, 34.

18   J. Bulman, 'Patterns of Pay: Results of the 2002 New Earnings Survey', ONS, UK, 2002.

19   Equal Opportunities Commission, 2005.

20   *Ibid.*

21   'Glass Ceiling Is a Heavy Barrier for Minorities, Blocking Them from Top Jobs', *The Wall Street Journal*, March 14, 1995, A1.

22   *The Economist*, 21 July 2005.

23   'Catalyst Report Outlines Unique Challenges Faced By African-American Women in Business', Catalyst News Release, February 18, 2004.

24   Maria Miguel Sierra, 'Anti-Discrimination Legislation in EU Member States', European Monitoring Centre on Racism and Xenophobia (EUMC), 2002.

25   S. Dixon, 'Implications of Population Ageing for the Labour Market', ONS, UK, 2003.

26   *Ibid.*

27   Equal Opportunities Commission, UK.

28   *Ibid.*

29   '2000 Catalyst Census of Women Corporate Officers and Top Earners of the Fortune 500', www.catalystwomen.org, October 21, 2001; S. Wellington, M. Brumit Kropf and P. R. Gerkovich, 'What's Holding Women Back?', *Harvard Business Review* (June 2003), 18–19; D. Jones, 'The Gender Factor', USAToday.com, December 30, 2003; '2002 Catalyst Census of Women Corporate Officers and Top Earners in the Fortune 500', www.catalystwomen.org, August 17, 2004.

30   http://www.employersjobs.com/news/3546991-recruitment-news-uk.html.

31   'Catalyst Census of Women Board Directors', www.catalystwomen.org, August 17, 2004.

32   Equal Opportunities Commission.

33   R. Sharpe, 'As Leaders, Women Rule', *BusinessWeek*, November 20, 2000, 75–84.

34   *Ibid.*

35   'New Catalyst Study Reveals Financial Performance Is Higher for Companies with More Women at the Top', Catalyst News Release, January 26, 2004.

36   Classification of Ethnic Groups, ONS, UK.

37   Government Actuary Department.

38   http://www.population-growth-migration.info/.

39   Government Report, 2003.

40   *Ibid.*

41   'Reports Says Disparities Abound Between Blacks, Whites', *Houston Chronicle*, March 24, 2004, 7A.

42   Runnymede Trust.

43   National Association of Realtors, 'Real Estate Industry Adapting to Increasing Cultural Diversity', *PR Newswire*, May 16, 2001.

44   'Toyota Apologizes to African Americans over Controversial Ad', Kyodo News Service, Japan, May 23, 2001.

45   http://www.homeoffice.gov.uk/comrace/faith/crime/.

46   J. H. Coplan, 'Putting a Little Faith in Diversity', *BusinessWeek*, December 21, 2000.

47   J. N. Cleveland, J. Barnes-Farrell and J. M. Ratz, 'Accommodation in the Workplace', *Human Resource Management Review* 7 (1997), 77–108; A. Colella, 'Coworker Distributive Fairness Judgements of the Workplace Accommodations of Employees with Disabilities', *Academy of Management Review* 26 (2001), 100–16.

48   M. S. West and R. L. Cardy, 'Accommodating Claims of Disability: The Potential Impact of Abuses', *Human Resource Management Review* 7 (1997), 233–46.

49   A. Smith and B. Twomay, 'Labour Market Experience of People with Disabilities', Office for National Statistics, UK, 2002.

50   M. Hirst and P. Thorne, 'Disabled People in Public Sector Employment', ONS, UK, 2004.

51   Colella, 'Coworker Distributive Fairness Judgements'; D. Stamps, 'Just How Scary Is the ADA', *Training* 32 (1995), 93–101.

52   'Notre Dame Disability Awareness Week 2004 Events', www.nd.edu/~bbuddies/daw.html, April 30, 2004.

53   P. Hewitt, 'UH Highlights Abilities, Issues of the Disabled', *Houston Chronicle*, October 22, 2001, 24A.

54   *Ibid.*

55   http://www.drc-gb.org/.

56   J. M. George, 'AIDS/AIDSRelated Complex', in L. H. Peters, C. R. Greer and S. A. Youngblood, eds., *The Blackwell Encyclopedic Dictionary of Human Resource Management* (Oxford: Blackwell, 1997), 6–7.

57   George, 'AIDS'.

58   S. Armour, 'Firms Juggle Stigma, Needs of More Workers with HIV', *USA Today*, September 7, 2000, B1.

59   http://www.businessfightsaids.org.

60   S. Vaughn, 'Career Challenge: Companies' Work Not Over in HIV and AIDS Education', *Los Angeles Times*, July 8, 2001.

61   ONS, UK.

62   B. Carton, 'Bedtime Stories: In 24-Hour Workplace, Day Care Is Moving to the Night Shift', *The Wall Street Journal*, July 6, 2001, A1, A4.

63   http://www.uk-nurseries.com/industry.html.

64   Carton, 'Bedtime Stories'.

65   http://www.gaytoz.com/btax.asp.

66   J. Hempel, 'Coming Out in Corporate America', *BusinessWeek*, December 15, 2003, 64–72.

67   http://www.stonewall.org.uk/stonewall/workplace/.

68   Hempel, 'Coming Out in Corporate America'.

69   J. Files, 'Study Says Discharges Continue Under "Don't Ask, Don't Tell"', *The New York Times*, March 24, 2004, A14; J. Files, 'Gay Ex-Officers Say "Don't Ask Doesn't Work"', *The New York Times*, December 10, 2003, A1.

70   J. Hempel, 'Coming Out in Corporate America'.

71   *Ibid.*

72   croner.co.uk.

73   'For Women, Weight May Affect Pay', *Houston Chronicle*, March 4, 2004, 12A.

74   For further statistics on other EEA countries see http://epp.eurostat.ec.europa.eu.

75   V. Valian, *Why So Slow? The Advancement of Women* (Cambridge, MA: MIT Press, 2000).

76   S. T. Fiske and S. E. Taylor, *Social Cognition*, 2nd ed. (New York: McGraw-Hill, 1991).

77 Valian, *Why So Slow?*

78 S. Rynes and B. Rosen, 'A Field Survey of Factors Affecting the Adoption and Perceived Success of Diversity Training', *Personnel Psychology* 48 (1995), 247–70.

79 V. Brown and F. L. Geis, 'Turning Lead into Gold: Leadership by Men and Women and the Alchemy of Social Consensus', *Journal of Personality and Social Psychology* 46 (1984), 811–24.

80 Valian, *Why So Slow?*

81 J. Cole and B. Singer, 'A Theory of Limited Differences: Explaining the Productivity Puzzle in Science', in H. Zuckerman, J. R. Cole and J. T. Bruer, eds., *The Outer Circle: Women in the Scientific Community* (New York: Norton, 1991), 277–310; M. F. Fox, 'Sex, Salary, and Achievement: Reward-Dualism in Academia', *Sociology of Education* 54 (1981), 71–84; J. S. Long, 'The Origins of Sex Differences in Science', *Social Forces* 68 (1990), 1297–1315; R. F. Martell, D. M. Lane and C. Emrich, 'Male–Female Differences: A Computer Simulation', *American Psychologist* 51 (1996), 157–58.

82 Valian, *Why So Slow?*

83 R. Folger and M. A. Konovsky, 'Effects of Procedural and Distributive Justice on Reactions to Pay Raise Decisions', *Academy of Management Journal* 32 (1989), 115–30; J. Greenberg, 'Organizational Justice: Yesterday, Today, and Tomorrow', *Journal of Management* 16 (1990), 399–402; O. Janssen, 'How Fairness Perceptions Make Innovative Behavior Much or Less Stressful', *Journal of Organizational Behavior* 25 (2004), 201–15.

84 Catalyst, 'The Glass Ceiling in 2000: Where Are Women Now?', www.catalystwomen.org, October 21, 2001; Bureau of Labor Statistics, 1999; Catalyst, '1999 Census of Women Corporate Officers and Top Earners'; Catalyst, '1999 Census of Women Board Directors of the Fortune 1000'; Catalyst, 'The Glass Ceiling in 2000'; Catalyst, 'Women of Color in Corporate Management: Opportunities and Barriers. 1999', www.catalystwomen.org, October 21, 2001.

85 ONS, Individual Income 1996/97–2003/04, 2005.

86 'Household Data Annual Averages', www.bls.gov, April 28, 2004.

87 businessweek.com 2004.

88 Greenberg, 'Organizational Justice'; M. G. Ehrhart, 'Leadership and Procedural Justice Climate as Antecedents of Unit-Level Organizational Citizenship Behavior', *Personnel Psychology* 57 (2004), 61–94; A. Colella, R. L. Paetzold and M. A. Belliveau, 'Factors Affecting Coworkers' Procedural Justice Inferences of the Workplace Accommodations of Employees with Disabilities', *Personnel Psychology* 57 (2004), 1–23.

89 G. Robinson and K. Dechant, 'Building a Case for Business Diversity', *Academy of Management Executive*, 3 (1997), 32–47.

90 bytestart.co.uk.

91 blink.org.uk.

92 blink.org.uk.

93 tescocorporate.com.

94 H. R. Schiffmann, *Sensation and Perception: An Integrated Approach* (New York: Wiley, 1990).

95 A. E. Serwer, 'McDonald's Conquers the World', *Fortune*, October 17, 1994, 103–16.

96 S. T. Fiske and S. E. Taylor, *Social Cognition* (Reading, MA: Addison-Wesley, 1984).

97 J. S. Bruner, 'Going Beyond the Information Given', in H. Gruber, G. Terrell and M. Wertheimer, eds., *Contemporary Approaches to Cognition* (Cambridge, MA: Harvard University Press, 1957).

98 Fiske and Taylor, *Social Cognition*.

99 S. Bird, 'Sex Composition, Masculinity Stereotype Dissimilarity and the Quality of Men's Workplace Social Relations', *Gender, Work and Organisation*, 10(5), 2003.

100 Valian, *Why So Slow?*

101 P. R. Sackett, C. M. Hardison and M. J. Cullen, 'On Interpreting Stereotype Threat as Accounting for African American–White Differences on Cognitive Tests', *American Psychologist* 59(1) (January 2004), 7–13; C. M. Steele and J. A. Aronson, 'Stereotype Threat Does Not Live by Steele and

Aronson', *American Psychologist* 59(1) (January 2004), 47–55; P. R. Sackett, C. M. Hardison and M. J. Cullen, 'On the Value of Correcting Mischaracterizations of Stereotype Threat Research', *American Psychologist* 59(1) (January 2004), 47–49; D. M. Amodio, E. Harmon-Jones, P. G. Devine, J. J. Curtin, S. L. Hartley and A. E. Covert, 'Neural Signals for the Detection of Unintentional Race Bias', *Psychological Science* 15(2) (2004), 88–93.

102 M. Loden and J. B. Rosener, *Workforce America! Managing Employee Diversity as a Vital Resource* (Burr Ridge, IL: Irwin, 1991).

103 E. D. Pulakos and K. N. Wexley, 'The Relationship Among Perceptual Similarity, Sex, and Performance Ratings in Manager-Subordinate Dyads', *Academy of Management Journal* 26 (1983), 129–39.

104 S. T. Fiske and S. E. Taylor, *Social Cognition*, 2nd ed. (New York: McGraw-Hill, 1991).

105 'Court Expands Sex Discrimination Lawsuit Against Wal-Mart Stores', walmart.walmartclass.com/clients/walmart/press_release/2002-09-10-067168, Press Release, May 1, 2004.

106 'Suit Alleges Gender Bias at Wal-Mart', *Houston Chronicle*, June 20, 2001, 10C.

107 National Organization for Women, 'Good News, Case Against Wal-Mart Gets a Green Light', www.now.org/issues/wfw/041904walmart.html, April 19, 2004; 'Wal-Mart: Merchant of Shame', www.now.org.issues/wfw/wal-mart.html, May 1, 2004; W. Zellner, 'Analyzing the "Sins" of Wal-Mart', *BusinessWeek Online* April 15, 2004, www.businessweek.com; 'Wal-Mart Tops Most Admired List', *CNNMoney*, February 24, 2004, money.cnn.com/2004/02/23/news/companies/fortune_best; National Organization for Women, 'Wal-Mart: The Facts', www.now.org/issues/wfw/wm-facts.html, May 1, 2004.

108 National Organization for Women.

109 M. Conlin and W. Zellner, 'Is Wal-Mart Hostile to Women?', *BusinessWeek*, July 16, 2001.

110 K. Capell, 'Sex-Bias Suits: the Fight gets Ugly', *BusinessWeek*, September 6, 2004.

111 *BusinessWeek Online*, September 6, 2004.

112 news.bbc.co.uk 03/02/05.

113 A. G. Greenwald and M. Banaji, 'Implicit Social Cognition: Attitudes, Self-Esteem, and Stereotypes', *Psychological Review* 102 (1995), 4–27.

114 A. Fisher, 'Ask Annie: Five Ways to Promote Diversity in the Workplace', *Fortune*, April 23, 2004, www.fortune.com/fortune/subs/print/0,15935,455997, 00.html; E. Bonabeau, 'Don't Trust Your Gut', *Harvard Business Review*, May 2003, 116–23.

115 A. P. Carnevale and S. C. Stone, 'Diversity: Beyond the Golden Rule', *Training & Development*, October 1994, 22–39.

116 Fisher, 'Ask Annie'.

117 B. A. Battaglia, 'Skills for Managing Multicultural Teams', *Cultural Diversity at Work* 4 (1992).

118 A. P. Brief, R. T. Buttram, R. M. Reizenstein, S. D. Pugh, J. D. Callahan, R. L. McCline and J. B. Vaslow, 'Beyond Good Intentions: The Next Steps Toward Racial Equality in the American Workplace', *Academy of Management Executive*, November 1997, 59–72.

119 Valian, *Why So Slow?*

120 A. P. Brief, R. T. Buttram, R. M. Reizenstein, S. D. Pugh, J. D. Callahan, R. L. McCline, and J. B. Vaslow, 'Beyond Good Intentions'.

121 *Ibid.*

122 http://www.arbeitsagentur.de/.

123 A. P. Brief, R. T. Buttram, R. M. Reizenstein, S. D. Pugh, J. D. Callahan, R. L. McCline, and J. B. Vaslow, 'Beyond Good Intentions'.

124 T. Cole, 'Linking Diversity to Executive Compensation', *Diversity Inc.*, August–September 2003, 58–62.

125 B. Mandell and S. Kohler-Gray, 'Management Development That Values Diversity', *Personnel*, March 1990, 41–47.

126 B. Filipczak, '25 Years of Diversity at UPS', *Training*, August 1992, 42–46.

127 D. A. Thomas, 'Race Matters: The Truth About Mentoring Minorities', *Harvard Business Review*, April 2001, 99–107.

128 *Ibid.*

129 S. N. Mehta, 'Why Mentoring Works', *Fortune*, July 9, 2000.

130 *Ibid.*

131 T. Segal, 'Getting Serious About Sexual Harassment', *BusinessWeek*, November 9, 1992, 78–82.

132 US Equal Employment Opportunity Commission, 'Facts About Sexual Harassment', www.eeoc.gov/facts/fs-sex.html, May 1, 2004.

133 R. L. Paetzold and A. M. O'Leary-Kelly, 'Organizational Communication and the Legal Dimensions of Hostile Work Environment Sexual Harassment', in G. L. Kreps, ed., *Sexual Harassment: Communication Implications* (Cresskill, NJ: Hampton Press, 1993).

134 M. Galen, J. Weber and A. Z. Cuneo, 'Sexual Harassment: Out of the Shadows', *Fortune*, October 28, 1991, 30–31.

135 A. M. O'Leary-Kelly, R. L. Paetzold and R. W. Griffin, 'Sexual Harassment as Aggressive Action: A Framework for Understanding Sexual Harassment', Paper presented at the annual meeting of the Academy of Management, Vancouver, August 1995.

136 B. S. Roberts and R. A. Mann, 'Sexual Harassment in the Workplace: A Primer', http:www3.uakron.edu/lawrev/robert1.html, May 1, 2004.

137 S. J. Bresler and R. Thacker, 'Four-Point Plan Helps Solve Harassment Problems', *HR Magazine*, May 1993, 117–24.

138 'Du Pont's Solution', *Training*, March 1992, 29.

139 B. S. Roberts and R. A. Mann, 'Sexual Harassment in the Workplace'.

Chapter 6

Managing in the Global Environment

LEARNING OBJECTIVES

After studying this chapter, you should be able to:

☑ Explain why the ability to perceive, interpret and respond appropriately to the organisational environment is crucial for managerial success.

☑ Identify the main forces in a global organisation's task and general environments, and describe the challenges that each force presents to managers.

☑ Explain why the global environment is becoming more open and competitive and why barriers to the global transfer of goods and services are falling, increasing the opportunities, complexities, challenges and threats that managers face.

A Manager's Challenge

Nestlé's Global Food Empire

The history

In 1867 Henri Nestlé, a pharmacist living in Vevey, Switzerland, invented an infant formula made from cow's milk and wheat flour and saved the life of a neighbour's child. That formula then became a well-known and trusted substitute for mother's milk and the Nestlé Company was founded. Since then, the company has been committed to building its business on sound human values and has become a pioneer in food product innovation. The first UK sales office was set up a year later and in 1901 Nestlé's first UK factory was opened and then merged with Anglo-Swiss company to produce condensed milk. In 1939 a later innovation was Nescafé instant coffee, which is still the best-selling brand in the world. During the 1950s and 1960s, other brands of coffee (e.g. Blend 37 and Gold Blend were introduced). Throughout the 1980s and 1990s Nestlé made major acquisitions such as the British chocolate maker Rowntree and UK Spillers (1988), and the French bottle water company Perrier (1990). During 1990, Nestlé also joined with General Mills to create 'Cereal Partners Worldwide' which now commands the market in most cereal products. The company has continued its development into the twenty-first century with the acquisition of Ralston Purina Pet Food internationally and the Ski and Munch Bunch brands in the UK.

Many of Nestlé's brands have been household names for generations – think of Nescafé, Quality Street, Aero, Kit Kat, After Eight, Polo, Black Magic and Smarties. These successes and others demonstrate that Nestlé UK has unrivalled expertise in developing strong brands and keeping them in the public eye. Ireland also boasts Nestlé as one of their top branded names.

Why is managing the global environment so complex today?

Today Nestlé is the world's largest food company, with over £28 billion in annual sales, 224,000 employees and 500 factories in 80 countries. In 2004, it made and sold over 8,000 food products, including such popular brands as Kit Kat chocolate bars, Taster's Choice coffee, Carnation Instant milk and Stouffer's Foods. At its corporate headquarters in Vevey, CEO Peter Brabeck-Latmathe, who has been in charge since 1997, is responsible for boosting Nestlé's global performance. He has faced many challenges.[1] Brabeck-Latmathe has been working to increase Nestlé's revenues and profits by entering attractive markets in both developed and emerging nations.

Under his leadership, Nestlé spent £10 billion to acquire US companies Ralston Purina, Dreyer's Ice-cream and Chef America, although it also intends to modify these products to suit the tastes of customers in countries throughout the world. He is particularly anxious to enter emerging markets such as those in Eastern Europe and Asia to take advantage of the enormous numbers of potential new customers in these regions. In this way Nestlé can leverage its well-known products and brand image around the world to increase its performance.

Increasing global revenues from increased product sales is only the first part of his global business model, however. He is also anxious to increase Nestlé's operating efficiency and reduce the cost of managing its global operations. Obviously the global costs involved in managing 224,000 employees and running 500 factories are enormous. The CEO benchmarked its operating costs to those of competitors such as Kraft Foods and Unilever and found that Nestlé's costs were significantly higher. He has cut the workforce by 15 per cent, closed 114 factories and reduced operating costs by over 10 per cent, and plans to make more sizable cuts by 2010.

As another way to reduce global operating costs, Nestlé is investing £28 billion to install a companywide global information system to link all its companies to the corporate headquarters in Vevey and to their global suppliers. The goal is to automate and integrate all of Nestlé's operations including purchasing, manufacturing, distribution and marketing. Nestlé began its overhaul by signing a £112 million contract with SAP, the world's leading enterprise management software supplier. It will use SAP software to monitor its purchasing activities around the globe to ensure that it is achieving the lowest-priced and highest-quality inputs possible. Nestlé is also using IT both to reduce the number of its global suppliers and to negotiate more favourable supply contracts with them. Such changes in management processes should result in a significant drop in purchasing costs. To improve the efficiency of its purchasing and retailing functions, Nestlé has developed e-business websites where it lists the detailed specifications of the inputs it requires from suppliers.

Brabeck-Latmathe hopes that the new IT system will result in an increased flow of information that will allow Nestlé to capitalise on what has always been its main source of competitive advantage: *superior innovation*. His goal is to use Nestlé's new IT system to share knowledge between its global food divisions and thus enhance their ability to innovate a flow of new and improved products for markets around the world. His global vision for Nestlé is therefore driven by three main goals:

- To expand Nestlé's range of products and offer them to new and existing customers in countries throughout the world
- To find lower-cost ways to make and sell these products
- To speed up Nestlé's product innovation by leveraging its expertise across its food businesses to create more attractive food products that will increase its global market share.

By implementing these strategies, he will then be well on the way to making Nestlé not only the largest but also the most profitable global food company.

Overview

Senior managers of a global company like Nestlé are always operating in an environment where they are competing with other companies for scarce and valuable resources. Managers of large and small companies have concluded that in order to survive in the twenty-first century most organisations must become *global organisations*, organisations that operate and compete not only domestically, at home, but also globally, in countries around the world. Operating in a global environment is uncertain and unpredictable because it is *complex* and *constantly changing*.

If organisations are to adapt to this changing environment, their managers must learn to understand the forces that operate in it and how these forces can give rise to both opportunities and threats. This chapter examines why the environment, both domestically and globally, has become more open, vibrant and competitive. It examines how forces in the task and general environments affect both global organisations and their managers. By the end of this chapter, you will appreciate the changes that have been taking place in the environment and understand why it is important for managers to develop a *global perspective* as they strive to increase their organisational efficiency and effectiveness.

What is the Organisational Environment?

The *organisational environment* is a set of forces and conditions outside the organisation's boundaries that have the potential to affect the way it operates.[2] These forces change over time and thus present managers with both *opportunities* and *threats*. Changes in the environment – such as the introduction of new technology or the opening of global markets – create opportunities for managers to obtain resources or enter new markets and thereby strengthen their organisations. In contrast, the rise of new competitors, a global economic recession or an oil shortage pose threats that can devastate an organisation if managers are unable to obtain resources or sell the organisation's goods and services. The quality of managers' understanding of organisational environment forces and their ability to respond appropriately to those forces, such as Brabeck-Lamathe's plans for Nestlé, are critical factors affecting organisational performance.

In this chapter the nature of these forces and how managers can respond to them are explored. To identify the opportunities and threats caused by forces in the organisational environment, it is helpful for managers to distinguish between the **task environment** and the more encompassing **general environment** (Fig. 6.1).

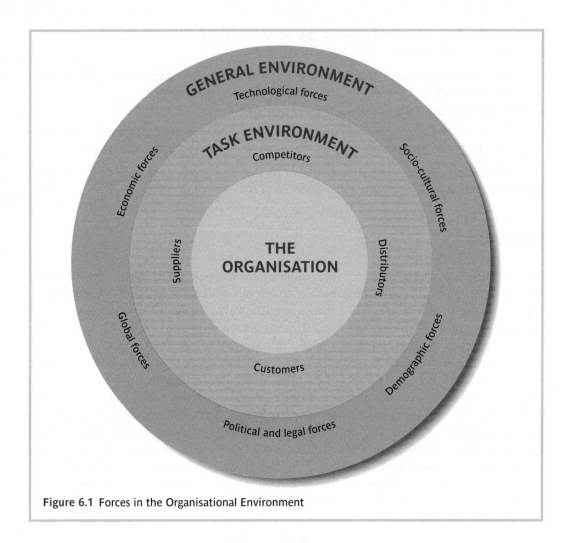

Figure 6.1 Forces in the Organisational Environment

The *task environment* is the set of forces and conditions that originate with suppliers, distributors, customers and competitors; these forces and conditions affect an organisation's ability to obtain inputs and dispose of its outputs. The task environment contains the forces that have the most immediate and direct effect on managers because they pressurise and influence managers on a *daily basis*. When managers turn on the radio or television, arrive at their offices in the morning, open their mail or look at their computer screens, they are likely to learn about problems because of changing conditions in their organisation's task environment.

The *general environment* includes the wideranging economic, technological, socio-cultural, demographic, political and legal and global forces that affect the organisation and its task environment. For the individual manager, the opportunities and threats resulting from changes in the general environment are often more difficult to identify and respond to than events in the task environment. However, changes in these forces, such as the ageing of the workforce outlined in Chapter 5, can have major impacts on managers and their organisations.

The Task Environment

Forces in the task environment result from the actions of suppliers, distributors, customers and competitors (Fig. 6.1). These four groups affect a manager's ability to obtain resources and dispose of outputs on a daily, weekly and monthly basis and thus have a significant impact on *short-term decision making*.

Suppliers

Suppliers are the individuals and companies that provide an organisation with the *input resources* (such as raw materials, component parts or employees) that it needs to produce goods and services. In return, the supplier receives compensation for those goods and services. An important aspect of a manager's job is to ensure a reliable supply of input resources.

Take Dell Computer, for example, the company that was discussed in Chapter 1. Dell has many suppliers of component parts such as microprocessors (Intel and AMD) and disk drives (Quantum and Seagate Technologies). It also has suppliers of preinstalled software, including the operating system (Microsoft) and specific applications software (IBM, Oracle and AOL). Dell's providers of capital, such as banks and financial institutions, are also important suppliers. Cisco Systems and Oracle are important providers of Internet hardware and software for dot-coms.

Dell has several suppliers of labour. One source is the educational institutions that train future Dell employees and therefore provide the company with skilled workers. Another is trades unions, organisations that represent employee interests and can control the supply of labour by exercising the right of unionised workers to strike. Unions can also influence the terms and conditions under which labour is employed. Dell's workers are not unionised; when redundancies became necessary due to an economic slowdown in the early 2000s, Dell had few problems making workers redundant to reduce costs. In organisations and industries where unions are very strong, however, an important part of a manager's job is negotiating and administering agreements with unions and their representatives.

Changes in the nature, numbers or types of any supplier will result in forces that produce opportunities and threats to which managers must respond if their organisations are to prosper. For example, a major supplier-related threat that confronts managers arises when their suppliers' bargaining position is so strong that they can raise the prices of the inputs they supply to the organisation. A supplier's bargaining position is especially strong when (1) the supplier is the sole source of an input and (2) the input is vital to the organisation. One example is a contract that has been awarded to Ericsson, the Swedish technology company, as sole provider for all 3G mobile phone network solutions for the Finnish mobile phone network provider Finnet. Ericsson has been able to establish such a prominent position within the mobile and Internet communication market through its continuous innovation,[3] therefore providing a product that is vital to the organisation and is provided by only one source. Ericsson provides a similar service in the role of sole supplier to the Hungarian telecommunications provider Matav.[4]

A dominant supplier position can also be misused; such is the case of French-based drug company Orphan Europe. This company is licensing a drug that has so far been without a patent and thus gaining the exclusive marketing rights for ten years. The chemical in question is a vital component in the treatment of rare children's diseases. Since the process of licensing began, the price for the chemical has been raised from a maximum of £1,500 a year to over £100,000 a year.[5] Until the patent and licence run out, health providers will have to pay whatever price is demanded by the manufacturer. Russia's state-owned gas company Gazprom also misused its monopolistic position to decrease gas supply to Ukraine significantly until Ukraine was prepared to pay a much higher unit price.[6]

In contrast, when an organisation has many suppliers for a particular input, it is in a relatively strong bargaining position with those suppliers and can demand low-cost, high-quality inputs from them. An organisation can often use its power with suppliers to force them to reduce their prices, as Dell and ALDI frequently do.

ALDI, the German discount supermarket, for example, is constantly searching for low-cost suppliers to keep its prices competitive. At a global level, managers have the opportunity to buy products from foreign suppliers or to become their own suppliers and manufacture their own products abroad. It is important that managers recognise the opportunities and threats associated with managing the *global supply chain*. On the one hand, gaining access to low-cost products made abroad represents an opportunity for companies to lower their input costs. On the other hand, managers who fail to utilise low-cost foreign suppliers create a threat and put their organisations at a competitive disadvantage.[7] Levi Strauss, for example, was slow to realise that it could not compete with the low-priced jeans sold by some retailers, and it was eventually forced to close almost all of its US jean factories and utilise low-cost foreign suppliers to keep the price of its jeans competitive. Now it sells its low-priced jeans, called the Signature Line, in ASDA! The downside to global outsourcing is, of course, the loss of millions of jobs, an issue we have discussed in Chapters 4 and 5.

A common problem facing managers of large global companies such as Ford, Procter & Gamble and IBM is managing the development of a global network of suppliers that will allow their companies to keep costs down and quality high. For example, the building of Boeing's newest jet airliner, the 777, required 132,500 engineered parts produced around the world by 545 suppliers.[8] While Boeing makes the majority of these parts, eight Japanese suppliers make parts for the 777's fuselage, doors and wings; a Singapore supplier makes the doors for the plane's forward landing gear; and three Italian suppliers manufacture wing flaps. Boeing's rationale for buying so many inputs from foreign suppliers is that these suppliers are the best in the world at performing their particular activity and doing business with them helps Boeing to produce a high-quality final product, a vital requirement given the need for aircraft safety and reliability.[9]

The purchasing activities of global companies have become increasingly complicated as a result of the development of a whole range of skills and competences in different countries around the world. It is clearly in their interests to search out the lowest-cost, best-quality suppliers, no matter where they may be. The Internet also makes it possible for companies to co-ordinate complicated 'virtual exchanges' involving the purchasing of inputs and the disposal of outputs.

Global outsourcing is the process by which organisations purchase inputs from other companies or produce inputs themselves throughout the world to lower their production costs and improve the quality or design of their products.[10] To take advantage of national differences in the cost and quality of resources such as labour or raw materials, Vauxhall might build its own engines in one country, transmissions in another and brakes in a third and buy other components from hundreds of global suppliers. Trade expert Robert Reich once calculated that of the £10,778 that customers pay for a car, for example a Vauxhall Corsa, some £3,330 may go to South Korea, where the car may be assembled; £1,945 to Japan for advanced components such as engines, transaxles and electronics; £834 to Germany, where the Corsa is designed; £445 to Taiwan, Singapore and Japan for small components; £278 to Britain for advertising and marketing services; and some £56 to Ireland for data-processing services. The remaining £3,890 goes to Vauxhall – and to the lawyers, bankers and insurance agents.[11]

A study published in 2004 by LogicaCMG predicted that by 2009 global outsourcing would increase the UK gross domestic product (GDP) by £16 billion and that companies would potentially be outsourcing up to 46 per cent of their business, a move which would improve productivity by 2.7 per cent. The report also claimed that by increasing outsourcing, by 2010 British companies could benefit by £1.7 billion in profits.[12] Through 2003–04 British companies accounted for 54 per cent of the outsourcing deals signed across Europe,[13] however not all companies have been happy with the change. In a survey of 1,000 senior managers across nine different countries, 44 per cent of the British companies opted to keep all business operations 'at home'. The survey revealed that the UK currently had the lowest incidence of global outsourcing after Australia and Germany; South African businesses were increasingly outsourcing their business functions, with only 19 per cent deciding to keep operations in-house.[14]

The Outsourcing Debate

Deloittes[15] have reported that despite hostility from the public, 2 million European jobs are likely to be outsourced globally by 2008. During the early 2000s many British companies began the trend by outsourcing their call centre and back-office operations overseas. Large insurance companies (e.g. Royal &Sun Alliance, Norwich Union) outsourced many jobs to India and Sri Lanka. Financial services companies (e.g. Barclays and HSBC banks and Abbey plc) were also some of first companies to lead the way in outsourcing remote call centring operations, and have deployed staff to India, Malaysia and China. Citibank also employs over 3,000 people in Mumbai and Chennai. Companies from other industrial sectors have followed, including British Airways, British Telecom and Tesco.

However, companies expecting huge benefits including vast reduction of annual running costs, easier execution of administration and flexibility appear to have been disappointed. On a survey of 25 organisations, the Deloittes research reported that 25 per cent of the organisations were bringing operations back in-house. It seems that the whole outsourcing process is not only not cost-effective for large firms, but that there is also more management expertise and effort needed to make such a strategy successful. Lack of standardised methods in organising functions abroad and the complexity of the strategy, as well as the pressures put upon companies through loss of expertise and skill within the UK are making people rethink before relocating. Richard Punt, a strategy partner at Deloitte's noted that:

> 'Outsourcing can put at risk the desire for innovation, cost savings and quality. Moreover, the structural advantages envisioned do not always translate into cheaper, better, or faster services'.[16]

Today, such global exchanges are becoming so complex that specialised organisations are emerging to help manage global organisations' supply chains – that is, the flow of inputs necessary to produce a product. One example is Li & Fung, profiled in Case 6.1.

Case 6.1: **Global supply chain management**

Finding the foreign suppliers that offer the lowest-priced and highest-quality products is an important task facing the managers of global organisations. Since these suppliers are located in thousands of cities in many countries around the world, finding them is a difficult business. Often, global companies use the services of foreign intermediaries or brokers, located near these suppliers, to find the one that best meets their input requirements. Li & Fung, now run by brothers Victor and William Fung, is one of the brokers that has helped hundreds of global companies to locate suitable foreign suppliers, especially suppliers in mainland China.[17]

In the 2000s, however, managing global companies' supply chains became a more complicated task. To reduce costs, foreign suppliers were increasingly *specialising* in just one part of the task of producing a product. In the past, any company retailing shirts at low prices might have negotiated with a foreign supplier to manufacture 1 million units of some particular shirt at a certain cost per unit. But with specialisation, a company may find that it can reduce the costs of producing the shirt even further by splitting apart the operations involved in its production and having different foreign suppliers, often in different countries, perform each operation. For example, to get the lowest cost per unit, rather than negotiating with a single foreign supplier over the price of making a particular shirt, a company might first negotiate with a yarn manufacturer in Vietnam to make the yarn. It may then ship the yarn to a Chinese supplier to weave it into cloth, and then ship the cloth to several different factories in Malaysia and the Philippines to cut the fabric and sew the shirts. Another foreign company might then take responsibility for packaging and shipping the shirts to wherever in the world they were required. Because a company such as H&M or Topshop has thousands of different clothing products under production, and they change all the time, the problems of managing such a supply chain to get the full cost savings from global expansion are clearly difficult and costly.

Li & Fung capitalised on this opportunity. Realising that many global companies do not have the time or expertise to find such specialised low-price suppliers, its founders moved quickly to provide such a service. Li & Fung employs 3,600 agents who travel across 37 countries to locate new suppliers and inspect required suppliers to find new ways to help its global clients get lower prices or higher-quality products. Global companies are happy to outsource their supply chain management to Li & Fung because they realise significant cost savings. Even though they pay a hefty fee to Li & Fung, they avoid the costs of employing their own agents. As the complexity of supply chain management continues to increase, more and more companies like Li & Fung are appearing.

Distributors

Distributors are organisations that help other organisations sell their goods or services to customers. The decisions that managers make about how to distribute products to customers can have important effects on organisational performance. Package delivery companies such as DHL, UPS or Parcelforce UK, for example, became vital distributors for the millions of items bought online and shipped to customers by dot-com companies.

The changing nature of distributors and distribution methods can bring both opportunities and threats for managers. If distributors become so large and powerful that they can control customers' access to a particular organisation's goods and services, they can threaten the organisation by demanding that it reduce the prices of its goods and services.[18] For example, the huge retail distributor ASDA controls its suppliers' access to a great number of customers and thus often demands that its suppliers reduce their prices. If an organisation such as Procter & Gamble refuses to reduce its prices, ASDA might respond by buying products only from Procter & Gamble's competitors – companies such as Unilever. In 2004, ASDA announced that by 2006 all its suppliers had to adopt a new wireless scanning technology that would reduce its cost of distributing products to its stores or it would stop doing business with them.[19]

In contrast, the power of a distributor may be weakened if there are many options. The electricity consumer market in the UK, Spain[20] and in France[21] saw a decrease in prices due to the market liberalisation of the European electricity market in 2002.[22] The monopolistic nature of the energy market has thus been replaced by a competitive market structure, in which consumers can choose the best possible option for them, rather than having to use energy from a monopolistic distributor.

Similarly, because there are many package delivery companies, such as ParcelForce, UPS or DHL, online retailers such as Amazon would not really be threatened if one delivery firm tried to increase its prices; they could simply switch delivery companies.

Another force that creates both opportunities and threats for global managers is the nature of a country's distribution system. Japan's systems of distributing Japanese-made products caused problems for Toys 'R' Us managers when they were seeking to establish a chain of stores in Japan. Traditionally, Japanese manufacturers sold their products only by means of wholesalers with which they had developed long-term business relationships. Because the wholesalers added their own price mark-up, the price Toys 'R' Us had to pay for Japanese toys increased, and this thwarted the company's attempt to establish a competitive advantage in Japan based on price discounting. To keep its costs low, Toys 'R' Us insisted on buying directly from Japanese manufacturers, but the manufacturers refused.

This standoff was finally broken by Japan's deep recession in the early 1990s. Faced with slumping orders, computer-game maker Nintendo reversed its earlier decision and agreed to sell merchandise directly to Toys 'R' Us. Soon a host of other Japanese toy companies followed Nintendo's lead. With these major problems solved, average sales in Toys 'R' Us' Japanese stores increased to nearly double the sales per store in the US. As Toys 'R' Us discovered in Japan, the traditional means by which goods and services are distributed and sold to customers can present challenges to managers of organisations pursuing international expansion. Managers must identify the hidden problems surrounding the distribution and sale of goods and services – such as anti-competitive government regulations (discussed later) – in order to discover hidden threats early and find ways to overcome them before significant resources are invested.

Customers

Customers are the individuals and groups that buy the goods and services that an organisation produces. For example, Dell's customers can be segmented into several distinct groups: (1) individuals who purchase PCs for home use, (2) small companies, (3) large companies, (4) government agencies and (5) educational institutions. Changes in the number and types of customers or changes in customers' tastes and needs result in both opportunities and threats. An organisation's success depends on its response to customers: in the PC industry, customers are demanding lower prices and increased multimedia capability and PC companies must respond to the changing types and needs.[23] A school, too, must adapt to the changing needs of its customers: if more Spanish-speaking students enrol, for example, additional classes in English as a second language may need to be scheduled. A manager's ability to identify an organisation's main customers and produce the goods and services they want is a crucial factor affecting both organisational and managerial success.

The most obvious opportunity associated with expanding into the global environment is the prospect of selling goods and services to new customers, as Amazon.com's CEO Jeff Bezos discovered when he began to operate in many countries abroad. Today, once-distinct national markets are merging into one huge global marketplace where the same basic product can be sold to customers worldwide. This consolidation is occurring for both consumer goods and business products, and has created enormous opportunities for managers. The global acceptance of Coca-Cola, Sony Walkmans, McDonald's hamburgers, Doc Martin boots and Nokia cell phones is a sign that the tastes and preferences of consumers in different countries are beginning to become more similar.[24] Likewise, large global markets currently exist for business products such as telecommunications equipment, electronic components, computer services and financial services. Motorola sells its telecommunications equipment, Intel its microprocessors and SAP its business systems management software to customers throughout the world.

Nevertheless, despite evidence that the same goods and services are receiving acceptance from customers worldwide, it is important not to place too much emphasis on this development. Because national cultures differ in many ways, significant differences between countries in consumer tastes and preferences still remain, and these differences often require that managers customise goods and services to suit the preferences of local consumers. Despite McDonald's position as a leading global organisation, its management has recognised a need for local customisation. In Brazil, McDonald's sells a soft drink made from the guarana, an exotic berry that grows along the Amazon River: in Malaysia, it sells milk shakes flavoured with durian, a strong-smelling fruit that local people consider an aphrodisiac.[25] Similarly, when Mattel decided to begin selling Barbie dolls in Japan it had to redesign the doll's appearance (colour of hair, facial features, and so on) to suit the tastes of its prospective customers. Companies also have to be careful to design and select the right kind of information systems and websites to enable customers to buy their products (Case 6.2).

Case 6.2: Designing global information systems

As more and more customers buy products online, the importance of a company's website is increasing. Good design is essential for attracting not only domestic customers but also those overseas. Domestically, the problems involved in designing a good website caused even IT expert Wal-Mart, the mother company of ASDA, to close down its website for two weeks in 2000 while it reworked its search and ordering system.[26] Dell Computer, however, has one of the easiest-to-use and most popular websites, so imagine its surprise when, after creating a Japanese website, it found that Japanese customers were not attracted to it at all.

The reason? Dell's designers decided to give the website a thick black border around the outside of the screen, and in Japan black is a symbol of negative feelings and emotions.[27] Dell's designers moved quickly to solve this problem and now, whenever they create a website in a foreign country, they are careful to work with local managers to make sure that their screen colours or icons do not offend local tastes or customs. Another common problem is linguistic errors. To avoid embarrassing mistakes, companies must ensure that designers are correctly using the country's language. This is particularly important in Asia, where local scripts are easy to misinterpret. Companies must also take into consideration how customers like to pay for their online products. Unlike UK consumers, who make constant use of credit cards, consumers in Germany and Japan like to avoid debt and pay by cash or debit card.

To respond to these problems, companies such as Yahoo, Dell and SAP are increasingly developing local management teams based in each country in which they operate to oversee their businesses.[28] Often, this can involve giving domestic managers foreign assignments to help develop their global expertise. Managers can learn about each country's different regulatory environment; they can also help develop a strategy to customise products to suit local tastes. In this way, a company's global knowledge increases.

Beyond having websites directed at customers, companies also have to be sure they are developing information systems and intranets that are understandable and usable not only by domestic and foreign managers but also by their suppliers worldwide. Wal-Mart's push to become a global company has led it to develop a global knowledge management system that tells foreign suppliers what kinds of products Wal-Mart requires for its local markets and what it is willing to pay for them.[29] Foreign suppliers can then bid for Wal-Mart's business and Wal-Mart makes sure that it is securing the lowest prices. Its global knowledge system is also used to share merchandising information from country to country so that Wal-Mart can quickly take advantage of changing trends and ideas.

Competitors

One of the most important forces that an organisation confronts in its task environment is its **competitors**. *Competitors* are organisations that produce goods and services similar to a particular organisation's goods and services – in other words, competitors are organisations *vying for the same* customers. Dell's competitors include other domestic manufacturers of PCs (such as Apple, Compaq and Gateway) as well as foreign competitors (such as Sony and Toshiba in Japan and Group Bull in France). Dot-com stockbroker E*Trade has other dot-com competitors, like Ameritrade and TD Waterhouse, as well as bricks-and-clicks competitors, such as Merrill Lynch and Charles Schwab.

Rivalry between competitors is potentially the most threatening force that managers must deal with. A high level of rivalry often results in price competition, and falling prices reduce access to resources and so to lower profits. In the 2000s, competition in the PC industry became intense not only because of an economic slowdown but also because Dell was aggressively cutting costs and prices to try to increase its market share. Michael Dell announced that he wanted to increase Dell's market share from 13 to 40 per cent – and Dell was already the global leader.[30] By 2004 Dell had increased its global market share to 35 per cent;[31] unable to compete, IBM announced it was exiting the PC business because it was losing millions in its battle against low-cost rivals such as Dell and Gateway.

Although the rivalry between required competitors is a major threat, so is the potential for new competitors to enter the task environment. **Potential competitors** are organisations that are not presently in a task environment but could enter if they so chose. Amazon.com, for example, is not currently in the furniture business, but it could enter this business if its managers decided it could profitably sell such products; Amazon has done this with small electrical goods and appliances. When new competitors enter an industry, competition increases and prices decrease.

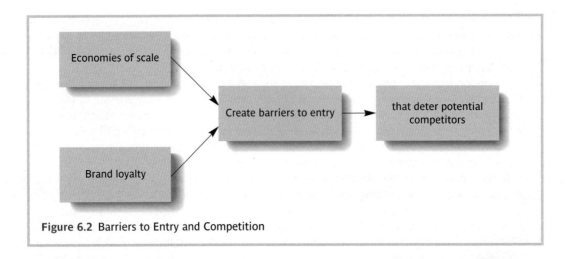

Figure 6.2 Barriers to Entry and Competition

In general, the potential for new competitors to enter a task environment (and thus boost the level of competition) is a function of **barriers to entry**.[32] *Barriers to entry* are factors that make it difficult and costly for an organisation to enter a particular task environment or industry:[33] in other words, the more difficult and costly it is to enter the task environment, the higher are the barriers to entry. The higher the barriers to entry, the fewer the competitors in an organisation's task environment and thus the lower the threat of competition. With fewer competitors, it is easier to obtain customers and keep prices high.

Barriers to entry result from three main sources: **economies of scale, brand loyalty** and government regulations that impede entry (Fig. 6.2). *Economies of scale* are the cost advantages associated with large operations and result from factors such as manufacturing products in very large quantities, buying inputs in bulk or making more effective use of organisational resources than do competitors by fully utilising employees' skills and knowledge. If organisations already in the task environment are large and enjoy significant economies of scale, then their costs are lower than the costs of potential entrants will be, and newcomers will find it very expensive to enter the industry. Amazon.com, for example, enjoys significant economies of scale relative to most other dot-com companies.[34]

Brand loyalty is customers' preference for the products of organisations currently existing in the task environment. If established organisations enjoy significant brand loyalty then a new entrant will find it extremely difficult and costly to obtain a share of the market. Newcomers must bear huge advertising costs to build customer awareness of the goods or services they intend to provide.[35] Both Amazon.com and Yahoo, for example, two of the first dot-coms to go online, enjoy a high level of brand loyalty and have some of the highest website hit rates of all dot-coms (which also allows them to increase their advertising revenues).

In some cases, *government regulations* function as a barrier to entry at both the industry and the country levels. Many industries that were deregulated in the 1980s and 1990s – such as air transport, trucking, utilities and telecommunications – experienced a high level of new entry after deregulation; this forced existing companies in those industries to operate more efficiently or risk being put out of business. An example is the emergence of low-cost airlines such as flybe, Easyjet, or AirBerlin, who have seriously threatened traditional carries like Lufthansa and British Airways.

At the national and global level, *administrative barriers* are government policies that create a barrier to entry and limit imports of goods by foreign companies. Japan is well known for the many ways in which it attempts to restrict the entry of foreign competitors or lessen their impact on Japanese firms. Why do Dutch companies export tulip bulbs to almost every country in the world except Japan? Japanese customs inspectors insist on checking every tulip bulb by cutting the stems vertically down the middle, and even Japanese ingenuity cannot put them back together.[36] Japan has come under intense pressure to relax and abolish such regulations, as Case 6.3 suggests.

Case 6.3: American rice invades Japan

The Japanese rice market, similar to many other Japanese markets, was closed to foreign competitors until 1993 to protect Japan's thousands of high-cost, low-output rice farmers. Rice cultivation is expensive in Japan because of the country's mountainous terrain, so Japanese consumers have always paid high prices for rice. Under foreign pressure, the Japanese government opened the market, and foreign competitors are now allowed to export to Japan 8 per cent of its annual rice consumption. Despite the still-present hefty foreign tariff on rice – £1.32 per Kg – foreign rice sells for around £8 per lb bag while Japanese rice sells for nearly £11. With the recession affecting Japan, price-conscious consumers are turning to foreign rice, which has hurt domestic farmers.

In 2001, however, an alliance between organic rice grower Lundberg Family Farms of California and the Nippon Restaurant Enterprise Co. found a new way to break into the Japanese rice market. Because there is no tariff on rice used in processed foods, Nippon takes the US organic rice and converts it into 'O-bento,' an organic hot boxed lunch packed with rice, vegetables, chicken, beef and salmon, all imported from the US. The new lunches, which cost about £2.30 compared to a Japanese rice bento that costs about £5, are sold at railway stations and other outlets throughout Japan. They are proving to be very popular and are creating a storm of protest from Japanese rice farmers, who have already been forced to leave 37 per cent of their rice fields idle and grow less-profitable crops because of the entry of foreign rice growers. Japanese and foreign companies are increasingly forming alliances to find new ways to break into the high-price Japanese market, and, little by little, Japan's restrictive trade practices are being whittled away.

In summary, intense rivalry among competitors creates a task environment that is highly threatening and causes difficulty for managers trying to gain access to the resources an organisation needs. Conversely, low rivalry results in a task environment where competitive pressures are more moderate and managers have greater opportunities to acquire the resources they need for their organisations to be effective.

Reaction Time

1. Why is it important for managers to understand the nature of the environmental forces that are acting on both them and their organisation?

2. Which organisation is likely to face the most complex task environment, a biotechnology company trying to develop a new cure for cancer or a large retailer like Tesco or Topshop? Why?

The General Environment

Economic, technological, socio-cultural, demographic, political and legal and global forces in an organisation's general environment can have profound effects on the organisation's task environment, effects that may not be immediately evident to managers. The sudden, dramatic upheavals in the Internet and dot-com industry environment were brought about by a combination of changing Internet technology, the 'softening' of stock markets and increasing fears about the health of the global economy. These changes triggered intense competition between dot-com companies that further worsened the industry situation.

The implication is clear: managers must constantly analyse forces in the general environment because these forces affect ongoing decision making and planning. We next discuss the major forces in the general environment, and examine their impacts on an organisation's task environment.

Economic Forces

Economic forces affect the general health and well-being of a country or world region. They include interest rates, inflation, unemployment and economic growth. Economic forces produce many opportunities and threats for managers. Low levels of unemployment and falling interest rates mean a change in the customer base: more people have more money to spend, and as a result organisations have an opportunity to sell more goods and services. Good economic times affect supplies: resources become easier to acquire, and organisations have an opportunity to flourish, as high-tech companies did throughout the 1990s. The high-techs made record profits as the economy boomed, mainly because of advances in IT and growing global trade.

In contrast, worsening macroeconomic conditions, as in the early 2000s, pose a major threat because they limit managers' ability to gain access to the resources their organisations need. Profit-oriented organisations such as retail stores and hotels have fewer customers for their goods and services during economic downturns and not-for-profit organisations, such as charities and colleges, receive fewer donations. Even a moderate deterioration in national or regional economic conditions can seriously affect performance. A relatively mild recession was a major factor in the staggering collapse of dot-com companies in the early 2000s; a rise in interest rates has partially been responsible for a slow housing and property market in the UK.[37]

Poor economic conditions make the environment more complex and managers' jobs more difficult and demanding. Managers may need to reduce the number of individuals in their departments and increase the motivation of the remaining employees, and both managers and workers may need to identify ways to acquire and utilise resources more efficiently. Successful managers realise the important effects that economic forces have on their organisations, and they pay close attention to what is occurring in the national and regional economies in order to respond appropriately.

Technological Forces

Technology is the combination of tools, machines, computers, skills, information and knowledge that managers use in the design, production and distribution of goods and services. **Technological forces** are the outcomes of changes in the technology that managers use to design, produce or distribute goods and services. The overall pace of technological change has accelerated greatly since the mid-1990s because of advances in microprocessors and computer hardware and software, and technological forces have increased in magnitude.[38] Technological forces can have profound implications for managers and organisations.

Technological change can make established products – for example, typewriters, black-and-white televisions, tape recorders – obsolete, forcing managers to find new ways to satisfy customer needs. Although technological change can threaten an organisation, it also can create a host of new opportunities for designing, making or distributing new and better kinds of goods and services. More powerful microprocessors, primarily developed by Intel, caused an IT revolution that spurred demand for PCs, contributed to the success of companies such as Dell and Compaq and led to the decline of others such as IBM.[39] IBM and other producers of mainframe computers saw demand for their products decrease as organisationwide networks of PCs replaced mainframes in many computing applications.[40] However, IBM responded in the 1990s by changing its emphasis from providing computer hardware to providing computer services and consulting, and is once again in a strong global position. Managers must move quickly to respond to such changes if their organisations are to survive and prosper.

Changes in IT are altering the very nature of work itself within organisations, including that of the managers. Telecommuting along the information superhighway and videoconferencing are now everyday activities that provide opportunities for managers to supervise and co-ordinate geographically dispersed employees. Salespeople in many companies work from home offices and 'commute' electronically to work. They communicate with other employees through company-wide electronic mail networks and use video cameras attached to PCs for 'face-to-face' meetings with co-workers who may be in another country.

Socio-cultural Forces

Socio-cultural forces are pressures emanating from the **social structure** of a country or society or from the national culture, pressures that were discussed at length in Chapter 5. Pressures from both sources can either constrain or facilitate the way organisations operate and managers behave. The *social structure* is the arrangement of relationships between individuals and groups in a society, and societies can differ substantially. In societies that have a high degree of *social stratification*, there are many distinctions among individuals and groups. Caste systems in India and Tibet and the recognition of numerous social classes in Great Britain and France produce a multi-layered social structure in each of those countries. In contrast, social stratification is lower in relatively egalitarian New Zealand and in Sweden, where the social structure reveals few distinctions among people. Most senior managers in France come from the upper classes of French society, but senior managers in egalitarian societies may come from any strata of society.

Societies also differ in the extent to which they emphasise the *individual* over the *group*. For example, the UK and US emphasise the primacy of the individual, and Japan emphasises the primacy of the group. This difference may dictate the methods managers need to use to motivate and lead employees. **National culture** is the set of values that a society considers important and the norms of behaviour that are approved or sanctioned in that society. Societies differ substantially in the values and norms that they emphasise. For example, in the UK individualism is highly valued, while in Korea and Japan individuals are expected to conform to group expectations.[41] National culture, discussed at length later in this chapter, also affects the way managers motivate and co-ordinate employees and the way organisations do business. Ethics, an important aspect of national culture, was discussed in detail in Chapter 4.

Social structure and national culture not only differ across societies but also change within societies over time. In the UK, attitudes toward the roles of women, love, sex and marriage change in every decade. Many people in Asian countries such as Hong Kong, Singapore, Korea and Japan think that the younger generation is far more individualistic and westernised than previous generations. Currently, throughout much of Eastern Europe, new values that emphasise individualism and entrepreneurship are replacing communist values based on collectivism and obedience to the state. The pace of change is accelerating.

Individual managers and organisations must be responsive to changes in, and differences among, the social structures and national cultures of all the countries in which they operate. In today's increasingly integrated global economy, managers are likely to interact with people from several countries, and many managers live and work abroad. Effective managers are sensitive to differences between societies and adjust their behaviours accordingly.

Managers and organisations also must respond to social changes within a society. In the last few decades, for example, Europeans have become increasingly interested in their personal health and fitness. Managers who recognised this trend early and exploited the opportunities that resulted from it were able to reap significant gains for their organisations. PepsiCo used the opportunity to take market share from arch-rival Coca-Cola by being the first to introduce diet colas and fruit-based soft drinks. Quaker Oats made Gatorade the most popular sports drink and brought out a whole host of low-fat food products. The health trend, however, did not offer opportunities to all companies: to some it posed a threat. Tobacco companies came under intense pressure due to consumers' greater awareness of negative health impacts from smoking. Nestlé and other manufacturers of candy bars were threatened by customers' desires for low-fat, healthy foods. The rage for 'low-carb' foods led to a huge increase in demand for meat and hurt bread and doughnut companies such as Kraft.

Demographic Forces

Demographic forces are outcomes of changes in – or changing attitudes toward – the characteristics of a population, such as age, gender, ethnic origin, race, sexual orientation and social class. Like the other forces in the general environment, demographic forces present managers with both opportunities and threats and can have major implications for organisations. We examined the nature of these challenges in depth in our discussion of diversity in Chapter 5, so we shall not discuss these forces again here.

Just note here one important change occurring today: most industrialised nations are experiencing the ageing of their populations as a consequence of falling birth and death rates and the ageing of the 'baby-boom' generation (children born in 1945–50). In Germany, for example, the percentage of the population over age 65 is expected to rise to 20.7 per cent by 2010, from 15.4 per cent in 1990. Comparable figures for Canada are 14.4 and 11.4 per cent; for Japan, 19.5 and 11.7 per cent; and for the US, 13.5 and 12.6 per cent.[42] For the UK it is predicted that by 2015 there will be more people over the age of 65 than under 16. However, the absolute number of older people has grown substantially and is increasing opportunities for organisations that cater to older people; home care and recreation industries, for example, are seeing an upswing in demand for their services.

The ageing of the population also has several implications for the workplace. The most significant are a relative decline in young people joining the workforce and an increase in the number of active employees willing to postpone retirement past the traditional retirement age of 60 or 65. These changes suggest that organisations need to find ways to motivate and utilise the skills and knowledge of older employees, an issue that many western societies have yet to tackle.

Political and Legal Forces

Political and legal forces are the outcomes of changes in laws and regulations. They result from political and legal developments within society, and significantly affect managers and organisations. Political processes shape a society's laws; laws constrain the operations of organisations and managers and thus create both opportunities and threats.[43] Throughout much of the industrialised world, for example, there has been a strong trend toward *deregulation* of industries previously controlled by the state and *privatisation* of organisations once owned by the state.

Deregulation of the airline industry ushered into the task environment of commercial airlines major changes that are still working themselves out. Deregulation allowed new airlines to enter the industry. The increase in airlines' passenger-carrying capacity after deregulation led to excess capacity on many routes, intense competition and 'fare wars'. To respond to this more competitive task environment, airlines in the 1980s looked for ways to reduce operating costs. The introduction of 'no-frills' discount services is a response to increased competition in the airlines' task environment. By the 1990s, once again in control of their environments, airlines were making record profits. However, soaring oil prices in the 2000s wiped these out, and airlines found themselves once again under pressure – some of them even close to bankruptcy. Privatisation in other transport industries, such as rail travel, has led to increased prices for customers, as market rules applied.

Deregulation and privatisation are just two examples of the political and legal forces that can challenge both organisations and managers. Others include increased emphasis on environmental protection and the preservation of endangered species, increased emphasis on safety in the workplace and legal constraints against discrimination on the basis of race, gender or age. Managers who want to take advantage of the opportunities created by changing global political and legal and economic forces face a major challenge, and nowhere has this been seen more clearly than in the global car industry (Case 6.4).

Case 6.4: Car manufacturing is changing around the world

In the 1990s, a huge wave of mergers and alliances between global car manufacturers resulted from changing economic and political conditions. Ford, for example, bought Jaguar and Volvo and owns a majority share in Mazda.[44] GM owns Germany's Opel, Sweden's Saab and Japan's Isuzu; Chrysler and Daimler-Benz merged and bought Mitsubishi in 2000; Renault bought Nissan in 2000.[45]

These global mergers occurred because car makers realised that they needed to have a strong presence in every region of the world if they were to obtain the full benefits from globalisation. Car companies were merging rapidly to achieve *global economies of scale*.[46] The goal of these companies was to design and produce cars that could be sold throughout the world, making it easier to recoup the huge costs of developing a new vehicle. Global car companies could also enjoy the low costs that could be obtained from having global supply chains, as discussed on p. 176. Moreover, they could obtain and share the valuable design or car-making skills

▶

▶ that might be present in one car company but not in another, such as Mercedes-Benz's safety features or Mitsubishi's low-cost, small-car design skills.

Some of these mergers were successful. The merger between Renault and Nissan paid off handsomely as Nissan introduced new global models of cars and SUVs in the 2000s that proved popular around the world; similarly, Ford's merger with Mazda worked out well.[47] Others were less successful. The DaimlerChrysler and Mitsubishi merger led to no cost savings and proved a disaster and the German company essentially abandoned its links with the Japanese company in 2004. Until 2004, many analysts felt that the merger between Daimler-Benz and Chrysler had also been a mistake, as costs rose and the company made record losses. In 2004, however, Chrysler began to introduce many innovative vehicles, so the merger might have a bright future after all. Nevertheless, to date DaimlerChrysler has lost billions, as has GM from its investments in Saab and Isuzu.[48]

Despite their short-term economic problems, however, these mergers were expected to pay off during the 2010s as car companies jockey for position as world leaders. Indeed, politically, as the world divides into economic regions, only a global presence will allow a car company to play in the world league. To enter new, largely untapped markets such as Eastern Europe and China, car companies have also to be able to respond to the different political and cultural forces that characterise business in different countries – hence, the need for operations on a truly global level. Indeed, the takeover of Japanese car companies was due to the combination of a severe recession in Japan and an increasing political willingness by the Japanese government to allow foreign firms to control Japanese companies.[49]

Global Forces

Global forces are the outcomes of changes in international relationships, changes in nations' economic, political and legal systems and changes in technology. Perhaps the most important global force affecting managers and organisations is the increasing *economic integration* of countries around the world that has been taking place since the 1980s.[50] Free trade agreements (FTAs) such as the General Agreement on Tariffs and Trade (GATT), the North American Free Trade Agreement (NAFTA), the World Trade Organisation (WTO) and the growth of the EU, have led to a lowering of barriers to the free flow of goods and services between nations.[51]

Falling trade barriers have created enormous opportunities for companies in one country to sell goods and services in others. By allowing companies from other countries to compete for domestic customers, however, falling trade barriers also pose a serious threat because they increase competition in the task environment. Between 1973 and 2004, for example, carmakers saw Japanese competitors increase their share of the western car market.[52] This growth would not have been possible without the relatively low trade barriers, which allowed producers in Japan to export cars to the US and other countries.

Competition from Toyota, Honda and other Japanese companies forced managers of the western car companies to find ways to improve their operations. To remain competitive, they had to transform the way their organisations designed and manufactured cars. However, if global forces had not increased the intensity of competition in the task environment of car companies, managers might have been slow to make such changes. The car industry used to be very conservative and slow-moving, but this is no longer the case: it has had to learn new global values and norms, such as product quality and reliability.

TIP FOR PRACTICE

1. Look at the forces of the (general or task) environment that affect your job most. Consider if changes in the environment are threats or opportunities.

The Changing Global Environment

In the twenty-first century, any idea that the world is composed of a set of distinct national countries and markets that are separated physically, economically and culturally from one another has vanished. Managers now recognise that companies exist and compete in a truly global market. Today, managers regard the *global environment* as a source of important opportunities and threats to which they must respond. Managers constantly confront the challenges of global competition – establishing operations in a country abroad or obtaining inputs from suppliers abroad – or the challenges of managing in a different national culture (Fig. 6.3).[53]

In essence, managers view the global environment as *open* – that is, as an environment in which they and their organisations are free to buy goods and services from, and sell goods and services to, whichever countries they choose. An open environment is also one in which global organisations are free not only to compete against each other to attract customers but also to establish operations or subsidiaries abroad to become the strongest competitors throughout the world. Coca-Cola and PepsiCo, for example, have competed aggressively for 20 years to develop the strongest global soft-drink empire.

In this section, we explain why the global environment has become more open and competitive and why this development is so significant for managers today. We examine how economic changes such as the lowering of barriers to trade and investment have led to greater interaction and exchanges between organisations and countries. We discuss how declines in barriers of distance and culture have increased the interdependencies between organisations and countries. And we consider the specific implications of these changes for both managers and organisations.

Weakening Barriers to Trade and Investment

During the 1920s and 1930s, many countries erected formidable barriers to international trade and investment in the belief that this was the best way to promote their economic well-being. Many of these barriers were high **tariffs** on imports of manufactured goods. A *tariff* is a tax that a government imposes on imported or, occasionally, exported goods. The aim of *import tariffs* is to protect domestic industries and jobs, such as those in the auto or steel industry, from foreign competition by raising the price of goods from abroad. In 2001, for example, the US government increased the tariffs on the import of foreign steel to protect US steel makers; under pressure from the EU, however, these tariffs were significantly reduced in 2003.

The reason for removing tariffs is that very often, when one country imposes an import tariff, others follow suit and the result is a series of retaliatory moves as countries progressively raise tariff barriers against each other. In the 1920s this behaviour depressed world demand and helped usher in the *Great Depression* of the 1930s and massive unemployment. It was to avoid tariffs on US goods entering Europe that the steel tariffs were reduced. In short,

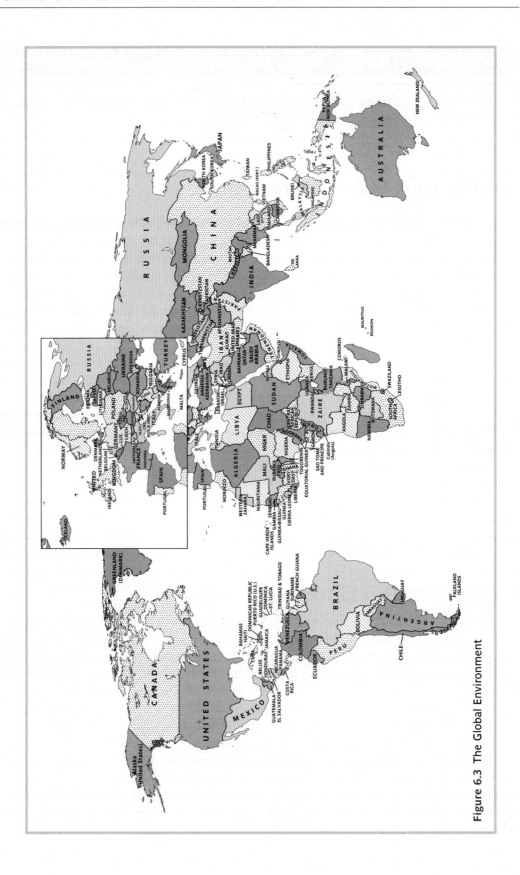

Figure 6.3 The Global Environment

rather than protecting jobs and promoting economic well-being, governments of countries that resort to raising high tariff barriers ultimately reduce employment and undermine economic growth.[54]

Gatt and the rise of free trade

After the Second World War, advanced western industrial countries, having learned from the Great Depression, committed themselves to the goal of removing barriers to the free flow of resources between countries. This commitment was reinforced by acceptance of the principle that *free trade*, rather than tariff barriers, was the best way to foster a healthy domestic economy and low unemployment.[55]

The **free-trade doctrine** predicts that if each country agrees to specialise in the production of the goods and services that it can produce most efficiently, this will make the best use of global resources and will result in lower prices.[56] If Indian companies are highly efficient in the production of textiles and US companies are highly efficient in the production of computer software, for example, then under an FTA production of textiles would shift to India and that of computer software to the US. Consequently, prices of both textiles and software should fall, because each good is being produced in the location where it can be made at the lowest cost, benefiting consumers and making the best use of scarce resources. This doctrine is, of course, responsible for the increase in *global outsourcing* and the loss of millions of UK jobs in textiles and manufacturing. However, the aim was to create millions of jobs in high-tech, in IT and in the service sector that, in theory, should in the long run more than offset these job losses.

Historically, countries that accepted this free-trade doctrine set as their goal the removal of barriers to the free flow of goods between countries. They attempted to achieve this through an international treaty known as the GATT. In the years since the Second World War, there have been eight rounds of GATT negotiations aimed at lowering tariff barriers. The last round, the Uruguay Round, involved 117 countries and was completed in December 1993. This round succeeded in lowering tariffs by over 30 per cent from the previous level. It also led to the dissolving of GATT and its replacement by the World Trade Organisation (WTO), which continues the struggle to reduce tariffs and has more power to sanction countries that break global agreements.[57] Further liberalisation of trade and more advantage for third world countries is part of the current Doha round of trade talks that were agreed upon in 2001. On average, the tariff barriers among the governments of developed countries declined from over 40 per cent in 1948 to about 3 per cent in 2000, causing a dramatic increase in world trade.[58]

The EU has a common trade policy and where trade is concerned, the EU acts as a single entity (the Single Economic Market, or SEM). This policy is governed by a representative body of all 25 member states.[59] Its current aim is to harness globalisation and increase fair trade, which the EU commission sees as best achieved through its strong support of the WTO.[60]

Weakening Barriers of Distance and Culture

Barriers of distance and culture also closed the global environment and kept managers looking inward. The management problems that Unilever, the huge British-based, global soap and detergent maker, experienced in the 1990s illustrate the effect of these barriers.

Founded in London during the 1880s by William Lever, a Quaker, Unilever had a worldwide reach by the early 1900s and operated subsidiaries in most major countries of the British Empire, including India, Canada and Australia. Lever had a very 'hands-on', autocratic management style and found his far-flung business empire difficult to control because communication over great distances was difficult: it took six weeks to reach India by ship from England, and international telephone and telegraph services were very unreliable.

Another problem that Unilever encountered was the difficulty of doing business in societies that were separated from Britain by barriers of language and culture. Different countries, as we know, have different sets of national beliefs, values and norms, and Lever found that a management approach that worked in Britain did not necessarily work in India or Persia (now Iran). As a result, management practices had to be tailored to suit each unique national culture. After Lever's death in 1925, senior management at Unilever *decentralised* (Chapter 10) decision-making authority to the managers of the various national subsidiaries so that they could develop a management approach that suited their own country. One result of this strategy was that the subsidiaries grew distant and remote from one another, which reduced Unilever's performance.[61]

Since the end of the Second World War, major advances in communications and transportation technology have reduced the barriers of distance and culture that affected both Unilever and other global organisations. Global communications have been revolutionised by developments in satellites, digital switching and optical-fibre telephone lines – and, most recently, by the exploding growth of the Internet and global computer networks. Satellites and optical fibres can carry hundreds of thousands of messages simultaneously, making possible global video teleconferencing and allowing companies to develop global intranets that are company-specific information and decision-making systems.[62]

As a result of such developments, reliable, secure and instantaneous communication is now possible with almost any location in the world. Fax machines in Sri Lanka, cellular phones in the Brazilian rain forest, satellite dishes in Russia, video phones in Manhattan and videoconferencing facilities in Japan are all part of the communications revolution that is changing the way the world works. This revolution has made it possible for a global organisation – a tiny garment factory in Li & Fung's network (see p. 178) or a huge company such as Nestlé or Unilever – to do business anywhere, anytime and to search for customers and suppliers around the world. The way in which retailers have used the possibilities of e-commerce to expand globally is very instructive (Case 6.5).

Case 6.5: E-commerce and global customer responsiveness

The senior managers of dot-com companies such as Amazon.co.uk and eBay were quick to understand the potential of the Internet as a new way to reach customers and create a competitive advantage. These companies' managers quickly built their virtual storefronts and began to offer their products to customers. Amazon, for example, is the acknowledged leader in designing an online storefront that offers its customers an easy-to-use, personalised shopping experience. Its ability to offer customers every book in publication, and at a low price, wiped out thousands of small bookstores. Similarly, eBay's ability to connect buyers and sellers and create a market in which fair prices could be determined revolutionised the auction business.

Having developed the companies' appeal in the US, it seemed natural to dot-com managers that they should expand their operations globally to take advantage of the huge number of potential customers worldwide. They also believed they could develop a global business model quite inexpensively. With the US storefront up and running, all they would need to do was transfer it to an overseas market. There, it could be easily customised to the needs of consumers in a particular country. Amazon.com was particularly aggressive in its expansions plans. In 1996 it established an online bookstore in the UK; in 1998 it entered the German market; and since then it has entered countries such as Japan and France. Similarly, E*Trade, the stock brokerage and banking company, entered the Japanese market and expanded into Europe. Because of their successful expansion, it is now difficult to know exactly where those companies originated from, as they have managed to integrate so successfully into local markets.

Developing a successful global business model, however, was much more difficult and expensive than the dot-com managers had anticipated. As Amazon discovered, having a successful 'virtual store' is only one of the many pieces of a viable global business model. Creating a sophisticated purchasing and distribution network to get the product to the customer is also vital, and globally this is an expensive proposition. Indeed, because of the enormous investment needed to establish its overseas operations, Amazon could not declare its second quarterly profit until the spring of 2003. Similarly, E*Trade found that customising its brokerage and banking services to the legal and tax regulations that differ from country to country was much more time-consuming and costly than it expected.

It turned out that the dot-coms that performed the best on a global level were those like Lands' End and Avon that had been catalogue sellers. These companies had well-managed overseas sales and distribution networks and were in a strong position to profit from them when they took their catalogues online. Other companies that also performed well were those whose products did not require a high investment in a physical business infrastructure. eBay, for example, provides an electronic platform that links buyers and sellers and allows them to trade. All the actual time and cost involved in shipping products globally is borne by the buyers and sellers, so eBay needed to invest far less in building operations overseas. The job of its managers was to tailor its operating system to the local national culture. Similarly, today most stocks are sold electronically, so companies like E*Trade, which have also created storefronts that match the needs of customers in a particular national culture, seem likely to fare particularly well in the future.

One of the most important innovations in transportation technology that has made the global environment more open has been the growth of commercial jet travel, which reduced the time it takes to get from one location to another. Because of jet travel, New York is now closer to Tokyo than it was to Philadelphia in the days of the 13 colonies in seventeenth- and eighteenth-century America – a fact that makes control of far-flung international businesses much easier today than in William Lever's era.

In addition to making travel faster, modern communications and transportation technologies have also helped reduce the *cultural distance* between countries. The Internet and its millions of websites facilitates the development of global communications networks and media that are helping to create a worldwide culture above and beyond unique national cultures. Moreover, television networks such as the BBC, CNN, HBO, MTV and RTL can now be received in many countries, and Hollywood films are shown throughout the world.

Effects of Free Trade on Managers

The lowering of barriers to trade and investment and the decline of distance and cultural barriers has created enormous opportunities for companies to expand the market for their goods and services through exports and investments in foreign countries. Although managers at some organisations have shied away from trying to sell their goods and services overseas, the situation of Wal-Mart/ASDA and Lands' End, which have developed profitable global operations, is more typical. The shift toward a more open global economy has created not only more opportunities to sell goods and services in markets abroad but also the opportunity to buy more from other countries. Indeed, the success in the US of Lands' End has been based in part on its managers' willingness to import low-cost clothes and bedding from foreign manufacturers. Lands' End purchases clothing from manufacturers in Hong Kong, Malaysia, Taiwan and China because US textile makers often do not offer the same quality, styling, flexibility or price. Indeed, most clothing companies such as Levi Strauss, ASDA and BhS are major players in the global environment by virtue of their purchasing activities, even if BhS sells only in the UK.

The manager's job is more challenging in a dynamic global environment because of the increased intensity of competition that goes hand in hand with the lowering of barriers to trade and investment. Thus, as discussed above, the job of the average manager in a car company became a lot harder from the mid-1970s on as a result of the penetration of the market by efficient Japanese competitors. Recall (p. 176) that Levi Strauss closed its last US clothing factory in 2001 because it could not match the prices of low-cost foreign jeans manufacturers that compete with Levi's to sell to clothing chains such as ASDA.

NAFTA

The growth of regional trade agreements (RTAs) such as NAFTA also presents opportunities and threats for managers and their organisations. NAFTA, which became effective on 1 January 1994, had the aim of abolishing the tariffs on 99 per cent of the goods traded between Mexico, Canada and the US by 2004. Although it has not achieved this lofty goal, NAFTA has removed most barriers on the cross-border flow of resources, giving, for example, financial institutions and retail businesses in Canada and the US unrestricted access to the Mexican marketplace. After NAFTA was signed, there was a flood of investment into Mexico from the US, as well as many other countries.

The three current NAFTA members have announced that they hope to expand the treaty in the future to include countries in Central and South America and thus increase economic prosperity throughout the Americas. Chile is a possible future member, as are Brazil and Argentina. However, the currency and economic problems that these countries have been experiencing have slowed down the attempt to expand NAFTA, as has political resistance within the US because of jobs lost to Mexico and Canada.

In essence, the shift toward a more open, competitive global environment has increased both the opportunities that managers can take advantage of, and the threats they must respond to, in performing their jobs effectively.

The Role of National Culture

Despite evidence that countries are becoming more similar to one another and that the world is on the verge of becoming a 'global village', the cultures of different countries still vary widely because of critical differences in their values, norms and attitudes. As noted in Chapter 3, national culture includes the values, norms, knowledge, beliefs, moral principles, laws, customs and other practices that unite the citizens of a country.[63] National culture shapes individual behaviour by specifying appropriate and inappropriate behaviour and interaction with others. People learn national culture in their everyday lives by interacting with those around them. This learning starts at an early age and continues throughout a person's life.

Values and norms

The basic building blocks of national culture are *values* and *norms*. Values are ideas about what a society believes to be good, right, desirable or beautiful. They provide the basic underpinnings for notions of individual freedom, democracy, truth, justice, honesty, loyalty, social obligation, collective responsibility, the appropriate roles for men and women, love, sex, marriage and so on. Values are more than merely abstract concepts; they are invested with considerable *emotional significance*. People argue, fight and even die over values such as freedom.

Although deeply embedded in society, values are not static; however, change in a country's values is likely to be slow and painful. For example, the value systems of many formerly communist states, such as Russia, are undergoing significant changes as those countries move away from a value system that emphasised the state and toward one that emphasises individual freedom. Social turmoil often results when countries undergo major changes in their values.

Norms are unwritten rules and codes of conduct that prescribe appropriate behaviour in particular situations and shape the behaviour of people toward one another. Two types of norms play a major role in national culture: folkways and mores. Folkways are the routine social conventions of everyday life: they concern customs and practices such as dressing appropriately for particular situations, good social manners, eating with the correct utensils and neighbourly behaviour. Although folkways define the way people are expected to behave, violation of folkways is not a serious or moral matter. People who violate folkways are often thought to be eccentric or ill-mannered, but they are not usually considered to be evil or bad. In many countries, foreigners may initially be excused for violating folkways because they are unaccustomed to local behaviour, but repeated violations are not excused because foreigners are expected to learn appropriate behaviour.

Mores are norms that are considered to be central to the functioning of society and to social life. They have much greater significance than folkways and the violation of mores can be expected to bring serious retribution. Mores include proscriptions against theft, adultery and incest. In many societies mores have been enacted into law: all advanced societies, for example, have laws against theft and incest. However, there are many differences in mores from one society to another. In the European countries, for example, drinking alcohol is widely accepted but in Saudi Arabia the consumption of alcohol is viewed as a violation of social norms and is punishable by imprisonment (some foreigners have experienced this when working in Saudi Arabia).

Hofstede's Model of National Culture

Researchers have spent considerable time and effort identifying similarities and differences in the values and norms of different countries. One model of national culture was developed by Geert Hofstede.[64] As a psychologist for IBM, Hofstede collected data on employee values and norms from more than 100,000 IBM employees in 64 countries. Based on his research, Hofstede developed five dimensions along which national cultures can be placed (Fig. 6.4).[65]

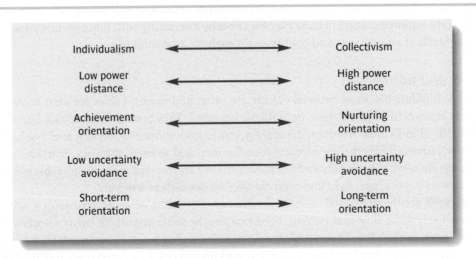

Figure 6.4 Hofstede's Model of National Culture

Source: Geert Hofstede, Bram Nevijen, Denise Daval Ohayv and Geert Sanders, 'Measuring Organisational Cultures: A Qualitative and Quantitative Study Across Twenty Cases', *Administrative Science Quarterly* 35 (2) (June 1990), 286–316. Approval of Request for Permission to Reprint. © Johnson Graduate School of Management, Cornell University.

Individualism versus collectivism

The first dimension, which Hofstede labelled 'individualism versus collectivism', has a long history in human thought. **Individualism** is a worldview that values individual freedom and self-expression and adherence to the principle that people should be judged by their individual achievements rather than by their social background. In western countries, individualism usually includes admiration for personal success, a strong belief in individual rights and high regard for individual entrepreneurs.[66]

In contrast, **collectivism** is a worldview that values subordination of the individual to the goals of the group and adherence to the principle that people should be judged by their contribution to it. Collectivism was widespread in communist countries but has become less prevalent since the collapse of communism in most of those countries. Japan is a non-communist country where collectivism is highly valued. Collectivism in Japan traces its roots to the fusion of Confucian, Buddhist and Shinto thought that occurred during the Tokugawa period in Japanese history (1600–1870s).[67] One of the central values that emerged during this period was strong attachment to the group – whether a village, a work group or a company. Strong identification with the group is said to create pressures for collective action in Japan, as well as strong pressure for conformity to group norms and a relative lack of individualism.[68]

Managers must realise that organisations and organisational members reflect their national culture's emphasis on individualism or collectivism. Indeed, one of the major reasons why Japanese and American management practices differ is that Japanese culture values collectivism and US culture values individualism.

Power distance

By **power distance**, Hofstede meant the degree to which societies accept the idea that inequalities in the power and well-being of their citizens are due to differences in individuals' physical and intellectual capabilities and heritage. This concept also encompasses the degree to which societies accept the economic and social differences in wealth, status and well-being that result from differences in individual capabilities.

Societies in which inequalities are allowed to persist or grow over time have *high* power distance. In high-power-distance societies, workers who are professionally successful amass wealth and pass it on to their children and, as a result, inequalities may grow over time. In such societies, the gap between rich and poor, with all the attendant political and social consequences, grows very large. In contrast, in societies with *low* power distance large inequalities between citizens are not allowed to develop. In low-power-distance countries, the government uses taxation and social welfare programmes to reduce inequality and improve the welfare of the least fortunate. These societies are more attuned to preventing a large gap between rich and poor and minimising discord between different classes of citizens.

Advanced western countries such as the US, Germany, the Netherlands and the UK have relatively low power distance and high individualism. Economically poor Latin American countries such as Guatemala and Panama, and Asian countries such as Malaysia and the Philippines, have high power distance and low individualism. These findings suggest that the cultural values of richer countries emphasise protecting the rights of individuals and, at the same time, provide a fair chance of success to every member of society.

Achievement versus nurturing orientation

Societies that have an **achievement orientation** value assertiveness, performance, success, competition and results. Societies that have a **nurturing orientation** value the quality of life, warm personal relationships and services and care for the weak. Japan and the US tend to be achievement-oriented; the Netherlands, Sweden and Denmark are more nurturing-oriented.

Uncertainty avoidance

Societies as well as individuals differ in their tolerance for uncertainty and risk. Societies low on **uncertainty avoidance** (such as the US and Hong Kong) are easygoing, value diversity and tolerate differences in personal beliefs and actions. Societies high on uncertainty avoidance (such as Japan and France) are more rigid and sceptical about people whose behaviours or beliefs differ from the norm. In these societies, conformity to the values of the social and work groups to which a person belongs is the norm, and structured situations are preferred because they provide a sense of security.

Long-term versus short-term orientation

The last dimension that Hofstede described is orientation toward life and work. A national culture with a **long-term orientation** rests on values such as thrift (saving) and persistence in achieving goals. A national culture with a **short-term orientation** is concerned with maintaining personal stability or happiness and living for the present. Societies with a long-term orientation include Taiwan and Hong Kong, well known for their high rate of *per capita* savings. The US and France have a short-term orientation, and their citizens tend to spend more and save less.

A more recent project looked at the issue of national culture in more detail. The GLOBE project was set up across 61 countries and aimed to refine earlier work on national cultures. The project includes a larger number of European countries within their studies.[69] Their findings show similarities with Hofstede's work.

National Culture and Global Management

Differences among national cultures have important implications for managers. First, because of cultural differences, management practices that are effective in one country may be troublesome in another. General Electric's managers learned this while trying to manage Tungsram, a Hungarian lighting products company it had acquired. GE was attracted to Tungsram, widely regarded as one of Hungary's best companies, because of Hungary's low wage rates and the possibility of using the company as a base from which to export lighting products to western Europe. GE transferred some of its best managers to Tungsram and hoped that it would soon become a leader in Europe. Unfortunately, many problems arose.

One of the problems resulted from major misunderstandings between the US managers and the Hungarian workers. The Americans complained that the Hungarians were lazy; the Hungarians thought the Americans were pushy. The Americans wanted strong sales and marketing functions that would pamper customers; in the earlier Hungarian command economy, sales and marketing activities were unnecessary. In addition, the Hungarians expected GE to deliver western-style wages, but GE came to Hungary to take advantage of the country's low wage structure.[70] As Tungsram's losses mounted, GE managers had to admit that, because of differences in the basic attitudes between the countries, they had under-estimated the difficulties they would face in turning Tungsram around. Nevertheless, by 2001, these problems had been solved, and the increased efficiency of GE's Hungarian operations made the company a major player in the European lighting market, so that it could invest more money.[71]

Management practices must often be tailored to suit the cultural context within which an organisation operates. An approach effective in the UK might not work in Japan, Hungary or Sweden because of differences in national culture. Managers doing business with individuals from another country must be sensitive to the value systems and norms of that country, and behave accordingly. For example, Fridays are religiously significant days within Islamic and Jewish culture so it would be impolite and inappropriate for a western manager to schedule a busy day of activities for Saudi Arabian or Israeli managers visiting on a Friday.

A culturally diverse management team can be a source of strength for an organisation participating in the global marketplace. Organisations that employ managers from a variety of cultures appreciate better than do organisations with culturally homogeneous management teams how national cultures can differ, and they tailor their management systems and behaviours accordingly. Indeed, one of the advantages that many western companies have over their Japanese competitors is greater willingness to build an international team of senior managers.[72]

Reaction Time

1. The population is 'greying' because of declining birth rates, declining death rates and the ageing of the 'baby-boom' generation. What might some of the implications of this demographic trend be for (a) a pharmaceutical company, (b) the home construction industry?

2. How do political, legal and economic forces shape national culture? What characteristics of national culture do you think have the most important effect on how successful a country is in doing business abroad?

TIPS FOR PRACTICE

1. Think about the countries you are interacting with and how their culture may influence your business practice.

2. Be aware of your own behaviour and reflect on how business partners from other countries may perceive it.

Summary and Review

What is the organisational environment? The organisational environment is the set of forces and conditions that operate beyond an organisation's boundaries but affect a manager's ability to acquire and utilise resources. The organisational environment has two components – the task environment and the general environment.

The task environment The task environment is the set of forces and conditions that originates with suppliers, distributors, customers and competitors that influence managers on a daily basis. The opportunities and threats associated with forces in the task environment become more complex as a company begins to operate in more than one country and expands globally.

The general environment The general environment is the set of wideranging economic, technological, socio-cultural, demographic, political and legal and global forces that affect an organisation and its task environment.

The changing global environment In recent years there has been a marked shift away from a closed global environment, in which countries are cut off from one another by barriers to international trade and investment and by barriers of distance and culture, and toward a more open global environment. The emergence of an open global environment and the reduction of barriers to the free flow of goods, services and investment owes much to the rise of global trade agreements such as the GATT, to the growing global acceptance of a free-market philosophy and to the poor performance of countries that protected their markets from international trade and investment.

Topic for Action

■ Choose an organisation, and ask a manager to list the number and strengths of forces in the organisation's task environment. Ask the manager to pay particular attention to identifying the opportunities and threats that result from pressures and changes in customers, competitors and suppliers.

Applied Independent Learning

Building Management Skills

Analysing an Organisation's Task and General Environments

Pick an organisation with which you are familiar. It can be an organisation in which you have worked or currently work or one that you interact with regularly as a customer (such as the college that you are currently attending). For this organisation do the following:

1. Describe the main forces in the task environment that are affecting the organisation.
2. Describe the main forces in the general environment that are affecting the organisation.
3. Describe the main global forces that are affecting the organisation.
4. Explain how environmental forces affect the job of an individual manager within this organisation. How do they determine the opportunities and threats that its managers must confront?

Managing Ethically

In recent years, the number of companies that buy their inputs from low-cost foreign suppliers has been growing, and concern about the ethics associated with employing young children in factories has been increasing. In Pakistan and India, children as young as six years old work long hours to make rugs and carpets for export to western countries or clay bricks for local use. In countries like Malaysia and in Central America, children and teenagers routinely work long hours in factories and sweat shops to produce the clothing that is found in most High street stores.

Questions

1. Either by yourself or in a group, discuss whether it is ethical to employ children in factories and whether companies should buy and sell products made by these children. What are some arguments for and against child labour?
2. If child labour is an economic necessity, what ways could be employed to make it as ethical a practice as possible? Or is it simply unethical?

Small Group Breakout Exercise

How to Enter the Copying Business

Form groups of three to five people, and appoint one group member as the spokesperson who will communicate your findings to the whole class when called on by the instructor. Then discuss the following scenario.

You and your partners have decided to open a small printing and copying business in a college town of 100,000 people. Your business will compete with companies like the US online printers Kinko's. You know that over 50 per cent of small businesses fail in their first year, so to increase your chances of success you have decided to do a detailed analysis of the task environment of the copying business to discover what opportunities and threats you will encounter. As a group:

1. Decide what you must know about (a) your future customers, (b) your future competitors and (c) other critical forces in the task environment if you are to be successful.

2. Evaluate the main barriers to entry into the copying business.

3. Based on this analysis, list some of the steps you would take to help your new copying business succeed.

Exploring the World Wide Web

Go to an international company of your choice and find out about its global activities.

1. How would you characterise the way your chosen company manages the global environment? For example, how has the company responded to the needs of customers in different countries?

2. How have increasing global competition and weakening barriers of distance and culture been affecting the company's operations?

Application in Today's Business World

Posco: One Sharp Steelmaker

Korea these days enjoys a well-deserved reputation for its digital prowess: a land where lab-coated engineers and scientists work with delicate wafer chips, while pink-haired youths write software for the latest cell phone. But you don't have to dig too deep to find another Korea, one where hardbodied workers labour in factories to produce the stuff that makes the physical world go. To get an idea of the vibrancy of this part of the economy, visit the Posco steelworks in Pohang, on the peninsula's east coast. Here, in sweltering heat, sparks fly as molten iron is ladled into vast bins and ribbons of fiery metal roll through milling machines.

Old Economy? Sure. But Posco is no rust-belt relic. True, with $12 billion in sales, it isn't the biggest steel maker on earth. That title belongs to Luxembourg-based Arcelor, more than double Posco's size. But where it really counts, Posco is in a class all its own. The company enjoys the biggest profits in the global steel industry, raking in enough cash to make many a high-tech outfit envious. Thanks to robust demand at home and in China, net earnings from Posco's array of steel products – used in everything from screws to skyscrapers – shot up 80 per cent in 2003, to $1.66 billion. Daewoo Securities Co. forecast a 61 per cent jump in profits, to $2.7 billion, on $15.6 billion in sales in 2003. 'As far as efficiency is concerned, Posco stands taller than any other steelmaker in the world,' says Daewoo analyst Yang Ki In.

In fact, Posco isn't as different from South Korea's New Economy innovators as all the sweat and sparks might lead you to believe. The company is considered one of the industry's high-tech paladins. In August 2004, Posco enhanced that reputation when it broke ground on a $1.1 billion mill that could boost productivity even higher. The mill will use a new technology, called Finex, that will help cut costs by nearly a fifth and harmful emissions by more than 90 per cent, says Chairman and CEO Lee Ku Taek. For decades, steel makers have used highly polluting ovens to turn powdery coal and iron ore into chunks called coke and sinter, which are melted with superheated air to make iron. With Finex, coal and ore are turned into

▶ iron without coking and sintering. After the plant opens, in 2006, Posco plans to roll out the technology in other mills. 'I want to be remembered as the CEO who started another leap forward,' says Lee, a 35-year Posco veteran who has become the project's champion since taking over the top job in 2003.

Posco has put plenty of slick IT to work, too. The company has invested $179 million to network its 80 Korean plants so that it can take orders online and co-ordinate production and deliveries. So, as molten steel slabs wend their way through the mills at Posco's two major steelworks – in Pohang and at Gwangyang, on the southern coast – each is pressed to a specified weight and width depending on a particular customer's needs. This mill-level customisation helps push steel out the door faster, which has enabled Posco to halve delivery times and slash inventories by 60 per cent.

Like the rest of Korea, Inc., Posco believes that its future lies across the Yellow Sea in China. The country has become the world's biggest steel market as well as the biggest producer, with more than 1,000 mills, from giants such as Shanghai BaoSteel Group and Wuhan Iron & Steel Group to tiny operations in outlying provinces. To cash in on this vast opportunity, Posco has invested $800 million in China, its biggest export market. One joint venture, with Benxi Iron & Steel (Group) Co., near Shenyang, will churn out 1.8 million tons of coldrolled sheets annually for autos and home appliances when it opens in 2006. Another, with Jiangsu Shagang Group, already produces 280,000 tons of stainless coldrolled coils and some 100,000 tons of galvanized steel every year. In all, Posco has 14 joint ventures in China. By 2006, Posco plans some $1.4 billion in fresh investment on the mainland, especially in galvanized and stainless steel to supply the global auto and appliance makers that have opened plants there.

Questions

1. In what ways is Posco responding to the changing forces in its task environment?

2. In what ways is Posco responding to the changing forces in its general environment?

Source: Brian Bremmer, Moon Ihlwan and Dexter Roberts, 'Posco: One Sharp Steelmaker', adapted and reprinted from *BusinessWeek*, August 30, 2004 by special permission. Copyright © 2004 by the McGraw-Hill Companies, Inc.

Notes and References

1   http://www.nestle.co.uk/Home.

2   L. J. Bourgeois, 'Strategy and Environment: A Conceptual Integration', *Academy of Management Review* 5 (1985), 25–39.

3   www.3G.co.uk.

4   www.rednova.com.

5   www.guardian.co.uk/Archive.

6   'Russia Turns off Gas Supply in Payment Row, and EU feels the chill', *Guardian*, 2 October 2006, http://www.guardian.co.uk/.

7   A. K. Gupta and V. Govindarajan, 'Cultivating a Global Mindset', *Academy of Management Executive* 16 (February 2002), 116–27.

8   'Boeing's Worldwide Supplier Network', *Seattle Post-Intelligence*, April 9, 1994, 13.

9   I. Metthee, 'Playing a Large Part', *Seattle Post-Intelligence*, April 9, 1994, 13.

10 R. J. Trent and R. M. Monczke, 'Pursuing Competitive Advantage Through Integrated Global Sourcing', *Academy of Management Executive* 16 (May 2002), 66–81.

11   R. B. Reich, *The Work of Nations* (New York: Knopf, 1991).

12   www.theregister.co.uk.

13   www.computeractive.co.uk.

14   www.personneltoday.com.

15   *Management issues*, 2005.

16   www.management-issues.com, April 2005.

17   'Business: Link in the Global Chain', *The Economist*, June 2, 2001, 62–63.

18   M. E. Porter, *Competitive Advantage* (New York: Free Press, 1985).

19   www.walmart.com, 2004.

20   http://www.econ.cam.ac.uk/.

21   D. Finon, 'Introducing Competition in the French Electricity Supply Industry: The Destabilisation of a Public Hierarchy in an Open Institutional Environment', Conference of the International Society for New Institutional Economics (ISNIE), Cambridge, MA, 27–29 September 2002.

22   *Ibid.*

23   'The Tech Slump Doesn't Scare Michael Dell', *BusinessWeek*, April 16, 2001, 48.

24   T. Levitt, 'The Globalization of Markets', *Harvard Business Review*, May–June 1983, 92–102.

25   T. Deveny *et al.*, 'McWorld?' *BusinessWeek*, October 13, 1986, 78–86.

26   www.walmart.com, 2004.

27   A. Chen and M. Hicks, 'Going Global? Avoid Culture Clashes', *PC Week*, April 3, 2000, 65.

28   T. W. Malnight, 'Emerging Structural Patterns Within Multinational Corporations: Toward Process-Based Structures', *Academy of Management Journal*, 44 (December 2001), 1187–1211.

29   M. Troy, 'Global Group Ready for New Growth Phase', *DSN Retailing Today*, June 5, 2000, 11.

30   'Dell CEO Would Like 40 Per cent PC Market Share', www.daily news.yahoo.com, June 20, 2001.

31   www.dell.com.

32   For views on barriers to entry from an economics perspective, see Porter, *Competitive Advantage*. For the sociological perspective, see J. Pfeffer and G. R. Salancik, *The External Control of Organization: A Resource Dependence Perspective* (New York: Harper & Row, 1978).

33   Porter, *Competitive Advantage*; J. E. Bain, *Barriers to New Competition* (Cambridge, MA: Harvard University Press, 1956); R. J. Gilbert, 'Mobility Barriers and the Value of Incumbency', in R. Schmalensee and R. D. Willig, eds., *Handbook of Industrial Organization*, 1 (Amsterdam: North-Holland, 1989).

34   www.amazon.com, Press Release, May 2001.

35   C. W. L. Hill, 'The Computer Industry: The New Industry of Industries', in C. W. L. Hill and G. R. Jones, *Strategic Management: An Integrated Approach* (Boston: Houghton Mifflin, 2003).

36   J. Bhagwati, *Protectionism* (Cambridge, MA; MIT Press, 1988).

37   http://www.findaproperty.com.

38   J. Schumpeter, *Capitalism, Socialism and Democracy* (London: Macmillan, 1950), 68. Also see R. R. Winter and S. G. Winter, *An Evolutionary Theory of Economic Change* (Cambridge MA: Harvard University Press, 1982).

39   'The Coming Clash of Logic', *The Economist*, July 3, 1993, 21–23.

40   S. Sherman, 'The New Computer Revolution', *Fortune*, June 14, 1993, 56–84.

41   N. Goodman, *An Introduction to Sociology* (New York: HarperCollins, 1991); C. Nakane, *Japanese Society* (Berkeley: University of California Press, 1970).

42   The Economist, *The Economist Book of Vital World Statistics* (New York: Random House, 1990).

43   For a detailed discussion of the importance of the structure of law as a factor explaining economic change and growth, see D. C. North, *Institutions, Institutional Change and Economic Performance* (Cambridge: Cambridge University Press, 1990).

44   www.ford.com, 2004.

45   www.gm.com, 2004; www.daimlerchrysler.com, 2004; www.renault.com, 2004.

46   J. Green, 'Riding Together', *BusinessWeek*, February 26, 2001, 46–49.

47   www.nissanusa.com, 2004; www.mazdausa.com, 2004.

48   L. Cohn, 'GM Tries to Show Who's Boss', *BusinessWeek*, March 12, 2001, 54–56.

49   C. Tierney, A. Bowden and I. M. Kunii, 'Who Says It's Iffy Now', *BusinessWeek*, October 23, 2001, 64.

50   R. B. Reich, *The Work of Nations* (New York: Knopf, 1991).

51   Bhagwati, *Protectionism*.

52   www.cnn.com, 2004.

53   M. A. Carpenter and J. W. Fredrickson, 'Top Management Teams, Global Strategic Posture, and the Moderating Role of Uncertainty', *Academy of Management Journal* 44 (June 2001), 533–46.

54   Bhagwati, *Protectionism*.

55   For a summary of these theories, see P. Krugman and M. Obstfeld, *International Economics: Theory and Policy* (New York: HarperCollins, 1991). See also C. W. L. Hill, *International Business* (New York: McGraw-Hill, 1997), Chapter 4.

56   A. M. Rugman, 'The Quest for Global Dominance', *Academy of Management Executive* 16 (August 2002), 157–60.

57   www.wto.org.com, 2004.

58   www.wto.org.

59   http://ec.europa.eu/comm/trade/issues/newround/index_en.htm.

60   http://ec.europa.eu/comm/trade/whatwedo/beginners/begin05_en.htm.

61   C. A. Bartlett and S. Ghoshal, *Managing Across Borders* (Boston: Harvard Business School Press, 1989).

62   C. Arnst and G. Edmondson, 'The Global Free-for-All', *BusinessWeek*, September 26, 1994, 118–26.

63   E. B. Tylor, *Primitive Culture* (London: Murray, 1971).

64   G. Hofstede, B. Neuijen, D. D. Ohayv and G. Sanders, 'Measuring Organizational Cultures: A Qualitative and Quantitative Study Across Twenty Cases', *Administrative Science Quarterly* 35 (1990), 286–316.

65   M. H. Hoppe, 'Introduction: Geert Hofstede's Culture's Consequences: International Differences in Work-Related Values', *Academy of Management Executive* 18 (February 2004), 73–75.

66   R. Bellah, *Habits of the Heart: Individualism and Commitment in American Life* (Berkeley: University of California Press, 1985).

67   R. Bellah, *The Tokugawa Religion* (New York: Free Press, 1957).

68   Nakane, *Japanese Society*.

69   http://www.thunderbird.edu/wwwfiles/ms/globe/index.htm.

70   J. Perlez, 'GE Finds Tough Going in Hungary', *The New York Times*, July 25, 1994, C1, C3.

71   www.ge.com.

72   J. P. Fernandez and M. Barr, *The Diversity Advantage* (New York: Lexington Books, 1994).

Chapter 7

The Manager as a Decision Maker

LEARNING OBJECTIVES

After studying this chapter, you should be able to:

☑ Differentiate between programmed and non-programmed decisions, and explain why non-programmed decision making is a complex, uncertain process.

☑ Describe the six steps that managers should take to make the best decisions.

☑ Explain how cognitive bias can affect decision making and lead managers to make poor decisions.

☑ Identify the advantages and disadvantages of group decision making, and describe techniques that can improve it.

☑ Explain the role that organisational learning and creativity play in helping managers to improve their decisions.

A Manager's Challenge

Yamada Transforms GlaxoSmithKline

How can senior managers in large corporations encourage effective decision making, creativity and entrepreneurship?

By all accounts, Tadataka (Tachi) Yamada faced a challenging task. Yamada was a senior manager at SmithKline Beecham, one of the world's largest pharmaceutical companies, when things couldn't seem more dismal.[1] Not enough potential drugs were in the pipeline, patents on top-selling drugs like Zovirax were nearing their expiration dates and Smith-Kline Beecham was in the process of merging with Glaxo Wellcome, a pharmaceutical company with similar challenges.[2] Yamada's task was no less than daunting – reinvent the 15,000-people-strong research and development (R&D) function of the merged company, GlaxoSmithKline, to fill the company's pipeline with promising new drugs. The new CEO of the just merged company put it: 'We can't keep doing what we're doing . . . So start thinking about something radical.'[3]

Yamada was up for the challenge and made bold decisions to reinvent R&D at GlaxoSmithKline (Glaxo). Interestingly, his efforts focused on changing the way decisions were traditionally made in the company. This was not an easy process – it took three years, the support and commitment of the CEO and his own courage. It was challenging during much of this period, but by 2004 Yamada's reorientation of decision making started to pay off. While only a few new drugs were under development in 2001, by 2004 Glaxo had over 40 drugs in phases 2 and 3 of their clinical trials.[4]

What did Yamada decide that changed the fate of Glaxo? Taking a bold step, he decided not to do what typically is done after such a mega-merger – consolidate R&D across the newly merged companies, lay off employees and focus on cutting costs. Rather, Yamada went back to his research roots (he has an MD degree).[5] He decided that to develop new drugs, R&D employees need to think and act like entrepreneurs – making decisions that they believed in and being highly motivated to follow through to make them a success.[6]

Yamada restructured R&D at Glaxo by forming autonomous, entrepreneurial startup laboratories to develop new drugs. Rather than consolidating decision making at the top, which usually happens after a merger, he empowered researchers in the laboratories to make the decisions that would hopefully revive Glaxo, or seal its fate. Yamada's bold experiment was a testament to his belief that the research scientists responsible for discovering and developing new drugs should be making the key decisions – not senior executives, who are a step removed from the research process on a day-to-day basis. Given the huge investments and lengthy time horizons involved, developing a new drug and getting it approved by the authorities, such as the National Institute for Clinical Excellence (NICE) in the UK, can take up to 10 years and costs about £454 million. Giving research scientists the final say on what new drugs to pursue was a dramatic departure from the tradition of having senior managers make such decisions.[7]

Yamada divided R&D at Glaxo into six small, semi-autonomous laboratories, each with a primary research focus, such as cardiovascular disease or cancer. Rather than operating as R&D typically does in a large company, these laboratories resemble biotech startups: each has its own senior managers, budget and staff (kept deliberately at no more than 400 employees). Not only do the laboratories decide what drugs to pursue, but they also follow through with their decisions into the clinical testing phase. Previously, as is typical in large pharmaceutical companies, once R&D discovered new drugs, it passed them on to other units responsible for getting the drugs into clinical testing. Yamada wanted the researchers who were closest to the new discoveries to take ownership of them, make key decisions on how to proceed and be responsible for their success (or failure). Importantly, researchers are rewarded for their expanded role in drug development; those who succeed at discovering a new drug and moving it into clinical testing are rewarded with bonuses and royalties.[8]

This restructuring of R&D was a major change from the status quo at Glaxo, a change that during the first two years seemed doomed to failure. Setting up the new laboratory structure, redesigning jobs, dismantling the decision-making hierarchy and empowering scientists to make key decisions resulted in ownership battles, chaos and high levels of uncertainty and stress. Many R&D scientists and executives fled to work for other companies, and the price of Glaxo shares declined by almost 20 per cent.[9]

The CEO and Yamada believed in what they were doing and were willing to carry on making tough decisions to make it a success. While the ultimate outcome of their bold decisions will take years to crystallise in terms of approved, effective new drugs for treating diseases, things are now looking bright. In 2003, Glaxo approximately doubled their number of new drugs it was advancing into phase 1 and 2 trials compared to 2001. They had also accelerated earlier-stage discovery efforts with new automated drug-screening facilities.[10] Yamada's willingness to take risks to enhance long-term viability, innovation and success seems to be paying off. It has convinced many, including a top research executive recruited from rival Merck to head a new cancer laboratory,[11] that Yamada has successfully reinvented R&D. The wisdom of his efforts has not gone unnoticed at the very highest levels of the company. In 2004, the 58-year-old was named executive director/chairman of R&D and became a member of Glaxo's board of directors.[12]

Overview

The discussion has described how the ways in which decisions are made in an organisation, and who makes them, can have a profound influence on organisational effectiveness and innovation. Glaxo was floundering, and the bold decisions Yamada made to reinvent R&D and push decision-making authority down the hierarchy to the research labs has paid off in terms of a rich pipeline of promising new drugs. In contrast, Merck, another large pharmaceutical company, is currently suffering the consequences of a series of poor decisions such as halting the development of promising new drugs, and faces a number of large law suits (see Chapter 1).[13] The decisions managers make, and the effects that these decisions have on the decision making process throughout an organisation, can profoundly influence organisational effectiveness.[14] Yet such decisions can be very difficult to make because they are fraught with uncertainty.

In this chapter, the focus is on how people make decisions and how individual, group and organisational factors can affect the quality of the decisions they make and ultimately determine organisational performance. The nature of managerial decision making and some models of the decision-making process that help reveal the complexities of successful decision making will be discussed. The main steps of the decision-making process are then examined. In addition, there is an exploration of the biases that may cause people to make poor decisions both as individuals and as members of a group. Finally, the chapter will examine how managers can promote organisational learning and creativity and improve the quality of decision making. By the end of this chapter, you will appreciate the critical role decision making plays in creating a high-performing organisation.

The Nature of Managerial Decision Making

Individuals are making decisions every day from the moment they get up – what clothes to wear, what to eat, where to go. Every time managers plan, organise, lead or control organisational activities, they also make a stream of decisions. In opening a new restaurant, for example, managers have to decide where to locate it, what kinds of food to provide to customers, which people to employ and so on. Decision making is a basic part of everyday life and thus of every task managers perform.

As discussed in Chapters 4–6, one of the main tasks facing a manager is to manage the *organisational environment*. Forces in the external environment give rise to many opportunities and threats for managers and their organisations; inside an organisation managers must address the many opportunities and threats that may arise during the course of utilising organisational resources. To deal with these opportunities and threats, managers must make decisions – that is, they must select one solution from a set of alternatives. **Decision making** is the process by which managers respond to the opportunities and threats that confront them by analysing the options and making determinations, or *decisions*, about specific organisational goals and courses of action. Good decisions result in the selection of appropriate goals and courses of action that increase organisational performance; bad decisions result in lower performance.

Decision making in response to opportunities occurs when managers search for ways to improve organisational performance to benefit customers, employees and other stakeholder groups. Tachi Yamada saw an opportunity to fill Glaxo's pipeline with promising new drugs by restructuring R&D into entrepreneurial biotech labs. *Decision making in response to threats* occurs when events inside or outside the organisation adversely affect organisational performance and managers search for ways to increase performance.[15] At Glaxo, Yamada realised that being the world's second-largest pharmaceutical company in a 'brutal industry' was proving to be a liability for R&D. Pharmaceuticals like Glaxo must have a pipeline of new drugs to remain competitive because even when they develop best-sellers like Zovirax and Combivir, once their patent protection expires, revenues plummet as generic forms of the drugs hit the market. As Yamada puts it: 'The answer to the pipeline problem is to be big and small at the same time. . . . You need people who think like entrepreneurs and play the hunches. That's what the industry lost when it got too big.'[16] Decision making is central to being a manager, and whenever managers engage in planning, organising, leading and controlling they are constantly making decisions.

Managers are always searching for ways to make better decisions to improve organisational performance. At the same time, they do their best to avoid costly mistakes that will hurt it. Examples of spectacularly good decisions include Stelios Haji-Ioannou's decision to create a low-cost carrier that flies to existing, large airports, doing 90 per cent of its trade online; and acquiring GO airlines, made it arguably the biggest and most successful 'no-frills' airline.[17] Bill Gates' decision to buy a computer operating system for £28,600 from a small company in Seattle and sell it to IBM for the new IBM personal computer turned Gates and Microsoft, respectively, into the richest man and richest software company in the world. Examples of spectacularly bad decisions include the decision by managers at NASA and Morton Thiokol to launch the *Challenger* space shuttle – a decision that resulted in the deaths of six astronauts in 1986. The decision of Compass, a UK FTSE 100 catering group, to buy the Granada catering group in 2002 was not a sustainable decision and almost ruined the company's UK operations.[18]

Information and Decisions

Much of management (planning, organising, leading and controlling) is about *making decisions*. The marketing manager must decide what price to charge for a product, what distribution channels to use and what promotional messages to emphasise. The manufacturing manager must decide how much of a product to make and how to make it. The purchasing manager must decide from whom to purchase inputs and what inventory of inputs to hold. The human relations (HR) manager must decide how much employees should be paid, how they should be trained and what benefits they should be given. The engineering manager must make decisions about new product design. Senior managers must decide how to allocate scarce financial resources among competing projects, how best to structure and control the organisation and what business-level strategy the organisation should be pursuing. Regardless of their functional orientation, all managers have to make decisions about matters such as what performance evaluation to give to a subordinate.

Decision making cannot be effective in an information vacuum: to make effective decisions, managers need information, from both inside the organisation and from external stakeholders. When deciding how to price a product, for example, marketing managers need information about how consumers will react to different prices. They need information about unit costs because they do not want to set the price below the cost of production. And they need information about competitive strategy, since pricing strategy should be consistent with an organisation's competitive strategy. Some of this information will come from outside the organisation (for example, from consumer surveys) and some from inside the organisation (information about unit production costs will come from manufacturing). Managers' ability to make effective decisions thus rests on their ability to *acquire and process information*.

Information and Control

Chapter 11 will discuss *controlling* as the process whereby managers regulate how efficiently and effectively an organisation and its members are performing the activities necessary to achieve their organisational goals.[19] Managers achieve control over organisational activities by taking four steps: (1) They establish *measurable standards of performance* or *goals*. (2) They measure *actual performance*. (3) They compare *actual performance* against *established goals*. (4) They *evaluate* the result and take *corrective action* if necessary.[20] The package delivery company DHL (bought by Deutsche Post, the German Mail delivery company), for example, has a delivery goal: to deliver 95 per cent of the packages it picks up by noon the next day.[21] Throughout the world, DHL has thousands of ground stations (branch offices that co-ordinate the pickup and delivery of packages in a particular area) that are responsible for the physical pickup and delivery of packages. DHL managers monitor the delivery performance of these stations on a regular basis; if they find that the 95 per cent goal is not being attained, they determine why and take corrective action if necessary.[22]

To achieve control over any organisational activity, managers must have information. To control a ground station, a manager at DHL needs to know how many of that station's packages are being delivered by noon. To acquire information, managers often rely on IT. Packages to be shipped by DHL are scanned with a hand-held scanner by the DHL driver who first picks them up. The pickup information is sent by a wireless link to a central computer at DHL's headquarters. The packages are scanned again by the van driver when they are delivered. The delivery information is also transmitted to DHL's central computer. By accessing the central computer, a manager can quickly find out not only what percentage of packages have been delivered by noon of the day after they were picked up but also how this information breaks down on a station-by-station basis.

Information and Co-ordination

Co-ordinating department and divisional activities to achieve organisational goals is another basic task of management. As an extreme example of the size of the co-ordination task that managers face, consider the effort involved in building Boeing's commercial jet aircraft, the 777. The 777 is composed of 3 million individual parts and thousands of major components. Managers at Boeing have to co-ordinate the production and delivery of all of these parts so that every part arrives at Boeing's Everett, Washington, facility exactly when it is needed (for example, the wings should arrive before the engines). Boeing managers jokingly refer to this task as 'co-ordinating 3 million parts in flying formation'.[23] To achieve this high level of co-ordination, managers need information about which supplier is producing what, when it is to be produced and when it is to be delivered. Managers also need this information so that they are able to track the delivery performance of suppliers against expectations and receive advance warning of any likely problems. To meet these needs, managers at Boeing established a computer-based information system that links Boeing to all its suppliers and can track the flow of 3 million component parts through the production process – an immense task.

While some companies have sophisticated systems, sometime employees, especially managers, have to make decisions based on incomplete information; an issue discussed in more detail in the remainder of this chapter.

Programmed and Non-programmed Decision Making

Regardless of the specific decisions that managers make, the decision-making process is either *programmed* or *non-programmed*.[24]

Programmed decision making

Programmed decision making is a routine, virtually automatic process. Programmed decisions are decisions that have been made so many times in the past that managers have developed *rules* or *guidelines* to be applied when certain situations inevitably occur. Programmed decision making takes place when a school principal asks the school board to hire a new teacher whenever student enrolment increases by 40 students; when a manufacturing supervisor hires new workers whenever existing workers' overtime increases by more than 10 per cent; and when an office manager orders basic office supplies, such as paper and pens, whenever the inventory of supplies on hand drops below a certain level. In the last example, the office manager probably also orders the same amount of supplies each time.

This decision making is called *programmed* because office managers, for example, do not need to repeatedly make new judgements about what should be done. They can rely on long-established decision rules:

- *Rule 1*: When the storage shelves are three-quarters empty, order more copy paper.
- *Rule 2*: When ordering paper, order enough to fill the shelves.

Managers can develop rules and guidelines to regulate all routine organisational activities. For example, rules can specify how a worker should perform a certain task, and rules can specify the quality standards that raw materials must meet to be acceptable. Most decision making that relates to the day-to-day running of an organisation is programmed decision making. Examples include decision making about how much inventory to hold, when to pay bills, when to bill customers and when to order materials and supplies. Programmed decision making occurs when managers have the information they need to create rules that will guide decision making. There is little ambiguity involved in assessing when the stockroom is empty, or counting the number of new students in a class.

Non-programmed decision making

Suppose, however, that managers are not at all certain that a course of action will lead to a desired outcome. Or, in even more ambiguous terms, suppose managers are not even clear about what they are really trying to achieve. Obviously, rules cannot be developed to predict uncertain events. **Non-programmed decision making** is required for these non-routine decisions. Non-programmed decisions are made in response to unusual or novel opportunities and threats. Non-programmed decision making occurs when there are no ready-made decision rules that managers can apply to a situation. Rules do not exist because the situation is unexpected or uncertain, and managers lack the information they need to develop rules to cover it. Examples of non-programmed decision making include decisions to invest in a new technology, develop a new product, launch a new promotional campaign, enter a new market, expand internationally or restructure an organisation or function (as Yamada had to for his R&D).

How do managers make decisions in the absence of decision rules? They may rely on their **intuition** – feelings, beliefs and hunches that come readily to mind, require little effort and information gathering and result in on-the-spot decisions.[25] Or they may make a **reasoned judgement** – a decision that takes time and effort to make and results from careful information gathering, generation of alternatives and evaluation of alternatives. 'Exercising' one's judgement is a more rational process than 'going with' one's intuition. For reasons that we examine later in this chapter, both intuition and judgement often are flawed, and can result in poor decision making. The likelihood of error is much greater in non-programmed decision making than in programmed decision making,[26] and the remainder of this chapter refers to *non-programmed* decision making because it is inherently challenging and causes the most problems for managers.

Sometimes managers have to make rapid decisions and do not have the time for careful consideration of the issues involved; or they lack the necessary information to make reasoned judgements. They must rely on their intuition to respond quickly to a pressing concern. For example, when fire chiefs manage fire fighters battling a dangerous, out-of-control fire, they often need to rely on their expert intuition to make on-the-spot decisions that will protect the lives of the fire fighters and save the lives of others, contain the fires and preserve property – decisions made in emergency situations entailing high uncertainty, high risk and rapidly changing conditions.[27] On other occasions, managers do have the time available to make reasoned judgements but there are no established rules to guide their decisions, such as when deciding whether or not to proceed with a proposed merger. Regardless of the circumstances, making non-programmed decisions can result in effective or ineffective decision making. As indicated in Case 7.1, managers have to be on their guard to avoid being over-confident in decisions that result from their intuition and reasoned judgement.

Case 7.1: Curbing overconfidence

Should managers be confident in their intuition and reasoned judgements? Decades of research by Nobel Prize winner Daniel Kahneman, his long-time collaborator the late Amos Tversy and other researchers suggests that, if anything, managers (like all people) tend to be over-confident in the decisions they make (whether based on intuition or reasoned judgement). With over-confidence comes the failure to evaluate and rethink the wisdom of the decisions one makes and to learn from one's mistakes.[28]

▶

Kahneman distinguishes between the intuitions of managers who are truly expert in the content domain of a decision and the intuition of managers who have some knowledge and experience but are not true experts. While the intuition of both types can be faulty, that of experts is less likely to be flawed. This is why fire captains can make good decisions and why expert chess players can make good moves, in both cases without spending much time and deliberation on what, for non-experts, is a very complicated set of circumstances. What distinguishes expert managers from those with 'some' expertise is that the experts have extensive experience under conditions in which they receive quick and clear feedback about the outcomes of their decisions.

Unfortunately, managers who have some experience in a content area but are not true experts tend to be overly confident in their intuition and their judgements.[29] As Kahneman puts it: 'People jump to statistical conclusions on the basis of very weak evidence. We form powerful intuitions about trends and about the replicability of results on the basis of information that is truly inadequate.'[30] Not only do managers, and all people, tend to be over-confident about their intuitions and judgements, but they also tend not to learn from their mistakes. Compounding this undue optimism is a very human tendency to be over-confident in one's own abilities and influence over unpredictable events. Surveys have found that the majority of people think they are above average, make better decisions and are less prone to making bad decisions than others (of course, it is impossible for most people to be above average on any dimension).[31]

A recent example of managerial over-confidence is particularly telling. Research has consistently found that mergers tend to turn out poorly – post-merger profitability declines, stock prices decline and so forth (think of AOL Time Warner, or Compass and Granada catering, p. 208). One would imagine that senior executives and boards of directors would learn from this research and from articles in the business press about the woes of merged companies. Evidently not! According to a study by Hewitt Associates, top executives and board members are, if anything, planning on increasing their involvement in mergers over the next few years. These senior managers, evidently, are over-confident in believing that they can succeed where others have failed.[32]

Jeffrey Pfeffer, a professor at Stanford University's Graduate School of Business, suggests that managers can avoid the perils of over-confidence by critically evaluating the decisions they have made and the outcomes of those decisions. They should admit to themselves when they have made a mistake and really learn from their mistakes (rather than dismissing them as flukes or situations out of their control). In addition, managers should be guarded against too much agreement at the top. As Pfeffer puts it: 'If two people agree all the time, one of them is redundant.'[33]

The classical and the administrative decision-making models reveal many of the assumptions, complexities and pitfalls that affect decision making. These models help reveal the factors that managers and other decision makers must be aware of to improve the quality of their decision making. Keep in mind, however, that the classical and administrative models are just guides that can help managers understand the decision-making process. In real life, the process is typically not as clear-cut and simplistic but these models can help a manager to reflect on the process of decision making and guide them through it.

The Classical Model

One of the earliest models, the **classical decision-making model**, is *prescriptive*, which means that it specifies how decisions *should* be made. Managers using the classical model make a series of simplifying assumptions about the nature of the decision-making process. The premise of the classical model is that once managers recognise the need to make a decision, they should be able to generate a complete list of all alternatives and consequences and make the best choice. In other words, the classical model assumes that managers have access to *all* the information they need to make the **optimum decision**. This decision is the most appropriate decision possible in light of what they believe to be the most desirable future consequences for the organisation. Furthermore, the classical model assumes that managers can easily list their own preferences for each alternative and rank them from least to most preferred.

While this model may be helpful, it seems obvious that managers or individuals in general do not always have all the necessary and vital information at hand. This model should thus not be seen as more than a guiding principle of how to approach decision making.

The Administrative Model

James March and Herbert Simon[34] disagreed with the underlying assumptions of the classical model of decision making. In contrast, they supported the idea that managers in the real world did *not* have access to all the information they needed to make a decision. Moreover, they pointed out that even if all information were readily available, many managers would lack the mental or psychological ability to absorb and evaluate it correctly. As a result, March and Simon developed the **administrative decision-making model** to explain why decision making is always an inherently *uncertain* and *risky* process – and why managers can rarely make decisions in the manner prescribed by the classical model. The administrative model is based on three important concepts: **bounded rationality**, **incomplete information** and **satisficing**.

Bounded rationality
March and Simon pointed out that human decision-making capabilities are bounded by people's *cognitive limitations* – that is, limitations in their ability to interpret, process and act on large amounts of information.[35] They argued that the limitations of human intelligence constrain the ability of decision makers to determine the optimum decision. They coined the term *bounded rationality* to describe the situation in which the number of alternatives a manager must identify is so great, and the amount of information so vast, that it is difficult for the manager to even come close to evaluating it all before making a decision.[36]

Incomplete information
Even if managers did have an unlimited ability to evaluate information, they still would not be able to arrive at the optimum decision because they would have incomplete information. Information is incomplete because the full range of decision-making alternatives is unknowable in most situations and the consequences associated with known alternatives are uncertain, as was true for Yamada at GlaxoSmithKline.[37] In other words, information is incomplete because of **risk** and uncertainty, ambiguous information and time constraints (Fig. 7.1).

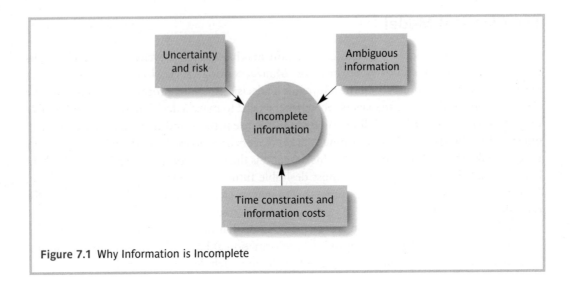

Figure 7.1 Why Information is Incomplete

Risk and Uncertainty

As described in Chapter 6, forces in the organisational environment are constantly changing. *Risk* is present when managers know the possible outcomes of a particular course of action, and can assign probabilities to them. Managers in the biotechnology industry, for example, know that new drugs have a 10 per cent probability of successfully passing advanced clinical trials and a 90 per cent probability of failing. These probabilities reflect the experiences of thousands of drugs that have gone through advanced clinical trials. Thus, when managers in the biotechnology industry decide to submit a drug for testing, they know that there is only a 10 per cent chance that the drug will succeed, but at least they have some information on which to base their decision.

When *uncertainty* exists, the probabilities of alternative outcomes *cannot* be determined and future outcomes are *unknown*: managers are working blind. Since the probability of a given outcome occurring is not known, managers have little information to use in making a decision. In 1993, when Apple Computer introduced the Newton, its personal digital assistant (PDA), managers had no idea what the probability of a successful product launch for a PDA might be. Because Apple was the first to market this totally new product, there was no body of well-known data that Apple's managers could draw on to calculate the probability of a successful launch. Uncertainty plagues most managerial decision making.[38] Although Apple's initial launch of its PDA was a disaster due to technical problems, an improved version was more successful. In fact, Apple created the PDA market that boomed during the 2000s as new and different wireless products such as the BlackBerry were introduced.

A major source of uncertainty for senior managers revolves around being unable to accurately predict or forecast future demand for products and services. One such example is Red Bull, the energy-giving soft drink created in 1984 after its founder, Dietrich Mateschitz, discovered a similar 'tonic drink' while travelling in Asia. He was one of the first to launch such a product in a different style, by applying different marketing techniques and by not diversifying the product (until 2003, when a sugar-free version was introduced). Nowadays the energy drinks market exceeds £1.6 billion a year, with Red Bull leading the market with 70 per cent even though every year a large number of new products is launched.[39] No one could have known that a single-product-line company would be the market leader in the functional drinks market. However, the future is unpredictable as more and more supermarkets launch their own branded products and health concerns are voiced over sugary and caffeinated drinks. Red Bull will have to think of new ways to attract new customers.

Ambiguous Information

A second reason why information is incomplete is that much of the information managers have at their disposal is *ambiguous* information. This means the information is not clear – it can be interpreted in multiple and often conflicting ways. Take a look at Fig. 7.2. Do you see a young woman or an old woman? Managers often interpret the same piece of information differently and make decisions based on their own interpretations.[40] Recall that Yamada perceived Glaxo's problems in 2001 in terms of too much top-down decision making and an R&D function that needed to be much more entrepreneurial. Merck is currently facing similar problems, but its CEO seems to perceive the company's troubles in terms of the need to cut costs – in November 2003, Merck lay off 4,400 Merck employees, 7 per cent of the workforce, the largest layoff the company had had in over 100 years.[41]

Figure 7.2 Ambiguous Information: Young Woman or Old Woman?

Time Constraints and Information Costs

The third reason why information is incomplete is that managers have neither the time nor the money to search for all possible alternative solutions and evaluate all their potential consequences. Consider the situation confronting a Ford Motor Company purchasing manager who has one month to choose a supplier for a small engine part. Of the thousands of potential suppliers for this part, there are 20,000 alone that are located nationally. Given the time available, the purchasing manager cannot contact all potential suppliers and ask each for its terms (price, delivery schedules, and so on). Moreover, even if the time were available, the costs of obtaining the information, including the manager's own time, would be prohibitive.

Satisficing

March and Simon argue that managers do not attempt to discover every alternative when faced with bounded rationality, an uncertain future, unquantifiable risks, considerable ambiguity, time constraints and high information costs. Rather, they use a strategy known as *satisficing*, exploring a limited sample of all the potential alternatives.[42] When managers satisfice, they search for and choose acceptable, or satisfactory, ways to respond to problems and opportunities rather than trying to make the optimal decision.[43] In the case of the Ford purchasing manager's search, for example, satisficing may involve asking a limited number of suppliers for their terms, trusting that they are representative of suppliers in general and making a choice based on that limited sample. Although this course of action is reasonable from the perspective of the purchasing manager, it may mean that a potentially superior supplier is overlooked.

March and Simon pointed out that managerial decision making is often more art than science. In the real world, managers must rely on their intuition and judgement to make what seems to them to be the best decision in the face of uncertainty and ambiguity.[44] Moreover, managerial decision making is often fast-paced, as managers use their experience and judgement to make crucial decisions under conditions of incomplete information. Although there is nothing wrong with this approach, decision makers should be aware that human judgement is often flawed: even the best managers sometimes end up making very poor decisions.[45]

Reaction Time

1. What are the main differences between programmed decision making and non-programmed decision making?
2. In what ways do the classical and administrative models of decision making help managers to appreciate the complexities of real-world decision making?

Steps in the Decision-Making Process

Using the work of March and Simon as a basis, researchers have developed a step-by-step model of the decision-making process. This model tries to address the issues and problems that managers confront at each step. Perhaps the best way to introduce this model is to examine the real-world non-programmed decision making that Chief Executive Paul Otellini at Intel had to make.

Intel is one of the most dominant producers of computer processors, with 80 per cent of desktop computer having 'Intel Inside'. However, Intel is facing some difficult decisions, as it has failed to enter the new, extensively growing market of small, mobile devices. Paul Otellini decided to change the engineering-led outlook of Intel into a more customer-focused one. In order to do this, he restructured the organisation – one of the biggest shakeups the company had ever experienced. He also decided in January 2005 to break up parts of the company to create new business units that addressed different customer segments.

The decisions made were difficult, as they changed the face of Intel. While Intel's stronghold on PCs is still growing, many assume that they need to move beyond this expertise. Thanks to this change in structure and a move to a more customer-centred approach, Intel has started to enter the new market, and was chosen to provide the processors for the new-generation

BlueBerry email devices.[46] No one can be sure where the market is heading. Intel has already achieved success with producing smaller and smaller but more powerful and energy-saving processors. But is that the future?

Many managers who must make important decisions with incomplete information face dilemmas similar to Otellini's. There are six steps that managers should consciously follow to make a good decision (Fig. 7.3),[47] and we review them in the remainder of this section.

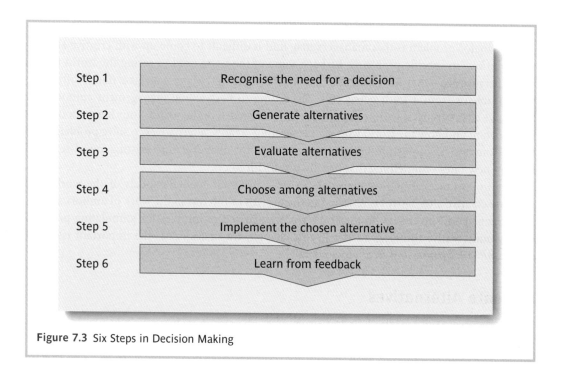

Figure 7.3 Six Steps in Decision Making

Recognise the Need for a Decision

The first step in the decision-making process is to *recognise the need* for a decision. Otellini recognised a need and realised that a decision had to be made quickly because it would take time to implement the changes that would secure Intel's future success.

Some stimuli usually spark the realisation that there is a need to make a decision. These stimuli often become apparent because changes in the organisational environment result in new kinds of opportunities and threats. For Intel, this meant addressing the need for smaller, maybe even less powerful, processors that met the need for more mobile technology beyond their Centrino product.

The stimuli that spark decision making are as likely to result from the actions of managers inside an organisation as they are from changes in the external environment.[48] An organisation possesses a set of skills, competencies and resources in its employees and in departments such as marketing, manufacturing and R&D. Managers who actively pursue opportunities to use these competencies create the need to make decisions. Managers thus can be *proactive* or *reactive* in recognising the need to make a decision, but that they must recognise this need and respond in a timely and appropriate way.[49]

Generate Alternatives

Having recognised the need to make a decision, a manager must generate a set of *feasible altern-ative courses of action* to take in response to the opportunity or threat. Management experts cite failure to properly generate and consider different alternatives as one reason why managers sometimes make bad decisions.[50] In the Intel scenario, the alternatives were obvious: stay engineering-led and lose out on new markets (for example, Intel missed out on the contract to supply the new Xbox with processors), or adapt and aim to provide products based on customer needs. Often, however, the alternatives are not so obvious or so clearly specified.

One major problem is that managers may find it difficult to come up with creative alterna-tive solutions to specific problems. Perhaps some of them are used to seeing the world from a single perspective – they have a certain 'managerial mind-set'. Many managers find it difficult to view problems from a fresh perspective. According to best-selling management author Peter Senge, we all are trapped within our *personal mental models* of the world – our ideas about what is important and how the world works.[51] Generating creative alternatives to solve problems and take advantage of opportunities may require that we abandon our existing mind-sets and develop new ones – something that usually is difficult to do.

The importance of getting managers to set aside their mental models of the world and generate creative alternatives is reflected in the growth of interest in the work of authors such as Peter Senge and Edward de Bono, who have popularised techniques for stimulating problem solving and creative thinking.[52] Later in this chapter, we shall discuss the important issues of *organisational learning and creativity* in detail.

Evaluate Alternatives

Once managers have generated a set of alternatives, they must evaluate the advantages and dis-advantages of each.[53] The key to a good assessment of the alternatives is to define the oppor-tunity or threat exactly and then specify the criteria that should influence the selection of alternatives for responding to the problem or opportunity. One reason for bad decisions is that managers often fail to specify the criteria that are important in reaching a decision.[54] In general, successful managers use four criteria to evaluate the pros and cons of alternative courses of action (Fig. 7.4):

1. *Legality*   Managers must ensure that a possible course of action is legal, and will not violate any domestic and international laws or government regulations.

2. *Ethicalness*   Managers must ensure that a possible course of action is ethical, and will not unnecessarily harm any stakeholder group. Many of the decisions that managers make may help some organisational stakeholders and harm others (see Chapter 3). When examining alternative courses of action, managers need to be very clear about the potential effects of their decisions.

3. *Economic feasibility*   Managers must decide whether the alternatives are economically feasible – that is, whether they can be accomplished given the organisation's performance goals. Typically, managers perform a **cost-benefit analysis** of the various alternatives to determine which one will have the best net financial payoff.

4. *Practicality*   Managers must decide whether they have the capabilities and resources required to implement the alternative, and they must be sure that it will not threaten the attainment

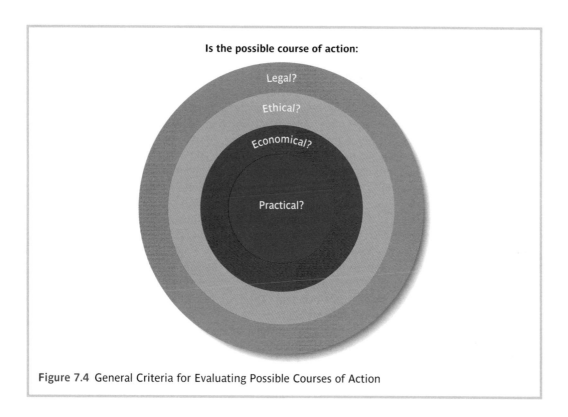

Figure 7.4 General Criteria for Evaluating Possible Courses of Action

of other organisational goals. At first glance, an alternative might seem to be economically superior to other alternatives, but if managers realise that it is likely to threaten other important projects, they might decide that it is not practical after all.

Very often, a manager must consider these four criteria simultaneously. The problems at Intel were clearly framed with regard to the criteria that influenced Ontellini's decision. The decision to break up parts of the company was to ensure viability (*economic criterion*). Intel is also facing some legal threats from a competitor, Advanced Micro Devices (AMD), which claims that Intel has not behaved ethically within various countries, and AMD has filed anti-trust lawsuits against Intel. Ontellini has to ensure that his restructuring and his approaches to enter new markets adhere to the criteria of *legality and ethicalness*. At times, criteria can conflict: entering new markets or aggressively pursuing new business ventures may be economically important, but may raise serious questions about the legality and ethicalness of the actions undertaken.

Some of the worst managerial decisions can be traced to poor assessment of the alternatives, such as the decision to launch the *Challenger* space shuttle, mentioned on p. 208. In that case, the desire of NASA and Morton Thiokol managers to demonstrate to the public the success of the US space programme in order to ensure future funding (*economic feasibility*) conflicted with the need to ensure the safety of the astronauts (*ethicalness*). Managers deemed the economic criterion more important and decided to launch the space shuttle even though there were unanswered questions about safety. Tragically, some of the same decision-making problems that resulted in the *Challenger* tragedy led to the demise of the *Columbia* space shuttle 17 years later in 2003, killing all seven astronauts on board (Case 7.2).[55]

Case 7.2: **NASA's flawed culture**

Seventeen years after the *Challenger* disaster, history repeated itself on 1 February 2003, when *Columbia* broke up over Texas on the final day of its mission, killing all seven astronauts on board.[56] While different specific causes resulted in each of these tragedies, they were both at least partially the result of a deeper, more widespread problem: a flawed safety culture at NASA where concerns with budgets and schedules were emphasised at the expense of safety.[57]

Both the Columbia Accident Investigation Board (CAIB) and a NASA team headed by Al Diaz, director of the Goddard Space Flight Centre, concluded – after intensive investigations involving employees at all ranks, outside contractors and engineering and scientific data – that NASA's flawed, 'can-do' culture, emphasising budgets and schedules over safety, was partially to blame for the *Columbia* tragedy. Commenting on the CAIB report and their own investigations, the Diaz team stated: 'Had the fate of STS-107 been the result of a small number of well-defined problems in a single program, finding solutions would be a relatively straightforward matter. But the CAIB determined that such is not the case . . . It was their conclusion that the mistakes made on STS-107 were not isolated failures but rather were indicative of systemic flaws that existed prior to the accident. The Diaz team believes that some of these systemic flaws exist beyond the shuttle programme.'[58]

In both the *Challenger* and the *Columbia* disasters, safety questions were raised before the shuttles were launched; safety concerns took second place to budgets, economic feasibility and schedules; top decision makers seemed to ignore or downplay the inputs of those with relevant technical expertise; and speaking up was discouraged.[59] Rather than making safety a top priority, decision makers seemed overly concerned with keeping on schedule and within budget.[60] The day before *Columbia* lifted off, mission managers were presented with data indicating that a ring that linked the rocket boosters to the external tank had failed to meet strength requirements. Rather than postponing the launch to address this problem, a shuttle manager temporarily waived the requirements based on what later turned out to be faulty data. After foam had broken loose the next day during lift-off (a recurring problem) and struck the left wing, NASA engineers repeatedly and doggedly requested that images of the area in which the foam had struck be obtained to assess the extent of the damage and perhaps plan a rescue mission. Mission managers actively opposed their requests and no images were obtained.

Bill Parsons, who now heads the troubled shuttle programme, is committed to changing the organisation's culture.[61] Among other things, he is trying to improve communication, encourage all employees to speak up without fear of retribution, make sure that all employees' inputs are heard, ensure that technical expertise is taken into account when making decisions and, above all, emphasise safety. Currently, NASA engineers are trying to develop fillers and wrappings that astronauts can use to repair unexpected cracks, gashes and holes on shuttles during space flights.[62] Efforts are under way to prevent foam insulation from breaking off fuel tanks when shuttles are launched. Above all else, Parsons is trying to change the culture so that safety is a top priority, technical expertise is respected and shuttles are not launched until all known problems have been addressed.

Choose Among Alternatives

Once a set of alternative solutions has been carefully evaluated, the next task is to *rank* the various alternatives (using the criteria discussed in the previous section) and make a decision.

When ranking alternatives, managers must be sure that *all* the information available is brought to bear on the problem or issue at hand. As the case indicates, however, identifying all *relevant* information for a decision does not mean that the manager has *complete* information: in most instances, information is incomplete.

Perhaps more serious than the existence of incomplete information, is the often-documented tendency of managers to ignore critical information – even when it is available. We discuss this tendency in detail below when we examine the operation of **cognitive bias** and **groupthink**.

Implement the Chosen Alternative

Once a decision has been made and an alternative has been selected, it must be *implemented*, and many subsequent and related decisions must be made. After a course of action has been decided – say, to develop a new processor – thousands of subsequent decisions are necessary to implement it. These decisions will involve recruiting experts in semiconduction, analysing the available material, finding high-quality manufacturers and signing contracts with the manufacturers who will use your product.

Although the need to make subsequent decisions to implement the chosen course of action may seem obvious, many managers make a decision and then fail to act on it. This is the same as not making a decision at all: to ensure that a decision is implemented, senior managers must assign to middle managers the responsibility for making the *follow-up decisions* necessary to achieve the goal. They must give middle managers sufficient resources to achieve the goal, and they must hold the middle managers accountable for their performance.

Learn from Feedback

The final step in the decision-making process is learning from feedback. Effective managers always conduct a *retrospective analysis* to see what they can learn from past successes or failures. Managers who do not evaluate the results of their decisions do not learn from experience; instead, they stagnate and are likely to make the same mistakes again and again.[63] To avoid this problem, managers must establish a formal procedure by which they can learn from the results of past decisions. The procedure should include three steps:

1. Compare what actually happened to what was expected to happen as a result of the decision.

2. Explore why any expectations for the decision were not met.

3. Derive guidelines that will help in future decision making.

Managers who always strive to learn from past mistakes and successes are likely to continuously improve the decisions they make. A significant amount of learning can take place when the outcomes of decisions are evaluated and this assessment can produce enormous benefits. Many companies identify *lessons learned* or *war stories*, which transmit individually held knowledge in order to inform future decision making.

TIPS FOR PRACTICE

1. Don't forget that it is impossible to make optimum or perfect decisions, but try to make the best decision possible!

2. Think about using intuition and judgement to reach the best possible solution – try to think of alternatives.

3. Be aware of what is going on in your environment to make appropriate, maybe even corrective, decisions.

Cognitive Bias and Decision Making

In the 1970s psychologists Daniel Kahneman and Amos Tversky suggested that because all decision makers are subject to bounded rationality, they tend to use **heuristics** – rules of thumb that simplify the process of making decisions.[64] Kahneman and Tversky argued that rules of thumb are often useful because they help decision makers make sense of complex, uncertain and ambiguous information. Sometimes, however, the use of heuristics can lead to **systematic errors** in the way decision makers process information about alternatives and make decisions. *Systematic errors* are errors that people make repeatedly and that result in poor decision making. Because of cognitive bias, which is caused by systematic errors, otherwise-capable managers may end up making bad decisions.[65] Four sources of bias that can adversely affect the way managers make decisions are:

- Prior hypotheses
- Representativeness
- The illusion of control
- Escalating commitment (see Fig. 7.5).

Prior-hypothesis Bias

Decision makers who have strong prior beliefs about the relationship between two variables tend to make decisions based on those beliefs *even when presented with evidence that their beliefs are wrong*. In doing so, they are falling victim to **prior-hypothesis bias**. Decision makers tend to seek and use information that is consistent with their prior beliefs, and to ignore information that contradicts them.

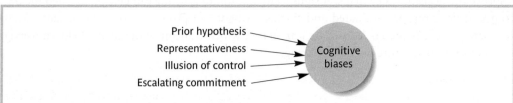

Figure 7.5 Sources of Cognitive Bias at the Individual and Group Levels

Representativeness Bias

Many decision makers inappropriately generalise from a small sample or even from a single vivid case or episode. An interesting example of the **representativeness bias** may be seen in Intel. While the computer market is moving away from desktop computers, Intel still believes that this market will keep on growing. No one can predict with any certainty, but many other processor manufacturers are moving towards the new markets of mobile technology.

Illusion of Control

Other errors in decision making result from the **illusion of control** – the tendency of decision makers to over-estimate their ability to control activities and events. Senior-level managers seem to be particularly prone to this bias. Having worked their way to the top of an organisation, they tend to have an exaggerated sense of their own worth and are over-confident about their ability to succeed and to control events.[66] The illusion of control causes managers to over-estimate the odds of a favourable outcome and, consequently, they may make inappropriate decisions. Nissan used to be controlled by Katsuji Kawamata, an autocratic CEO who thought he had the ability to run the car company single-handed. He made all the decisions, some of which resulted in a series of spectacular mistakes, including changing the company's name from Datsun to Nissan.

Escalating Commitment

Having already committed significant resources to a course of action, some managers commit more resources to the project *even if they receive feedback that the project is failing*.[67] Feelings of personal responsibility for a project apparently bias the analysis of decision makers and lead to this **escalating commitment**. The managers decide to increase their investment of time and money in a course of action and ignore evidence that it is illegal, unethical, uneconomical or impractical. Often, the more appropriate decision would be to cut the losses and run.

As we have seen, a tragic example of where escalating commitment can lead is the *Challenger* disaster. Managers at both NASA and Morton Thiokol were apparently so anxious to keep the shuttle programme on schedule that they ignored or discounted any evidence that would slow the programme down. The information offered by two Thiokol engineers, who warned about O-ring failure in cold weather, was discounted, and the shuttle was launched on a chilly day in January 1986.

Another example of escalating commitment occurred during the 1960s and 1970s when large steel makers responded to low-cost competition from mini-mills and foreign steel makers by increasing their investments in the technologically obsolete steelmaking facilities they already possessed, rather than investing in new, cutting-edge technology.[68] This decision was irrational because investment in obsolete technology would never enable them to lower their costs and compete successfully.

Be Aware of Your Biases

How can managers avoid the negative effects of cognitive bias and improve their decision-making and problem-solving abilities? Managers must become aware of biases and their effects, and they must identify their own personal style of making decisions. One useful way for managers to analyse their decision-making style is to review two decisions that they made recently – one decision that turned out well, and one that turned out poorly. Problem-solving experts recommend that managers start by determining how much time to spend on each of the decision-making steps, such as gathering information to identify the pros and cons of alternatives or ranking the alternatives, to make sure that they spend sufficient time on each step.[69]

Another recommended technique for examining decision-making style is for managers to list the *criteria* they typically use to assess and evaluate alternatives – the *heuristics* (rules of thumb) they typically employ, their personal biases, and so on – and then critically evaluate the appropriateness of these different factors.

Many individual managers are likely to have difficulty identifying their own biases, so it is often advisable for managers to scrutinise their own assumptions by working with other managers to help expose weaknesses in their decision-making style. In this context, the issue of *group decision making* becomes important.

Group Decision Making

Many, perhaps most, important organisational decisions are made by groups or teams of managers rather than by individuals, and group decision making is superior to individual decision making in several respects. When managers work as a team to make decisions and solve problems, their choices of alternatives are less likely to fall victim to the biases and errors already discussed. They are able to draw on the combined skills, competencies and accumulated knowledge of group members and thereby improve their ability to generate feasible alternatives and make good decisions. Group decision making also allows managers to process more information and to correct one another's errors. In the implementation phase, all managers affected by the decisions agree to co-operate: when a group of managers makes a decision (as opposed to one senior manager making a decision and imposing it on subordinate managers), the probability that it will be implemented successfully increases. (We discuss in Chapter 13 how to encourage employee participation in decision making.) Advances in IT can facilitate the group decision-making process, as indicated in Case 7.3.

Case 7.3: **Improving medical decision making to deliver better care**

Physicians and medical professionals are often sceptical about the ability of advances in IT to improve medical decision making. However, information is central to medical practice. Doctors manage information all the time: taking a history from a patient, communicating with colleagues, ordering investigations, checking test results, keeping up-to-date with research findings or monitoring their own performance. The NHS has rolled out the National Programme for Information Technology (NPfIT) that aims that by 2010 all patient records can be accessed from anywhere in England. The system is designed to link every GP's surgery and hospital in England and provide online records for up to 50 million patients. It will improve patient care by increasing the efficiency and effectiveness of clinicians and other NHS staff.[70] Since its inception in 2003, the NPfIT has already made a difference. The first e-prescriptions have been given out, more than 5,000 NHS sites are connected to the new N3 data network and several GPs have already connected to the national data spine. It is clear that in the future, IT will make an enormous difference to the care patients receive.

There are some potential disadvantages associated with group decision making. Groups often take much longer than individuals to make decisions. Getting two or more managers to agree to the same solution can be difficult because managers' interests and preferences are often different. In addition, just like decision making by individual managers, group decision making can be undermined by biases. A major source of group bias is *groupthink*.

The Perils of Groupthink

Groupthink is a pattern of faulty and biased decision making that occurs in groups whose members strive for agreement among themselves at the expense of accurately assessing the information relevant to a decision.[71] When managers are subject to groupthink, they collectively embark on a course of action without developing the appropriate criteria to evaluate alternatives. Typically, a group rallies around one central manager, such as the CEO, and the course of action that manager supports. Group members become blindly committed to that course of action without evaluating its merits. Commitment is often based on an *emotional*, rather than an objective, assessment of the optimal course of action.

When groupthink occurs, pressures for agreement and harmony within a group have the unintended effect of discouraging individuals from raising issues that run counter to majority opinion. As we have seen, when managers at NASA and Morton Thiokol fell victim to groupthink, they convinced each other that all was well and that there was no need to delay the launch of the *Challenger* space shuttle.

Devil's Advocacy and Dialectical Inquiry

The existence of cognitive bias and groupthink raises the question: how can we improve the quality of group and individual decision making? How can managers make decisions that are realistic and are based on a thorough evaluation of alternatives? Two techniques known to counteract groupthink and cognitive bias are **devil's advocacy** and **dialectic inquiry** (Fig. 7.6).[72]

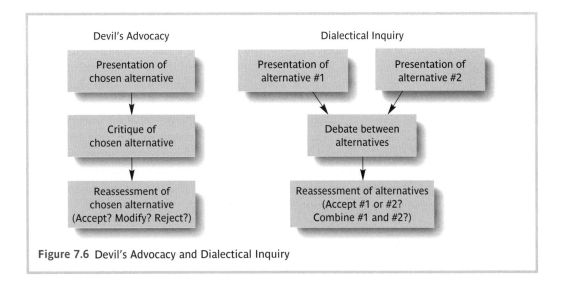

Figure 7.6 Devil's Advocacy and Dialectical Inquiry

Devil's advocacy is a critical analysis of a preferred alternative to ascertain its strengths and weaknesses before it is implemented.[73] Typically, one member of the decision-making group plays the role of 'devil's advocate' and critiques and challenges the way the group has evaluated alternatives and ranked their relevance. The purpose of devil's advocacy is to identify all the reasons that might make the preferred alternative *unacceptable* after all. In this way, decision makers can be made aware of the possible perils of recommended courses of action.

Dialectical inquiry goes one step further. Two groups of managers are assigned to a problem, and each is responsible for evaluating alternatives and selecting one of them. Senior managers hear each group present its preferred alternative, and then each group critiques the other's position. During this debate, senior managers challenge both groups' positions to uncover potential problems and perils associated with their solutions. The goal is to find an *even better alternative course of action* for the organisation to adopt.

Both devil's advocacy and dialectical inquiry can help counter the effects of cognitive bias and groupthink.[74] In practice, however, devil's advocacy is probably the easier method to implement because it involves less commitment in managerial time and effort.

Diversity Among Decision Makers

Another way to improve group decision making is to promote diversity in decision making groups (Chapter 5).[75] Bringing together managers of both genders from various ethnic, national and functional backgrounds broadens the range of life experiences and opinions – Senge's *mental models* – that group members can draw on as they generate, assess and choose among alternatives. Diverse groups are sometimes less prone to groupthink because group members already differ from each other and so are less subject to pressures for uniformity.

Organisational Learning and Creativity

The quality of managerial decision making ultimately depends on innovative responses to opportunities and threats. How can managers increase their ability to make non-programmed decisions, decisions that will allow them to adapt to, modify and even drastically alter their task environments so that they can continually increase organisational performance? The answer is by encouraging **organisational learning**.[76]

Organisational learning is the process through which managers seek to improve employees' desire and ability to understand and manage the organisation and its task environment so that they can make decisions that continuously raise organisational effectiveness. A **learning organisation** is one in which managers do everything possible to maximise the ability of individuals and groups to think and behave creatively and thus maximise the potential for organisational learning to take place. At the heart of organisational learning is **creativity**, the ability of a decision maker to discover original and novel ideas that lead to feasible alternative courses of action. Encouraging creativity among managers is such a pressing organisational concern that many organisations hire outside experts to help them develop programmes to train their managers in the art of creative thinking and problem solving.

Creating a Learning Organisation

How do managers go about creating a learning organisation? Learning theorist Peter Senge identified five key principles (Fig. 7.7):[77]

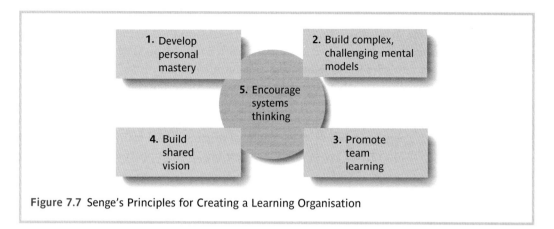

Figure 7.7 Senge's Principles for Creating a Learning Organisation

1. For organisational learning to occur, senior managers must allow every person in the organisation to develop a sense of *personal mastery*. Managers must empower employees and allow them to experiment and create and explore whatever they want.

2. As part of attaining personal mastery, organisations need to encourage employees to develop and use *complex mental models* – sophisticated ways of thinking that challenge them to find new or better ways of performing a task – to deepen their understanding of what is involved in a particular activity. Here Senge is arguing that managers must encourage employees to develop a taste for *experimenting* and *risk taking*.[78]

3. Managers must do everything they can to promote group creativity. Senge thinks that *team learning* (learning that takes place in a group or team) is more important than individual learning: he points out that many important decisions are made in subunits such as groups, functions and divisions.

4. Managers must emphasise the importance of *building a shared vision* – a common mental model that all organisational members use to frame problems or opportunities.

5. Managers must encourage *systems thinking* (a concept drawn from systems theory, discussed in Chapter 2). Senge emphasises that to create a learning organisation managers must recognise the effects of one level of learning on another. For example, there is little point in creating teams to facilitate team learning if managers do not also take steps to give employees the freedom to develop a sense of personal mastery.

Building a learning organisation requires that managers radically change their management assumptions. Developing a learning organisation is neither a quick nor an easy process. Senge has been working with Ford Motor Company to help managers make Ford a learning organisation. Why does Ford want this? Senior management believes that to compete successfully, the company must improve its members' ability to be creative and make the right decisions.

Increasingly, managers are being called on to promote global organisational learning. Managers at ASDA, for example, use the lessons derived from its failures and successes in one country to promote global organisational learning across the many countries in which it now operates. For instance, when Wal-Mart, owner of ASDA supermarkets, entered Malaysia, it was convinced customers there would respond to its one-stop shopping format. It found, however, that Malaysians enjoy the social experience of shopping in a lively market or bazaar and thus did not like the impersonal efficiency of the typical Wal-Mart store. Wal-Mart has learned the importance of designing store layouts to appeal specifically to the customers of each country in which it operates.

When purchasing and operating a chain of stores, such as the ASDA chain, in another country Wal-Mart now strives to retain what customers value in the local market while taking advantage of all of its own accumulated organisational learning. Wal-Mart improved ASDA's IT used for inventory and sales tracking in stores and enrolled ASDA in Wal-Mart's global purchasing operations, which has enabled the chain to pay less for certain products, sell them for less and, overall, significantly increase sales. At the same time, Wal-Mart empowered local ASDA managers to run the stores; as the president of ASDA indicates: 'This is still essentially a British business in the way it's run day to day.'[79] Clearly, global organisational learning is essential for companies such as Wal-Mart that have significant operations in multiple countries.

Promoting Individual Creativity

Research suggests that when certain conditions are met, managers are more likely to be creative. As just discussed, people must be given the opportunity and freedom to generate new ideas. Creativity declines when managers look over the shoulders of talented employees and try to 'hurry up' a creative solution: how would you feel if your boss said you had one week to come up with a new product idea to beat the competition? Creativity results when employees have an opportunity to experiment, to take risks and to make mistakes and learn from them. Employees must not fear that they will be looked down on or penalised for ideas that might at first seem peculiar: it is sometimes the ideas that initially seem strange that yield truly innovative products and services, as indicated in Case 7.4.

Case 7.4: Asking different questions and providing different answers

Ideas for truly creative goods, products and services sometimes come from asking different kinds of questions and seeking different kinds of answers. When George Ohr discovered the wonders of making clay pots at a potter's wheel in the late 1800s, he learned as much as he could about pots and then proceeded to question everything that people at the time thought pots should look like and provided answers in his own unique form of pottery art.[80]

Disdained at the time, Ohr's pottery is now so revered for its creativity and beauty that his pots command five-digit prices and famed architect Frank Gehry is designing a museum (opening in 2006) in Ohr's honour to display his work.[81] Ohr turned pot making on its head. Each of his pots was unique: he would form perfect shapes and then crumple them like newspaper; he would make delicate, paper-thin pots; he carved writings into his pots; and he used bright, bold colours – all unheard of at the time and hailed as innovations decades later. It was only after Ohr's death that the art world recognised the genius and beauty in his work, which came from his unique answers to the question of pottery as an art form.

Asking the right questions and providing different kinds of answers can lead to creativity in other arenas as well.[82] Denmark, the acclaimed design hotspot in Europe, has seen the launch of a design award with a difference. Usually design awards are given to people who create a new product with particularly appealing aesthetical features: the new INDEX: awards have taken a step back from the at times elitist world of design awards. Rather than limiting their definition of design, the INDEX: jury highlighted the fact that good design has to have a direct and immediate impact on improving our lives. So by asking the right question – i.e. to improve lives – but framing it in a design context, the organisers managed to attract over 500 entries. There were five winners that encapsulate the 'thinking outside the box' that underlines INDEX:

philosophy. Typically cool-looking, well-functioning products were amongst the winners, but most were far more unusual. One of the winners recognised by the INDEX: judges, for example, was a successful programme that helps Latin American craftspeople produce better products and sell them more successfully around the world. Even more surprising was the selection of a programme to build football fields in southern Africa whose clubhouses will double as local HIV/AIDS counselling and treatment centres (opening in late 2006). While some of the design and solutions may not yield immediate returns, the organisers feel that such creative ideas can serve as inspiration to others – taking design to a higher level.[83]

Highly innovative companies like 3M (who brought us the Post-it note) are well known for the wide degree of freedom they give their managers and employees to ask different questions and seek their own answers. At 3M, employees are expected to spend a certain percentage of their time on projects of their own choosing, a policy that fosters creativity. Once managers have generated alternatives, creativity can be fostered by providing them with constructive feedback so that they know how well they are doing. Ideas that seem to be going nowhere can be eliminated and creative energies refocused in other directions. Ideas that seem promising can be promoted, and help from other managers can also be obtained.[84]

Senior managers must also stress the importance of looking for alternative solutions and should visibly reward employees who come up with creative ideas. Being creative can be demanding and stressful: employees who believe that they are working on important, vital issues are motivated to give the high levels of effort that creativity demands. Creative people like to receive the acclaim of others, and innovative organisations have many kinds of ceremonies and rewards to recognise creative employees. 3M established the 'Carlton Hall of Fame' to recognise successful innovators. These employees not only become members of the Hall of Fame but also receive financial rewards through the Golden Step programme, a financial reward system for achieving sales of a new product over a specific target.

Source: A. Brand, 'Knowledge Management and Innovation at 3M', *Journal of Knowledge Management* 2 (1) (September 1998), 17–22.

Promoting Group Creativity

To encourage creativity at the group level, organisations can make use of *group problem solving techniques* that promote creative ideas and innovative solutions. These techniques can also be used to prevent groupthink and to help managers uncover bias. Here, three group decision-making techniques are examined: brainstorming, the **nominal group technique** and the **Delphi technique**.

Brainstorming

Brainstorming is a group problem-solving technique in which managers meet face-to-face to generate and debate a wide variety of alternatives from which to make a decision.[85] Generally, from 5 to 15 managers meet in a closed-door session and proceed as follows:

- One manager outlines the problem the group is to address.
- Group members then share their ideas and generate alternative courses of action.
- As each alternative is described, group members are not allowed to criticise it: everyone withholds judgement until all alternatives have been heard; one member of the group records the alternatives on a flip chart.
- Group members are encouraged to be as innovative and radical as possible: anything goes, and the greater the number of ideas put forward, the better; group members are encouraged to 'piggyback' or build on each other's suggestions.

- When all alternatives have been generated, group members debate the pros and cons of each and develop a short list of the best alternatives.

Brainstorming is very useful in some problem-solving situations – for example, when managers are trying to find a new name for a perfume or for a model of car. Sometimes, however, individuals working alone can generate more alternatives. The main reason for the loss of productivity in brainstorming appears to be **production blocking**, which occurs because group members cannot always simultaneously make sense of all the alternatives being generated, think up additional alternatives and remember what they were thinking.[86]

Nominal group technique

To avoid production blocking, the *nominal group technique* is often used. It provides a more structured way of generating alternatives in writing and gives each manager more time and opportunity to come up with potential solutions. The nominal group technique is especially useful when an issue is controversial and when different managers might be expected to champion different courses of action. Generally, a small group of managers meet in a closed-door session and adopt the following procedures:

- One manager outlines the problem to be addressed, and 30 or 40 minutes are allocated for group members, working individually, to write down their ideas and solutions. Group members are encouraged to be innovative.

- Managers take turns reading their suggestions to the group. One manager writes all the alternatives on a flip chart. No criticism or evaluation of alternatives is allowed until all alternatives have been read.

- The alternatives are then discussed, one by one, in the sequence in which they were first proposed. Group members can ask for clarifying information and critique each alternative to identify its pros and cons.

- When all alternatives have been discussed, each group member ranks all the alternatives from most preferred to least preferred, and the alternative that receives the highest ranking is chosen.[87]

Delphi technique

Both the nominal group technique and brainstorming require that managers meet together to generate creative ideas and engage in joint problem solving. What happens if managers are in different cities or in different parts of the world and cannot meet face to face? *Videoconferencing* is one way to bring distant managers together to brainstorm. Another way is to use the *Delphi technique*, a written approach to creative problem solving.[88] The Delphi technique works like this:

- The group leader writes a statement of the problem and a series of questions to which participating managers are to respond.

- The questionnaire is sent to the managers and departmental experts who are most knowledgeable about the problem; they are asked to generate solutions and mail the questionnaire back to the group leader.

- A team of senior managers records and summarises the responses; the results are then sent back to the participants, with additional questions to be answered before a decision can be made.

- The process is repeated until a consensus is reached and the most suitable course of action is apparent.

Promoting Creativity at the Global Level

The Delphi technique is particularly useful when barriers of time and distance – a situation that is common in the global environment – separate managers. Organisations are under increasing pressure to reduce costs and develop global products; to do so, they typically centralise their R&D expertise by bringing R&D managers together at one location. Encouraging creativity among teams of R&D experts from different countries, however, poses special problems. First, such experts often have difficulty communicating their ideas to one another because of language problems and cultural differences in their approaches to problem solving. Second, the decision making process differs from country to country. In Japan, for example, decisions tend to be made in a very participative manner and the group as a whole must agree on a course of action before a decision is made. In contrast, in Mexico decision making is very centralised; senior managers decide what to do with little input from subordinates.

Managers must take special steps to encourage creativity among people from different countries who are supposed to be working together. They must develop training programmes that promote awareness and understanding so that diverse individuals can co-operate and brainstorm new ideas and approaches to problems, opportunities and threats.

Summary and Review

The nature of managerial decision making Programmed decisions are routine decisions made so often that managers have developed decision rules to be followed automatically. Non-programmed decisions are made in response to situations that are unusual or novel; they are non-routine decisions. The classical model of decision making assumes that decision makers have complete information, are able to process that information in an objective, rational manner and can make optimum decisions. March and Simon argue that managers are boundedly rational, rarely have access to all the information they need to make optimum decisions and, consequently, satisfice and rely on their intuition and judgement when making decisions.

Steps in the decision-making process When making decisions, managers should take six steps: recognise the need for a decision, generate alternatives, assess alternatives, choose among alternatives, implement the chosen alternative and learn from feedback.

Cognitive bias and decision making Most of the time, managers are fairly good decision makers. On occasion, however, problems can result because human judgement can be adversely affected by the operation of cognitive bias that results in poor decisions. Cognitive bias is caused by systematic errors in the way decision makers process information and make decisions. Sources of such error include prior hypotheses, representativeness, the illusion of control and escalating commitment. Managers should undertake a *personal decision audit* to become aware of their biases and thus improve their decision making.

Group decision making Many advantages can be associated with group decision making, but there are also several disadvantages. One major source of poor decision making is groupthink. Afflicted decision makers collectively embark on a dubious course of action without questioning the assumptions that underlie their decision. Managers can improve ▶

▶ the quality of group decision making by using techniques such as devil's advocacy and dialectical inquiry and by increasing diversity in the decision-making group.

Organisational learning and creativity Organisational learning is the process through which managers seek to improve employees' desire and ability to understand and manage the organisation and its task environment so that they can make decisions that continuously raise organisational effectiveness. Managers must take steps to promote organisational learning and creativity at the individual and group levels to improve the quality of decision making.

Reaction Time

1. Why do capable managers sometimes make bad decisions? What can individual managers do to improve their decision-making skills?

2. In what kinds of groups is groupthink most likely to be a problem? When is it least likely to be a problem? What steps can group members take to avoid groupthink?

3. What is organisational learning, and how can managers promote it?

Topic for Action

- Ask a manager to recall the best and the worst decisions he or she ever made. Try to determine why these decisions were so good or so bad.

- Think about an organisation in your local community, your university or an organisation that you are familiar with that is doing poorly. Now come up with questions their managers in this organisation should ask stakeholders to elicit creative ideas for turning around the organisation's fortunes.

Applied Independent Learning

Building Management Skills

How Do You Make Decisions?

Pick a decision that you made recently and that has had important consequences for you. It may be your decision about which college to attend, which subject to select, whether to take a part-time job, or which part-time job to take. Using the material in this chapter, analyse the way in which you made the decision – in particular:

1. Identify the criteria you used, either consciously or unconsciously, to guide your decision making.

2. List the alternatives you considered. Were they all possible alternatives? Did you unconsciously (or consciously) ignore some important alternatives?

3. How much information did you have about each alternative? Were you making the decision on the basis of complete or incomplete information?

4. Try to remember how you reached the decision. Did you sit down and consciously think through the implications of each alternative, or did you make the decision on the basis of intuition? Did you use any rules of thumb to help you make the decision?

5. In retrospect, do you think that your choice of alternative was shaped by any of the types of cognitive bias discussed in this chapter?

6. Having answered questions 1–5, do you think in retrospect that you made a reasonable decision? What, if anything, might you do to improve your ability to make good decisions in the future?

Managing Ethically

Sometimes groups make *extreme decisions* – decisions that are either more risky or more conservative than they would have been if individuals acting alone had made them. One explanation for the tendency of groups to make extreme decisions is diffusion of responsibility. In a group, responsibility for the outcomes of a decision is spread among group members, so each person feels less than fully accountable: the group's decision is extreme because no individual has taken full responsibility for it.

Questions

1. Either alone or in a group, think about the ethical implications of extreme decision making by groups.

2. When group decision making takes place, should members of the group each feel fully accountable for outcomes of the decision? Why or why not?

Small Group Breakout Exercise

Brainstorming

Form groups of three or four people, and appoint one member as the spokesperson who will communicate your findings to the whole class when called on by the instructor. Then discuss the following scenario.

You and your partners are trying to decide which kind of restaurant to open in a centrally located shopping centre that has just been built in your city. The problem confronting you is that the city already has many restaurants that provide different kinds of food at all price ranges. You have the resources to open any type of restaurant. Your challenge is to decide which type is most likely to succeed.

Use the brainstorming technique to decide which type of restaurant to open. Follow these three steps:

1. As a group, spend 5 or 10 minutes generating ideas about the alternative restaurants that the members think will be most likely to succeed. Each group member should be as innovative and creative as possible, and no suggestions should be criticised.

▶

▶ 2. Appoint one group member to write down the alternatives as they are identified.

3. Spend the next 10 or 15 minutes debating the pros and cons of the alternatives. As a group, try to reach a consensus on which alternative is most likely to succeed.

After making your decision, discuss the pros and cons of the brainstorming method, and decide whether any production blocking occurred.

When called on by the instructor, the spokesperson should be prepared to share your group's decision with the class, as well as the reasons the group made its decision.

Application in Today's Business World

The Brains Behind BlackBerry

They are the odd couple of the wireless world. One is a Turkish-born whiz kid who grew up across the border from Detroit and later dropped out of college to build an industrial display network for General Motors Corp. (GM), the other, an ambitious tradesman's son from rural Ontario who glided through one of Canada's top colleges and Harvard Business School before settling into corporate life. But as co-chief executives of Research in Motion Ltd. (RIM), Mike Lazaridis and Jim Balsillie, both 43, are the quiet men behind the hottest wireless email gadget around: the BlackBerry. Among the million-plus subscribers are such reported fans as Jeb Bush, Bill Gates, Sarah Jessica Parker and Jack Welch. From the near-constant clicking in the halls of Congress to its spot on Oprah Winfrey's 'favourite things of 2003' list, the BlackBerry has become almost shorthand for wireless email itself.

The addictive little devices, introduced in early 1999, defy many of the stereotypes of high-tech. They were spawned far from Silicon Valley in Waterloo, Ont., a quiet university town of 99,000 about an hour's drive west of Toronto. And RIM is no glitzy startup; Lazaridis founded it two decades ago to consult and develop technologies like the film bar-code readers that would eventually win him a technical Emmy and an Oscar.

Still, nothing has ever rocked RIM and its hometown like the BlackBerry. The brand has become the industry standard, far better known than its cryptically named parent, and a cultural icon to boot. Every major carrier wants to offer it to its customers. Everyone wants to work there. And that stock price! It roared from $12.75 to $108 in 2002–03, and on 7 April the company announced a two-for-one split. Lazaridis' stake was worth $782 million, while Balsillie's came to $674 million. Even so, Balsillie banned staff from checking the price at the office.

Instead, the co-CEOs have obsessed over the core product: email that is automatically pushed to the BlackBerry as it's going to the desktop and can be instantly answered with an intuitive, thumb-operated keyboard. Notes Andy Brown, chief technology architect at Merrill Lynch & Co.: 'People don't want wireless email. They want a BlackBerry.' But that may not always be so. The duo have forged deals with companies ranging from Microsoft Corp. to Palm-Source, Inc. to license BlackBerry software. Think 'Intel Inside'. And they signed a deal with Sun Microsystems, Inc. to extend wireless Web services to BlackBerry customers. The goal, says Balsillie, is 'to enable wireless email whenever and on whatever device people want'.

But RIM's quirky duo are hardly alone in their passion for wireless email. They face competition ranging from pocket PC devices to similar hand-helds put out by Good Technology, Inc., which just settled a patent lawsuit with RIM and agreed to pay royalties for using its technology. And they have their own legal battles with Virginia's NTP, Inc., which alleges that RIM and numerous other wireless email operators infringed its 1990 patents. RIM lost the first round in court; the case is on appeal.

'Science is the Core'

Still, the company's main challenge at the moment may be gearing up for explosive growth. With added features like voice, colour screens and international roaming, analysts predict that the number of customers could easily double in 2003, to 2 million. On 7 April RIM said its subscriber base had increased by 24 per cent, to almost 1.1 million, in the fourth quarter ended 28 February. It also reported sales of $210.6 million, up 37 per cent from the previous quarter, while profits rose 255 per cent, to $41.5 million.

Those who know RIM attribute much of its success to the complementary relationship of its co-CEOs. Without Lazaridis, the silverhaired science buff who once won a special award from his public school for checking every science and maths book out of the library, RIM would have no technology. 'Science is the core of everything, yet we take it for granted,' he says. And without Balsillie, the business maven who as a young father mortgaged his house and poured much of his net worth into Lazaridis' fledgling operation in 1992, it would have far less commercial success. As he puts it: 'People capitalise on opportunities. They don't create them.' He is the corporate strategist, the financial wizard, the negotiator and the face of the company on Wall Street. Lazaridis is the science mastermind, the production guru, the dreamer and the one who solves customers' problems. He likes to frequent physics lectures and read books like *Sojourner: An Insider's View of the Mars Pathfinder Mission*. But his real hobby is, well, thinking about RIM. Balsillie coaches his son's basketball team, races into Toronto for the Maple Leafs' hockey games and cherishes time in his cottage on Georgian Bay.

Despite such obvious differences, though, the two men share some important similarities. First is their conviction, stretching back a decade, that people would one day want constant access to email through a device they could hook on their belts. Balsillie, who joined the then-tiny outfit when Lazaridis wooed him from a customer to manage the business in 1992, calls email 'one of the most profound medium shifts we'll ever see'. Lazaridis never doubted it for a minute. Even now, he gets visibly exasperated when RIM is treated like some kind of here-today-gone-tomorrow dot-com. 'We've passed all the initiation by fire to get to 20 years old,' he says, noting that RIM went public in 1998 and has a market capitalization of almost $10 billion.

They are equally relentless about pushing the BlackBerry. In 1999, they were so sure that it would just take a few days with one to get hooked that they hired 'evangelists' to lend the devices out to executives on Wall Street. That helped the no-name Canadian company win contracts with a number of big firms. 'You immediately saw everyone get it,' recalls Leonard G. Rosen, a technology banker and managing director at Lehman Brothers, Inc., which works with RIM. Soon, the company decided to let the network carriers offer BlackBerries to their customers. The payoff for RIM is clear: 65 per cent plus margins on the service and 35 per cent plus margins on the hardware, according to analyst Deepak Chopra of National Bank Financial.

Both men are building a legacy beyond the BlackBerry. Lazardis donated about $100 million (Canadian) in stock to start Waterloo's Perimeter Institute for Theoretical Physics in 2000, while Balsillie gave $30 million to start the Centre for International Governance Innovation two years later. But they're nowhere near retirement. Defending RIM's niche will take all of Balsillie's strategic smarts. This odd couple is smack in the middle of the hot zone.   ▶

> ▶ **Questions**
>
> 1. What factors are responsible for the success of BlackBerry?
>
> 2. What are Lazaridis' and Balsillie's distinctive qualities as senior managers and decision makers?
>
> 3. Up to this point, these two senior managers at RIM have seemed to make good decisions. Why do you think they have been successful?
>
> 4. Looking to the future, what challenges will RIM, BlackBerry and Lazaridis and Balsillie face? Do you think these co-CEOs are up for the challenge and will continue to make decisions that contribute to the success of RIM and BlackBerry? Why or why not?
>
> *Source*: D. Brady, 'The Brains Behind BlackBerry', adapted and reprinted from *BusinessWeek*, April 19, 2004 by special permission. Copyright © 2004 by the McGraw-Hill Companies, Inc.

Notes and References

1   M. Arndt, 'Pharmaceuticals: For Drugmakers, There's No Panacea', *BusinessWeek online*, January 12, 2004, www.businessweek.com:/print/magazine/content/04_02/b3865615.htm?mz; M. Boyle, 'AMGEN', *Fortune*, April 9, 2004, www.fortune.com/fortune/subs/print/0,15935,612314,00.html.

2   P. O'Connell, ed., 'What's Next for Pharma?' *BusinessWeek online* January 5, 2004, www.businessweek.com:/print/technology/content/jan2.../tc2004015_0769_tc074.htm?t.

3   K. Kelleher, 'The Drug Pipeline Flows Again', *Business 2.0*, April 2004, 50–51.

4   *Ibid.*

5   'Tachi Yamada, M.D.', www.forbes.com, Person Tearsheet, May 6, 2004, www.forbes.com/FromMktGuideIdPersonTearsheet.jhtml?passesMktGuided ID=47566.

6   Kelleher, 'The Drug Pipeline Flows Again'.

7   *Ibid.*

8   *Ibid.*

9   *Ibid.*

10 *Ibid.*

11 J. Simons, 'Merck's Man in the Hot Seat', *Fortune*, February 23, 2004, 111–14.

12 'Tadataka Yamada (Aged 58) Executive Director, Chairman Research & Development Appointed to the Board on 1st January 2004', GlaxoSmithKline, May 6, 2004, www.gsk.com/bios/bio_yamada.htm.

13 Simons, 'Merck's Man in the Hot Seat'.

14 Kelleher, 'The Drug Pipeline Flows Again'.

15 G. P. Huber, *Managerial Decision Making* (Glenview, IL: Scott, Foresman, 1993).

16 Kelleher, 'The Drug Pipeline Flows Again'.

17 http://www.bized.ac.uk/compfact/easyjet/easyindex.htm.

18 *Sunday Times*, 2 October 2005.

19 S. M. Dornbusch and W. R. Scott, *Evaluation and the Exercise of Authority* (San Francisco: Jossey-Bass, 1975).

20 J. Child, *Organization: A Guide to Problems and Practice* (London: Harper & Row, 1984).

21 www.dhl.com.

22 *Ibid.*

23 www.boeing.com.

24 H. A. Simon, *The New Science of Management* (Englewood Cliffs, NJ: Prentice Hall, 1977).

25 D. Kahneman, 'Maps of Bounded Rationality: A Perspective on Intuitive Judgment and Choice', Prize Lecture, December 8, 2002; E. Jaffe, 'What Was I Thinking? Kahneman Explains How Intuition Leads Us Astray', *American Psychological Society* 17 (5) (May 2004), 23–26.

26   P. Senge, *The Fifth Discipline: The Art and Practice of the Learning Organization* (New York: Doubleday, 1990).

27   Kahneman, 'Maps of Bounded Rationality'; Jaffe, 'What Was I Thinking?'.

28   J. Smutniak, 'Freud, Finance and Folly: Human Intuition Is a Bad Guide to Handling Risk', *The Economist* 24 (January 2004), 5–6.

29   J. Pfeffer, 'Curbing the Urge to Merge', *Business 2.0*, July 2003, 58.

30   Smutniak, 'Freud, Finance and Folly'.

31   Pfeffer, 'Curbing the Urge to Merge'; Smutniak, 'Freud, Finance and Folly'.

32   Pfeffer, 'Curbing the Urge to Merge'.

33   *Ibid.*

34   H. A. Simon, *Administrative Behavior* (New York: Macmillan, 1947).

35   *Ibid.*

36   H. A. Simon, *Models of Man* (New York: Wiley, 1957).

37   K. J. Arrow, *Aspects of the Theory of Risk Bearing* (Helsinki: Yrjo Johnssonis Saatio, 1965).

38   *Ibid.*

39   http://www.speedace.info/red_bull.htm; http://www.bized.ac.uk/.

40   R. L. Daft and R. H. Lengel, 'Organizational Information Requirements, Media Richness and Structural Design', *Management Science* 32 (1986), 554–71.

41   Simons, 'Merck's Man in the Hot Seat'.

42   R. Cyert and J. March, *Behavioral Theory of the Firm* (Englewood Cliffs, NJ: Prentice Hall, 1963).

43   J. G. March and H. A. Simon, *Organizations* (New York: Wiley, 1958).

44   H. A. Simon, 'Making Management Decisions: The Role of Intuition and Emotion', *Academy of Management Executive* 1 (1987), 57–64.

45   M. H. Bazerman, *Judgment in Managerial Decision Making* (New York: Wiley, 1986). See also Simon, *Administrative Behavior*.

46   *Sunday Times*, 9 October 2005.

47   Bazerman, *Judgment in Managerial Decision Making*; Huber, *Managerial Decision Making*; J. E. Russo and P. J. Schoemaker, *Decision Traps* (New York: Simon & Schuster, 1989).

48   M. D. Cohen, J. G. March and J. P. Olsen, 'A Garbage Can Model of Organizational Choice', *Administrative Science Quarterly* 17 (1972), 1–25.

49   *Ibid.*

50   Bazerman, *Judgment in Managerial Decision Making*.

51   Senge, *The Fifth Discipline*.

52   E. de Bono, *Lateral Thinking* (London: Penguin, 1968); Senge, *The Fifth Discipline*.

53   Russo and Schoemaker, *Decision Traps*.

54   Bazerman, *Judgment in Managerial Decision Making*.

55   B. Berger, 'NASA: One Year After *Columbia* – Bush's New Vision Changes Agency's Course Mid-stream', *Space News Business Report*, January 26, 2004, www.space.com/spacenews/businessmonday_040126.html.

56   *Ibid.*

57   P. Reinert, 'Study by NASA Executives Supports *Columbia* Panel', *Houston Chronicle*, February 11, 2004, 6A.

58   *Ibid.*

59   J. Glanz and J. Schwartz, 'Dogged Engineer's Effort to Assess Shuttle Damage', *The New York Times*, September 26, 2003, A1.

60   M. L. Wald and J. Schwartz, 'NASA Chief Promises a Shift in Attitude', *The New York Times*, August 28, 2003, A23.

61   M. Dunn, 'Remaking NASA One Step at a Time', July 3, 2004, www.msnbc.msn.com/id/3158779, July 3, 2004.

62   M. Dunn, 'NASA Lags in Shuttle Patch Development', www.sunherald.com/mld/sunherald/news/photos/8966629.htm?template=cont, June 19, 2004.

63 Russo and Schoemaker, *Decision Traps*.

64 D. Kahneman and A. Tversky, 'Judgment Under Uncertainty: Heuristics and Biases', *Science* 185 (1974), 1124–31.

65 C. R. Schwenk, 'Cognitive Simplification Processes in Strategic Decision Making', *Strategic Management Journal* 5 (1984), 111–28.

66 An interesting example of the illusion of control is Richard Roll's hubris hypothesis of takeovers. See R. Roll, 'The Hubris Hypothesis of Corporate Takeovers', *Journal of Business* 59 (1986), 197–216.

67 B. M. Staw, 'The Escalation of Commitment to a Course of Action', *Academy of Management Review* 6 (1981), 577–87.

68 M. J. Tang, 'An Economic Perspective on Escalating Commitment', *Strategic Management Journal* 9 (1988), 79–92.

69 Russo and Schoemaker, *Decision Traps*.

70 http://www.bma.org.uk/ap.nsf/Content/ITNatprog.

71 I. L. Janis, *Groupthink: Psychological Studies of Policy Decisions and Disasters*, 2nd ed. (Boston: Houghton Mifflin, 1982).

72 C. R. Schwenk, *The Essence of Strategic Decision Making* (Lexington, MA: Lexington Books, 1988).

73 R. O. Mason, 'A Dialectic Approach to Strategic Planning', *Management Science* 13 (1969), 403–14; R. A. Cosier and J. C. Aplin, 'A Critical View of Dialectic Inquiry in Strategic Planning', *Strategic Management Journal* 1 (1980), 343–56; I. I. Mitroff and R. O. Mason, 'Structuring III – Structured Policy Issues: Further Explorations in a Methodology for Messy Problems', *Strategic Management Journal* 1 (1980), 331–42.

74 D. M. Schweiger and P. A. Finger, 'The Comparative Effectiveness of Dialectic Inquiry and Devil's Advocacy', *Strategic Management Journal* 5 (1984), 335–50.

75 Mary C. Gentile, *Differences That Work: Organizational Excellence Through Diversity* (Boston: Harvard Business School Press, 1994); F. Rice, 'How to Make Diversity Pay', *Fortune*, August 8, 1994, 78–86.

76 B. Hedberg, 'How Organizations Learn and Unlearn', in W. H. Starbuck and P. C. Nystrom, eds., *Handbook of Organizational Design*, 1 (New York: Oxford University Press, 1981), 1–27.

77 Senge, *The Fifth Discipline*.

78 P. M. Senge, 'The Leader's New Work: Building Learning Organizations', *Sloan Management Review*, Fall 1990, 7–23.

79 W. Zellner, K. A. Schmidt, M. Ihlwan and H. Dawley, 'How Well Does Wal-Mart Travel?', *BusinessWeek*, September 3, 2001, 82–84.

80 B. Watson, 'The Mad Potter of Biloxi', *Smithsonian*, February 2004, 88–94.

81 *Ibid.*

82 'Expect the Unexpected', *Economist Technology Quarterly*, September 6, 2003, 5.

83 *BusinessWeek online*, 27 September 2005.

84 R. W. Woodman, J. E. Sawyer and R. W. Griffin, 'Towards a Theory of Organizational Creativity', *Academy of Management Review* 18 (1993), 293–321.

85 T. J. Bouchard, Jr., J. Barsaloux and G. Drauden, 'Brainstorming Procedure, Group Size, and Sex as Determinants of Problem Solving Effectiveness of Individuals and Groups', *Journal of Applied Psychology* 59 (1974), 135–38.

86 M. Diehl and W. Stroebe, 'Productivity Loss in Brainstorming Groups: Towards the Solution of a Riddle', *Journal of Personality and Social Psychology* 53 (1987), 497–509.

87 D. H. Gustafson, R. K. Shulka, A. Delbecq and W. G. Walster, 'A Comparative Study of Differences in Subjective Likelihood Estimates Made by Individuals, Interacting Groups, Delphi Groups, and Nominal Groups', *Organizational Behavior and Human Performance* 9 (1973), 280–91.

88 N. Dalkey, *The Delphi Method: An Experimental Study of Group Decision Making* (Santa Monica, CA: Rand Corp., 1989).

Chapter 8

The Manager as a Planner and Strategist

LEARNING OBJECTIVES

After studying this chapter, you should be able to:

☑ Describe the three steps of the planning process and the relationship between planning and strategy.

☑ Explain the role of planning in predicting the future and in mobilising organisational resources to meet future contingencies.

☑ Outline the main steps in SWOT analysis.

☑ Differentiate among corporate-, business- and functional-level strategies.

☑ Describe the vital role played by strategy implementation in determining managers' ability to achieve an organisation's mission and goals.

A Manager's Challenge

How to Compete in the Soft-Drink Business

What is the best way to compete in an industry?

Coca-Cola and Pepsi-Cola are household names worldwide. Together they control over 70 per cent of the global soft-drink market. Their success can be attributed in part to the overall strategy that Coca-Cola and PepsiCo developed to produce and promote their products. Both companies decided to build global brands by manufacturing the soft-drink concentrate that gives cola its flavour and then selling the concentrate in a syrup form to bottlers throughout the world. Coca-Cola and PepsiCo charge the bottlers a premium price for the syrup; they then invest part of the proceeds in advertising to build and maintain brand awareness. The bottlers are responsible for producing and distributing the product. They add carbonated water to the syrup, package the resulting drink and distribute it to vending machines, supermarkets, restaurants and other retail outlets.

The bottlers leave all the advertising to Coca-Cola and PepsiCo. In addition, the bottlers must sign an exclusive agreement that prohibits them from distributing competing cola brands. A Coke or Pepsi bottler cannot bottle any other cola drink. This strategy has two major advantages for Coca-Cola and PepsiCo. First, it forces bottlers to enter into exclusive agreements, which create a high barrier to entry into the industry; any potential competitors that might want to produce and distribute a new cola product must create their own distribution network rather than use the existing network. Second, the large amount of money spent on advertising (in 2003, both companies spent over £287 million each) to develop a global brand name has helped Coca-Cola and PepsiCo differentiate their products so that consumers are more likely to buy a Coke or a Pepsi rather than a lesser-known cola. This is further enhanced by using celebrity endorsements that are relevant for each country (for example the use of David Beckham, who, during the 2002 World Cup, was advertising both soft drinks[1]), or Pepsi's football table advert, using a number of famous international players that widens the country-specific appeal. Brand loyalty allows both companies to charge a premium or comparatively high price for what is, after all, merely coloured water and flavouring. This differentiation strategy has made Coca-Cola and PepsiCo two of the most profitable companies in the world.

In the last decade the global soft-drink environment has undergone major changes due to the entrepreneurial skills of the then CEO of Cott Corporation, Gerald Pencer. Cott is one of the world's largest suppliers of retailer-branded carbonated soft drinks and supplies some of the biggest food retailers and wholesalers in the UK, as well as a large number of leading retailers throughout Europe. It has 19 manufacturing facilities in Canada, the US, Mexico and the UK and a syrup concentrate production plant in Columbus, Georgia, that supplies most of the private-label grocery stores, chemist outlets, mass-merchandising and convenience store chains in these countries. In successfully capturing the retailer brands, Cott has created a leadership position in the international soft drinks market by providing high-quality retailer brand drinks to the benefit of discerning customers.[2]

The UK/European division of Cott now employs over 700 employees and operates three beverage production facilities in the UK. In 2005 Cott UK/Europe led the company's sales growth with an increase of 30 per cent with sales of £228 million. This was partly due to a diversification strategy of including the production of Hi-energy drinks and a premium organic fruit carbonate. Such changes led to the acquisition of Macaw Soft Drinks Company in 2005 and Cott grossed £163 million at the year end. The UK CEO, John Sheppard, announced that '2006 will be an important transition year, as we are pursuing a number of specific initiatives including a disciplined and strategic approach to pricing, sourcing and supply chain efficiencies etc.'.

In the early 1990s Pencer came up with a new plan for competing in the cola market and created a new strategy to attract customers. Pencer's strategy was to produce a high-quality, low-priced cola, manufactured and bottled by the Cott Corporation, and sell directly to major retail establishments (such as supermarket chains) as a private-label 'house brand', thus bypassing the bottlers. Retailers were attracted to Cott's cola and other soft-drink flavours because its low cost allowed them to make more profit than they received from selling Coke or Pepsi while building their store brand image.

To implement his strategy, Pencer decided to spend no money on advertising (so that he could charge a lower price for the soft drinks) but instead took advantage of efficient national distribution systems that giant retailers such as ASDA have created in recent years. This low-cost strategy enabled Cott to circumvent the barrier to entry created by the exclusive distribution agreements that Coca-Cola and PepsiCo had signed with their bottlers. Pencer went on to supply an international market by offering to sell soft-drinks concentrate at prices lower than Coca-Cola and PepsiCo charged. In April 1994, for example, Cott launched a cola product in Britain for Sainsbury's, one of Britain's largest supermarkets. The product was sold as 'Sainsbury's Classic Cola' and was priced 30 per cent below Coke and Pepsi.[3]

Overview

As the beginning of the chapter suggests, there is more than one way to compete in an industry, and to find a viable way to enter and compete in an industry, managers must study the way other organisations behave and identify their strategies. By studying the strategies of Coca-Cola and PepsiCo, Cott were able to devise a strategy that allowed them to enter the cola industry and take on these global giants; so far, Cott has had considerable success.

In an uncertain competitive environment, managers must engage in thorough planning to find a strategy that will allow them to compete effectively. This chapter explores the manager's role both as *planner* and as *strategist*. The different elements involved in the planning process will be discussed, including its three major steps: (1) determining an organisation's mission and major goals, (2) choosing strategies to realise the mission and goals and (3) selecting the appropriate way of organising resources to implement the strategies. Further discussion points in this chapter concern two important techniques that managers can use in their analysis of situations: scenario planning and SWOT analysis. By the end of this chapter, you will understand the role managers play in the planning and strategy making process to create high-performing organisations.

The Nature of the Planning Process

Planning, as was noted in Chapter 1, is a process that managers use to identify and select appropriate goals and courses of action for an organisation.[4] The *organisational plan* that results from the planning process details the goals of the organisation and specifies how managers intend to attain them. The cluster of decisions and actions that managers take to help an organisation attain its goals is its **strategy**. Planning is thus both a goal making and a strategy making process.

In most organisations, planning is a three-step activity (Fig. 8.1). The first step is determining the organisation's *mission* and *goals*. A **mission statement** is a broad declaration of an organisation's overarching purpose, intended to identify an organisation's products and customer base, as well as distinguish the organisation in some way from its competitors. The second step is *formulating strategy*. Managers analyse the organisation's current situation and then conceive and develop the strategies necessary to attain the organisation's mission and goals. The third step is *implementing strategy*: managers decide how to allocate the resources and responsibilities that are required to implement the strategies for people and groups within the organisation.[5] In subsequent sections of this chapter, each of these steps will be examined in detail. The general nature and purpose of planning, which is one of the four managerial functions identified by Henri Fayol (p. 5), will also be revisited.

Levels of Planning

In large organisations, planning usually takes place at three levels of management: corporate, business or division and department or functional. Figure 8.2 shows the link between the three

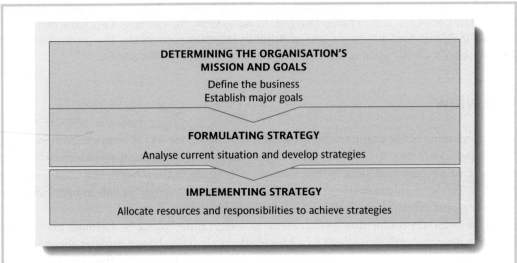

Figure 8.1 Three Steps in Planning

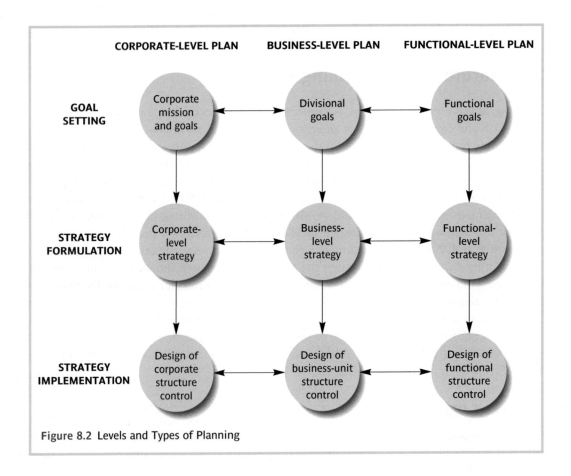

Figure 8.2 Levels and Types of Planning

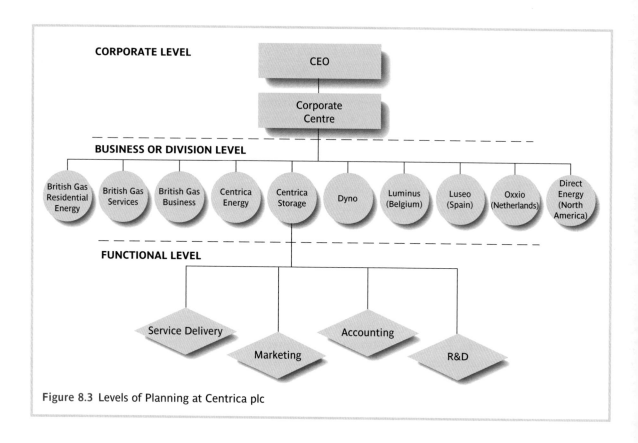

Figure 8.3 Levels of Planning at Centrica plc

steps in the planning process and these three levels. To understand this model, consider how Centrica, a large UK-based organisation that competes in many different businesses, operates.[6]

Centrica provides many different products and services, from gas and electrical to insurance and telephone services across Europe. Centrica has three main levels of management: corporate level, business level and functional level (Fig. 8.3). At the Board or corporate level are the Chairman Roger Carr and CEO, Sir Roy Gardener, three other senior directors and non-executive directors. Below the Board level is the business or division level: *a division* is a business unit that competes in a distinct industry.

Each division has its own set of divisional managers and its own set of functions or departments – manufacturing, marketing, human resource management (HRM), R&D and so on. British Gas which is part of BG Group plc, for example, has its own marketing function, as do Transco (part of Centrica plc) and Dyno (part of British Gas).

At Centrica, as at other large organisations, planning takes place at each level. The corporate-level plan contains senior management's decisions pertaining to the organisation's mission and goals, overall (corporate-level) strategy and structure (Fig. 8.2). Corporate-level strategy indicates in which industries and national markets an organisation intends to compete. One of the goals stated in Centrica's corporate-level plan is to be the leading supplier of energy and related services throughout the UK and Europe. With this overall goal in mind and the 2003 EU Energy Directives enabling open competition for the energy market across Europe by 2007, Centrica has already started to extend its energy supply business.[7] It now has a joint energy supply business in Belgium with the creation of Luminus Energy. It has entered Spain where it has created a Spanish subsidiary company (Centrica Energia SL) who supply electricity to SMEs across Spain. With the acquisition of Oxxio (a low-cost energy supplier in the Netherlands) another step in the development of Centrica's European long-term strategy has taken place. A large conglomerate such as Centrica has to respond and plan at a corporate level for divisional goals as well as changes across the industry. If a division cannot attain its goals then a company may be sold or demerged. Once gas supply became competitive in May 1998, British Gas plc demerged and formed two separate companies: Centrica plc is responsible for gas trading and supply, and BG plc focuses on gas transportation, storage, exploration/production and R&D.

The corporate-level plan provides the framework within which divisional managers create their **business-level plans**. At the business level, the managers of each division create a *business-level plan* that details (1) the long-term goals that will allow the division to meet corporate goals and (2) the division's **business-level strategy** and structure. The *business-level strategy* states the methods that a division or business intends to use to compete against its rivals in an industry. For example, Bruce Walker, the Managing Director of Centrica Storage, was committed to meeting the highest achievable health, safety and environmental standards in operations, both offshore and onshore. This was aligned with the company's priority of improving the reliability of facilities and in excess of £20 million was spent over 2004–05 in capital and revenue projects. Centrica Storage has benefited from this high-level investment as they are ahead of their competitors in that all firm-storage capacity for 2006 has been sold and customers are now focusing on requirements for 2007–08.

A *function* is a unit or department in which people have the same skills or use the same resources to perform their jobs: examples include manufacturing, accounting and sales. The business-level plan provides the framework within which **functional managers** devise their plans. A **functional-level plan** states the goals that functional managers propose to pursue to help the division attain its business-level goals – which, in turn, allow the organisation to achieve its corporate goals. The **functional-level strategy** sets out the actions that managers intend to take at the level of departments such as manufacturing, marketing and R&D to allow the organisation to attain its goals.

An important issue in planning is ensuring *consistency* in planning across the three different levels. Functional goals and strategies should be consistent with divisional goals and strategies, which in turn should be consistent with corporate goals and strategies. Once complete, each function's plan is normally linked to its division's business-level plan which, in turn, is linked to the corporate plan. Although few organisations are as large and complex as Centrica, most plan as Centrica does and have written plans to guide managerial decision making.

Who Plans?

In general, corporate-level planning is the primary responsibility of senior managers.[8] At Centrica, the corporate-level goals of being a leader in energy supply and related services were the vision of CEO Sam Laidlaw. The CEO and his corporate-level management team decide in which industries Centrica should compete. Corporate-level managers are responsible for approving business- and functional-level plans to ensure that they are consistent with the corporate plan.

Corporate planning decisions are not made in a vacuum: other managers have input. At Centrica, and many other companies, divisional and functional managers are encouraged to submit proposals for new business ventures to the CEO and senior managers, who evaluate the proposals and decide whether or not to fund them. Thus, even though corporate-level planning is the responsibility of senior managers, lower-level managers can be, and usually are, given the opportunity to become involved in the process.

This approach is common not only at the corporate level but also at the business and functional levels. At the business level, planning is the responsibility of divisional managers, who also review functional plans. Functional managers also typically participate in business-level planning. Similarly, although the functional managers bear primary responsibility for functional-level planning, they can and do involve their subordinates in this process. Thus, although ultimate responsibility for planning may lie with certain select managers within an organisation, all managers and many non-managerial employees typically participate in the planning process.

Time Horizons of Plans

Plans differ in their **time horizons**, or intended durations. Managers usually distinguish among *long-term plans*, with a horizon of five years or more; *intermediate-term plans*, with a horizon between one and five years; and *short-term plans*, with a horizon of one year or less. Typically, corporate- and business-level goals and strategies require long- and intermediate-term plans, and functional-level goals and strategies require intermediate- and short-term plans.

Although most organisations operate with planning horizons of five years or more, it would be inaccurate to infer from this that they undertake major planning exercises only once every five years and then 'lock in' a specific set of goals and strategies for that time period. Most organisations have an *annual planning cycle*, which is usually linked to the annual financial budget (although a major planning effort may be undertaken only every few years).

Although a corporate- or business-level plan may extend over five years or more, it is typically treated as a *rolling plan*, a plan that is updated and amended every year to take account of changing conditions in the external environment. Thus, the time horizon for an organisation's 2006 corporate-level plan might be 2011; for the 2007 plan 2012; and so on. The use of rolling plans is essential because of the high rate of change in the environment and the difficulty of predicting competitive conditions five years in the future. Rolling plans allow managers to make *mid-course corrections* if environmental changes warrant, or to change the thrust of the plan altogether if it no longer seems appropriate. The use of rolling plans allows managers to plan flexibly, without losing sight of the need to plan for the long term.

Why Planning Is Important

Essentially, planning is ascertaining where an organisation *is* at the present time and deciding where it *should be* in the future, and how to move it forward. When managers plan, they must consider the future and forecast what may happen in order to take actions in the present and mobilise organisational resources to deal with future opportunities and threats. As discussed in Chapter 6, however, the external environment is uncertain and complex, and managers must typically deal with *incomplete information* and *bounded rationality*. This is one reason why planning is so complex and difficult.

Almost all managers engage in planning, and all should participate because they must try to predict future opportunities and threats. The absence of a plan often results in hesitations, false steps and mistaken changes of direction that can hurt an organisation or even lead to disaster. Planning is important for four main reasons:

1. Planning is a useful way of getting managers to participate in decision making about the *appropriate goals and strategies* for an organisation. Effective planning gives all managers the opportunity to participate in decision making. At Intel, for example, senior managers, as part of their annual planning process, regularly request input from lower-level managers to determine what the organisation's goals and strategies should be.

2. Planning is necessary to give the organisation a *sense of direction and purpose*.[9] A plan states what goals an organisation is trying to achieve, and what strategies it intends to use to achieve them. Without the sense of direction and purpose that a formal plan provides, managers may interpret their own tasks and roles in ways that best suit themselves. The result will be an organisation that is pursuing multiple and often conflicting goals and a set of managers who do not co-operate and work well together. By stating which organisational goals and strategies are important, a plan keeps managers on track so that they can use the resources under their control effectively.

3. A plan helps co-ordinate managers of the different functions and divisions of an organisation to ensure that they *all pull in the same direction*. Without a good plan, it is possible that the members of the manufacturing function will produce more products than the members of the sales function can sell, resulting in a mass of unsold inventory. Implausible as this might seem, it happened to the high-flying Internet router supplier Cisco Systems in the early 2000s. The company suddenly found it had over £1.2 billion of unsold routers because of the combination of an economic recession and customers' demands for new kinds of optical routers that Cisco did not have in stock.

4. A plan can be used as a device for *controlling managers* within an organisation. A good plan specifies not only to which goals and strategies the organisation is committed, but also who is responsible for putting the strategies into action to attain the goals. When managers know that they will be held accountable for attaining a goal, they are motivated to do their best to make sure the goal is achieved.

Henri Fayol, the originator of the model of management (Chapter 1), said that effective plans should have four qualities: unity, continuity, accuracy and flexibility.[10] *Unity* means that at any one time only one central guiding plan is put into operation to achieve an organisational goal; more than one plan to achieve a goal would cause confusion and disorder. *Continuity* means that planning is an ongoing process in which managers build and refine previous plans and continually modify plans at all levels – corporate, business and functional – so that they fit together into one broad framework. *Accuracy* means that managers need to make every attempt to collect and utilise all the available information at their disposal in the planning process. Of course, managers must recognise the fact that uncertainty exists and that information is almost always incomplete (for the reasons discussed in Chapter 7). Despite the need for continuity and accuracy, however, Fayol emphasised that the planning process should be *flexible* enough so that plans can be altered and changed if the situation changes: managers must not be bound to a static plan.

Scenario Planning

One way in which managers can try to create plans that have the four qualities that Fayol described is by utilising **scenario planning**, one of the most widely used planning techniques. Scenario planning (also known as *contingency planning*) is the generation of multiple forecasts of future conditions followed by an analysis of how to respond effectively to each of them.

As noted previously, planning is about trying to forecast and predict the future in order to be able to anticipate future opportunities and threats. The future, however, is inherently *unpredictable*. How can managers best deal with this unpredictability?

Scenario planning was first developed by Pierre Wack and Edward Newland for strategic purposes at Royal Dutch/Shell in 1971.[11] Research revealed that Shell's survival depended upon its senior management teams being able to pre-empt changes in the market and act accordingly, and be able to 'learn quicker than their competitors'.[12] However, little research has been done on how scenario planning can affect company performance over time.[13]

At the World Economic Forum in January 2005, the Chief Executive of Royal Dutch Shell, Jeroen van der Veer, stated that global scenario planning was vital for energy companies that are highly complex. World events such as 11 September 2001, the fall of Enron, terrorism, etc. have highlighted the *vulnerability* of our globalised world. This has led Shell to re-think their 'futures planning' in an attempt to promote continuity and flexibility for strategic planning in a complex and changing environment. Since the 1970s, Shell have developed *Global Scenarios* in order to identify emerging challenges and foster adaptability to change. The current Global Scenarios to 2025 (released in 2005) took a more robust view and addressed broader planning and strategic requirements. They have moved from a three-year planning cycle to an annual one, and van Der Veer has adopted a new analytical framework involving three potential Global Scenarios. The first is known as 'Low Trust Globalisation' which emphasises security and efficiency. The second possible futures scenario is 'Open Doors', which emphasises social cohesion and efficiency where the market provides 'built-in' solutions to the crises of trust and security within the industry. The third, called 'Flags', is a scenario where security and community values are emphasised at the expense of efficiency.[14]

Because the future is unpredictable, the only reasonable approach to planning is first to generate 'multiple futures' – or scenarios of the future – based on different assumptions about conditions that *might* prevail in the future and then to develop different plans that detail what a company *should* do in the event that one of these scenarios actually occurs. Scenario planning is a *learning tool* that raises the quality of the planning process and can bring real benefits to an organisation.[15] Shell's success with scenario planning has influenced many other companies to adopt similar systems: by 1990, more than 50 per cent of Fortune 500 companies were using some version of scenario planning, and the number has increased since then.[16] The great strength of scenario planning is its ability not only to anticipate the challenges of an uncertain future but also to educate managers to think about the future – to *think strategically*.[17]

TIPS FOR PRACTICE

1. Even if it is not always appropriate, try to use some of the structured techniques, such as scenario planning, when planning your work. The more you use it, the easier it gets.

2. Don't feel that plans are rigid. They are guides to action, but need to be flexible enough to be adaptable if changes in the environment occur.

3. Always ensure that your plans match and are compatible with those at the other organisational levels. The aim of an organisation is to achieve a common goal, so all plans need to move in the same direction.

4. Be as participative as possible when planning. This ensures commitment and allows for a broad range of perspectives to inform your plans.

Reaction Time

1. Describe the three steps of planning. Explain how they are related.
2. How can scenario planning help managers to predict the future?

Determining the Organisation's Mission and Goals

Determining the organisation's mission and goals is the first step of the planning process. Once the mission and goals are agreed upon and formally stated in the corporate plan, they guide the next steps by defining which strategies are appropriate and which are inappropriate.[18]

Defining the Business

To determine an organisation's mission, managers must first *define its business* so that they can identify what kind of value they will provide to customers. To define the business, managers must ask three questions: (1) Who are our customers? (2) What customer needs are being satisfied? (3) How are we satisfying customer needs?[19] These questions identify the customer needs that the organisation satisfies and the way that the organisation satisfies those needs. Answering these questions helps managers to identify not only the customer needs they are satisfying now but the needs they should try to satisfy in the future and who their true competitors are. All of this information helps managers plan and establish appropriate goals. Case 8.1, on the Lego Group, shows the important role that defining the business has in the planning process.

Case 8.1: Ups and downs at The LEGO Group

LEGO was founded in 1932 in Denmark and in 2000 the LEGO brick was announced the 'toy of the century' by the British Association of Toy Retailers. However most toy manufacturers and suppliers have recently witnessed difficult times, primarily due to rapid changes in consumer behaviour through the escalation of technology. Consumer electronics, MP3 players, video games and interactive soft toys have overtaken 'imaginative playing' and children now tend to grow out of traditional toys at a younger age. Consequently, LEGO has had to change its strategy in order to keep up with competitors, as well as think about how they are going to tackle the future. After suffering financial losses in 2003–04, the company changed its CEO and the corporate management team has developed and implemented new strategies which are now beginning to bear fruit. Initially, LEGO decided to cut their labour costs and closed down factories in Korea along with some closures in Denmark and Switzerland. By outsourcing their labour to Eastern Europe they were able to cut production costs considerably.

Throughout the 1990s the LEGO group launched a constant flow of new products including the LEGO Technic, LEGO Belville (fairytale toys for girls) and LEGO Primo (LEGO designed for 0–2 year olds). During this period they also opened a number of LEGOLAND parks (in the US, Denmark, the UK and a fourth in Germany in 2002). This diversification was boosted by a licensing agreement with Lucas-film Ltd, which allowed LEGO to develop, manufacture and market a series of LEGO based on the Star Wars trilogy. Further expansion included the BIONICLE range, which was a whole building system using LEGO in the development of story themes using construction and action figures. Financial losses made the company 'rethink its strategy', to rationalise its business in terms of defining exactly on what it was going to concentrate. LEGO has now reverted to what it knows best in terms of production and is focused once again on the core business, 'the LEGO brick'. The new corporate team made up of Chairman, Vice Chairman and CEO stated in their 2005 annual report that 'LEGO has for generations given children a very special playing experience and stirs children's imagination'.[20]

LEGO has developed its markets around these values and has concentrated on building good quality, effectively costed bricks. A third strategy has been to develop financial stability. LEGO decided to sell assets, including its majority shareholding in the LEGOLAND parks, thus releasing financial and management resources so that the group could survive. Since 2006 they have downsized the structure of the company in order to increase focus on both the operational and strategic challenges that the company still faces. Jorgen Vig Knudstorp, LEGO Group CEO, commented that 'it is important for us to build on the unique advantages we have. The LEGO brick and system are proving their ability to cater for the modern world – continuing to represent creativity, fun and quality and these are precisely the values that consumers associate with the LEGO brand.'[21]

In the fast-paced toy market where customers' needs change and evolve, and where new groups of customers emerge as new technologies result in new kinds of toys, toy companies like LEGO must learn to define and redefine their businesses to satisfy such needs (see Table 8.1). The results of the company's radical strategic planning has turned the LEGO group around and having suffered a £154 million loss in 2004 they announced pre-tax profits of £64 million in 2005. The CEO maintains that nurturing and building good customer relationships and continuing to adapt the Group to the changing market conditions is the key to enabling them to achieve their medium-term goal of creating sustainable value and increasing profitability.

Table 8.1 Three mission statements

Company	Mission statement
LEGO[22]	Our mission is to nurture the child in each of us, and this means that we actively encourage self-expression through creation, thus enabling children of all ages to bring endless ideas to life. The LEGO® experience is playing, learning, interacting, exploring, expressing, discovering, creating and imagining – all with a heavy dose of fun. We will do this as the world leader in providing quality products and experiences that stimulate creativity, imagination, fun and learning.
ASDA[23]	Our customers have always expected us to deliver a great range of quality goods and services at our famous 'everyday low prices' . . . but not at any cost. That's why we believe we have a responsibility not only to 'do the right thing' for our customers and colleagues, but also for the wider community.
IKEA[24]	The IKEA Concept is based on offering a wide range of well-designed, functional home furnishing products at prices so low that as many people as possible will be able to afford them. Rather than selling expensive home furnishings that only a few can buy, the IKEA Concept makes it possible to serve the many by providing low-priced products that contribute to helping more people live a better life at home.

Establishing Major Goals

Once the business is defined, managers must establish a set of *primary goals* to which the organisation is committed. Developing these goals gives the organisation a sense of direction or purpose. In most organisations, articulating major goals is the job of the CEO, although other managers have an input into the process.

The best statements of organisational goals are ambitious – they stretch the organisation's imagination and require that managers improve its performance capabilities.[25]

In 2005 the CEO of Britain's oldest family-owned jam maker outlined some very challenging goals.[26] Mark Duerr, of F. Duerr & Sons, had to face a shrinking market of 'jam eaters'. Since the 1950s, British jam manufacturing has declined from over 40 companies to three in 2006, one of which is Duerr & Sons, still remaining independent. The reasons for such rapid decline in jam sales have been factors such as increased awareness of obesity in both adults and children, competition with other foods such as snacks, cereal bars, etc. and the general consciousness of people about reducing sugar intake. The challenge for this small company was how to expand when sales were falling. Fortunately Duerr was forward-thinking in his strategy, and saw such changes in the environment coming and changed the emphasis of his business from making jam under his own name to making jams and other products under own-label supermarket names such as Morrisons, Tesco and Sainsbury's, which now makes up 60 per cent of Duerr's business. At the top end of the jam market, branded names are still popular, and profit margins are higher; however, costs in production are high due to the investment in machinery and marketing. The competition, particularly from European companies (e.g. Bonne Maman), also has a stronghold in this market.

Duerr has therefore used a *diversification strategy* and begun making other products such as peanut butter and condiments: peanut butter sales have increased dramatically since the 1980s and now represent 20 per cent of Duerr's sales. Duerr has survived so far, but realises that any diversification will remove him from his core strengths. Another way that Duerr has strategically enhanced its business arm is to embark on a joint venture with a Welsh spring water company to make unfrozen spring-water ice-cubes, to encourage consumers to make their own ice-cubes but with the added benefit of using spring water. Duerr owns 51 per cent of the company and they already have contracts with the four main British supermarkets. Duerr is still an independent family-owned business that is self-funded, but if these latest strategies do not succeed the company may be tempted to sell out or merge.

Although goals should be challenging, they should also be *realistic*. Challenging goals give managers an incentive to look for ways to improve an organisation's operation, but a goal that is unrealistic and impossible to attain may prompt managers to give up.[27] For example, Duerr set the challenging, realistic goal of being able to increase sales by diversifying by maintaining their main product but reducing costs and increasing profit margins by producing own-label products for larger conglomerates. Duerr is a small company, but it is surviving due to forward planning and innovative strategies, while keeping their main product intact. The time period in which a goal is expected to be achieved should be stated. Time constraints are important because they emphasise that a goal must be attained within a reasonable period; they inject a sense of urgency into goal attainment and act as a motivator.

Formulating Strategy

In **strategy formulation**, managers analyse an organisation's current situation and then develop strategies to accomplish its mission and achieve its goals.[28] Strategy formulation begins with managers analysing the factors within an organisation and outside (in the global environment) that affect or may affect the organisation's ability to meet its goals now and in the future. SWOT

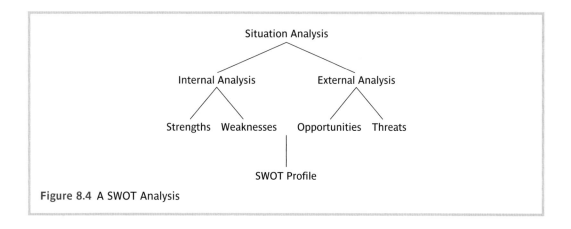

Figure 8.4 A SWOT Analysis

analysis and the five forces model (p. 255) are two useful techniques that managers can use to analyse these factors.

SWOT Analysis

SWOT analysis is a simple framework for generating strategic alternatives from a situation analysis. SWOT stands for Strengths, Weaknesses, Opportunities and Threats. The SWOT framework was formulated in the late 1960s[29] and focuses on issues that have potentially most impact. It is a useful tool when a very limited amount of time is available to address a complex strategic situation.

Figure 8.4 shows how a SWOT analysis fits into a strategic situation analysis.

The internal and external situation analysis can produce a large amount of information, much of which may not be highly relevant. The SWOT analysis can serve as an *interpretative filter* to reduce the information to a manageable quantity of key issues. The SWOT analysis classifies the internal aspects of the company as strengths or weaknesses and the external situational factors as opportunities or threats. *Strengths* can serve as a foundation for building a competitive advantage, and *weaknesses* may hinder it. By understanding these four aspects of its situation, an organisation can better leverage its strengths, correct its weaknesses, capitalize on opportunities and deter potentially devastating threats.

The internal analysis is a comprehensive evaluation of the internal environment's potential strengths and weaknesses. An evaluation of areas across the organisation may include factors such as:

- Company culture
- Company image
- Organisational structure
- Key staff
- Access to natural resources
- Position on the experience curve
- Operational efficiency
- Operational capacity
- Brand awareness

- Market share
- Financial resources
- Exclusive contracts
- Patents and trade secrets.

The SWOT analysis summarises the internal factors of the firm as a list of strengths and weaknesses.

Within an organisation, opportunities that may arise to introduce a new product or service are often the result of a change in the external environment. Such changes can sometimes be seen as threats to the market position of existing products and may necessitate a change in product specifications or the development of new products in order for the company to remain competitive. Changes in the external environment may be related to:

- Customers
- Competitors
- Market trends
- Suppliers
- Partners
- Social changes
- New technology
- Economic environment
- Political and regulatory environment.

Based on a SWOT analysis, managers at the different levels of the organisation select the corporate-, business- and functional-level strategies to best position the organisation to achieve its mission and goals (Fig. 8.5). SWOT analysis is the first step in strategy formulation at any level and is examined first, before turning specifically to corporate-, business- and functional-level strategies.

In Chapter 6 forces in the task and general environments that have the potential to affect an organisation were discussed. It was noted that changes in these forces can produce opportunities that an organisation might take advantage of and consider threats that may harm its current

Figure 8.5 Planning and Strategy Formulation

situation. The first step in SWOT analysis is to identify an organisation's strengths and weaknesses. Table 8.2 lists many important strengths (such as high-quality skills in marketing and in R&D) and weaknesses (such as rising manufacturing costs and outdated technology). The task facing managers is to identify the strengths and weaknesses that characterise the *present state* of their organisation.

The second step in SWOT analysis begins when managers embark on a full-scale SWOT planning exercise to identify potential opportunities and threats in the environment that affect the organisation at the present, or may affect it in the future. Examples of possible opportunities and threats that must be anticipated (many of which were discussed in Chapter 5) are listed in Table 8.2.

Table 8.2 Questions for SWOT analysis

Potential strengths	Potential opportunities	Potential weaknesses	Potential threats
Well-developed strategy?	Expand core business(es)?	Poorly developed strategy?	Attacks on core business(es)?
Strong product lines?	Exploit new market segments?	Obsolete, narrow product lines?	Increase in domestic competition?
Broad market coverage?			
Manufacturing competence?	Widen product range?	Rising manufacturing costs?	Increase in foreign competition?
Good marketing skills?	Extend cost or differentiation advantage?	Decline in R&D innovations?	Change in consumer tastes?
Good materials management systems?	Diversify into new growth businesses?	Poor marketing plan?	Fall in barriers to entry?
R&D skills and leadership?	Expand into foreign markets?	Poor materials management systems?	Rise in new or substitute products?
HR competencies?	Apply R&D skills in new areas?	Loss of customer goodwill?	Increase in industry rivalry?
Brand-name reputation?		Inadequate human resources?	New forms of industry competition?
Cost of differentiation advantage?	Enter new related businesses?	Loss of brand name?	Potential for takeover?
Appropriate management style?	Vertically integrate forward?	Growth without direction?	Changes in demographic factors?
Appropriate organisational structure?	Vertically integrate backward?	Loss of corporate direction?	Changes in economic factors?
Appropriate control systems?	Overcome barriers to entry?	Infighting among divisions?	Downturn in economy?
Ability to manage strategic change?	Reduce rivalry among competitors?	Loss of corporate control?	Rising labour costs? Slower market growth?
Others?	Apply brand-name capital in new areas? Seek fast market growth?	Inappropriate organisational structure and control systems?	Others?
	Others?	High conflict and politics? Others?	

With the SWOT analysis completed and strengths, weaknesses, opportunities and threats identified, managers can begin the planning process and determine strategies for achieving the organisation's mission and goals. The resulting strategies should enable the organisation to attain its goals by taking advantage of opportunities, countering threats, building strengths and correcting organisational weaknesses. To appreciate how managers can use SWOT analysis, consider how Douglas Conant, CEO of Campbell Soup, has used it to try to find strategies to turn around the troubled food products maker (Case 8.2).

Case 8.2: Douglas Conant is in the soup

Campbell Soup Co. is one of the oldest and best-known companies in the world. However, in recent years it has seen demand for its major products such as condensed soup plummet as customers have switched from high-salt, processed soups to healthier low-fat, low-salt varieties. Indeed, its condensed soup business fell by 30 per cent between 1998 and 2004. By the early 2000s Campbell's market share and profits were falling, and its new CEO Douglas Conant decided it was necessary to devise a three-year turnaround plan to help the company maintain its market position.

One of Conant's first actions was to initiate a thorough SWOT planning exercise. An analysis of the environment identified the growth of the organic- and health-food segment of the food market and the increasing number of other kinds of convenience foods as a threat to Campbell's core soup business. The analysis of the environment also revealed three growth opportunities: (1) the growing market for health and sports drinks, in which Campbell was already a competitor with its V8 juice, (2) the growing market for salsas, in which Campbell competed with its Pace salsa and (3) chocolate products, where Campbell's Godiva brand had enjoyed increasing sales throughout the 1990s.

With the analysis of the environment complete, Conant turned his attention to his organisation's resources and capabilities. His internal analysis of Campbell identified a number of major weaknesses. These included staffing levels that were too high relative to its competitors and high costs associated with manufacturing its soups because of the use of outdated machinery. Conant also noted that Campbell had a very conservative culture in which people seemed to be afraid to take risks – something that was a real problem in the fast-changing food industry where customer tastes are always changing and new products must constantly be developed. At the same time, the SWOT analysis identified an enormous strength. Campbell enjoyed huge economies of scale because of the vast quantity of food products that it makes. It also had a first-rate R&D division that had the capability to develop exciting new food products.

Using the information gained from this SWOT analysis, Conant and his managers decided that Campbell needed to use its product development skills to revitalise its core products and modify or reinvent them in ways that would appeal to increasingly health-conscious and busy consumers who did not want to take the time to prepare old-fashioned condensed soup. Moreover, it needed to expand its franchise in the health-, sports-, snack- and luxury-food segments of the market. Another major need that managers saw was to find new ways to deliver Campbell's products to customers. Campbell's needed to tap into new food outlets, such as corporate cafeterias, college dining halls and other mass eateries to expand consumers' access to its foods. Finally, Conant decided that it was necessary to decentralise authority to managers at lower levels in the organisation and give them the responsibility of bringing new kinds of soups, salsas and chocolate products to the market. In this way, he hoped to revitalise Campbell's slow-moving culture and speed the flow of improved and new products to the market.

Conant put his new plan into action – sales of soup started to rise and he began to put more emphasis on sales of soup at outlets such as Subway and less on supermarket sales.[30] By 2004, analysts felt that he had made a significant difference in Campbell's performance but that there was still a lot to do as operating margins were still shrinking. Carrying on the SWOT analysis, Conant decided Campbell should produce more products to meet the challenge of the 'low-carb diet', such as new kinds of low-carb bread and cookies. He also decided to shrink the company's operations to lower costs. His goal is to raise profit margins to the level of his major competitor (Kraft) by 2007, using a new three-year plan based on his SWOT analysis.[31]

The Five Forces Model

A well-known model that helps managers isolate the particular forces in the external environment that are potential threats is Michael Porter's **five forces model** (the first four of which were discussed in Chapter 5). Porter identified these five factors as major threats because they affect how much profit organisations competing within the same industry can expect to make:

- *The level of rivalry among organisations in an industry*   The more that companies compete against one another for customers – for example, by lowering the prices of their products or by increasing advertising – the lower is the level of industry profits (low prices mean less profit).

- *The potential for entry into an industry*   The easier it is for companies to enter an industry – because, for example, barriers to entry, such as brand loyalty, are low – the more likely it is for industry prices (and therefore industry profits) to be low.

- *The power of suppliers*   If there are only a few suppliers of an important input, then suppliers can drive up the price of that input, and expensive inputs result in lower profits for the producer.

- *The power of customers*   If only a few large customers are available to buy an industry's output, they can bargain to drive down the price of that output. As a result, producers make lower profits.

- *The threat of substitute products*   Often, the output of one industry is a substitute for the output of another industry (plastic may be a substitute for steel in some applications, for example; similarly, bottled water is a substitute for cola). Companies that produce a product with a known substitute cannot demand high prices for their products, and this constraint keeps their profits low.

Porter argued that when managers analyse opportunities and threats they should pay particular attention to these five forces because they are the major threats that an organisation will encounter. It is the job of managers at the corporate, business and functional levels to formulate strategies to counter these threats so that an organisation can respond to its task and general environments, perform at a high level and generate high profits. At Campbell, Conant performed such an analysis to identify the opportunities and threats stemming from the actions of its food industry rivals.

Formulating Corporate-level Strategies

Corporate-level strategy, as previously discussed, is a *plan of action* concerning the industries and countries in which an organisation should invest its resources to achieve its mission and goals.

In developing a corporate-level strategy, managers must ask: how should the growth and development of the company be managed in order to increase its ability to create value for its customers (and thus increase performance) over the long run? Managers of most organisations have the goal of growing their companies, and actively seek out new opportunities to use the organisation's resources to create more goods and services. Examples of organisations growing rapidly are Google, Hyundai, Innocent Drinks and Toyota, whose managers pursue any feasible opportunity to use their companies' skills to provide customers with new products.

In addition, some managers must help their organisations respond to threats due to changing forces in the task or general environment. Customers may no longer be buying the kinds of goods and services a company is producing (bulky computer monitors or televisions), or other organisations may have entered the market and attracted away customers (this happened to Intel when AMD began to produce more powerful chips). Senior managers aim to find the best strategies to help the organisation respond to these changes and improve performance.

The principal corporate-level strategies that managers use to help a company grow, to keep it on top of its industry and to help it retrench and reorganise to stop its decline are (1) concentration on a single business, (2) diversification, (3) international expansion and (4) vertical integration. These four strategies are all based on one idea: an organisation benefits from pursuing any one of them only when the strategy helps *further increase the value of the organisation's goods and services for customers*. To increase the value of goods and services, a corporate-level strategy must help an organisation, or one of its divisions, differentiate and add value to its products either by making them unique or special, or by lowering the costs of value creation.

Concentration on a Single Business

Most organisations begin their growth and development with a corporate-level strategy aimed at concentrating resources in one business or industry in order to develop a strong competitive position within that industry. Innocent Drinks started as a stall at a music festival, and has now become a major player in the healthy-drinks market, with an annual growth of 50–60 per cent.[32]

Concentration on a single business can become an appropriate corporate-level strategy when managers see the need to reduce the size of their organisations to increase performance. Managers may decide to get out of certain industries, for example, when particular divisions lose their competitive advantage: managers may sell off those divisions, lay off workers and concentrate remaining organisational resources in another market or business to try to improve performance. This happened to electronics maker Hitachi when it was forced to get out of the CRT computer monitor business. Intense low-price competition existed in the computer monitor market because customers were increasingly switching from bulky CRT monitors to the newer, flat, LCD monitors. Hitachi announced it was closing three factories in Japan, Singapore and Malaysia that produced CRT monitors and would use its resources to invest in the new LCD technology. In contrast, when organisations are performing effectively, they often decide to enter new industries in which they can use their resources to create more value.

Diversification

Diversification is the strategy of expanding operations into a new business or industry and producing new goods or services.[33] Examples of diversification include Tesco or Sainsbury's which diversified into financial products, or British Petroleum (BP), which diversified into convenience stores on the US West coast. There are two main kinds of diversification: **related** and **unrelated**.

Related diversification

Related diversification is the strategy of entering a new business or industry to create a competitive advantage in one or more of an organisation's existing divisions or businesses. Related diversification can add value to an organisation's products if managers can find ways for its various divisions or business units to share their valuable skills or resources so that *synergy* is created.[34] Synergy is obtained when the value created by two divisions co-operating is greater than the value that would be created if the two divisions operated separately. For example, suppose two or more divisions within a diversified company can utilise the same manufacturing facilities, distribution channels, advertising campaigns and so on. Each division that shares resources has to invest less in the shared functions than it would have to invest if it had full responsibility for the activity. In this way, related diversification can be a major source of cost savings.[35] Similarly, if one division's R&D skills can be used to improve another division's products, the second division's products may receive a competitive advantage.

Procter & Gamble's disposable diaper and paper towel businesses offer one of the best examples of the successful production of synergies. These businesses share the costs of procuring inputs such as paper and developing new technology to reduce manufacturing costs. In addition, a joint sales force sells both products to supermarkets and both products are shipped by means of the same distribution system. This resource-sharing has enabled both divisions to reduce their costs, and as a result, they can charge lower prices than their competitors and thus attract more customers.[36]

In pursuing related diversification, managers often seek to find new businesses where they can use the existing skills and resources in their departments to create synergies, add value to the new business and hence improve the competitive position of the company. Alternatively, managers may acquire a company in a new industry because they believe that some of the skills and resources of the acquired company may improve the efficiency of one or more of their existing divisions. If successful, such skill transfers can help an organisation to lower its costs or better differentiate its products because they create synergies between divisions.

Unrelated diversification

Managers pursue *unrelated diversification* when they enter new industries or buy companies in new industries that are not related in any way to their current businesses or industries. One main reason for pursuing unrelated diversification is that, sometimes, managers can buy a poorly performing company, transfer their management skills to that company, turn around its business and increase its performance, all of which creates value.

Another reason for pursuing unrelated diversification is that purchasing businesses in different industries lets managers engage in a *portfolio strategy*, which is apportioning financial resources among divisions to increase financial returns or spread risks among different businesses. For example, managers may transfer funds from a rich division to a new and promising division and, by appropriately allocating money between them, create value. Though used as a popular explanation in the 1980s for unrelated diversification, portfolio strategy ran into increasing criticism in the 1990s.[37]

Indeed, more and more companies and their managers have abandoned the strategy of unrelated diversification because there is evidence that too much diversification can cause managers to lose control of their organisation's *core business*. Management experts suggest that although unrelated diversification may initially create value for a company, managers sometimes use portfolio strategy to expand the scope of their organisation's businesses too much. When this happens, it becomes difficult for senior managers to be knowledgeable about all of the organisation's diverse businesses. Managers do not have the time to process all of the information required to adequately assess the strategy and performance of each division objectively, and organisational performance often suffers.

Thus, although unrelated diversification can create value for a company, research evidence suggests that many diversification efforts have reduced value rather than created it.[38] As a consequence, there was a trend during the 1990s among many diversified companies to divest many of their unrelated divisions. Managers sold off divisions and concentrated organisational resources on their core business, focusing more on related diversification.[39]

International Expansion

As if planning the appropriate level of diversification were not a difficult enough decision, corporate-level managers must also decide on the appropriate way to *compete internationally*. A basic question confronts the managers of any organisation that competes in more than one national market: to what extent should the organisation customise features of its products and marketing campaign to different national conditions?[40]

If managers decide that their organisation should sell the same standardised product in each national market in which it competes, and use the same basic marketing approach, they adopt a **global strategy**.[41] Such companies undertake very little, if any, customisation to suit the specific needs of customers in different countries. However, if managers decide to customise products and marketing strategies to specific national conditions, they adopt a **multi-domestic strategy**.

Matsushita, with its Panasonic brand, has traditionally pursued a global strategy, selling the same basic TVs and VCRs in every market in which it does business and often using the same basic marketing approach. Unilever, the European food and household products company, has pursued a multi-domestic strategy. To appeal to German customers, Unilever's German division sells a different range of food products and uses a different marketing approach than its North American division or even its UK division.

Global and multi-domestic strategies have both advantages and disadvantages. The major advantage of a global strategy is the significant cost savings associated with not having to customise products and marketing approaches to different national conditions. For example, Rolex watches, Ralph Lauren or Tommy Hilfiger clothing, Chanel or Armani accessories or perfume, Dell computers, Chinese-made plastic toys and buckets, and US-grown rice and wheat are all products that can be sold using the same marketing across many countries by simply translating it into a different language, saving companies a significant amount of money. The major disadvantage of pursuing a global strategy is that, by ignoring national differences, managers may leave themselves vulnerable to local competitors that do differentiate their products to suit local tastes. This occurred in the British consumer electronics industry. Amstrad, a British computer and electronics company, began by recognising and responding to local consumer needs. Amstrad captured a major share of the British audio market by ignoring the standardised inexpensive music centres marketed by companies pursuing a global strategy, such as Sony and Matsushita. Instead, Amstrad's product was encased in teak rather than metal and featured a control panel tailor-made to appeal to British consumers' preferences. To remain competitive in this market, Matsushita had to place more emphasis on local customisation of its Panasonic and JVC brands.

The advantages and disadvantages of a multi-domestic strategy are the opposite of those of a global strategy. The major advantage of a multi-domestic strategy is that by customising product offerings and marketing approaches to local conditions, managers may be able to gain market share or charge higher prices for their products. The major disadvantage is that custom-isation raises production costs and puts the multi-domestic company at a price disadvantage because it often has to charge prices higher than the prices charged by competitors pursuing a global strategy. Obviously, the choice between these two strategies calls for *trade-offs*.

Managers at Gillette, the well-known razor blade maker, created a strategy that combined the best features of both international strategies. Gillette was a global company from the beginning, as its managers quickly saw the advantages of selling its razor blades abroad. By 2004, 65 per cent of Gillette's revenues came from global sales, and this percentage was expected to increase.[42] Gillette's strategy over the years was pretty constant: find a new foreign country with a growing market for razor blades, form a strategic alliance with a local razor blade company and take a majority stake in it, invest in a large marketing campaign and then build a modern factory to make razor blades and other products for the local market. When Gillette entered Russia after the break-up of the Soviet Union, it saw a huge opportunity to increase sales. It formed a joint venture with a local company called Leninets Concern, which made a razor known as the Sputnik, and then with this base began to import its own brands into Russia. When sales growth rose sharply, Gillette decided to offer more products in the market and built a new plant in St Petersburg.[43]

Today, Gillette operates 50 manufacturing facilities in more than 20 countries.[44] It establishes its factories in countries where labour and other costs are low and then distributes and markets its products to countries in that region of the world. In this sense it pursues a global strategy. However, all of Gillette's research and development and design take place in one location. As it develops new kinds of razors, it equips its foreign factories to manufacture them when it decides that local customers are ready to trade up to the new product. So Gillette's latest razor, for example, may be introduced in a foreign country years later than in the US. Gillette is customising its product offering to the needs of different countries and also pursuing a multi-domestic strategy. By pursuing this international strategy, Gillette can achieve low costs and still differentiate and customise its product range to suit the needs of each country or world region. This strategy has proved very effective, and the company's global sales and profits continue to increase.

Choosing a way to expand internationally

As discussed above, a more competitive global environment has proven to be both an oppor-tunity and a threat for organisations and managers. The opportunity is that organisations that expand globally are able to open new markets, reach more customers and gain access to new sources of raw materials and to low-cost suppliers of inputs. The threat is that organisations that expand globally are likely to encounter new competitors in the foreign countries they enter, and must respond to new political, economic and cultural conditions.

Before setting up foreign operations, managers of companies such as Amazon.com, Lands' End, Toys 'R' Us and Volkswagen needed to analyse the forces in the environment of a particu-lar country (such as Korea or Brazil) in order to choose the right method to expand and respond to those forces in the most appropriate way. Four basic ways to operate in the global environ-ment are importing and exporting, licensing and franchising, strategic alliances and wholly owned foreign subsidiaries. Each one will be briefly discussed, moving from the lowest level of foreign involvement and investment required of a global organisation and its managers, and the least amount of risk, to the high end of the spectrum (Fig. 8.6).[45]

Figure 8.6 Four Ways of Expanding Internationally

Importing and exporting

The least complex global operations are **exporting** and **importing**. A company engaged in *exporting* makes products at home and sells them abroad. An organisation might sell its own products abroad or allow a local organisation in the foreign country to distribute its products. Few risks are associated with exporting because a company does not have to invest in developing manufacturing facilities abroad. It can further reduce its investment abroad if it allows a local company to distribute its products.

A company engaged in *importing* sells at home products that are made abroad (products it makes itself or buys from other companies). For example, most of the products that IKEA or ALDI sell are made abroad, and in many cases the appeal of a product is that it is made abroad. The Internet has made it much easier for companies to inform potential foreign buyers about their products; detailed product specifications and features are available online and informed buyers can communicate easily with prospective sellers. The way in which Levi Strauss was forced to change its international approach from exporting to importing (Case 8.3) illustrates how the growth of low-cost manufacturing abroad has changed competition in many industries.

Case 8.3: Levi Strauss's big problems

Levi Strauss, the well-known jeans maker, was once the global leader in the apparel industry. Its jeans commanded a premium price as customers the world over perceived that the value or status of wearing Levi jeans was worth paying extra for. Indeed, in Europe and Asia, Levi jeans were often sold at double or triple their US price. No more: Levi is now fighting to lower its costs to be able to survive in the fast-changing jeans industry.

Levi's problems arose because of changes in the international strategies of other jeans makers and apparel companies. In the early 1990s, other jeans makers such as VF Corp (which makes Wrangler jeans), Calvin Klein and Polo outsourced the production of jeans to countries abroad where labour costs were lowest. With their lower costs, these companies then began to charge lower prices for their products and customers began to switch to buying their jeans. Then, in a significant move, companies such as ASDA and Matalan began to wonder why they should pay Levi a premium price for selling its jeans when they could sell jeans under their own labels at a lower price and still make more profit than if they sold Levi's jeans. So they contracted with low-cost foreign producers to make jeans under their own in-house labels. The result was that sales of Levi jeans plummeted as many customers began to buy jeans on the basis of their price.

Levi, because it still produced most of its jeans in the US and exported them abroad, was caught unprepared and found it could no longer compete. It lost billions of dollars in the 1990s. To survive, it was forced to change from exporting its jeans to importing its jeans from abroad – it outsourced all production to manufacturers abroad. Since 1997 it has closed all 35 of its US manufacturing facilities and laid off over 30,000 employees.

Once it outsourced production abroad, Levi was able to reduce its prices to be competitive. Indeed, its prices fell so low that ASDA began to sell Levi jeans as part of its range in its stores. However, low prices mean low profits, and Levi's problems have continued into the 2000s as it struggles to find a way to compete successfully in a global market dominated by ruthless low-cost/price competition.

Licensing and franchising

In **licensing**, a company (the *licenser*) allows a foreign organisation (the *licensee*) to take charge of both manufacturing and distributing one or more of its products in the licensee's country or world region in return for a negotiated fee. German chemical maker BASF might license a local factory in India to produce glues. The advantage of licensing is that the licenser does not have to bear the development costs associated with opening up in a foreign country; the licensee bears the costs. The risks associated with this strategy are that the company granting the licence has to give its foreign partner access to its technological know-how, and so risks losing control over its secrets.

Whereas licensing is pursued primarily by manufacturing companies, **franchising** is pursued primarily by service organisations. In franchising, a company (the *franchiser*) sells to a foreign organisation (the *franchisee*) the rights to use its brand name and operating know-how in return for a lump-sum payment and share of the franchiser's profits. Hilton Hotels might sell a franchise to a local company in Chile to operate hotels under the Hilton name in return for a franchise payment. The advantage of franchising is that the franchiser does not have to bear the development costs of overseas expansion and avoids the many problems associated with setting up foreign operations. The downside is that the organisation that grants the franchise may lose control over the way in which the franchisee operates and product quality may fall. Franchisers, such as Hilton, Europcar and McDonald's, then risk losing their good names. Customers who buy McDonald's hamburgers in Korea may reasonably expect those burgers to be as good as the ones they get at home. If they are not, McDonald's reputation will suffer over time. Once again, the Internet facilitates communication between partners and allows them to better meet each other's expectations.

Strategic alliances

One way to overcome the loss-of-control problems associated with exporting, licensing and franchising is to expand globally by means of a **strategic alliance**. In a strategic alliance, managers pool or share their organisation's resources and know-how with those of a foreign company, and the two organisations share the rewards or risks of starting a new venture in a foreign country. Sharing resources allows a company, for example, to take advantage of the high-quality skills of foreign manufacturers and the specialised knowledge of foreign managers about the needs of local customers and to reduce the risks involved in a venture. At the same time, the terms of the alliance give the company more control over how the good or service is produced or sold in the foreign country than it would have as a franchiser or licenser.

A *strategic alliance* can take the form of a written contract between two or more companies to exchange resources, or it can result in the creation of a new organisation. A *joint venture* (JV) is a strategic alliance among two or more companies that agree to jointly establish and share the ownership of a new business.[46] An organisation's level of involvement abroad increases in a JV because the alliance normally involves a *capital investment* in production facilities abroad in order to produce goods or services outside the home country. Risk, however, is reduced. The Internet and global teleconferencing provide the increased communication and co-ordination necessary for partners to work together on a global basis. In 2001, for example, Coca-Cola and Nestlé announced that they would form a JV and co-operate in marketing their teas, coffees and health-oriented beverages to more than 50 countries in the world.[47] British Petroleum (BP), Amoco and Italy's ENI announced in the same year that they would form a JV to build a £1.4 billion gas-liquefaction plant in Egypt.[48]

Wholly-owned foreign subsidiaries

When managers decide to establish a **wholly-owned foreign subsidiary**, they invest in establishing production/service operations in a foreign country independent of any local direct involvement. For example, UK's Lloyds Pharmacy Ltd is a wholly-owned subsidiary of GEHE AG, now Celesio AG, Europe's largest pharmaceutical wholesaler based in Germany.[49] Being a subsidiary allows the pharmacy to compete on economies of scales.

Operating alone, without any direct involvement from foreign companies, an organisation receives all of the rewards and bears all of the risks associated with operating abroad.[50] This method of international expansion is much more expensive than the others because it requires a higher level of foreign investment and presents managers with many more threats. However, investment in a foreign subsidiary or division offers significant advantages. It gives an organisation high potential for returns because the organisation does not have to share its profits with a foreign organisation, and it reduces the level of risk because managers have full control over all aspects of their foreign subsidiary's operations. Moreover, this type of investment allows managers to protect their technology and know-how from foreign organisations. Large, well-known companies like Scottish Power and Gillette, which have ample resources, make extensive use of wholly-owned subsidiaries. No matter what means they choose to expand globally, however, companies have to be careful to design and select the right kind of information systems and websites to allow customers to buy their products.

Vertical Integration

When an organisation is doing well in its business, managers often see new opportunities to create value by either *producing* their own inputs or *distributing* their own outputs. The Spanish clothes retailer ZARA felt it was a waste of resources to source all its products from different suppliers such as H&M, who uses approximately 900 suppliers. In order to be more efficient, more than 50 per cent of its clotheslines are now made in-house, integrating marketing, design and manufacturing.[51]

Vertical integration is the corporate-level strategy through which an organisation becomes involved in producing its own inputs (*backward* vertical integration) or distributing and selling its own outputs (*forward* vertical integration).[52] A steel company that supplies its iron ore needs from company-owned iron ore mines is engaging in backward vertical integration. A PC company that sells its computers through company-owned distribution outlets has engaged in forward vertical integration.

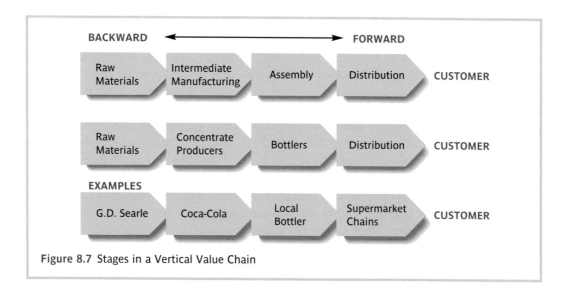

Figure 8.7 Stages in a Vertical Value Chain

Figure 8.7 illustrates the four main stages in a typical raw-material-to-consumer value chain: value is added at each stage. Typically, the primary operations of an organisation take place in one of these stages. For a company based in the assembly stage, backward integration would involve establishing a new division in intermediate manufacturing or raw-material production, and forward integration would involve establishing a new division to distribute its products to wholesalers or to sell directly to customers. A division at one stage receives the goods produced by the division in the previous stage, transforms it in some way – adding value – and then transfers the output at a higher price to the division at the next stage in the chain.

As an example of how the value chain works, consider the cola segment of the soft-drink industry. Raw-material suppliers include sugar companies and the manufacturer of the artificial sweetener NutraSweet, which is used in diet colas. These companies sell their products to companies that make concentrate – such as Coca-Cola and PepsiCo – which mix these inputs with others to produce the cola concentrate that they market. In the process, they add value to these inputs. The concentrate producers then sell the concentrate to bottlers, who add carbonated water to the concentrate and package the resulting drink – again adding value to the concentrate. Next, the bottlers sell the packaged product to various distributors, including retail stores such as Sainsbury's and ASDA and fast-food chains such as McDonald's. These distributors add value by making the product accessible to customers. Value is thus added by companies at each stage in the raw-material-to-consumer chain.

A major reason why managers pursue vertical integration is that it allows them either to add value to their products by making them special or unique or to lower the costs of value creation. For example, Coca-Cola and PepsiCo, in a case of forward vertical integration to build brand loyalty and enhance the differentiated appeal of their colas, decided to buy up their major bottlers to increase control over marketing and promotion efforts, which had been handled by the bottlers.[53] An example of using forward vertical integration to lower costs is Matsushita's decision to open company-owned stores to sell its Panasonic and JVC products and thus keep the profit that otherwise would be earned by independent retailers.[54]

Although vertical integration can help an organisation to grow rapidly, it can be a problem when forces in the environment counter the strategies of the organisation and make it necessary for managers to reorganise or retrench. Vertical integration can reduce an organisation's flexibility to respond to changing environmental conditions. IBM used to produce most of its own components for mainframe computers; while this made sense in the 1970s it became a major handicap in the fast-changing computer industry of the 1990s. The rise of organisation-wide networks of personal computers meant slumping demand for mainframes, as demand fell, IBM found itself with an excess-capacity problem not only in its mainframe assembly operations but also in component operations. Closing down this capacity cost IBM over £2.8 billion.[55]

When considering vertical integration as a strategy to add value, managers must take care because vertical integration can sometimes actually reduce an organisation's ability to create value when the environment changes. This is why so many companies now *outsource* the production of component parts to other companies. IBM, however, has found a new opportunity for forward vertical integration in the 1990s.[56] It decided to provide IT consulting services to mainframe users and to advise them on how to install and manage any software packages they chose on their mainframes. Providing such IT services was so profitable for IBM that by 2000 it had recovered its market position.

A second type of integration is called horizontal integration. This type of integration usually refers to an organisation that is expanding its business activities at the same level, mostly through mergers or acquisitions (M&As). While BP may own a number of distribution networks (vertical integration), it has also bought the German-based petrol stations chain ARAL; it has therefore bought into the same type of industry. The advantages of horizontal integration are economies of scale and greater market power. The disadvantages are similar to those associated with M&As – i.e. problems of the *realisation of economies of scale*.

Formulating Business-level Strategies

Michael Porter, the researcher who developed the five forces model discussed on p. 255, also formulated a theory of how managers can select a *business-level strategy*, a plan to gain a competitive advantage in a particular market or industry.[57] According to Porter, managers must choose between two basic ways of increasing the value of an organisation's products: *differentiating* the product to add value or lowering the costs of *value creation*. Porter also argues that managers must choose between serving the *whole* market and serving just one *segment* or *part* of a market. Based on those choices, managers choose to pursue one of four business-level strategies: low cost, differentiation, focused low cost, or focused differentiation (Table 8.3).

Low-Cost Strategy

With a **low-cost strategy**, managers try to gain a competitive advantage by focusing the energy of all the organisation's departments or functions on driving the organisation's costs down below the costs of its rivals. This strategy requires that manufacturing managers search for new ways to reduce production costs, R&D managers focus on developing new products that can be manufactured more cheaply and marketing managers find ways to lower the costs of attracting customers. According to Porter, organisations pursuing a low-cost strategy can sell a product for less than their rivals sell it and yet still make a profit because of their lower costs. Organisations that pursue a low-cost strategy thus hope to enjoy a competitive advantage based on their low prices. ALDI, the German supermarket discounter, for example, is able to offer low prices by

Table 8.3 Porter's business-level strategies

	Number of market segments served	
Strategy	**Many**	**Few**
Low cost	✓	
Focused low cost		✓
Differentiation	✓	
Focused differentiation		✓

only stocking a limited number of products and being able to exert pressures on its producers through economies of scale. This has led to Theo and Karl Albrecht, the owners of ALDI, being amongst the richest entrepreneurs in Europe.[58]

Differentiation Strategy

With a *differentiation strategy*, managers try to gain a competitive advantage by focusing all the energies of the organisation's departments or functions on distinguishing the organisation's products from those of competitors on one or more important dimensions, such as product design, quality or after-sales service and support. The process of making products unique and different is often expensive, and this strategy often requires that managers increase spending on product design or R&D to differentiate the product, and costs rise as a result. Organisations that successfully pursue a differentiation strategy may be able to charge a *premium price* for their products – a price usually much higher than the price charged by a low-cost organisation. The premium price allows organisations pursuing a differentiation strategy to recoup their higher costs. Large fashion brands like Gucci and Armani are some of the many well-known companies that pursue a strategy of differentiation. They spend enormous amounts of money on advertising to differentiate, and create a unique image for, their products. However, just because companies can differentiate their products does not mean that there cannot be intense competition between them, as Case 8.4 suggests.

Case 8.4: Strategy in the world package delivery business

In 1971, Federal Express (FedEx) turned the package delivery world upside down when it began to offer overnight package delivery by air. Its founder, Fred Smith, had seen the opportunity for next-day delivery because both the US Postal Service and United Parcel Service (UPS) were, at that time, taking several days to deliver packages. Smith was convinced there was pent-up demand for overnight delivery, and he was also convinced that customers would be willing to pay a high premium price to get such a unique new service, at least about £10 a package at that time.[59] Smith was right: customers were willing to pay high prices for fast, reliable delivery. By discovering and tapping into an unmet customer need, he redefined the package delivery industry.

Several companies imitated FedEx's new strategy and introduced their own air overnight service. None, however, could match FedEx's state-of-the-art information system that allowed continuous tracking of all packages in transit, and several of its competitors went out of business. A few, like Airborne Express, managed to survive by focusing or *specialising* on serving the ▶

▶ needs of one particular group of customers – corporate customers – and by offering lower prices than FedEx.

The well-known road delivery package company UPS initiated an overnight air delivery service of its own in 1998.[60] UPS managers realised that the future of package delivery lay both on the road and in the air because different customer groups, with different needs, were emerging. It began to aggressively imitate FedEx's state-of-the-art operating and information systems, especially its tracking system. Slowly and surely UPS increased the number of overnight packages that it was delivering. In 1999, UPS announced two major innovations. First, it introduced a new tracking and shipping information system that matched, and even exceeded, the sophistication of the FedEx system because it could work with any IT system used by corporate customers. (By contrast, customers had to install and use FedEx's proprietary IT, an approach that caused more work and cost for them.) Second, UPS integrated its overnight air service into its nationwide delivery service and created a seamless interface between these two different aspects of its business. This gave it a differentiation advantage over FedEx because UPS could deliver short-range and mid-distance packages, those being shipped within about 500 miles, more quickly than FedEx, as well as matching the speed and reliability of FedEx's long-range operations.

Competition between FedEx and UPS became intense in the early 2000s. Then, in 2003, both companies received a shock when the largest global package delivery company, the now German-owned DHL, announced that it would purchase Airborne Express and would thus become a direct competitor of FedEx and UPS. When DHL began a marketing campaign to emphasise the extent of its global reach and the speed of its operations, all three companies started to fight for customers and find new ways of differentiating their products. In 2003 FedEx announced that it would purchase Kinko's Copies and make each Kinko's store a base for its delivery operations. In doing so, it was following UPS' approach; UPS had purchased a chain of packaging stores and turned them into UPS stores. The fight is ongoing, and which company will turn out to be the global leader is still unclear.

'Stuck in the Middle'

According to Porter's theory, managers cannot simultaneously pursue both a low-cost strategy and a differentiation strategy. Porter identified a simple correlation: differentiation raises costs and thus necessitates premium pricing to recoup those high costs. If ALDI suddenly began to advertise heavily to try to build a strong global brand image for its products, costs would rise; the stores would then no longer make a profit simply by pricing their products lower than other supermarkets. According to Porter, managers must choose between a low-cost strategy and a differentiation strategy. He refers to managers and organisations that have not made this choice as being 'stuck in the middle'. Organisations 'stuck in the middle' tend to have lower levels of performance than do those that pursue either a low-cost or a differentiation strategy. To avoid being 'stuck in the middle', senior managers must instruct departmental managers to take actions that will result in either low cost or differentiation.

However, exceptions to this rule can be found. In many organisations managers have been able to drive costs below those of rivals and simultaneously differentiate their products from those offered by them.[61] Toyota's production system is reportedly the most efficient in the world. This efficiency gives Toyota a low-cost strategy *vis-à-vis* its rivals in the global car industry. At the same time, Toyota has differentiated its cars from those of rivals on the basis of superior design and quality. This superiority allows the company to charge a premium price for many of its popular models.[62] Toyota thus seems to be simultaneously pursuing both a low-cost and a differentiated business-level strategy. This example suggests that although Porter's ideas may be valid in most cases, very well managed companies such as Toyota may have both low costs and differentiated products.

Focused Low-cost and Focused Differentiation Strategies

Both the differentiation strategy and the low-cost strategy are aimed at serving many or most segments of a particular market, such as that for cars or computers. Porter identified two other business-level strategies that aim to serve the needs of customers in only one or a few market segments.[63] Managers pursuing a **focused low-cost strategy** serve one or a few segments of the overall market and aim to make their organisation the lowest-cost company serving that segment. For example, Cott Corporation is the world's leading supplier of retailer-brand-name carbonated soft drinks. With production facilities in North America and the UK, Cott produces, packages and distributes a wide selection of retailer-brand beverages for grocery, mass-merchandise and convenience store chains. All Sainsbury's soda sold under its own brand name is made by Cott, for example. However, while Cott is the world's leading supplier of retailer-brand-name sodas, it is focusing on a *low-cost strategy*: It makes no attempt to compete with Coke and Pepsi which, as noted earlier, pursue a differentiation strategy and whose brand-name sodas dominate the global soda market.

By contrast, managers pursuing a **focused differentiation strategy** serve just one or a few segments of the market and aim to make their organisation the most differentiated company serving that segment. BMW, for example, pursues a focused strategy, producing cars exclusively for higher-income customers. By contrast, Toyota pursues a differentiation strategy and produces cars that appeal to consumers in almost all segments of the car market, from basic transportation (Toyota AYGO), through the middle of the market (Toyota Avensis) to the high-income end of the market (Lexus).

As these examples suggest, companies pursuing either of these focused strategies have chosen to *specialise* in some way by directing their efforts at a particular kind of customer (such as serving the needs of babies or affluent customers) or even the needs of customers in a specific geographic region (customers in Eastern Europe or Western Europe).

Zara, the Spanish manufacturer of fashionable clothing, provides an excellent example of how a company can pursue both a low-cost and a differentiated focused strategy at the same time by using new IT. Well-known fashion houses like Channel, Dior and Armani can charge thousands of pounds for the fashionable collections of suits and dresses that they introduce twice yearly in the autumn and in the spring. Only the rich can afford such differentiated and expensive clothing, and this has opened up a gap in the fashion market for companies that can supply fashionable clothes at lower prices. Essentially, these companies have the capabilities to pursue a focused differentiation and cost-leadership strategy.

While many clothing companies, such as the The Gap and England's Jaeger and Laura Ashley, have attempted to supply fashionable clothes at lower prices, none has succeeded as well as Spanish clothes maker Zara, whose sales have soared in recent years.[64] Zara has managed to position itself as the low-price/cost leader in the fashion segment of the clothing market because of the way it uses IT. It has created an information system that allows it to manage its design and manufacturing process in a way that minimises the inventory it has to carry – the major cost borne by a clothing retailer. However, its IT also gives instantaneous feedback on which clothes are selling well and in which countries, and this gives it a competitive advantage from differentiation.

Zara can manufacture more of a particular kind of dress or suit to meet high customer demand, decide which clothing should be sold in its rapidly expanding network of global stores and constantly change the mix of clothes it offers customers to keep up with fashion. Moreover, it can do this at relatively small output levels, something which is also a part of a specialised, focused strategy. This is partly possible as Zara has *vertically integrated* some of its production.

Zara's IT also allows it to manage the interface between its design and manufacturing operations more efficiently. Zara only takes five weeks to design a new collection and then a week to make it. Other fashion houses, by contrast, can take six or more months to design the collection and then three more before it is available in stores.[65] This short *time to market* gives Zara great flexibility and allows the company to respond quickly to the rapidly changing fashion market in which fashions can change several times a year. Because of the quick manufacturing-to-sales cycle and just-in-time (JIT) fashion, Zara can offer its clothes collections at relatively low prices and still make a profit that is the envy of the fashion clothing industry.[66]

Formulating Functional-level Strategies

Zara has developed many kinds of strengths in functions such as clothing design and IT that have given it a competitive advantage. A *functional-level strategy* is a plan of action to improve the ability of an organisation's functions to create value. It involves the actions that managers of individual functions (such as manufacturing or marketing) can take to add value to an organisation's goods and services and thereby increase the value customers receive. The price that customers are prepared to pay for a product indicates how much they value an organisation's products: the more customers value a product, the more they are willing to pay for it.

There are two ways in which functions can add value to an organisation's products:

1. Functional managers can lower the costs of creating value so that an organisation can attract customers by keeping its prices lower than its competitors' prices.

2. Functional managers can add value to a product by finding ways to differentiate it from the products of other companies.

If customers see more value in one organisation's products than in the products of its competitors, they may be willing to pay a premium price. There must be a fit between functional- and business-level strategies if an organisation is to achieve its mission and goal of maximising the amount of value it gives customers. The better the fit between functional- and business-level strategies, the greater will be the organisation's *competitive advantage* – its ability to attract customers and the revenue they provide.

Each organisational function has an important role to play in the process of lowering costs or adding value to a product (Table 8.4). Manufacturing can find new ways to lower production costs or to build superior quality into the product to add value. Marketing, sales and after-sales service and support can add value by, for example, building brand loyalty (as Coca-Cola and PepsiCo have done in the soft-drink industry) and finding more effective ways to attract customers. Human resource management (HRM) can lower the costs of creating value by recruiting and training a highly productive workforce. The R&D function can lower the costs of creating value by developing more efficient production processes. R&D can also add value by developing new and improved products that customers value over established product offerings.

Creating value at the functional level requires the adoption of many state-of-the-art management techniques and practices that are discussed at length in Chapter 9. As discussed here, it

Table 8.4 How functions can lower the costs and create value or add value to create a competitive advantage

Value-creating function	Ways to lower the cost of creating value (low-cost advantage)	Ways to add value (differentiation advantage)
Sales and marketing	■ Find new customers	■ Promote brand-name awareness and loyalty
Materials management	■ Find low-cost advertising methods	
R&D		■ Tailor products to suit customers' needs
Manufacturing	■ Use JIT inventory system/ computerised warehousing	
HRM	■ Develop long-term relationships with suppliers and customers ■ Improve efficiency of machinery and equipment ■ Design products that can be made more cheaply ■ Develop skills in low-cost manufacturing ■ Reduce turnover and absenteeism ■ Raise employee skills	■ Develop long-term relationships with suppliers to provide high-quality inputs ■ Reduce shipping time to customers ■ Create new products ■ Improve existing products ■ Increase product quality and reliability ■ Hire highly skilled employees ■ Develop innovative training programmes

is the responsibility of managers at the functional level to identify these techniques and develop a functional-level plan that contains the strategies necessary to develop them. The important issue to remember is that all of these techniques can help an organisation achieve a competitive advantage by lowering the costs of creating value, or by adding value above and beyond that offered by rivals.

Reaction time

1. What is the role of divisional and functional managers in the formulation of strategy?

2. Why is it important for functional managers to have a clear grasp of the organisation's mission when developing strategies within their departments?

3. What is the relationship among corporate-, business- and functional-level strategies, and how can they create value for an organisation?

Planning and Implementing Strategy

After identifying the appropriate strategies to attain an organisation's mission and goals, managers must confront the challenge of putting those strategies into action. *Strategy implementation* is a five-step process:

1. Allocating responsibility for implementation to the appropriate individuals or groups
2. Drafting detailed action plans that specify how a strategy is to be implemented
3. Establishing a timetable for implementation that includes precise, measurable goals linked to the attainment of the action plan
4. Allocating appropriate resources to the responsible individuals or groups
5. Holding specific individuals or groups responsible for the attainment of corporate, divisional and functional goals.

The planning process goes beyond the mere identification of strategies; it also includes actions taken to ensure that the organisation actually puts its strategies into action. It should be noted that the plan for implementing a strategy may require radical redesign of the organisation's structure, the development of new control systems and the adoption of a programme for changing the organisation's culture. These are all issues that are addressed in Chapters 9–11.

TIPS FOR PRACTICE

1. Always remind yourself of the primary business of your organisation. Ask questions about how well the organisation is achieving this, and use this to decide future goals.
2. Make SWOT an automatic and integral part of any planning process.

Summary and Review

The nature of the planning process Planning is a three-step process: (1) determining an organisation's mission and goals; (2) formulating strategy; (3) implementing strategy. Managers use planning to identify and select appropriate goals and courses of action for an organisation and to decide how to allocate the resources they need to attain those goals and carry out those actions. A good plan builds commitment for the organisation's goals, gives the organisation a sense of direction and purpose, co-ordinates the different functions and divisions of the organisation and controls managers by making them accountable for specific goals. In large organisations planning takes place at three levels: corporate, business or divisional and functional or departmental. Although planning is typically the responsibility of a well-defined group of managers, the subordinates of those managers should be given every opportunity to have input into the process and to shape the outcome. Long-term plans have a time horizon of five years or more; intermediate-term plans, between one and five years; and short-term plans, one year or less.

Determining the organisation's mission and goals and formulating strategy Determining the organisation's mission requires that managers define the business of the organisation and establish major goals.

Formulating strategy Strategy formulation requires that managers perform a SWOT analysis and then choose appropriate strategies at the corporate, business and functional levels. At the corporate level, organisations use strategies such as concentration on a single business, diversification, international expansion and vertical integration to help increase the value of the goods and services provided to customers. At the business level, managers are responsible for developing a successful low-cost or differentiation strategy, either for the whole market or for a particular segment of it. At the functional level, departmental managers strive to develop and use their skills to help the organisation either to add value to its products by differentiating them or to lower the costs of value creation.

Planning and implementing strategy Strategy implementation requires that managers allocate responsibilities to appropriate individuals or groups, draft detailed action plans that specify how a strategy is to be implemented, establish a timetable for implementation that includes precise, measurable goals linked to the attainment of the action plan, allocate appropriate resources to the responsible individuals or groups and hold individuals or groups accountable for the attainment of goals.

Topic for Action

- Ask a manager about the kinds of planning exercises he or she regularly uses. What are the purposes of these exercises, and what are their advantages or disadvantages?
- Ask a manager to identify the corporate-, business- and functional-level strategies used by his or her organisation.

Applied Independent Learning

Building Management Skills

How to Analyse a Company's Strategy

Pick a well-known business organisation that has received recent press coverage and for which you can get the annual reports from their website. For this organisation, do the following:

1. From the annual reports, identify the main strategies pursued by the company over a 10-year period (if that many reports are available).
2. Try to identify why the company pursued these strategies. What reason was given in the annual reports, press reports and so on?
3. Document whether and when any major changes in the strategy of the organisation occurred. If changes did occur, try to identify the reason for them.
4. If changes in strategy occurred, try to determine the extent to which they were the result of long-term plans and the extent to which they were responses to unforeseen changes in the company's task environment.
5. What is the main industry that the company competes in?

▶

▶ 6. What business-level strategy does the company seem to be pursuing in this industry?

7. What is the company's reputation with regard to productivity, quality, innovation and responsiveness to customers in this industry? If the company has attained an advantage in any of these areas, how has it done so?

8. What is the current corporate-level strategy of the company? What is the company's stated reason for pursuing this strategy?

9. Has the company expanded internationally? If it has, identify its largest international market. How did the company enter this market? Did its mode of entry change over time?

Managing Ethically

A few years ago, IBM announced that it had fired the three senior managers of its Argentine division because of their involvement in a scheme to secure a large contract for IBM to provide and service the computers of one of Argentina's largest state-owned banks. The three executives paid millions of the contract money to a third company, CCR, which then paid nearly half to phantom companies. This money was then used to bribe the bank executives who agreed to give IBM the contract.

These bribes are not necessarily illegal under Argentine law. Moreover, the three managers argued that all companies have to pay bribes to get new business contracts, and they were not doing anything that managers in other companies were not doing.

Questions

1. Either by yourself or in a group decide if this business practice of paying bribes is ethical or unethical.

2. Should IBM allow its foreign divisions to pay bribes if all other companies are doing so?

3. If bribery is common in a particular country, what effect would this likely have on the nation's economy and culture?

Small Group Breakout Exercise

Low Cost or Differentiation?

Form groups of three or four people, and appoint one member as spokesperson who will communicate your findings to the class when called on by the instructor. Then discuss the following scenario.

You are a team of managers of a major national clothing chain, and you have been charged with finding a way to restore your organisation's competitive advantage. Recently, your organisation has been experiencing increasing competition from two sources. First, discount stores such as Wal-Mart and Target have been undercutting your prices because they buy their clothes from low-cost foreign manufacturers while you buy most of yours from high-quality domestic suppliers. Discount stores have been attracting your customers who buy at the low end of the price range. Second, small boutiques opening in malls provide high-price designer clothing and are attracting your customers at the high end of the market. Your company has become 'stuck in the middle', and you have to decide what to do.

Should you start to buy abroad so that you can lower your prices and begin to pursue a low-cost strategy? Should you focus on the high end of the market and become more of a differentiator? Or should you try to do both and pursue a low-cost strategy and a differentiation strategy?

1. Using scenario planning, analyse the pros and cons of each alternative.

2. Think about the various clothing retailers in your local malls and city, and analyse the choices they have made about how to compete with one another along the low-cost and differentiation dimensions.

Exploring the World Wide Web

Go to the corporate website of Google (www.google.com/corporate/execs.html), click on 'corporate info', and explore this site; in particular, click on 'Google's history' and 'The 10 Things' that guide Google's corporate philosophy.

1. How would you describe Google's mission and goals?

2. What is Google's business-level strategy?

3. What is Google's corporate-level strategy?

Application in Today's Business World

Volkswagen Slips Into Reverse

It has been a rough ride for Bernd Pischetsrieder since the former BMW boss took over as chief executive at Volkswagen (VW) in April 2002. VW's share price has fallen nearly 50 per cent since then, wiping out $11 billion in market capitalisation as profits plummeted at the $150 billion company.

On 23 July 2004, Pischetsrieder delivered more bad news – a 36 per cent net profit drop in the first half of the year. Profits for all of 2003 were already down by more than half, and just to take even more air out of VW's tyres the boss issued a grim earnings warning for 2004. In three years – just half a model life cycle in the auto business – the world's fourth-largest car maker had gone from Europe's showcase turnaround to major-league laggard.

What went wrong? Volkswagen's vaunted brand premium – the implicit guarantee of quality and innovation that for long allowed it to charge as much as 8 per cent more than the competition for mass-market cars – is eroding fast. French, Asian and even US rivals are improving quality, bolstering manufacturing efficiency and besting VW at design. The Golf compact lost out in 2003 to the Peugeot 206 as Europe's best-selling car for the second year in a row. The all-new, richly priced Golf is running neck-and-neck with its ageing French rival in 2004. To counter slow sales of its Golf in Europe, VW was forced in January to offer a $1,500 air-conditioning system for free and hefty dealer rebates on used-car trade ins. In the US, meanwhile, VW has slapped a $3,000 rebate on its ageing Passat and joined the 0 per cent financing game. US losses were expected to reach $1.4 billion in 2004, due to falling sales and the weak dollar's impact on reported earnings.

▶

▶   Another nasty surprise was in China, which until recently accounted for up to 24 per cent of VW's operating profit. In late May 2004, General Motors Corp., keen to dethrone VW as China's market leader, cut prices by 11 per cent. VW matched the move. GM's sales doubled in the first half of 2004, while VW's fell 4.2 per cent. VW commanded half the mainland market in 1999; now it controls just over a quarter. Pischetsrieder now expected China sales to grow only 5 per cent to 7 per cent in 2004, down from over 30 per cent in recent years. 'Our prime objective is profitability, not maintaining market share,' he said in a 23 July 2004 conference call with financial analysts and journalists.

What is the way out? Pischetsrieder has launched a cost-savings programme called ForMotion aimed at trimming $2.6 billion over two years, on top of the company's existing effort to squeeze costs by $1.1 billion a year. The plan seeks to cut $970 million in purchasing costs, $600 million in reduced staffing and $360 million in restructured sales activities. VW is also beefing up its lucrative auto-finance business by buying a leading Dutch car-leasing company.

More models are coming, too: a souped-up Golf was due later in 2004, with the debut of Passat and Jetta remakes. In China, Pischetsrieder is investing $6 billion over the next four years and aims to double VW's production capacity, to 1.6 million cars, by 2008. VW is also introducing fresher models to the Chinese market – the Touareg sport utility, the Phaeton luxury sedan, the Audi A6 and a car that will be expressly designed for China. Pischetsrieder is shifting decision making from VW's Wolfsburg headquarters to Beijing and sending out experienced managers.

Pischetsrieder also has a winner in the Audi, VW's $28 billion-in-revenue premium brand. Strong sales of Audi's luxury A8, the new A6 midsize sedan and the hot A3 compact helped drive a 10 per cent increase in operating profit, to $666 million, in the first half of 2004. Audi introduced the rugged Pike's Peak SUV in 2005.

Cost cuts, new models, new focus, a strong luxury brand: sounds good. So why aren't investors impressed? Analysts who had expected 2004 to be a comeback year now say that earnings will remain anemic through 2006. 'VW is a huge ship. You can't turn it for miles and miles,' says George C. Peterson, president of AutoPacific, Inc. in Tustin, CA.

One problem is that achieving big efficiencies is like shooting at a moving target. Pischetsrieder's cuts will help, but analysts say the effort pales in comparison with the thorough streamlining already achieved at Renault, Peugeot and Chrysler. Besides, 'VW has never faced up to its fundamental cost problem. It has never faced up to the unions,' says John Wormald, a partner at London-based consultant Autopolis. While rivals retooled, VW dallied. Labour costs at VW's factories are 17.4 per cent of revenues, versus a European average of 15 per cent, according to a 27 July 2004 report by Dresdner Kleinwort Wasserstein. Since closing a plant in Germany is politically impossible, analysts say, Pischetsrieder needs to accelerate cost-cutting dramatically and boost sales while improving plant flexibility. 'The group is far from being on a sound recovery path,' says Bruno Lapierre, an Exane BNP Paribas analyst, in a 23 July 2004 report.

VW has also blundered by neglecting to develop a stable of minivans and SUVs, which make up over 54 per cent of industry sales in the US. So far, VW's only offering is the Touareg SUV. 'In the United States, it's playing with one hand behind its back. It has no lineup to match Honda and Toyota,' says Peterson. 'How did that escape them?'

Slow-Moving Managers

Pischetsrieder, who has a consensus-driven management style, is making little headway against a bureaucracy that is resistant to change. Insiders say that VW's chronically weak management and poor execution were aggravated by the nine-year tenure of former CEO Ferdinand K. Piëch, a brilliant but autocratic engineer. 'Of the top 100 managers, 50 are not used to making their own decisions or thinking on their own. They wait for the phone to ring to get their orders. They are used to being told what to do,' says an auto-industry expert who is close to the company.

Pischetsrieder has sought to set up more democratic decision-making structures, but many say the pace of change is glacial. 'What Pischetsrieder wants to do is right – to transform the organisation, processes and behaviour,' says one consultant. 'The question is whether there is enough time to survive the tough period ahead.' Looks like it's time for a radical shift of gears.

Questions

1. What is the source of Volkswagen's problems?

2. What strategies is it adopting to solve these problems?

Source: Gail Edmundson and Dexter Roberts, 'Volkswagen Slips into Reverse', adapted and reprinted from *BusinessWeek*, August 9, 2004 by special permission. Copyright © 2004 by the McGraw-Hill Companies, Inc.

Notes and References

1 *Evening Standard*, 'Pepsi vs Coke over Beckham', April 2002.

2 www.cott.com, 2004.

3 htpp://www.cnw.ca/en/releases/archive/January2006/26/c0838.html; http://www.cott.com/.

4 A. Chandler, *Strategy and Structure: Chapters in the History of the American Enterprise* (Cambridge, MA: MIT Press, 1962).

5 *Ibid.*

6 http://www.centrica.co.uk/index.asp?pageid=5.

7 www.edf.fr.

8 F. J. Aguilar, 'General Electric: Reg Jones and Jack Welch', in F. J. Aguilar, *General Managers in Action* (Oxford: Oxford University Press, 1992).

9 H. Fayol, *General and Industrial Management* (1884; New York: IEEE Press, 1984).

10 *Ibid.*

11 P. Wack, 'Scenarios – Shooting the Rapids', *Harvard Business Review* 85. (November–December 1985), 131–50; P. Wack, 'Scenarios – Uncharted Waters Ahead', *Harvard Business Review* 85 (September–October 1985), 73–89.

12 A. P. De Geus, 'Planning as Learning'. *Harvard Business Review* 88 (March–April 1988), 70–74.

13 R. Phelps, C. Chan and S. C. Kapsalis, 'Does Scenario Planning Affect Performance? Two Exploratory Studies', *Journal of Business Research*, 51(3) (2001), 223–32.

14 http://www.shell.com/home/Framework. http://www.shell.com/static/royal-en/downloads/scenarios/exsum_23052005.pdf.

15 Wack, 'Scenarios – Shooting the Rapids'.

16 P. J. H. Schoemaker, 'Multiple Scenario Development: Its Conceptual and Behavioral Foundation', *Strategic Management Journal* 14 (1993), 193–213.

17 Phelps, Chan and Kapsalis, 'Does Scenario Planning Affect Performance?'.

18 J. A. Pearce, 'The Company Mission as a Strategic Tool', *Sloan Management Review*, (Spring 1992), 15–24.

19 D. F. Abell, *Defining the Business: The Starting Point of Strategic Planning* (Englewood Cliffs, NJ: Prentice Hall, 1980).

20   http://www.lego.com/info/pdf/annualreport2005UK.pdf.

21   http://www.lego.com/info/pdf/annualreport2005UK.pdf. http://www.lego.com/eng/info/default.asp?page=pressdetail&contentid=18853&countrycode=2057.

22   G. Hamel and C. K. Prahalad, 'Strategic Intent', *Harvard Business Review*, (May–June 1989), 63–73.

23   *Sunday Times*, 6 March 2005.

24   www.lego.com.

25   www.asda.co.uk.

26   http://franchisor.ikea.com/showContent.asp?swfId=concept2.

27   E. A. Locke, G. P. Latham and M. Erez, 'The Determinants of Goal Commitment', *Academy of Management Review* 13 (1988), 23–39.

28   K. R. Andrews, *The Concept of Corporate Strategy* (Homewood, IL: Irwin, 1971).

29   Edmund P. Learned, C. Roland Christiansen, Kenneth Andrews and William D. Guth, *Business Policy, Text and Cases* (Homewood, IL: Irwin, 1969).

30   G. Mulvihill, 'Campbell Is Really Cooking', San Diego Tribune.com, August 5, 2004.

31   W. D. Crotty, 'Campbell Soup Is Not So Hot', MotleyFool.com, May 24, 2004.

32   http://www.bcentral.co.uk/startingup/formingacompany/innocent-drinks.mspx.

33   E. Penrose, *The Theory of the Growth of the Firm* (Oxford: Oxford University Press, 1959).

34   M. E. Porter, 'From Competitive Advantage to Corporate Strategy', *Harvard Business Review* 65 (1987), 43–59.

35   D. J. Teece, 'Economies of Scope and the Scope of the Enterprise', *Journal of Economic Behavior and Organization* 3 (1980), 223–47.

36   M. E. Porter, *Competitive Advantage: Creating and Sustaining Superior Performance* (New York: Free Press, 1985).

37   For a review of the evidence, see C. W. L. Hill and G. R. Jones, *Strategic Management: An Integrated Approach*, 5th ed. (Boston: Houghton Mifflin, 2003), Chapter 10.

38   V. Ramanujam and P. Varadarajan, 'Research on Corporate Diversification: A Synthesis', *Strategic Management Journal* 10 (1989), 523–51. See also A. Shleifer and R. W. Vishny, 'Takeovers in the 1960s and 1980s: Evidence and Implications', in R. P. Rumelt, D. E. Schendel and D. J. Teece, *Fundamental Issues in Strategy* (Boston: Harvard Business School Press, 1994).

39   J. R. Williams, B. L. Paez and L. Sanders, 'Conglomerates Revisited', *Strategic Management Journal* 9 (1988), 403–14.

40   C. A. Bartlett and S. Ghoshal, *Managing Across Borders* (Boston: Harvard Business School Press, 1989).

41   C. K. Prahalad and Y. L. Doz, *The Multinational Mission* (New York: Free Press, 1987).

42   www.gillette.com, 2004.

43   'Gillette Co.'s New $40 Million Razor Blade Factory in St Petersburg Russia', *Boston Globe*, June 7, 2000, C6.

44   www.gillette.com, 2004.

45   R. E. Caves, *Multinational Enterprise and Economic Analysis* (Cambridge: Cambridge University Press, 1982).

46   B. Kogut, 'Joint Ventures: Theoretical and Empirical Perspectives', *Strategic Management Journal* 9 (1988), 319–33.

47   'Venture with Nestle SA Is Slated for Expansion', *The Wall Street Journal*, April 15, 2001, B2.

48   B. Bahree, 'BP Amoco, Italy's ENI Plan $2.5 Billion Gas Plant', *The Wall Street Journal*, March 6, 2001, A16.

49   http://www.lloydspharmacy.co.uk/home-page/about-us/who_are_we.htm.

50   N. Hood and S. Young, *The Economics of the Multinational Enterprise* (London: Longman, 1979).

51   http://www.betterproductdesign.net/npi/products/zara.htm.

52   M. K. Perry, 'Vertical Integration: Determinants and Effects', in R. Schmalensee and R. D. Willig, *Handbook of Industrial Organization*, 1 (New York: Elsevier Science, 1989).

53 T. Muris, D. Scheffman and P. Spiller, 'Strategy and Transaction Costs: The Organization of Distribution in the Carbonated Soft Drink Industry', *Journal of Economics and Management Strategy* 1 (1992), 77–97.

54 'Matsushita Electric Industrial (MEI) in 1987', Harvard Business School Case, 388–444.

55 P. Ghemawat, *Commitment: The Dynamic of Strategy* (New York: Free Press, 1991).

56 www.ibm.com.

57 M. E. Porter, *Competitive Strategy* (New York: Free Press, 1980).

58 http://archives.cnn.com/.

59 www.federalexpress.com.

60 www.ups.com.

61 C. W. L. Hill, 'Differentiation Versus Low Cost or Differentiation and Low Cost: A Contingency Framework', *Academy of Management Review* 13 (1988), 401–12.

62 For details, see J. P. Womack, D. T. Jones and D. Roos, *The Machine That Changed the World* (New York: Rawson Associates, 1990).

63 Porter, *Competitive Advantage.*

64 www.zara.com.

65 C. Vitzthum, 'Just-in-Time-Fashion', *The Wall Street Journal*, May 18, 2001, B1, B4.

66 www.zara.com.

Chapter 9

Value-chain Management: Functional Strategies to Increase Quality, Efficiency and Responsiveness to Customers

LEARNING OBJECTIVES

After studying this chapter, you should be able to:

- ☑ Explain the role of value-chain management in achieving superior quality, efficiency and responsiveness to customers.

- ☑ Describe what customers want, and explain why it is so important for managers to be responsive to their needs.

- ☑ Explain why achieving superior quality is important.

- ☑ Describe the challenges facing managers and organisations that seek to implement quality management programmes.

- ☑ Explain why achieving superior efficiency is so important.

- ☑ Differentiate among facilities layout, flexible manufacturing, just-in-time (JIT) inventory and process reengineering.

A Manager's Challenge

Bricks, Clicks or Bricks-and-Clicks Supermarkets

How can managers increase operating performance?

The potential uses of IT and the Internet for improving responsiveness to customers became clear to companies in many industries in the late 1990s. One of these industries was the food delivery/supermarket industry. Many supermarkets decided that developing an online ordering system that allowed customers to use the Internet to order their food online and creating an operating system to deliver the food to their homes had enormous potential. An American virtual grocer raised more than £57 million to develop both the information system and the physical infrastructure of warehouses and hot and cold delivery trucks that it needed to deliver food to customers.

However, the world's largest online grocery retailer, the UK-based supermarket giant Tesco, opted for less investment by providing a store-based model. Because Tesco used its already established outlets, it reached a market coverage across England of 90 per cent. This is rivalled only by frozen food retailer Iceland, which has 95 per cent coverage across the UK.

The UK food market is worth between £80 and £100 billion and is dominated by a small number of large supermarket chains. The ongoing competition between Tesco, Sainsbury's, ASDA and Morrisons is only going to intensify away from the 'bricks & mortar' (B&M) of traditional in-store supermarket shopping. The competition has gained momentum; the UK is the global leader in online grocery shopping, overtaking the US and leaving other western European countries such as Spain, France and Italy trailing behind. The e-grocery business in the UK has experienced an annual growth of over 250 per cent; this has already forced smaller retailers such as Budgens and Somerfield to withdraw from selling their groceries online.

One of the first responses by B&M supermarkets was to take steps to make their customers' shopping experience more enjoyable. First, they improved their operations by building large, new, attractive stores that contained a wide variety of produce. Second, they increasingly incorporated IT into their operations to improve customer satisfaction with their stores: most supermarkets, for example, are now offering self-service tills. These IT improvements are seen to help operations because they eliminate lengthy checkout lines and help the company focus more on customer service. These moves have helped B&M supermarkets improve responsiveness to customers and increase the quality of their produce and service. They have also helped reduce operating costs, because customers perform their own services – including of course selecting their own produce and delivering it to their homes.

In Sweden the market share of e-grocers is the largest with approximately 2 per cent, whereby the supply chain model is mainly store-based. The UK has an approximate market share of 0.3–0.7 per cent and in the US the market share is approximately 0.2 per cent. The US operates mainly on a warehouse-based, purely online-based retail model, whereas most UK e-grocers are store-based and associated with established supermarket brands.

However, the question of which operating system is the most successful is difficult to predict. Most online grocery stores do not yet cover all their operating costs, which will, slowly, force some smaller retailers out of the e-grocery market, especially those focusing primarily on online sales. Datamonitor argues that, in order to survive, specialisation in either B&M or online will not be sufficient, and an amalgam of both is needed. Why? First, unlike their well-established B&M rivals, the new e-grocers did not possess the experience and ability to master the complex inventory management, sourcing, transportation, distribution, warehousing and logistics necessary to operate successfully in this market. Second, e-grocers totally underestimated the problems and costs of operating the production and physical delivery service necessary to get products to customers. Tesco opted for a store-based model, arguing that a warehouse-based model would require a minimum of 5,000 orders a week, with each order exceeding £100.

Virtual grocers need to take a careful look at how they are designing their operating systems. While it is still the fastest growing e-commerce market, many players collapsed after initial success in the late 1990s.

Overview

Virtual grocers use IT and the Internet to develop an operating system that may be very responsive to customers but can be very costly and inefficient compared to the systems used by the B&M supermarket chains. Some also failed to develop functional strategies that could have helped their operating systems work more efficiently – such as smaller, warehouse-based e-grocers such as Webvan, an American e-grocer that went bankrupt. The B&M supermarkets, on the other hand, made innovations in their materials management, sales and information systems that allowed them to achieve superior quality, efficiency and responsiveness to customers. Possessing these sources of competitive advantage, they retain control of the £80–£100 billion grocery market.

In this chapter the focus is on **value-chain management** and the functional (or operational) strategies that managers can use to increase the performance of a company's **operating system** – specifically, to improve the quality of a company's goods and services, the efficiency with which they are produced and the level of responsiveness to its customers. By the end of this chapter, you will understand the vital role value-chain management plays in building competitive advantage and creating a high-performing organisation.

Value-chain Management and Competitive Advantage

Value-chain management is the development of a set of functional-level strategies that can increase the performance of the operating system a company uses to transform inputs into finished products and services. An *operating system* is composed of the various different *functional activities* (marketing, materials management or production) an organisation uses to acquire inputs, convert inputs into outputs and dispose of the outputs (products or services). Functional managers are responsible for managing an organisation's operating system; they are the ones who decide what kind of functional strategies each function should pursue to build competitive advantage. Specifically, their job is to manage the value chain to determine where operating improvements might be made to increase quality, efficiency and responsiveness to customers – and so give an organisation a competitive advantage.

The Value Chain

The **value chain** refers to the idea that a company is a *chain of functional activities* that transforms inputs into an output of products or services that are valued by the customer. The process of transforming inputs into outputs is composed of a number of functional operating activities, or an *operating system*, beginning with the need to acquire inputs, to design and control conversion processes and to distribute and sell products and services. Each activity adds value to the product and so increases the price a company can charge for its products. A value chain is illustrated in Fig. 9.1, in which several important functional activities are represented.

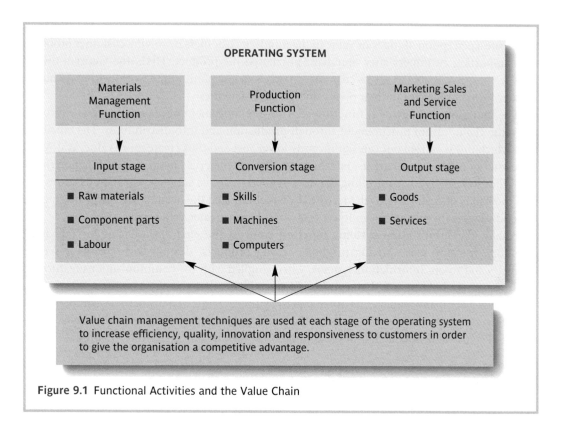

OPERATING SYSTEM

| Materials Management Function | Production Function | Marketing Sales and Service Function |

| Input stage | Conversion stage | Output stage |

- Raw materials
- Component parts
- Labour

- Skills
- Machines
- Computers

- Goods
- Services

Value chain management techniques are used at each stage of the operating system to increase efficiency, quality, innovation and responsiveness to customers in order to give the organisation a competitive advantage.

Figure 9.1 Functional Activities and the Value Chain

The **production function** is responsible for the *creation of a product or service*. For physical products, when we talk about production, we generally mean manufacturing. For services such as banking or retailing, production typically takes place when the service is actually delivered to the customer (when a bank provides a loan to a customer, for example it is engaged in 'production' of the loan). By performing its activities efficiently, the production function of a company helps to lower its cost structure. The efficient production operations of some Japanese companies, such as Honda and Toyota, are helping those companies achieve higher profitability relative to competitors such as Volkswagen, Saab or Volvo. The production function of a company can also perform its activities in a way that is consistent with high product quality, which may also lead to differentiation (and higher value) and lower costs.

There are several ways in which the **marketing/sales functions** of a company can help to create value. By *positioning* and *advertising* a brand appropriately, the marketing function can increase the value that customers perceive to be contained in a company's product. As branding aids in creating a favourable impression of the company's product in the minds of customers, they increase value. In the 1980s, the French company Perrier persuaded customers that slightly carbonated bottled water was worth £0.90 for 750 ml, rather than the £0.87 it cost to purchase 5 litres of spring water from the supermarket's own brand. Perrier's marketing function essentially developed marketing strategies that increased the perception of value that customers ascribed to the product. In the 1990s, major companies such as Coca-Cola and PepsiCo rushed to bring out their own bottled-water labels to capitalise on customers' growing appetite for bottled water. The total UK market for bottled water is worth in the region of 50 million litres which equates to about £30 million.

The role of the **service function** is to provide *after-sales service and support*. This function can create a perception of superior value in the minds of customers by solving customer problems and supporting customers after they have purchased the product. DHL, the German-owned logistic company, is able to get its customers' parcels to any point in the world within 24 hours, thereby lowering the cost of their own value-creation activities.

The **materials management function** controls the movement of *physical materials* through the value chain – from procurement through production and into distribution. The efficiency with which this is carried out can significantly lower cost and thus create more value. Wal-Mart, the owner of ASDA supermarkets, has the most efficient materials management function in the retail industry. By tightly controlling the flow of goods from its suppliers through its stores and into the hands of customers, Wal-Mart/ASDA has eliminated the need to hold large inventories of goods. Lower inventories mean lower costs, and hence greater value creation.

Finally, the **information systems function** controls the *electronic systems* for managing inventory, tracking sales, pricing products, selling products, dealing with customer service enquiries and so on. Information systems, when coupled with the communications features of the Internet, are holding out the promise of being able to alter the efficiency and effectiveness with which a company manages its other value-creation activities. Many delivery companies are now allowing you to track your parcels on the Internet, for example. However, the implementation of IT adds value only if all other functions are efficiently and effectively organised.

Functional Strategies and Competitive Advantage

In managing the value chain to create a high-performing operating system, functional managers need to attend to the four major goals discussed in Chapter 1:[1]

1. *To attain superior efficiency*   Efficiency is a measure of the amount of *inputs* required to produce a given *amount* of outputs. The fewer the inputs required to produce a given output, the higher is the efficiency and the lower the cost of outputs. In 1990, it took the average Japanese auto company 16.8 employee-hours to build a car, while the average American car company took 25.1 employee-hours. Japanese companies at that time were more efficient and had lower costs than their western rivals.[2] By 2004, US companies, and many European manufacturers, had adopted more efficient manufacturing methods and narrowed the gap significantly; matching Japanese quality levels, however, has been more difficult.

2. *To attain superior quality*   'Quality' here means producing goods and services that are reliable – they do what they were designed for, and do it well.[3] Providing high-quality products creates a *brand-name reputation* for an organisation's products. In turn, this enhanced reputation allows the organisation to charge a higher price. In the automobile industry, for example, not only does Toyota have an efficiency-based cost advantage over many European competitors, but the higher quality of Toyota's products has also enabled the company to earn more money because customers are willing to pay a premium price for its cars.

3. *To attain superior speed, flexibility and innovation*   Anything new or better about the way an organisation operates or the goods and services it produces is the result of innovation. Innovation leads to advances in the kinds of products, production processes, management systems, organisational structures and strategies that an organisation develops. Successful innovation gives an organisation something *unique* that its rivals lack. This uniqueness may enhance value added and thereby allow the organisation to differentiate itself from its rivals

and attract customers who will pay a premium price for its product. Toyota, for example, is widely credited with pioneering a number of critical innovations in the way that cars are built, and these innovations have helped Toyota achieve superior productivity and quality, the basis of the company's competitive advantage. VW tried a similar innovation by creating their modular consortium plant for the production of HGVs in Brazil.[4] Rather than using a large number of suppliers, an expensive manufacturing process and a large number of employees, VW created an *integrated assembly plant* that incorporated the seven major contributors. Each of those contributors assembled a particular modular for the vehicles, but all seven at the same assembly line. VW's investment was a contribution to the plant and infrastructure and its remaining responsibility was quality control, marketing and sales of the vehicles.

4. *To attain superior responsiveness to customers* An organisation that is responsive to customers tries to satisfy their needs and give them exactly what they want. An organisation that treats customers better than its rivals provides a valuable service, for which customers may be willing to pay a higher price.

In managing the value chain to add value, or lower the costs of creating value, functional managers need to find ways to attain superior quality, efficiency, innovation and responsiveness to customers. Functional managers are responsible for ensuring that an organisation has sufficient supplies of high-quality, low-cost inputs, and they are also responsible for designing an operating system that creates high-quality, low-cost products that customers are willing to buy. Notice, however, that achieving superior efficiency, quality and innovation is part of attaining superior responsiveness to customers. Customers want value for their money, and an organisation that develops functional strategies that lead to a high-performing operating system creates new high-quality, low-cost products that best deliver this value. For this reason, the chapter begins by discussing how functional managers can design the operating system to increase responsiveness to customers.

Improving Responsiveness to Customers

Organisations create outputs – products or services – that are consumed by customers. All organisations, profit-seeking or not-for-profit, have customers: without customers, most organisations would cease to exist. Because customers are vital to the survival of most organisations, managers must correctly identify their customers and pursue the strategies that respond to their needs. This is why the marketing function plays such an important part in the value chain. Management writers recommend that marketing managers should focus on defining their company's business in terms of the customer needs they are satisfying, and not simply the type of products they make or provide.[5] The credo of the pharmaceutical company Johnson & Johnson, for example, begins: 'We believe our first responsibility is to the doctors, nurses and patients, to mothers and fathers and all others who use our products and services'.[6] Through this credo, Johnson & Johnson's managers emphasise their commitment to exemplary customer service.

In contrast, in the early 2000s, Lucent Technologies, a spin-off of AT&T, decided that, given its expertise in transistor technology, it would focus on producing transistor-based Internet routers that could handle vast quantities of information. When it became clear that customers were choosing optical Internet routers because these routers could transfer information extremely quickly, Lucent lost a large part of its business, and by 2004 had radically altered its strategies to focus on a narrow range of high-speed networking devices that allow Internet ser-vice providers to offer their business customers high-speed, secure Internet access.[7]

What Do Customers Want?

Given that satisfying customer demands is central to the survival of an organisation, an important question is: What do customers want? Specifying exactly what they want is usually not possible because wants vary from industry to industry. However, it is possible to identify some *universal product attributes* that most customers in most industries want. Generally, other things being equal, most customers prefer:

1. A lower price to a higher price
2. High-quality products to low-quality products
3. Quick service to slow service (they will always prefer good after-sales service and support to poor after-sales service and support)
4. Products with many features to products with few features (they will prefer a personal com-puter with a CD-ROM drive, lots of memory and a powerful microprocessor to one without these features)
5. Products that are, as far as possible, customised or tailored to their unique needs.

Of course, the problem is that other things are not equal. Providing high-quality, quick service and after-sales service and support, products with many features and products that are customised raises operating costs and thus the price that must be charged to cover these costs.[8] So customer demand for these attributes typically conflicts with their demand for low prices. Customers must thus make a *trade-off* between price and preferred attributes, and so must managers. This price/attribute trade-off is illustrated in Fig. 9.2.

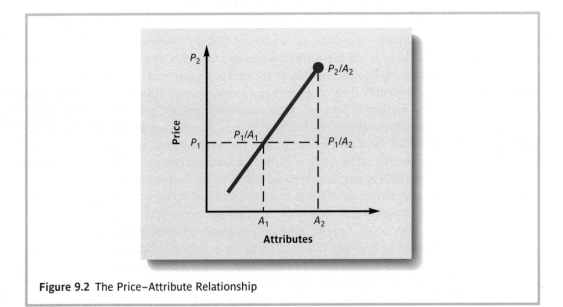

Figure 9.2 The Price–Attribute Relationship

The desired attributes of a product – such as high quality, service, speed, after-sales support, features and customisation – are plotted on the horizontal axis in Fig. 9.2. Price is plotted on the vertical axis. The solid line shows the price–attribute relationship – i.e. the combination of price and attributes an organisation can offer and still make a profit. As Fig. 9.2 illustrates, the higher the price the customer is willing to pay for a product, the more desired attributes the customer is able to get. In other words, the more desired attributes that an organisation can build into its products, the higher is the price that the organisation will have to charge to cover its costs. At price P_1 managers can offer a product with A_1 attributes. If managers offer a product with A_2 attributes at price P_1, they will lose money because the price is too low to cover costs. A product with A_2 attributes needs a price of P_2 to be profitable for the organisation. The nature of the organisation's operating system thus *limits* how responsive managers can be to customers.

Given the limits imposed on managers by their existing operating system, what can the managers of a customer-responsive organisation try to do? They can try to develop functional strategies to push or shift the price–attribute curve to the right (toward the vertical dotted line in Fig. 9.2) by developing new or improved operating systems that are able to deliver either more desired product attributes for the same price, or the same product attributes for a lower price.[9]

Figure 9.3 shows the price-attribute curves for a supermarket chain in the 1990s, before the introduction of customer-oriented IT. The second line represents the same supermarket chain in the 2000s, when new self-service tills and new store design were put in place. By accommodating customer demands for a greater variety of foods, increased quality and quicker customer service, the new operating system allowed the supermarket to offer more product attributes at a similar or even lower price to customers. The shift from a traditional to a modern, IT-oriented store operation thus increased its responsiveness to customers and did so without imposing higher costs.

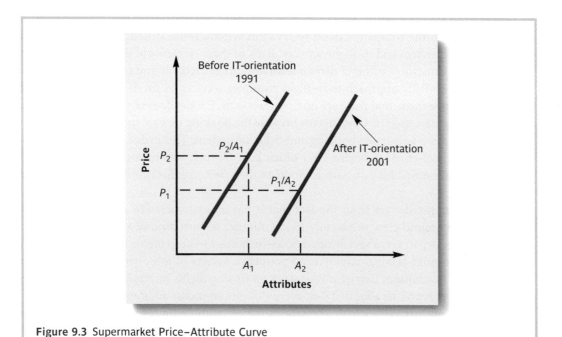

Figure 9.3 Supermarket Price–Attribute Curve

Designing Operating Systems Responsive to Customers

Because satisfying customers is so important, managers try to design operating systems that can produce the outputs that have the attributes customers desire. The attributes of an organisation's outputs – their quality, cost and features – are determined by the organisation's operating system.[10] As discussed earlier, the need to respond to customer demands for competitively priced, quality food drove managers of supermarkets to choose a new store operation system. The imperative of satisfying customer needs shaped Sainsbury's 'production' system. When managers focus on being responsive to their customers, and not just on producing or providing a product, they find new ways to reduce costs and increase quality – such as the introduction of faster self-service tills.

Since the ability of an organisation to satisfy the demands of its customers derives from its operating system, managers need to devote considerable attention to *value-chain management*. Managers' desire to attract customers by shifting the price–attribute line to the right explains their adoption of many new functional strategies to build competitive advantage into their operating systems. These include total quality management (TQM), flexible manufacturing systems, JIT inventory and, of course, new information systems and technologies that can accelerate the sale and delivery of products to customers.

As an example of the link between responsiveness to customers and an organisation's operating system, consider the success of low-cost airlines such as Easyjet or Flybe. One of the most consistently successful airlines, Easyjet expanded rapidly in the early 2000s.[11] One reason for Easyjet's success is that its managers created an operating system uniquely tailored to satisfy the demands of its customers for low-priced, reliable (on-time) and convenient air travel. Easyjet commands high customer loyalty precisely because its operating system delivers products – such as flights from and to most major cities in Europe – that have all the desired attributes: reliability, convenience and low price.

Easyjet's low-cost operating system focuses not only on improving the maintenance of aircraft but also on the company's ticket reservation system, route structure, flight frequency, baggage-handling system and in-flight services. Each of these elements of the operating system is geared toward satisfying customer demands for low-priced, reliable and convenient air travel. Easyjet offers a 'no-frills' approach to in-flight customer service: no meals are served onboard unless you purchase them, and there are no first-class seats. Easyjet does not subscribe to the big reservation computers used by travel agents because the booking fees are too costly, and instead predominantly uses a web-based booking and ticketing system. The airline originally only flew one aircraft, the fuel-efficient Boeing 737, which kept training and maintenance costs down, although they have now added an Airbus model to their fleet. All this translates into low prices for customers.

Easyjet's reliability derives from the fact that it has an extremely fast aircraft turnaround time. An Easyjet ground crew needs only 15–30 minutes to turn around an incoming aircraft and prepare it for departure, a speedy operation which helps to keep flights on time. Easyjet can also deploy their multi-tasking employees to perform a variety of jobs, which keeps employee numbers down. In addition, Easyjet is very strict on closing flights on time to ensure that each flight is able to depart on its allocated slot; every slot missed incurs additional cost.

Easyjet's convenience comes from the scheduling of multiple flights every day between its popular locations and the use of airports that are close to downtown instead of more distant airports (a model that is applied by other no-frills airlines in Europe and North America).[12] Easyjet, unlike other low-cost carriers such as Ryanair, uses main airports that have the infrastructure to allow passengers a quick and efficient onward journey. In sum, Easyjet's excellent value-chain management has given it a competitive advantage in the airline industry.

Although managers must seek to improve their responsiveness to customers by improving their organisations' operating systems, they should not offer a level of responsiveness to customers that is more than can *profitably be sustained*. The company that customises every product to the unique demands of individual customers is likely to see its cost structure become so high that unit costs exceed unit revenues. This happened to Toyota in the 1990s when its managers tried to provide customers with many choices of car models and specifications. This increased costs faster than it generated additional revenues: at one point, Toyota factories were producing literally thousands of variations of Toyota's basic models, such as the Avensis and Corolla. Managers at Toyota concluded that the costs of extreme customisation were exceeding the benefits, and cut back on the number of models and specifications of its cars.[13]

Improving Quality

As noted earlier, high-quality products are reliable, dependable and satisfying. They do the job they were designed for, and meet customer requirements.[14] *Quality* is a concept that can be applied to the products of both manufacturing and service organisations – goods such as a Toyota car or a Tesco ready meal, or services such as Easyjet's flight service or customer service at your local bank. Why do managers seek to control and improve the quality of their organisations' products?[15] There are two reasons (Fig. 9.4).

First, customers usually prefer a higher-quality product to a lower-quality product. So an organisation that is able to provide, *for the same price*, a product of higher quality than a competitor's product is serving its customers better – it is being more responsive to its customers. Often, providing high-quality products creates a brand-name reputation for an organisation's products. In turn, this enhanced reputation may allow the organisation to charge more for its products than its competitors, and thus it makes even greater profits. In 2005, the most reliable car in the UK was a Honda. The only European manufacturers in the Top 10 were Skoda and Mercedes-Benz.[16] The high quality of Honda vehicles enabled the company to charge higher prices for its cars than the prices charged by rival auto makers.

Figure 9.4 The Impact of Increased Quality on Organisational Performance

The second reason for trying to boost product quality is that higher product quality can increase *efficiency* and thereby lower operating costs and boost profits. Achieving high product quality lowers operating costs because of the effect of quality on employee productivity: higher product quality means that less employee time is wasted in making defective products that must be discarded or in providing substandard services, and thus less time has to be spent fixing mistakes. This translates into *higher employee productivity*, which means lower costs.

Total Quality Management

At the forefront of the drive to improve product quality is a technique known as *total quality management* (TQM).[17] TQM focuses on improving the quality of an organisation's products and services and stresses that all of an organisation's value-chain activities should be directed toward this goal. Conceived as an organisation-wide management programme, TQM requires the co-operation of managers in every function of an organisation. The TQM concept was developed by a number of American consultants, including the late W. Edwards Deming, Joseph Juran and A. V. Feigenbaum.[18]

What actions should managers take to implement a successful TQM programme? Ten steps are necessary to make a TQM control system work.

1. *Build organisational commitment to quality* TQM will do little to improve the performance of an organisation unless all employees embrace it, and this often requires a change in an organisation's *culture*.[19] At Citibank, discussed in detail in Case 9.1, the process of changing culture began at the top. First, a group of senior managers, including the CEO, received training in TQM from consultants from Motorola. Each member of the senior management group was then given the responsibility of training a group at the next level in the hierarchy, and so on down through the organisation until all 100,000 employees had received basic TQM training.

2. *Focus on the customer* TQM practitioners see a focus on the customer as the starting point.[20] According to TQM philosophy, the *customer*, not managers in quality control or engineering, defines what quality is. The challenge is fourfold: (1) to identify what customers want from the good or service that the company provides; (2) to identify what the company actually provides to customers; (3) to identify the gap that exists between what customers want and what they actually get (the *quality gap*); and (4) to formulate a plan for closing the quality gap. The efforts of Citibank managers to increase responsiveness to customers illustrate this aspect of TQM well (Case 9.1).

Case 9.1: Citibank uses TQM to increase customer loyalty

Citibank is one of the leading financial institutions, operating in a large number of countries, including Germany and the UK, where it was voted best Internet bank. Citibank's goal is to become *the* premier institution in the twenty-first century. To achieve this goal, Citibank has started to use TQM to increase its responsiveness to customers, recognising that, ultimately, it is its customer base and customer loyalty that will determine its future success.

As the first step in its TQM effort, Citibank identified the factors that *dissatisfied* its customers. When analysing complaints, it found that most concerned the time it took to complete a customer's request, such as responding to an account problem or getting a loan. So Citibank's managers began to examine how they handled each kind of customer request. For each distinct request, they formed a cross-functional team that broke down a specific request into the steps between people and departments that were needed to complete it. Teams found that many steps in the process were often unnecessary and could be replaced by using the right information systems. They also found that delays often occurred because employees simply did not know how to handle a request: they were not being given the right kind of training. When they couldn't handle a request, they simply put it aside until a supervisor could deal with it.

Citibank's second step to increase its responsiveness was to implement an organisation-wide TQM programme. Managers and supervisors were charged with reducing the complexity of the work process and finding the most effective way to process each particular request, such as a request for a loan. Managers were also charged with training employees to answer each specific request. The results were remarkable. In the loan department the TQM programme reduced the number of handoffs necessary to process a request by 75 per cent. The department's average response time dropped from several hours to 30 minutes. By 2000, more than 92,000 employees worldwide had been trained in the new TQM processes, and Citibank could easily measure effectiveness by the increased speed with which it was handling an increased volume of customer requests.

3. *Find ways to measure quality*   Another crucial element of any TQM programme is the creation of a *measuring system* that managers can consistently use to evaluate quality. Devising appropriate measures is relatively easy in manufacturing companies, where quality can be measured by criteria such as defects per million parts. It is more difficult in service companies, where outputs are less tangible. However, with a little creativity, suitable quality measures can be devised, as they were by managers at Citibank. The common theme is that managers must identify what 'quality' means from a *customer's* perspective and devise some measure that can capture this.

4. *Set goals and create incentives*   Once a measure has been devised, managers' next step is to set a *challenging quality goal* and to create *incentives* for reaching it. At Citibank, the CEO set an initial goal of reducing customer complaints by 50 per cent. One way of creating incentives to attain a goal is to link rewards, such as bonus pay and promotional opportunities, to it.

5. *Solicit input from employees*   Employees can be a major source of information about the causes of poor quality. It is therefore important for managers to establish a framework for soliciting employee suggestions about improvements that can be made. **Quality circles (QCs)** – groups of employees who meet regularly to discuss ways to increase quality – are often created to achieve this goal. Companies also create self-managed teams to further quality improvement efforts. Whatever the means chosen to solicit input from lower-level employees, managers must be open to receiving, and acting on, bad news and criticism from employees.

6. *Identify defects and trace them to their source*   A major source of product defects is the *operating system*. TQM preaches the need for managers to identify defects in the work process, trace those defects back to their source, find out why they occur and make corrections so that they do not occur again. To identify defects, the use of statistical procedures to spot variations in the quality of goods or services may be used, and IT makes the measurement of quality much easier.

7. *Introduce JIT inventory systems*   **Inventory** is the stock of raw materials, inputs and component parts that an organisation has at its disposal at a particular time. **JIT inventory systems** play a major role in the process of identifying and finding the source of defects in inputs. When the materials management function designs a JIT inventory system, parts or supplies arrive at the organisation when they are needed, and not before. With a JIT inventory system component parts travel from suppliers to the assembly line in a small-wheeled container known as a *kanban*. Assembly-line workers empty the kanbans and the empty container is then sent back to the supplier as the signal to produce another small batch of component parts, and so the process repeats itself. This system can be contrasted with a *just-in-case* view of inventory, which leads an organisation to stockpile excess inputs in a warehouse just in case it needs them to meet sudden upturns in demand.

   Under a JIT inventory system, defective parts enter an organisation's operating system immediately; they are not warehoused for months before use. This means that *defective inputs* can be quickly spotted. Materials managers can then trace the problem to the supply source and fix it before more defective parts are produced.

8. *Work closely with suppliers*   A major cause of poor-quality finished goods is poor-quality *component parts*. To decrease product defects, materials managers must work closely with suppliers to improve the quality of the parts they supply. Managers at Xerox worked closely with suppliers to get them to adopt TQM programmes, and the result was a huge reduction in the defect rate of component parts. Managers also need to work closely with suppliers to get them to adopt the JIT inventory system necessary for high quality.

   To implement JIT systems with suppliers, and to get suppliers to set up their own TQM programmes, two steps are necessary. First, managers must reduce the *number of suppliers* with which their organisations do business. Second, managers need to develop *co-operative long-term relationships* with remaining suppliers. Over the years, managers at Dell Computer reduced the number of suppliers they needed to a minimum, which greatly streamlined their interactions with suppliers and led to increased quality and lower-cost inputs. The modular consortium approach adopted by VW also reduced the number of direct suppliers. VW is responsible only for the assembly and quality control so they reduced the number of direct suppliers from over 200 to seven modular manufacturers.

9. *Design for ease of production*   The more steps required to assemble a product or provide a service, the more opportunities there are for making a mistake. It follows that designing products that have fewer parts, or finding ways to simplify providing a service, should be linked with fewer defects or customer complaints. Dell continually redesigns the way it assembles its computers to reduce the number of assembly steps required and to search for new ways to reduce the number of components that have to be linked together. The consequence of these redesign efforts has been a fall in assembly costs and a marked improvement in product quality that has led to Dell's becoming the Number One global PC maker. Dell also has striven to improve its procedures for helping customers who experience problems with their new PCs.

10. *Break down barriers between functions*   Successful implementation of TQM requires substantial co-operation between the different functions of an organisation. Materials managers have to co-operate with manufacturing managers to find high-quality inputs that reduce manufacturing costs; marketing managers have to co-operate with manufacturing so that customer problems identified by marketing can be acted on; information systems have to

co-operate with all of the other functions of the company to devise suitable IT training programmes; and so on.

In essence, to increase quality, all functional managers need to co-operate to develop strategic plans that state goals precisely and spell out how they will be achieved. Managers should embrace the philosophy that mistakes, defects and poor-quality materials are not acceptable, and should be eliminated. Functional managers should spend more time working with employees and providing them with the tools they need to do the job. Managers should create an environment in which employees will not be afraid to report problems or recommend improvements. Output goals and targets need to include not only numbers or quotas but also some notion of quality to promote the production of *defect-free output*. Functional managers also need to train employees in new skills to keep pace with changes in the workplace. Achieving better quality also requires that managers develop *organisational values* and *norms* centred on improving quality.

TQM is now an established model and has been implemented widely across the world. Like other management theories, other models have been developed. Another quality model is the **EFQM model** that was introduced in the early 1990s and has been widely adopted across Europe. It differs from the traditional TQM model as it is an excellence model that focuses on a number of different areas – such as leadership, customer focus, results, employee involvement, continuous learning, partnership involvement and corporate social responsibility. It is a process model that is easily combinable with other quality initiatives such as Investors in People.[21]

Reaction Time

1. What are the main challenges to be overcome in implementing a successful TQM programme?

2. Widespread dissatisfaction with the results of TQM programmes has been reported in the popular press. Why do you think TQM programmes frequently fail to deliver their promised benefits?

Improving Efficiency

The third goal of value-chain management is to increase the efficiency of an organisation's operating system. The fewer the inputs required to produce a given output, the higher will be the operating system's efficiency. Managers can measure efficiency at the organisation level in two ways. The measure known as **total factor productivity** (TFP) looks at how well an organisation utilises all of its resources – such as labour, capital, materials or energy – to produce its outputs. It is expressed in the following equation:

$$TFP = \frac{Outputs}{All\ inputs}$$

The problem with TFP is that each input is typically measured in *different units*: labour's contribution to producing an output is measured by hours worked; the contribution of materials is measured by the amount consumed (for example, tons of iron ore required to make a ton of steel); the contribution of energy is measured by the units of energy consumed (for example, kilowatt-hours, kWh); and so on. To compute TFP, managers must convert all the inputs to a *common unit*, such as pounds sterling (£), before they can work the equation.

Although sometimes a useful measure of efficiency overall, TFP can obscure the precise contribution of an individual input – such as labour – to the production of a given output. Consequently, most organisations focus on a specific measure of efficiency, known as *partial productivity*, which measures the efficiency of an *individual unit*. For example, the efficiency of labour inputs can be expressed as:

$$\text{Labour productivity} = \frac{\text{Outputs}}{\text{Direct labour}}$$

Labour productivity is most commonly used to draw efficiency comparisons between different organisations. One study found that in 1994 it took the average Japanese automobile components supplier half as many labour hours as the average British company to produce a part such as a car seat or exhaust system.[22] The study concluded that Japanese companies used labour more efficiently than British companies. In the 1990s car companies throughout the world strove to catch up with the Japanese and many, such as Vauxhall and Ford, closed the efficiency gap significantly.

The *management of efficiency* is an extremely important issue in most organisations, because increased efficiency lowers production costs, thereby allowing the organisation to make a greater profit or to attract more customers by lowering its price. In 1990, the price of the average PC was £1,700; by 1995 it was about £1,000; in 2004 it was about £500. This decrease occurred despite the fact that the power and capabilities of the average PC increased dramatically during this period (microprocessors became more powerful, memory increased, modems were built in and multimedia capability was added).

Why was the decrease in price possible? PC makers such as Dell focused on quality and used TQM to boost their efficiency by improving the quality of their components and making PCs easier to assemble. This allowed them to lower their costs and prices and still make a profit.[23] While TQM is an important step in the drive to raise efficiency, several other factors are also important.

Facilities Layout, Flexible Manufacturing and Efficiency

Another factor that influences efficiency is the way managers decide to lay out or design an organisation's physical work facilities. This is important for two reasons. First, the way in which machines and workers are organised or grouped together into workstations affects the efficiency of the operating system. Second, a major determinant of efficiency is the cost associated with setting up the equipment needed to make a particular product. **Facilities layout** is the process of designing the machine–worker interface to increase operating system efficiency. **Flexible manufacturing** is the set of techniques, usually IT-based, that attempts to reduce the costs associated with an operating system. This might be the way computers are made on a production line, or the way patients are routed through a hospital.

Facilities layout

The way in which machines, robots and people are grouped together affects how *productive* they can be. Figure 9.5 shows three basic ways of arranging workstations: product layout, process layout and fixed-position layout.

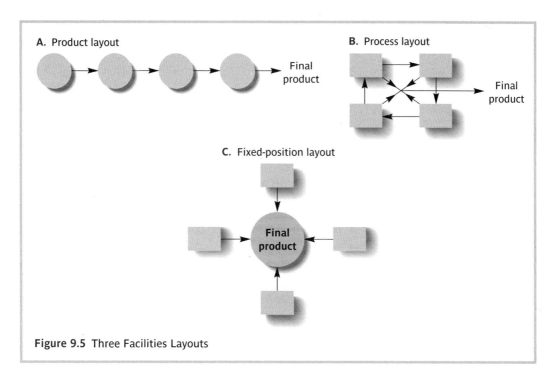

Figure 9.5 Three Facilities Layouts

In a *product layout*, machines are organised so that each operation needed to manufacture a product is performed at workstations arranged in a fixed sequence. Within less tangible products, processes are arranged in a similarly fixed sequence: workers are stationary in this arrangement, and a moving conveyor belt takes the product being worked on to the next workstation so that it is progressively assembled. *Mass production* is the familiar name for this layout, and car assembly lines are probably the best-known example. Product layout used to be efficient only when products were created in large quantities; however, the introduction of *modular assembly lines* controlled by computers is making it efficient to make products in small batches.

In a *process layout*, workstations are not organised in a fixed sequence. Each workstation is relatively self-contained, and a product goes to whichever workstation is needed to perform the next operation to complete the product. Process layout is often suited to manufacturing settings that produce a variety of custom-made products, each tailored to the needs of a different kind of customer. A custom furniture manufacturer might use a process layout so that different teams of workers can produce different styles of chairs or tables made from different kinds of woods and finishes. Such a layout also describes how a patient might go through a hospital from emergency room, to X-ray room, to operating theatre and so on. A process layout provides the flexibility needed to *change* a product, whether it is a PC or a patient. Such flexibility, however, often reduces efficiency because it is expensive.

In a *fixed-position layout*, the product stays in a fixed position. Its component parts are produced in remote workstations and are brought to the production area for final assembly. Increasingly, *self-managed teams* are using fixed-position layouts: different teams assemble each component part and then send the parts to the final assembly team, which makes the final product. A fixed-position layout is commonly used for products such as jet airlines, mainframe computers and gas turbines – products that are complex and difficult to assemble or are so large that moving them from one workstation to another is difficult. The effects of moving from one facilities layout to another can be dramatic (Case 9.2).

Case 9.2: **Paddy Hopkirk improves facilities layout**

Paddy Hopkirk established his car accessories business in Bedfordshire, England, shortly after he had shot to car-racing fame by winning the Monte Carlo Rally. Sales of Hopkirk's accessories, such as bicycle racks and axle stands, were always brisk, but Hopkirk was the first to admit that his operating system left a lot to be desired, so he invited consultants to help reorganise it.

After analysing his factory's operating system, the consultants realised that the source of the problem was the *facilities layout* that Hopkirk had established. Over time, as sales grew, Hopkirk simply added new workstations to the operating system as they were needed. The result was a process layout in which the product being assembled moved in the irregular sequences shown in the 'Before Change' section of Fig. 9.6. The consultants suggested that to save time and effort, the workstations should be reorganised into the sequential product layout shown in the 'After Change' section of Fig. 9.6.

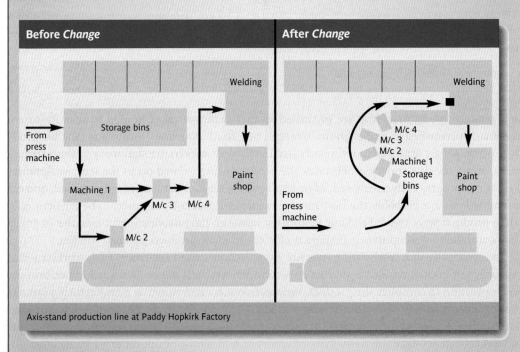

Axis-stand production line at Paddy Hopkirk Factory

Figure 9.6 Changing a Facilities Layout

Source: 'The Application of Kaizen to Facilities Layout', *Financial Times*, 4 January 1994, 12. Reprinted by permission of Financial Times Syndication, London.

Once this change was made, the results were dramatic. One morning the factory was an untidy sprawl of workstations surrounded by piles of crates holding semi-finished components. Two days later, when the 170-person workforce came back to work, the machines had been brought together into tightly grouped workstations arranged in the fixed sequence shown in Fig. 9.6. The piles of components had disappeared and the newly cleared floor space was neatly marked with colour-coded lines mapping out the new flow of materials between workstations.

In the first full day of production, efficiency increased by 30 per cent. The space needed for some operations had been cut in half, and work-in-progress had been cut considerably. Moreover, the improved layout allowed for some jobs to be combined, freeing operators for deployment elsewhere in the factory. An amazed Hopkirk exclaimed: 'I was expecting a change but nothing as dramatic as this . . . it is fantastic'.[24]

Flexible manufacturing

In a manufacturing company, a major source of expenditure is the costs associated with setting up the equipment needed to make a particular product. One of these costs is the cost of production that is forgone because nothing is produced while the equipment is being set up. Components manufacturers often need as much as half a day to set up automated production equipment when switching from production of one component part (such as a washer ring for the steering column of a car) to another (such as a washer ring for the steering column of a truck). During this half-day, a manufacturing plant is not producing anything, but employees have to be paid for this 'non-productive' time.

If setup times for complex production equipment can be reduced, so can setup costs and efficiency will rise. In other words, if setup times can be reduced, the time that plant and employees spend in actually producing the product will increase. This simple insight has been the driving force behind the development of *flexible manufacturing techniques*.

Flexible manufacturing aims to reduce the time required to set up production equipment.[25] By redesigning the manufacturing process so that the production equipment for manufacturing one product can be quickly replaced with the equipment to manufacture another, setup times and costs can be dramatically reduced. Another favourable outcome from flexible manufacturing is that a company is able to produce many more varieties of a product than before, in the same amount of time. Flexible manufacturing thus increases a company's ability to be responsive to its customers.

Increasingly, organisations are experimenting with new designs for operating systems that not only allow workers to be more productive but also make the work process more flexible, thus reducing setup costs. Some Japanese companies are experimenting with facilities layouts arranged as a spiral, as in the letter Y, and as in the number 6, to see how these various configurations affect setup costs and worker productivity. At a camcorder plant in Kohda, Japan, for example, Sony changed from a fixed-position layout in which 50 workers sequentially built a camcorder to a flexible spiral process design in which four workers performed all the operations necessary. This new layout allowed the most efficient workers to work at the highest pace, and it reduced setup costs because workers could easily switch from one model to another, increasing efficiency by 10 per cent.[26]

An interesting example of a company that built a new factory to obtain the benefits from flexible manufacturing is Igus, Inc., headquartered in Cologne, Germany. Igus makes over 28,000 polymer bearings and energy supply cable products used in applications the world over. In the 1990s, Igus' managers realised that they needed to build a new factory that could handle the company's rapidly growing product line. The product line was changing constantly as new products were innovated and old ones became obsolete. At Igus, new products are often introduced on a daily basis, so this need for flexibility is the company's prime requirement:

because many of its products are highly customised, the specific and changing needs of its customers also drive new product development.

Igus' new factory was designed with the need for flexibility in mind. As big as three football fields, nothing in the factory is tied down or bolted to the floor. All the machines, computers and equipment can be moved and repositioned to suit changing product requirements. Moreover, all Igus' employees are trained to be flexible and can perform many of the necessary production tasks. When one new product line proved popular with customers, its employees and production operations were relocated four times as it grew into larger spaces. Igus can change its operating system at a moment's notice and with minimal disruption, and since the company operates seven days a week, 24 hours a day, these changes are occurring constantly.

To facilitate these changes, workers are equipped with power scooters to move around the plant quickly and reconfigure operations. This also allows them to move quickly to wherever in the factory their skills are most needed. Employees are also equipped with mobile phones so that they are always on call.

Igus' decision to create a flexible factory of the future has paid off: in the 1990s its global sales tripled.

Just-in-time Inventory and Efficiency

Although JIT systems, such as Toyota's *kanban* system, were originally developed as part of the effort to improve product quality, they have major implications for efficiency. Major cost savings can result from increasing *inventory turnover* and reducing inventory *holding costs* – such as warehousing and storage costs and the cost of capital tied up in inventory. Although companies that manufacture and assemble products can obviously use JIT to great advantage, so can service organisations. ASDA, one of the biggest grocers in the UK, uses JIT systems to replenish the stock in its stores at least twice a week. Many ASDA stores receive daily deliveries; ASDA can maintain the same service levels as competitors but has a lower inventory holding cost, a major source of cost saving. Faster inventory turnover has helped ASDA achieve an efficiency-based competitive advantage in the retailing industry.[27]

One drawback of JIT systems is that they can leave an organisation without a buffer stock of inventory.[28] Although such stocks can be expensive to store, they can help an organisation when it is affected by shortages of inputs brought about by a supply disruption (such as a labour dispute at a key supplier). Buffer stocks can also help an organisation respond quickly to increases in customer demand – that is, they can increase an organisation's responsiveness to customers.

Self-managed Work Teams and Efficiency

Another efficiency-boosting technique is the use of self-managed work teams.[29] The typical team consists of 5–15 employees who produce an entire product instead of just parts of it.[30] Team members learn all the team tasks and move from job to job. The result is a flexible workforce, because team members can fill in for absent co-workers. The members of each team also assume responsibility for scheduling work and vacations, ordering materials and hiring new members – previously all responsibilities of first-line managers. Because people often respond well to being given greater autonomy and responsibility, the use of empowered self-managed teams can increase productivity and efficiency. Cost savings also arise from eliminating supervisors and creating a 'flatter' organisational hierarchy, which further increases efficiency. The side-effects of self-managed teams are the demise of 'social loafing' and an increase in motivation through the reduction of isolated workers (i.e. workers who usually do not feel part of a team).[31]

The effect of introducing self-managed teams is often an increase in efficiency of 30 per cent or more – sometimes much more. After the introduction of self-managed teams at a UK day surgery unit, a 15-month study showed improvement in patient satisfaction, improvement in staff morale (measured in less absenteeism) and an increase of efficiency of 36 per cent. The day surgery provided more surgeries than national targets dictated and was financially viable.[32]

Process Re-engineering and Efficiency

Think of the value chain as a collection of functional activities or business processes that takes one or more kinds of inputs and transforms them to create an output that is of value to the customer.[33] **Process re-engineering** is the fundamental *rethinking* and radical *redesign* of business processes (and thus the value chain) to achieve dramatic improvements in critical measures of performance such as cost, quality, service and speed.[34] Order fulfilment, for example, can be thought of as a business process: when a customer's order is received (the input), many different functional tasks must be performed to process the order, and then the ordered goods must be delivered to the customer (the output). Process re-engineering boosts efficiency when it reduces the number of order fulfilment tasks that must be performed, or reduces the time they take, and so reduces operating costs.

For an example of process re-engineering in practice, consider the Ford Motor Company. One day, a manager from Ford was working in its Japanese partner Mazda and discovered by accident that Mazda had only five people in its accounts payable department. The Ford manager was shocked, since Ford's operation in other countries had up to 500 employees in accounts payable. He reported his discovery to Ford's managers, who decided to form a task force to figure out why the difference existed.

Ford managers discovered that procurement began when the purchasing department sent a purchase order to a supplier and sent a copy of the purchase order to Ford's accounts payable department. When the supplier shipped the goods and they arrived at Ford, a clerk at the receiving dock completed a form describing the goods and sent the form to accounts payable. The supplier, meanwhile, sent accounts payable an invoice. Accounts payable thus received three documents relating to these goods: a copy of the original purchase order, the receiving document and the invoice. If the information in all three was in agreement (most of the time it was), a clerk in accounts payable issued payment. Occasionally, however, all three documents did not agree, and Ford discovered that accounts payable clerks spent most of their time straightening out the 1 per cent of instances in which the purchase order, receiving document and invoice contained conflicting information.[35]

Ford managers decided to re-engineer the procurement process to simplify it. Now, when a buyer in the purchasing department issues a purchase order to a supplier, that buyer also enters the order into an online database. As before, suppliers send goods to the receiving dock. When the goods arrive, the clerk at the receiving dock checks a computer terminal to see whether the received shipment matches the description on the purchase order. If it does, the clerk accepts the goods and pushes a button on the terminal keyboard that tells the database the goods have arrived. Receipt of the goods is recorded in the database and a computer automatically issues and sends a cheque to the supplier. If the goods do not correspond to the description on the purchase order in the database, the clerk at the dock refuses the shipment and sends it back to the supplier.

Payment authorisation, which used to be performed by accounts payable, is now accomplished at the receiving dock. The new process has come close to eliminating the need for an accounts payable department: in some parts of the company, the size of the accounts payable department has been cut by 95 per cent. By reducing the head count in accounts payable, the re-engineering effort reduced the amount of time wasted on unproductive activities, thereby increasing the efficiency of the total organisation.

Information Systems, the Internet and Efficiency

With the rapid spread of computers, the explosive growth of the Internet and corporate intranets (internal corporate computer networks based on Internet standards) and the spread of high-bandwidth fibre optics and digital wireless technology, the information systems function is moving to centre stage in the quest for operating efficiencies and a lower cost structure. The impact of information systems on productivity is wideranging and potentially affects all the other activities of a company. Cisco Systems has been able to realise significant cost savings by moving its ordering and customer service functions online: the company has just 300 service agents handling its customer accounts, compared to the 900 it would need if sales were not handled online, and the difference represents an annual saving of £11.5 million a year. Without automated customer service functions, Cisco calculates that it would need at least 1,000 additional service engineers, which would cost around £43 million. Dell Computer also makes extensive use of the Internet to lower its cost structure and differentiate itself from rivals, as Case 9.3 shows.

Case 9.3: **How to make use of the Internet**

By 2004, more than 90 per cent of Dell's computers were sold online.[36] According to Michael Dell: 'As I saw it, the Internet offered a logical extension of the direct [selling] model, creating even stronger relationships with our customers. The Internet would augment conventional telephone, fax and face-to-face encounters, and give our customers the information they wanted faster, cheaper, and more efficiently.'[37]

Dell's website allows customers to customise their orders to get the system that best suits their particular requirements. By allowing customers to configure their orders, Dell increases its customer responsiveness. Dell has also put much of its customer service function online, reducing the need for telephone calls to customer service representatives and saving costs in the process. Each week, some 200,000 people access Dell's troubleshooting tips online. Each of these visits to Dell's website saves the company a potential £8.50, which is the average cost of a technical support call. If just 10 per cent of these online visitors were to call Dell by telephone instead, it would cost the company nearly £9 million per year.

Dell uses the Internet to manage its value chain, feeding real-time information about order flow to its suppliers, which use this information to schedule their own production, providing components to Dell on a JIT basis. Dell's ultimate goal is to drive all inventories out of the supply chain apart from inventory in transit between suppliers and Dell, effectively replacing *inventory* with *information*. In that way, Dell can drive significant costs out of its system.

Companies like Dell use Web-based information systems to reduce the costs of *co-ordination* between the company and its customers and between the company and its suppliers. By using Web-based programmes to automate customer and supplier interactions, the number of people required to manage these interfaces can be substantially reduced, thereby reducing costs. This trend extends beyond high-tech companies. Banks and financial service companies are finding that they can substantially reduce costs by moving customer accounts and support functions online. Such a move reduces the need for customer service representatives, bank tellers, stockbrokers, insurance agents and others. The costs to execute a transaction at a bank, such as shifting money from one account to another, for example, can be reduced by a tenth using online technology.

Managers at all levels thus have important roles to play in developing functional strategies to improve the way a company's value chain operates to boost efficiency. Senior management's role is to encourage efficiency improvements by, for example, emphasising the need for continuous improvement or reengineering. Senior management also must ensure that managers from different functions work together to find ways to increase efficiency. However, while senior managers might recognise the need for such actions, functional-level managers are in the best position to identify opportunities for making efficiency-enhancing improvements to an organisation's operating system. They are the managers who are involved in an organisation's operating system on a day-to-day basis. Improving efficiency, like quality, is an ongoing, never-ending process.

However, not all of those reengineering processes are about the reduction of labour. Most of the time, the expertise that is held by employees is difficult to substitute through technology or better processes. These improvements and increases in efficiency have their roots in the way these changes impact on the interaction of suppliers and manufacturers or service providers. Making those interactions more efficient and customer-focused is a way to improve overall performance.

Value-chain Management: Some Remaining Issues

Achieving improved quality, efficiency and responsiveness to customers often requires a profound change in the way that managers perform the four functions of management. The ways managers plan, organise, lead and control work activities all change as a company searches for ways to increase its competitive advantage. Planning often involves managers at all levels, and customers are brought into the planning process, the use of self-managed teams and empowered workers changes the way that managers lead and organise employees, and employees become responsible for controlling many more dimensions of their work activities.

Obtaining the information necessary to improve the value chain becomes an important and never-ending task for functional managers. It is their job to collect the relevant information about the competitive environment, such as (1) the future intentions of competitors, (2) the identity of new customers for the organisation's products and (3) the identity of new suppliers of crucial or low-cost inputs. They also need to seek out new ways to use resources more efficiently to hold down costs, or to get close to customers and learn what they want.

Two issues that arise from the constant need to improve a company's operating system are, first, the need to use *boundary-spanning roles* to obtain valuable functional information and, second, the need to consider the ethical implications of adopting advanced value-chain management techniques.

Boundary-spanning Roles

The ability of functional managers to gain access to the information they need to improve *value-chain management* is critical. The history of business is littered with numerous once-great companies whose managers did not recognise, and adapt their value chains to respond to, significant changes taking place in the competitive environment. Examples include Digital Equipment, a former leading computer maker now defunct because its CEO believed that 'personal computers are just toys', and Pan-Am, which was unable to survive because of its high operating costs in a competitive airline industry. History is also marked by companies whose managers made the wrong value-chain choices because they misinterpreted the competitive environment. Examples include the Motorola managers who invested more than £1.72 billion in the Iridium satellite project that was abandoned in 2000 and the managers of the thousands of dot-coms, like European online fashion retailer boo.com,[38] who failed to understand the competitive dynamics of the online marketplace and under-estimated the problems associated with delivering online products and services reliably to customers.

Managers can learn to perceive, interpret and appreciate better the competitive environments by practising **boundary spanning** – interacting with individuals and groups outside the organisation to obtain valuable information from the environment.[39] Managers who engage in boundary-spanning activities seek ways not only to respond to forces in the environment but also to *directly influence and manage* the perceptions of suppliers and customers in that environment to increase their organisations' access to resources.

To understand how boundary spanning works, look at Fig. 9.7. A functional manager in a boundary-spanning role in organisation *X* establishes a personal or virtual link with a manager in a boundary-spanning role in organisation *Y*. The two managers communicate and share information that helps both of them understand the changing forces and conditions in the environment. These managers then share this information with other functional managers in their

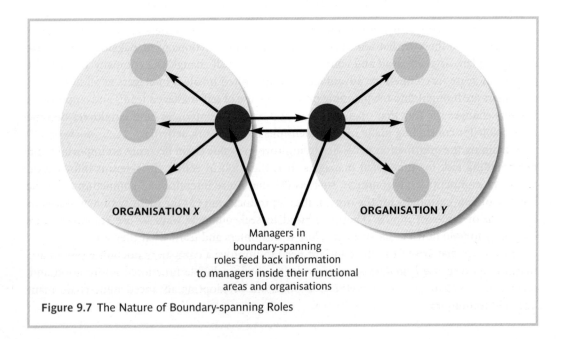

ORGANISATION *X*

ORGANISATION *Y*

Managers in
boundary-spanning
roles feed back information
to managers inside their functional
areas and organisations

Figure 9.7 The Nature of Boundary-spanning Roles

respective organisations so that all managers become better informed about events outside their own organisation's boundaries. As a result, the managers in both organisations can make value-chain decisions that lead to a higher-performing operating system.

For an example of a manager performing a boundary-spanning role, consider the situation of a purchasing manager for Burger King. The purchasing manager is charged with finding the lowest-cost supplier of low-fat cheese and lettuce. To perform this task, the manager could write to major food companies and ask for price quotes. Or the manager could phone food company managers personally, develop an informal yet professional relationship with them, and, over time, learn from them which food companies are active in the low-fat food and vegetable area and what they envision for the future. By developing such a relationship, the purchasing manager will be able to provide Burger King with valuable information that will allow the purchasing department to make well-informed choices. This flow of information from the environment may, in turn, allow marketing to develop more effective sales campaigns or product development to develop better-looking and better-tasting burgers. Note that *personal communication* is often necessary to supplement the information provided by IT.

What would happen if managers in *all* an organisation's functions performed boundary-spanning roles? The richness of the information available to managers throughout the organisation probably would lead to an increase in the quality of managers' decision making and planning, enabling them to produce goods and services that customers preferred or to create advertising campaigns that attracted new customers.

Searching for and collecting information to understand how changing trends and forces in the environment are affecting a company's operating system is an important boundary-spanning activity. Many organisations employ functional experts whose only job is to scan professional journals, trade association publications and newspapers to identify changes in technology, government regulations, fashion trends and so on, that will affect the way their organisation operates. However, merely collecting information is not enough for the boundary-spanning manager. He or she must interpret what the information means and then practise **gatekeeping** – deciding what information to allow into the organisation and what information to keep out. The nature of the information that the gatekeeper chooses to pass on to other managers will influence the decisions they make. Accurate information processing is vital, and utilising IT can obviously help here.[40]

Managers as agents of change

Note that although many of the outside forces affecting a company's value chain are independent of a particular organisation (for example, basic advances in biotechnology or microprocessors), the actions managers of a particular organisation take to change their company's operating system can have a significant effect on competition in their industry.[41] The choices functional managers make about which products to produce, and even about how to compete with other organisations, often affect all the companies in an industry. A good example of how the decisions of functional managers (or, in this case, of just one manager) can result in profound changes in the competitive environment is discussed in Case 9.4.

Despite the performance-enhancing advantages of value-chain management, many reports have appeared in the popular press about widespread disillusionment with techniques such as TQM, JIT, flexible manufacturing and reengineering. It is possible that many of the disillusioned organisations are those that have failed to understand that implementing these value-chain techniques requires a marked shift in *organisational culture* – in the way managers think and act.[42]

Case 9.4: IBM's Bill Lowe changes the rules of the game

In 1980, Bill Lowe was a manager at IBM's entry systems division. Lowe had watched the growth of the PC industry – dominated by Apple, Atari and Radio Shack – with growing interest and apprehension. He believed that IBM, the dominant force in the mainframe computer industry, should also be a leading player in the fast-growing PC segment. In mid-1980, acting on his own initiative, he assembled a team of managers to draft a proposal describing how IBM could build a viable PC within a year.

Lowe's plan called for IBM to adopt an open-system architecture for the new PC. This meant that he proposed a departure from the company's normal practice of producing key components and software in-house so that other companies could not buy them. He recommended that IBM buy components 'off the shelf' from other producers. The key components that Lowe proposed to buy included Intel's 8088 microprocessor and a software operating system known as MS-DOS from Microsoft, then a little-known Seattle-based company. The advantage of this approach was that it would enable IBM to get a PC to market quickly. The disadvantage was that it would allow other companies to produce IBM-compatible PCs by simply buying the same Intel microprocessor and MS-DOS operating system. Such a strategy represented a radical departure for IBM, which in the past, as we have seen, had tried to stop imitation of its products by producing all key components in-house.[43]

Lowe's team submitted the plan to IBM's powerful corporate management committee. In August 1980 he received the authorisation to go ahead. Just over a year later the first IBM PC was introduced into the marketplace. It was an overnight sensation and quickly grabbed the market lead from Apple. More important, however, Lowe's decision to go with an open-system architecture enabled a flood of imitators to enter the market.

Within two years, the imitators were producing PCs that were compatible with the IBM standard. The first of these imitators was Compaq Computer. Compaq was soon followed by a myriad of other companies, including current industry stars such as Dell and Gateway. The result was the creation of today's highly competitive PC industry, an industry of which IBM is no longer a part, having exited in 2000 after experiencing huge losses. Lowe's fateful decision to adopt open-system architecture changed competition in the personal computer industry forever.

None of these techniques is a panacea that can be taken once, like a pill, to cure industrial ills. Making these techniques work within an organisation can pose a significant challenge that calls for hard work and years of persistence by the sponsoring managers. Changing the way an organisation works is a difficult and demanding task, and we shall discuss how an organisation can achieve this in later chapters.

Reaction Time

1. What is efficiency, and what are the techniques that managers can use to increase it?

2. Why is it important for managers to pay close attention to their organisation's operating system if they wish to be responsive to their customers?

3. 'Total customer service is the goal toward which most organisations should strive.' To what degree is this statement correct?

Ethical Implications

Managers also need to understand the ethical implications of the adoption of many of the value-chain management techniques discussed in this chapter. Although TQM, JIT, flexible manufacturing and reengineering can all increase quality, efficiency and responsiveness to customers, they may do so at great cost to employees. Employees may see the demands of their jobs increase as the result of TQM – or, worse, may see themselves reengineered out of a job. Toyota is the most efficient car manufacturer in the world, but some of its gains have been achieved at a significant cost to its employees, as discussed in Case 9.5. The example is poignant, as Japan is seen as a superior manufacturer of cars compared to its few remaining European competitors.

Case 9.5: **The human cost of improving productivity**

Hisashi Tomiki is the leader of a four-man self-managed team in a Toyota production plant, 200 miles south of Tokyo, Japan. Tomiki and his team work at a gruelling pace to build cowls (steel chambers onto which the windshields and steering columns are attached). Consider this description of Tomiki at work:

> In two minutes Tomiki fits 24 metal pieces into designated slots on three welding machines; runs two large metal sheets through each of the machines, which weld on the parts; and fuses the two sheets together with two spot welds. There is little room for error. Once or twice an hour a mistake is made or a machine sticks, causing the next machine in line to stop. A yellow light flashes. Tomiki runs over. The squad must fix the part and work faster to catch up. A red button halts the production line if the problems are severe, but there is an unspoken rule against pushing it. Only once this day does Tomiki call in a special maintenance worker.[44]

The experience of workers like Tomiki has become increasingly common – especially in the 2000s when the threat of outsourcing led workers to accept management's demand for a faster work pace. Workers are heard to complain that constant attempts to increase quality and reduce costs really means continuous speedup and added job stress from the increase in the pressure put on employees to perform. Although some pressure is good, beyond a certain point it can seriously harm employees. Consider the following quote from Jerry Miller, whose team of billing clerks reengineered themselves out of a job:

> When we first formed our teams, the company came in talking teams and empowerment and promised that we wouldn't lose any jobs. It turns out all this was a big cover. The company had us all set up for reengineering. We showed them how to streamline the work, and now 9,000 people are gone. It was cut-your-own-throat. It makes you feel used.[45]

Is it ethical to continually increase the demands placed on employees, regardless of the human cost in terms of job stress? It is obvious that the answer is 'no'. Employee support is vital if the organisation is to function effectively. What kinds of work pressures are legitimate, and what pressures are excessive? There is no clear answer to this question; ultimately the issue comes down to the judgement of responsible managers seeking to act ethically.

TIPS FOR PRACTICE

1. Always remember the links between superior customer responsiveness and the production system of an organisation.
2. Think about balancing customer responsiveness with financial viability of the product: if it's too expensive to produce, it's not worth it!
3. Be aware that the organisation needs to ensure that appropriate quality assurance procedures are in place.

Summary and Review

Value-chain management and competitive advantage To achieve high performance, managers try to improve their responsiveness to customers, the quality of their products and the efficiency of their organisation. To achieve these goals, managers can use a number of value-chain management techniques to improve the way an organisation's operating system operates.

Improving responsiveness to customers To achieve high performance in a competitive environment, it is imperative that the operating system of an organisation respond to customer demands. Managers try to design operating systems that produce outputs that have the attributes customers desire. One of the central tasks of value-chain management is to develop new and improved operating systems that enhance the ability of the organisation to economically deliver more of the product attributes that customers desire for the same price. Techniques such as TQM, JIT, flexible manufacturing and process reengineering are popular because they promise to do this. Managers should carefully analyse the links between responsiveness to customers and the operating system of an organisation. The ability of an organisation to satisfy the demands of its customers for lower prices, acceptable quality, better features and so on, depends critically on the nature of the organisation's operating system. As important as responsiveness to customers is, however, managers need to recognise that there are limits to how responsive an organisation can be and still cover its costs.

Improving quality Managers seek to improve the quality of their organisation's output because doing so enables them to better serve customers, to raise prices and to lower production costs. TQM focuses on improving the quality of an organisation's products and services and stresses that all of an organisation's operations should be directed toward this goal. Putting TQM into practice requires having an organisationwide commitment, having a strong customer focus, finding ways to measure quality, setting quality improvement goals, soliciting input from employees about how to improve product quality, identifying defects and tracing them to their source, introducing JIT inventory systems, getting suppliers to adopt TQM practices, designing products for ease of manufacture and breaking down barriers between functional departments.

Improving efficiency Improving efficiency requires one or more of the following: the introduction of a TQM programme, the adoption of flexible manufacturing technologies, the introduction of JIT inventory systems, the establishment of self-managed work teams and the application of process reengineering. Senior management is responsible for setting the context within which efficiency improvements can take place by, for example, emphasising the need for continuous improvement. Functional-level managers bear the prime responsibility for identifying and implementing efficiency-enhancing improvements in operating systems.

Topic for Action

- Ask a manager how quality, efficiency and responsiveness to customers are defined and measured in his or her organisation.

- Go into a local store, restaurant or supermarket and list the ways in which you think the organisation is being responsive or unresponsive to the needs of its customers. How could this business's responsiveness to customers be improved?

Applied Independent Learning

Building Management Skills

Managing an Operating System

Choose an organisation with which you are familiar – one that you have worked in or have used as a customer or one that has received extensive coverage in the popular press. The organisation should be involved in only one industry or business. Answer these questions about the organisation:

1. What is the output of the organisation?
2. Describe the operating system that the organisation uses to produce this output.
3. What product attributes do customers of the organisation desire?
4. Does its operating system allow the organisation to deliver the desired product attributes?
5. Try to identify improvements that might be made to the organisation's operating system to boost its responsiveness to customers, quality and efficiency.

Managing Ethically

Go back and review Case 9.5 on the human costs of Toyota's production system. After implementing efficiency-improving techniques, many companies commonly lay off employees who are no longer needed. Frequently, the remaining employees must then perform more tasks more quickly, a situation that can generate employee stress and other work-related problems.

▶

▶ ## Questions

1. Either by yourself or in a group think through the ethical implications of using some new functional strategy to improve organisational performance.

2. What criteria would you use to decide what kind of strategy is ethical to adopt and/or how far to push employees to raise the level of their performance?

3. How big a layoff, if any, is acceptable? If layoffs are acceptable, what can be done to reduce their harm to employees?

Small Group Breakout Exercise

How to Compete in the Sandwich Business

Form groups of three or four people, and appoint one member as the spokesperson who will communicate your findings to the whole class when called on by the instructor. Then discuss the following scenario.

You and your partners are thinking about opening a new kind of sandwich shop that will compete head-to-head with Subway. Because this chain has good brand-name recognition, it is vital that you find some source of competitive advantage for your new sandwich shop, and you are meeting to brainstorm ways of obtaining one.

1. Identify the product attributes that a typical sandwich shop customer wants the most.

2. In what ways do you think you will be able to improve on the operations and processes of existing sandwich shops and achieve a competitive advantage through better (a) product quality, (b) efficiency, or (c) responsiveness to customers?

Exploring the World Wide Web

Find a manufacturer who uses TQM and explore how it is employed in that organisation. Find a different organisation that uses EFQM and compare the difference.

Application in Today's Business World

Europe's Fastest Cars

The Continent invented the fast car: It still does it better than anyone

Lavish amenities and high-end appointments are no longer the privilege of luxury cars. These days, even basic Toyotas and low-end Hondas can be equipped with wood trim, heated seats and multi-speaker sound systems at modest consequence to the final cost tally. Korean manufacturers, in particular, are advancing cabin quality in their bargain-basement offerings rapidly enough to startle even the most entrenched auto snob.

But the big European auto makers aren't worried. As the mainstream has moved downmarket over the past decade, the biggest (and some of the smallest) in European autos have been working on supercars so powerful, fast and beautiful they zoom past and completely redefine the top end.

The criteria for supercar status is debatable. Indeed, prices range from a mere $250,000 to well over $1 million. Top speeds hover around 200 miles per hour, with a few notable models pushing far past that. Rarity is another important mark of distinction. Many manufacturers produce worldwide runs that number in the mere hundreds.

Rising Stars

If the definition is flexible, it's because there have never been so many supercars to choose from. Nearly every major global brand, from Ford to Ferrari, features at least one high-performance offering. Big European brands have enthusiastically hopped on the speed bandwagon, both for profit and PR.

Newer stars of the superfast firmament include the Porsche Carrera GT and the Mercedes-Benz SLR McLaren, both of which cost more than $500,000. The Carrera's 600-plus horses propel it to over 200 miles per hour, and from 0 to 60 in 3.8 seconds. Mercedes' offering, meanwhile, harkens back to an esteemed racing pedigree, bearing the names of not one but two racing legends – 'SLR' for the famed 1950s model series and 'McLaren' for the Formula 1 giant with which it partners.

But the Germans are treading on hallowed ground. Companies such as Ferrari and Lamborghini have been at the supercar game for decades. Ferrari, in particular, is regarded as the long-haul champ in the arena, having produced classics like the F40, F50 and the current 660 horsepower, V12 Ferrari Enzo.

What's more, the 2006 model year marks what may very well be an apex in supercar history. That's because the long-awaited and much-vaunted Bugatti Veyron will finally be rolling off the assembly line to a lucky few. Its 1,001 horses take it to 60 in 2.5 seconds and make it, most likely, the fastest car in the world – capable of besting 250 miles per hour.

Bully for Billionaires

But why so many new models? For one thing, the supercar market is increasingly lucrative and growing rapidly. Not only do analysts expect annual worldwide sales to increase to $6 billion by 2010 but the number of eligible buyers is expanding as well. Cap Gemini reported that in 2005 the number of high-net-worth individuals – i.e. millionaires and billionaires – grew at a record-setting pace of nearly 10 per cent, to 8.3 million people.

Christoph Grenier, head of sales at Ferrari France, welcomes the growing number of potential supercar customers. 'More and more people have more and more money, which helps us', he says. 'It's true we have many more competitors than before, but to some extent they're all emulating us.' He adds: 'We're a monopoly no more.'

That's partly because the economics of small-run, high-cost vehicles have never been more generous. Phillipp Rosengarten of Global Insight in Frankfurt, Germany, notes: 'The high-quality parts market has never been better or more plentiful. It has become possible for smart manufacturers to return healthy profits from even very small, limited-production runs.'

Plethora of Parts

The availability of performance parts has also led to the rise of small, independent shops – often in unexpected places – that produce vehicles capable of competing with the oldest and most recognized manufacturers. Sweden's Koenigsegg CCR model hails from the snowy land of Volvos and yet holds the Guinness World Record for speed in a production vehicle (see *BW Online*, 'A Revolution in Swede Speed', March 24, 2006). And Holland's Spyker is on an ▶

▶ astonishingly rapid path to profit, announcing that it was doubling production and had increased profits in 2005 by 62 per cent.

Christian von Koenigsegg, the CEO of the company that bears his name and the man behind the marvel of the world's fastest vehicle emanating from Sweden, not Italy, attributes a great deal of his company's success to the availability of high-performance parts. He says: 'They definitely allow us to achieve a performance envelope, from raw horsepower to electronic stabilisation controls, that wasn't possible previously.'

Manufacturers large and small also benefit from significant technological advancements. The use of carbon fibre – which, on average, reduces weight by 60 per cent and fuel consumption by 10 per cent to 30 per cent – is ubiquitous. It's not uncommon to find production materials from jet fighters and the space shuttle being used as well.

California's Cutting Edge

But perhaps the biggest recent change has been the steadily increasing requirements that manufacturers must meet to sell roadworthy cars. Emissions and crash-safety standards – the most restrictive of which happen to emanate from the biggest market in the world, California – force designers to add performance-reducing weight to today's models. Indeed, some contend that the golden age of supercars was 15 years ago, with milestone models like the Jaguar XJ220 and the original McLaren F1 of the early 1990s. Nevertheless, in terms of sheer range and power, today's car cognoscenti have never had so many *à la mode* options.

Ferrari's Grenier sums it up: 'People are following the vogue. And the vogue is towards very fast and very expensive.'

Questions:

1. Why have traditional manufacturers of exclusive high-speed cars lost their monopoly for supercars?

2. How can small producers compete with the traditional supercar manufacturers?

Source: Matt Vella, 'Europe's fastest cars', adapted and reprinted from *BusinessWeek*, April 13, 2006 by special permission. Copyright © 2006 by the McGraw-Hill Companies, Inc.

Notes and References

1. C. W. L. Hill and G. R. Jones, *Strategic Management: An Integrated Approach* (Boston MA: Houghton-Mifflin, 2004).

2. J. Womack, D. Jones and D. Roos, *The Machine That Changed the World* (New York: HarperCollins, 1991).

3. See D. Garvin, 'What Does Product Quality Really Mean?', *Sloan Management Review* 26 (Fall 1984), 25–44; P. B. Crosby, *Quality Is Free* (New York: Mentor Books, 1980); A. Gabor, *The Man Who Discovered Quality* (New York: Times Books, 1990).

4. S. R. I. Pires, 'Managerial Implication of a Modular Consortium Model in a Brazilian Automotive Plant', *International Journal of Operations and Production Management* 18(3) (1998), 221–32.

5. D. F. Abell, *Defining the Business: The Starting Point of Strategic Planning* (Englewood Cliffs, NJ: Prentice Hall, 1980).

6. For details, see 'Johnson & Johnson (A)', Harvard Business School Case, 384–053.

7. www.lucent.com.

8. M. E. Porter, *Competitive Advantage* (New York: Free Press, 1985).

9 According to Richard D'Aveni, the process of pushing price-attribute curves to the right is a characteristic of the competitive process. See R. D'Aveni, *Hypercompetition* (New York: Free Press, 1994).

10 This is a central insight of the modern manufacturing literature. See R. H. Hayes and S. C. Wheelwright, 'Link Manufacturing Process and Product Life Cycles', *Harvard Business Review* (January–February 1979), 127–36; R. H. Hayes and S. C. Wheelwright, 'Competing Through Manufacturing', *Harvard Business Review* (January–February 1985), 99–109.

11 www.easyjet.com.

12 B. O'Brian, 'Flying on the Cheap', *The Wall Street Journal*, October 26, 1992, A1; B. O'Reilly, 'Where Service Flies Right', *Fortune*, August 24, 1992, 116–17; A. Salpukas, 'Hurt in Expansion, Airlines Cut Back and May Sell Hubs', *The Wall Street Journal*, April 1, 1993, A1, C8.

13 K. Done, 'Toyota Warns of Continuing Decline', *Financial Times*, November 23, 1993, 23.

14 The view of quality as reliability goes back to the work of Deming and Juran; see Gabor, *The Man Who Discovered Quality*.

15 See Garvin, 'What Does Product Quality Really Mean?'; Crosby, *Quality Is Free*; Gabor, *The Man Who Discovered Quality*.

16 http://www.jonfry.com/2005/08/what-car-reveals-uks-most-reliable.html.

17 See J. W. Dean and D. E. Bowen, 'Management Theory and Total Quality: Improving Research and Practice Through Theory Development', *Academy of Management Review* 19 (1994), 392–418.

18 For general background information, see J. C. Anderson, M. Rungtusanatham and R. G. Schroeder, 'A Theory of Quality Management Underlying the Deming Management Method', *Academy of Management Review* 19 (1994), 472–509; 'How to Build Quality', *The Economist*, September 23, 1989, 91–92; Gabor, *The Man Who Discovered Quality*; Crosby, *Quality Is Free*.

19 Bowles, 'Is American Management Really Committed to Quality?', *Management Review* (April 1992), 42–46.

20 Gabor, *The Man Who Discovered Quality*.

21 http://www.efqm.org/.

22 J. Griffiths, 'Europe's Manufacturing Quality and Productivity Still Lag Far Behind Japan's', *Financial Times*, November 4, 1994, 11.

23 S. McCartney, 'Compaq Borrows Wal-Mart's Idea to Boost Production', *The Wall Street Journal*, June 17, 1994, B4.

24 R. Gourlay, 'Back to Basics on the Factory Floor', *Financial Times*, January 4, 1994, 12.

25 P. Nemetz and L. Fry, 'Flexible Manufacturing Organizations: Implications for Strategy Formulation', *Academy of Management Review* 13 (1988), 627–38; N. Greenwood, *Implementing Flexible Manufacturing Systems* (New York: Halstead Press, 1986).

26 M. Williams, 'Back to the Past', *The Wall Street Journal*, October 24, 1994, A1.

27 G. Stalk and T. M. Hout, *Competing Against Time* (New York: Free Press, 1990).

28 For an interesting discussion of some other drawbacks of JIT and other 'Japanese' manufacturing techniques, see S. M. Young, 'A Framework for Successful Adoption and Performance of Japanese Manufacturing Practices in the United States', *Academy of Management Review* 17 (1992), 677–701.

29 B. Dumaine, 'The Trouble with Teams', *Fortune*, September 5, 1994, 86–92.

30 See C. W. L. Hill, 'Transaction Cost Economizing as a Source of National Competitive Advantage: The Case of Japan', *Organization Science*, 2, 1994; M. Aoki, *Information, Incentives, and Bargaining in the Japanese Economy* (Cambridge: Cambridge University Press, 1989).

31 http://news.bbc.co.uk/1/hi/uk/341328.stm.

32 V. M. Steelman and N. Quinlan, *AORN Journal* (December 1999).

33 M. Hammer and J. Champy, *Re-engineering the Corporation* (New York: HarperBusiness, 1993), 35.

34 *Ibid.*

35 *Ibid.*

36 www.dell.com.

37   Michael Dell, *Direct from Dell: Strategies That Revolutionized an Industry* (New York: HarperBusiness, 1999), 91.

38   http://news.bbc.co.uk/1/hi/business/752293.stm.

39   J. S. Adams, 'The Structure and Dynamics of Behavior in Boundary Spanning Roles', in M. D. Dunnette, ed., *The Handbook of Industrial and Organizational Psychology* (Chicago: Rand McNally, 1976).

40   For a discussion of sources of organizational inertia, see M. T. Hannah and J. Freeman, 'Structural Inertia and Organizational Change', *American Sociological Review* 49 (1984), 149–64.

41   Not everyone agrees with this assessment. Some argue that organizations and individual managers have little impact on the environment. See Hannah and Freeman, 'Structural Inertia and Organizational Change'.

42   R. X. Cringeley, *Accidental Empires* (New York: HarperBusiness, 1993).

43   For example, see V. Houlder, 'Two Steps Forward, One Step Back', *Financial Times*, 31 October 1994; Kumar Naj, 'Shifting Gears', *The Wall Street Journal*, May 7, 1993, A1; and D. Greising, 'Quality: How to Make It Pay', *BusinessWeek*, August 8, 1994, 54–59.

44   L. Helm and M. Edid, 'Life on the Line: Two Auto Workers Who Are Worlds Apart', *BusinessWeek*, September 30, 1994, 76–78.

45   Dumaine, 'The Trouble with Teams'.

10

Managing Organisational Structure

LEARNING OBJECTIVES

After studying this chapter, you should be able to:

- ☑ Identify the factors that influence managers' choice of an organisational structure.

- ☑ Explain how managers group tasks into jobs that are motivating and satisfying for employees.

- ☑ Describe the types of organisational structures managers can design, and explain why they choose one structure over another.

- ☑ Explain why there is a need to both centralise and decentralise authority.

- ☑ Explain why managers must co-ordinate and integrate among jobs, functions and divisions as an organisation grows.

- ☑ Explain why managers who seek new ways to increase efficiency and effectiveness are using strategic alliances and network structures.

A Manager's Challenge

Nokia, Dow and the LEGO Company Revamp Their Global Structures to Raise Performance

How should managers organise to improve performance?

In 2004, suffering from its worst-ever annual losses, caused by a 25 per cent decline in global sales (see p. 248), the LEGO company decided that it needed to restructure its European operations.[1] Until 2004, the LEGO company had operated with three global subdivisions inside its European division – central, northern and southern. Many problems had arisen with this structure: first, each subdivision was performing many of the same activities, so the duplication was raising operating costs. Second, the subdivisions often did not co-operate and share information on new product developments or changes in customer needs. As a result, many opportunities were being lost, especially because this structure made it even more difficult to communicate with LEGO's US and Asian divisions.

The LEGO company's solution was to abolish these subdivisions and reunite them all into one European division under the control of its former top global marketer, Henrik Poulsen.[2] Poulsen reports to the LEGO company's CEO, just as do the heads of the LEGO company's other global divisions, and the company is hoping that this will lead to an increase in co-operation among its divisions around the world. The goal of the reorganisation is to help LEGO's global divisions to learn from one another and work together to develop toys that better suit the changing needs of customers throughout the world.

While the LEGO company is trying to solve its problem by combining its three European units into one, in 2004 US giant Dow Chemicals decided that the best way to leverage the skills and resources of its global chemicals division was to split it into three different global product groups – the plastics, chemicals and intermediates and performance chemicals groups.[3] Dow believes that when each group acts as a self-contained unit, this will make it easier for managers to focus on one range of chemical products that can then be delivered to customers around the world.[4] Note that in Dow's case the issue was to create more product divisions, while the issue facing the LEGO company was to reduce the number of its market divisions.

Finally, Nokia, the Finnish company that is the world's leader in cellular phones, also made a change to its global structure in 2004. Nokia recognised that it had an important weakness in its product line, wireless business communications, by means of which a company can communicate with its workforce through some form of wireless communication such as laptops, Palms and other PDAs, or wireless phones that allow employees to share information and communicate.

Since this part of the wireless market was rapidly growing, Nokia chairman Jornma Ollila decided to create a new global division to innovate wireless communication products and a new global product division, the Enterprise Solutions group. To give the new divisions the autonomy to innovate products quickly, he set them up in New York and appointed a former Hewlett-Packard (HP) manager, Mary McDowell, to develop an entry technology that would offer everything from server software to handsets and compete with giants like HP and IBM. Since the potential market in this area was expected to grow from £15.5 to £24 billion by 2007, Nokia hoped to obtain a significant share of this lucrative market to help boost its performance.[5]

Overview

The challenge facing managers in all three companies was to identify the best way to operate in a new, more competitive environment. Managers in all three companies were forced to radically change the way they organised their employees and other resources to meet that challenge.

Managers need to know how to organise and control human and other resources to create high-performing organisations. To organise and control (two of the four managerial functions), managers must design an **organisational architecture** that makes the best use of resources to produce the goods and services customers want. Organisational architecture is the combination of organisational structure, control systems, culture and human resource management

(HRM) systems that together determine how efficiently and effectively organisational resources are used.

By the end of this chapter, you will be familiar with various organisational structures and with a range of factors that determine the organisational design choices that managers make. In Chapters 11–12 the issues surrounding the design of an organisation's control systems, culture and HRM systems will be explored.

Designing Organisational Structure

Organising is the process by which managers establish the structure of *working relationships* among employees to allow them to achieve *organisational goals* efficiently and effectively. *Organisational structure* is the formal system of task and job reporting relationships that determines how employees use resources to achieve organisational goals.[6] **Organisational design** is the process by which managers make specific organising choices about tasks and job relationships that result in the construction of a particular organisational structure.[7]

As noted in Chapter 2, according to *contingency theory* managers design organisational structures to fit the factors or circumstances that are impacting the company the most and causing them the most uncertainty.[8] Thus, there is no one best way to design an organisation. Design reflects each organisation's specific situation, and researchers have argued that in some situations stable, mechanistic structures may be most appropriate while in a different industry or a different situation, flexible, organic structures may be the most effective. Four factors are important determinants of the type of organisational structure or organising method managers select: the nature of the organisational environment, the type of strategy the organisation pursues, the technology (this includes the IT) the organisation uses and the characteristics of the organisation's HR (Fig. 10.1).[9]

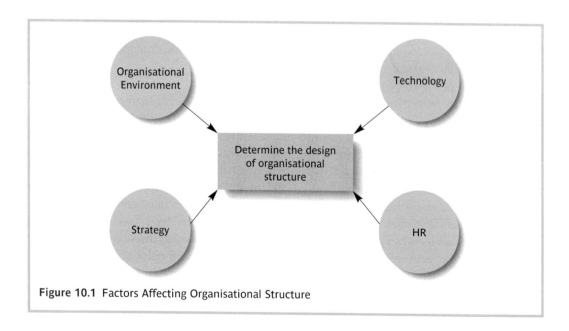

Figure 10.1 Factors Affecting Organisational Structure

The Organisational Environment

In general, a causal relationship can be found between the *speed of change* within an organisation's environment and the speed in which an organisation has to *adapt* to these changes. The quicker an external environment is changing, the greater the uncertainty. This results in greater problems for managers to gain access to scarce resources. To accelerate decision making and communication, and make it easier to obtain resources, managers typically make organising choices that bring *flexibility* to the organisational structure.[10] They are likely to decentralise authority and empower lower-level employees to make important operating decisions – a more *organic structure*. In contrast, if the external environment is stable, resources are readily available and uncertainty is low, then less co-ordination and communication among people and functions is needed to obtain resources. Managers can make organising choices that bring more *stability* or *formality* to the organisational structure. Managers in this situation prefer to make decisions within a clearly defined hierarchy of authority and use extensive rules and standard operating procedures to govern activities – a more *mechanistic structure*.

As we discussed in Chapter 6, change is rapid in today's marketplace, and increasing competition both at home and abroad is putting greater pressure on managers to attract customers and increase efficiency and effectiveness. Interest in finding ways to structure organisations – such as through empowerment and self-managed teams – to allow people and departments to behave flexibly has been rapidly increasing.

Strategy

As discussed in Chapter 8, once managers decide on a strategy, they must choose the right means of *implementing* it. Different strategies often call for the use of different organisational structures: a differentiation strategy, for example, aimed at increasing the value customers perceive in an organisation's products and services, usually succeeds best in a flexible structure. Flexibility facilitates a differentiation strategy because managers can develop new or innovative products quickly – an activity that requires extensive co-operation among functions or departments. In contrast, a low-cost strategy, aimed at driving down costs in all functions, usually sits best in a more formal structure, which gives managers greater control over the expenditures and actions of the organisation's various departments.[11]

In addition, at the corporate level, when managers decide to expand the scope of organisational activities by vertical integration or diversification, for example, they need to design a flexible structure to provide sufficient co-ordination among the different business divisions.[12] As discussed in Chapter 8, many companies have been *divesting* businesses because managers have been unable to create a competitive advantage to keep them up to speed in fast-changing industries. By moving to a more flexible structure, such as a product division structure, divisional managers gain more control over their different businesses. Expanding internationally and operating in many different countries challenges managers to create organisational structures that allow organisations to be flexible on a global level.[13] As will be discussed in this chapter, managers can group their departments or functions and divisions in several ways to allow them to effectively pursue an international strategy, or sell parts of their business to make them more successful ventures. The Motorola example in Case 10.1 shows that restructuring can sometimes mean selling off parts of an organisation for the business to retain its strength.

Case 10.1: Motorola succeeds in Freescale spin-off

In 2004, Motorola spun off one of its businesses in a move to make this 'redheaded stepchild'[14] a large, independent company even though it had been part of the Motorola family for 50 years. The move to restructuring was led by Freescale's (a £3.3 billion semiconductor business) poor performance as part of the Motorola Group. In the early 2000s Motorola downsized the business by closing nearly half of Freescale's plants and making 13,000 people redundant. After all this effort, Freescale still did not produce the desired results and was operating at a non-profitable margin of 29 per cent and making losses of up to £210 million. What could be done?

Motorola had to decide if spinning off Freescale was a viable option, considering that spin-offs are not always a successful way of restructuring an organisation. However, Motorola, which makes up 25 per cent of Freescale's revenue, needed the company to be a strong contender in the market in order to maintain a sustainable strategic partnership. Motorola's decision to distribute all shares and not retain any ownership was one important decision to Freescale's success. However, the most cunning decision was to hire the energetic Frenchman Michel Mayer who managed to turn around Freescale's performance within 15 months of his arrival. One of the major changes Mayer introduced was the refocusing of an engineering-led company to a customer focused and responsive one. Mayer also adapted the company's manufacturing to include technology and smarter operations. Mayer also retained the Motorola spirit by encouraging strong communication across its plants to ensure everyone was pulling in the same direction. For example, if production fell behind in order to respond to an emergency order in one plant, this was considered acceptable in order to be customer-focused. Mayer's arrival saw Freescale's performance soaring: its earnings jumped threefold and the share price rose by nearly 70 per cent.[15]

Technology

Technology is the combination of skills, knowledge, tools, machines, computers and equipment that is used in the design, production and distribution of goods and services. As a rule, the more complicated the technology that an organisation uses, the more difficult it is for managers and workers to impose strict control on it or to regulate it efficiently. The more complicated the technology, the greater is the need for a flexible structure to enhance managers' ability to respond to unexpected situations and give them the freedom to work out new solutions to the problems they encounter. In contrast, the more routine the technology, the more appropriate is a formal structure, because tasks are simple and the steps needed to produce goods and services have been worked out in advance.

What makes a technology routine or complicated? One researcher who investigated this issue, Charles Perrow, argued that two factors determine how complicated or non-routine technology is: *task variety* and *task analysability*.[16] Task variety is the number of new or unexpected problems or situations that a person or function will encounter in performing tasks or jobs. Task analysability is the degree to which programmed solutions are available to people or functions to solve the problems they encounter. Non-routine or complicated technologies are characterised by high task variety and low task analysability; this means that many varied problems occur and that solving them requires significant non-programmed decision making. In contrast, routine technologies are characterised by low task variety and high task analysability; the problems encountered do not vary much and are easily resolved through programmed decision making.

Examples of non-routine technology are found in the work of R&D units which develop new drugs or new compound materials, such as new forms of carbon fibre or plastic. Examples of routine technology include typical mass-production or assembly operations, where workers perform the same task repeatedly and where managers have already identified the programmed solutions necessary to perform a task efficiently. Similarly, in service organisations such as fast-food restaurants, the tasks that crew members perform in making and serving fast food are very routine.

The extent to which the process of actually producing or creating goods and services is dependent on people or machines, is another factor that determines how non-routine a technology is. The more the technology used to produce goods and services is based on individuals' skills, knowledge and abilities of working together on an ongoing basis and not on automated machines that can be programmed in advance, the more complex the technology is. Joan Woodward, a professor who investigated the relationship between technology and organisational structure, differentiated among three kinds of technology on the basis of the relative contribution made by people or machines.[17]

Small-batch technology is used to produce small quantities of customised, one-of-a-kind products and is based on the skills of people who work together in small groups. Examples of goods and services produced by small-batch technology include custom-built cars, such as Lamborghinis and Rolls Royces, highly specialised metals and chemicals that are produced by the pound rather than by the ton and the process of auditing in which a small team of auditors is sent to a company to evaluate and report on its accounts. Because small-batch goods or services are customised and unique, workers need to respond to each situation as required. A structure that decentralises authority to employees and allows them to respond flexibly is most appropriate with small-batch technology.

Woodward's second kind of technology, **mass-production technology**, is based primarily on the use of automated machines that are programmed to perform the same operations time and time again. Mass production works most efficiently when each person performs a repetitive task; there is less need for flexibility, and a formal organisational structure is the preferred choice because it gives managers the most control over the production process. Mass production results in an output of large quantities of standardised products such as tin cans, washing machines and light bulbs, or even services such as a car wash or dry cleaning.

The third kind of technology that Woodward identified, **continuous-process technology**, is almost totally mechanised. Goods are produced by automated machines working in sequence and controlled through computers from a central monitoring station. Examples of continuous-process technology include large steel mills, oil refineries, nuclear power stations and large-scale brewing operations. The role of workers in continuous-process technology is to watch for problems that may occur unexpectedly and cause dangerous or even deadly situations. The possibility of a machinery or computer breakdown, for example, is a major source of uncertainty associated with this technology. If an unexpected situation occurs, employees must be able to respond quickly and appropriately to prevent a disaster from resulting. An example could be a technological fault in a nuclear power station's cooling system, which could result in a potentially fatal accident. The need for a flexible response makes a flexible organisational structure the preferred choice for this kind of technology.

Information technology

As seen in previous chapters, new technologies have profound effects on the way an organisation operates. At the level of organisational structure, IT is changing methods of organising. An *IT-enabled organisational structure* allows for new kinds of tasks and job reporting relationships among electronically connected people that promotes superior communication and co-ordination. One type of IT-enabled organisational relationship is *knowledge management*, the sharing and integrating of expertise within and between functions and divisions through real-time, inter-connected IT.[18] Some benefits from these arrangements include the development of synergies that may result in competitive advantage in the form of product or service differentiation – something LEGO, Dow and Nokia were seeking to achieve. Unlike the case with more rigid, bureaucratic organising methods, new IT-enabled organisations can respond more quickly to changing environmental conditions such as increased global competition.

Other examples include more flexible, interactive ways for teams to interact. For example, Dresdner Kleinwort Wasserstein, a financial services firm, has encouraged the use of interactive technologies, such as wikis and blogs (virtual spaces), after realising that email is not an effective tool for collaborative working. Since its introduction, this technology has been used by 1,500 employees. The email volume on projects is down by three-quarters, meeting times have halved and a general increase in productivity has been recorded.[19]

The nature of an organisation's technology is an important determinant of its structure. Today, many companies are trying to use IT in innovative ways to make their structures more flexible and to take advantage of its value-creating benefits. Many of the ways in which IT affects organising are discussed in this and later chapters.

Human Resources

A final important factor affecting an organisation's choice of structure are the characteristics of the *human resources* (HR) it employs. In general, the more highly skilled an organisation's workforce is, and the more people are required to work together in groups or teams to perform tasks, the more likely an organisation is to use a flexible, decentralised structure. Highly skilled employees or employees who have internalised strong professional values and norms of behaviour as part of their training usually desire freedom and autonomy and dislike close supervision. Accountants, for example, have learned the need to report company accounts honestly and impartially, and doctors and nurses have absorbed the obligation to give patients the best care possible.

Flexible structures, characterised by decentralised authority and empowered employees, are well suited to the needs of highly skilled people. Similarly, when people work in teams, they must be allowed to interact freely, which also is possible in a flexible organisational structure. When designing an organisational structure, managers must pay close attention to both the *workforce* and to the *work itself*.

An organisation's external environment, strategy, technology and HR are all factors to be considered by managers in seeking to design the best structure for an organisation. The greater the level of uncertainty in the organisation's environment, the more complex its strategy and technologies and the more highly qualified and skilled its workforce, the more likely managers are to design a structure that is flexible and that can change quickly. The more stable the organisation's environment, the less complex and more well understood its strategy or technology and the less skilled its workforce, the more likely managers are to design an organisational structure that is formal and controlling.

How do managers design a structure to be either flexible or formal? The way an organisation's structure works depends on the organising choices managers make about four issues:

- How to group tasks into *individual jobs*
- How to group jobs into *functions* and *divisions*

- How to *allocate authority* in the organisation among jobs, functions and divisions
- How to co-ordinate or integrate among jobs, functions and divisions.

Grouping Tasks into Jobs: Job Design

The first step in organisational design is **job design**, the process by which managers decide how to divide into specific jobs the tasks that have to be performed to provide customers with products and services. Managers at McDonald's, for example, have decided how best to divide the tasks required to provide customers with fast, cheap food in each McDonald's restaurant. After experimenting with different job arrangements, McDonald's managers decided on a basic division of labour among chefs and food servers. Managers allocated all the tasks involved in actually cooking the food (putting oil in the fat fryers, opening packages of frozen french fries, putting beef burgers on the grill, making salads and so on) to the job of chef. They allocated all the tasks involved in giving the food to customers (such as greeting customers, taking orders, putting fries and burgers into bags, adding salt, pepper and napkins and taking money) to food servers. In addition, they created other jobs – the job of dealing with drive-in customers, the job of keeping the restaurant clean and the job of overseeing employees and responding to unexpected events. The result of the job design process is a *division of labour* among employees, one that McDonald's managers have discovered through experience.

Establishing an appropriate division of labour among employees is a critical part of the organising process, vital to increasing efficiency and effectiveness. At McDonald's, the tasks associated with chef and food server were split into different jobs because managers found that, for the kind of food McDonald's serves, this approach was most efficient: when each employee is given fewer tasks to perform (so that each job becomes more *specialised*), employees become more productive at performing the tasks that constitute each job.

At the US Subway sandwich shops, however, managers chose a different kind of job design. At Subway, there is no division of labour among the people who make the sandwiches, wrap the sandwiches, give them to customers and take the money. The roles of chef and food server are combined into one. This different division of tasks and jobs is efficient for Subway and not for McDonald's because Subway serves a limited menu of mostly submarine-style sandwiches that are prepared to order. Subway's production system is far simpler than McDonald's, because McDonald's menu is much more varied and its chefs must cook many different kinds of foods.

Managers of every organisation need to analyse the range of tasks to be performed and then create the jobs that best allow the organisation to give customers the products and services they want. In deciding how to assign tasks to individual jobs, however, managers must be careful not to take **job simplification** – the process of reducing the number of tasks that each worker performs – too far.[20] Too much job simplification may reduce efficiency rather than increase it: if workers find their simplified jobs boring and monotonous, they become demotivated and unhappy, and as a result, perform at a low level.

Job Enlargement and Job Enrichment

In an attempt to create a division of labour and design individual jobs to encourage workers to perform at a higher level and be more satisfied with their work, several researchers have proposed two other ways to group tasks into jobs: **job enlargement** and **job enrichment**.

Job enlargement is increasing the number of different *tasks* in a given job by changing the division of labour.[21] For example, because Subway food servers make the food as well as serve it, their jobs are 'larger' than the jobs of McDonald's food servers. Increasing the range of tasks performed by a worker will reduce boredom and fatigue and may increase motivation to perform at a high level – increasing both the quantity and the quality of products and services provided.

Job enrichment is increasing the degree of *responsibility* a worker has over a job by, for example, (1) empowering workers to experiment to find new or better ways of doing the job, (2) encouraging workers to develop new skills, (3) allowing workers to decide how to do the work and giving them the responsibility for deciding how to respond to unexpected situations and (4) allowing workers to monitor and measure their own performance.[22] Increasing workers' responsibility increases their involvement in their jobs and thus increases their interest in the quality of the products they manufacture, or the services they provide.

In general, managers who make design choices that increase job enrichment and job enlargement are likely to increase the degree to which people behave flexibly rather than rigidly or mechanically. Narrow, specialised jobs are likely to lead people to behave in predictable ways; workers who perform a variety of tasks and who are allowed and encouraged to discover new and better ways to perform their jobs are likely to act flexibly and creatively. Managers who enlarge and enrich jobs create a flexible organisational structure, and those who simplify jobs create a more formal structure. If workers are grouped into self-managed work teams, the organisation is likely to be flexible because team members provide support for each other and can learn from one another.

The Job Characteristics Model

J. R. Hackman and G. R. Oldham's *job characteristics model* is an influential model of job design that explains in detail how managers can make jobs more interesting and motivating.[23] Hackman and Oldham's model (Fig. 10.2) also describes the likely *personal* and *organisational* outcomes that will result from enriched and enlarged jobs.

According to Hackman and Oldham, every job has five characteristics that determine how motivating the job is. These characteristics determine how employees *react to* their work and lead to outcomes such as high performance and satisfaction, low absenteeism and turnover:

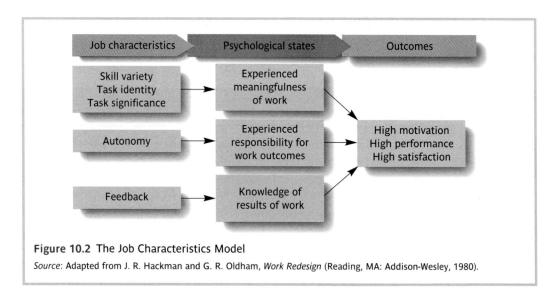

Figure 10.2 The Job Characteristics Model

Source: Adapted from J. R. Hackman and G. R. Oldham, *Work Redesign* (Reading, MA: Addison-Wesley, 1980).

- *Skill variety*   The extent to which a job requires that an employee use a wide range of different skills abilities or knowledge. *Example*: the skill variety required by a family doctor is higher than that called for by the job of a McDonald's food server.

- *Task identity*   The extent to which a job requires that a worker perform all the tasks necessary to complete the job from the beginning to the end of the production process. *Example*: a crafts worker who takes a piece of wood and transforms it into a custom-made piece of furniture such as a desk has higher task identity than does a worker who performs only one of the numerous operations required to assemble a television.

- *Task significance*   The degree to which a worker feels that their job is meaningful because of its effect on people inside the organisation such as co-workers or on people outside the organisation such as customers. *Example*: a teacher who sees the effect of their efforts in a well-educated and well-adjusted student enjoys high task significance compared to a dishwasher who monotonously washes dishes as they come to the kitchen.

- *Autonomy*   The degree to which a job gives an employee the freedom and discretion needed to schedule different tasks and decide how to carry them out. *Example*: salespeople who have to plan their schedules and decide how to allocate their time among different customers have relatively high autonomy compared to assembly-line workers whose actions are determined by the speed of the production line.

- *Feedback*   The extent to which actually doing a job provides a worker with clear and direct information about how well they have performed the job. *Example*: an air traffic controller whose mistakes may result in a mid-air collision receives immediate feedback on job performance; a person who compiles statistics for a business magazine often has little idea of when he or she makes a mistake or does a particularly good job.

Hackman and Oldham argue that these five job characteristics affect an employee's motivation because they affect three critical psychological states (Fig. 10.2). The more employees feel that their work is *meaningful* and that they are *responsible for work outcomes* and *responsible for knowing how those outcomes affect others*, the more motivating work becomes, and the more likely employees are to be satisfied and to perform at a high level. Moreover, employees who have jobs that are highly motivating are called on to use their skills more and to perform more tasks. Usually, they are given more responsibility for doing their job. These are all characteristics of jobs and employees in flexible structures where authority is decentralised and where employees commonly work with others and must learn new skills to complete the range of tasks for which their group is responsible.

TIPS FOR PRACTICE

1. Be aware that the organisational structure should be appropriate for the organisational environment, strategy, technology and HR.
2. Formal structures require detail: if this is the preferred structure, remember to draw up specific job descriptions and evaluate performance.
3. If a flexible structure is more appropriate, then concepts such as job enrichment and enlargement, which encourage collaboration, should be employed.
4. Think about how you could make every job as motivating and satisfying as possible. Try to use the job characteristic model or other tools to think about this.

Grouping Jobs into Functions and Divisions

Once managers have decided which tasks to allocate to which jobs, they face the next organising decision: how to *group jobs together* to best match the needs of the organisation's environment, strategy, technology and HR. Most senior management teams decide to group jobs into *departments* and develop a *functional structure* to use organisational resources. As the organisation grows, managers design a *divisional structure* or a more complex *matrix or product team structure*.

Choosing a structure and then designing it so that it works as intended is a significant challenge. As noted earlier, managers reap the rewards of a well-thought-out strategy only if they choose the right type of structure to implement and execute the strategy. The ability to make the right kinds of organising choices is often what differentiates effective from ineffective managers.

Functional Structure

A *function* is a group of people, working together, who possess similar skills or use the same kind of knowledge, tools or techniques to perform their jobs. Manufacturing, sales and R&D are often organised into functional departments. A **functional structure** is an organisational structure composed of all the departments that an organisation requires to produce its goods or services. Figure 10.3 shows the functional structure of Telehouse Europe, a London-based IT housing and management service.[24]

Telehouse's main functions are finance, technical services and European sales and marketing. Each job inside a function exists because it helps the function perform the activities necessary for high organisational performance. Within the Sales and Marketing department, for example, are all the jobs necessary to efficiently distribute the service, to increase business awareness and to market the service appropriately.

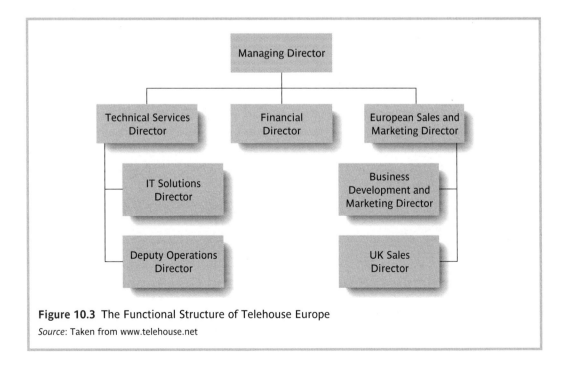

Figure 10.3 The Functional Structure of Telehouse Europe

Source: Taken from www.telehouse.net

There are several advantages to grouping jobs according to function. First, when people who perform similar jobs are grouped together, they can learn from observing one another and thus become more *specialised* and can perform at a higher level. The tasks associated with one job often are related to the tasks associated with another, which encourages *co-operation* within a function.

Second, when people who perform similar jobs are grouped together, it is easier for managers to *monitor* and *evaluate their performance*.[25] Imagine if marketing experts, purchasing experts and real-estate experts were grouped together in one function and supervised by a manager from merchandising. Obviously, the merchandising manager would not have the expertise to evaluate all these different people appropriately. However, a functional structure allows co-workers to evaluate how well their colleagues are performing their jobs, and if some are performing poorly, more experienced co-workers can help them develop new skills.

Finally, managers appreciate a functional structure because it allows them to create the set of functions they need in order to *scan and monitor the competitive environment* and obtain information about the way it is changing. With the right set of functions in place, managers are in a good position to develop a strategy that allows the organisation to respond to its changing situation. Employees in marketing, for example, can specialise in monitoring new marketing developments that will allow Telehouse Europe to better target its customers.

As an organisation grows, and particularly as its task environment and strategy change because it is beginning to produce a wider range of goods and services for different kinds of customers, several problems can make a functional structure less efficient and effective.[26] First, managers in different functions may find it more difficult to *communicate* and *co-ordinate* with one another when they are responsible for several different kinds of products, especially as the organisation grows both domestically and internationally. Second, functional managers may become so preoccupied with supervising their own specific departments and achieving their departmental goals that they lose sight of *organisational goals*. If that happens, organisational effectiveness will suffer because managers will be viewing issues and problems facing the organisation only from their own, relatively narrow, departmental perspectives.[27] Both of these problems can reduce efficiency and effectiveness.

Reaction Time

1. Would a flexible or a more formal structure be appropriate for these organisations: (a) a large department store, (b) a 'Big Five' accountancy firm, (c) a biotechnology company? Explain your reasoning.

2. Using the job characteristics model as a guide, discuss how a manager can enrich or enlarge subordinates' jobs.

3. How might a sales assistant's job or a secretary's job be enlarged or enriched to make it more motivating?

Divisional Structures: Product, Market and Geographic

As the problems associated with growth and diversification increase over time, managers must search for new ways to organise their activities to overcome the problems associated with a functional structure. Most managers of large organisations choose a **divisional structure** and create a series of business units to produce a specific kind of product for a specific kind of customer. Each division is a collection of functions or departments that work together to produce the product. The goal behind the change to a divisional structure is to create smaller, more manageable units within the organisation. There are three forms of divisional structure (Fig. 10.4).[28] When managers organise divisions according to the type of product or service they provide, they adopt a **product structure**. When managers organise divisions according to the area of the country or world they operate in, they adopt a **geographic structure**. When

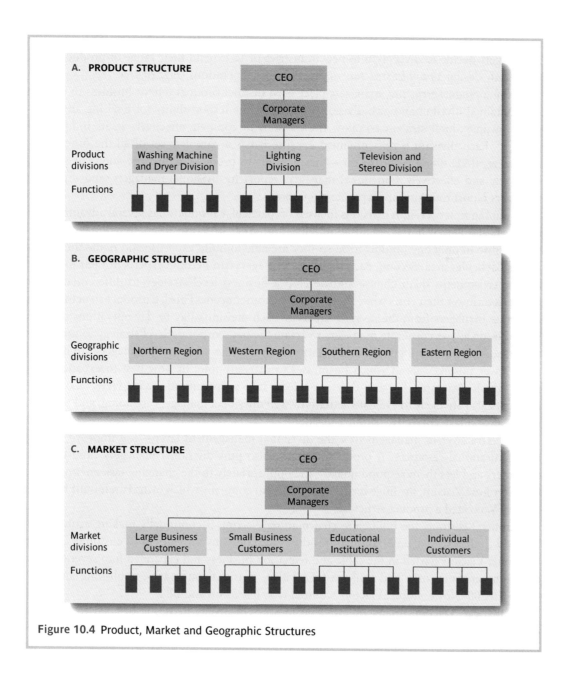

Figure 10.4 Product, Market and Geographic Structures

managers organise divisions according to the type of customer they focus on, they adopt a **market structure.**

Product structure

Imagine the problems that managers at IKEA would encounter if they decided to diversify into producing and selling cars, PCs and health insurance – in addition to home furnishings. They could try to use their existing set of functional managers to oversee the production of all four kinds of products. However, no manager would have the necessary skills or abilities to oversee them all. No individual marketing manager, for example, could effectively market cars, PCs, health insurance and home furnishings at the same time. To perform a functional activity successfully, managers must have experience in specific markets or industries. Consequently, if managers decide to diversify into new industries or to expand their range of products, they commonly design a *product structure* to organise their operations (Fig. 10.4A).

Using a *product structure*, managers place each distinct product line or business in its own self-contained division and give divisional managers the responsibility for devising an appropriate business-level strategy to allow the division to compete effectively in its industry or market.[29] Each division is self-contained because it has a complete set of all the functions – marketing, R&D, finance and so on – that it needs to produce or provide goods or services efficiently and effectively. Functional managers report to divisional managers, and divisional managers report to senior or corporate managers.

Grouping functions into divisions focused on particular products has several advantages for managers at all levels in the organisation. First, a product structure allows functional managers to specialise in only one product area, so they are able to build expertise and refine their skills in this particular area. Second, each division's managers can become experts in their industry; this expertise helps them choose and develop a business-level strategy to differentiate their products or lower their costs while meeting the customer needs. Third, a product structure frees corporate managers from the need to supervise each division's day-to-day operations directly. This latitude allows corporate managers to create the best corporate-level strategy to maximise the organisation's future growth and ability to create value. Corporate managers are likely to make fewer mistakes about which businesses to diversify into, or how best to expand internationally, for example, because they are able to take an organisationwide view.[30] Corporate managers also are likely to evaluate better how well divisional managers are doing, and they can intervene and take corrective action as needed.

The extra layer of management – the divisional management layer – can improve the use of organisational resources. A product structure also puts divisional managers close to their customers and lets them respond quickly and appropriately to the changing task environment. Consider how Viacom, the huge media entertainment company which owns Paramount Pictures and MTV, created a product structure.

Sumner Redstone, the billionaire chairman of Viacom, is continually making acquisitions that add to the range of entertainment products the company provides to its customers. Under Redstone, Viacom started in the cable and television business and expanded into several fields: entertainment, networks and broadcasting, video, music, theme parks, publishing and television. In 2000, for example, Viacom acquired CBS television and BET.[31]

To manage Viacom's many different businesses effectively, Redstone decided to design a product structure (Fig. 10.5). He put each business in a separate division and gave managers in each division responsibility for making their business the Number One performer in its

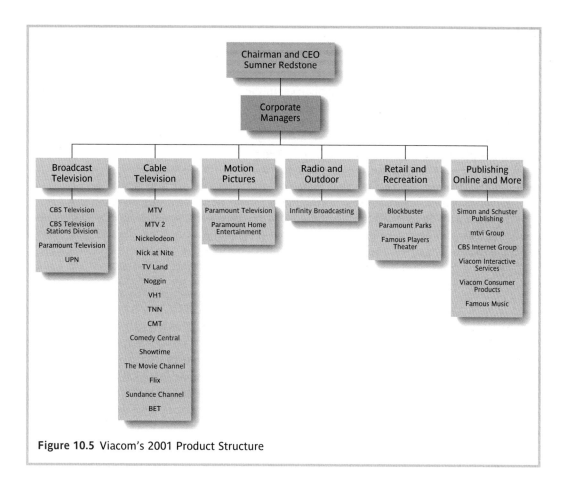

Figure 10.5 Viacom's 2001 Product Structure

industry. Redstone recognised, however, that the different divisions could help each other and create *synergies* for Viacom by sharing their skills and resources. Blockbuster, for example, could launch a major advertising campaign to publicise the movies that Paramount makes and thus boost the visibility of both divisions' products. Simon & Schuster, a publisher, could produce and publish specific books to tie in with the opening of a movie and thus boost ticket and book sales. To achieve these synergies, Redstone created a team of corporate managers who were responsible for working with the different divisional managers to identify new opportunities to create value. So far, this method of organising has served Viacom well, and it has become one of the 'Top Four' media and entertainment companies.[32]

A pharmaceutical company that has recently adopted a new product structure to better organise its activities is profiled in Case 10.2.

Geographic structure

When organisations expand rapidly both at home and abroad, functional structures can create special problems because managers in one central location may find it increasingly difficult to deal with the different problems and issues that may arise in each of the regions – whether these are countries or areas of the world. In these cases, a *geographic structure*, in which divisions are broken down by geographic location, is often chosen (Fig. 10.4B). To achieve the corporate mission of providing a next-day postage service, Fred Smith, CEO of Federal Express, chose a

Case 10.2: GlaxoSmithKline's new product structure

The need to innovate new kinds of prescription drugs in order to boost performance is a continual battle for pharmaceutical companies. In the 2000s, many of these companies have been merging to try to increase their research productivity, and one, GlaxoSmithKline, was created from the merger between Glaxo Wellcome and SmithKline Beechum.[33] Prior to the merger, both companies had experienced a steep decline in the number of new prescription drugs that their scientists were able to invent. The problem facing the new company's senior managers was how to best use and combine the talents of the scientists and researchers from both of the former companies to allow them to quickly innovate exciting new drugs.

Senior managers realised that after the merger there would be enormous problems associated with co-ordinating the activities of the thousands of research scientists who were working on hundreds of different kinds of drug research programmes. Understanding the problems associated with large size, the senior managers decided to group the researchers into eight smaller product divisions to allow them to focus on particular clusters of diseases, such as heart disease or viral infections. The members of each product division were told that they would be rewarded based on the number of new prescription drugs they were able to invent and the speed with which they could bring these new drugs to the market.

To date, GlaxoSmithKlein's new product structure has worked well. The company claimed that by 2004 research productivity had more than doubled since the reorganisation. The number of new drugs moving into clinical trials had doubled from 10 to 20, and the company had 148 new drugs that were being tested.[34] Moreover, the company claimed that the morale of its researchers had increased and turnover had fallen because the members of each division enjoyed working together and collaborating to innovate lifesaving new drugs. The company expected to have the best new drug pipeline in its industry in the next three to four years.

geographic structure and divided up operations by creating a division in each region. Since the needs of retail customers differ by region a geographic structure gives retail regional managers the flexibility they need to choose the range of products that best meets the needs of regional customers. Tesco has adopted such a structure to ensure that local customers are provided with the goods they need – for example, the product range in Malaysia differs from the product range in the UK.

In adopting a *global geographic structure*, such as shown in Fig. 10.6A, managers locate different divisions in each of the world regions where the organisation operates. Managers are most likely to do this when they pursue a *multi-domestic strategy*, because customer needs vary widely by country or world region. For example, if products that appeal to US customers do not sell in Europe, the Pacific Rim or South America, then managers must customise the products to meet the needs of customers in those different world regions; a global geographic structure with global divisions will allow them to do this.

In contrast, to the degree that customers abroad are willing to buy the same kind of product, or slight variations of it, managers are more likely to pursue a global strategy. In this case they are more likely to use a *global product structure*. In such a structure, each product division, not the country and regional managers, takes responsibility for deciding where to manufacture its products and how to market them in foreign countries worldwide (Fig. 10.6B). Product division managers manage their own global value chains and decide where to establish foreign

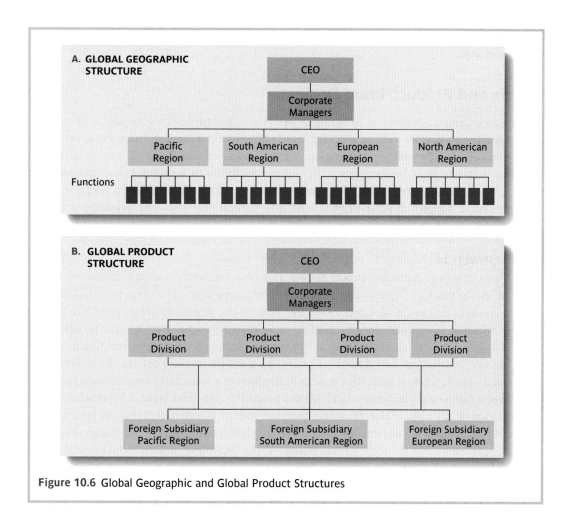

Figure 10.6 Global Geographic and Global Product Structures

subsidiaries to distribute and sell their products to customers in foreign countries. As we noted at the beginning of this chapter, an organisation's strategy is a major determinant of its structure both at home and abroad.

Market structure

Sometimes the pressing issue facing managers is to group functions according to the type of customer buying the product, in order to tailor the products the organisation offers to each customer's unique demands. A computer company like Dell, for example, has several kinds of customers, including large businesses (which might demand networks of computers linked to a mainframe computer), small companies (which may need just a few PCs linked together), educational users in schools and universities (which might want thousands of independent PCs for their students) and individual users (who may want a high-quality multimedia PC so that they can play the latest video games).

To satisfy the needs of diverse customers, a company might adopt a *market structure* (also called a *customer structure*), which groups divisions according to the particular kinds of customers they serve (Fig. 10.4C). A market structure allows managers to be responsive to the needs of their customers and allows them to act flexibly in making decisions in response to customers' changing needs.

Matrix and Product Team Designs

Moving to a product, market or geographic divisional structure allows managers to respond more quickly and flexibly to the particular set of circumstances they confront. However, when the environment is dynamic and changing rapidly and uncertainty is high, even a divisional structure may not provide managers with enough flexibility to respond to the environment quickly. When customer needs or IT is changing rapidly, and the environment is very uncertain, managers must design the most flexible kind of organisational structure available: a **matrix structure** or a **product team structure** (Fig. 10.7).

Matrix structure

In a *matrix structure*, managers group people and resources in two ways simultaneously: by function and by product.[35] Employees are grouped by *functions* to allow them to learn from one another and become more skilled and productive. In addition, employees are grouped into *product teams* in which members of different functions work together to develop a specific product. The result is a complex network of reporting relationships among product teams and functions that make the matrix structure very flexible (Fig. 10.7A). Each person in a product team reports to two bosses: (1) a functional boss, who assigns individuals to a team and evaluates their performance from a functional perspective, and (2) the boss of the product team, who evaluates their performance on the team. Thus, team members are known as *two-boss employees* because they report to two managers. The functional employees assigned to product teams change over time as the specific skills that the team needs change. At the beginning of the product development process, for example, engineers and R&D specialists are assigned to a product team because their skills are needed to develop new products. When a provisional design has been established, marketing experts are assigned to the team to assess how customers will respond to the new product. Manufacturing personnel join when it is time to find the most efficient way to produce the product. As their specific jobs are completed, team members leave and are reassigned to new teams. In this way the matrix structure makes the most use of HR.

To keep the matrix structure flexible, product teams are empowered and team members are responsible for making most of the important decisions involved in product development.[36] The product team manager acts as a *facilitator*, controlling the financial resources and trying to keep the project on time and within budget. The functional managers try to ensure that the product is the best that it can be in order to maximise its differentiated appeal.

High-tech companies that operate in environments where new product development takes place on a regular basis have used matrix structures successfully for many years, and the need to innovate quickly is vital to the organisation's survival. The flexibility afforded by a matrix structure allows managers to keep pace with a changing and increasingly complex environment.[37]

Product team structure

The dual reporting relationships that are at the heart of a matrix structure have always been difficult for managers and employees to deal with. The functional boss and the product boss often make conflicting demands on team members, who do not know which boss to satisfy first. Functional and product team bosses may also come into conflict over precisely who is in charge

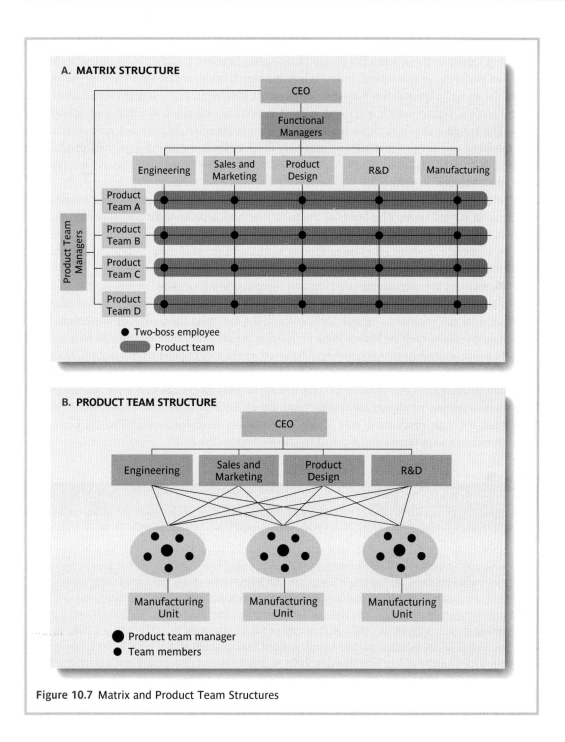

Figure 10.7 Matrix and Product Team Structures

of which team members, and for how long. To avoid these problems, managers have devised a way of organising people and resources that still allows an organisation to be flexible but make its structure easier to operate: a product team structure.

The *product team structure* differs from a matrix structure in two ways: (1) it eliminates dual reporting relationships and two-boss employees, and (2) functional employees are permanently assigned to a cross-functional team that is empowered to bring a new or redesigned product to market. A *cross-functional team* is a group of managers brought together from different departments to perform organisational tasks. When managers are grouped into cross-departmental teams, the artificial boundaries between departments disappear, and a narrow focus on departmental goals is replaced with a general interest in working together to achieve organisational goals. The results of such changes have been dramatic: DaimlerChrysler can now introduce a new model of car in two years, down from five; Black & Decker can innovate new products in months, not years; Hallmark Cards can respond to changing customer demand for types of cards in weeks, not months.

Members of a cross-functional team report only to the *product team manager* or to one of his or her direct subordinates. The heads of the functions have only an informal, advisory relationship with members of the product teams – the role of functional managers is only to counsel and help team members, share knowledge among teams and provide new technological developments that can help improve each team's performance (Fig. 10.7B).[38]

Organisations are increasingly making empowered cross-functional teams an essential part of their organisational architecture to help them gain a competitive advantage in fast-changing organisational environments. Newell Rubbermaid, for example, the maker of more than 5,000 household products such as Parker Pens or Rotring writing implements, moved to a product team structure because its managers wanted to speed up the rate of product innovation. Managers created 20 cross-functional teams composed of five–seven people from marketing, manufacturing, R&D, finance and other functions.[39] Each team focuses its energies on a particular product line, such as garden products, bathroom products or kitchen products. These teams develop more than 365 new products a year. Case 10.3 describes developments at Oxford University, which is facing a long-term commitment to change and restructure.

Case 10.3: Oxford faces its toughest challenge in its 900-year history

The university sector is changing. Global competition for academics, students and money has replaced the idealistic notion of an eternally curious and scholarly search for knowledge and scientific advancement. While these ideas are still alive, universities are now facing increasing pressure to maintain financial viability and expand. This development does not even stop at the gates of such prestigious institutions as Oxford. For the fourth year running, Oxford held the Number One spot in the UK's league tables for universities in 2005.[40] In a 2004 review of the top 200 universities in the world, Oxford was placed at Number 5.[41] However, its current Vice-Chancellor was employed in 2004 to overhaul and restructure the university.[42]

John Hood, who prior to his appointment was Vice-Chancellor at the University of Auckland, has a reputation for turning around conflict-ridden institutions and obtaining substantial investments; in the case of the University of Auckland he managed to lay the foundations for a £290 million investment. His aim of initiating and achieving change at Oxford is different from commercial companies. Hood argues he holds little power other than the 'power of persuasion'. His job is to move Oxford to an improved standing in the globalised academic market and achieve outstanding leadership in research by attracting international scientists. Oxford, like many other organisations, be they universities or private companies, is now competing against American counterparts: for Oxford, these are Yale, Harvard, or Stanford.

In order to achieve this, Hood plans, among other things, to restructure both finances and governance.

However, restructuring a 900-year-old institution is challenging. Oxford is extremely decentralised, with the Congregation, a 3,500-body strong institution of academics and administrators, at its centre. This Congregation can call votes on important decisions within the university. Alongside this structure are some 39 autonomous colleges that are trying to ensure their independence. These colleges at present control their finances, student admissions, etc.

Another area that Hood feels needs restructuring is Oxford's 28-member council, that includes only four external members, to provide a more objective viewpoint. Hood plans to restructure the council into two boards. One will be responsible for all academic and scholarly matters that arise at Oxford University. The second will resemble a more business-oriented board of directors. It is anticipated that this board will be 15 strong, comprising seven outside trustees, seven internal members and the University Chancellor as the Chair. These suggestions, nevertheless, did not receive positive feedback, as some people felt that it was undermining the democracy of Oxford University and that Hood was managing the institution like a large corporation.

Few, however, doubt that Hood will be able to restructure Oxford in time, as he has good intentions and knows where Oxford needs to be to compete successfully with its national and international rivals.[43]

Hybrid Structure

A large organisation that has many divisions and simultaneously uses many different structures has a **hybrid structure**. Most large organisations use product division structures and create self-contained divisions; each division's managers then select the structure that best meets the needs of the particular environment, strategy and so on. One product division may choose to operate with a functional structure, a second may choose a geographic structure and a third may choose a product team structure because of the nature of the division's products or the desire to be more responsive to customers' needs. Target, a US-based retailer which has very similar characteristics to the UK-based Argos, uses a hybrid structure based on grouping by customer and by geography.

As shown in Fig. 10.8, Target operates its different store chains as four independent divisions in a market division structure. Its four market divisions are Mervyn's and Marshall Field's, which cater to the needs of affluent customers; Target Stores, which competes in the low-price segment; and target direct, Target's Internet division, which manages online sales.

Beneath this organisational layer is another layer of structure because both Target Stores and Marshall Field's operate with a geographic structure that groups stores by region. This applies also to Argos, which is organised in a similar way. Individual stores are under the direction of a regional office, which is responsible for co-ordinating the market needs of the stores in its region and for responding to regional customer needs. The regional office feeds information back to divisional headquarters, where centralised merchandising functions make decisions for all Target or Marshall Field's stores.

Organisational structure may thus be likened to the layers of an onion. The outer layer provides the overarching organisational framework – most commonly a product or market division structure – and each inner layer is the structure that each division selects for itself in response to

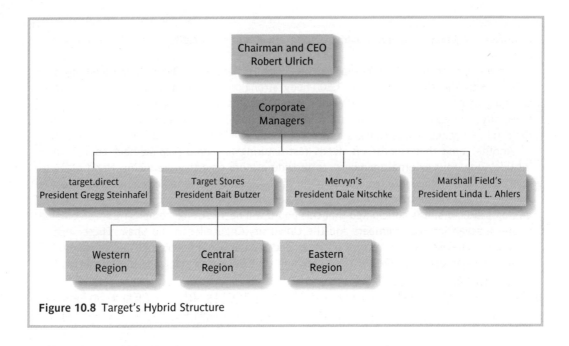

Figure 10.8 Target's Hybrid Structure

the contingencies it faces – such as a geographic or product team structure. The ability to break a large organisation into smaller units or divisions makes it much easier for managers to change structure when the need arises – for example, when a change in technology or an increase in competition in the environment necessitates a change from a functional to a product team structure.

Reaction Time

1. When and under what conditions might managers change from a functional to (a) a product, (b) a geographic, or (c) a market structure?

2. How do matrix structure and product team structure differ? Why is product team structure more widely used?

Co-ordinating Functions and Divisions

In organising, managers have several tasks. The first is to group functions and divisions and create the organisational structures best suited to the contingencies they face. The next task is to ensure that there is sufficient co-ordination or integration among functions and divisions so that organisational resources are used efficiently and effectively. Having discussed how managers divide organisational activities into jobs, functions and divisions to increase efficiency and effectiveness, we now need to look at how they put the parts back together.

We look first at the way in which managers design the **hierarchy of authority** to co-ordinate functions and divisions so that they work together effectively. Then we focus on *integration*, and examine the many different **integrating mechanisms** that managers can use to co-ordinate functions and divisions.

Allocating Authority

As organisations grow and produce a wider range of goods and services, the size and number of their functions and divisions increase. To co-ordinate the activities of people, functions and divisions and to allow them to work together effectively, managers must develop a clear hierarchy of authority.[44] **Authority** is the power vested in a manager to make decisions and use resources to achieve organisational goals by virtue of his or her position in an organisation. The *hierarchy of authority* is an organisation's chain of command – the relative authority that each manager or employee has – extending from the CEO at the top, down through the middle managers and first-line managers, to the non-managerial employees who actually make goods or provide services. Every manager, at every level of the hierarchy, supervises one or more subordinates. The term **span of control** refers to the number of subordinates who report directly to a manager.

Figure 10.9 shows a simplified picture of the hierarchy of authority and the span of control of managers in McDonald's in 2004. At the top of the hierarchy is Charlie Bell, CEO and chairman of McDonald's board of directors, who took control in 2004.[45] Bell is the manager who has ultimate responsibility for McDonald's performance, and he has the authority to decide how to use organisational resources to benefit McDonald's stakeholders.[46] Both Mike Roberts and Jim Skinner report directly to Bell. Roberts is the CEO of McDonald's domestic operations; Vice Chairman Skinner is the head of McDonald's overseas operations. They are next in the chain of command under Bell. Of special mention is Ralph Alvarez, who in July 2004 was appointed as president of domestic operations, reporting to Roberts. Also depicted is CFO Mathew Paull, who also reports directly to Bell; however, unlike the others, he is not a **line manager**, someone in the direct line or chain of command who has formal authority over people and resources. Rather, Paull is the **staff manager**, responsible for one of McDonald's specialist functions, finance.

Managers at each level of the hierarchy give managers at the next level down the authority to make decisions about how to use organisational resources. Accepting this authority, those lower-level managers then become responsible for their decisions and are accountable for how well they make them. Managers who make appropriate, sustainable and effective decisions are typically promoted. Organisations often motivate managers with the prospects of promotion and increased responsibility within the chain of command.

Below Roberts are the other main levels or layers in the McDonald's chain of command – executive vice presidents, zone managers, regional managers and supervisors. A hierarchy is also evident in each company-owned McDonald's restaurant. At the senior is the store manager; at lower levels are the first assistant, shift managers and crew personnel. McDonald's managers have decided that this hierarchy of authority best allows the company to pursue its business-level strategy of providing fast food at reasonable prices.

Tall and flat organisations

As an organisation grows in size (normally measured by the *number of employees*), its hierarchy of authority normally lengthens in order to decrease the span of control, making the organisational structure taller. A *tall* organisation has many levels of authority relative to company size; a *flat* organisation has fewer levels relative to company size (Fig. 10.10).[47] As a hierarchy becomes

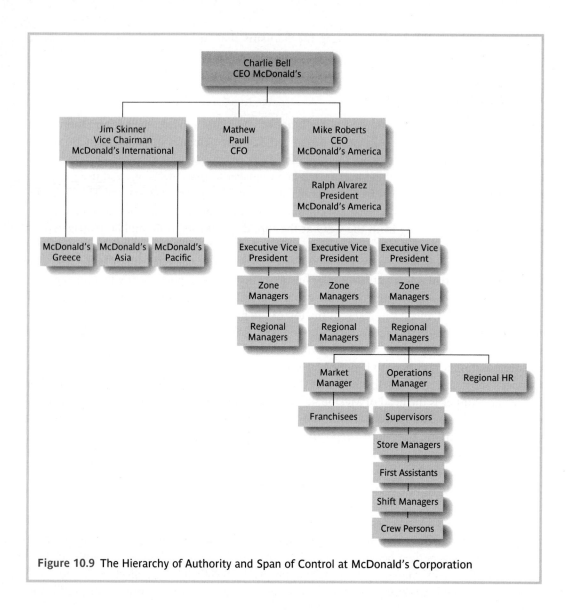

Figure 10.9 The Hierarchy of Authority and Span of Control at McDonald's Corporation

taller, an organisation's structure is likely to become less flexible and a slower response from managers to changes in the organisational environment may be the result.

Communication problems may arise when an organisation has many levels in the hierarchy: it can take a long time for the decisions and orders of upper-level managers to reach managers further down. It can also increase the time for senior managers to learn how well their decisions have worked. Feeling out of touch, senior managers may want to verify that lower-level managers are following orders and may require written confirmation from them. Middle managers, who know they will be held strictly accountable for their actions, start devoting more time to the process of decision making to improve their chances of making appropriate decisions; they may even try to avoid responsibility by making senior managers decide what actions to take.

Another communication problem that can result is the distortion of commands and orders being transmitted up and down the hierarchy, which may cause managers at different levels to

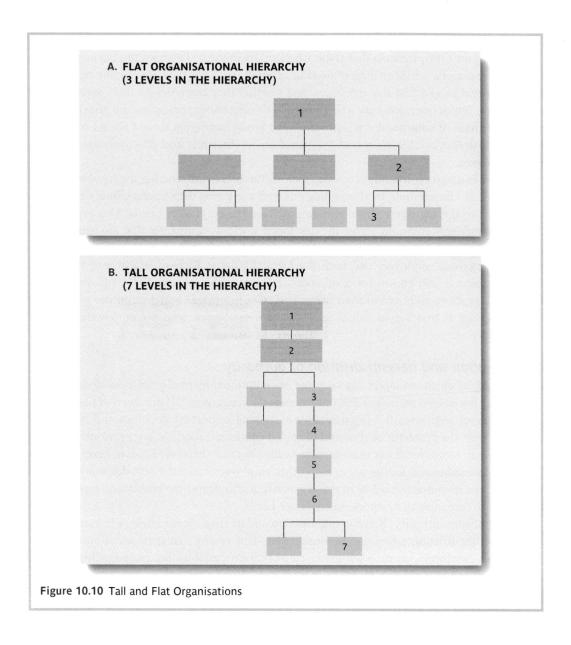

Figure 10.10 Tall and Flat Organisations

interpret the messages differently. Distortion of orders and messages can be accidental, occurring because different managers interpret messages from their own narrow, functional perspectives. Distortion may even be intentional, because managers lower in the hierarchy decide to interpret information in a way that increases their own personal advantage.

Another problem with tall hierarchies is that they usually indicate that an organisation is employing many managers, and managers are expensive. Managerial salaries, benefits, offices and secretaries are a huge expense. Large companies such as IBM and GM pay their managers billions of dollars a year. In the early 2000s, hundreds of thousands of middle managers were laid off as dot-coms collapsed and high-tech companies such as Hewlett-Packard, or manufacturers such as Volkswagen, attempted to reduce costs by restructuring and downsizing their workforces.

The minimum chain of command

To protect against the problems that result when an organisation becomes too tall and employs too many managers, senior managers need to ascertain whether they are employing the right number of middle and first-line managers, and whether they can redesign their organisational architecture. Senior managers may well follow a basic organising principle – the principle of the **minimum chain of command** – which states that senior managers should always construct a hierarchy with the *fewest levels of authority necessary* to efficiently and effectively use organisational resources.

Effective managers constantly scrutinise their hierarchies to see whether the number of levels can be reduced – for example, by eliminating one level and giving the responsibilities of managers at that level to the managers above and empowering the employees below. This practice has become increasingly common across the developed world as companies that are battling low-cost foreign competitors search for new ways to reduce costs. One manager who is constantly trying to empower employees and keep the hierarchy flat is Richard Branson of the Virgin Group. Branson is well known for continually reaffirming the message that employees should feel free to go above and beyond their prescribed roles to provide better customer service. His central message is that Virgin values and trusts its employees, who are empowered to take responsibility.

Centralisation and decentralisation of authority

Another way in which managers can keep the organisational hierarchy flat is by decentralising authority to lower-level managers and non-managerial employees.[48] If managers at higher levels give lower-level employees the responsibility of making important decisions and manage by exception, then the problems of slow and distorted communication we saw previously are kept to a minimum. Moreover, fewer managers are needed because their role is not to make decisions but to act as *coaches* and *facilitators* to help other employees make the best decisions. In addition, when decision making is low in the organisation and nearer the customer, employees are better able to recognise and respond to customer needs.

Decentralising authority allows an organisation and its employees to behave in a flexible way even as the organisation grows and becomes taller. This is why managers are so interested in empowering employees, creating self-managed work teams, establishing cross-functional teams and even moving to a product team structure. These design innovations help keep the organisational architecture flexible and responsive to complex task and general environments, complex technologies and complex strategies.

Although more and more organisations are taking steps to decentralise authority, *too much decentralisation* may also have negative impacts. If divisions, functions or teams are given too much decision-making authority, they may begin to pursue their own goals at the expense of organisational goals. Managers in engineering design or R&D, for example, may become so focused on making the best possible product that they fail to realise that the best product may be so expensive that few people will be willing or able to buy it. With too much decentralisation, lack of communication among functions or among divisions may also prevent possible synergies among them from ever materialising, and organisational performance suffers.

Senior managers must seek the balance between centralisation and decentralisation of authority that best meets the four major contingencies an organisation faces (Fig. 10.1). If managers are in a stable environment, are using well-understood technology and are producing staple kinds of products (such as cereal, canned soup, books or televisions), then there is no pressing need to decentralise authority, and managers at the top can maintain control of much of the organisational decision making.[49] However, in uncertain, changing environments where high-tech companies are producing state-of-the-art products, senior managers must empower employees and allow teams to make important strategic decisions so that the organisation can keep up with the changes taking place.

Case 10.4: Decentralisation to become one of the UK's best DIY stores

Homebase is the Number Two DIY retailer in the UK, serving more than 1.5 million customers weekly. Homebase has approximately 300 stores and a 12 per cent current market share.[50] In order to get to this position, Homebase had to adapt to new ways of organising its stores.

Homebase employees are organised into teams. Each team has a team leader who is responsible for holding regular team meetings, team building exercises and fun activities. These bonding activities are used to encourage employees to contribute to all kinds of decisions about the company and its processes, improvement of sales or improvements to customer service. Homebase emphasises the knowledge and expertise held by its shop floor workers, who are closest to customer needs. Empowerment in Homebase means that employees are not only encouraged to make their own decisions, but are expected to. The empowerment and team work is underpinned by a simple but effective philosophy. Employees go beyond simple decisions – they take full responsibility for their actions. They are expected to act confidently on problems they encounter and appreciate each other's contribution to the company's overall achievements.

But Homebase does not only place expectations on its employees. Part of the decentralisation is a Recognition Award that is given to employees who deliver outstanding customer service and go beyond their call of duty.[51]

Types of Integrating Mechanisms

Much co-ordination takes place through the hierarchy of authority. In addition, managers can use various *integrating mechanisms* to increase communication and co-ordination among functions and divisions. The greater the complexity of an organisation's structure, the greater is the need for co-ordination among people, functions and divisions to make the organisational structure work efficiently and effectively.[52] Thus, when managers choose to adopt a divisional, matrix or product team structure, they must use complex kinds of integrating mechanisms to achieve organisational goals. UPS and FedEx, for example, have complex geographic structures that need an enormous amount of co-ordination among regions to achieve the goal of next-day package delivery. They achieve this through the innovative use of integrating mechanisms such as computer-controlled tracking equipment and customer-liaison personnel to manage transactions quickly and efficiently.

Six integrating mechanisms are available to managers to increase communication and co-ordination.[53] These mechanisms – arranged on a continuum from simplest to most complex – are listed in Fig. 10.11, with examples of the individuals or groups that might use them. In the remainder of this section we examine each one.

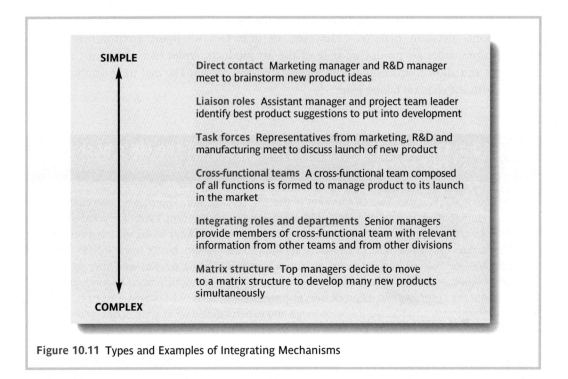

Figure 10.11 Types and Examples of Integrating Mechanisms

Direct contact

Direct contact among managers creates a context within which managers from different functions or divisions can work together to solve mutual problems. However, several problems are associated with establishing contact among managers in different functions or divisions. Managers from different functions may have different views about what must be done to achieve organisational goals. But if the managers have equal authority (as functional managers typically do), the only manager who can tell them what to do is the CEO: if functional and divisional managers cannot reach agreement, no mechanism exists to resolve the conflict apart from the authority of the boss. The need to solve everyday conflicts, however, wastes senior management time and effort and slows decision making. In fact, one sign of a poorly performing organisational structure is the number of problems sent up the hierarchy for senior managers to solve. To increase co-ordination among functions and divisions and to prevent these problems from emerging, senior managers can incorporate more complex integrating mechanisms into their organisational architecture.

Liaison roles

Managers can increase co-ordination among functions and divisions by establishing liaison roles. When the volume of contacts between two functions increases, one way to improve co-ordination is to give one manager in each function or division the responsibility for co-ordinating with the other. These managers may meet daily, weekly, monthly or as needed. Figure 10.12A depicts a liaison role; the small dot represents the person within a function who has responsibility for co-ordinating with the other function. The responsibility for co-ordination is part of the liaison

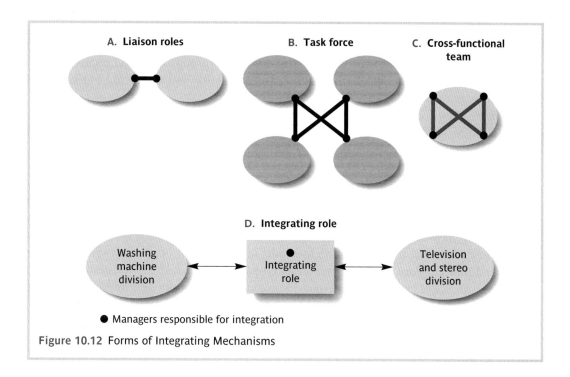

Figure 10.12 Forms of Integrating Mechanisms

person's full-time job, and usually an informal relationship forms between the people involved, greatly easing strains between functions. Furthermore, liaison roles provide a way of transmitting information across an organisation, which is important in large organisations whose employees may know no one outside their immediate function or division.

Task forces

When more than two functions or divisions share many common problems, direct contact and liaison roles may not provide sufficient co-ordination. In these cases, a more complex integrating mechanism, a **task force**, may be appropriate (Fig. 10.12B). One manager from each relevant function or division is assigned to a task force that meets to solve a specific, mutual problem; members are responsible for reporting back to their departments on the issues addressed and the solutions recommended. Task forces are often called ad hoc committees because they are temporary: they may meet on a regular basis or only a few times. When the problem or issue is solved, the task force is no longer needed; members return to their normal roles in their departments or are assigned to other task forces. Typically, task force members also perform many of their normal duties while serving on the task force.

Cross-functional teams

In many cases, the issues addressed by a task force are recurring problems, such as the need to develop new products or find new kinds of customers. To address recurring problems effectively, managers are increasingly using permanent integrating mechanisms such as cross-functional teams (Fig. 10.12C). An example of a cross-functional team is a new product development committee that is responsible for the choice, design, manufacturing and marketing of a new product. Such an activity obviously requires a great deal of integration among functions if new products are to be successfully introduced, and using a complex integrating mechanism such as a cross-functional team accomplishes this. Intel, for instance, emphasises cross-functional teamwork. Its structure consists of over 90 cross-functional groups that meet regularly to set functional strategy in areas such as engineering and marketing and to develop business-level strategy.

The more complex an organisation, the more important cross-functional teams become. As discussed previously, the product team structure is based on cross-functional teams to speed products to market. These teams assume responsibility for all aspects of product development.

Integrating roles and departments

An **integrating role** is a role whose only function is to increase co-ordination and integration among functions or divisions to achieve performance gains from *synergies* (Fig. 10.12D). Usually, managers who perform integrating roles are experienced senior managers who can envisage how to use the resources of the functions or divisions to obtain new synergies. One study found that Du Pont, the giant chemical company, had created 160 integrating roles to provide co-ordination among the different divisions of the company and improve corporate performance. Once again, the more complex an organisation and the greater the number of its divisions, the more important are integrating roles.

Matrix structure

When managers must be able to respond quickly to a task and general environment, they often use a matrix structure. The reason for choosing a matrix structure is clear. It contains many of the integrating mechanisms already discussed: the two-boss managers integrate between functions and product teams; the matrix is built on the basis of temporary teams or task forces; and each member of a team performs a liaison role. The matrix structure is flexible precisely because it is formed from *complex integrating mechanisms*.

To keep an organisation responsive to changes in its task and general environments as the organisation grows and becomes more complex, managers must increase co-ordination among functions and divisions by using complex integrating mechanisms. Managers must decide on the best way to organise their structures to create an organisational architecture that allows them to make the best use of organisational resources.

Strategic Alliances, B2B Network Structures and IT

Increasing globalisation and the use of new IT have brought about two innovations in organisational architecture that are sweeping through European companies: *strategic alliances* and **business-to-business (B2B) network** structures. A strategic alliance is a formal agreement that commits two or more companies to exchange or share their resources in order to produce and market a product.[54] Most commonly, strategic alliances are formed because the companies share similar interests and believe that they can benefit from co-operating. Japanese car companies such as Toyota and Honda for example, have formed many strategic alliances with particular suppliers of inputs such as car axles, gearboxes and air-conditioning systems. Over time, these car companies work closely with their suppliers to improve the efficiency and effectiveness of the inputs so that the final product – the car produced – is of higher quality and can very often be produced at lower cost. Toyota and Honda have also established alliances with suppliers throughout the world, because both companies now build several models of cars in other countries.

Throughout the 1990s, the growing sophistication of IT, with global intranets and tele-conferencing, has made it much easier to manage strategic alliances and allow managers to share information and co-operate. One outcome of this has been the growth of strategic alliances into a **network structure**. A network structure is a series of global strategic alliances that one or several organisations create with suppliers, manufacturers and/or distributors to produce and market a product. Network structures allow an organisation to manage its global value chain in order to find new ways to reduce costs and increase the quality of products – without incurring the high costs of operating a complex organisational structure (such as the costs of employing many managers). More and more European companies are relying on *global network structures* to gain access to low-cost foreign sources of inputs, as discussed in Chapter 6. Shoe makers such as Nike and Adidas are two companies that have extensively used this approach.

Nike is the largest and most profitable sports shoe manufacturer in the world. The key to the company's success is the network structure that Nike founder and CEO Philip Knight created to allow his company to produce and market shoes. As noted in Chapter 8, the most successful companies today are trying to pursue simultaneously *low-cost* and a *differentiation* strategy. Knight decided early that to do this at Nike he needed an organisational architecture that would allow his company to focus on some functions (such as design) and leave others (such as manufacturing) to other organisations.

By far the largest function at Nike's headquarters is the design function, composed of talented designers who pioneered innovations in sports shoe design such as the air pump and Air Jordans that Nike introduced so successfully. Designers used computer-aided design (CAD) to design Nike shoes, and they electronically stored all new product information, including manufacturing instructions. When the designers finished their work, they electronically transmitted all the blueprints for the new products to a network of Southeast Asian suppliers and manufacturers with which Nike had formed strategic alliances.[55] Instructions for the design of a new sole may be sent to a supplier in Taiwan; instructions for the leather uppers to a supplier in Malaysia. The suppliers produce the shoe parts and send them for final assembly to a manufacturer in China with which Nike has established another strategic alliance. From China, the shoes are shipped to distributors throughout the world: 99 per cent of the 99 million pairs of shoes that Nike makes each year are made in Southeast Asia.

This network structure gives Nike two important advantages. First, Nike is able to respond to changes in sports shoe fashion very quickly. Using its global IT system, Nike can literally change the instructions it gives each of its suppliers overnight, so that within a few weeks its foreign manufacturers are producing new kinds of shoes.[56] Any alliance partners that fail to perform up to Nike's standards are replaced with new ones.

Second, Nike's costs are very low because wages in Southeast Asia are a fraction of what they are in developed countries, and this difference gives Nike a low-cost advantage. Also, Nike's ability to **outsource** and use foreign manufacturers to produce all its shoes abroad allows Knight to keep the organisation's structure flat and flexible. Nike is able to use a relatively inexpensive functional structure to organise its activities. However, sports shoe manufacturers' attempts to keep their costs low have led to many charges that Nike and others are supporting sweatshops that harm foreign workers, as Case 10.5 suggests.

Case 10.5: Of shoes and sweatshops

As the production of all kinds of goods and services is being increasingly outsourced to poor regions and countries of the world, the behaviour of companies that outsource production to subcontractors in these countries has come under increasing scrutiny. Nike, the giant sports shoe maker, with sales of more than £5.2 billion a year, was one of the first to experience a backlash when critics revealed how workers in these countries were being treated. Indonesian workers were stitching together shoes in hot, noisy factories for about 50 pence a day or about £10 a month.[57] Workers in Vietnam and China fared better; they could earn approximately £1 a day. In all cases, however, critics charged that at least £1.75 a day was needed to maintain an adequate living standard.

These facts generated an outcry, and Nike was attacked for its labour practices; a backlash against sales of Nike products forced Phil Knight, Nike's billionaire owner, to re-evaluate. Nike announced that henceforth all the factories producing its shoes and clothes would be independently monitored and inspected. After its competitor Reebok, which also had been criticised for similar labour practices, announced that it was raising wages in Indonesia by 20 per cent, Nike raised them by 25 per cent to over £13 a month.[58] Small though this may seem, it was a huge increase to workers in these countries.

In Europe, another sportswear company, Adidas, largely escaped such criticism, but in 1999 it was reported that in El Salvador a Taiwan-based Adidas subcontractor was employing girls as young as 14 in its factories and making them work for more than 70 hours a week. They were allowed to go to the restroom only twice a day, and if they stayed longer than three minutes, they lost a day's wages.[59] Adidas moved swiftly to avoid the public relations nightmare that Nike had experienced, by announcing that henceforth its subcontractors would be required to abide by more strict labour standards.

What happened in the sports shoe industry happened throughout the clothing industry as well as other industries like electronics and toys in the 2000s. Companies such as ASDA, Gap, Sony and Mattel were all forced to re-evaluate the ethics of their labour practices and to promise to keep a constant watch on subcontractors in the future. A statement to this effect can be found on many of these companies' Web pages – for example, Nike (www.nikebiz.com) and Unilever (www.unilever.co.uk/ourvalues), as mentioned in Chapter 4.

The ability of managers to develop a network structure to produce or provide the goods and services customers want, rather than create a complex organisational structure to do so, has led many researchers and consultants to popularise the idea of a **boundaryless organisation**. Such an organisation is composed of people linked by IT – computers, faxes, CAD systems and video teleconferencing – who may rarely, if ever, see one another face to face. People are utilised when their services are needed, much as in a matrix structure, but they are not formal members of an organisation; they are *functional experts* who form an alliance with an organisation, fulfil their contractual obligations and then move on to the next project.

Large consulting companies, such as PricewaterhouseCooper and McKinsey & Co., utilise their global consultants in this way. Consultants are connected by laptops to an organisation's **knowledge management system**, its company-specific information system that systematises the knowledge of its employees and provides them with access to other employees who have the expertise to solve the problems that they encounter as they perform their jobs.

The use of outsourcing and the development of network structures are increasing rapidly as organisations recognise the opportunities they offer to reduce costs and increase organisational flexibility. The current push to lower costs has led to the development of electronic *business-to-business (B2B) networks* in which most or all of the companies in an industry (for example, car makers) use the same software platform to link to each other and establish industry specifications and standards. These companies then jointly list the quantity and specifications of the inputs they require and invite bids from the thousands of potential suppliers around the world. Suppliers also use the same software platform, so that electronic bidding, auctions and transactions are possible between buyers and sellers around the world. The idea is that high-volume standardised transactions can help drive down costs at the industry level.

Today, with advances in IT, designing organisational architecture is becoming an increasingly complex management function. To maximise efficiency and effectiveness, managers must assess carefully the relative benefits of having their own organisation perform a functional activity versus forming an alliance with another organisation to perform the activity. It is still not clear how B2B networks and other forms of electronic alliances between companies will develop in the future.

TIPS FOR PRACTICE

1. Always ensure that the organisation you are working for adapts its structure to its business – i.e. if you diversify your product range, move to a product structure; if you diversify geographically, move to a geographic structure, etc.

2. Remember that there are a variety of structures available that have an impact on efficiency, quality, innovation and responsiveness, such as matrix or product teams, or a decentralised or centralised structure.

3. Do not allow organisations to become too tall. Assess the hierarchy frequently and check if alliances or networks can improve your structure.

Summary and Review

Designing organisational structure The four main determinants of organisational structure are the external environment, strategy, technology and HR. In general, the higher the level of uncertainty associated with these factors, the more appropriate is a flexible, adaptable structure as opposed to a formal, rigid one.

Grouping tasks into jobs: job design Job design is the process by which managers group tasks into jobs. To create more interesting jobs, and to get workers to act flexibly, managers can enlarge and enrich jobs. The job characteristics model provides a tool managers can use to measure how motivating or satisfying a particular job is.

Grouping jobs into functions and divisions Managers can choose from many kinds of organisational structures to make the best use of organisational resources. Depending on the specific organising problems they face, managers can choose from functional, product, geographic, market, matrix, product team and hybrid structures.

▶

► **Co-ordinating functions and divisions** No matter which structure managers choose, they must decide how to distribute authority in the organisation, how many levels to have in the hierarchy of authority and what balance to strike between centralisation and decentralisation to keep the number of levels in the hierarchy to a minimum. As organisations grow, managers must increase integration and co-ordination among functions and divisions. Six integrating mechanisms are available to facilitate this: direct contact, liaison roles, task forces, cross-functional teams, integrating roles and the matrix structure.

Strategic alliances, B2B network structures and IT To avoid many of the communication and co-ordination problems that emerge as organisations grow, managers are attempting to use IT to develop new ways of organising. In a strategic alliance, managers enter into an agreement with another organisation to provide inputs or to perform a functional activity. If managers enter into a series of these agreements, they create a network structure. A network structure, most commonly based on some shared form of IT, can be formed around one company, or a number of companies can join together to create an industry B2B network.

Topic for Action

- Compare the pros and cons of using a network structure to perform organisational activities and performing all activities in-house or within one organisational hierarchy.

- What are the advantages and disadvantages of B2B networks?

- Find a manager, and identify the kind of organisational structure that his or her organisation uses to co-ordinate its people and resources. Why is the organisation using that structure? Do you think a different structure would be more appropriate? Which one?

- With the same or another manager, discuss the distribution of authority in the organisation. Does the manager think that decentralising authority and empowering employees is appropriate?

Applied Independent Learning

Building Management Skills

Understanding Organising

Think of an organisation with which you are familiar, perhaps one you have worked in – such as a shop, restaurant, office, church or school. Then answer the following questions:

1. Which contingencies are most important in explaining how the organisation is organised? Do you think it is organised in the best way?

2. Using the job characteristics model, how motivating do you think the job of a typical employee in this organisation is?

3. Can you think of any ways in which a typical job could be enlarged or enriched?

4. What kind of organisational structure does the organisation use? If it is part of a chain, what kind of structure does the entire organisation use? What other structures discussed in the chapter might allow the organisation to operate more effectively? For example, would the move to a product team structure lead to greater efficiency or effectiveness? Why or why not?

5. How many levels are there in the organisation's hierarchy? Is authority centralised or decentralised? Describe the span of control of the senior manager and of middle or first-line managers.

6. Is the distribution of authority appropriate for the organisation and its activities? Would it be possible to flatten the hierarchy by decentralising authority and empowering employees?

7. What are the principal integrating mechanisms used in the organisation? Do they provide sufficient co-ordination among individuals and functions? How might they be improved?

8. Now that you have analysed the way this organisation is organised, what advice would you give its managers to help them improve the way it operates?

Managing Ethically

Suppose an organisation is downsizing and laying off many of its middle managers. Some senior managers charged with deciding who to terminate might decide to keep the subordinates they like, and who are obedient to them, rather than the ones who are difficult or the best performers. They might also decide to lay off the most highly paid subordinates even if they are high performers. Think of the ethical issues involved in designing a hierarchy, and discuss the following issues.

Questions

1. What ethical rules (see Chapter 4) should managers use to decide which employees to terminate when redesigning their hierarchy?

2. Some people argue that employees who have worked for an organisation for many years have a claim on the organisation at least as strong as that of its shareholders. What do you think of the ethics of this position – can employees claim to 'own' their jobs if they have contributed significantly to its past success? How does a socially responsible organisation behave in this situation?

Small Group Breakout Exercise

Bob's Appliances

Form groups of three or four people, and appoint one member as the spokesperson who will communicate your findings to the whole class when called on by the instructor. Then discuss the following scenario.

Bob's Appliances sells and services household appliances such as washing machines, dishwashers, ovens and refrigerators. Over the years, the company has developed a good reputation for the quality of its customer service, and many local builders patronise the store.

▶

▶ Recently, some new appliance retailers, including Comet and Dixons, have opened stores that also provide numerous appliances. In addition to appliances, however, to attract more customers these stores carry a complete range of consumer electronics products – televisions, stereos and computers. Bob Lange, the owner of Bob's Appliances, has decided that if he is to stay in business he must widen his product range and compete directly with the chains.

In 2002, he decided to build a 20,000 ft^2 store and service centre, and he is now hiring new employees to sell and service the new line of consumer electronics. Because of his company's increased size, Lange is not sure of the best way to organise the employees. Currently, he uses a functional structure; employees are divided into sales, purchasing and accounting and repair. Bob is wondering whether selling and servicing consumer electronics is so different from selling and servicing appliances that he should move to a product structure (see below) and create separate sets of functions for each of his two lines of business.

You are a team of local consultants whom Bob has called in to advise him as he makes this crucial choice. Which structure do you recommend? Why?

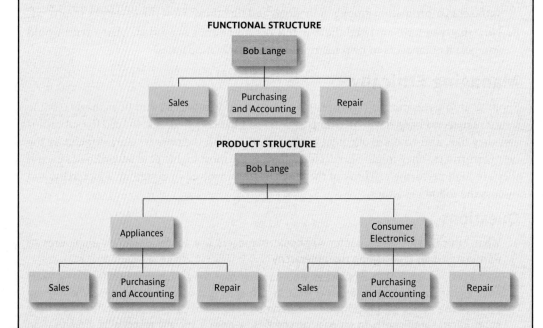

FUNCTIONAL STRUCTURE

PRODUCT STRUCTURE

Exploring The World Wide Web

Go to the website of Kraft, the food services company (www.kraft.com). Click on 'brands', and then click on 'Europe' and answer the following questions:

1. What kind of international structure do you think Kraft uses to manage its food operations?

2. What kind of organisational structure do you think Kraft uses to manage its European operations? Why do you think it uses this structure?

3. What do you think are the main challenges Kraft faces in managing its food business to improve performance?

Application in Today's Business World

Making Barclays Sparkle

Bob Diamond discusses how he restructured the venerable institution's investment-banking unit, turning it into a leading fixed-income firm

One of the reasons London now rivals New York as a financial centre is the city's openness to a diverse, talented group of people. Bob Diamond, 54, is one of those Americans who has made a big impression in the UK. Diamond, a graduate of Colby College in Maine and the University of Connecticut School of Business, first came to London in early 1988 to run Morgan Stanley's Europe and Asia fixed-income trading business. But he found his calling in 1996 when he was recruited to reverse the fortunes of the floundering investment banking wing, then known as BZW, of Barclays PLC, one of Britain's largest banks.

Diamond survived the turmoil unleashed by the restructuring of the investment bank, and went on to forge its successor, Barclays Capital, into a world-class fixed-income player. Last year he also took on the additional title of president of the parent company. He talked in his Canary Wharf office to *BusinessWeek*'s London bureau chief, Stanley Reed. Edited excerpts from their conversation follow:

How did you get started on Wall Street?

After business school, I took a job at a company called US Surgical. I worked for a guy who is still a good friend, named Bill Cook, the head of administration. After two years, Bill Cook was hired by Morgan Stanley, in 1979. That was just when Morgan Stanley was moving from a pure advisory firm into secondary sales and trading. They needed someone to build all the IT and systems. Bill was hired for that, and he asked me to join him.

After a year as assistant to the CFO, I took a job on the fixed-income floor. It would be a bit excessive to say I fell in love with the markets. But given my personality, that's not far off. Although the markets are harsh, they are a very, very fair judge of what you do. I played sports throughout high school and some college, and I enjoy the competitive aspects. I also enjoy the fairness where we are all in competition with the same information and where the guy who works hardest or works smartest wins.

As long as the coach puts them out there . . .

That's a very good point. Markets are very fair, but who gets a shot is not necessarily fair. Some of the things that make me most proud of this organisation are the meritocracy – the feeling that we really put a lot of time and a lot of process into giving all people an equal shot and measuring them based on how they perform – not who they know or how long they have been here or what connections they have.

I made a decision in early 1996 to leave Credit Suisse First Boston. What was intriguing to me about the discussions I had with Martin Taylor (then-CEO of Barclays PLC) were that I believed very strongly in the single currency. It was going to be a reality – and change the balance of power between Europe and the US. The second thing was that [the] Glass–Steagall [the law separating commercial and investment banking] was eroding. Frankly, European and British banks were more comfortable with the universal banking, integrated model and would benefit big-time by that shift.

You found yourself in a pretty tough situation

It was clear pretty quickly that the all-singing, all-dancing, US bulge-bracket lookalike model was unsustainable. I knew it had to change, and Martin knew it had to change. But it was very ▶

▶ important that we restructure quietly as opposed to announcing to the market that were going to sell M&A and equities. Frankly, that ended up hurting the organisation, because we didn't get the price we should have gotten for it, and it created a lot of internal drama. What was happening was that at the parts of the business that were for sale, everyone was out interviewing; no one was working.

How was the decision to sell made?

There were always four choices. One, ignore all these problems and just keep going. I wasn't going to be part of that, because it simply wasn't sustainable.

The second was to buy a US firm. My feeling was that Barclays couldn't manage that integration at that time, and, frankly, the success rates of deals in investment banking are very poor. The third option was to sell everything, but to sell the entire organisation would be ludicrous because we would be selling our access to clients and the capital markets. The fourth view, which I supported, was to dramatically restructure and take advantage of the fact that we are Barclays and that we are European. We have one of the world's best brands, AA+ credit rating, and a huge balance sheet. Take advantage of being in [Britain] and European time zones, and create a structure that we know will work.

That was the beginning of financing and risk management. We don't have to compete with the US firms in M&A. We don't have to have a large-scale cash equity business, where the model doesn't work and where one after another foreign firm and one after another US firm went through the same thing – trying and failing to mimic the US bulge-bracket firms. It was pouring good money after bad.

Why is the business working so well now?

The model of investment banking has changed radically to a more integrated model. It is the best of commercial banking and the best of investment banking. It is not just Barcap any more, but UBS, BNP Paribas, JP Morgan, Citigroup – most of the successful firms now have the integrated model. Goldman, too, has changed its model as a result of not doing a deal with a bank, which would have allowed it to adopt an integrated model.

The best example I can give you is virtually any league table of capital raising for corporates: ten years ago, Goldman, Merrill and Morgan Stanley would dominate. Now the top players are Deutsche Bank (DB), Barclays Capital, JP Morgan, Citigroup – all universal banks. Goldman is not even in the top 15. That doesn't mean it is not a great firm, but the model has changed.

So the direction of interest rates doesn't matter that much?

Our business is risk management. If you look at our results with value at risk down, corporate issuance down and the yield curve trade gone, you would say, 'How the hell did you drive up revenues?' The answer is what we have been preaching: relentless, rigorous focus on clients around risk management. If you are a German car manufacturer selling in the US, your exposure to the dollar is enormous. You may need to hedge your income. You may need to hedge the price of steel. If you are an airline you have a massive exposure to the price of fuel. All of the large corporates now manufacture in multiple locations. They have people in multiple locations. They sell in multiple locations. They have exposure to a multiplicity of risks, which they have to manage.

When you try to fix a business, what is your approach?

The thing that is most important of all is being very clear about the strategy and keeping it pretty simple. Once that is established, you need to make the tough decisions and implement them quickly. My style has been to spend an awful lot of time with the business until I have tremendous confidence that I have the right people, who understand the plan. At that point, it is equally important to step away and delegate.

Questions:

1. What were the main influences to change the structure of Barclay's investment bank?

2. What does Bob Diamond think are the most important aspects that make the structure effective?

Source: Online Extra, 'Making Barclay's Sparkle', adapted and reprinted from *Business Week*, April 10 2006. Copyright © 2006 by the McGraw-Hill Companies, Inc.

Notes and References

1   www.lego.com.

2   B. Carter, 'Lego Centralizes European Activity to Combat Losses', *Marketing*, January 15, 2004, 1.

3   'Dow Revamps Its Corporate Structure', *Chemical Market Reporter*, December 15, 2003, 3.

4   www.dow.com.

5   A. Reinhardt, 'Can Nokia Capture Mobile Workers?', *BusinessWeek*, February 9, 2004, 80.

6   G. R. Jones, *Organizational Theory, Design and Change: Text and Cases* (Upper Saddle River: Prentice Hall, 2003).

7   J. Child, *Organization: A Guide for Managers and Administrators* (New York: Harper & Row, 1977).

8   P. R. Lawrence and J. W. Lorsch, *Organization and Environment* (Boston: Graduate School of Business Administration, Harvard University, 1967).

9   R. Duncan, 'What Is the Right Organizational Design?', *Organizational Dynamics*, Winter 1979, 59–80.

10 T. Burns and G. R. Stalker, *The Management of Innovation* (London: Tavistock, 1966).

11 D. Miller, 'Strategy Making and Structure: Analysis and Implications for Performance', *Academy of Management Journal* 30 (1987), 7–32.

12 A. D. Chandler, *Strategy and Structure* (Cambridge, MA: MIT Press, 1962).

13 J. Stopford and L. Wells, *Managing the Multinational Enterprise* (London: Longman, 1972).

14 *BusinessWeek* November 14, 2005.

15 *BusinessWeek* November 14, 2005.

16 C. Perrow, *Organizational Analysis: A Sociological View* (Belmont, CA: Wadsworth, 1970).

17 J. Woodward, *Management and Technology* (London: Her Majesty's Stationery Office, 1958).

18 *Ibid.*

19 *BusinessWeek* November 21, 2005.

20 F. W. Taylor, *The Principles of Scientific Management* (New York: Harper, 1911).

21 R. W. Griffin, *Task Design: An Integrative Approach* (Glenview, IL: Scott, Foresman, 1982).

22 *Ibid.*

23 J. R. Hackman and G. R. Oldham, *Work Redesign* (Reading, MA: Addison-Wesley, 1980).

24 http://www.telehouse.net/company_profile.asp.

25 J. R. Galbraith and R. K. Kazanjian, *Strategy Implementation: Structure, System, and Process*, 2nd ed. (St. Paul, MN: West, 1986).

26 Jones, *Organizational Theory, Design and Change*.

27 Lawrence and Lorsch, *Organization and Environment*.

28 R. H. Hall, *Organizations: Structure and Process* (Englewood Cliffs, NJ: Prentice Hall, 1972); R. Miles, *Macro Organizational Behavior* (Santa Monica, CA: Goodyear, 1980).

29 Chandler, *Strategy and Structure*.

30 G. R. Jones and C. W. L. Hill, 'Transaction Cost Analysis of Strategy-Structure Choice', *Strategic Management Journal* 9 (1988), 159–72.

31 www.viacom.com.

32 *Ibid.*

33 www.gsk.com.

34 *Ibid.*

35 S. M. Davis and P. R. Lawrence, *Matrix* (Reading, MA: Addison-Wesley, 1977); J. R. Galbraith, 'Matrix Organization Designs: How to Combine Functional and Project Forms', *Business Horizons* 14 (1971), 29–40.

36 L. R. Burns, 'Matrix Management in Hospitals: Testing Theories of Matrix Structure and Development', *Administrative Science Quarterly* 34 (1989), 349–68.

37 C. W. L. Hill, *International Business* (Homewood, IL: Irwin, 2003).

38 Jones, *Organizational Theory*.

39 A. Farnham, 'America's Most Admired Company', *Fortune*, February 7, 1994, 50–54.

40 www.timesonline.co.uk.

41 http://www.ccer.pku.edu.cn/ss/world-rankingsUnis.pdf.

42 *BusinessWeek*, December 5, 2005.

43 *Ibid.*

44 P. Blau, 'A Formal Theory of Differentiation in Organizations', *American Sociological Review* 35 (1970), 684–95.

45 S. Grey, 'McDonald's CEO Announces Shifts of Top Executives', *The Wall Street Journal*, July 16, 2004, A11.

46 www.mcdonalds.com.

47 Child, *Organization*.

48 P. M. Blau and R. A. Schoenherr, *The Structure of Organizations* (New York: Basic Books, 1971).

49 Jones, *Organizational Theory*.

50 www.homebase.co.uk.

51 http://www.thetimes100.co.uk/case_study.

52 Lawrence and Lorsch, *Organization and Environment*, 50–55.

53 J. R. Galbraith, *Designing Complex Organizations* (Reading, MA: Addison-Wesley, 1977), Chapter 1; Galbraith and Kazanjian, *Strategy Implementation*, Chapter 7.

54 B. Kogut, 'Joint Ventures: Theoretical and Empirical Perspectives', *Strategic Management Journal* 9 (1988), 319–32.

55 G. S. Capowski, 'Designing a Corporate Identity', *Management Review* (June 1993), 37–38.

56 J. Marcia, 'Just Doing It', *Distribution*, January 1995, 36–40.

57 'Nike Battles Backlash from Overseas Sweatshops', *Marketing News*, November 9, 1998, 14.

58 J. Laabs, 'Mike Gives Indonesian Workers a Raise', *Workforce*, December 1998, 15–16.

59 W. Echikson, 'It's Europe's Turn to Sweat About Sweatshops', *BusinessWeek*, July 19, 1999, 96.

Chapter 11

Organisational Control and Change

LEARNING OBJECTIVES

After studying this chapter, you should be able to:

☑ Define organisational control, and describe the steps of the control process.

☑ Identify the main output controls, and discuss their advantages and disadvantages as a means of co-ordinating and motivating employees.

☑ Identify the main behaviour controls, and discuss their advantages and disadvantages as a means of co-ordinating and motivating employees.

☑ Explain the role of clan control or organisational culture in creating an effective organisational architecture.

☑ Discuss the relationship between organisational control and change, and explain why managing change is a vital management task.

A Manager's Challenge

B&Q Going from Strength to Strength

How should managers control to improve performance?

B&Q, originally called Block & Quayle, was founded in 1969 in Southampton and is the largest home improvement retailer in Europe and the third largest in the world. It has an annual turnover of £4.1 billion, holds 14.7 per cent market share within its industry within the UK and has now opened 341 stores, 60 of which are overseas. Having begun in an old, dilapidated movie theatre, the growth to one of the biggest home improvement retailers involved a continuous drive to control and improve performance.

B&Q's rise to the top was accompanied by an astute understanding of the need to monitor and control information about products, stock and margins. The company recognised early on the need to implement IT to control and improve performance. While the initial electronic point-of-sale (EPOS) system was soon replaced by a more sophisticated, mainframe-based data warehouse system that contributed greatly to effective control and decision making, only a few people held the knowledge and access privileges to the large amounts of data that were available.

It became apparent that this could not be sustained if the company wanted more growth. It was thus decided to move away from the current system and implement a new one that allowed more people access to vital company information. To initiate the change, the buying function of B&Q was reviewed, as it controlled the range of products, the profit margins and their prices and thus had a significant impact on the performance of the company. In order to develop this new system, B&Q senior management felt that it was necessary to involve users, senior managers and external experts in database design and business process analysis. This approach by B&Q senior management created a level of buy-in that improved the likelihood of success.

Since the introduction of the new system the number of users has risen sharply and has already brought great benefits to B&Q by providing general access to important business information throughout the company. It has increased the ability to manage stock, driving down inventory and ensuring appropriate stock cover.

But improvements in the management of inventory and access to information is not the only way in which B&Q has achieved better control and improvement of performance. The streamlining of these processes to make them more efficient is only one aspect of successful performance management.

One aspect that anecdotally influences business performance is the involvement and satisfaction of staff. Because of rapid growth, B&Q was somewhat obsessed with staying competitive, considering that they have over 38,000 employees. Further change had to be undertaken to align staffing issues with the improved information access and supply chain management.

In 1998 B&Q engaged a consultancy company that had devised a robust tool measuring employee engagement. A pilot project involving 3,500 employees exposed them to a questionnaire measuring their perceived engagement with the company. The results were disappointing to the Board, who had until that point not been convinced that a focus on employee involvement would make a difference to the bottom line. After reviewing the low scores, managers and employees co-operatively designed improvement and change strategies to increase perceived employee engagement by assessing their needs: these were often simple things like missing aprons, pencils or staplers, but they led to frustration and disengagement.

As part of the pilot, the questionnaire was repeated after six months. Few innovative changes had been implemented and the results showed minor improvements. By 2002 80 per cent of the workforce had undertaken the survey and B&Q had amassed significant and robust data to prove the influence of employee engagement in controlling and improving performance. Managers realised that attitudes had to change in order to affect employee engagement, which in turn influenced customer service and general performance. In some stores, successful changes brought about through the questionnaire generated £3.4 million more in sales and £1 million in profits.

But there is still a lot of variation and more has to be done. While a large number of stores are successful in implementing new ways of engaging staff and are thus better in controlling and improving performance, some stores still lag behind. The reasons are said to emanate from the difference in managers. One of the board members suggested that 'Great managers make the difference'. Because senior management at B&Q recognised this, the questionnaire is now part of their management training scheme.

Such approaches to improving and controlling performance are not unique to B&Q: they could be replicated by any company or industry.[1]

Overview

As the experience of B&Q suggests, the ways in which managers control the behaviour of their employees can have very different effects on the way employees behave. When managers make choices about how to influence and regulate their employees' behaviour and performance, they establish the second foundation of organisational architecture, *organisational control*. Control is the essential ingredient needed to bring about and manage organisational change efficiently and effectively.

As discussed in Chapter 10, the first task facing managers is to establish the *structure of task and job reporting relationships* that allows organisational members to use resources most efficiently and effectively. Structure alone, however, does not provide the incentive or motivation for people to behave in ways that help to achieve organisational goals. The purpose of organisational control is to provide managers with a means of directing and motivating subordinates to work toward achieving organisational goals and to provide managers with specific feedback on how well an organisation and its members are performing. B&Q's changes to the way employees felt about the company and the changes made to the access to important performance information were intended to direct and motivate employee behaviour; B&Q's market share, profits and customer satisfaction ratings are measures that give feedback on how well it is performing.

Organisational structure provides an organisation with a skeleton, and control and culture give it the muscles, sinews, nerves and sensations that allow managers to regulate and govern its activities. The managerial functions of organising and controlling are inseparable, and effective managers must learn to make them work together harmoniously.

In this chapter, the nature of organisational control and the steps in the control process will be considered. This is followed by a discussion of the three types of control available to managers to control and influence organisational members – **output control**, **behaviour control** and **clan control** (which operates through the values and norms of an organisation's culture).[2] Finally, the important issue of organisational change – change that is possible only when managers have put in place a control system that allows them to alter the way people and groups behave – is examined. By the end of this chapter, you will appreciate the rich variety of control systems available to managers, and understand why developing an appropriate control system is vital to increasing the performance of an organisation and its members.

What is Organisational Control?

As noted in Chapter 1, *controlling* is the process whereby managers monitor and regulate how efficiently and effectively an organisation and its members are performing the activities necessary to achieve organisational goals. When planning and organising, managers develop the organisational strategy and structure that they hope will allow the organisation to use resources most effectively to create value for customers. In controlling, managers monitor and evaluate whether the organisation's strategy and structure are working as intended, how they could be improved and how they might be changed if they are not working.

Control, however, does not mean just reacting to events after they have occurred. It also means being *proactive*, anticipating events that might occur and then changing the organisation to respond to whatever opportunities or threats have been identified. Control is concerned with keeping employees motivated, focused on the important problems confronting the organisation and working together to make the changes that will help an organisation perform increasingly better over time.

The Importance of Organisational Control

To understand the importance of organisational control, consider how it helps managers obtain superior efficiency, quality, responsiveness to customers and innovation – the four building blocks of competitive advantage.

To determine how efficiently they are using their resources, managers must be able to accurately measure how many *units of inputs* (raw materials, human resources and so on) are being used to produce a unit of output. Managers also must be able to measure how many *units of outputs* (goods and services) are being produced. A control system contains the measures that allow managers to assess how efficiently the organisation is producing goods and services. If managers experiment with changing the way the organisation produces goods and services to find a more efficient way of producing them, measures can tell managers how successful they have been. When managers at Ford decided to adopt a product team structure to design, engineer and manufacture new car models, for example, they used measures such as time taken to design a new car and cost savings per car produced to evaluate how well the new structure was working in comparison with the old structure. They found that the new structure resulted in improved performance. Without a control system in place, managers have no idea how well their organisation is performing and how its performance can be improved – information that is becoming increasingly important in today's highly competitive environment.

Today, much of the competition among organisations revolves around increasing the *quality* of goods and services. In the car industry, for example, cars within each price range compete against one another in features, design and reliability. Whether a customer will buy a Ford Mondeo, Vauxhall Vectra, Toyota Avensis or Honda Accord depends significantly on the quality of each product. Organisational control is important in determining the quality of products and services because it gives managers feedback on product quality. If the managers of car makers consistently measure the number of customer complaints and the number of new cars returned for repairs, or if heads of schools measure how many students drop out of school or how achievement scores compared to national averages vary over time, they have a good indication of how much quality they have built into their product – be it a car that does not break down or an educated student. Effective managers create a **control system** that consistently monitors the quality of goods and services so that they can make continuous improvements to quality – an approach to change that gives them a *competitive advantage*.

Managers can also help make their organisations more responsive to customers if they develop a control system that allows them to evaluate how well customer service staff are performing their jobs, as B&Q now does by looking at their needs and aiming to address them. Monitoring employee behaviour can help managers find ways to increase employees' performance levels. Perhaps by revealing areas in which skill training can help employees, by finding new procedures that allow employees to perform their jobs better, or by providing them with the necessary materials to perform their task, levels of performance increase. To improve customer service, for example, Citroen Germany always follows up with customers who purchase a new vehicle about their experiences with the particular dealer. Ford undertakes similar surveys to ensure quality. If too many complaints are received, managers at Ford, for example, investigate the dealership to uncover the sources of the problems and suggest solutions; if necessary, they may even threaten to reduce the number of cars a dealership receives to force the dealer to improve the quality of its customer service.

Finally, controlling may raise the level of *innovation* in an organisation. Successful innovation takes place when managers create an organisational setting in which employees feel empowered to be creative and in which authority is decentralised to employees so that they feel free to experiment and take risks. Deciding on the appropriate control systems to *encourage risk taking* is an important management challenge; organisational culture (discussed later in this chapter) is very important in this regard.

Control Systems and IT

Control systems are formal target-setting, monitoring, evaluation and feedback systems that provide managers with information about whether the organisation's strategy and structure are working efficiently and effectively.[3] Effective control systems alert managers when something is going wrong and give them time to respond to opportunities and threats. An effective control system has three characteristics: it is *flexible* enough to allow managers to respond as necessary to unexpected events; it provides *accurate* information and gives managers a true picture of organisational performance; and it provides managers with the information in a *timely manner*, because making decisions on the basis of outdated information is likely to result in bad decisions.

New forms of IT have revolutionised control systems because they facilitate the flow of accurate and timely information up and down the organisational hierarchy and between functions and divisions. Today, employees at all levels of the organisation routinely feed information into a company's information system or network and start the chain of events that affects decision making in some other part of the organisation. This could be the department store clerk whose scanning of purchased clothing tells merchandise managers what kinds of clothing need to be reordered or the salesperson in the field who feeds into a wireless laptop information about customers' changing needs or problems. The introduction of the new system at B&Q is a successful example of how an improved IT structure can foster better control throughout a company.

Control and information systems are developed to measure performance at each stage in the process of transforming inputs into finished products and services (Fig. 11.1). At the input stage, managers use **feedforward control** to anticipate problems before they arise so that problems do not occur later, during the conversion process.[4] For example, by giving stringent product specifications to suppliers in advance (a form of *performance target*), an organisation can control the quality of the inputs it receives from its suppliers and thus avoid potential problems during the conversion process. In general, the development of *management information systems* (MISs) promotes feedforward control that provides managers with timely information about changes in the task and general environments that may impact their organisation later. Effective managers always monitor trends and changes in the external environment to try to anticipate problems. (We discuss MISs in more detail in Chapter 18.)

At the conversion stage, **concurrent control** gives managers immediate feedback on how efficiently inputs are being transformed into outputs so that they can correct problems as they arise. Concurrent control through IT alerts managers to the need to react quickly to whatever is the source of the problem – be it a defective batch of inputs, a machine that is out of alignment, or a worker who lacks the skills necessary to perform a task efficiently. Concurrent control is at the heart of TQM programmes (see p. 288), in which workers are expected to constantly monitor

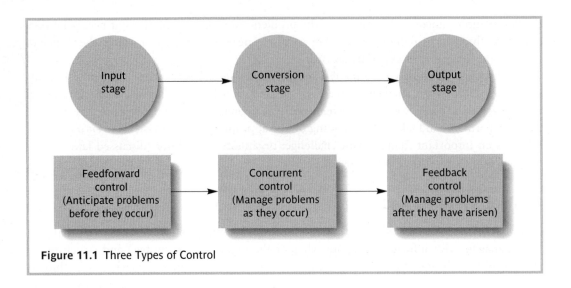

Figure 11.1 Three Types of Control

the quality of the products or services they provide at every step of the production process, and inform managers as soon as they discover problems. One of the strengths of Toyota's production system, for example, is that individual workers are given the authority to push a button to stop the assembly line whenever they discover a quality problem. When all problems have been corrected, the result is a finished product that is much more reliable.

At the output stage, managers use **feedback control** to provide information about customers' reactions to products and services so that if necessary corrective action can be taken. For example, a feedback control system that monitors the number of customer returns alerts managers when defective products are being produced, and an MIS that measures increases or decreases in relative sales of different products alerts managers to changes in customer tastes so that they can increase or reduce the production of specific products.

The Control Process

The control process, whether at the input, conversion or output stage, can be broken down into four steps: *establishing* standards of performance, then *measuring* the performance, *comparing* this performance against the standard, and *evaluating* actual performance (Fig. 11.2).[5]

■ *Step 1: Establish the standards of performance, goals or targets against which performance is to be evaluated*   At step 1 in the control process managers decide on the standards of performance, goals or targets that they think ought to be achieved by a division, a function or an individual. The standards of performance that managers select measure efficiency, quality, responsiveness to customers and innovation.[6] If managers decide to pursue a low-cost strategy, for example, then they need to measure efficiency at all levels in the organisation.

At the corporate level, a standard of performance that measures efficiency is *operating costs* – the actual costs associated with producing goods and services, including all employee-related costs. Senior managers might set a corporate goal of 'reducing operating costs by 10 per cent for the next three years' to increase efficiency. Corporate managers might then evaluate divisional managers for their ability to reduce operating costs within their respective divisions,

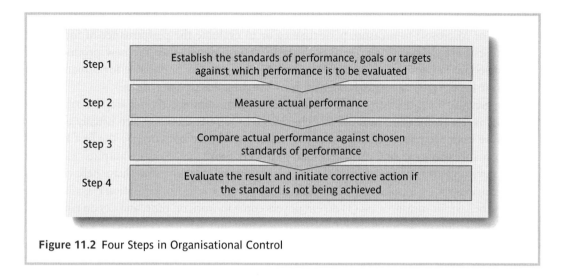

Figure 11.2 Four Steps in Organisational Control

and divisional managers might set cost-savings targets for functional managers. Performance standards selected at one level thus affect those at other levels. Ultimately the performance of individual managers is evaluated in terms of their ability to *reduce costs*. AIXTRON AG was a leading German provider of equipment to the semiconductor industry. It had been able to establish a leading market position but needed to consider costs in order to remain a dominant player. CEO Paul Hyland implemented a stringent cost-saving plan that was highly successful in maintaining the company's market position.

The number of standards of performance that an organisation's managers use to evaluate efficiency, quality and so on, can run into thousands or hundreds of thousands. Managers at each level are responsible for selecting those standards that will best allow them to evaluate how their area of responsibility is performing.[7] Managers must be careful to choose the standards of performance that allow them to assess how well they are doing with all four of the building blocks of competitive advantage. If managers focus on just one (such as efficiency) and ignore others (such as determining what customers really want and innovating a new line of products to satisfy them), managers may cause imbalances that can eventually lead to bad performance.

■ *Step 2: Measure actual performance*   Once managers have decided which standards or targets they will use to evaluate performance, the next step in the control process is to measure *actual performance*. In practice, managers can measure or evaluate two things: (1) the actual *outputs* that result from the behaviour of their members and (2) the *behaviours* themselves (hence the terms *output control* and *behaviour control* used below).[8]

Sometimes both outputs and behaviours can be easily measured. Measuring outputs and evaluating behaviour is relatively easy in a fast-food restaurant, for example, because employees are performing routine tasks: managers can count how many customers their employees serve and how much money customers spend. They can easily observe each employee's behaviour and quickly take action to solve any problems that may arise. Output control was easily achieved in B&Q, as technology allowed detailed assessment of product flows.

When an organisation and its members perform complex, non-routine activities that are intrinsically difficult to measure, it is much harder for managers to measure outputs or behaviour.[9] It is very difficult, for example, for managers in charge of R&D departments at Merck or Microsoft to measure performance or to evaluate the performance of individual members because it can take 5 or 10 years to determine whether the new products that scientists are developing are going to be profitable. It is also impossible for a manager to measure how creative a research scientist is by watching his or her actions.

In general, the more non-routine or complex organisational activities are, the harder it is for managers to measure outputs or behaviours.[10] Outputs, however, are usually easier to measure than behaviours because they are more *tangible* and *objective*. So the first kinds of performance measures that managers tend to use are those that measure outputs. Managers then develop performance measures or standards that allow them to evaluate behaviours to determine whether employees at all levels are working toward organisational goals. Some simple behaviour measures are (1) do employees come to work on time, and (2) do employees consistently follow the established rules for greeting and serving customers? Each type of output and behaviour control and the way it is used at the different organisational levels – corporate, divisional, functional and individual – is discussed in detail below.

- *Step 3: Compare actual performance against chosen standards of performance*   During step 3, managers evaluate if performance has deviated from the standards of performance chosen in step 1. If performance is higher than expected, managers may decide that they have set performance standards too low and may raise them for the next time period to challenge their subordinates.[11] Managers that adopt Japanese management practices are well known for the way they try to increase performance in manufacturing settings by constantly raising performance standards to motivate managers and workers to find new ways to reduce costs or increase quality.

  However, if performance is too low and standards have not been reached, or if standards have been set so high that employees cannot achieve them, managers must decide whether to take corrective action.[12] It is easy to do this when the reasons for poor performance can be identified – high labour costs, for instance. To reduce costs, managers can search for low-cost foreign sources of supply, invest more in technology, or implement cross-functional teams. More often, however, the reasons for poor performance are hard to identify. Changes in the environment, such as the emergence of a new global competitor, a recession, or an increase in interest rates, may be the source of the problem. Within an organisation, perhaps the R&D function has under-estimated the problems it encountered in developing a new product or the extra costs of doing unforeseen research. If managers are to take any form of corrective action, step 4 is critical.

- *Step 4: Evaluate the result and initiate corrective action (that is, make changes) if the standard is not being achieved*   The final step in the control process is to evaluate the results from steps 1–3 and bring about change as appropriate. Independent of the achievement or non-achievement of performance targets, this step is an important *learning source* for managers. If managers decide that the level of performance is unacceptable, they must try to change the way work activities are performed. Sometimes, performance problems occur because the work standard is too high – for example, a sales target is too optimistic and impossible to achieve. In this case, adopting more realistic standards can reduce the gap between *actual* performance and *desired* performance.

  However, if managers determine that something in the process is causing the problem, then they will need to change the way resources are being utilised[13] and how the process is being managed. Perhaps the latest technology is not being used; perhaps workers lack the advanced training needed to perform at a higher level; perhaps the organisation needs to buy its inputs or assemble its products abroad to compete against low-cost rivals; perhaps it needs to restructure itself or reengineer its work processes to increase efficiency.

The simplest example of a control system is the thermostat in a home. By setting the thermostat, you establish the standard of performance with which actual temperature is to be compared. The thermostat contains a sensing or monitoring device, which measures the actual temperature against the desired temperature. Whenever there is a difference between them, the boiler or air-conditioning unit is activated to bring the temperature back to the standard. In other words, *corrective action* is initiated. This is a simple control system, for it is entirely self-contained and the target (temperature) is easy to measure.

Establishing targets and designing measurement systems is much more difficult for managers because the high level of uncertainty in the organisational environment often means that managers do not know what may happen. It is thus vital for managers to design control systems to alert them to problems so that they can be dealt with before they become threatening. Managers should not just be concerned with bringing the organisation's perform-ance up to some predetermined standard; they should want to push that standard forward, to encourage employees at all levels to find new ways to raise performance.

In the following sections, we consider the three most important types of control that managers can use to co-ordinate and motivate employees to ensure superior efficiency, quality, innovation and responsiveness to customers: *output* control, *behaviour* control and *organisational culture* or *clan* control (Fig. 11.3). Managers use all three to govern and regulate organisational activities, no matter what specific organisational structure is in place.

Type of control	Mechanisms of control
Output control	Financial measures of performance Organisational goals Operating budgets
Behaviour control	Direct supervision Management by objectives Rules and standard operating procedures
Organisational culture/clan control	Values Norms Socialisation

Figure 11.3 Three Organisational Control Systems

Output Control

All managers develop a system of *output control* for their organisations. First, they choose the goals or output performance standards or targets that they think will best measure efficiency, quality, innovation and responsiveness to customers. Then they measure to see whether the

Table 11.1 Four measures of financial performance

Profit ratios

Return on investment	$= \dfrac{\text{net profit before taxes}}{\text{total assets}}$	Measures how well managers are using the organisation's resources to generate profits.
Gross profit margin	$= \dfrac{\text{sales revenues} - \text{cost of goods sold}}{\text{sales revenues}}$	The difference between the amount of revenue generated from the product and the resources used to produce the product.

Liquidity ratios

Current ratio	$= \dfrac{\text{current assets}}{\text{current liabilities}}$	Do managers have resources available to meet claims of short-term creditors?
Quick ratio	$= \dfrac{\text{current assets} - \text{inventory}}{\text{current liabilities}}$	Can managers pay off claims of short-term creditors without selling inventory?

Leverage ratios

Debt-to-assets ratio	$= \dfrac{\text{total debt}}{\text{total assets}}$	To what extent have managers used borrowed funds to finance investments?
Times-covered ratio	$= \dfrac{\text{profit before interest and taxes}}{\text{total interest charges}}$	Measures how far profits can decline before managers cannot meet interest changes. If ratio declines to less than 1, the organisation is technically insolvent.

Activity ratios

Inventory turnover	$= \dfrac{\text{cost of goods sold}}{\text{inventory}}$	Measures how efficiently managers are turning inventory over so that excess inventory is not carried.
Days sales outstanding	$= \dfrac{\text{current accounts receivable}}{\text{sales for period divided by days in period}}$	Measures how efficiently managers are collecting revenues from customers to pay expenses.

performance goals and standards are being achieved at the corporate, divisional or functional, and individual levels of the organisation. The three main mechanisms that managers use to assess output or performance are **financial measures, organisational goals** and **operating budgets**.

Financial Measures of Performance

Senior managers are most concerned with overall organisational performance and use various financial measures to evaluate performance. The most common are profit ratios, liquidity ratios, leverage ratios and activity ratios. These are discussed below and summarised in Table 11.1.[14]

- **Profit ratios** measure how efficiently managers are using the organisation's resources to generate profits. **Return on investment (ROI)**, an organisation's net income before taxes divided by its total assets, is the most commonly used financial performance measure because it allows managers of one organisation to compare performance with that of others. ROI allows managers to assess an organisation's competitive advantage. **Gross profit margin** is the difference between the amount of revenue generated by a product and the resources used to produce the product. This measure provides managers with information about how efficiently an organisation is utilising its resources and about how attractive customers find the product. It also provides managers with a way to assess how well an organisation is building a competitive advantage.

- **Liquidity ratios** measure how well managers have protected organisational resources to be able to meet short-term obligations. The *current ratio* (current assets divided by current liabilities) tells managers whether they have the resources available to meet the claims of short-term creditors. The *quick ratio* tells them whether they can pay these claims without selling inventory.

- **Leverage ratios** such as the *debt-to-assets ratio* and the *times-covered ratio* measure the degree to which managers use debt (borrow money) or equity (issue new shares) to finance ongoing operations. An organisation is highly leveraged if it uses more debt than equity, and debt can be very risky when profits fail to cover the interest on the debt.

- **Activity ratios** provide measures of how well managers are creating value from organisational assets. **Inventory turnover** measures how efficiently managers are turning inventory over so that excess inventory is not carried. **Days sales outstanding** provides information on how efficiently managers are collecting revenue from customers to pay expenses.

The *objectivity* of financial measures of performance is the reason why so many managers use them to assess the efficiency and effectiveness of their organisations. When an organisation fails to meet performance standards such as ROI, revenue or stock price targets, managers know that they must take corrective action. Financial controls tell managers when a corporate reorganisation might be necessary, when they should sell off divisions and exit from businesses, or when they should rethink their corporate strategies.[15]

Although financial information is an important output control, financial information by itself does not provide managers with all the information they need about the four building blocks of competitive advantage. Financial results inform managers about the results of decisions they have already made: they do not tell managers how to find new opportunities to build competitive advantage in the future. To encourage a future-oriented approach, senior managers must establish organisational goals that encourage middle and first-line managers to achieve superior efficiency, quality, innovation and responsiveness to customers.

Organisational Goals

Once senior managers consult with lower-level managers and set the organisation's overall goals, they establish performance standards for the divisions and functions. These standards specify for divisional and functional managers the level at which their units must perform if the organisation is to achieve its overall goals.[16] Each division is given a set of specific goals to achieve (Fig. 11.4). Divisional managers develop a business-level strategy (based on achieving superior efficiency or innovation) that they hope will allow them to achieve that goal.[17] In consultation with functional managers, they specify the functional goals that the managers of different functions need to achieve to allow the division to achieve its goals. Sales managers might be evaluated for their ability to increase sales; materials management managers, for their ability to increase the quality of inputs or lower their costs; R&D managers, for the number of products they innovate or the number of patents they receive. In turn, functional managers establish the goals that first-line managers and non-managerial employees need to achieve to allow the function to achieve its overall goals.

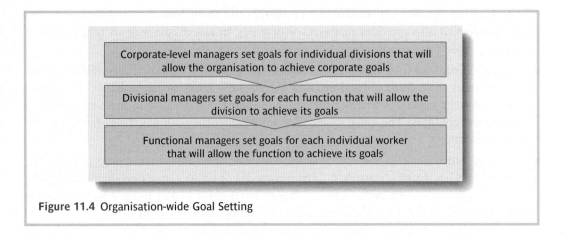

Figure 11.4 Organisation-wide Goal Setting

Output control is used at every level of the organisation, and it is vital that the goals set at one level harmonise with the goals set at other levels so that managers and other employees throughout the organisation work together to attain the corporate goals that senior managers have set.[18] It is also important that goals are set *appropriately*, so that managers are motivated to accomplish them. If goals are set too high, managers may work only half-heartedly to achieve them because they are certain they will fail. In contrast, if goals are set so low that they are easy to achieve, managers will not be motivated to use all their resources as efficiently and effectively as possible. Research suggests that the best goals are *specific, difficult goals* – goals that challenge and stretch managers' ability but are not out of reach and do not require an impossibly high expenditure of managerial time and energy. Such goals are often called **stretch goals**.

Deciding what is a specific, difficult goal and what is a goal that is too difficult or too easy is a skill that managers must develop. Based on their judgement and work experience, managers at all levels must assess how difficult a certain task is and must assess the ability of a particular subordinate manager to achieve it. If they do so successfully, challenging, interrelated goals – goals that reinforce one another and focus on achieving overall corporate objectives – will energise the organisation.

Operating Budgets

Once managers at each level have been given a goal or target to achieve, the next step in developing an output control system is to establish *operating budgets* that regulate how managers and workers attain their goals. An operating budget is a blueprint that states how managers intend to use organisational resources to achieve organisational goals efficiently. Typically, managers at one level allocate to subordinate managers a specific amount of resources to use for the production of goods and services. Once they have been given a budget, these lower-level managers must decide how to allocate money for different organisational activities. They are then evaluated for their ability to stay within the budget and to make the best use of available resources. Managers at Dyson, for example, may have a budget of £20 million to spend on developing and selling a new line of vacuum cleaners. They must decide how much money to allocate to the various functions such as R&D, engineering and sales so that the division generates the most customer revenue and makes the biggest profit.

Large organisations often treat each division as a singular or stand-alone *responsibility centre*. Corporate managers can then evaluate each division's contribution to corporate performance. Managers of a division may be given a fixed budget for resources and be evaluated on the amount of goods or services they can produce using those resources (this is a *cost* or *expense* budget approach). Managers may be asked to maximise the revenues from the sales of goods and services produced (a *revenue* budget approach). A different approach could be that managers are evaluated on the difference between the revenues generated by the sales of products and services and the budgeted cost of making those products and services (a *profit* budget approach). Japanese-style management, which uses operating budgets and challenging goals to increase efficiency, is instructive in this context.

Three components – objective financial measures, challenging goals and performance standards and appropriate operating budgets – are thus the essence of effective output control. Most organisations develop sophisticated *output control systems* to allow managers at all levels to keep accurate account of the organisation so that they can move quickly to take corrective action as needed.[19] Output control is an essential part of management: the way in which Carrefour, the French supermarket chain, uses IT to support its control mechanisms to expand internationally is discussed in Case 11.1.

Case 11.1: The need for smarter control when expanding internationally

Europe's largest retailer, Carrefour, has not only expanded massively in Europe but has taken to the world with over 1,200 hypermarkets, supermarkets and discount stores in Asia and Middle and South America. One of its latest acquisitions was Italian Hyparlo hypermarkets in 2003.[20]

Carrefour has been extremely successful in its expansion, having established itself as the world's second largest supermarket chain. Unlike other retail giants, such as Tesco, Carrefour does not change the names of supermarket chains it takes over, as then-CEO Bernard believed that this would maintain customer loyalty. Carrefour aims to stay true to the local markets that it enters. However, as part of this development, Carrefour had to start thinking about how to maintain output control across such a diverse range of countries.

In 2003, Carrefour signed a contract with one of the world's largest supply chain software providers, Finland's Aldata Solution.[21] With a successful roll-out of the new technology in its Thailand, Brazil and Poland stores, Carrefour managed to streamline control over the entire supply chain through implementing Aldata's integrated applications. By 2007 the programme will be implemented in more than 15 central offices around the world. Aldata says that the global reach of Carrefour and the associated requirements for output control were challenging but have been successfully addressed.

The new technology includes a central application for head offices and a shop module for stores themselves. This integrated nature of the system allows Carrefour's local, national and international managers to access large amounts of information about the company's performance. It is anticipated that more than 900 stores will be connected to this new system; once additional components or applications are needed, they can just be added.

However, Carrefour, besides its good understanding of the necessity to maintain control over the outputs and performance of a company, realises that global recessions and increasing market pressures impact on its overall performance. In 2005 its share prices fell to half its value of 1999: different and new ways have to be found to address increased performance.

Problems with Output Control

When designing an output control system, managers must be careful to avoid some pitfalls. They must be sure, for example, that the output standards they create motivate managers at all levels and do not cause them to behave in inappropriate ways to achieve organisational goals.

Suppose senior managers give divisional managers the goal of doubling profits over a three-year period. This goal seems challenging and reachable when it is jointly agreed upon, and in the first two years profits go up by 70 per cent. In the third year, however, an economic recession hits and sales plummet. Divisional managers think it is increasingly unlikely that they will meet their profit goal, and failure will mean losing the substantial monetary bonus tied to achieving the goal. How might managers behave to try to preserve their bonuses?

One course of action they might take is to find ways to reduce costs, since profit can be increased either by raising revenues or reducing costs. Divisional managers might cut back on expensive R&D activities, delay maintenance on machinery, reduce marketing expenditures and lay off middle managers and workers to reduce costs so that at the end of the year they will make their target of doubling profits and receive their bonuses. This tactic might help them achieve a short-run goal – doubling profits – but such actions could hurt long-term profitability or ROI (because a cutback in R&D can reduce the rate of product innovation, a cutback in marketing will lead to the loss of customers and so on).

Problems of this sort occurred at Gillette when its new chairman, James M. Kilts, announced that the poorly performing company would not be experiencing a turnaround any time in the near future. He attributed a large part of the company's problems to the overly ambitious sales and profit goals that his predecessor had set for managers of its divisions (razors and toiletries, Braun appliances and Duracell batteries). To achieve these ambitious sales targets, divisional managers had slashed advertising budgets and loaded up on inventory hoping to sell it quickly and generate large revenues. However, this had backfired when customer demand dropped and a recession occurred.

Kilts saw that Gillette's managers had not been focusing on the right ways to reduce costs. Because managers' salaries and bonuses were based on their ability to meet the ambitious goals that had been set for them, they had acted with a short-term mind-set. Managers had not been thinking about the long-term goal of trying to find the best balance between keeping costs under control, keeping customers happy and keeping the pipeline of new products full.

Kilts announced that henceforth Gillette would no longer provide specific and unrealistic sales and earning targets that created a 'circle of doom' and led managers to behave in precisely the ways that would prevent them from achieving company goals – by reducing advertising to reduce costs, for example. Kilts decided that Gillette would set long-term goals based on carefully drawn marketing plans that targeted the products customers wanted and would lead to long-term sales growth. Gillette would also carefully examine its product line to focus its resources on products that offered the most payoffs and to discontinue poorly performing products that did not contribute much to the bottom line. The changes worked; in 2004 Gillette announced record sales and profits.[22]

As Gillette's experience suggests, *long-run effectiveness* is what managers should be most concerned about. Managers must consider carefully how flexible they should be when using output control. If conditions change (as they will because of uncertainty in the task and general environments), it is probably better for senior managers to communicate to managers lower in the hierarchy that they are aware of the changes taking place and are willing to revise and lower goals and standards. Indeed, many organisations schedule yearly revisions of their five-year plan and goals and use scenario planning to avoid the problems Gillette experienced.

The message is clear: although output control is a useful tool for keeping managers and employees at all levels motivated and the organisation on track, it is only a guide to appropriate action. Managers must be sensitive to how they use output control and must constantly monitor its effects at all levels in the organisation.

Behaviour Control

Organisational structure by itself does not provide any mechanism that motivates managers and non-managerial employees to behave in ways that make the structure work or even improve the way it works – hence the need for control. Put another way, managers can develop an elegant organisational structure with highly appropriate task and reporting relationships, but the design will work only if managers also establish control systems that allow them to motivate and shape employee behaviour.[23] Output control is one method of motivating employees; behaviour control is another method. This section examines three mechanisms of behaviour control that managers can use to keep subordinates on track and make organisational structures work as they are designed to work: *direct supervision, management by objectives (MBO)* and *rules and standard operating procedures (SOPs)* (Fig. 11.3).

Direct Supervision

The most immediate and potent form of behaviour control is *direct supervision* by managers who actively monitor and observe the behaviour of their subordinates, teach subordinates the behaviours that are appropriate and inappropriate and intervene to take any corrective action that is needed. When managers personally supervise subordinates, they lead by example, and in this way can help subordinates develop and increase their own skill levels. Leading by example is one aspect of *leadership*, which will be discussed in Chapter 14.

Control through personal supervision can be a very effective way of motivating employees and promoting behaviours that increase efficiency and effectiveness.[24]

Nevertheless, certain problems are associated with direct supervision. First, it is very expensive, because a manager can personally manage only a small number of subordinates effectively. If direct supervision is the main kind of control being used in an organisation, a lot of managers will be needed, and costs will increase. Output control is therefore usually preferred to behaviour control; indeed, output control tends to be the first type of control that managers at all levels use to evaluate performance.

Second, direct supervision can demotivate subordinates if they feel that they are under such close scrutiny that they are not free to make their own decisions. Subordinates may start to shy away from responsibility if they feel that their manager is waiting for an opportunity to reprimand anyone who makes the slightest error.

Third, as noted previously, for many jobs direct supervision is simply not feasible. The more complex a job is, the more difficult it is for a manager to evaluate how well a subordinate is performing. The performance of divisional and functional managers, for example, can be evaluated only over relatively long time periods (this is why an output control system is developed), so it makes little sense for senior managers to continually monitor their performance.

Management by Objectives

To provide a framework within which to evaluate subordinates' behaviour and, in particular, to allow managers to monitor progress toward achieving goals, many organisations implement some version of *MBO*. MBO is a system of evaluating subordinates for their ability to achieve specific organisational goals or performance standards and to meet operating budgets.[25] Most organisations make some use of MBO because there is little sense in establishing goals and then failing to evaluate whether or not they are being achieved. MBO involves three specific steps:

- *Step 1: Specific goals and objectives are established at each level of the organisation*   MBO starts when senior managers establish *overall organisational objectives*, such as financial or other performance targets. Objective setting 'cascades down' throughout the organisation as managers at the divisional and functional levels set their objectives to achieve corporate objectives.[26] Finally, first-level managers and workers jointly set objectives that will contribute to achieving functional goals.

- *Step 2: Managers and their subordinates together determine the subordinates' goals*   An important characteristic of MBO is its *participatory nature*. Managers at every level sit down with each of the subordinate managers who reports directly to them, and together they determine appropriate and feasible goals for the subordinate and bargain over the budget that the subordinate will need to achieve his or her goals. The participation of subordinates in the objective-setting process is a way of strengthening their commitment to achieving their goals and meeting their budgets.[27] Another reason why it is so important for subordinates (both individuals and teams) to participate in goal-setting is that doing so enables them to tell managers what they think they can *realistically achieve*.[28]

- *Step 3: Managers and their subordinates periodically review the subordinates' progress toward meeting goals*   Once specific objectives have been agreed on for managers at each level, managers are *accountable* for meeting them. Periodically, reviews with their subordinates to evaluate their progress are undertaken. This may take place as part of standardised, yearly *appraisal cycles*. In certain industries, salary rises may be linked to the goal-setting process, and managers who achieve their goals receive greater rewards than those who fall short. Promotions are usually based on successfully achieving goals. (The issue of how to design *reward systems* to motivate managers and other organisational employees is discussed in Chapter 13.)

In the companies that have decentralised responsibility for the production of goods and services to empowered teams and cross-functional teams, MBO works somewhat differently. Managers ask each team to develop a set of goals and performance targets that the team hopes to achieve – goals that are consistent with organisational objectives. Managers then negotiate with each team to establish its final goals and the budget the team will need to achieve them. The reward system is linked to *team performance*, not to the performance of any one team member.

Cypress Semiconductor offers an interesting example of how IT can be used to manage the MBO process quickly and effectively. In the fast-moving semiconductor business a premium is placed on organisational adaptability. At Cypress, CEO T. J. Rodgers was facing a problem. How could he control his growing, 1,500-employee organisation without developing a bureaucratic management hierarchy? Rodgers believed that a 'tall' hierarchy hindered the ability of an organisation to adapt to changing conditions. He was committed to maintaining a 'flat' and decentralised organisational structure with a minimum of management layers. At the same time, he needed to control his employees to ensure that they performed in a manner consistent with the goals of the company.[29] How could he achieve this without resorting to direct supervision and the management hierarchy that it implies?

Rodgers implemented an online information system through which he could manage what every employee and team was doing in his fast-moving and decentralised organisation. Each employee maintained a list of 10–15 goals, such as 'Meet with marketing for new product launch' or 'Make sure to check with customer X'. Noted next to each goal are when it was agreed upon, when it was due to be finished and whether it had been finished. All of this information is stored on a central computer. Rodgers claims that he can review the goals of all employees in about four hours and that he does so each week.[30] How is this possible? He *manages by exception* and looks only for employees who are falling behind. He then calls them, not to blame but to ask whether there is anything he can do to help them get the job done. It takes only about half an hour each week for employees to review and update their lists. This system allows Rodgers to exercise control over his organisation without resorting to the expensive layers of a management hierarchy and direct supervision.

Bureaucratic Control

When direct supervision is too expensive and management by objectives is inappropriate, managers may turn to another mechanism to shape and motivate employee behaviour: **bureaucratic control**. Bureaucratic control is control by means of a comprehensive system of rules and SOPs that shapes and regulates the behaviour of divisions, functions and individuals. Weber's theory of bureaucracy was introduced in Chapter 2 and it was noted that while all organisations use bureaucratic rules and procedures, some use them more than others.[31]

Rules and SOPs guide behaviour and specify what employees are to do when they confront a problem that needs a solution. It is the responsibility of a manager to develop rules that allow employees to perform their activities efficiently and effectively. When employees follow the rules that managers have developed, their behaviour is *standardised* – actions are performed the same way time and time again – and the outcome of their work is *predictable*. This suggests that managers can make employees' behaviour predictable. It is assumed that there is no need to monitor the outputs of behaviour because standardised behaviour will lead to standardised outputs.

Suppose a worker at BMW comes up with a way to attach exhaust pipes that reduces the number of steps in the assembly process and increases efficiency. Always on the lookout for ways to standardise procedures, managers make this idea the basis of a new rule that says: 'From now on, the procedure for attaching the exhaust pipe to the car is as follows.' If all workers follow the rule to the letter, every car will come off the assembly line with its exhaust pipe attached in the new way and there will be no need to check exhaust pipes at the end of the line. In practice, mistakes and lapses of attention do happen, so output control is used at the end of the line, and each car's exhaust system is given a routine inspection. However, the number of quality problems with the exhaust system is minimised because the rule (bureaucratic control) is being followed.

Service organisations such as retail stores, fast-food restaurants and home improvement stores attempt to standardise the behaviour of employees by instructing them on the correct way to greet customers or the appropriate way to serve and bag food. Employees are trained to follow the rules that have proved to be most effective in a particular situation. The better trained the employees are, the more standardised is their behaviour and the more trust managers can have that outputs (such as food quality) will be consistent. An interesting example of how creating rules can enhance performance is discussed in Case 11.2.

Case 11.2: How to enhance customer satisfaction the French way

In 1969 Dominique Mondonnaud established Sephora in France, and it has now become a symbol for the worldwide beauty industry. In 1997 it was acquired by the French luxury conglomerate Louis Vuitton Moet Hennessy (LVMH) and has gone from strength to strength ever since. It has now more than 400 stores worldwide, operating in Europe, North America and some parts of Asia.[32] In America it revolutionised cosmetic merchandising and purchasing. Entering the American market as a European business was not easy, but Sephora's concept paid off.[33]

What did they do that inspired customers?

Especially in America, cosmetic retailing was primarily 'look but don't touch'. Before Sephora entered the market, customers either had to buy their cosmetic products without trying them, or they had the choice to be served by sales personnel whose commission was driven by pushing one particular brand. None of those approaches left customers much choice.

Sephora was different. First of all, the French chain impressed with its minimalist shop designs which set off the products they were trying to sell. Most stores were like Sephora's flagship store in Paris. Secondly, the company offered a variety of products including some luxury brands that were usually reserved for exclusive department stores. It further extended its range by providing access to smaller beauty companies, which were usually struggling to gain access to such a wide distribution channel. With its product range, Sephora broadened the customer base of its stores: its senior vice president for marketing noted that the age range of customers was between 15 and 70. Sephora also managed to make their stores attractive to men.

Thirdly, Sephora changed its approach to selling its products. Its stores offered an environment to browse and sample the product. Customers were encouraged to try one of the 11,000 items from 250 brands. Sephora's shops were organised and orderly, allowing customers to easily find and try the products they were interested in. In addition, the sales assistants were encouraged to offer help only on request. One of the rules created by Sephora's management was that the stores were 'assisted self-service stores'. By creating this rule, customers felt less intimidated to shop and browse a variety of brands.

This French approach to cosmetic retailing and the rules for the staff and store layouts challenged the American market and Sephora has become a serious threat to department stores.

Daniel Richard, CEO of Sephora, argued that everything about Sephora stores – be it the layout or the background music – was designed with the purpose of enhancing and underlining that the shopping experience for each customer in Sephora would emphasise 'freedom, exploration, discovery and a personal definition of beauty'.[34]

Problems with Bureaucratic Control

Many organisations make extensive use of bureaucratic control because rules and SOPs effectively control routine organisational activities. With a bureaucratic control system in place, managers can manage by exception and intervene and take corrective action only when necessary. However, managers need to be aware of a number of problems associated with bureaucratic control, because they can reduce organisational effectiveness.[35]

First, *establishing* rules is always easier than discarding them. Organisations tend to become overly bureaucratic over time as managers do everything 'according to the book'. If the amount of red tape becomes too great, decision making slows and managers react sluggishly to changing conditions. This can imperil an organisation's survival if agile new competitors emerge. US department stores that do not allow their customers to try their limited product range are an example of how operating procedures can hinder organisational success.

Second, because rules constrain and standardise behaviour and lead people to behave in predictable ways, there is a danger that people become so used to automatically following rules that they *stop thinking for themselves*. Too much standardisation can actually reduce the level of learning taking place in an organisation and get the organisation off track if managers and workers focus on the wrong issues. An organisation thrives when its members are constantly thinking of new ways to increase efficiency, quality and customer responsiveness: by definition, new ideas do not come from blindly following standardised procedures. Similarly, the pursuit of innovation implies a commitment by managers to discover new ways of doing things; innovation, however, is incompatible with the use of extensive bureaucratic control.

Managers must therefore be sensitive about the way they use bureaucratic control. It is most useful when organisational activities are routine and well understood and when employees are making programmed decisions – for example, in mass-production settings such as Ford or in routine service settings such as stores like McDonald's. Bureaucratic control is much less useful in situations where non-programmed decisions have to be made and managers have to react quickly to changes in the organisational environment.

To use output control and behaviour control, managers must be able to identify the outcomes they want to achieve and the behaviours they want employees to perform to achieve those outcomes. For many of the most important and significant organisational activities, however, output control and behaviour control are inappropriate:

- A manager cannot evaluate the performance of workers such as doctors, research scientists or engineers by observing their behaviour on a day-to-day basis.

- Rules and SOPs are of little use in telling a doctor how to respond to an emergency situation, or a scientist how to discover something new.

- Output controls such as the amount of time a surgeon takes for each operation or the costs of making a discovery are very crude measures of the quality of performance.

How can managers attempt to control and regulate the behaviour of their subordinates when personal supervision is of little use, when rules cannot be developed to tell employees what to do, and when outputs and goals cannot be measured at all or can be measured usefully only over long periods? One source of control increasingly being used by organisations is a strong organisational culture.

Reaction Time

1. What is the relationship between organising and controlling?
2. How do output control and behaviour control differ?
3. Why is it important for managers to involve subordinates in the control process?

Organisational Culture and Clan Control

Organisational culture is another important control system that regulates and governs employee attitudes and behaviour. As discussed in Chapter 3, *organisational culture* is the shared set of beliefs, expectations, values, norms and work routines that influences how members of an organisation relate to one another and work together to achieve organisational goals. *Clan control* is the control exerted on individuals and groups in an organisation by shared values, norms, standards of behaviour and expectations. Organisational culture is not an externally imposed system of constraints, such as direct supervision or rules and procedures. Rather, employees *internalise* organisational values and norms and then let these values and norms guide their decisions and actions. Just as people in society usually behave in accordance with socially acceptable values and norms – such as the norm that people join the end of a check-out queue when waiting to pay – so individuals in an organisational setting are mindful of the force of organisational values and norms.

Organisational culture is an important source of control for two reasons. First, it makes control possible in situations where managers cannot use output or behaviour control. More importantly, when a strong and cohesive set of organisational values and norms is in place, employees focus on thinking about what is best for the organisation in the long run – all their decisions and actions become oriented toward helping the organisation perform well. For example, a teacher spends personal time after school coaching and counselling students; an R&D scientist works 80 hours a week, evenings and weekends to help speed up an over-running project; a sales assistant at a department store runs after a customer who has left a credit card at the till. An interesting example of a company that has built a strong culture based on close attention to developing the right set of output and behaviour controls is Siemens, profiled in Case 11.3.

Case 11.3: **Von Pierer changes the culture at Siemens**

Siemens, one of the world largest German-based companies, was founded in 1847 (see Chapter 1). It has, through various restructurings, become one of the leading electronic engineering companies in the world, working in transport systems, medical equipment, energy generation, business services and communication technology. Dr Heinrich von Pierer became CEO in 1992, and sparked a continuous programme of change at Siemens in the 1990s.

From the beginning, von Pierer realised that the ingrained culture of strong hierarchies, over-reliance on bureaucracy and general inflexible perfectionism was preventing Siemens from keeping up with the competition. In order to change this, von Pierer stopped at nothing, combining traditional cost-cutting with a 'cultural revolution'.

First, he changed the *management structure* from large, hierarchical teams to smaller groups that were encouraged to be entrepreneurial. New management techniques were introduced and a culture of knowledge-sharing and collaboration was encouraged in order to drive innovation forward, endorsed by incentives. Von Pierer eliminated a significant number of middle managers to achieve this. In order to keep up entrepreneurial and innovative thinking, von Pierer also introduced performance-related pay and made senior managers directly responsible for their division's bottom line.

An additional part of this cultural change was the *freedom* given to employees. Employees, who were used to doing what management told them, were now encouraged to give feedback to their managers. 'Bottom-up' reviews were introduced, in which staff are able to critique the performance of their mangers. In R&D von Pierer also gave employees more freedom – and responsibility. R&D costs Siemens nearly 10 per cent of its revenues and two-thirds of the products the company sells are less than five years old. In order to maintain a constant stream of new and innovative products and systems in all of its diverse markets, Siemens now allows researchers to choose their own area of research. However, they will get a budget only if a product division is willing to endorse or manufacture the product or system.

While already successful, von Pierer is aware that this is just the beginning and that this entrepreneurial and innovative thinking needs to continue for Siemens to maintain its market position. However, after initial difficulties and some inevitable human tragedies of employees who had difficulty adapting to the new way of doing things, the result of von Pierer's efforts has been a different approach to product development and manufacturing and more collaboration in all levels of the organisation. This change has impacted on all Siemens' business areas, too, from hearing aids to power plants.[36]

TIPS FOR PRACTICE

1. Think about building and evaluating control systems related to a company's competitive edge and business goals.
2. Remember that employee participation in goal-setting and MBO creates commitment.
3. Be aware that there is a balance between matching the supervisory style used, the individual employees and the organisational design and culture.

Adaptive Cultures versus Inert Cultures

Many researchers and managers believe that some employees go out of their way to help the organisation because it has a strong and cohesive organisational culture. These cultures are referred to as **adaptive cultures**. An adaptive culture is a culture whose values and norms help an organisation to build momentum and to grow and change as needed to achieve its goals and be effective. By contrast, an **inert culture** is one that leads to values and norms that fail to motivate or inspire employees; it leads to stagnation and often failure over time. What leads to an adaptive or inert culture?

Researchers have found that organisations with strong adaptive cultures, like UPS, Microsoft and IBM, *invest in their employees*. They demonstrate their commitment by, for example, emphasising the long-term nature of the employment relationship and trying to avoid redundancies. These companies develop long-term career paths for their employees and invest heavily in training and development to increase their employees' value to the organisation. In these ways, terminal and instrumental values pertaining to the worth of HR encourage the development of supportive work attitudes and behaviours.

In adaptive cultures, employees often receive rewards linked directly to their performance and to the performance of the company as a whole. Sometimes, **employee stock ownership plans (ESOPs)** are developed, in which workers as a group are allowed to buy a significant percentage of their company's stock. Workers who are owners of the company have an additional incentive to develop skills that allow them to perform highly and search actively for ways to improve quality, efficiency and performance. At John Lewis, employees are trustees of the company and thus own their share in the business and its success.

Some organisations, however, develop cultures with values that do not include protecting and increasing the worth of their HR as a major goal. Their employment practices are based on short-term employment according to the needs of the organisation and on minimal investment in employees who perform simple, routine tasks. Moreover, employees are often not rewarded based on their performance and thus have little incentive to improve their skills or otherwise invest in the organisation. If a company has an inert culture, poor working relationships frequently develop between the organisation and its employees; this usually results in instrumental values of non-co-operation, laziness and loafing, and work norms of output restriction are common.

An adaptive culture also develops an emphasis on entrepreneurship and respect for the employee and allows the use of organisational structures, such as cross-functional teams, that empower employees to make decisions and motivate them to succeed. By contrast, in an inert culture, employees are content to be told what to do and have little incentive or motivation to perform beyond the minimum work requirements. As you might expect, the emphasis is on close supervision and hierarchical authority, which results in a culture that makes it difficult to adapt to a changing environment.

Nokia, the world's largest mobile phone producer, headquartered in Finland, is a good example of a company in which managers strove to create an adaptive culture.[37] Nokia's president, Matti Alahuhta, believes that Nokia's cultural values are based on the Finnish character: Finns are down-to-earth, rational, straightforward people. They are also very friendly and democratic people who do not believe in a rigid hierarchy based either on a person's authority or on social class. Nokia's culture reflects these values because innovation and decision making are pushed right down to the bottom line, to teams of employees who take up the challenge of developing the ever-smaller and more sophisticated phones for which the company is known. Bureaucracy is kept to a minimum at Nokia; its adaptive culture is based on informal and personal relationships and norms of co-operation and teamwork.

To help strengthen its culture, Nokia has built a futuristic open-plan steel and glass building just outside Helsinki. Here, in an open environment, its R&D people can work together to innovate new kinds of mobile phones. More than one in three of Nokia's 60,000 employees works in research; what keeps these people together and focused is Nokia's company mission to produce phones that are better, cheaper, smaller and easier to use than competitor's phones.[38] This is the 'Nokia Way', a system of *cultural values and norms* that cannot necessarily be written down, but is always present in the values that cement people together and in the language and stories that its members use to orient themselves to the company.

Another company with an adaptive culture is Merck & Co., one of the largest producers of prescription drugs in the world. Much of Merck's success can be attributed to its ability to attract the very best research scientists, who come because its adaptive culture nurtures scientists and emphasises values and norms of innovation. Scientists are given great freedom to pursue intriguing ideas, even if a commercial payoff is not guaranteed. Researchers are also inspired to think of their work as a quest to alleviate human disease and suffering worldwide, and Merck has a reputation as an ethical company whose values put people above profits.

Although the experience of Nokia and Merck suggests that organisational culture can give rise to managerial actions that ultimately benefit the organisation, this is not always the case. The cultures of some organisations become *dysfunctional*, encouraging managerial actions that harm the organisation and discouraging action that might lead to an improvement in performance.[39]

Reaction Time

1. What is organisational culture, and how does it affect the way employees behave?
2. What kind of controls would you expect to find most used in (a) a hospital, (b) the Navy, (c) a city police force? Why?

Organisational Control and Change

As discussed, many problems can arise if an organisation's control systems are not designed correctly. One of these problems is that an organisation cannot change or adapt in response to a changing environment unless it has effective control over its activities. Companies can lose this control over time, or they can change in ways that make them more effective.

There is a fundamental tension or need to balance two opposing forces in the control process that influences the way organisations change. As just noted, organisations and their managers need to be able to control their activities and make their operations routine and predictable. At the same time, however, organisations have to be responsive to the need to change, and managers and employees have to think quickly to realise when they need to depart from routines to be responsive to unpredictable events. In other words, even though adopting the right set of output and behaviour controls is essential for improving efficiency, because the environment is dynamic and uncertain, employees also need to feel that they have the autonomy to depart from routines as necessary to increase effectiveness (Fig. 11.5).

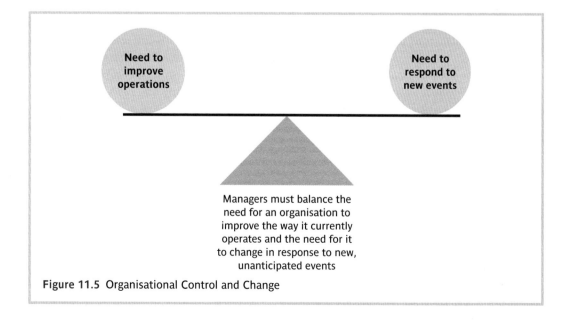

Managers must balance the need for an organisation to improve the way it currently operates and the need for it to change in response to new, unanticipated events

Figure 11.5 Organisational Control and Change

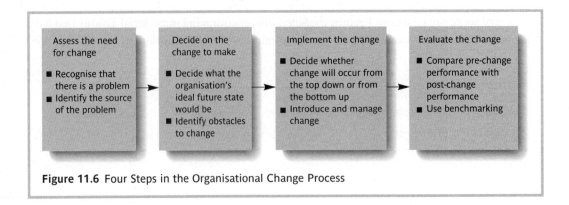

Figure 11.6 Four Steps in the Organisational Change Process

It is for this reason that many researchers believe that the highest-performing organisations are those that are constantly changing – and thus become experienced at doing so – in their search to become more efficient and effective. Companies like B&Q are constantly changing the mix of their activities to move forward, even as they are seeking to make their existing operations more efficient. B&Q did not only improve its IT systems, for example, but also ensured that the staff were sufficiently trained and prepared to perform their tasks.

The need to constantly search for ways to improve efficiency and effectiveness makes it vital that managers develop the skills necessary to manage change effectively. Several experts have proposed a model that managers can follow to implement change successfully.[40] **Organisation change** is the movement of an organisation away from its present state and toward some desired future state to increase its efficiency and effectiveness. Figure 11.6 outlines the steps that managers must take to manage change effectively. In the following section, we examine each step more carefully.

Assessing the Need for Change

Organisation change can affect practically all aspects of organisational functioning, including organisational structure, culture, strategies, control systems and groups and teams, as well as the human resource management (HRM) system and critical organisational processes such as communication, motivation and leadership. Organisation change can bring alterations in the ways managers carry out the critical tasks of planning, organising, leading and controlling, and the ways they perform their managerial roles.

Deciding how to change an organisation is a complex matter because change disrupts the status quo and poses a threat, prompting employees to resist attempts to alter work relationships and procedures. *Organisational learning* – the process through which managers try to increase organisational members' abilities to understand and appropriately respond to changing conditions – can be an important impetus for change. It can help all members of an organisation, including managers, to effectively make decisions about required changes.

Assessing the need for change involves two important activities: recognising that there is a *problem* and identifying the *source*. Sometimes the need for change is obvious, such as when an organisation's performance is suffering. Often, however, managers have trouble determining that something is going wrong because problems develop gradually; organisational performance may slip for a number of years before a problem becomes obvious. During the first step in the change process, managers thus need to recognise that there is a problem that requires change.

A gap between *desired* performance and *actual* performance often brings to the fore a potential problem. To detect such a gap, managers need to look at performance measures – such as falling market share or profits, rising costs, or employees' failure to meet their established goals or stay within budgets – which indicate whether change is needed. These measures are provided by organisational control systems, discussed earlier in the chapter (p. 355).

To discover the source of the problem, managers need to look both inside and outside the organisation. *Outside* the organisation, they must examine how changes in environmental forces may be creating opportunities and threats that are affecting internal work relationships. The emergence of low-cost competitors abroad may have led to conflict among different departments that are trying to find new ways to gain a competitive advantage. Managers also need to look *inside* the organisation to see whether its structure is causing problems between departments. Perhaps a company does not have the integrating mechanisms in place to allow different departments to respond to low-cost competition.

Deciding on the Change to Make

Once managers have identified the source of the problem, they must decide what they think the organisation's ideal future state should be. In other words, they must decide where they would like their organisation to be in the future – what kinds of goods and services it should be making, what its business-level strategy should be, how the organisational structure should be changed and so on. During this step, managers also must engage in planning how they are going to attain the organisation's *ideal future state*.

This step in the change process also includes identifying *obstacles* or *sources of resistance* to change. Managers must analyse the factors that may prevent the company from reaching its ideal future state: obstacles to change can be found at the corporate, divisional, departmental and individual level of the organisation.

Corporate-level changes in an organisation's strategy or structure – even seemingly trivial changes – may significantly affect how divisional and departmental managers behave. Suppose that to compete with low-cost foreign competitors senior managers decide to increase the resources spent on state-of-the-art machinery and reduce the resources spent on marketing or R&D. The power of manufacturing managers will increase, and the power of marketing and R&D managers will fall. This decision will alter the *balance of power* among departments and may lead to increased conflict as departments start jostling to retain their status in the organisation. An organisation's present strategy and structure are powerful obstacles to change.

If a company's culture is adaptive it is likely to facilitate change. However, if the culture is inert, change is likely to be obstructed. Organisations with entrepreneurial, flexible cultures, such as high-tech companies, are much easier to change than are organisations with more rigid cultures, such as those sometimes found in large, bureaucratic organisations like the military or Siemens before its 'cultural change'.

The same obstacles to change exist at the *divisional and departmental levels*. Division managers may differ in their attitudes toward the changes that senior managers propose and, if their interests and power seem threatened, will resist those changes. Managers at all levels usually fight to protect their power and control over resources. Given that departments have different goals and time horizons, they may also react differently to the changes that other managers propose. When senior managers are trying to reduce costs, for example, sales managers may resist attempts to cut back on sales expenditures if they believe that problems stem from manufacturing managers' inefficiencies.

At the *individual level*, too, people are often resistant to change because change brings uncertainty, and uncertainty brings stress. Individuals may resist the introduction of a new technology because they are uncertain about their abilities to learn it and effectively use it. At times, the fear of being replaced by evolving technology makes individuals resist change.

These obstacles make organisation change a slow process. Managers must recognise the potential obstacles to change, and take them into consideration. Some obstacles can be overcome by *improving communication* so that all organisational members are aware of the need for change and of the nature of the change being made. Empowering employees and inviting them to participate in the planning for change also can help overcome resistance and allay employees' fears. Managers can sometimes overcome resistance by emphasising group or shared goals, such as increased organisational efficiency and effectiveness. In Siemens' case, the company's inflexibility and ongoing, but ineffective, change programmes made employees aware that von Pierer's overall approach to change was ultimately in everyone's best interests because it would increase organisational performance. However, some managers left the company because they didn't like its new culture and operating system, or were unable to adapt to the new ways of thinking. The larger and more complex an organisation is, the more complex will the change process be.

Implementing the Change

Generally, managers *implement* – that is, introduce and manage – change from the top down or from the bottom up.[41] '**Top-down change**' is implemented quickly: senior managers identify the need for change, decide what to do and then move quickly to implement the changes throughout the organisation. Senior managers may decide to restructure and downsize the organisation, and then give divisional and departmental managers specific goals to achieve. With top-down change, the emphasis is on making the changes quickly and dealing with problems as they arise; it is revolutionary in nature.

'**Bottom-up change**' is typically more gradual or evolutionary. Senior managers consult with middle and first-line managers about the need for change; over time, managers at all levels work to develop a detailed plan for change. A major advantage of bottom-up change is that it can co-opt resistance to change from employees. Because the emphasis in bottom-up change is on participation and on keeping people informed about what is going on, uncertainty and resistance are minimised. By giving employees more freedom and allowing them to critique their managers, employees in Siemens felt part of the change process and commitment was likely to be stronger.

Evaluating the Change

The last step in the change process is to evaluate how successful the change effort has been in improving organisational performance.[42] Using measures such as changes in market share, in profits, or in the ability of managers to meet their goals, managers can compare how well an organisation is performing after the change with how well it was performing before. Managers also can use **benchmarking** – comparing their performance on specific dimensions with the performance of other high-performing organisations – to decide how successful a change effort has been. When Xerox was doing poorly in the 1980s, it benchmarked the efficiency of its distribution operations against that of L. L. Bean, the efficiency of its central computer operations against that of John Deere and the efficiency of its marketing abilities against Procter & Gamble. These three companies were renowned for their skills in those different areas, and by studying how they performed, Xerox was able to dramatically increase its own performance. Benchmarking is a key tool in TQM, an important change programme discussed in Chapter 9.

Organisational control and change are closely linked because organisations operate in environments that are constantly changing and so managers must be alert to the need to alter their strategies and structures. High-performing organisations are those whose managers are attuned to the need to continually modify the way they operate and which adopt techniques – like empowered work groups and teams, benchmarking, and global outsourcing – to remain competitive in a global world.

Summary and Review

What is organisational control? Controlling is the process whereby managers monitor and regulate how efficiently and effectively an organisation and its members are performing the activities necessary to achieve organisational goals. Controlling is a four-step process: (1) establishing performance standards, (2) measuring actual performance, (3) comparing actual performance against performance standards and (4) evaluating the results and initiating corrective action if needed.

Output control To monitor output or performance, managers choose goals or performance standards that they think will best measure efficiency, quality, innovation and responsiveness to customers at the corporate, divisional, departmental or functional and individual level. The main mechanisms that managers use to monitor output are financial measures of performance, organisational goals and operating budgets.

Behaviour control In an attempt to shape behaviour and induce employees to work toward achieving organisational goals, managers utilise direct supervision, MBO and bureaucratic control by means of rules and standard operating procedures.

Organisational culture and clan control Organisational culture is the set of values, norms, standards of behaviour and common expectations that control the ways individuals and groups in an organisation interact with one another and work to achieve organisational goals. Clan control is the control exerted on individuals and groups by shared values, norms, standards of behaviour and expectations. Organisational culture is transmitted to employees through the values of the founder, the process of socialisation, organisational ceremonies and rites and stories and language. The way managers perform their management functions influences the kind of culture that develops in an organisation.

Organisational control and change There is a need to balance two opposing forces in the control process that influences the way organisations change. On the one hand, managers need to be able to control organisational activities and make their operations routine and predictable. On the other hand, organisations have to be responsive to the need to change, and managers must understand when they need to depart from routines to be responsive to unpredictable events. The four steps in managing change are (1) assessing the need for change, (2) deciding on the changes to make, (3) implementing change and (4) evaluating the results of change.

Topic for Action

- Ask a manager to list the main performance measures that he or she uses to evaluate how well the organisation is achieving its goals.

- Ask the same or a different manager to list the main forms of output control and behaviour control that he or she uses to monitor and evaluate employee behaviour.

- Interview some employees of an organisation, and ask them about the organisation's values, norms, socialisation practices, ceremonies and rites and special language and stories. Referring to this information, describe the organisation's culture.

Applied Independent Learning

Building Management Skills

Understanding Controlling

For this exercise you will analyse the control systems used by a real organisation such as a department store, restaurant, hospital, police department or small business. It can be the organisation that you investigated in Chapter 10 or a different one. Your objective is to uncover all the different ways in which managers monitor and evaluate the performance of the organisation and employees.

1. At what levels does control take place in this organisation?

2. Which output performance standards (such as financial measures and organisational goals) do managers use most often to evaluate performance at each level?

3. Does the organisation have an MBO system in place? If it does, describe it. If it does not, speculate about why not.

4. How important is behaviour control in this organisation? For example, how much of managers' time is spent directly supervising employees? How formalised is the organisation? Do employees receive a book of rules to instruct them about how to perform their jobs?

5. What kind of culture does the organisation have? What are the values and norms? What effect does the organisational culture have on the way employees behave or treat customers?

6. Based on this analysis, do you think there is a 'fit' between the organisation's control systems and its culture? What is the nature of this fit? How could it be improved?

Managing Ethically

Some managers and organisations go to great lengths to monitor their employees' behaviour, and they keep extensive records about behaviour and performance. Some organisations also seem to possess norms and values that cause their employees to behave in certain ways.

Questions

1. Either by yourself or in a group, think about the ethical implications of organisations' monitoring and collecting information about their employees. What kind of information is it ethical to collect or unethical to collect? Why? Should managers and organisations inform subordinates they are collecting such information?

2. Similarly, some organisations' cultures, like those of Arthur Andersen, the accounting firm, and of Enron, developed norms and values that caused their members to behave in unethical ways. When and why does a strong norm that encourages high performance become one that can cause people to act unethically? How can organisations keep their values and norms from becoming 'too strong'?

Small Group Breakout Exercise

How Best to Control the Sales Force?

Form groups of three or four people, and appoint one member as the spokesperson who will communicate your findings to the whole class when called on by the instructor. Then discuss the following scenario.

You are the regional sales managers of an organisation that supplies high-quality windows and doors to building supply centres nationwide. Over the last three years, the rate of sales growth has slackened. There is increasing evidence that, to make their jobs easier, salespeople are primarily servicing large customer accounts and ignoring small accounts. In addition, the salespeople are not dealing promptly with customer questions and complaints, and this inattention has resulted in a drop in after-sales service. You have talked about these problems, and you are meeting to design a control system to increase both the amount of sales and the quality of customer service.

1. Design a control system that you think will best motivate salespeople to achieve these goals.

2. What relative importance do you put on (a) output control, (b) behaviour control and (c) organisational culture in this design?

Exploring the World Wide Web

Go to the website of a company you could imagine working for. Try and discover what the organisational culture of this organisation is (most organisations now tell you about this on their website).

1. How would you expect the values and norms of this company to affect its employees' behaviour?

2. How would you describe design of the organisational structure, and how do you think it matches with its culture?

Application in Today's Business World

The 'Constant Challenge' at eBay

Online auction site eBay finished its annual member conference, eBay Live!, on 26 June 2004, bringing together more than 10,000 of its sellers and buyers in New Orleans. It was a chance for the most fanatic of eBay's 45 million active members to trade ideas, take classes in how to sell better and lobby the online marketplace's staff for changes.

Part love fest and part bitch session, the show was an annual highlight for eBay CEO Margaret C. Whitman, who took the opportunity to mingle with the masses. As she gazed down on the show floor, Whitman shared her thoughts with *BusinessWeek* Silicon Valley bureau chief Robert D. Hof about how she copes with the contentious hordes on eBay and why, despite rumours that she might leave the company before long, she was happy with her job. Edited excerpts of their conversation follow:

Q: Is it difficult to manage sellers, many of whom seem to have little business experience?

A: Actually, most of these sellers know more about eBay than most [eBay] employees. They use it every single day. They're the experts. Folks have basically quit their day jobs to sell full-time on eBay. They do eBay before their kids come home from school. The businesses that have been built on this platform are remarkable.

Q: Some veteran sellers are fed up with eBay's constant tinkering with the site. How are you responding?

A: The community right now has seen a lot of change. We probably need to slow down that pace of change just a tad. It's hard for folks to adapt to so much change. That said, the underlying technology is changing, and the competitive landscape provides some new challenges. We want to make sure we strike the right balance between keeping pace with what's new and what's important in online commerce, and at the same time empower the people who are making their living on eBay.

Q: In particular, some sellers are very unhappy about how eBay recently changed the organisation of several product categories, which made it tougher for buyers to browse and thus hurt sales in some categories. Did their complaints hit home?

A: Absolutely. We think that books and apparel went really well, helping buyers search for specific products more easily. Music was pretty good, too. As we ventured into pottery and glass, I think we may have moved too fast. There are still a lot of consumers in pottery and glass who like to browse, and that was disrupted somewhat by the category changes. We're going to slow down [those types of changes] until we determine the exact business impact on our sellers.

Q: How do you balance the competing demands of buyers and sellers?

A: It's an art, not a science. We've gotten pretty experienced at it now. We can anticipate the reaction because we ask both buyers and sellers. Then it comes back to: what's the right thing for the marketplace? Sometimes we come down on the side of the sellers, sometimes we come down on the side of the buyers. We really think hard about it.

We rarely make a big change without running a beta, where we run a new site in parallel with the existing one. We never used to do that, because we didn't have the technical capability. We do now.

Q: On eBay's own discussion boards, sellers aren't shy about pointing out what they view as problems. How do you sift through those complaints to determine what's really important?

A: The scale of this user base is so large that part of [managing it] is being able to parse what one ought to do based on the feedback. We have community development teams who know each discussion-board poster.

We think most of our sellers are very happy. But they're like the silent majority. We do extensive surveys of the community. For example, we surveyed 50,000 people on the changes to My eBay [a customised page for buyers and sellers]. About 80 per cent liked it. If we get 80 per cent approval, we're good to go.

Q: eBay's international business is growing much faster than in the US. How does that change the nature of the company?

A: It used to be that the US was largely the innovation engine. Now, it is the US and Germany. And Germany has a very significant say in how this platform develops. So I think that as more countries get to that scale, we will include them even more in product-development strategy.

Q: Has the proliferation of eBay around the world changed how people buy and sell?

A: I hear all the time that Germans trade on the Italy site. They may not speak much Italian, but the site is laid out the same way, so they kind of know how to do it. And it's the same with French [going] to the Italian site, and Germans to the UK one. In the long run, the way the site works consistently across geographies is going to be really important to global trade.

Q: The rumour on the floor of eBay Live! Is that you might leave eBay before long, possibly for Walt Disney, where CEO Michael Eisner has been under fire.

A: [Laughs] As far as I know, there isn't a vacancy at Disney. People speculate a lot. But I have to tell you, I have one of the best jobs in Corporate America. It's this unique blend of commerce and community. The community of users is endlessly interesting and endlessly surprising. That's what I love the most.

Questions

1. In what ways does eBay design its IT to control its relationships with buyers and sellers?

2. How does e-Bay make sure that changes to its control systems over time improve interactions between buyers and sellers?

Source: Robert Hof, 'The Constant Challenge at eBay', adapted and reprinted from *BusinessWeek*, June 30, 2004 by special permission. Copyright © 2004 by the McGraw-Hill Companies, Inc.

Notes and References

1   Theresa Tritch 'B&Q boosts employee involvement – and profits', *Gallup Management Journal*, May 2003; http://www.zyra.org.uk/b-and-q.htm; http://www.diy.com; http://www.tdwi.org/research/display.aspx?ID=5486.

2   W. G. Ouchi, 'Markets, Bureaucracies, and Clans', *Administrative Science Quarterly* 25 (1980), 129–41.

3   P. Lorange, M. Morton and S. Ghoshal, *Strategic Control* (St. Paul, MN: West, 1986).

4 H. Koontz and R. W. Bradspies, 'Managing Through Feedforward Control', *Business Horizons*, June 1972, 25–36.

5 E. E. Lawler, III and J. G. Rhode, *Information and Control in Organizations* (Pacific Palisades, CA: Goodyear, 1976).

6 C. W. L. Hill and G. R. Jones, *Strategic Management: An Integrated Approach*, 6th ed. (Boston: Houghton Mifflin, 2003).

7 E. Flamholtz, 'Organizational Control Systems as a Management Tool', *California Management Review* (Winter 1979), 50–58.

8 W. G. Ouchi, 'The Transmission of Control Through Organizational Hierarchy', *Academy of Management Journal* 21 (1978), 173–92.

9 W. G. Ouchi, 'The Relationship Between Organizational Structure and Organizational Control', *Administrative Science Quarterly* 22 (1977), 95–113.

10 Ouchi, 'Markets, Bureaucracies, and Clans'.

11 W. H. Newman, *Constructive Control* (Englewood Cliffs, NJ: Prentice Hall, 1975).

12 J. D. Thompson, *Organizations in Action* (New York: McGraw-Hill, 1967).

13 R. N. Anthony, *The Management Control Function* (Boston: Harvard Business School Press, 1988).

14 Ouchi, 'Markets, Bureaucracies, and Clans'.

15 Hill and Jones, *Strategic Management*.

16 R. Simons, 'Strategic Orientation and Top Management Attention to Control Systems', *Strategic Management Journal* 12 (1991), 49–62.

17 G. Schreyogg and H. Steinmann, 'Strategic Control: A New Perspective', *Academy of Management Review* 12 (1987), 91–103.

18 B. Woolridge and S. W. Floyd, 'The Strategy Process, Middle Management Involvement, and Organizational Performance', *Strategic Management Journal* 11 (1990), 231–41.

19 J. A. Alexander, 'Adaptive Changes in Corporate Control Practices', *Academy of Management Journal* 34 (1991), 162–93.

20 http://www.carrefour.com/.

21 http://www.cimtalk.com/news/ald/ald104.html.

22 www.gillette.com.

23 Hill and Jones, *Strategic Management*.

24 G. H. B. Ross, 'Revolution in Management Control', *Management Accounting* 72 (1992), 23–27.

25 P. F. Drucker, *The Practice of Management* (New York: Harper & Row, 1954).

26 S. J. Carroll and H. L. Tosi, *Management by Objectives: Applications and Research* (New York: Macmillan, 1973).

27 R. Rodgers and J. E. Hunter, 'Impact of Management by Objectives on Organizational Productivity', *Journal of Applied Psychology* 76 (1991), 322–26.

28 M. B. Gavin, S. G. Green and G. T. Fairhurst, 'Managerial Control Strategies for Poor Performance over Time and the Impact on Subordinate Reactions', *Organizational Behavior and Human Decision Processes* 63 (1995), 207–21.

29 www.cypress.com.

30 B. Dumaine, 'The Bureaucracy Busters', *Fortune*, June 17, 1991, 46.

31 D. S. Pugh, D. J. Hickson, C. R. Hinings and C. Turner, 'Dimensions of Organizational Structure', *Administrative Science Quarterly* 13 (1968), 65–91.

32 http://www.sephora.com.

33 http://www.cosmeticsdesign.com.

34 'Sephora: Liberating Beauty Products', *BusinessWeek*, January 25, 2006.

35 P. M. Blau, *The Dynamics of Bureaucracy* (Chicago: University of Chicago Press, 1955).

36 'Siemens Shapes up', *BusinessWeek*, May 1995.

37 www.nokia.com.

38 P. de Bendern, 'Quirky Culture Paves Nokia's Road to Fortune', www.yahoo.com.

39 K. E. Weick, *The Social Psychology of Organization* (Reading, MA: Addison-Wesley, 1979).

40 L. Brown, 'Research Action: Organizational Feedback, Understanding and Change', *Journal of Applied Behavioral Research* 8 (1972), 697–711; P. A. Clark, *Action Research and Organizational Change* (New York: Harper & Row, 1972); N. Margulies and A. P. Raia, eds., *Conceptual Foundations of Organizational Development* (New York: McGraw-Hill, 1978).

41 W. L. French and C. H. Bell, *Organizational Development* (Englewood Cliffs, NJ: Prentice Hall, 1990).

42 W. L. French, 'A Checklist for Organizing and Implementing an OD Effort', in W. L. French, C. H. Bell and R. A. Zawacki, eds., *Organizational Development and Transformation* (Homewood, IL: Irwin, 1994), 484–95.

Chapter 12

Human Resource Management

LEARNING OBJECTIVES

After studying this chapter, you should be able to:

☑ Explain why strategic human resource management (HRM) can help an organisation gain a competitive advantage.

☑ Describe the steps managers take to recruit and select organisational members.

☑ Discuss the training and development options that ensure that organisational members can effectively perform their jobs.

☑ Explain why performance appraisal and feedback is such a crucial activity and list the choices managers must make in designing effective performance appraisal and feedback procedures.

☑ Explain the issues that managers face in determining levels of pay and benefits.

A Manager's Challenge

Democracy in Action at W.L. Gore & Associates

How can managers provide employees with freedom and flexibility at work while ensuring their company's survival and profitability?

W.L. Gore & Associates was first founded by William (Bill) and Genevieve Gore on New Year's Day 1958 in Newark, Delaware, in their basement. Bill had learned from working in a hard and male-oriented engineering environment for seventeen years that the only time anyone communicated 'was in the car park'. Bill also realised, however, that when there was a crisis then the bureaucratic hierarchical organisation would actually 'soften up' and managers would begin talking to employees. Task forces would be set up to deal with the problems and suddenly risks were being taken and problems were getting solved. So he mused that rules could be broken and the company would survive! It was his son Bob's innovative idea of producing plastic coating for insulating cables while at university that sparked his father's idea for the company. When Bill Gore created his own company, he set it up with very few rules, hardly any hierarchy and very few ranks and titles. He built his company on small task forces within limited-sized teams where people could get to know one another both personally and what they were good at. This way, people were self-motivated to share knowledge, work to their strengths and achieve their own goals, whether it was a new product or managing the process.[1]

Today, Gore ranks Number One in the '100 best places to work in the UK'.[2] The company produces everything from GORE-TEX® outerwear to fibre optic cable and medical implants. Their manufacturing operations cover the US, Germany, Scotland, Japan and China and they have sales and customer service sites located all over the world.

The company has also earned a position on the US *Fortune* list of best companies. Gore ranked fifth in the best small- and medium-sized enterprises (SMEs) to work for in Germany in 2005 and amongst the top 20 in Italy in 2004. In 2006, sales topped £1.5 billion and yet it is still a privately owned company, employing over 7,000 people across 40 plants and sales office worldwide. Bill Gore (who died in 1986) would be the first to admit that this family business owes its phenomenal success to its HR – its employees – or 'associates', as they are familiarly known. His son Bob Gore took over as CEO in the early 1980s and has kept the same culture built on strong family values. In fact, Gore so firmly believe in their employees that they are reluctant to tell employees what to do. Gore has no rules, regulations or organisational charts; hierarchy is eschewed; workplace democracy rules. Although the structure is not completely 'flat', the current organisational hierarchy hardly represents a pyramid. CEO Chuck Carroll, who succeeded Bob Gore in 2002, now heads up four main divisions: fabrics, medical, industrial and electronic products. Each division has a number of teams where each member or associate gradually builds their own role to match their skills base: no-one is expected to fit into a 'black box'. Each team has a recognised leader, a person who naturally evolves or exists through their innovativeness and passion for what they do. At Gore, leaders become leaders by leading and they then attract follows and others with similar talents and passions. Leaders are known as 'talent magnets' in the company and are elected by their own credibility for what they do and what they contribute to the company. Employees have levels of freedom and autonomy unheard of in other companies, and flexibility and trust are built into every aspect of HRM at Gore. The company believes in employees' willingness and desire to be productive and efficient, make significant contributions and ensure its continued profitability (which also benefits the employees in terms of their own compensation). Each employee when they start at the company is given a mentor – there is no such thing as a boss nor are there standard job descriptions, but each team member has a different set of commitments, depending on their expertise and skill level. However, this takes time to develop and within the first six months you do nothing but get to know your team. This means you observe, ask questions, learn and find out where you can best adapt your skills to fit into the whole. That's why it takes time to build credibility and trust, but that's also why Gore has a very low staff turnover (7 per cent worldwide). Compensation and reward is attached to how much you contribute and is decided by a committee, who examine your past and present performance as well as your future potential. Excellent benefits underpin this progressive style; Gore encourages risk takers and innovative thinkers and also rewards its employees with stock, equivalent to 15 per cent of their salary after they have worked there for more than one year, and it contributes double their 5 per cent pension contribution. There is free private health care and a heavily subsidised canteen. Most impressive, though, is 26 weeks' fully paid maternity leave, with a further six months off unpaid, throughout which holiday accrues.[3]

Within the UK group there are three sites in Scotland. Each 'associate' or employee is accountable to each other, even to the extent that team mates influence each other's pay.

'You've got to be a team player at Gore,' says lab engineer Dave Thompson. 'Your team rates your contribution on a scale of one to six, and that's one of the things salaries are based on.'

However, as Gore hits double-figure growth rates every year, and for the second time around is voted Number One in the '100 best places to work in the UK', it needs to take on the challenges of its large hierarchical competitors. The leader of the Dundee plant in Scotland UK, Bob Doak, says of the company: 'Gore has immense patience about the time it takes to get it right and get it to market. If there's a glimmer of hope, you're encouraged to keep a project going to see if it could become a big thing.' The culture is that of nurturing ideas and excellence and allowing people to progress in their own strengths and talents through total autonomy and empowerment. However, this may not be easy to maintain as the company grows from a £1.5 billion organisation and employs 14,000 rather than 7,000 people. Most Europeans are used to, and actually prefer, tighter structures, in terms of where they are in the status hierarchy, who their boss is and what their role is. As *Fast Company* writer, Alan Deutchman, explains, Gore's culture has been likened to its most famous product – Gore-Tex – and as the company continues to grow it must continue to invent ways to protect its people from the harsh outside elements, even as it lets their big and creative ideas breathe and prosper.[4]

HR practices at Gore revolve around maximising the contributions employees can make to the company, and this begins by hiring individuals who want to, can and will contribute. Everyone chooses a sponsor who helps them develop, and each division has a leader but no-one is called 'the boss'. Plant production leader John House explains: 'I was voted into this job. That was a really special moment.'

According to research, it seems that this approach works: nine in every 10 employees think their manager trusts their judgement; associates feel that they can communicate openly with their leaders and feel that they are cared about; 84 per cent say the principles of the firm would not alter if the leader changed – all are the highest scores for these questions among the 100 best companies.

Further accelerating Gore to its Number One position are the exceptionally high 'my company' scores: 92 per cent believe they make a valuable contribution to the firm's success, and 93 per cent would miss it if they left.[5] The man who is responsible for all the UK associates explains that the secret of Gore's success is 'its belief in the individual . . . we try to let people do the things that they are good at as opposed to forcing them into things they are not good at. Its all down to the way people are treated', and they react accordingly!

Overall, Gore is a great democratic company to work for and although its two founders are now dead, the legacy of their company remains durable and watertight – just like its products!

Overview

Managers are responsible for acquiring, developing, protecting and utilising the resources that an organisation needs to be efficient and effective. One of the most important resources in all organisations is human resources (HR) – the people involved in the production and distribution of goods and services. HR include all members of an organisation, ranging from senior managers to entry-level employees. Effective managers realise how valuable HR are and take active steps to make sure that their organisations build and fully utilise their HR to gain a competitive advantage.

This chapter examines how managers can tailor their HRM system to their organisation's strategy and structure. The discussion will examine the major components of HRM: recruitment and selection, training and development, performance appraisal, pay and benefits and labour relations. By the end of this chapter, you will understand the central role that HRM can play in creating a high-performing organisation.

Strategic Human Resource Management

Organisational architecture (see Chapter 10) is the combination of organisational structure, control systems, culture and an HRM system that managers develop to use resources efficiently and effectively. *HRM* includes all the activities that managers engage in to attract and retain employees and to ensure that they perform at a high level and contribute to the accomplishment of organisational goals. These activities make up an organisation's HRM system, which has five major components: *recruitment and selection, training and development, performance appraisal and feedback, pay and benefits* and **labour relations** (Fig. 12.1).

Strategic HRM is the process by which managers design the components of an HRM system to be consistent with each other, with other elements of organisational architecture and with the organisation's strategy and goals.[6] The objective of strategic HRM is the development of an HRM system that enhances an organisation's efficiency, quality, innovation and responsiveness to customers – the four building blocks of competitive advantage.

As part of strategic HRM, some managers have adopted '*Six Sigma*' quality improvement plans. These plans ensure that an organisation's products and services are as free of error or defects as possible through a variety of HR-related initiatives. The Six Sigma concept provides a rigorous and quantitative way of measuring error prevention, cycle time reduction and cost savings. Six Sigma thus identifies and eliminates wastage which is of no value to customers. The model can be identified as a simple performance improvement model known as *DMAIC* (or Define, Measure, Analyse, Improve and Control).[7]

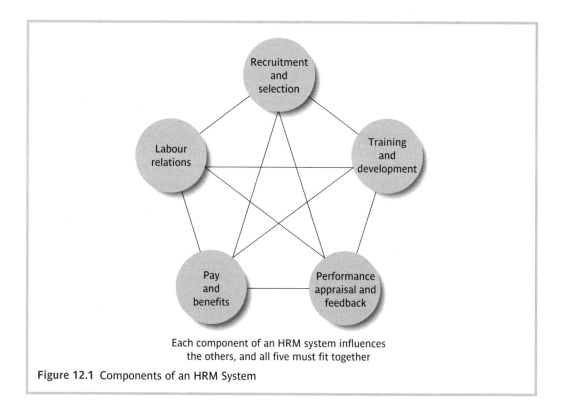

Each component of an HRM system influences
the others, and all five must fit together

Figure 12.1 Components of an HRM System

Six Sigma was the backbone of Motorola's quality management strategy during the 1980s. The then CEO, Bob Galvin, embarked on a quality programme, becoming a business icon through turning the company around so that Motorola today is a global leader in quality and success. The Six Sigma concept literally saved Motorola and other companies, such as Whirlpool, millions of pounds.[8] In order for such initiatives to be effective, however, senior managers have to be committed to Six Sigma, employees must be motivated and there must be demand for the products or services of the organisation in the first place. David Fitzpatrick, head of Deloitte Consulting's Lean Enterprise Practice, estimates that most Six Sigma plans are not effective because the conditions for effective Six Sigma are not in place. If senior managers are not committed to the quality initiative, for example, they may not devote the necessary time and resources to make it work and may lose interest in it prematurely.[9]

Effective strategic HRM can not only help organisations be responsive to customers but also help corporate customers develop their own strategies and effectively utilise their own human resources, as indicated in Case 12.1.

Case 12.1: IBM researchers help corporate customers achieve their goals

As a global leader within the information technology industry, IBM and its R&D division has been shifting its focus from making mainframe computers to providing customers with complex technological services.[10] As part of this strategic change in focus, IBM has begun putting its scientists, mathematicians and researchers in close contact with major corporate customers so that these specialists can learn first-hand the major challenges customers face in their technology needs. Today, researchers spend more than a quarter of their time working with customers and learning about customers' businesses and challenges. This enables the IBM specialists to develop solutions, based on their expertise, that customers might not be aware of or even think possible. Their OnDemand Innovation Services groups will also spend up to 50 per cent of their time talking and working with customers directly to conceive and develop future generation on-demand services.[11]

IBM mathematician, Howard Sacher, spent over a year meeting with senior managers in charge of technology at J.P. Morgan Chase, learning about the current state of banking and future challenges and exploring how IBM could develop technological solutions to put Chase ahead of its competition in terms of responsiveness to customers.[12] Sacher determined that Chase should act like a single bank with its customers so that any Chase employee interacting with a customer at any branch would be able to pull up all relevant information about that customer instantly. Developing the technology to make the 'one-bank' mentality a reality is actually a complicated problem due to Chase's multitude of services, ways of interacting with customers, record-keeping procedures and so forth.[13] Moreover, the technology needs to be in step with future developments and the new technologies that banks will be unfolding to provide better service in the future. Sacher's efforts paid off when Chase awarded IBM a contract worth several billion pounds to develop and manage its technological infrastructure.[14]

IBM have now set up their Industry Solutions Labs (ISLx) which are collaborative partnerships between researchers and customers to embark on collaborative leading-edge technologies and innovative solutions that can help solve customers' business problems. Customers can visit the labs located in either New York or Zurich, where they can view demonstrations of new projects and talk to the scientists and researchers so that each solution to the company is geared to their bespoke requirements.

Overview of the Components of HRM

Managers use *recruitment* and **selection**, the first component of an HRM system, to attract and hire new employees who have the abilities, skills and experiences that will help an organisation achieve its goals. Oxford University, for example, has the goal of remaining the premier higher education provider in the UK and competing in a global market (see Case 10.3). To achieve this goal, Oxford University realises the importance of hiring only the best researchers and lecturers. When any company with such expectations hires new employees, hundreds of highly qualified candidates with excellent CVs and references are interviewed and rigorously tested; only the very best are hired. This careful attention to selection has contributed to Oxford's competitive advantage. While Oxford may face difficulties in recruiting, any lecturer and researcher knows that they are working at one of the most prestigious universities in the world with large resources available.

After recruiting and selecting employees, managers use the second component, *training* and **development**, to ensure that organisational members develop the skills and abilities that will enable them to perform their jobs effectively in the present and the future. Training and development is an ongoing process: changes in technology and the environment, as well as in an organisation's goals and strategies, often require that organisational members learn new techniques and ways of working. At Microsoft, for example, newly hired programme designers receive on-the-job training by joining small teams that include experienced employees who serve as mentors or advisers. New recruits learn first-hand from team members how to develop computer systems that are responsive to customers' programming needs.[15]

The third component, *performance appraisal* and *feedback,* serves two different purposes in HRM. First, performance appraisal can provide managers with the information they need to make good HR decisions – decisions about how to train, motivate and reward organisational members. The performance appraisal and feedback component is thus a kind of *control system* that can be used with MBO (discussed in Chapter 10). Second, feedback from performance appraisal serves a developmental purpose for members of an organisation. When managers regularly evaluate their subordinates' performance, they can provide employees with valuable information about their strengths and weaknesses and the areas in which they need to concentrate.

On the basis of performance appraisals, managers distribute *pay* to employees, part of the fourth component of an HRM system. By rewarding high-performing organisational members with pay rises, bonuses etc., managers increase the likelihood that an organisation's most valued HR will be motivated to continue their high levels of contribution to the organisation. By linking pay to performance, high-performing employees are more likely to stay with the organisation, and managers are more likely to fill positions that become open with highly talented individuals. *Benefits* such as health insurance are important outcomes that employees receive by virtue of their membership in an organisation.

Last, but not least, *labour relations* encompass the steps that managers take to develop and maintain good working relationships with the labour unions that may represent their employees' interests. An organisation's labour relations component can help managers establish safe working conditions and fair labour practices in their offices and plants.

Managers must ensure that all five of these components fit together and complement their company's structure and control systems.[16] If managers decide to decentralise authority and empower employees, they need to invest in training and development to ensure that lower-level employees have the knowledge and expertise they need to make the decisions that senior managers would make in a more centralised structure.

Each of the five components of HRM influences the others (Fig. 12.1).[17] The kinds of people that the organisation attracts and hires through recruitment and selection, for example, determine (1) the kinds of training and development that are necessary, (2) the way performance is appraised and (3) the appropriate levels of pay and benefits. Managers at Microsoft ensure that their organisation has highly qualified programme designers by (1) recruiting and selecting the best candidates, (2) providing new hires with the guidance of experienced team members so that they learn how to be responsive to customers' needs when designing programmes and systems, (3) appraising programme designers' performance in terms of their individual contributions and their team's performance and (4) basing programmers' pay on individual and team performance.

The Legal Environment of HRM

The remaining sections of this chapter focus in detail on the choices managers must make in strategically managing HR to attain organisational goals and gain a competitive advantage. Managing HR is a complex undertaking for managers, and we provide an overview of some of the major issues they face. Before we do, however, we need to look at how the legal environment affects HRM. This book takes the UK as an example for how HRM is placed within a legal context: other European countries have similar legislation and its focus and strength are often determined by national cultures and labour relations history. Members of the EU have specific employment regulations that must be adhered to with the aim of fostering equal treatment and a fair deal for employees.

The local, state and national laws and regulations that managers and organisations must abide by add to the complexity of HRM. The UK government's commitment to **equal employment opportunities** was manifested in the *Equal Opportunities Commission (EOC)* that was established in 1975. In the same year, the Sex Discrimination Act was passed and the Equal Pay Act came into force. This legislation meant that certain rules and laws have to be abided by within organisations. The goal of the EOC was to ensure that everyone had an equal opportunity to obtain employment regardless of their gender. Other organisations lobby for equality in regard to race and country of origin, religion, age or disabilities. Although the UK can celebrate some achievements, we could ask: what has really changed? There still exists a pay gap of up to 18 per cent in favour of men and although women make up 45 per cent of the workforce, only 9 per cent sit on executive boards or are directors on the FTSE 100 companies.[18] According to the EOC Annual Report 2003–04[19] nearly two-thirds of women were unaware of differences in rates of pay for jobs mainly done by women and those mainly done by men. By April 2007, the *gender equality duty* for public bodies will come into force which will make all organisations responsible for demonstrating fair treatment of women and men in the delivery of policy and services as well as in their employment.[20]

Table 12.1 summarises some of the major laws affecting HRM. Other laws, such as the Occupational Safety and Health Act (1970), require that managers ensure that employees are protected from workplace hazards and safety standards are met.

In Chapter 5, it was explained how effectively managing diversity is both an *ethical* and a *business* imperative and discussed the many issues surrounding diversity. The EOC rules and their enforcement make the effective management of diversity a legal imperative as well. Contemporary challenges that managers face related to the legal environment include how to eliminate sexual harassment (see Chapter 5 for an in-depth discussion of sexual harassment), how to make accommodation for employees with disabilities, how to deal with employees who have substance abuse problems and how to manage HIV-positive employees and employees with AIDS.[21] HIV-

Table 12.1 Major equal employment opportunity laws affecting HRM

Year	Law	Description
1970	Equal Pay Act (EPA)	Requires employers to pay men and women on the same terms where: 1. A woman is employed on like work with a man in the same employment 2. A woman is employed on work rates equivalent with that of a man in the same employment 3. The work is of equal value
1983	EPA amended	
1992	Trade Union and Labour Relations (Consolidation) Act (TULRA)	Makes it illegal to refuse to employ someone on the grounds of membership or non-membership of a trade union
1999	Employment Relations Act	Brings in new rights to take unpaid leave of up to 13 weeks per child for parents in the event of family or domestic emergencies
2002	Employment Act	Introduces equal pay questionnaires that employees could use to obtain information from their employers about their pay and that of similar employees
2002	Employment Act	Entitles women to 26 weeks' ordinary maternity leave and 26 weeks' additional leave where they have been employed for 26 weeks at the 15th week before the child is due; the first 6 weeks of ordinary leave are paid at 90 per cent of average weekly earnings and the remaining 20 weeks at the statutory rate
		Paternity leave is also available at two weeks' leave at the statutory rate and is available to same-sex partners
		The Act also allows rights for parents with a disabled child either under six or 18 to request flexible working arrangements when they have been employed for 26 weeks
2003	Employment Equality Regulations	Outlaws discrimination in employment and vocational training on grounds of sexual orientation and religion or belief; they also outlaw harassment
2005	Disability Discrimination Amendment Act (in force from December 2006)	Promotes equality of opportunity between disabled and other people
		Encourages participation of disabled people in public life and promotes positive attitudes towards disabled people
		Some public authorities have specific duties to include the introduction of a disability equality scheme in higher and further education institutions
2006	Employment Equality (Age) Regulations	Allows people to have the right to request working beyond their retirement age

positive employees are infected with the virus that causes AIDS but may show no AIDS symptoms and may not develop AIDS in the near future. Often, such employees are able to perform their jobs effectively, and managers must take steps to ensure that they are allowed to do so and are not discriminated against in the workplace.[22] Employees with AIDS may or may not be able to perform their jobs effectively, and, once again, managers need to ensure that they are not unfairly discriminated against. Many organisations have instituted AIDS awareness training programmes to educate organisational members about HIV and AIDS, dispel unfounded myths about how HIV is spread and ensure that individuals infected with the HIV virus are treated fairly and are able to be productive as long as they can be while not putting others at risk.[23]

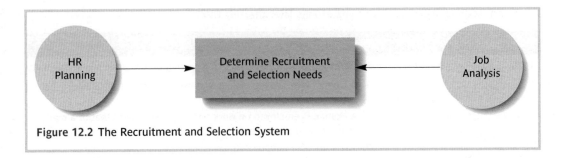

Figure 12.2 The Recruitment and Selection System

Recruitment and Selection

Recruitment includes all the activities in which managers engage to develop a pool of qualified candidates for open positions.[24] *Selection* is the process by which managers determine the relative qualifications of job applicants and their potential for performing well in a particular job. Prior to actually recruiting and selecting employees, managers need to engage in two important activities: HR planning and job analysis (Fig. 12.2).

Human Resource Planning

HR planning includes all the activities in which managers engage to predict their current and future *HR needs*. Current HR are the employees an organisation needs today to provide high-quality goods and services to customers. Future HR needs are the employees the organisation will need at some later date to achieve its longer-term goals.

As part of HR planning, managers must make both *demand predictions* and *supply predictions*. Demand predictions estimate the qualifications and numbers of employees an organisation will need given its goals and strategies. Supply predictions estimate the availability and qualifications of current employees now and in the future, as well as the supply of qualified workers in the external labour market.

As a result of their HR planning, managers sometimes decide to *outsource* to fill some of their HR needs. Instead of recruiting and selecting employees to produce goods and services, managers contract with people who are not members of their organisation to produce goods and services. Managers in publishing companies, for example, frequently contract people who are freelance editors to copyedit new books that they intend to publish. Kelly Services is an organisation that provides temporary keying, clerical and secretarial workers to managers who want to use outsourcing to fill some of their HR requirements in these areas.

Two reasons why HR planning sometimes leads managers to outsource are *flexibility* and *cost*. Outsourcing can give managers increased flexibility, especially when accurately forecasting HR needs is difficult, HR needs fluctuate over time, or finding skilled workers in a particular area is difficult. Outsourcing can also sometimes allow managers to make use of HR at a lower cost. When work is outsourced, costs can be lower for a number of reasons: the organisation does not have to provide benefits to workers; managers are able to contract for work only when the work is needed; and managers do not have to invest in training.

Outsourcing can be used for functional activities such as after-sales service on appliances and equipment, legal work and the management of information systems. Outsourcing does have its disadvantages, however. When work is outsourced, managers may lose some control over the quality of goods and services. Individuals performing outsourced work may have less knowledge of organisational practices, procedures and goals, and less commitment to an organisation than regular employees. Unions resist outsourcing because it has the potential to eliminate some of their members. To gain some of the flexibility and cost savings of outsourcing and avoid some of the disadvantages, a number of organisations, such as Microsoft and IBM, rely on a pool of temporary employees to debug programmes, for example.

A major trend reflecting the increasing globalisation of business is the outsourcing of office work, computer programming and technical jobs from the UK and countries in western Europe, with high labour costs, to countries like India and China, with low labour costs.[25] Computer programmers in India and China earn a fraction of what their UK counterparts earn. In 2003, India alone provided over £5.2 billion worth of software and technological outsourcing services to companies in North America, western Europe, Latin America, Asia and the Pacific Rim, and Japan; North American companies accounted for the majority of outsourcing to India.[26]

Sodexho is one of the world's largest service providers of catering and management services, spanning 72 countries, and has outsourced its telecommunications successfully since 2003. However, in 2004 they took outsourcing one step further and contracted IBM to manage their financial and accounting systems. Since embarking on this project, the company has noticed significant improvements in the speed of financial and accounting role performance.[27]

The director of finance for Asia-Pacific, Garen Azoyn, believes that this is just the beginning and that their pioneering five-year project with IBM, who will support and host all the e-business for the company, will be used as a model for other Sodexho locations to outsource their financial systems. Having had different systems in place in every location, they have now introduced one common platform and one application which is used everywhere across the Asia Pacific locations. This allows them to shift their resources to their core business activity – to provide catering and a range of support services to clients in the business and industry, education, health care, leisure and defence sectors.

Sodexho has also outsourced its HR and payroll function to Automatic Data Processing (ADP). Garen Azoyn stated: 'Before this we were doing all hosting of password authentication protocol (PAP), maintenance and support ourselves, at each location. We had difficulties with untimely management reporting and communication problems with different finance teams in each organisation that came about from the use of different systems, plus it was taking time and energy away from our core business functions.'[28]

The flexible contract Sodexho now has with IBM gives the company the benefit of managing all its costs out of one centralised office in Sydney. This eliminates the need for highly paid permanent finance staff in every location and allows the same application to be run from Thailand to China. As Azoyan explains: 'This means all our directors can see all the reporting on time everywhere, regardless of their location.' Costs are also cut with reduced staffing levels. While IBM has the majority of staff running the finance application, Sodexho has put two of its key staff, as employees of the company, on the project to work with IBM solely on its implementation. 'These are the only staff changes – these people have been replaced with temporary staff within their departments to make sure your day-to-day business does not suffer.'[29]

As companies gain experience in outsourcing software and technological services, managers are learning what kinds of work can be effectively outsourced and what work should probably not be outsourced. In India, for example, the workforce is highly trained and motivated, and cities like Bangalore are bustling with high-tech jobs and companies such as Infosys Technologies, providing software services to companies abroad. Managers who have outsourcing experience have found that outsourcing works best for tasks that can be rule-based, do not require closeness/familiarity with customers and/or the customs and culture of the country in which the company is based and do not require creativity.[30] When the work requires the recognition and solution of problems rather than the application of pre-required algorithms, creativity in developing solutions and independent thinking and judgement without the guidance of SOPs, performance may suffer from outsourcing. Essentially, the more complex and uncertain the work and the more it depends on being close to customers and the company itself, the less advantageous outsourcing tends to be. As indicated in Case 12.2, these *trade-offs* between gaining the cost advantages of outsourcing and being responsive to customers, providing effective services and developing innovative products have led some managers to cease outsourcing certain kinds of tasks that might be better performed by an organisation's own employees.[31]

Case 12.2: **Beware of the pitfalls of outsourcing**

In an IT consulting report in November 2004 it was announced that outsourcing is not always the way forward, that a third of UK businesses had not benefited from outsourcing HRM activities and that many companies are now rethinking their outsourcing strategies and bringing services back in-house.[32] One point in case is the supermarket retailer, J. S. Sainsbury, who suffered massive losses during 2004–05 as a result of their disastrous outsourcing experiences. In an attempt to turn around their sales, they attempted to automate their depot and supply chain activities using IT systems. Unfortunately this project failed to bring products to the shelves quickly enough, and they had to rethink their £1.8 billion IT outsourcing contract with Accenture. Sainsbury had to write off £140 million of IT assets and £120 million for automated equipment. They also lost £30 million in stock due to disruptions in the new depots with IT systems and it is estimated that they will have to spend another £200 million in 2006 for the clear-up process, together with capital needed for new IT systems and supply chain systems. The CEO, Justin King, pointed out that the business transformation project had distracted them from their customer focus and the aim now was to put a recovery plan together that would include going back to basics. King admitted that 'IT systems have also failed to deliver the anticipated increase in productivity and the costs today are a greater proportion of sales than they were four years ago. IT systems will now be simplified and some areas of business process will revert to using manual processes where current IT systems have failed. It is considered that the IT and supply chain costs account for 25 per cent of total operational savings which are targeted to be £400 million by the end of 2007–08.'

The lessons learned from such a disaster are that companies should research the pros and cons of outsourcing some business processes and consider strategies that are workable and cost-effective. Outsourcing should not be driven by a 'sticking plaster' philosophy – a quick way to fix a problem. For outsourcing to be successful, organisations need to consider the cost, skill base and expertise, but also how potential changes 'fit' with the *culture of the company*; users and suppliers must match culturally as well as for business reasons. The chairman of the user and supplier industry body, the UK National Outsourcing Association, maintained that 'Outsourcing is not a one-off purchase: it can be a long-term close partnership'. As the CEO of Sainsbury warns: 'Business benefits don't necessarily follow from IT infrastructure renewal unless the business itself is well run and the two sides are properly connected. New IT infrastructure can't compensate for poor business management.' In that sense, Sainsbury shows us the limits of transformational outsourcing.[33]

Job Analysis

Job analysis is a second important activity that managers need to undertake prior to recruitment and selection.[34] Job analysis is the process of identifying (1) the tasks, duties and responsibilities that make up a job (the *job description*), and (2) the knowledge, skills and abilities needed to perform the job (the *job specifications*).[35] For each job in an organisation, a job analysis needs to be done.

A job analysis can be done in a number of ways, including observing current employees as they perform the job, or interviewing them. Managers often rely on questionnaires compiled by jobholders and their managers. The questionnaires ask about the skills and abilities needed to perform the job, job tasks and the amount of time spent on them, responsibilities, supervisory activities, equipment used, reports prepared and decisions made.[36] The Position Analysis Questionnaire (PAQ) is a comprehensive standardised questionnaire that many managers rely on to conduct job analyses.[37] It focuses on behaviours jobholders perform, working conditions and job characteristics, and can be used for a variety of jobs.[38] The PAQ contains 194 items organised into six divisions: (1) information input (where and how the jobholder acquires the information to perform the job), (2) mental processes (the reasoning, decision making, planning and information processing activities that are part of the job), (3) work output (the physical activities performed on the job and the machines and devices used), (4) relationships with others (interactions with other people that are necessary to perform the job), (5) job context (the physical and social environment of the job) and (6) other job characteristics (such as work pace).[39] A trend, in some organisations is toward more flexible jobs in which tasks and responsibilities change and cannot be clearly specified in advance. For these kinds of jobs, job analysis focuses more on determining the *skills* and *knowledge* workers need to be effective and less on specific duties.

However, research has now begun to question the accuracy of such methods in attempting to quantify jobs. Globalisation and technology, for example, are factors that are significantly influencing the way that we work and the nature of jobs performed by employees can change rapidly over a short period of time, particularly if jobs are project- or contract-based. Sanchez and Levine argue that jobs are *socially constructed*, and rather than simply analysing the tasks, job analysis should include the opinions and predispositions of the job constructor. They therefore conclude that it is impossible to achieve an unquestionably correct description of any job. Organisations should not assume that all jobs are static entities, and should be wary of the validity of job analyses. Morgeon and Campion discussed how some of the problems of validity of job analysis may be solved and in an attempt to move away from a 'one-test-fits-all' approach they developed a model that looks at the *inferences* between job descriptions and job specifications made in the analysis process. Their model identifies a different approach towards job analysis and includes a *conceptual* and *operational* level. Initially, under job description, analysts need to know what the job entails and whether the tasks involved are representative of the job performance. Secondly, examining the job specification is necessary and the extent to which knowledge, skills, ability and other characterstics (KSAO) adequately represent the psychological constructs that underlie job-related capabilities. Finally, one needs to know to what degree KSAOs are needed to perform the job tasks and activities. Morgeon and Campion conclude that their model emphasises the inferences between the different job components and the type of evidence used to validate such inferences, as in many cases evidence is not observable from job incumbents. Such a model appears to incorporate the many different facets attached to jobs, and also highlights the problems that analysts have in portraying an accurate and valid account of a job.[40]

Once the HR planning and job analyses have been completed then managers will be better informed as to their HR needs and the jobs they need to fill. They will also know the knowledge, skills and abilities that potential employees need to perform those jobs. At this point, recruitment and selection can begin.

External and Internal Recruitment

Recruitment involves gathering together a number of qualified candidates for the available positions within the company. Traditionally, two main types of recruiting have been used: *external* and *internal*, which is now supplemented by recruiting over the *Internet*.

External recruiting

When managers recruit externally to fill positions, they look outside the organisation for people who have not worked for it previously. There are multiple means through which managers can recruit externally – advertisements in newspapers and magazines, open days for students and career counsellors at high schools and colleges or on-site at the organisation, career fairs at colleges and recruitment meetings with groups in the local community.

Many large organisations send teams of interviewers to university campuses to recruit new employees. External recruitment can also take place through informal networks, as occurs when current employees inform friends about positions in their companies or recommend people they know to fill vacant spots. Some organisations use employment agencies for external recruitment, and some external recruitment takes place simply through 'walk-ins' – job hunters coming to an organisation and inquiring about employment possibilities.

With all the downsizings and corporate redundancies that have taken place in recent years, you may think that external recruiting would be a relatively easy task for managers. However, it rarely is, because even though many people may be searching for employment many of the jobs that are opening up require skills and abilities that these job hunters do not have. Managers needing to fill vacant positions and job hunters seeking employment opportunities increasingly rely on the Web to make connections with each other through employment websites such as Monster.com[41] and Jobline International, Europe's largest electronic recruiting site, with operations in 12 countries.[42] Major corporations such as Coca-Cola, Cisco, Ernst & Young, Canon and Telia have relied on Jobline to fill global positions.[43]

In the UK, the academic fraternity also utilise Web technology to search for positions throughout the world as the idea of armchair job-change appeals to many who either want to move for promotional reasons, have just entered the higher education market after newly qualifying or are just looking for new opportunities. The Jobs.ac.uk site claims to have 345,000 unique user visits per month and advertises 40,000 jobs per year; the claim is that 84 per cent of users confirm that online selection is their preferred method of recruitment.[44]

External recruiting has both advantages and disadvantages for managers. The advantages include having access to a potentially large applicant pool; being able to attract people who have the skills, knowledge and abilities that an organisation needs to achieve its goals; and being able to bring in newcomers who may have a fresh approach to problems and be up-to-date on the latest technology. These advantages have to be weighed against the disadvantages, including the relatively high costs of external recruitment. Employees recruited externally also lack knowledge about the inner workings of the organisation and may need to receive more training than those recruited internally. Finally, when employees are recruited externally, there is always uncertainty concerning whether they will actually be good performers.

Internal recruiting

When recruiting is internal, managers turn to existing employees to fill positions. Employees recruited internally are either seeking **lateral moves** (job changes that entail no major changes in responsibility or authority levels) or promotions. Internal recruiting has several advantages. Internal applicants are already familiar with the organisation (including its goals, structure, culture, rules and norms). Managers already know the candidates; they have considerable information about their skills and abilities and actual behaviour on the job. Internal recruiting can also help boost levels of employee motivation and morale, both for the employee who gets the job and for other workers. Those who are not seeking a promotion or who may not be ready for one can see that promotion is a possibility for the future; a lateral move can alleviate boredom once a job has been fully mastered and can also be a useful way to learn new skills. Internal recruiting is also normally less time-consuming and expensive than external recruiting.

Given the advantages of internal recruiting, why do managers rely on external recruiting as much as they do? The answer is because of the disadvantages of internal recruiting – among them, a limited pool of candidates and a tendency among those candidates to be set in the organisation's ways. Often, the organisation simply does not have suitable internal candidates. Even when suitable internal applicants are available, managers may sometimes rely on external recruiting to find the very best candidate or to help bring new ideas and approaches into their organisation. When organisations are in trouble and performing poorly, external recruiting is often relied on to bring in managerial talent with a fresh approach. When IBM's performance was suffering in the 1990s and the board of directors was looking for a new CEO, rather than consider any of IBM's required senior managers for this position the board recruited Lou Gerstner, an outsider who had no previous experience in the computer industry.

Honesty in recruiting

At times, when trying to recruit the most qualified applicants, managers may be tempted to paint overly rosy pictures of both the position and the organisation as a whole. They may worry that if they are totally honest about the advantages and disadvantages they will either not be able to fill positions, or will have fewer or less qualified applicants. A manager trying to fill a secretarial position, for example, may emphasise the high level of pay and benefits the job offers and fail to mention the fact that the position is usually a dead-end job offering few opportunities for promotion.

Research suggests that painting an overly positive image of a job and the organisation is not a wise recruiting strategy. Recruitment is more likely to be effective when managers provide potential applicants with an honest assessment of both the advantages and the disadvantages of the job and organisation. Such an assessment is called a **realistic job preview** (RJP).[45] RJPs can reduce the number of new appointments who later leave when their jobs and organisations fail to meet their unrealistic expectations, and they help applicants decide for themselves whether the job is right for them.

The manager who promotes the positive while avoiding the negative aspects of any job may have an easy time filling the position, but may end up with an employee who expects to be promoted quickly. After a few weeks on the job, the new recruit may realise that a promotion is highly unlikely no matter how good his or her performance, becomes dissatisfied and looks for and accepts another job. The manager then has to recruit, select and train another new employee. The manager could have avoided this waste of valuable organisational resources by using an RJP. The RJP would have increased the likelihood of hiring someone who was comfortable with few promotional opportunities and subsequently would have been satisfied to remain on the job.

The Selection Process

Once managers develop a pool of applicants for positions through the recruitment process, they need to find out whether each applicant is qualified for the position and likely to be a good performer. If more than one applicant meets these two conditions, managers must further determine which applicants are likely to be better performers than others. They have several *selection tools* to help them sort out the relative qualifications of job applicants and appraise their potential for being good performers in a particular job. These tools include background information known as biographical data, interviews, psychometric tests, physical ability tests, work sample tests, performance tests (such as assessment centres) and references (Fig. 12.3).[46]

Background information

To aid in the selection process, managers obtain background information from job applications and from curriculum vitaes. Such information might include the highest levels of education obtained, degrees and postgraduate degrees, type of college or university attended, years and type of work experience and mastery of foreign languages. Background information can be helpful both to screen out applicants who are lacking key qualifications (such as a college degree) and to determine which qualified applicants are more promising than others – for example, applicants with a BSc may be acceptable, but those who also have an MBA are preferable.

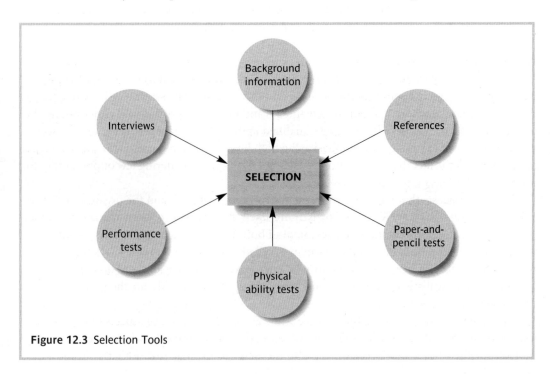

Figure 12.3 Selection Tools

Interviews

Virtually all organisations use interviews during the selection process. The interview can represent a significant and valid method of employee selection, providing that it is *structured*. This means that the questions asked at the interview should be based on an appropriate job analysis; the questions are consistent across interviewers and interviewees and interviewers use a standardised method of evaluating candidates' responses. Interviews may be structured or unstructured. In a *structured interview*, managers ask each applicant the same standard questions (e.g. 'What are your unique qualifications for this position?' and 'What characteristics of a job are most important for you?'). Particularly informative questions may be those that prompt an interviewee to demonstrate the skills and abilities needed for the job. Sometimes called *situational interview questions*, these often present interviewees with a scenario that they would likely encounter on the job and ask them to indicate how they would handle it. For example, applicants for a sales job may be asked to indicate how they would respond to a customer who complains about waiting too long for service, a customer who is indecisive and a customer whose order is lost. Hunter and Hirsch found that that structured interviews such as the situational interview are more valid and argue that when structured interviews are used for lateral transfer or promotion – e.g. with experienced existing employees – then the format is exactly that of a job knowledge or work sample test. Furthermore, when candidates are being asked hypothetical scenarios that contain a mixture of specific job knowledge and general mental ability then the interview can be seen as having a similar function to an intelligence test.[47]

An *unstructured interview*, however, is conducted rather like an ordinary conversation. The interviewer feels free to ask probing questions to discover what the applicant is like and does not ask a fixed set of questions determined in advance. In general, structured interviews are superior to unstructured interviews because they are more likely to yield information that will help identify qualified candidates and are less subjective. Evaluations based on structured interviews may be less influenced by the interviewer's biases than evaluations based on unstructured interviews.

Even when structured interviews are used, however, the potential exists for the interviewer's biases to influence his or her judgement. Recall from Chapter 5 how the 'similar-to-me' effect can cause people to perceive others who are similar to themselves more positively than those who are different and how stereotypes can result in inaccurate perceptions. Interviewers must be trained to avoid these biases and sources of inaccurate perceptions as much as possible. Many of the approaches to increasing diversity awareness and diversity skills described in Chapter 5 are used to train interviewers to avoid the effects of biases and stereotypes. In addition, using *multiple interviewers* can be advantageous, as their individual biases and idiosyncrasies may cancel each other out.[48]

When conducting interviews, managers cannot ask questions that are irrelevant to the job in question, otherwise their organisations run the risk of being discriminatory, which could ultimately lead to a costly lawsuit. It is inappropriate and illegal, for example, to inquire about an interviewee's spouse or to ask questions about whether an interviewee plans to have children. Because questions such as these are irrelevant to job performance, they are discriminatory and violate EOC rules (see Table 12.1). All interviewers need to be instructed in EOC rules and informed about questions that may violate them.

Managers can use interviews at various stages in the selection process. Some use interviews as *initial screening devices*; others use them as a *final hurdle* that applicants must jump. Regardless of when they are used, managers typically use other selection tools in conjunction with interviews because of the potential for bias and for inaccurate assessment of interviewees.

Even though training and using structured rather than unstructured interviews can eliminate the effects of some biases, interviewers can still come to erroneous conclusions about interviewees' qualifications. Interviewees, for example, who make a bad initial impression or are overly nervous in the first minute or two of an interview, tend to be judged more harshly than other, less nervous candidates, even if the rest of the interview goes well.

Ability tests or *cognitive tests* assess the extent to which applicants possess the skills necessary for job performance, such as verbal comprehension or numerical skills. The use of testing and assessments has become an integral part of the recruitment process for a large proportion of UK organisations, and their use is increasing. Over three-quarters of UK organisations rely on *psychometric profiling* when recruiting graduates:[49] even if a candidate has outstanding educational attainments, most employers will still use psychometric testing.

Companies are increasingly realising that there is a significant business benefit from using a thorough and well-planned programme of assessment in order to accurately identify candidates with the experience, knowledge and skills necessary for success. Seven key benefits for organisations are:

■ More accurate representation of the candidate across many competencies – candidates are tested on *actual demonstrated ability* rather than their self-report of ability

■ Candidates who more accurately match *organisational culture* and individual roles

■ Improved *in-job performance*

■ Increased *staff morale and commitment*

■ Reduced *turnover of staff*

■ Can be used as part of an *organisational change process*

■ Provide an equal opportunity to all candidates to demonstrate relevant skills – less opportunity for one assessor's assessment to unfairly influence a selection decision.

Ability tests improve the validity and reliability of the recruiting process and help to reduce interview bias and error in selection. They provide objective, fair and quantifiable data to the organisation and can assist managers in appointing the right person.[50]

Personality tests measure personality traits and characteristics relevant to job performance. Some retail organisations, for example, give job applicants honesty tests to determine how trustworthy they are. The use of personality tests (including honesty tests) for hiring purposes is controversial: some critics maintain that honesty tests do not really measure honesty (that is, they are not valid) and can be faked by job applicants. Before using any psychometric measurement for selection purposes, managers must have sound evidence that the tests are actually good predictors of performance on the job in question. Managers who use tests without such evidence may be subject to costly discrimination lawsuits.

Physical ability tests

For jobs requiring physical abilities, such as firefighting, garbage collecting and package delivery, managers use physical ability tests that measure physical strength and stamina as selection tools. Autoworkers are typically tested for mechanical dexterity because this physical ability is an important skill for high job performance in many auto plants.[51]

Performance tests

Performance tests measure job applicants' performance on actual job tasks. These are also referred to as *work sample tests* in some industries. Applicants for secretarial positions, for example, are typically required to complete a keyboard test that measures how quickly and accurately they can type. Applicants for management positions are sometimes given short-term projects to complete – projects that mirror the kinds of situations that arise in the job being filled – to assess their knowledge and problem-solving capabilities.[52]

Assessment centres are used to gather additional information from candidates that cannot be tested at an interview. People are analysed how they handle situations under pressure, and their ability to talk through problems. Over the course of three or four days, potential candidates may be tested on their team skills or leadership style. PricewaterhouseCooper are known leaders in utilising such methods for recruiting, especially for graduates. Candidates are assessed for the skills an effective manager needs – problem-solving skills, organisation skills, communication skills and conflict resolution skills. Some of the activities are performed individually; others are performed in groups. Throughout the process, current managers observe the candidates' behaviour and measure performance. Summary evaluations are then used as a selection tool.

References

Applicants for many jobs are required to provide references from former employers or other knowledgeable sources (such as a college tutor or adviser) who know the applicants' skills, abilities and other personal characteristics and are asked to provide candid information. References are often used at the end of the selection process to confirm a decision to hire, yet the fact that many former employers are reluctant to provide negative information sometimes makes it difficult to interpret what a reference is really saying about an applicant.

Several lawsuits filed by applicants who felt that they had been unfairly denigrated or had had their privacy invaded by unfavourable references from former employers have caused managers to be increasingly wary of providing any negative information in a reference, even if it is accurate. For jobs in which the jobholder is responsible for the safety and lives of other people, however, failing to provide accurate negative information in a reference does not just mean that the wrong person may get hired; it may also mean that other people's lives could be at risk.

The importance of reliability and validity

Whatever selection tools a manager uses, these tools need to be both reliable and valid. **Reliability** is the degree to which a tool or test measures the same thing each time it is administered. Scores on a selection test should be very similar if the same person is assessed with the same tool on two different days; if there is quite a bit of variability, the tool is unreliable. For interviews, determining reliability is more complex because the dynamic is personal interpretation. That is why the reliability of interviews can be increased if two or more different qualified interviewers interview the same candidate. If the interviews are reliable, the interviewers should come to similar conclusions about the interviewee's qualifications.

Validity is the degree to which a tool measures what it purports to measure – for selection tools, it is the degree to which the test predicts performance on the tasks or job in question. Does a physical ability test used to select firefighters, for example, actually predict on-the-job performance? Do assessment centre ratings actually predict managerial performance? Do keyboarding tests predict secretarial performance? These are all questions of validity. Honesty tests, for example, are controversial because it is not clear that they validly predict honesty in such jobs as retailing and banking.

Managers have an ethical and legal obligation to use reliable and valid selection tools; yet reliability and validity are matters of degree rather than all-or-nothing characteristics. Managers should strive to use selection tools in such a way that they can achieve the greatest degree of reliability and validity. For ability tests of a particular skill, managers should keep up to date on the latest advances in the development of valid psychometric tests and use the test with the highest reliability and validity ratings possible for their purposes. Managers can improve reliability, as we have seen, by having more than one person interview job candidates.

Training and Development

Training and *development* help to ensure that organisational members have the knowledge and skills needed to perform jobs effectively, take on new responsibilities and adapt to changing conditions. Training primarily focuses on teaching organisational members how to perform their current jobs and helping them acquire the knowledge and skills they need to be effective performers. Development focuses on building the knowledge and skills of organisational members so that they are prepared to take on new responsibilities and challenges. Training tends to be used more frequently at lower levels of an organisation; development tends to be used more frequently with professionals and managers.

Before creating training and development programmes, managers should perform a **needs assessment** to determine which employees need training or development and what type of skills or knowledge they need to acquire (Fig. 12.4).[53]

Types of Training

There are two types of training: *classroom instruction* and **on-the-job training**.

Classroom instruction
Through classroom instruction, employees acquire knowledge and skills in a classroom setting. This instruction may take place within the organisation or outside it, such as courses at local

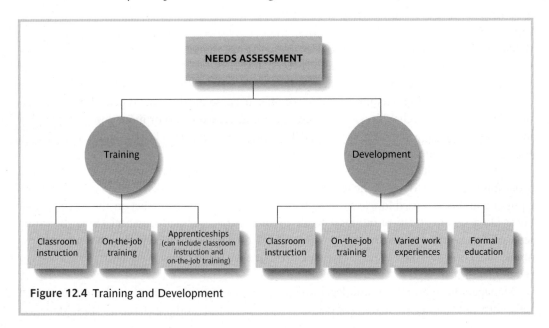

Figure 12.4 Training and Development

colleges and universities. Many organisations actually establish their own formal instructional divisions – some are even called 'colleges' – to provide the necessary classroom instruction. Hospital trusts, for example, may commission short, one-day programmes with universities to up-skill their staff. Such courses may cover particular skills that are needed to provide adequate care to patients, such as how to work specific equipment.

Classroom instruction frequently includes the use of videos and role playing in addition to traditional written materials, lectures and group discussions. *Videos* can be used to demonstrate appropriate and inappropriate job behaviours – for example, by watching an experienced salesperson effectively deal with a loud and angry customer in a video clip inexperienced sales-people can develop skills in handling similar situations. During *role playing*, trainees either directly participate in or watch others perform actual job activities in a simulated setting. At McDonald's Hamburger University, for example, role playing helps franchisees acquire the knowledge and skills they need to manage their restaurants.

Simulations also can be part of classroom instruction, particularly for complicated jobs that require an extensive amount of learning and in which errors carry a high cost. In a simulation, key aspects of the work situation and job tasks are duplicated as closely as possible in an artificial setting. Air traffic controllers are trained by simulations because of the complicated nature of the work, the extensive amount of learning involved and the very high costs of air traffic control errors.

On-the-job training

In *on-the-job training*, learning occurs in the work setting as employees perform their job tasks. On-the-job training can be provided by co-workers or supervisors, or can occur simply as jobholders gain experience and knowledge from doing the work – as is the case at Gore (p. 384).

The National Air Traffic Services (NATS) is responsible for all air traffic control services to aircraft flying in UK airspace and over the eastern part of the North Atlantic. Safety is NATS' first and foremost priority which means that excellent ongoing and continuous training is essential for all employees. New recruits go through intense training using simulators, advanced techno-logy as well as role play exercises and classroom training. Air traffic controllers, once qualified, are also expected to attend continuous on-the-job training, to keep up their level of expertise as well as test their reactions to 'what if' scenarios.[54]

Types of Development

Although both classroom instruction and on-the-job training can be used for development pur-poses as well as training, development often includes additional activities such as *varied work experiences* and *formal education*.

Varied work experiences

Senior managers need to develop an understanding of, and expertise in, a variety of functions, products and services and markets. To develop executives who will have this expertise, managers frequently make sure that employees with high potential have a wide variety of different job experiences, some in line positions and some in staff positions. Varied work experiences broaden employees' horizons and help them think more about the 'big picture'. For example, one- to three-year stints overseas are being used increasingly to provide managers with international work experience. With organisations becoming more global, managers need to develop an understanding of the different values, beliefs, cultures, regions and ways of doing business in different countries.

Having a *mentor* (recall from Chapter 3 that a mentor is an experienced member of an organisation who provides advice and guidance to a less experienced member, called a *protégé,*) can help managers seek out work experiences and assignments that will contribute to their development.[55] While some mentors and protégés meet informally, organisations have found that formal *mentorship programmes* can be valuable, as indicated in Case 12.3. As in Gore, all employees are an associate and all have a sponsor or mentor who is responsible for their ongoing development.

Case 12.3: **Development through mentoring**

British Telecom has a mentoring scheme in order to enhance the opportunities for its staff. The mentoring scheme aims to develop individuals and help them discover their capabilities, understand the culture of the organisation, remove barriers, break the 'glass ceiling', enhance their careers and help them to achieve their full potential. In order to facilitate those aims further BT set-up an e-mentoring scheme as part of their ethinic minority network. The traditional mentoring programme resourced facilitators from a range of organisations across the UK. The e-mentoring programme aimed to achieve similar results but on a global scale.

The programme aims to be one of the largest company sponsored e-mentoring networks in the world and builds on the success of the traditional mentoring programme in BT.[56]

BT's mentoring schemes are seen as a good example within the industry. BT does not only address the concerns of its ethnic minorities, it has also set up networks for disabled staff, women and women executives and gay and lesbian employees. All of these networks are supported through mentoring schemes, development programmes, senior management support and exposure to conferences and international debates within this area.[57]

Such schemes are moving the company closer to its goals; even though BT did not meet its diversity targets in 2005, it has achieved excellent feedback from its employees who are proud to work for the company. BT Spain has been voted one of the best companies to work for.[58]

Transfer of Training and Development

Whenever training and development take place off the job or in a classroom setting, it is vital for managers to promote the transfer of the knowledge and skills acquired to *the actual work situation.* Trainees should be encouraged and expected to use their new-found expertise on the job.

Performance Appraisal and Feedback

The recruitment/selection and training/development components of an HRM system ensure that employees have the knowledge and skills needed to be effective now and in the future. *Performance appraisal* and *performance feedback* complement recruitment, selection, training and development. Performance appraisal is the evaluation of employees' job performance and contributions to the organisation. Performance feedback is the process through which managers share performance appraisal information with their subordinates, give them an opportunity to reflect on their own performance and develop, with subordinates, plans for the future. Before performance feedback, performance appraisal must take place. Performance appraisal could take place without providing performance feedback, but wise managers are careful to provide feedback because it can contribute to employee motivation and performance.

Performance appraisal and feedback contribute to the effective management of HR in several ways. Performance appraisal gives managers important information on which to base HR decisions.[59] Decisions about pay rises, bonuses, promotions and job moves all hinge on the accurate appraisal of performance. Performance appraisal can also help managers determine which workers are candidates for training and development, and in what areas. Performance feedback encourages high levels of employee motivation and performance. It lets good performers know that their efforts are valued and appreciated; it also lets poor performers know that their performance needs improvement. Performance feedback can provide both good and poor performers with insight on their strengths and weaknesses, and the ways in which they can improve their performance in the future.

Types of Performance Appraisal

Performance appraisal focuses on the evaluation of *traits, behaviours* and *results*.[60]

Trait appraisals

When *trait appraisals* are used, managers assess subordinates on personal characteristics that are relevant to job performance – such as skills, abilities or personality. A factory worker, for example, may be evaluated based on his or her ability to use computerised equipment and perform numerical calculations. Social workers may be appraised based on their empathy and communication skills.

Three disadvantages of trait appraisals often lead managers to rely on other appraisal methods. Possessing a certain personal characteristic does not ensure that the characteristic will actually be used on the job and result in high performance. For example, a factory worker may possess superior computer and numerical skills but be a poor performer due to low motivation. The second disadvantage of trait appraisals is linked to the first. Because traits do not always show a *direct association with performance*, workers and courts of law may view them as unfair and potentially discriminatory. The third disadvantage of trait appraisals is that they often do not enable managers to provide employees with *feedback* that they can use to improve performance. Because trait appraisals focus on relatively enduring human characteristics that change only over the long term, employees can do little to change their behaviour in response to performance feedback from a trait appraisal. Telling a social worker that they lack empathy provides little guidance about how to improve interactions with clients, for example. These disadvantages suggest that managers should use trait appraisals only when they can demonstrate that the assessed traits are accurate and important indicators of job performance.

Behaviour appraisals

Through *behaviour appraisals*, managers can assess how workers perform their jobs – the actual actions and behaviours that workers exhibit on the job. Whereas trait appraisals assess what workers are *like*, behaviour appraisals assess what workers *do*. For example, with a behaviour appraisal, a manager might evaluate a social worker on the extent to which he or she looks a client in the eye when talking with them, expresses sympathy when they are upset and refers them to community counselling and support groups geared toward the specific problem they are encountering. Behaviour appraisals are especially useful when *how* workers perform their jobs is important. In educational organisations such as schools, for example, the number of classes and students taught is important, but how they are taught, or the methods teachers use to ensure that learning takes place, is also important.

Behaviour appraisals have the advantage of providing employees with clear information about what they are doing right and wrong, and how they can improve their performance. And because behaviours are much easier for employees to change than traits, performance feedback from behaviour appraisals is more likely to lead to performance improvements.

Result appraisals

For some jobs, *how* people perform the job is not as important as *what* they accomplish, or the results they obtain. With result appraisals, managers appraise performance by the results or the actual outcomes of work behaviours, as is the case at Gore. Take the case of two new-car salespersons. One salesperson strives to develop personal relationships with her customers; she spends hours talking to them and frequently calls them up to see how their decision making process is going. The other salesperson has a much more hands-off approach. He is very knowledgeable, answers customers' questions and then waits for them to come to him. Both salespersons sell, on average, the same number of cars, and the customers of both are satisfied with the service they receive, according to postcards that the dealership mails to customers asking for an assessment of their satisfaction. The manager of the dealership appropriately uses result appraisals (sales and customer satisfaction) to evaluate the salespeople's performance because it does not matter which behaviour salespeople use to sell cars, as long as they sell the desired number and satisfy customers. If one salesperson sells too few cars, however, the manager can give that person performance feedback about his or her low sales.

Objective and subjective appraisals

Whether managers appraise performance in terms of traits, behaviours or results, the information they assess is either *objective* or *subjective*. **Objective appraisals** are based on facts and are likely to be numerical – the number of cars sold, the number of meals prepared, the number of times late, the number of audits completed. Managers often use objective appraisals when results are being appraised because results tend to be easier to quantify than traits or behaviours. When *how* workers perform their jobs is important, however, subjective behaviour appraisals are more appropriate than result appraisals.

Subjective appraisals are based on managers' perceptions of traits, behaviours or results. Because subjective appraisals rest on managers' perceptions, there is always the chance that they may be inaccurate. This is why both researchers and managers have spent considerable time and effort on determining the best way to develop reliable and valid subjective measures of performance.

Some of the more popular subjective measures such as the *graphic rating scale*, the *behaviourally anchored rating scale (BARS)* and the *behaviour observation scale (BOS)* are illustrated in Fig. 12.5.[61] When graphic rating scales are used, performance is assessed along a *continuum with specified intervals*. When using BARS, performance is assessed along a *scale with clearly defined scale points* containing examples of specific behaviours. A BOS assesses performance by how often specific behaviours are performed. Many managers may use both objective and subjective appraisals. For example, a salesperson may be appraised both on the monetary value of sales (*objective*) and the quality of customer service (*subjective*).

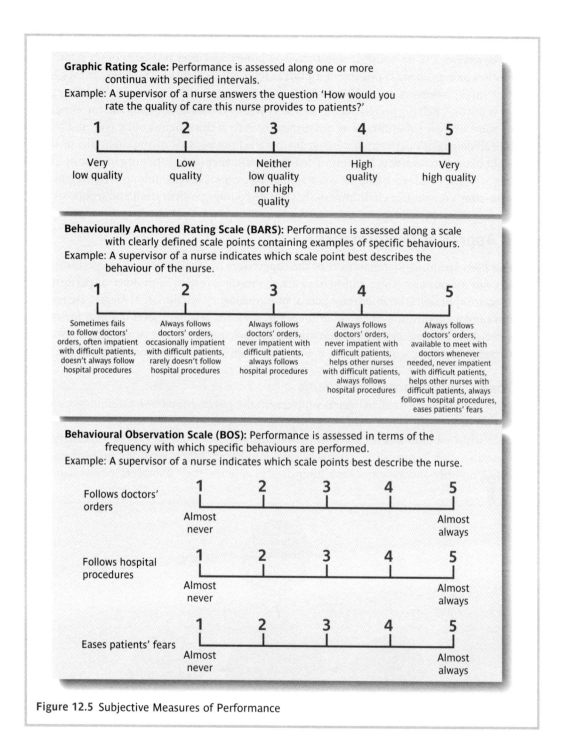

Figure 12.5 Subjective Measures of Performance

In addition to subjective appraisals, some organisations employ *forced rankings* where supervisors must rank their subordinates and assign them to different categories according to their performance (which is subjectively appraised). For example, middle managers at Ford Motor Company are ranked by their supervisors in a forced distribution from *A* to *C*, with 10 per cent of them receiving *A*s, 80 per cent receiving *B*s, and 10 per cent receiving *C*s.[62] The first year an employee receives a *C*, he or she does not receive a bonus, and after two years of *C* performance, a demotion or even firing is possible. Employees tend not to like these systems, as they believe they are unfair; managers at Ford have filed a class-action lawsuit because they feel the ranking system is unfair.[63] Relying on relative performance through ranking systems can force managers to rate some of their subordinates as unsatisfactory even if this might not be true and can also result in an employee's performance being downgraded not because of any change he or she has made but because co-workers have improved their performance. In other organisations that use ranking systems, employees tend to voice similar concerns. Forced-ranking systems can result in a **zero-sum**, competitive environment that can discourage co-operation and teamwork.[64]

Who Appraises Performance?

We have been assuming that managers or the supervisors of employees evaluate performance – a pretty fair assumption, since supervisors are the most common appraisers of performance. Performance appraisal is an important part of most managers' job duties. Managers are responsible not only for motivating their subordinates to perform at a high level but also for making many decisions hinging on performance appraisals, such as pay rises or promotions. Appraisals by managers, however, can be usefully augmented by appraisals from other sources (Fig. 12.6).

Self, peers, subordinates and clients

When *self-appraisals* are used, managers supplement their evaluations with an employee's assessment of his or her own performance. *Peer appraisals* are provided by an employee's co-workers. Especially when subordinates work in groups or teams, feedback from peer appraisals can motivate team members while providing managers with important information for decision making. A growing number of companies have subordinates appraise their managers' performance and

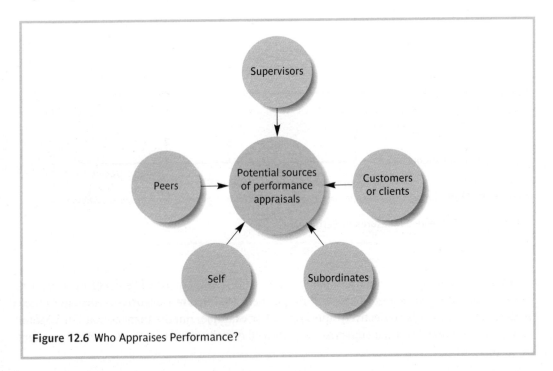

Figure 12.6 Who Appraises Performance?

leadership as well. Customers or clients can provide assessments of employee performance in terms of responsiveness to customers and quality of service. Although appraisals from each of these sources can be useful, managers need to be aware of potential issues that may arise when they are used. Subordinates sometimes may be inclined to inflate self-appraisals, especially if organisations are downsizing and they are worried about their job security. Managers who are appraised by their subordinates may fail to take necessary but unpopular actions out of fear that their subordinates will appraise them negatively.

Within Social Services departments across the UK, appraisal is part of the *Measures of Success* that are part of the Health Authorities Strategic Statement for Performance Management. This means that each department has a clear and specific *national performance management agenda* throughout all Social Services. All staff participate in appraisals against agreed objectives and then set new objectives for the following year. The appraisal will be from self-reports, peers, team leaders, clients and managers. The appraisal is all evidence-based and such evaluation of performance is then used as feedback to reflect on whether the department has met its measurable objectives and departmental aims. The definition of appraisal within such a context is about assessing how well people are doing, and how they are seeking ways to continuously improve.[65]

360-degree performance appraisals

To improve motivation and performance, some organisations include 360-degree performance appraisals and feedback in their appraisal systems, especially for managers. In a *360-degree appraisal*, a variety of people, beginning with the manager and including peers or co-workers, subordinates, superiors and sometimes even customers or clients, appraise a manager's performance. The manager receives feedback based on evaluations from these multiple sources.

For 360-degree appraisals and feedback to be effective, there has to be *trust* throughout an organisation. Trust is in fact a critical ingredient in any performance appraisal and feedback procedure. Research suggests that 360-degree appraisals should focus on *behaviours* rather than traits or results, and that managers need to carefully select appropriate raters. Appraisals also tend to be more honest when made anonymously. This method of feedback is multi-faceted and allows an employee to gain a complete picture of how well they are performing, contributing and interacting with their managers, peers and customers. The whole aim of the 360-degree feedback system is to help individuals to be more aware of their own strengths and weaknesses so that they can monitor their own behaviour and interactions more accurately in the future. For instance if from peer reviews, someone becomes more aware that they seldom listen to or act on ideas from others, then they may have to try harder to be a better listener or peers may stop bringing ideas to them.

Even when 360-degree appraisals are used, it is sometimes difficult to design an effective process by which subordinates' feedback can be communicated to their managers. Advances in IT provide organisations with a potential solution to this problem. The Victoria & Albert Museum in London, England, is embracing new technologies in order to build on its already excellent reputation for high commitment and level of expertise of its staff. This organisation has introduced a Web-based 360-degree feedback process in order to focus on key skills and behaviours. The Director of HR commented that this appraisal system has made a real difference to development and training opportunities for employees: it was made clear that the system would be used as a personal development tool, which reduced any potential anxiety or suspicion from employees. Senior management found that this on-line system has been a very successful tool in driving training and development programmes for staff, as it is easy to use and results are produced quickly.[66]

Effective Performance Feedback

For the performance appraisal and feedback component of an HRM system to encourage and motivate high performance, managers must provide their subordinates with *performance feedback*. To generate useful information to feed back to their subordinates, managers can use both formal and informal appraisals. **Formal appraisals** are conducted at set times during the year and are based on performance dimensions and measures that have been specified in advance. A salesperson, for example, may be evaluated by his or her manager twice a year on the performance dimensions of sales and customer service, sales being objectively measured from sales reports and customer service being measured with a BARS (Fig. 12.5).

Managers in most large organisations use formal performance appraisals on a fixed schedule dictated by company policy – such as every six months or every year. An integral part of a formal appraisal is a meeting between the manager and the subordinate in which the subordinate is given feedback on performance. Such feedback lets subordinates know which areas they are excelling in and which areas need improvement; it also should provide them with guidance for *improving performance*.

Realising the value of formal appraisals, managers in many large corporations have committed substantial resources to updating their performance appraisal procedures and training low-level managers in how to use them and provide accurate feedback to employees. Senior managers at the pharmaceutical company Hoffmann-La Roche, for example, spent £0.86 million updating and improving their performance appraisal procedures. Alan Rubino, Vice President of HR for Hoffmann-La Roche, believes that this was money well spent because 'people need to know exactly where they stand and what's required of them'. Before Hoffmann-La Roche's new system was implemented, managers attended a three-day training and development session to improve their performance appraisal skills. The new procedures call for every manager and subordinate to develop a performance plan for subordinates for the coming year – a plan that is linked to the company's strategy and goals and approved by the manager's own superiors. Formal performance appraisals are conducted every six months, during which actual performance is compared to planned performance.[67]

Formal performance appraisals supply both managers and subordinates with valuable information but subordinates often want feedback on a more frequent basis, and managers often want to motivate subordinates as the need arises. For these reasons many companies, including Hoffman-La Roche, supplement formal performance appraisal with frequent **informal appraisals,** for which managers and their subordinates meet as the need arises to discuss ongoing progress and areas for improvement. When job duties, assignments or goals change, informal appraisals can provide workers with timely feedback concerning how they are handling their new responsibilities.

Managers often dislike providing performance feedback, especially when the feedback is negative, but doing so is an important managerial activity.[68] Here are some guidelines for giving effective performance feedback that can contribute to employee motivation and performance:

- *Be specific and focus on behaviours or outcomes that are correctable and within a worker's ability to improve*   Telling a salesperson that he is too shy when interacting with customers is likely to do nothing other than lower his self-confidence and prompt him to become defensive. A more effective approach would be to give the salesperson feedback about specific behaviours to engage in – greeting customers as soon as they enter the store, asking customers whether they need help and volunteering to help customers find items if they seem to be having trouble.

- *Approach performance appraisal as an exercise in problem solving and solution finding, not criticising*   Rather than criticising a financial analyst for turning in reports late, the manager helps the analyst determine why the reports are late and identify ways to better manage her time.

- *Express confidence in a subordinate's ability to improve*   Instead of being sceptical, a first-level manager tells a subordinate that he is confident that he or she can increase quality levels.

- *Provide performance feedback both formally and informally*   The staff of a pre-school receives feedback from formal performance appraisals twice a year. The director of the school also provides frequent informal feedback such as complimenting staff members on creative ideas for special projects, noticing when they do a particularly good job handling a difficult child and pointing out when they provide inadequate supervision.

- *Praise instances of high performance and areas of a job in which a worker excels*   Rather than focusing on just the negative, a manager discusses the areas her subordinate excels in as well as the areas in need of improvement.

- *Avoid personal criticisms and treat subordinates with respect*   An engineering manager acknowledges her subordinates' expertise and treats them as professionals. Even when the manager points out performance problems to subordinates, she refrains from criticising them personally.

- *Agree to a timetable for performance improvements*   A first-level manager and his subordinate decide to meet again in one month to determine if quality levels have improved.

In following these guidelines, managers need to remember *why* they are giving performance feedback: to encourage high levels of *motivation* and *performance*. The information that managers gather through performance appraisal and feedback helps them determine how to distribute pay rises and bonuses.

Pay and Benefits

Pay includes employees' base salaries, pay rises and bonuses and is determined by a number of factors such as characteristics of the organisation and the job and levels of performance. *Benefits* are based on membership in an organisation (and not necessarily on the particular job held) and include sick days, vacation days and medical and life insurance. In Chapter 13, motivational factors such as pay and the different kinds of pay plans managers can use to help an organisation achieve its goals and gain a competitive advantage are discussed. In any organisation it is important for pay to be linked to behaviours or results that contribute to *organisational effectiveness*, as is true at Gore. We now focus on establishing an organisation's **pay level** and **pay structure**.

Pay Level

The *pay level* is a broad comparative concept that refers to how an organisation's pay incentives compare, in general, to those of other organisations in the same industry employing similar kinds of workers. Managers must decide if they want to offer relatively high wages, average wages or relatively low wages. High wages help ensure that an organisation is going to be able to recruit, select and retain high performers, but high wages also raise costs. Low wages give an organisation a cost advantage but may undermine the organisation's ability to select and recruit high performers and to motivate current employees to perform at a high level. Either of these situations may lead to inferior quality or inadequate customer service.

In determining pay levels, managers should take into account their organisation's strategy. A high pay level may prohibit managers from effectively pursuing a low-cost strategy; but a high pay level may be well worth the added costs in an organisation whose competitive advantage lies in superior quality and excellent customer service. As one might expect, hotel and motel chains with a low-cost strategy, such as Premier Travellodge, have lower pay levels than chains striving to provide high-quality rooms and services, such as Four Seasons and Hyatt Regency.

Pay Structure

After deciding on a pay level, managers have to establish a *pay structure* for the different jobs in the organisation. A pay structure clusters jobs into categories reflecting their relative importance to the organisation and its goals, levels of skill required and other characteristics managers consider to be important. Pay ranges are established for each job category. Individual jobholders' pay within job categories is then determined by factors such as performance, seniority and skill levels.

There are some interesting global differences in pay structures. Large corporations based in the US tend to pay their CEOs and senior managers higher salaries than do their European or Japanese counterparts. There also is a much greater **pay differential** between employees at the bottom of the corporate hierarchy and those higher up in US companies than in European or Japanese companies (Case 12.4).[69]

Case 12.4: **Is CEO pay over the top?**

Over the last ten years Britain's CEOs have been overpaid and have awarded themselves pay increases six times or more those of average wage earners, according to a BBC news survey in October 2003. 'CEOs have enjoyed pay rises of an average 288 per cent compared to 45 per cent for the average British worker.'[70] There was media hype and protest about the then British Gas CEO, Cedric Brown, in 1994, who got a massive 75 per cent pay increase; over a decade later, nothing has changed.

Even more mind-boggling are the severance packages some CEOs and senior managers receive when they leave their organisations. Steven Heyer was President and COO for Coca-Cola for three years; on leaving the company in June 2004, he received a £13.7 million severance package. Departing Coca-Cola CEO Douglas Daft received over £17.2 million in a severance package in 2004 even though the company's performance was less than stellar during his leadership. Douglas Ivestor, CEO of Coca-Cola prior to Daft, continues to receive 386,000 per year from a consulting contract with the company, even though he received over £57 million in his severance package.[71]

Another example is the departure of Sven Goran Eriksson. He left his job as coach of England's national football team in 2006 with a financial package nearing £5 million.[72]

Why do companies pay departing executives so excessively? Some say offering such 'golden parachutes' is necessary to recruit top talent. For some companies, generous departing payouts help ensure that confidential company information stays confidential and that ex-CEOs do not damage the reputation of the company with negative statements to the press. In an era in which many workers are struggling to find and keep jobs and make ends meet, however, more and more people are questioning whether it is ethical for senior managers to be making so much money. Some very highly paid CEOs have done wonders for their companies and created real value,[73] but what about those poorly performing CEOs who are pushed from their jobs with millions in severance pay to break their fall?

Benefits

In some countries, organisations are legally required to provide certain benefits to their employees, including *workers' compensation*, *Social Security* and *unemployment insurance*. Workers' compensation provides employees with financial assistance if they become unable to work due to a work-related injury or illness. Social Security provides financial assistance to retirees and disabled former employees. Unemployment insurance provides financial assistance to workers who lose their jobs due to no fault of their own. However, such benefits are country-specific and in the UK, for example, no such benefits exist directly. In Germany, however, taxes and insurance contributions by the employer and employee are made to insure people for unemployment.

Other benefits such as health insurance, dental insurance, holiday time, pension plans, life insurance, flexible working hours, company-provided day care and employee assistance and 'wellness' programmes are provided at the option of employers. Benefits enabling workers to simultaneously balance the demands of their jobs and of their lives away from the office or factory are of growing importance for many workers who have competing demands on their all-too-scarce time and energy. In some organisations, senior managers determine which benefits might best suit the employees and the organisation and offer the same benefit package to all employees. Other organisations, realising that employees' needs and desires may differ, offer **cafeteria-style benefit plans** that let the employees themselves choose the benefits they want. Cafeteria-style benefit plans sometimes assist managers in dealing with employees who feel unfairly treated because they are unable to take advantage of certain benefits available to other employees who, for example, have children. Some organisations have success with cafeteria-style benefit plans; others find them difficult to manage.

More and more managers are viewing benefits as a means of attracting and retaining valued employees and helping these employees stay healthy, as indicated in Case 12.5.

Case 12.5: Keeping employees happy and healthy with benefits

Working for the Royal Bank of Scotland (RBS) means that you are respected, understood and supported in every area of your work. Over 9,000 staff look after 3.5 million customers and are proud to work for RBS, earning the company 77 per cent in a survey on the best company to work for; 82 per cent of employees felt that their employer had worthy values that people could believe in and 79 per cent said they felt they made a healthy contribution. These positive scores may be because RBS looks after its employees and prides itself on caring and camaraderie. Some of the benefits that RBS offers are flexible working hours, final salary pensions, share options and profit-related pay. Rewarding and incentivising staff with such tangible benefits pays off; RBS has a very low staff turnover – one in three people have been at the bank for 15 years or more and half the staff for at least three years. RBS also scores high on the positive scale for balancing work life and happiness (70 per cent) and job security (79 per cent). Managing Director Ewen Munro, who has worked for RBS for 28 years, reported to *The Times* that RBS stood for pride and care in its staff and that one of the key factors in keeping staff happy was to work continuously in creating a positive working environment.[74]

Reaction Time

1. Discuss why it is important for HRM systems to be in line with an organisation's strategy and goals, and with each other.

2. Discuss why training and development must be ongoing activities for all organisations.

3. Describe the type of development activities that you think middle managers are most in need of.

4. Evaluate the pros and cons of 360-degree performance appraisals and feedback. Would you like your performance to be appraised in this manner? Why or why not?

Labour Relations

Labour relations are the activities that managers engage in to ensure that they have effective working relationships with the labour unions that represent their employees' interests. Although the UK government has responded to the potential for unethical organisations and unfair treatment of workers by creating and enforcing laws regulating employment (including the EOC rules listed in Table 12.1), some workers believe that a union will ensure that their interests are fairly represented in their organisations.

The 1970 Equal Pay Act makes it unlawful for employers to discriminate between men and women in terms of their pay and conditions where they are doing the same or similar work; work rated as equivalent in a job evaluation study by the employer; or work of equal value. Under the 1975 Sex Discrimination Act it is unlawful for an employer to discriminate against you because of your sex or because you are married (Table 12.1). The Management of Health and Safety at Work Regulations (1992) mandated procedures for managers to follow to ensure workplace safety. These are just a few of the UK government's efforts to protect workers' rights. The Employment Equality (Sex Discrimination) Regulations 2005 amended the Sex Discrimination Act 1975 and Equal Pay Act 1970 so that they are compatible with the requirements of EU legislation, including harassment and discrimination towards women who are pregnant or entitled to or taking maternity leave.[75]

Unions

Unions exist to represent workers' interests in the organisation. Given that managers have more power than rank-and-file workers and that organisations have multiple stakeholders, there is always the potential that managers might take steps that benefit one set of stakeholders (such as shareholders) while hurting another (such as employees). Managers may decide to speed up a production line to lower costs and increase production in the hopes of increasing returns to shareholders. Speeding up the line, however, could hurt employees forced to work at a rapid pace and might increase the risk of injuries. Employees would also receive no additional pay for the extra work they performed. Unions would represent workers' interests in a scenario such as this.

Throughout the world trades unions exist across a range of industries to protect the rights and advance the interests of their members. A trade union is an organised group of workers which often negotiates agreements with employers on pay and conditions. It may also provide legal and financial advice, sickness benefits and education facilities to its members. Employers which recognise any union(s), will negotiate with those union(s) over members' pay and conditions. Many recognition agreements are reached voluntarily, sometimes with the help of the Arbitration and Conciliation Service (Acas). If agreement can't be reached and the organisation employs more than 20 people, a union may apply for *statutory recognition*. To do so, it must first request recognition from the employer in writing. If this is unsuccessful, the union can apply to the Central Arbitration Committee (CAC) for a decision. In considering the union's application, the CAC must assess many factors including the level of union membership and the presence of any other unions. Often, the CAC will organise a ballot among the affected workforce to decide whether recognition should be awarded: throughout the process, the emphasis is on reaching voluntary agreement.[76]

Collective Bargaining

Collective bargaining is negotiation between trades unions and managers to resolve conflicts and disputes and important issues such as working hours, wages, working conditions and job security. Before sitting down with management to negotiate, union members sometimes go on strike to drive home their concerns. Once an agreement that union members support has been reached (sometimes with the help of a neutral third party called a **mediator**), union leaders and managers sign a contract spelling out the terms of the collective bargaining agreement. We discuss conflict and negotiation in depth in Chapter 16, but some brief observations are in order here because collective bargaining is an ongoing consideration in labour relations.

The signing of a contract, for example, does not bring the collective bargaining process to a halt. Disagreement and conflicts can arise over the interpretation of the contract. In such cases, a neutral third party called an **arbitrator** is usually called in to resolve the conflict. An important component of a collective bargaining agreement is a *grievance procedure* through which workers who believe they are not being fairly treated are allowed to voice their concerns and have their interests represented by the union. Workers who think that they have been unjustly fired in violation of a union contract, for example, may file a grievance, have the union represent them and get their jobs back if an arbitrator agrees with them.

Union members often go on strike to force the employer into 'listening to them'. This is how the firefighters' dispute started in 2002 when there was a disagreement over pay and conditions between the employer and the Fire Brigades Union (FBU). The fire brigade went out on strike in the UK for the first time in 25 years and the army was drafted in for several weeks to give emergency cover. Eventually, after much wrangling, negotiating and a long-drawn-out battle, the FBU, headed by Andy Gilchrist, accepted a deal of a two-tiered pay increase over the course of nine months from November 2003 to July 2004. In 2005, however, there were still disputes and several regional fire brigades had to strike in order to get what they had been promised.[77]

TIPS FOR PRACTICE

1. If you are in a supervisory role, ensure that you provide frequent informal appraisal and performance feedback. It is important for employees to know if they are doing well – and it will help to correct potential problems early!

2. Focus on results when appraising performance. People work in different ways and exhibit different behaviours – the same result can be achieved by different means.

3. Hone your personal skills and avoid personal criticism: challenge processes and opinions.

4. Ensure that you receive appropriate feedback and performance appraisals.

Summary and Review

Strategic human resource management HRM includes all the activities that managers engage in to ensure that their organisations are able to attract, retain and effectively utilise human resources. Strategic HRM is the process by which managers design the components of an HR management system to be consistent with each other, with other elements of organisational architecture and with the organisation's strategies and goals.

Recruitment and selection Before recruiting and selecting employees, managers must engage in HR planning and job analysis. HR planning includes all the activities managers engage in to forecast their current and future HR needs. Job analysis is the process of identifying (1) the tasks, duties and responsibilities that make up a job and (2) the knowledge, skills and abilities needed to perform the job. Recruitment includes all the activities that managers engage in to develop a pool of qualified applicants for vacant positions. Selection is the process by which managers determine the relative qualifications of job applicants and their potential for performing well in a particular job.

Training and development Training focuses on teaching organisational members how to perform effectively in their current jobs. Development focuses on broadening organisational members' knowledge and skills so that they will be prepared to take on new responsibilities and challenges.

Performance appraisal and feedback Performance appraisal is the evaluation of employees' job performance and contribution to the organisation. Performance feedback is the process through which managers share performance appraisal information with their subordinates, give them an opportunity to reflect on their own performance, and develop with them plans for the future. Performance appraisal provides managers with useful information for decision-making purposes. Performance feedback can encourage high levels of motivation and performance.

Pay and benefits The pay level is the relative position of an organisation's pay incentives in comparison with those of other organisations in the same industry employing similar workers. A pay structure clusters jobs into categories according to their relative importance to the organisation and its goals, the levels of skills required and other characteristics. Pay ranges are then established for each job category. Organisations are legally required to provide certain benefits to their employees; other benefits are provided at the discretion of employers.

Labour relations Labour relations include all the activities that managers engage in to ensure that they have effective working relationships with the labour unions that may represent their employees' interests. Collective bargaining is the process through which labour unions and managers resolve conflicts and disputes and negotiate agreements.

Topic for Action

- Interview a manager in a local organisation to determine how that organisation recruits and selects employees.

Applied Independent Learning

Building Management Skills

Analysing HR Systems

Think about your current job or a job that you have had in the past. If you have never had a job, then interview a friend or family member who is currently working. Answer the following questions about the job you have chosen:

1. How are people recruited and selected for this job? Are the recruitment and selection procedures that the organisation uses effective or ineffective? Why?
2. What training and development do people who hold this job receive? Is it appropriate? Why or why not?
3. How is performance of this job appraised? Does performance feedback contribute to motivation and high performance on this job?
4. What levels of pay and benefits are provided on this job? Are these levels of pay and benefits appropriate? Why or why not?

Managing Ethically

Some managers do not want to become overly friendly with their subordinates because they are afraid that, if they do so, their objectivity when conducting performance appraisals and making decisions about pay raises and promotions will be impaired. Some subordinates resent it when they see one or more of their co-workers being very friendly with the boss; they are concerned about the potential for favouritism. Their reasoning runs something like

▶

▶ this: if two subordinates are equally qualified for a promotion and one is a good friend of the boss and the other is a mere acquaintance, who is more likely to receive the promotion?

Questions

1. Either individually or in a group, think about the ethical implications of managers becoming friendly with their subordinates.

2. Do you think that managers should feel free to socialise and become good friends with their subordinates outside the workplace if they so desire? Why or why not?

Small Group Breakout Exercise

Building an HRM System

Form groups of three or four people, and appoint one group member as the spokesperson who will communicate your findings to the whole class when called upon by the instructor. Then discuss the following scenario.

You and your two or three partners are engineers who minored in business at college and have decided to start a consulting business. Your goal is to provide manufacturing-process engineering and other engineering services to large and small organisations. You forecast that there will be an increased use of outsourcing for these activities. You discussed with managers in several large organisations the services you plan to offer, and they expressed considerable interest. You have secured funding to start your business and now are building the HRM system. Your HR planning suggests that you need to hire between five and eight experienced engineers with good communication skills, two clerical/secretarial workers and two MBAs who between them have financial, accounting and HR skills. You are striving to develop your HR in a way that will enable your new business to prosper.

1. Describe the steps you will take to recruit and select (a) the engineers, (b) the clerical/secretarial workers and (c) the MBAs.

2. Describe the training and development the engineers, the clerical/secretarial workers and the MBAs will receive.

3. Describe how you will appraise the performance of each group of employees, and how you will provide feedback.

4. Describe the pay level and pay structure of your consulting firm.

Application in today's business world

Merck's Outside Man

CEO Richard Clark broke with tradition by looking beyond the company walls to find a new chief for its global pharma business

If there were any doubts that Merck Chief Executive Officer Richard Clark means to shake up the ailing drug giant, his first major hire dispelled them. On 3 April, the company announced Clark had hired Peter Loescher, president and CEO of GE Healthcare Bio-Sciences, to run Merck's global pharmaceutical business. In that newly created position, Loescher will have Merck's four main sales units reporting to him, including the US operation and Merck's growing vaccines division.

The move is a major shift for two reasons: Loescher is an outsider, and he has little in the way of Big Pharma experience in the US, Merck's biggest market. Right now, the ranks of the $22-billion drug maker are filled with long-time Merck managers, including Clark, a Merck lifer. So observers say bringing in an outsider is a clear sign that Clark wants to change the somewhat insular, academic culture at the company (see BW Online, 'Merck's Plan for a Comeback', December 16, 2005).

Marketing Maven

At the same time, while the Austrian-born Loescher spent years in Japan for drug maker Aventis and before that in Europe for Hoechst, he hasn't run a major US pharmaceutical operation. 'Clark is bringing in an outsider to challenge the status quo at Merck,' says Trevor Polischuk, an analyst at fund manager OrbiMed Advisors.

Those who know Loescher say he has strengths that will more than offset his lack of experience in the US pharmaceutical market. Loescher came to GE when it bought Amersham, a diagnostics and drug discovery tool company. GE Vice-Chairman Bill Castell, who recruited Loescher to Amersham in 2002, says that he was adept at improving the efficiency of operations while also enhancing the company's marketing strategy.

Kai Lindholst, a senior partner at executive search firm Egon Zehnder, who knows Loescher well, points out that he is fluent in German, English, Italian, French and Spanish: 'He's one of a very small group of individuals in Big Pharma with that kind of big company experience and extensive multicultural track record who can move into a position of this size with the issues [Merck] is facing.'

Recovery Mode

Loescher's challenge at Merck is sizable. Faced in recent years with a raft of patent expirations on big drugs and a weak pipeline, industry pros say Merck has lost a lot of talent in its management ranks. The withdrawal of arthritis drug Vioxx from the market in September 2004, because of stroke and heart attack risks – and a subsequent flood of lawsuits – seriously hurt morale at the company (see BW Online, 'A Weak Tonic for Merck', March 11, 2005).

The company has recovered since Clark took over in May 2004, with a number of promising new products moving toward the market, including a much-anticipated vaccine against cervical cancer. Still, Clark is looking to completely overhaul Merck's sales and marketing machine, including reducing the reliance on expensive sales reps and looking for ways to use the Internet

▶ to communicate with patients and doctors. The task for crafting and executing that reinvention will now fall to Loescher.

The question is whether he will face management turmoil as he attempts the overhaul. Lindholst says the Loescher appointment was most likely a 'bombshell' in the corridors of Merck's senior management. If successful in his new role, the 48-year-old Loescher will be widely viewed as an heir to the 60-year-old Clark (the mandatory retirement age at Merck is 65). In fact, Loescher's salary was set at $1.1 million, the same as CEO Clark's.

Loescher's hiring is widely viewed as a setback for ambitious executives in the company, including 49-year-old Bradley Sheares, who runs the US pharma operation. No doubt the changes are only beginning at Merck.

Questions

1. Why was the controversial decision taken to hire someone who had not been 'groomed' by Merck?

2. What are the potential challenges for the newly hired executive joining Merck as an outsider?

Source: Amy Barrett, 'Merck's Outside Man', adapted and reprinted from *BusinessWeek*, April 4, 2006. Copyright © 2006 by the McGraw-Hill Companies, Inc.

Notes and References

1 http://www.gore.com/en_xx/index.html.
2 http://www.gore.com/en_xx/aboutus/fastfacts/index.html.
3 http://business.timesonline.co.uk/article/0,,12190-1501908,00.html.
4 http://www.fastcompany.com/magazine/89/.
5 http://business.timesonline.co.uk/article/0,,12190-1501908,00.html.
6 J. E. Butler, G. R. Ferris and N. K. Napier, *Strategy and Human Resource Management* (Cincinnati: Southwestern Publishing, 1991); P. M. Wright and G. C. McMahan, 'Theoretical Perspectives for Strategic Human Resource Management', *Journal of Management* 18 (1992), 295–320.
7 J. O. Westgard, *Basic Method Validation*, Chapter 12 (Madison, WI: Westgard QC, Inc., 1999), 125–34.
8 http://www.qualityamerica.com/knolwedgecente/articles/.
9 L. Clifford, 'Why You Can Safely Ignore Six Sigma', *Fortune*, January 22, 2001, 140.
10 S. J. Palmisano, 'How the US Can Keep Its Innovation Edge', *BusinessWeek*, November 17, 2003, 34.
11 http://www.research.ibm.com/about/work_customers.shtml.
12 F. Warner, 'Brains for Sale', *Fast Company*, January 2004, 88–89.
13 *Ibid.*
14 *Ibid.*
15 J. B. Quinn, P. Anderson and S. Finkelstein, 'Managing Professional Intellect: Making the Most of the Best', *Harvard Business Review*, March–April 1996, 71–80.
16 Wright and McMahan, 'Theoretical Perspectives'.
17 L. Baird and I. Meshoulam, 'Managing Two Fits for Strategic Human Resource Management', *Academy of Management Review* 14, 116–28; J. Milliman, M. Von Glinow and M. Nathan, 'Organizational Life Cycles and Strategic International Human Resource Management in Multinational Companies: Implications for Congruence Theory', *Academy of Management Review* 16 (1991), 318–39; R. S. Schuler and S. E. Jackson, 'Linking Competitive Strategies with Human Resource Management Practices', *Academy of Management Executive* 1 (1987), 207–19; P. M. Wright and S. A. Snell, 'Toward an Integrative View of Strategic Human Resource Management', *Human Resource Management Review* 1 (1991), 203–25.

18 http://www.eoc.org.uk/.

19 http://www.eoc.org.uk/PDF/annual_report_2003_04.pdf.

20 http://www.eoc.org.uk/Default.aspx?page=15016.

21 R. Stogdill II, R. Mitchell, K. Thurston and C. Del Valle, 'Why AIDS Policy Must Be a Special Policy', *BusinessWeek*, February 1, 1993, 53–54

22 J. M. George, 'AIDS/AIDS-Related Complex', in L. Peters, B. Greer and S. Youngblood, eds., *The Blackwell Encyclopedic Dictionary of Human Resource Management* (Oxford: Blackwell, 1997).

23 J. M. George, 'AIDS Awareness Training', in Peters, Greer and Youngblood, eds., *The Blackwell Encyclopedic Dictionary*. Stogdill *et al.*, 'Why AIDS Policy Must Be a Special Policy'.

24 S. L. Rynes, 'Recruitment, Job Choice, and Post-Hire Consequences: A Call for New Research Directions', in M. D. Dunnette and L. M. Hough, eds., *Handbook of Industrial and Organizational Psychology*, v. 2 (Palo Alto, CA: Consulting Psychologists Press, 1991), 399–444.

25 D. Wessel, 'The Future of Jobs: New Ones Arise; Wage Gap Widens', *The Wall Street Journal*, April 2, 2004, A1, A5; 'Relocating the Back Office', *The Economist*, December 13, 2003, 67–69.

26 E. Porter, 'Send Jobs to India? US Companies Say It's Not Always Best', *The New York Times*, April 28, 2004, A1, A7.

27 http://www.sodexho.com/SodexhoCorp/jump_page_en.

28 http://insight.zdnet.co.uk/business/management/0,39020490,39183276-2,00.htm.

29 *Ibid.*

30 Porter, 'Send Jobs to India? US Companies Say It's Not Always Best'.

31 *Ibid.*

32 http://www.silicon.com/research/specialreports/consulting/0,3800004.

33 http://news.zdnet.co.uk/business/management/0,39020654,39170616,00.htm.

34 R. J. Harvey, 'Job Analysis', in M. D. Dunnette and L. M. Hough, eds., *Handbook of Industrial and Organizational Psychology*, 2 (Palo Alto, CA: Consulting Psychologists Press, 1991), 71–163

35 E. L. Levine, *Everything You Always Wanted to Know About Job Analysis: A Job Analysis Primer* (Tampa, FL: Mariner Publishing, 1983).

36 R. L. Mathis and J. H. Jackson, *Human Resource Management*, 7th ed. (Minneapolis: West, 1994).

37 E. J. McCormick, P. R. Jeannerette and R. C. Mecham, *Position Analysis Questionnaire* (West Lafayette, IN: Occupational Research Center, Department of Psychological Sciences, Purdue University, 1969).

38 C. D. Fisher, L. F. Schoenfeldt and J. B. Show, *Human Resource Management* (Boston: Houghton Mifflin, 1990); Mathis and Jackson, *Human Resource Management*; R. A. Noe, J. R. Hollenbeck, B. Gerhart and P. M. Wright, *Human Resource Management: Gaining a Competitive Advantage* (Burr Ridge, IL: Irwin, 1994).

39 Fisher *et al.*, *Human Resource Management*; E. J. McCormick, *Job Analysis: Methods and Applications* (New York: American Management Association, 1979); E. J. McCormick and P. R. Jeannerette, 'The Position Analysis Questionnaire', in S. Gael, ed., *The Job Analysis Handbook for Business, Industry, and Government* (New York: Wiley, 1988); Noe *et al.*, *Human Resource Management*.

40 J. L. Sanchez and E. L. Levine, 'Accuracy of Consequential Validity: Which is the Better Standard for Job Analysis Data?', *Journal of Organizational Behaviour*, 21 (2000), 809–18; Frederick P. Morgeon and Michael A. Campion, 'Accuracy in Job Analysis: Toward an Inference-Based Model', *Journal of Organizational Behaviour* 21, 819–27.

41 R. Sharpe, 'The Life of the Party? Can Jeff Taylor Keep the Good Times Rolling at Monster.com?', *BusinessWeek*, June 4, 2001.

42 www.monster.com, June 2001.

43 www.jobline.org/, June 2001; www.jobline.org, Jobline Press Releases, June 20, 2001, May 8, 2001.

44 http://www.jobs.ac.uk/recruiters/.

45 S. L. Premack and J. P. Wanous, 'A Meta-Analysis of Realistic Job Preview Experiments', *Journal of Applied Psychology*, 70 (1985), 706–19; J. P. Wanous, 'Realistic Job Previews: Can a Procedure to

Reduce Turnover also Influence the Relationship between Abilities and Performance?', *Personnel Psychology* 31 (1978), 249–58; J. P. Wanous, *Organizational Entry: Recruitment, Selection, and Socialization of Newcomers* (Reading, MA: Addison-Wesley, 1980).

46 R. M. Guion, 'Personnel *Assessment*, Selection, and Placement', in M. D. Dunnette and L. M. Hough, *Handbook of Industrial and Organizational Psychology*, 2 (Palo Alto, CA: Consulting Psychologists Press, Inc., 1991), 327–97.

47 J. E. Hunter and H. R. Hirsch, 'Applications of Meta-Analysis', in C. L. Cooper and I. T. Robertson, eds., *International Review of Industrial and Organisational Psychology* (Chichester: John Wiley: 1987), p. 330.

48 Noe, *et al.*, *Human Resource Management*.

49 *The Times*, August 2002.

50 http://www.grb.uk.com/psychometric_testing.0.html.

51 J. Flint, 'Can You Tell Applesauce from Pickles?', *Forbes*, October 9, 1995, 106–08

52 'Wanted: Middle Managers, Audition Required', *The Wall Street Journal*, December 28, 1995, A1.

53 I. L. Goldstein, 'Training in Work Organizations', in M. D. Dunnette and L. M. Hough, *Handbook of Industrial and Organizational Psychology*, 2 (Palo Alto, CA: Consulting Psychologists Press, Inc., 1991), 507–619.

54 http://www.nats.co.uk/.

55 T. D. Allen, L. T. Eby, M. L. Poteet, E. Lentz and L. Lima, 'Career Benefits Associated with Mentoring for Protégés: A Meta-Analysis', *Journal of Applied Psychology* 89 (1) (2004), 127–36.

56 http://www.coachingnetwork.org.uk/resourcecentre/CaseStudies/BTEMN.htm.

57 www.btplc.com/Societyandenvironment/Socialandenvironmentreport/.

58 *Ibid.*

59 Fisher *et al.*, *Human Resource Management*.

60 *Ibid.*; G. P. Latham and K. N. Wexley, *Increasing Productivity Through Performance Appraisal* (Reading, MA: Addison-Wesley, 1982).

61 T. A. DeCotiis, 'An Analysis of the External Validity and Applied Relevance of Three Rating Formats', *Organizational Behavior and Human Performance* 19 (1977), 247–66; Fisher *et al.*, *Human Resource Management*.

62 J. Muller, K. Kerwin, D. Welch, P. L. Moore and D. Brady, 'Ford: It's Worse Than You Think', *BusinessWeek*, June 25, 2001.

63 *Ibid.*

64 L. M. Sixel, 'Enron Rating Setup Irks Many Workers', *Houston Chronicle*, February 26, 2001, 1C.

65 http://www.hants.gov.uk/scrmxn/c27312.html.

66 http://www.emmettandsmith.com/features/va.htm.

67 J. S. Lublin, 'It's Shape-Up Time for Performance Reviews', *The Wall Street Journal*, October 3, 1994, B1, B2.

68 S. E. Moss and J. I. Sanchez, 'Are Your Employees Avoiding You? Managerial Strategies for Closing the Feedback Gap', *Academy of Management Executive* 18 (1) (2004), 32–46.

69 J. Flynn and F. Nayeri, 'Continental Divide over Executive Pay', *BusinessWeek*, July 3, 1995, 40–41.

70 http://news.bbc.co.uk/1/hi/business/3179550.stm.

71 C. Terhune, B. McKay, C. Mollenkamp and J. S. Lublin, 'Coke Tradition: CEOs Go Better with a Fat Send-Off', *The Wall Street Journal*, June 11, 2004, B1, B3.

72 *Guardian*, 'Eriksson Takes Golden Handshake to Walk Away after World Cup', 26 January 2006.

73 'Executive Pay'.

74 http://www.rbs.co.uk/default.htm; http://business.timesonline.co.uk/.

75 http://www.opsi.gov.uk/.

76 http://www.direct.gov.uk/Employment/Employees/TradeUnions/.

77 http://news.bbc.co.uk/1/hi/in_depth/uk/2002/firefighter_dispute/default.stm.

Chapter 13

Motivation and Performance

LEARNING OBJECTIVES

After studying this chapter, you should be able to:

☑ Explain what motivation is, and why managers need to be concerned about it.

☑ Describe from the perspectives of expectancy theory and equity theory what managers should do to have a highly motivated workforce.

☑ Explain how goals and needs motivate people, and what kinds of goals are especially likely to result in high performance.

☑ Identify the motivation lessons that managers can learn from operant conditioning theory and social learning theory.

☑ Explain why and how managers can use pay as a major motivation tool.

A Manager's Challenge

Consistently Ranking as a Best Company to Work For: Sandwell Community Caring Trust

How can managers motivate employees in an industry known for high levels of turnover and low levels of motivation?

Sandwell Community Caring Trust was founded in 1996. The trust, which is a registered charity, looks after people in three of the most deprived areas of the Midlands. The charity serves more than 350 severely disabled adults and children, and also runs a residential home for the elderly. The services offered include residential care, day care and support for people in their own home, and the trust actively helps in building specialist properties for disabled people.

Geoff Walker, CEO of the Trust, believes that it is important to treat its most important resource, the trust's staff, well for the charity to deliver the best service. His opinion is that 'they [staff] are mirror images. How you treat your workforce is the experience the service users get.' This motto includes an appreciation that in order to empower service users, treat them with dignity and make them feel good about themselves requires that the staff experiences a similar treatment.

This attitude has been rewarded by a continuous ranking as one of the best organisations to work for within the UK. So how does Geoff Walker manage to retain staff in an industry that is usually plagued by high staff turnover and low morale?

Sandwell Community Caring Trust ranks highest in a *Times* survey for delivering the best work–life balance. The charity offers a generous holiday allowance of up to 39 days and staff are extremely satisfied with the pay that they receive. Salaries for staff within the Trust are higher than the industry average, a deliberate choice to attract only the best people. The excellent pay packages offered by the charity are further enhanced by bonus schemes which, in effect, increase the salary by 6 per cent for an average member of staff. Staff turnover within the Trust is less than half of the industry's average.

But these rewards are just part of the Trust's success. The survey showed that most of the staff felt that the management of the charity was excellent and that senior managers were good role models. The staff also trusted the leadership that was given by the charity's senior managers. All this is underlined by the attitude of Geoff Walker and his team, who have reduced administration and thus kept a large proportion of their diaries free to work 'out there' where leadership is needed. Geoff Walker, for example, remains very hands-on. He performs care duties or drives the minibus, just like any other employee.[1]

Overview

Even with the best strategy in place and an appropriate organisational architecture, an organisation will be effective only if its members are motivated to perform at a high level. Walker clearly realises this. One reason why leading is such an important managerial activity is that it entails ensuring that each member of an organisation is motivated to perform highly and help the organisation achieve its goals. When managers are effective, the outcome of the leading process is a highly motivated workforce. A key challenge for managers of organisations both large and small is to encourage employees to perform at a high level.

This chapter describes what **motivation** is, where it comes from and why managers need to promote high levels of it for an organisation to be effective and achieve its goals. It examines important theories of motivation – **expectancy theory**, **need theories**, **equity theory**, **goal-setting theory** and **learning theories**. Each provides managers with important insights about how to motivate organisational members and the theories are complementary in that each focuses on a somewhat different aspect of motivation. Considering all of the theories together helps managers gain a rich understanding of the many issues and problems involved in encouraging high levels of motivation throughout an organisation. The chapter finally considers the use of pay as a motivation tool. By the end of this chapter, you will understand what it takes to have a highly motivated workforce.

The Nature of Motivation

Motivation may be defined as the psychological forces that determine the direction of a person's behaviour in an organisation, a person's level of effort and a person's level of persistence in the face of obstacles.[2] The *direction of a person's behaviour* refers to the many possible behaviours that a person could engage in. Employees at Sandwell Community Caring Trust know that they should do whatever is required to meet a customer's needs and don't have to ask permission to do something out of the ordinary.[3] *Effort* refers to how hard people work. Employees at the Trust exert high levels of effort to provide superior customer service. *Persistence* refers to whether, when faced with roadblocks and obstacles, people keep trying or give up.

Motivation is central to management because it explains *why* people behave the way they do in organisations[4] – why employees at the Trust provide such excellent customer service, and enjoy doing so. Motivation also explains why a waiter is polite or rude and why a kindergarten teacher really tries to get children to enjoy learning or just goes through the motions. It explains why some managers truly put their organisation's best interests first whereas others are more concerned with maximising their salaries and why – more generally – some workers put forth twice as much effort as others.

Motivation can come from *intrinsic* or *extrinsic* sources. **Intrinsically motivated behaviour** is behaviour that is performed for its own sake. The source of motivation is actually performing the behaviour, and motivation comes from doing the work itself. Many managers are intrinsically motivated; they derive a sense of accomplishment and achievement from helping the organisation to achieve its goals and gain competitive advantage. Jobs that are interesting and challenging or high on the five characteristics described by the job characteristics model in Chapter 9 are more likely to lead to intrinsic motivation than are jobs that are boring or do not make use of a person's skills and abilities. An elementary school teacher who really enjoys teaching children, a computer programmer who loves solving programming problems and a commercial photographer who relishes taking creative photographs are all intrinsically motivated. For these individuals, motivation comes from performing their jobs whether it be teaching children, finding bugs in computer programmes or taking pictures.

Extrinsically motivated behaviour is behaviour that is performed to acquire material or social rewards or to avoid punishment. The source of motivation is the consequences of the behaviour, not the behaviour itself. A salesperson who is motivated by receiving a commission on units sold, a lawyer who is motivated by the high salary and status that go along with the job and a factory worker who is motivated by the opportunity to earn a secure income are all extrinsically motivated. Their motivation comes from the consequences they receive as a result of their work behaviours.

People can be intrinsically motivated, extrinsically motivated, or both intrinsically and extrinsically motivated.[5] A senior manager who derives a sense of accomplishment and achievement from managing a large corporation and strives to reach year-end targets to obtain a hefty bonus is both intrinsically and extrinsically motivated. Similarly, a nurse who enjoys helping and taking care of patients and is motivated by having a secure job with good benefits is both intrinsically and extrinsically motivated. At the Trust, employees are both extrinsically motivated because they receive relatively high salaries and generous benefits and intrinsically motivated because they genuinely enjoy and get a sense of satisfaction out of doing their work and serving customers and look forward to coming to work each day: a senior care assistant, for example is excited about the change that he can observe in the people he works with, their growing confidence and happiness. Whether workers are intrinsically motivated, extrinsically motivated or both depends on a wide variety of factors. First of all, a worker's *own personal characteristics* (such as their personalities, abilities, values, attitudes and needs) are factors to be considered. Secondly, the *nature of the jobs* that are performed need to be taken into consideration – such as whether they have been enriched or where they are on the five core characteristics of the job characteristics model. Lastly, the *nature of the organisation* (such as its structure, its culture, its control systems, its HRM system and the ways in which rewards such as pay are distributed to employees) are likely to play a role in the way individuals are motivated.

Regardless of whether people are intrinsically or extrinsically motivated, they join and are motivated to work in organisations to obtain certain **outcomes**. An outcome is anything a person gets from a job or organisation. Some outcomes, such as autonomy, responsibility, a feeling of accomplishment and the pleasure of doing interesting or enjoyable work, result in intrinsically motivated behaviour. Other outcomes, such as pay, job security, benefits and annual leave allowances, result in extrinsically motivated behaviour.

Organisations hire people to obtain important **inputs**. An input is anything a person contributes to the job or organisation – such as time, effort, education, experience, skills, knowledge and actual work behaviours. Inputs such as these are necessary for an organisation to achieve its goals. Managers strive to motivate members of an organisation to contribute inputs – through their behaviour, effort and persistence – that help the organisation achieve its goals. How do managers do this? They ensure that members of an organisation obtain the outcomes they desire when they make valuable contributions to the organisation. Managers use outcomes to motivate people to contribute their inputs to the organisation: giving people outcomes when they contribute inputs and perform well aligns the interests of employees with the goals of the organisation as a whole because when employees do what is good for the organisation, they personally benefit.

This alignment between employees and organisational goals as a whole can be described by the *motivation equation* depicted in Fig. 13.1. Managers seek to ensure that people are motivated to contribute important inputs to the organisation, that these inputs are put to good use or focused in the direction of high performance and that high performance results in workers obtaining the outcomes they desire.

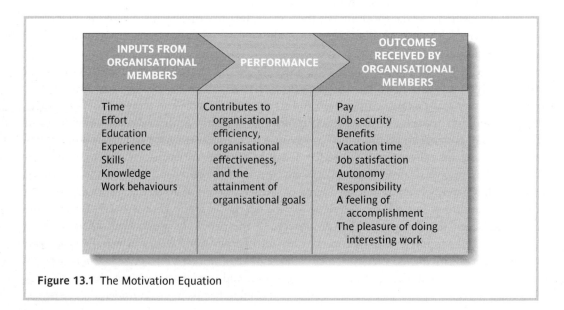

Figure 13.1 The Motivation Equation

Each of the theories of motivation discussed in this chapter focuses on one or more aspects of this equation. Each theory concentrates on a different set of issues that managers need to address to have a highly motivated workforce. Together, the theories provide a comprehensive set of guidelines for managers to follow in promoting high levels of employee motivation. Effective managers, such as Geoff Walker, tend to follow many of these guidelines, whereas ineffective managers often fail to follow them and seem to have trouble motivating organisational members.

Expectancy Theory

Expectancy theory, formulated by Victor H. Vroom in the 1960s, posits that motivation is high when workers believe that high levels of effort lead to high performance and high performance leads to the attainment of desired outcomes. Expectancy theory is one of the most popular theories of work motivation because it focuses on all three parts of the motivation equation: *inputs*, *performance* and *outcomes*. Expectancy theory identifies three major factors that determine a person's motivation: **expectancy**, **instrumentality** and **valence** (Fig. 13.2).[6]

Expectancy

Expectancy is a person's perception about the extent to which effort (an *input*) results in a certain level of performance. A person's level of expectancy determines whether he or she believes that a high level of effort results in a high level of performance. People are motivated to exert a

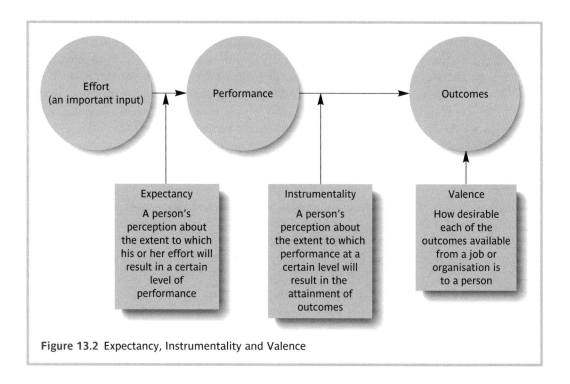

Figure 13.2 Expectancy, Instrumentality and Valence

lot of effort on their jobs only if they think that their effort will pay off in high performance – that is, if they have high expectancy. Think about how motivated you would be to study for a test if you thought that no matter how hard you tried, you would get a low mark. Think about how motivated a marketing manager would be who thought that no matter how hard he or she worked, there was no way to increase sales of an unpopular product. In these cases, expectancy is low, so overall motivation is also low.

Members of an organisation are motivated to put forth a high level of effort only if they think that doing so leads to high performance.[7] In other words, in order for people's motivation to be high, expectancy must be high. Thus, in attempting to influence motivation, managers need to make sure that their subordinates believe that if they try hard, they can actually succeed. One way managers can boost expectancies is through expressing confidence in their subordinates' capabilities.

One way for managers to boost subordinates' expectancy levels and motivation is by providing training so that people have all the expertise needed for high performance.

Instrumentality

Expectancy captures a person's perceptions about the relationship between effort and performance. *Instrumentality*, the second major concept in expectancy theory, is a person's perception about the extent to which performance at a certain level results in the attainment of outcomes (Fig. 13.2). According to expectancy theory, employees are motivated to perform at a high level only if they think that high performance will lead to (or is *instrumental* for attaining) outcomes such as pay, job security, interesting job assignments, bonuses or a feeling of accomplishment. In other words, instrumentalities must be high for motivation to be high – people must perceive that because of their high performance they will receive outcomes.[8]

Managers promote high levels of instrumentality when they clearly link performance to desired outcomes. In addition, managers must clearly communicate this linkage to subordinates. By making sure that outcomes available in an organisation are distributed to organisational members on the basis of their performance, managers promote high instrumentality and motivation. When outcomes are linked to performance in this way, high performers receive more outcomes than low performers. CEO Geoff Walker raises levels of instrumentality and motivation for the Trust employees by linking a bonus scheme to performance.

Valence

Although all members of an organisation must have high expectancies and instrumentalities, expectancy theory acknowledges that people differ in their preferences for outcomes. For many people, pay is the most important outcome of working. For others, a feeling of accomplishment or enjoying one's work is more important than pay. The term *valence* refers to how desirable each of the outcomes available from a job or organisation is to a person. To motivate organisational members, managers need to determine which outcomes have high valence for them – are highly desired – and make sure that those outcomes are provided when members perform at a high level. It appears that not only pay but also intrinsic rewards such as a stimulating work environment, observable change in patients and generous benefits are highly important outcomes for many employees at the Trust.

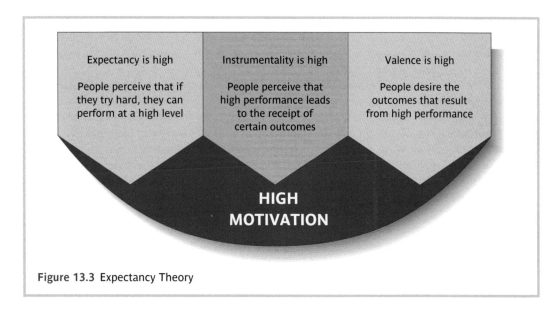

Figure 13.3 Expectancy Theory

Bringing it All Together

According to expectancy theory, high motivation results from high levels of expectancy, instrumentality and valence (Fig. 13.3). If any one of these factors is low, motivation is likely to be low. No matter how tightly desired outcomes are linked to performance, if a person thinks that it is practically impossible to perform at a high level, then motivation to perform at a high level is exceedingly low. Similarly, if a person does not think that outcomes are linked to high performance, or if a person does not desire the outcomes that are linked to high performance, then motivation to perform at a high level is low.

A key challenge for managers is encouraging high levels of motivation when trying to expand into new markets or trying out new products. Change needs enthusiastic people who drive the change and make it happen – even if similar attempts have been unsuccessful. As indicated in Case 13.1, maintaining high levels of expectancy, instrumentality and valence and learning from past failures are essential.

Case 13.1: **Nike's efforts to appeal to diverse customers**

Nike had some failures in the 1980s and 1990s trying to make inroads into new markets. Bowling shoes that left bowlers sliding down bowling alleys, a commercial for women's clothing that turned women off rather than on to Nike, and a golf shoe that was so uncomfortable employees nicknamed it 'air-blister' were among Nike's missteps in trying to appeal to diverse customers in new markets.[9] Fast-forward to 2004, and Nike was once again trying to win over diverse customers in new markets. But this time around, managers had learned from their mistakes and were taking a new approach.[10]

A key element of Nike's new approach was motivating employees to develop products in non-traditional markets (for Nike) in ways that would lead to high expectancy and instrumentality as well as to products that diverse customers would want to buy. Nike is a huge brand, embraced both by athletes playing team sports and consumers young and old looking for athletic clothing ▶

▶ and gear.[11] However, skateboarder or other extreme and alternative sporting groups would loathe having the Nike *swoosh* adorning their shoes or clothes. Skateboarders, for example, have their own subculture and brands.[12]

How could employees be motivated to enter this challenging market and woo diverse customers who prided themselves on having their individual style and were unconventional? Nike tried the approach of working in a small 'company' that knew the skateboarding subculture. This group's task was to take time to develop products that they were confident would appeal to skateboarders. Nike Skate, headed by a Vice President, a ski-racing coach, was an autonomous unit that began with 11 skateboarding employees. They took their time to develop products that would appeal to skateboarders, such as URL, E-Cue, Dunk SB and Air Angus shoes.[13] They also took pains to win over owners of skate shops who were initially reluctant to carry Nike merchandise out of fear that they would ultimately lose some of their customers when discount stores started selling the same Nike merchandise at lower prices. Offering skate shops exclusive rights to stock Nike's skate products helped to disperse such fears.[14]

Nike Skate employees were immersed in the skateboarding culture, listening to music and paging through skateboarding magazines on the job. Managing the new product development process in this manner helped managers and employees alike have high expectancy that they would be able to develop products that appealed to skateboarders, products instrumental for the growth and revenues of the unit.

Need Theories

A **need** is a requirement or necessity for survival and well-being. The basic premise of *need theories* is that people are motivated to obtain outcomes at work that will satisfy their needs. Need theory complements expectancy theory by exploring in depth which outcomes motivate people to perform at a high level. Need theories suggest that to motivate a person to contribute valuable inputs to a job and perform at a high level, a manager must determine what needs the person is trying to satisfy at work and ensure that the person receives outcomes that help to satisfy those needs when the person performs at a high level and helps the organisation achieve its goals.

There are several need theories. The chapter discusses **Maslow's hierarchy of needs, Alderfer's ERG theory, Herzberg's motivator-hygiene theory** and **McClelland's needs for achievement, affiliation and power**. These theories describe needs that people try to satisfy at work; in doing so, they provide managers with insights about what outcomes motivate members of an organisation to perform at a high level and contribute inputs to help the organisation achieve its goals.

Maslow's Hierarchy of Needs

One of the most widely used theories about needs is by psychologist *Abraham Maslow*, who proposed that all people seek to satisfy five basic kinds of needs: *physiological needs, safety needs, belongingness needs, esteem needs* and *self-actualisation needs* (Table 13.1).[15] He suggested that these needs constitute a *hierarchy of needs* (Fig. 13.4), with the most basic or compelling needs – physiological and safety needs – at the bottom. Maslow argued that these lowest-level needs must be met before a person strives to satisfy needs higher up in the hierarchy, such as self-esteem needs. Once a need is satisfied, Maslow proposed, it ceases to operate as a source of motivation. The lowest level of unmet needs in the hierarchy is the prime motivator of behaviour; if and when this level is satisfied, needs at the next-highest level in the hierarchy motivate behaviour.

Table 13.1 Maslow's hierarchy of needs

	Needs	Description	Examples of how managers can help people satisfy these needs at work
Highest-level needs	**Self-actualisation needs**	The needs to realise one's full potential as a human being	By giving people the opportunity to use their skills and abilities to the fullest extent possible
	Esteem needs	The needs to feel good about oneself and one's capabilities, to be respected by others, and to receive recognition and appreciation	By granting promotions and recognising accomplishments
	Belongingness needs	Needs for social interaction, friendship, affection and love	By promoting good interpersonal relations and organising social functions such as company picnics and holiday parties
	Safety needs	Needs for security, stability and a safe environment	By providing job security, adequate medical benefits and safe working conditions
Lowest-level needs (most basic or compelling)	**Physiological needs**	Basic needs for things such as food, water and shelter that must be met in order for a person to survive	By providing a level of pay that enables a person to buy food and clothing and have adequate housing

The lowest level of unsatisfied needs motivates behaviour; once this level of needs is satisfied, a person tries to satisfy the needs at the next level

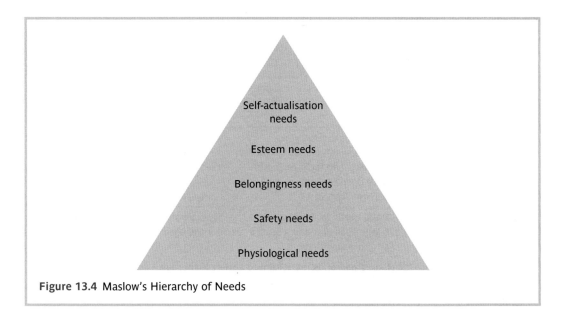

Figure 13.4 Maslow's Hierarchy of Needs

Although Maslow's theory identifies needs that are likely to be important sources of motivation for many people, research does not support his contention that there is a *need hierarchy* or his notion that only one level of needs is motivational at a time.[16] Nevertheless, a key conclusion can be drawn from Maslow's theory: individuals try to satisfy different needs at any one time – at work or in their private life. In the workplace, managers must determine which needs employees are trying to satisfy and then make sure that individuals receive outcomes that satisfy their needs when they perform at a high level and contribute to organisational effectiveness. By doing this, managers align the interests of individual members with the interests of the organisation as a whole. By doing what is good for the organisation (that is, performing at a high level), employees receive outcomes that satisfy their needs.

In our increasingly global economy, managers must realise that citizens of different countries may differ in the needs they seek to satisfy through work. Some research suggests, for example, that people in Greece and Japan are especially motivated by safety needs and that people in Sweden, Norway and Denmark are motivated by belongingness needs.[17] In less developed countries with low standards of living, physiological and safety needs are likely to be the prime motivators of behaviour. As countries become wealthier and have higher standards of living, needs related to personal growth and accomplishment (such as esteem and self-actualisation) become important as motivators of behaviour.

Alderfer's ERG Theory

Clayton Alderfer's ERG theory collapses the five categories of needs in Maslow's hierarchy into three universal categories – *existence*, *relatedness* and *growth* – also arranged in a hierarchy (Table 13.2). Alderfer agrees with Maslow that as lower-level needs become satisfied, a person seeks to satisfy higher-level needs. Unlike Maslow, however, Alderfer believes that a person can be motivated by needs at more than one level at the same time. A cashier in a supermarket, for

Table 13.2 Alderfer's ERG theory

	Needs	Description	Examples of how managers can help people satisfy these needs at work
Highest-level needs	**Growth needs**	The needs for self-development and creative and productive work	By allowing people to continually improve their skills and abilities and engage in meaningful work
	Relatedness needs	The needs to have good interpersonal relations, to share thoughts and feelings and to have open two-way communication	By promoting good interpersonal relations and by providing accurate feedback
Lowest-level needs	**Existence needs**	Basic needs for food, water, clothing, shelter and a secure and safe environment	By promoting enough pay to provide for the basic necessities of life and safe working conditions

As lower-level needs are satisfied, a person is motivated to satisfy higher-level needs; when a person is unable to satisfy higher-level needs (or is frustrated), motivation to satisfy lower-level needs increases

example, may be motivated both by existence needs and by relatedness needs. The existence needs motivate the cashier to come to work regularly and not make mistakes so that his job will be secure and he will be able to pay his rent and buy food. The relatedness needs motivate the cashier to become friends with some of the other cashiers and have a good relationship with the store manager. Alderfer also suggests that when people experience *need frustration* or are unable to satisfy needs at a certain level, they will focus all the more on satisfying the needs at the next-lowest level in the hierarchy.[18]

As with Maslow's theory, research does not support some of the specific ideas outlined in ERG theory, such as the existence of the three-level need hierarchy that Alderfer proposed.[19] However, for managers, the important message from ERG theory is the same as that from Maslow's theory: determine what needs your subordinates are trying to satisfy at work, and make sure that they receive outcomes that satisfy these needs when they perform at a high level to help the organisation achieve its goals.

Herzberg's Motivator–Hygiene Theory

Adopting an approach different from Maslow's and Alderfer's, *Frederick Herzberg* focuses on two factors: (1) outcomes that can lead to high levels of motivation and job satisfaction and (2) outcomes that can prevent people from being dissatisfied. According to Herzberg's *motivator–hygiene theory*, people have two sets of needs or requirements: *motivator needs* and *hygiene needs*.[20]

Motivator needs are related to the *nature of the work itself* and how challenging it is. Outcomes, such as interesting work, autonomy, responsibility, being able to grow and develop on the job and a sense of accomplishment and achievement, help to satisfy motivator needs. To have a highly motivated and satisfied workforce, Herzberg suggests, managers should take steps to ensure that employees' motivator needs are being met.

Hygiene needs are related to the *physical* and *psychological context* in which the work is performed. Hygiene needs are satisfied by outcomes such as pleasant and comfortable working conditions, pay, job security, good relationships with co-workers and effective supervision. According to Herzberg, when hygiene needs are not met, workers are dissatisfied, and when hygiene needs are met, workers are not dissatisfied. Satisfying hygiene needs, however, does not result in high levels of motivation or even high levels of job satisfaction. For motivation and job satisfaction to be high, motivator needs must be met.

Many research studies have tested Herzberg's propositions and, by and large, the theory has failed to receive support.[21] Nevertheless, Herzberg's formulations have contributed to our understanding of motivation in at least two ways. First, Herzberg helped to focus researchers' and managers' attention on the important distinction between *intrinsic* motivation (related to *motivator needs*) and *extrinsic* motivation (related to *hygiene needs*), covered earlier in the chapter. Second, his theory prompted researchers and managers to study how jobs could be designed or redesigned so that they were *intrinsically motivating*.

McClelland's Needs for Achievement, Affiliation and Power

Psychologist *David McClelland* has extensively researched the needs for achievement, affiliation and power.[22] The *need for achievement* is the extent to which an individual has a strong desire to perform challenging tasks well and to meet personal standards for excellence. People with a high need for achievement often set clear goals for themselves and like to receive performance feedback. The *need for affiliation* is the extent to which an individual is concerned with establishing and maintaining good interpersonal relations, being liked and having the people around him or her get along with each other. The *need for power* is the extent to which an individual desires to control or influence others.[23]

While each of these needs is present in each of us to some degree, their importance in the workplace depends upon the position one occupies. Research suggests that high needs for achievement and for power are assets for first-line and middle managers and that a high need for power is especially important for upper-level managers.[24] One study found that US presidents with a relatively high need for power tended to be especially effective during their terms of office.[25] A high need for affiliation may not always be desirable in managers and other leaders, because it may lead them to try too hard to be liked by others (including subordinates), rather than doing all they can to ensure that performance is as high as it can and should be. Although most research on these needs has been done in the US, some studies suggest that the findings may be applicable to people in other countries as well, such as India and New Zealand.[26]

Other Needs

Clearly more needs motivate workers than the needs described by the above four theories. More and more workers, for example, are feeling the need for a work–life balance and time to take care of their loved ones while simultaneously being highly motivated at work. Interestingly enough, research suggests that being exposed to nature (even just being able to see some trees from your office window) has many salutary effects and a lack of such exposure can actually impair well-being and performance.[27] Having some time during the day when one can at least see nature may thus be another important need.

Managers of successful companies often strive to ensure that as many of their valued employees' needs as possible are satisfied in the workplace. This is illustrated by Case 13.2, concerning an Essex-based fresh produce supplier.

Case 13.2: **High motivation rules at Hart Worldwide**

Hart Worldwide is a small privately owned business that still has representatives of the founder among its senior management team. The company is based in Harlow, Essex, UK, and has some 50 staff. The current Managing Director uses a 'one-team' approach, which means that staff support each other not only in the workplace but also in their home lives.

Hart Worldwide addresses the various needs of its employees by using different approaches. Extrinsic award is offered with excellent pay packages and a profit-sharing scheme of 10 per cent of basic salary. Staff are also entitled to free private health care and gym membership. The latter two address some of the basic needs, which make staff feel safe and secure. This feeling is also apparent when looking at the staff turnover rate; Hart Worldwide has only 10 per cent staff turnover.

However, as outlined above, not all employees are purely motivated by external, financial rewards. Hart Worldwide also offers a wide range of other incentives to motivate their staff. One of the initiatives that encourage staff to aim for self-actualisation is the heavy investment of the company in off-the-job training. The Managing Director also runs a scheme that allows employees to take any course that they think might be relevant as part of their 'try new things' initiative. Hart Worldwide gives each employee £100 to spend on any type of training course the employee might be interested in. Such schemes allow employees to do things that they feel are important to themselves.

But Hart Worldwide goes even further. A *Times* survey on the best SME to work for shows that Hart Worldwide has managed to create an organisational culture that fosters needs for belonging. More than 90 per cent of the employees say they care for their team mates and enjoy working with them. The employees also spend time together at social gatherings that are as diverse as paintballing and opera.

It thus seems that Hart Worldwide has been able to balance the provision of incentives for staff that have diverse needs – catering for basic needs, extrinsically and intrinsically motivated staff.[28]

Equity Theory

Equity theory is a theory of motivation that concentrates on people's perceptions of the fairness of their work *outcomes* relative to, or in proportion to, their work *inputs*. Equity theory complements expectancy and need theories by focusing on how people perceive the relationship between the outcomes they receive from their jobs and organisations and the inputs they contribute. Equity theory was formulated in the 1960s by *J. Stacy Adams*, who stressed that what is important in determining motivation is the *relative* rather than the *absolute* levels of outcomes a person receives and inputs a person contributes. Specifically, motivation is influenced by the comparison of one's own outcome–input ratio with the outcome–input ratio of a referent.[29] The *referent* could be another person or a group of people who are perceived to be similar to oneself; the referent also could be oneself in a previous job or one's expectations about what outcome–input ratios should be. In a comparison of one's own outcome–input ratio to a referent's outcome–input ratio, one's *perceptions* of outcomes and inputs (not any objective indicator of them) are critical.

Equity

Equity exists when a person perceives his or her own outcome–input ratio to be equal to a referent's outcome–input ratio. Under conditions of equity (Table 13.3), if a referent receives more outcomes than you receive, the referent contributes proportionally more inputs to the organisation, so his or her outcome–input ratio still equals your outcome–input ratio. Surinda Partel and Claudia King, for example, both work in a shoe shop. Partel is paid more per hour than King but also contributes more inputs, including being responsible for some of the shop's bookkeeping, closing the shop and periodically depositing cash in the bank. When King compares her outcome–input ratio to Partel's (her referent's), she perceives the ratios to be equitable because Partel's higher level of pay (an outcome) is proportional to her higher level of inputs (bookkeeping, closing the shop and going to the bank).

Similarly, under conditions of equity, if you receive more outcomes than a referent, then your inputs are perceived to be proportionally higher. Continuing with our example, when Partel compares her outcome–input ratio to King's (her referent's) outcome–input ratio, she perceives them to be equitable because her higher level of pay is proportional to her higher level of inputs.

When equity exists, people are motivated to continue contributing their current levels of inputs to their organisations to receive their current levels of outcomes. If people wish to increase their outcomes under conditions of equity, they are motivated to increase their inputs.

Inequity

Inequity, lack of fairness, exists when a person's outcome–input ratio is not perceived to be equal to a referent's. Inequity creates pressure or tension in people and motivates them to restore equity by bringing the two ratios back into balance.

There are two types of inequity: underpayment inequity and overpayment inequity (Table 13.3). **Under-payment inequity** exists when a person's own outcome–input ratio is perceived to be *less* than that of a referent. In comparing yourself to a referent, you think that you are *not* receiving the outcomes you should be, given your inputs. **Over-payment inequity** exists when a person perceives that his or her own outcome–input ratio is *greater* than that of a referent. In comparing yourself to a referent, you think that you are receiving *more* outcomes than you should be, given your inputs.

Table 13.3 Equity theory

Condition	Person		Referent	Example
Equity	$\dfrac{\text{Outcomes}}{\text{Inputs}}$	$=$	$\dfrac{\text{Outcomes}}{\text{Inputs}}$	An engineer perceives that he contributes more inputs (time and effort) and receives proportionally more outcomes (a higher salary and choice job assignments) than his referent
Under-payment inequity	$\dfrac{\text{Outcomes}}{\text{Inputs}}$	$<$ (less than)	$\dfrac{\text{Outcomes}}{\text{Inputs}}$	An engineer perceives that he contributes more inputs but receives the same outcomes as his referent
Over-payment inequity	$\dfrac{\text{Outcomes}}{\text{Inputs}}$	$>$ (greater than)	$\dfrac{\text{Outcomes}}{\text{Inputs}}$	An engineer perceives that he contributes the same inputs but receives more outcomes than his referent

Ways to Restore Equity

According to equity theory, both under-payment inequity and over-payment inequity create a tension that motivates most people to restore equity by bringing the ratios back into balance.[30] When people experience *under-payment* inequity, they may be motivated to lower their inputs by reducing their working hours, putting forth less effort on the job, or being absent, or they may be motivated to increase their outcomes by asking for a rise or a promotion. Susan Richie, a financial analyst at a large corporation, noticed that she was working longer hours and getting more work accomplished than a co-worker who had the same position, yet they both received the exact same pay and other outcomes. To restore equity, Richie decided to stop coming in early and staying late. Alternatively, she could have tried to restore equity by trying to increase her outcomes – say, by asking her boss for a rise.

When people experience under-payment inequity and other means of equity restoration fail, they can change their perceptions of their own or the referent's inputs or outcomes. For example, they may realise that their referent is really working on more difficult projects than they are, or that they really take more time off from work than their referent does. Alternatively, if people who feel that they are underpaid have other employment options, they may leave the organisation. John Steinberg, a deputy head of a secondary school, experienced under-payment inequity when he realised that all of the other deputy head teachers of secondary schools in his local authority (LA) had received promotions to the position of head teacher, even though they had been in their jobs for a shorter time than he had been. Steinberg's performance had always been appraised as being high, so after his repeated requests for a promotion went unheeded, he found a job as a head teacher in a different LA.

When people experience *over-payment* inequity, they may try to restore equity by changing their perceptions of their own or their referent's inputs or outcomes. Equity can be restored when people realise that they are contributing more inputs than they originally thought. Equity also can be restored by perceiving the referent's inputs to be lower or the referent's outcomes to be higher than one originally thought. When equity is restored in this way, actual inputs and outcomes are unchanged and the person being over-paid takes no real action. What is changed is how people think about or view their or the referent's inputs and outcomes. Mary McMann experienced over-payment inequity when she realised that she was being paid £1.50 an hour more than a co-worker who had the same job as she did in a record store and who contributed the same amount of inputs. McMann restored equity by changing her perception of her inputs. She recognised that she worked harder than her co-worker and solved more problems that came up in the store.

Experiencing either over-payment or under-payment inequity, you may decide that your referent is not appropriate because, for example, it is too different from yourself. Choosing a more appropriate referent may bring the ratios back into balance. Angela Martinez, a middle manager in the engineering department of a chemical company, experienced over-payment inequity when she realised that she was being paid quite a bit more than her friend who was a middle manager in the marketing department of the same company. After thinking about the discrepancy for a while, Martinez decided that engineering and marketing were so different that she should not be comparing her job to her friend's job even though they were both middle managers. Martinez restored equity by changing her referent; she picked a fellow middle manager in the engineering department as a new one.

Motivation is highest when as many people as possible in an organisation perceive that they are being equitably treated – their outcomes and inputs are in balance. Top contributors and performers are motivated to continue contributing a high level of inputs because they are receiving the outcomes they deserve. Mediocre contributors and performers notice that if they want to increase their outcomes, they have to increase their inputs. Managers of effective organisations are aware of the importance of equity for motivation and performance and continually strive to ensure that employees believe that they are being equitably treated.

The dot-com boom, subsequent bust and a recession, along with increased global competition, have resulted in some workers putting in longer and longer working hours (i.e. increasing their inputs) without any kind of increase in their outcomes. For those whose referents are not experiencing a similar change, perceptions of inequity are likely. According to a 2001 study, people in the UK work the longest hours in Europe with an average of 44.7 hours per week, compared to 39.9 in Germany and 38.0 in Belgium.[31] Moreover, advances in IT, such as email and cell phones, have resulted in work intruding on home time, vacation time and even special occasions.[32]

Goal-setting Theory

Goal-setting theory focuses on motivating workers to contribute their inputs to their jobs and organisations; in this way, it is similar to expectancy theory and equity theory. But goal-setting theory takes this focus a step further by considering as well how managers can ensure that organisational members *focus their inputs* in the direction of high performance and the achievement of organisational goals.

Ed Locke and Gary Latham, the leading researchers on goal-setting theory, suggest that the goals that organisational members strive to attain are prime determinants of their motivation and subsequent performance. A *goal* is what a person is trying to accomplish through his or her efforts and behaviours.[33] Just as you may have a goal to get a good mark in your university courses, so do members of an organisation have goals that they strive to meet. Salespeople at Dyson strive to meet sales targets, while senior managers at HP pursue market share and profitability goals.

Goal-setting theory suggests that to stimulate high motivation and performance, goals must be *specific* and *difficult*.[34] Specific goals are often quantitative – a salesperson's goal to sell £500 worth of merchandise per day, a scientist's goal to finish a project in one year, a Managing Director's goal to reduce debt by 40 per cent and increase revenues by 20 per cent, a restaurant manager's goal to serve 150 customers per evening. In contrast to specific goals, vague goals such as 'doing your best' or 'selling as much as you can' do not have much motivational impact.

Difficult goals are hard but not impossible to attain. In contrast, easy goals are those that practically everyone can attain and moderate goals are goals that about half of the people can attain. Both easy and moderate goals have less motivational power than difficult goals.

Regardless of whether specific, difficult goals are set by managers, workers or teams of managers and workers, they lead to high levels of motivation and performance. When managers set goals for their subordinates, they must accept the goals or agree to work toward them; they should also be committed to them or really want to attain them. Some managers find having subordinates participate in the actual setting of goals boosts their acceptance of, and commitment to, them. A *participative approach* to goal-setting can be advocated as it is likely to result in higher levels of *ownership* from the subordinates. A study in the automotive industry found that participative goal-setting had a significant influence on performance.[35] Organisational members also need to receive *feedback* about how they are doing; this can often be provided by the performance appraisal and feedback component of an organisation's HR management system (Chapter 12). Goals and feedback are integral components of performance management systems in organisations, such as MBO (Chapter 11).

Specific, difficult goals affect motivation in two ways. First, they motivate people to contribute more inputs to their jobs. Specific, difficult goals cause people to put forth high levels of effort: just as you would study harder if you were trying to get 80 per cent or an A in a course instead of a getting below 40 per cent or a C, so will a salesperson work harder to reach a £500 sales goal instead of a £250 goal. Specific, difficult goals also cause people to be more persistent than easy, moderate or vague goals when they run into difficulties. Salespeople who are told to sell as much as possible might stop trying on a slow day, whereas having a specific, difficult goal to reach causes them to keep trying.

A second way in which specific, difficult goals affect motivation is by helping people focus their inputs in the right direction. These goals let people know what they should be focusing their attention on – be it increasing the quality of customer service or sales or lowering new product development times. The fact that the goals are specific and difficult also frequently causes people to develop *action plans* for reaching them.[36] Action plans can include the strategies to attain the goals and timetables or schedules for the completion of different activities crucial to goal attainment. Like the goals themselves, action plans also help ensure that efforts are focused in the right direction and that people do not get sidetracked along the way.

When senior managers take over troubled companies, it is often important for them to set specific, difficult goals for themselves and their employees in order to focus and direct their own efforts and the efforts of the company.

Although specific, difficult goals have been found to increase motivation and performance in a wide variety of jobs and organisations, research suggests that they may *detract from performance* under certain conditions. When people are performing complicated and very challenging tasks that require a considerable amount of learning, specific, difficult goals may actually impair performance.[37] All of a person's attention needs to be focused on learning complicated and difficult tasks. Striving to reach a specific, difficult goal may detract from performance because some of a person's attention is directed away from learning about the task and toward trying to figure out how to achieve the goal. Once a person has learned the task and it no longer seems complicated or difficult, then the assignment of specific, difficult goals is likely to have its usual effects. Specific, difficult goals may also be detrimental for work that is very creative and uncertain.

Learning Theories

The basic premise of *learning theories* as applied to organisations is that managers can increase employee motivation and performance by the ways they link the outcomes that employees receive to the performance of desired behaviours in an organisation and the attainment of goals. Learning theory focuses on the linkage between performance and outcomes in the motivation equation (Fig. 13.1).

Learning can be defined as a relatively permanent change in a person's knowledge or behaviour that results from practice or experience.[38] Learning takes place in organisations when people learn to perform certain behaviours to receive certain outcomes. A person learns to perform at a higher level than in the past or to come to work earlier because he or she is motivated to obtain the outcomes that result from these behaviours, such as a pay rise or praise from a supervisor. The emphasis on training by Hart Worldwide (Case 13.2) ensures that all employees continue their learning throughout their careers.

Of the different learning theories, **operant conditioning theory** and **social learning theory** provide the most guidance to managers in their efforts to have a highly motivated workforce.

Operant Conditioning Theory

According to *operant conditioning theory*, developed by psychologist B. F. Skinner, people learn to perform behaviours that lead to desired consequences and learn not to perform behaviours that lead to undesired consequences.[39] Skinner's theory means that people will be motivated to perform at a high level and attain their work goals to the extent that high performance and goal attainment allow them to obtain outcomes they desire. Similarly, people avoid performing behaviours that lead to outcomes they do not desire. By linking the performance of *specific behaviours* to the attainment of *specific outcomes*, managers can motivate organisational members to perform in ways that help an organisation achieve its goals.

Operant conditioning theory provides four tools that managers can use to motivate high performance and prevent workers from engaging in absenteeism and other behaviours that detract from organisational effectiveness. These tools are **positive reinforcement, negative reinforcement, extinction** and **punishment**.[40]

Positive reinforcement

Positive reinforcement gives people outcomes they desire when they perform organisationally functional behaviours. These desired outcomes, called *positive reinforcers*, include any outcomes that a person desires, such as pay, praise or a promotion. Organisationally functional behaviours are behaviours that contribute to organisational effectiveness; they can include producing high-quality goods and services, providing high-quality customer service and meeting deadlines. By linking positive reinforcers to the performance of functional behaviours, managers motivate people to perform the desired behaviours.

Negative reinforcement

Negative reinforcement also can encourage members of an organisation to perform desired or organisationally functional behaviours. Managers using negative reinforcement actually eliminate or remove undesired outcomes once the functional behaviour is performed. These undesired outcomes, called *negative reinforcers*, can range from a manager's constant nagging or criticism to unpleasant assignments to the ever-present threat of losing one's job. When negative reinforcement is used, people are motivated to perform behaviours because they want to stop receiving or avoid undesired outcomes. Managers who try to encourage salespeople to sell more by threatening them with being fired are using negative reinforcement. In this case, the negative reinforcer is the threat of job loss, which is removed once the functional behaviour is performed.

Whenever possible, managers should try to use positive reinforcement. Negative reinforcement can create a very unpleasant work environment and even a *negative culture* in an organisation. No one likes to be nagged, threatened or exposed to other kinds of negative outcomes. The use of negative reinforcement sometimes causes subordinates to resent managers and try to get back at them.

Identifying the right behaviours for reinforcement

Even managers who use positive reinforcement (and refrain from using negative reinforcement) can get into trouble if they are not careful to identify the *right behaviours to reinforce* – behaviours that are truly functional for the organisation. Doing this is not always as straightforward as it may seem. First, it is crucial for managers to choose behaviours over which subordinates have control; in other words, subordinates must have the freedom and opportunity to perform the behaviours that are being reinforced. Second, it is crucial that these behaviours contribute to organisational effectiveness.

Extinction

Sometimes members of an organisation are motivated to perform behaviours that actually detract from organisational effectiveness. According to operant conditioning theory, all behaviour is controlled or determined by its consequences; one way for managers to curtail the performance of dysfunctional behaviours is to eliminate whatever is reinforcing the behaviours. This process is called *extinction*.

Suppose a manager has a subordinate who frequently stops by his office to chat – sometimes about work-related matters but more often about various topics ranging from politics to last night's football game. The manager and the subordinate share certain interests and views, so these conversations can get quite involved, and both seem to enjoy them. The manager, however, realises that these frequent and sometimes lengthy conversations are actually causing him to stay at work later in the evenings to make up for the time lost during the day. The manager also recognises that he is actually reinforcing his subordinate's behaviour by showing interest in the topics the subordinate brings up and responding at length to them. To extinguish this behaviour, the manager stops acting interested in these non-work-related conversations and keeps his responses polite and friendly but brief. No longer being reinforced with a pleasurable conversation, the subordinate eventually ceases to be motivated to interrupt the manager during working hours to discuss non-work-related issues.

Punishment

Sometimes managers cannot rely on extinction to eliminate dysfunctional behaviours because they do not have control over whatever is reinforcing the behaviour or because they cannot afford the time needed for extinction to work. When employees are performing dangerous behaviours or behaviours that are illegal or unethical, the behaviour needs to be eliminated immediately. Sexual harassment, for example, is an organisationally dysfunctional behaviour that cannot be tolerated. In such cases managers often rely on *punishment*, administering an undesired or negative consequence to subordinates when they perform the dysfunctional behaviour. Punishments used by organisations range from verbal reprimands to pay cuts, temporary suspensions, demotions and firings. Punishment, however, can have some unintended side-effects – resentment, loss of self-respect, a desire for retaliation – and should be used only when absolutely necessary.

To avoid the unintended side-effects of punishment, managers should keep in mind three guidelines:

- Downplay the *emotional element* involved in punishment. Make it clear that you are punishing a person's performance of a dysfunctional behaviour, not the person himself or herself.

- Try to punish dysfunctional behaviours as soon after they occur as possible, and make sure the negative consequence is a source of punishment for the individuals involved. Be certain that organisational members know exactly *why* they are being punished.

- Try to avoid punishing someone in front of others, as this can hurt a person's self-respect and lower esteem in the eyes of co-workers as well as make co-workers feel uncomfortable.[41] Even so, making organisational members aware that an individual who has committed a serious infraction has been punished can sometimes be effective in preventing future infractions and teaching all members of the organisation that certain behaviours are *unacceptable*. For example, when organisational members are informed that a manager who has sexually harassed subordinates has been punished, they learn or are reminded of the fact that sexual harassment is not tolerated and illegal.

Both managers and students often confuse negative reinforcement and punishment. To avoid such confusion, keep in mind the two major differences between them. First, negative reinforcement is used to *promote* the performance of functional behaviours in organisations; punishment is used to *stop* the performance of dysfunctional behaviours. Second, negative reinforcement entails the *removal* of a negative consequence when functional behaviours are performed; punishment entails the *administration* of negative consequences when dysfunctional behaviours are performed.

Organisational behaviour modification

When managers systematically apply operant conditioning techniques to promote the performance of organisationally functional behaviours and discourage the performance of dysfunctional behaviours, they are engaging in **organisational behaviour modification (OB MOD)**.[42] OB MOD has been successfully used to improve productivity, efficiency, attendance, punctuality, safe work practices, customer service and other important behaviours in a wide variety of organisations such as banks, department stores, factories, hospitals and construction sites.[43] The five basic steps in OB MOD are described in Fig. 13.5.

OB MOD works best for behaviours that are specific, objective and countable – such as attendance and punctuality, making sales or putting telephones together – all of which lend themselves to careful scrutiny and control. OB MOD may be questioned because of its lack of relevance to certain work behaviours (for example, the many work behaviours that are not specific, objective and countable). Some people also have questioned it on ethical grounds. Critics of OB MOD suggest that it is overly controlling and robs workers of their dignity, individuality, freedom of choice and even creativity. Supporters counter that OB MOD is a highly effective means of promoting organisational efficiency. There is some merit to both sides of this argument; what is clear, however, is that when used appropriately OB MOD provides managers with a technique to motivate the performance of at least some organisationally functional behaviours.[44]

Social Learning Theory

Social learning theory proposes that motivation results not only from the direct experience of rewards and punishments but also from a person's thoughts and beliefs. Social learning theory extends operant conditioning's contribution to managers' understanding of motivation by explaining (1) how people can be motivated by observing other people perform a behaviour and be reinforced for doing so (**vicarious learning**), (2) how people can be motivated to control their behaviour themselves (**self-reinforcement**) and (3) how people's beliefs about their ability to successfully perform a behaviour affect motivation (**self-efficacy**).[45] We now look briefly at each of these motivators.

Vicarious learning

Vicarious learning, often called *observational learning*, occurs when a person (the *learner*) becomes motivated to perform behaviour by watching another person (the *model*) perform the behaviour and be positively reinforced for doing so. Vicarious learning is a powerful source of motivation on many jobs in which people learn to perform functional behaviours by watching others. Salespeople learn how to be helpful to customers, medical school students learn how to treat patients, junior lawyers learn how to practise law and non-managers learn how to be managers, in part, by observing experienced members of an organisation perform these behaviours properly and be reinforced for them. In general, people are more likely to be motivated

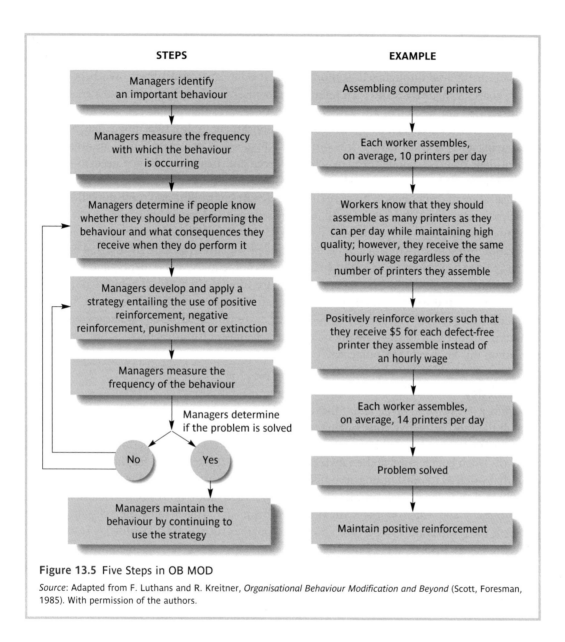

Figure 13.5 Five Steps in OB MOD

Source: Adapted from F. Luthans and R. Kreitner, *Organisational Behaviour Modification and Beyond* (Scott, Foresman, 1985). With permission of the authors.

to imitate the behaviour of models who are highly competent, are (to some extent) experts in the behaviour, have high status, receive attractive reinforcers and are friendly or approachable.[46]

To promote vicarious learning, managers should strive to have the learner meet five key conditions:

■ The learner observes the model performing the behaviour.

■ The learner accurately perceives the model's behaviour.

■ The learner remembers the behaviour.

■ The learner has the skills and abilities needed to perform the behaviour.

■ The learner sees or knows that the model is positively reinforced for the behaviour.[47]

Self-reinforcement

Although managers are often the providers of reinforcement in organisations, people sometimes motivate themselves through self-reinforcement. People can control their own behaviour by setting goals for themselves and then reinforcing themselves when they achieve the goals.[48] **Self-reinforcers** are any desired or attractive outcomes or rewards that people can give to themselves for good performance, such as a feeling of accomplishment, going to a movie, having dinner out, buying a new CD, or taking time out for a golf game. When members of an organisation control their own behaviour through self-reinforcement, managers do not need to spend as much time as they ordinarily would trying to motivate and control behaviour through the administration of consequences because subordinates are controlling and motivating themselves. In fact, this self-control is often referred to as the *self-management of behaviour.*

Chinese students at the prestigious Jiaotong University in Shanghai exemplify how strong motivation through self-control can be. These students, many of whom are aspiring engineers, live in spartan conditions (a barely lit small room is home for seven students) and take exceptionally heavy course loads. They spend their spare time reading up on subjects not covered in their classes, and many ultimately hope to obtain engineering jobs overseas with high-tech companies. 22-year-old Yan Kangrong spends his spare time reading computer textbooks and designing software for local companies: 'We learn the basics from teachers . . . But we need to expand on this knowledge by ourselves.'[49]

Self-efficacy

Self-efficacy is a person's belief about his or her ability to perform behaviour successfully. Even with all the most attractive consequences or reinforcers hinging on high performance, people are not going to be motivated if they do not think that they can actually perform at a high level. Similarly, when people control their own behaviour, they are likely to set for themselves difficult goals that will lead to outstanding accomplishments only if they think that they have the capability to reach those goals. Self-efficacy thus influences motivation both when managers provide reinforcement and when workers themselves provide it.[50] The greater the self-efficacy, the greater is the motivation and performance. In companies such as Hart Worldwide (Case 13.2), where managers believe and openly declare that employees are responsible and trustworthy enough to handle their workload, self-efficacy is boosted. Such verbal persuasion, as well as a person's own past performance and accomplishments and the accomplishments of other people, plays a role in determining a person's self-efficacy.

Pay and Motivation

Chapter 12 discussed how managers establish a pay level and structure for an organisation as a whole. Here the focus is on how, once a pay level and structure are in place, managers can use pay to motivate employees to perform at a high level and attain their work goals. Pay is used to motivate at all levels of an organisation, from entry-level personnel to senior managers. Pay can be used to motivate people to perform behaviours that help an organisation achieve its goals, and it can be used to motivate people to join and remain with an organisation.

Each of the theories described in this chapter alludes to the importance of pay and suggests that pay should be based on performance:

- *Expectancy theory*   Instrumentality, the association between performance and outcomes such as pay, must be high for motivation to be high. In addition, pay is an outcome that has high valence for many people

- *Need theories*   People should be able to satisfy their needs by performing at a high level; pay can be used to satisfy several different kinds of needs

- *Equity theory*   Outcomes such as pay should be distributed in proportion to inputs (including performance levels)

- *Goal-setting theory*   Outcomes such as pay should be linked to the attainment of goals

- *Learning theories*   The distribution of outcomes such as pay should be contingent on the performance of organisationally functional behaviours.

As these theories suggest, to promote high motivation managers should base the distribution of pay to organisational members on performance levels so that high performers receive more pay than low performers (other things being equal).[51] There are companies in which the pay of all employees, ranging from post room staff to senior managers, is based, at least in part, on performance.[52] A compensation plan basing pay on performance is often called a **merit pay plan**. Once managers have decided to use a merit pay plan, they face two important choices: whether to base pay on individual, group or organisational performance or to use salary increases or bonuses. Before commencing the discussion on pay as a motivator, caution is necessary: financial reward is an *extrinsic motivator* and thus not all people will be motivated this way. Financial rewards should be seen as a contributing factor to a motivated workforce, not the only way in which to motivate employees.

Basing Merit Pay on Individual, Group or Organisational Performance

Managers can base merit pay on individual, group or organisational performance. When individual performance (such as the value of merchandise a salesperson sells, the number of loudspeakers a factory worker assembles and a lawyer's billable hours) can be accurately determined, individual motivation is likely to be highest when pay is based on *individual performance*.[53] When members of an organisation work closely together and individual performance cannot be accurately determined (as in a team of computer programmers developing a single software package), pay cannot be based on individual performance, and a group- or organisation-based plan must be used. When the attainment of organisational goals hinges on members working closely together and co-operating with each other (as in a small construction company that builds custom homes), group- or organisation-based plans may be more appropriate than individual-based plans.[54]

It is possible to combine elements of an individual-based plan with a group- or organisation-based plan to motivate each individual to perform highly and, at the same time, motivate all individuals to work well together, co-operate with one another and help one another as needed. Lincoln Electric, a very successful company and a leading manufacturer of welding machines, uses a combination of individual- and organisation-based plans.[55] Pay is based on individual performance; in addition, each year the size of a bonus fund depends on organisational performance. Money from the bonus fund is distributed to people on the basis of their contributions to the organisation, attendance, levels of co-operation and other indications of performance. Lincoln Electric employees are motivated to co-operate and help one another because when the firm as a whole performs well, everybody benefits by having a larger bonus fund. Employees also are motivated to contribute their inputs to the organisation because their contributions determine their share of the bonus fund.

Salary Increase or Bonus?

Managers can distribute merit pay to people in the form of a salary increase or a bonus on top of regular salaries. Although the monetary amount of a salary increase or bonus may be identical, bonuses tend to have more motivational impact, for at least three reasons. First, salary levels are typically based on performance levels, cost-of-living increases and so forth, from the day people start working in an organisation, which means that the absolute level of the salary is based largely on factors unrelated to *current* performance: a 5 per cent merit increase in salary, for example, may seem relatively small in comparison to one's total salary. Second, a current salary increase may be affected by other factors in addition to performance, such as cost-of-living increases or across-the-board market adjustments. Third, because organisations rarely reduce salaries, salary levels tend to vary less than performance levels do. Bonuses also give managers more flexibility in distributing outcomes. If an organisation is doing well, bonuses can be relatively high to reward employees for their contributions. However, unlike salary increases, bonus levels can be reduced when an organisation's performance lags. Bonus plans have more motivational impact than salary increases because the amount of the bonus can be directly and exclusively based on performance.[56]

Consistent with the lessons from motivation theories, bonuses can be linked directly to performance and vary from year to year and employee to employee. Another organisation that successfully uses bonuses is Hart Worldwide (Case 13.2) and with low staff turnover and extremely satisfied employees, it is possible to argue that their success is based on receiving bonuses.

In addition to receiving pay rises and bonuses, high-level managers and executives are sometimes granted employee stock options. *Employee stock options* are financial instruments that entitle the bearer to buy shares of an organisation's stock at a certain price during a certain period of time or under certain conditions.[57] Stock options are sometimes used to attract high-level managers. The exercise price is the stock price at which the bearer can buy the stock, and the vesting conditions specify when the bearer can actually buy the stock at the exercise price. The option's exercise price is generally set equal to the market price of the stock on the date it is granted, and the vesting conditions may specify that the manager has to have worked at the organisation for 12 months or perhaps met some performance target (increase in profits) before being able to exercise the option. In high-technology firms and startups, options are sometimes used in a similar fashion for employees at various levels in the organisation.

From a motivation standpoint, stock options are used not so much to reward past individual performance but rather to motivate employees to work in the future for the good of the company as a whole. Stock options issued at current stock prices have value in the future only if an organisation does well and its stock price appreciates; giving employees stock options should thus encourage them to help the organisation improve its performance over time. At high-technology startups and dot-coms, stock options have often motivated potential employees to leave promising jobs in larger companies and work for the startups. In the late 1990s and early 2000s, many dot-commers were devastated to learn not only that their stock options were worthless, because their companies went out of business or were doing poorly, but also that they were unemployed.

Reaction Time

1. Discuss why two people with similar abilities may have very different expectancies for performing at a high level.
2. Describe why some people have low instrumentalities even when their managers distribute outcomes based on performance.
3. Analyse how professors can try to promote equity to motivate students.
4. Describe three techniques or procedures that managers can use to determine whether or not a goal is difficult.
5. Discuss why managers should always try to use positive reinforcement instead of negative reinforcement.

Summary and Review

The nature of motivation Motivation encompasses the psychological forces within a person that determine the direction of the person's behaviour in an organisation, the person's level of effort and the person's level of persistence in the face of obstacles. Managers strive to motivate people to contribute their inputs to an organisation, to focus these inputs in the direction of high performance and to ensure that people receive the outcomes they desire when they perform at a high level.

Expectancy theory According to expectancy theory, managers can promote high levels of motivation in their organisations by taking steps to ensure that expectancy is high (people think that if they try, they can perform at a high level), instrumentality is high (people think that if they perform at a high level, they will receive certain outcomes) and valence is high (people desire these outcomes).

Need theories Need theories suggest that to motivate their workforces, managers should determine what needs people are trying to satisfy in organisations and then ensure that people receive outcomes that satisfy these needs when they perform at a high level and contribute to organisational effectiveness.

Equity theory According to equity theory, managers can promote high levels of motivation by ensuring that people perceive that there is equity in the organisation, or that outcomes are distributed in proportion to inputs. Equity exists when a person perceives that his or her own outcome–input ratio equals the outcome–input ratio of a referent. Inequity motivates people to try to restore equity.

Goal-setting theory Goal-setting theory suggests that managers can promote high motivation and performance by ensuring that people strive to achieve specific, difficult goals. It is important for people to accept the goals, be committed to them and receive feedback about how they are doing.

▶

► **Learning theories** Operant conditioning theory suggests that managers can motivate people to perform highly by using positive reinforcement or negative reinforcement (positive reinforcement being the preferred strategy). Managers can motivate people to avoid performing dysfunctional behaviours by using extinction or punishment. Social learning theory suggests that people can also be motivated by observing how others perform behaviours and receive rewards, by engaging in self-reinforcement and by having high levels of self-efficacy.

Pay and motivation Each of the motivation theories discussed in this chapter alludes to the importance of pay and suggests that pay should be based on performance. Merit pay plans can be individual-, group- or organisation-based and can entail the use of salary increases or bonuses.

Topic for Action

■ Interview three people who have the same kind of job (such as salesperson, waiter/waitress or teacher), and determine what kinds of needs they are trying to satisfy at work.

■ Interview a manager in an organisation in your community to determine the extent to which he or she takes advantage of vicarious learning to promote high motivation among subordinates.

Applied Independent Learning

Building Management Skills

Diagnosing Motivation

Think about the ideal job that you would like to obtain upon graduation. Describe this job, the kind of manager you would like to report to, and the kind of organisation you would be working in. Then answer the following questions:

1. What would be your levels of expectancy and instrumentality on this job? Which outcomes would have high valence for you on this job? What steps would your manager take to influence your levels of expectancy, instrumentality and valence?

2. Whom would you choose as a referent on this job? What steps would your manager take to make you feel that you were being equitably treated? What would you do if, after a year on the job, you experienced under-payment inequity?

3. What goals would you strive to achieve on this job? Why? What role would your manager play in determining your goals?

4. What needs would you strive to satisfy on this job? Why? What role would your manager play in helping you satisfy these needs?

5. What behaviours would your manager positively reinforce on this job? Why? What positive reinforcers would your manager use?

6. Would there be any vicarious learning on this job? Why or why not?

7. To what extent would you be motivated by self-control on this job? Why?

8. What would be your level of self-efficacy on this job? Why would your self-efficacy be at this level? Should your manager take steps to boost your self-efficacy? If not, why not? If so, what would these steps be?

Managing Ethically

Sometimes pay is so contingent upon performance that it creates stress for employees. Imagine a salesperson who knows that if sales targets are not met, she or he will not be able to make a house mortgage payment or pay the rent.

Questions

1. Either individually or in a group, think about the ethical implications of closely linking pay to performance.

2. Under what conditions might contingent pay be most stressful, and what steps can managers take to try to help their subordinates perform effectively and not experience excessive amounts of stress?

Small Group Breakout Exercise

Increasing Motivation

Form groups of three or four people, and appoint one member as the spokesperson who will communicate your findings to the whole class when called on by the instructor. Then discuss the following scenario.
You and your partners own a chain of 15 dry-cleaning stores in a medium-size town. All of you are concerned about a problem in customer service that has surfaced recently. When any one of you spends the day, or even part of the day, in a particular store, clerks seem to provide excellent customer service, spotters are making sure all stains are removed from garments and pressers are doing a good job of pressing difficult items such as silk blouses. Yet during those same visits customers complain to you about such things as stains not being removed and items being poorly pressed in some of their previous orders; indeed, several customers have brought garments in to be redone. Customers also sometimes comment on having waited too long for service on previous visits. You and your partners are meeting today to address this problem.

1. Discuss the extent to which you believe that you have a motivation problem in your stores.

2. Given what you have learned in this chapter, design a plan to increase the motivation of clerks to provide prompt service to customers even when they are not being watched by a partner.

3. Design a plan to increase the motivation of spotters to remove as many stains as possible even when they are not being watched by a partner.

4. Design a plan to increase the motivation of pressers to do a top-notch job on all clothes they press, no matter how difficult.

▶ ## Exploring the World Wide Web

If you had the chance to choose which well-known corporation you would like to work for, which would it be? Now go to the website of that company and find out as much as you can about how it motivates employees. Also, using Google and other search engines, try to find articles in the news about this company. Based upon what you have learned, would this company still be your top choice? Why or why not?

Application in Today's Business World

Coverup at Boeing?

More than a decade ago, Boeing Co. quietly began investigating a sensitive internal issue: whether female employees were paid less than men. Several sophisticated salary studies concluded that the answer was 'yes'. One 1998 report said: 'Men are more likely to be hired into the high paying positions.' A statistical analysis completed the same year noted that the pay gap for entry-level managers was $3,741.04.

Although she knew nothing of these sensitive analyses, Carol Jensen would not have found them surprising. The 64-year-old technical drafter had long complained that women were under-paid. 'We were treated with little respect,' recalls the mother of nine, who started working at Boeing in 1967 and was laid off in 2000. 'The men believed that the only work for women at Boeing was behind a desk as a secretary.'

In 2000, 38 women filed a class action in Seattle for pay discrimination against the company. The potential cost to Boeing exceeded $100 million. All of those salary studies Boeing had done through the years, of course, would have been dynamite evidence for the aggrieved women. But when their lawyers made routine pre-trial requests for any statistical data the company might have compiled on gender pay differentials, the aerospace giant said it had no obligation to turn the studies over. Why? Because they had allegedly been prepared at the direction of Boeing's lawyers and were therefore protected by attorney–client privilege, a legal doctrine that shields confidential communications between executives and their attorneys from public disclosure. It's intended to allow managers to be candid with their legal team.

Behind the scenes, meanwhile, Boeing employees removed payroll-planning documents about pay discrimination from the company's files. In an email dated 27 August 2001, compensation manager Paul A. Wells advised colleagues to get rid of drafts of these types of documents on the Salary Administration server because 'that which is retained can potentially be subpoenaed and . . . those with access [to] the files can be called on to testify about the content'. Wells declined to comment.

Systematic Campaign

It's a classic scenario – the type of confrontation that has served as dramatic fodder for countless movies: a big, powerful company bullies small, weak individuals. *Erin Brockovich, A Civil Action* and many other legal thrillers tell this tale from the point of view of the victims. But *BusinessWeek* obtained a rare view of the other side of the story: what takes place at the company. The federal judge overseeing the class action, Marsha J. Pechman, agreed to unseal more than 12,000 pages of internal Boeing documents on 11 February after *BusinessWeek* attorneys argued that they should be disclosed. This hidden corporate history raises questions as to whether the company and its lawyers had engaged in a systematic campaign to hide evidence and take advantage of attorney–client privilege.

Having witnessed Boeing's intransigence for more than four years, highlighted by a ferocious battle to avoid disclosure of its salary studies, Judge Pechman dropped an even bigger bombshell on the company on 11 May. Citing 'an evolving awareness, as more facts come to light, of how Boeing had inappropriately tried to shield [the documents] from discovery', she ordered Boeing to hand over the series of salary analyses it had fought hardest to withhold – those that left little room for doubting the company's knowledge of its pay disparities. That was only one of several rebukes Boeing received from the judge, as well as from a special master assigned to referee discovery disputes, during the course of the lawsuit. Though many questions remain about the company's conduct during the case, and a complete picture of the role played by Boeing's various managers and lawyers is still unavailable, Judge Pechman's rulings suggest that the company went beyond standard aggressive legal defence tactics.

Now that Boeing was faced with the prospect of telling jurors why its own internal documents seemingly contradicted its legal theory, the company suddenly became accommodating. Two days before the case was scheduled to go to trial, on 17 May, Boeing made a settlement offer. While the two teams hammer out the details of the deal, which neither side will discuss, the case has been postponed. . . .

Spokesman Kenneth B. Mercer says Boeing is committed to honest business practices and equal opportunity. Because settlement talks in the Beck lawsuit aren't complete, he refuses to discuss the underlying facts of the case, the conduct of the company's attorneys, or any of the individual documents obtained by *BusinessWeek* – beyond saying that Boeing thinks that its hiring and promotion practices are fair. Mercer adds that the statistical studies Judge Pechman forced the company to turn over were intended to help eliminate pay disparities and that they 'can't capture all of the critical factors that go into pay or promotion decisions'.

Boeing's Mercer also noted that federal judges tossed out three similar gender-discrimination class actions filed against Boeing in Southern California, Kansas and Missouri. A fourth suit, in Oklahoma, has been granted class-action status. The company says its high batting average against female pay-discrimination suits is proof that its compensation practices were legal. But the plaintiffs' attorneys claim Boeing won mainly because it successfully suppressed the evidence that ultimately entered the Beck case.

Record Output of Jets

Troubling headlines are a comparatively new problem for Boeing. A company dominated by engineers, it traditionally focused on innovation and design. Executives believed that profits would naturally follow. During the Pentagon over-billing scandals of the late 1980s, Boeing was the least tarnished of the major contractors. But the culture started to change after its merger with the more aggressive McDonnell Douglas in 1997. That deal, along with tougher competition for government dollars in the Clinton years, shifted Boeing's emphasis to the bottom line.

Women first entered Boeing's workforce in large numbers during the Second World War – and they enabled the company to roll out record fleets of B-17 bombers. But when the war ended, Boeing's male-dominated culture returned in full force. When Carol Jensen joined in 1967, she was one of the first females to draw technical blueprints. 'Men were getting the plum designing assignments,' recalls Jensen. 'It was out-and-out discrimination, and a woman couldn't do anything about it.'

▶

▶   Despite the anger of Jensen and others, female pay did not become a serious concern at Boeing until 1996, when the US Labor Department's Office of Federal Contract Compliance Programme (OFCCP) ran a routine investigation of Boeing's mammoth Philadelphia plant. Under government contracting rules, the OFCCP has the right to audit whether federal contractors are complying with anti-discrimination laws. The agency does this by using a statistical method known as 'median analysis'. In broad terms, it compares the relationship between the median pay of male and female employees and their median job experience.

After informing Boeing that the OFCCP had discovered 'a prima facie case of systemic discrimination concerning compensation of females and minorities' in Philadelphia, the agency audited nine other plants nationwide. The stakes for Boeing, the country's Number Two federal contractor, were huge. With defence and space representing nearly half of its revenues and growing, the loss of federal contracts would be devastating.

Recognizing the seriousness of the inquiry, Boeing wasted no time launching a counterattack. It hired Jon A. Geier, a partner in the Washington (DC) office of Paul, Hastings, Janofsky & Walker LLP. One of his top priorities, he said in a declaration submitted in the Beck case, was developing a 'legally defensible' statistical analysis of Boeing's pay practices to counter the one OFCCP used to evaluate pay discrimination. But there was one big problem: the findings of Geier's own Diversity Salary Analysis project, or DSA, also found pay disparities. Its 1997 report determined that females 'are paid less'. The 1998 report noted that 'gender differences in starting salaries generally continue and often increase as a result of salary planning decisions'. Geier did not respond to requests for comment. . . .

'There Was a Lot More'

Despite Boeing's 'extensive efforts', in the words of one in-house lawyer, not to forfeit the attorney–client privilege, the company did do a few things to jeopardise its eligibility for that legal protection. Its attorneys, for instance, gave DSA documents to managers outside their tightly guarded legal team. These executives used the information not just to fight the OFCCP inquiry but also to make broader salary decisions.

The OFCCP settled with Boeing for $4.5 million in November 1999. Boeing did not admit liability. On 1 December, relieved HR executives and attorneys gathered to discuss their victory over the federal government, according to a meeting transcription obtained by *BusinessWeek*. Boeing's former director for employee relations, Marcella Fleming, declared that the company got off easy. 'We thought that there was a lot more potential financial liability out there,' Fleming told her colleagues. 'And so, what we're paying for this deal in the long run is a lot less than we think we could have potentially paid.' Fleming declined to comment for this story.

Boeing officials had little time to dwell on their triumph. On 25 February 2000, Seattle attorney Michael D. Helgren filed the *Beck* v. *Boeing* class action after some female employees told him their stories. The company enlisted the help of its chief outside law firm, Seattle-based Perkins Cole LLP. . . .

Almost immediately, the company resumed the aggressive strategies that had worked so well in the OFCCP investigation. After being deposed by attorney Helgren in September 2000, Boeing compensation manager Jeffrey K. Janders told colleagues in a memo that he wanted the Salary Planning Team to 'delete the concept of target salaries' – the hypothetical pay increases Boeing executives believed would be necessary to create salary parity – 'to prevent an audit trail where a substantial difference exists between target and planned salaries'. Because Janders could not be reached for comment, *BusinessWeek* does not know the full context of the email.

Helgren did not find out about these manoeuvres until years later, but from the start he suspected that the company was not turning over all of the salary infromation it had. After Boeing's Hannah claimed that many of the pay-related documents his rival wanted were covered by attorney–client privilege, Helgren requested a so-called privilege log – a list containing a brief description of every document the company was withholding. A common tool in US courts, these logs are intended to give plaintiffs' attorneys an idea of what material the defendant is holding back and why it is privileged without revealing any sensitive secrets. . . .

Suspecting that many of these documents did not deserve attorney–client privilege, Helgren asked for a judicial review of those covered by the privilege log. Judge Pechman assigned retired state court judge George Finkle the job of managing the pre-trial discovery disputes. After studying a 1,400-page sample of Boeing's DSA documents, Finkle rejected the claim that the studies were protected simply because attorneys were involved in producing them. The documents 'served business purposes extending well beyond providing assistance in . . . anticipation of litigation', Finkle ruled on 25 October 2000. 'Legal departments are not citadels in which public business or technical information may be placed to defeat discovery and thereby ensure confidentiality.'

That should have been the end of Helgren's quest. Still, Boeing dragged its feet. The documents Judge Finkle ordered Boeing to give to plaintiffs' attorneys came slowly and in small batches. It wasn't until early 2004 that Boeing attorneys handed over some damning internal statistical salary studies that executives had not even previously acknowledged. For Helgren, these late-released documents proved that Boeing not only knew about the pay discrimination but refused to take serious steps to eliminate it. 'These pay disparities were caused by their own practices,' Helgren says. 'None of this was by chance. And they continued for years and years to avoid the problem.'

Suddenly Amenable

In a last-ditch effort to prevent a jury from seeing these potential smoking guns, Boeing attorneys appealed Finkle's discovery order. They claimed that disclosing these documents would 'materially and unfairly' bias the case. On 11 March, Pechman denied Boeing's appeal. It was a huge boost for Helgren, who started gearing up for the trial, scheduled to begin on 17 May. But on 13 May, he got an unexpected call. A third party representing Boeing phoned to say the company was willing to talk settlement. Negotiations proceeded almost continuously until the next day at noon, when the two sides reached a tentative settlement.

While she is happy about the potential deal, plaintiff Jensen is reserving judgement about the company. Among her nine children are six adult daughters, and she currently 'wouldn't let any of them work at Boeing'. The pay gap there may disappear one day. But one thing Boeing will never be able to erase is its long history of under-paying women.

Questions

1. What inequities did women and minorities at Boeing experience?

2. What were the consequences of these inequities?

3. When managers became aware of the inequities, what did they do? Why didn't they do more?

4. What are the broader implications of the discrimination suits for Boeing and its future?

Source: S. Holmes and M. France, 'Coverup at Boeing?', adapted and reprinted from *BusinessWeek*, June 28, 2004 by special permission. Copyright © 2004 by the McGraw-Hill Companies, Inc.

Notes and References

1   *The Times*, 100 Best Companies, 5 March 2006, TimesOnline; www.tridos.co.uk.

2   R. Kanfer, 'Motivation Theory and Industrial and Organizational Psychology', in M. D. Dunnette and L. M. Hough, eds., *Handbook of Industrial and Organizational Psychology*, 1, 2nd ed. (Palo Alto, CA: Consulting Psychologists Press, 1990), 75–170.

3   T. A. Stewart, 'Just Think: No Permission Needed', *Fortune*, January 8, 2001.

4   G. Latham, 'The Study of Work Motivation in the 20th Century', in L. Koppes, ed., *The History of Industrial and Organizational Psychology* (Hillsdale, NJ: Laurence Erlbaum, 2006).

5   N. Nicholson, 'How to Motivate Your Problem People', *Harvard Business Review*, January 2003, 57–65.

6   J. P. Campbell and R. D. Pritchard, 'Motivation Theory in Industrial and Organizational Psychology', in M. D. Dunnette, ed., *Handbook of Industrial and Organizational Psychology* (Chicago: Rand McNally, 1976), 63–130; T. R. Mitchell, 'Expectancy-Value Models in Organizational Psychology', in N. T. Feather, ed., *Expectations and Actions: Expectancy-Value Models in Psychology* (Hillsdale, NJ: Erlbaum, 1982), 293–312; V. H. Vroom, *Work and Motivation* (New York: Wiley, 1964).

7   N. Shope Griffin, 'Personalize Your Management Development', *Harvard Business Review* 8 (10) (2003), 113–19.

8   T. J. Maurer, E. M. Weiss and F. G. Barbeite, 'A Model of Involvement in Work-Related Learning and Development Activity: The Effects of Individual, Situational, Motivational, and Age Variables', *Journal of Applied Psychology* 88 (4) (2003), 707–24.

9   B. Stone, 'Nike's Short Game', *Newsweek*, January 26, 2004, 40–41.

10 Holloway, 'The Man Who Put the Boing in Nike', *CB Media Limited*, March 15, 2004.

11 D. Edwards, 'Adultescents: The Over-40s Trying to Be Teens', *The Mirror*, February 3, 2004.

12 R. A. Martin, 'The Rebirth of the New York Sneakerhead', *The New York Times*, July 11, 2004, www.nytimes.com; R. J. Moody, 'Nike Puts Faith in Savier', *American City Business Journal* 20 (52) (February 20, 2004), 1.

13 Stone, 'Nike's Short Game'.

14 *Ibid.*

15 A. H. Maslow, *Motivation and Personality* (New York: Harper & Row, 1954); Campbell and Pritchard, 'Motivation Theory in Industrial and Organizational Psychology'.

16 Kanfer, 'Motivation Theory and Industrial and Organizational Psychology'.

17 N. J. Adler, *International Dimensions of Organizational Behavior*, 2nd ed. (Boston: P.W.S.-Kent, 1991); G. Hofstede, 'Motivation, Leadership and Organization: Do American Theories Apply Abroad?', *Organizational Dynamics*, Summer 1980, 42–63.

18 C. P. Alderfer, 'An Empirical Test of a New Theory of Human Needs', *Organizational Behavior and Human Performance* 4 (1969), 142–75; C. P. Alderfer, *Existence, Relatedness, and Growth: Human Needs in Organizational Settings* (New York: Free Press, 1972); Campbell and Pritchard, 'Motivation Theory in Industrial and Organizational Psychology'.

19 Kanfer, 'Motivation Theory and Industrial and Organizational Psychology'.

20 F. Herzberg, *Work and the Nature of Man* (Cleveland: World, 1966).

21 N. King, 'Clarification and Evaluation of the Two-Factor Theory of Job Satisfaction', *Psychological Bulletin* 74 (1970), 18–31; E. A. Locke, 'The Nature and Causes of Job Satisfaction', in M. D. Dunnette, ed., *Handbook of Industrial and Organizational Psychology* (Chicago: Rand McNally, 1976), 1297–1349.

22 D. C. McClelland, *Human Motivation* (Glenview, IL: Scott, Foresman, 1985); D. C. McClelland, 'How Motives, Skills, and Values Determine What People Do', *American Psychologist* 40 (1985), 812–25; D. C. McClelland, 'Managing Motivation to Expand Human Freedom', *American Psychologist* 33 (1978), 201–10.

23 D. G. Winter, *The Power Motive* (New York: Free Press, 1973).

24 M. J. Stahl, 'Achievement, Power, and Managerial Motivation: Selecting Managerial Talent with the Job Choice Exercise', *Personnel Psychology* 36 (1983), 775–89; D. C. McClelland and D. H. Burnham, 'Power Is the Great Motivator', *Harvard Business Review* 54 (1976), 100–10.

25 R. J. House, W. D. Spangler and J. Woycke, 'Personality and Charisma in the US Presidency: A Psychological Theory of Leader Effectiveness', *Administrative Science Quarterly* 36 (1991), 364–96.

26 G. H. Hines, 'Achievement, Motivation, Occupations, and Labor Turnover in New Zealand', *Journal of Applied Psychology* 58 (1973), 313–17; P. S. Hundal, 'A Study of Entrepreneurial Motivation: Comparison of Fast- and Slow-Progressing Small Scale Industrial Entrepreneurs in Punjab, India', *Journal of Applied Psychology* 55 (1971), 317–23.

27 R. A. Clay, 'Green Is Good for You', *Monitor on Psychology*, April 2001, 40–42.

28 *The Times*, 'Hart Worldwide', 6 March 2005, TimesOnline.

29 J. S. Adams, 'Toward an Understanding of Inequity', *Journal of Abnormal and Social Psychology* 67 (1963), 422–36.

30 *Ibid.*; J. Greenberg, 'Approaching Equity and Avoiding Inequity in Groups and Organizations', in J. Greenberg and R. L. Cohen, eds., *Equity and Justice in Social Behavior* (New York: Academic Press, 1982), 389–435; J. Greenberg, 'Equity and Workplace Status: A Field Experiment', *Journal of Applied Psychology* 73 (1988), 606–13; R. T. Mowday, 'Equity Theory Predictions of Behavior in Organizations', in R. M. Steers and L. W. Porter, eds., *Motivation and Work Behavior* (New York: McGraw-Hill, 1987), 89–110.

31 Health & Safety Executive, 'Working Long Hours', 2003, HSL/2003/02.

32 A. Goldwasser, 'Inhuman Resources', ecompany.com, March 2001, 154–55.

33 E. A. Locke and G. P. Latham, *A Theory of Goal Setting and Task Performance* (Englewood Cliffs, NJ: Prentice Hall, 1990).

34 J. J. Donovan and D. J. Radosevich, 'The Moderating Role of Goal Commitment on the Goal Difficulty–Performance Relationship: A Meta-Analytic Review and Critical Analysis', *Journal of Applied Psychology* 83 (1998), 308–15; M. E. Tubbs, 'Goal Setting: A Meta-Analytic Examination of the Empirical Evidence', *Journal of Applied Psychology* 71 (1986), 474–83.

35 C. O. Longenecker, J. A. Scazzero and T. T. Stansfield, 'Quality Improvement through Team Goal Setting, Feedback, and Problem Solving: A Case Study', *International Journal of Quality & Reliability Management*, 11 (4) (1994), 45–52.

36 E. A. Locke, K. N. Shaw, L. M. Saari and G. P. Latham, 'Goal Setting and Task Performance: 1969–1980', *Psychological Bulletin* 90 (1981), 125–52.

37 P. C. Earley, T. Connolly and G. Ekegren, 'Goals, Strategy Development, and Task Performance: Some Limits on the Efficacy of Goal Setting', *Journal of Applied Psychology* 74 (1989), 24–33; R. Kanfer and P. L. Ackerman, 'Motivation and Cognitive Abilities: An Integrative/Aptitude–Treatment Interaction Approach to Skill Acquisition', *Journal of Applied Psychology* 74 (1989), 657–90.

38 W. C. Hamner, 'Reinforcement Theory and Contingency Management in Organizational Settings', in H. Tosi and W. C. Hamner, eds., *Organizational Behavior and Management: A Contingency Approach* (Chicago: St Clair Press, 1974).

39 B. F. Skinner, *Contingencies of Reinforcement* (New York: Appleton-Century-Crofts, 1969).

40 H. W. Weiss, 'Learning Theory and Industrial and Organizational Psychology', in M. D. Dunnette and L. M. Hough, *Handbook of Industrial and Organizational Psychology*, 1, 2nd ed. (Palo Alto, CA: Consulting Psychologists Press, 1990), 171–221.

41 Hamner, 'Reinforcement Theory and Contingency Management'.

42 F. Luthans and R. Kreitner, *Organizational Behavior Modification and Beyond* (Glenview, IL: Scott, Foresman, 1985); A. D. Stajkovic and F. Luthans, 'A Meta-Analysis of the Effects of Organizational Behavior Modification on Task Performance, 1975–95', *Academy of Management Journal* 40 (1997), 1122–49.

43 A. D. Stajkovic and F. Luthans, 'Behavioral Management and Task Performance in Organizations: Conceptual Background, Meta-Analysis, and Test of Alternative Models', *Personnel Psychology* 56 (2003), 155–94.

44 *Ibid.*; F. Luthans and A. D. Stajkovic, 'Reinforce for Performance: The Need to Go Beyond Pay and Even Rewards', *Academy of Management Executive* 13 (2) (1999), 49–56; G. Billikopf Enciina and M. V. Norton, 'Pay Method Affects Vineyard Pruner Performance', www.cnr.berkeley.edu/ucce50/ag-labor/7research/7calag05.htm.

45 A. Bandura, *Principles of Behavior Modification* (New York: Holt, Rinehart & Winston, 1969); A. Bandura, *Social Learning Theory* (Englewood Cliffs, NJ: Prentice Hall, 1977); T. R. V. Davis and F. Luthans, 'A Social Learning Approach to Organizational Behavior', *Academy of Management Review* 5 (1980), 281–90.

46 A. P. Goldstein and M. Sorcher, *Changing Supervisor Behaviors* (New York: Pergamon Press, 1974); Luthans and Kreitner, *Organizational Behavior Modification and Beyond*.

47 Bandura, *Social Learning Theory*; Davis and Luthans, 'A Social Learning Approach to Organizational Behavior'; Luthans and Kreitner, *Organizational Behavior Modification and Beyond*.

48 A. Bandura, 'Self-Reinforcement: Theoretical and Methodological Considerations', *Behaviorism* 4 (1976), 135–55.

49 P. Engardio, 'A Hothouse of High-Tech Talent', *BusinessWeek/21st Century Capitalism* (1994), 126.

50 A. Bandura, 'Self-Efficacy Mechanism in Human Agency', *American Psychologist* 37 (1982), 122–27; M. E. Gist and T. R. Mitchell, 'Self-Efficacy: A Theoretical Analysis of Its Determinants and Malleability', *Academy of Management Review* 17 (1992), 183–211.

51 E. E. Lawler, III, *Pay and Organization Development* (Reading, MA: Addison-Wesley, 1981).

52 'The Risky New Bonuses', *Newsweek*, January 16, 1995, 42.

53 Lawler, III, *Pay and Organization Development*.

54 *Ibid.*

55 J. F. Lincoln, *Incentive Management* (Cleveland: Lincoln Electric Company, 1951); R. Zager, 'Managing Guaranteed Employment', *Harvard Business Review* 56 (1978), 103–15.

56 Lawler, III, *Pay and Organization Development*.

57 'Stock Option', *Encarta World English Dictionary*, www.dictionary.msn.com.

14

Leadership

LEARNING OBJECTIVES

After studying this chapter, you should be able to:

☑ Explain what leadership is, when leaders are effective and ineffective and the sources of power that enable managers to be effective leaders.

☑ Identify the traits that show the strongest relationship to leadership, the behaviours leaders engage in and the limitations of the trait and behaviour models of leadership.

☑ Explain how contingency models of leadership enhance our understanding of effective leadership and management in organisations.

☑ Describe what transformational leadership is, and explain how managers can engage in it.

☑ Characterise the relationship between gender and leadership.

A Manager's Challenge

Steve Ballmer at Microsoft

For years, the business world has centred on who the best leaders are. Many executives strive to be the leader of a company to show their abilities and to gain the rewards that are often associated with effective leadership – on both sides of the Atlantic. Every year, business executives across the world nominate companies that they respect and are leaders in business. In 2005 a study by PricewaterhouseCoopers and the *Financial Times* asked 954 executives in 25 countries which they thought was the most respected company, and who the most respected business leaders. For the first time, Microsoft was top of the poll banishing the seven times winner GE to second place. While 24 out of the most respected companies were US-based, Europe was catching up. Germany was the second most-represented country with six businesses in the top 50 (Siemens ranked 10th and BMW 16th). The UK overtook Japan to take third place with four places in the top 50 (Virgin 27th and BA 28th). For the first time in the history of this poll, a UK company (BP) made it to the top 10. France was represented with L'Oréal at 17 and Sweden has, among others, IKEA at 26.

The measures that seemed to dominate were financial success and the quality of the product. Below we describe the exceptional leadership exhibited at Microsoft, which was described as 'innovative . . . and fulfilling the needs of society'. Bill Gates was voted the most admired business leader, and below we outline the leadership skills of Microsoft's chairman, who holds much of the responsibility for making Microsoft 'the company [that] is the first and best in the world'.[1]

How can a manager remake a 55,000-strong company to simultaneously promote efficiency and innovation?

When Steve Ballmer became CEO of Microsoft in 2000, he faced a daunting task that became even more daunting a few months into his tenure when the dot-com bust hit the IT world. With over 55,000 employees, Microsoft had grown into a huge corporation. Yet, under Bill Gates's leadership since its founding as a two-person start-up, Microsoft had been run and managed in a very centralised fashion from its earliest days through the 1990s.[2] When Ballmer took over as CEO, he realised that Microsoft needed to become more efficient, employees and managers needed to be empowered to make decisions, and internal structures and processes needed to be put in place to promote efficiency, timely decision making and innovation. Employee morale also needed a boost.[3] Microsoft needed a new vision – a vision for a new era in which stock options had lost much of their value, competition was fierce and Microsoft was a huge corporation that needed a new kind of leadership.

Ballmer has been described as 'the quintessential, larger-than-life, rah-rah leader, and the perfect foil for his geeky and erudite best buddy, Bill Gates'.[4] His extraverted nature led to many an antic at employee gatherings, and his excitement is infectious. Above all else, Ballmer really cares about Microsoft and its future, and dynamism, passion and enthusiasm are his trademarks.[5]

Ballmer has other important qualities that make him ideally suited to transform Microsoft. He is disciplined, process-oriented and analytical, and he is driven to find ways to measure and maximise performance, innovation and customer responsiveness and make sure that all employees receive important feedback, including that from customers. Most importantly, Ballmer realises that instituting processes to transform Microsoft and promote innovation and employee motivation is a complex and delicate task that must allow for both autonomy and empowerment and enable different units to co-ordinate their efforts to achieve synergies. One of the reasons decision making was so centralised under Gates' leadership was the overarching need for integration across units.[6] Gates feared that giving unit managers autonomy would result in a lack of co-ordination across units, co-ordination essential for developing integrated technologies to achieve Microsoft's vision of 'seamless computing'.[7]

By 2004, Ballmer had led sweeping changes at Microsoft. Microsoft had been divided into seven operating divisions, with division managers not only empowered to make decisions that would formerly be made by the CEO but also accountable for the financial performance of their divisions. Integration across divisions was achieved by a matrix type of organisation called *integrated innovation*. Software developers in each of the divisions know and keep in close contact with developers in other divisions, and a process called *software engineering strategy* laid out how responsibility for implementing a creative idea should be distributed among members of a development team from different divisions. An online performance appraisal system for employees was put in place (in the past, there was no formal performance appraisal process); stock options were replaced with grants of restricted stock; and employees were able to cash in some of their 'underwater' options through an arrangement with J. P. Morgan Chase, which led to over £185 million being distributed to employees with otherwise worthless options.[8]

Ballmer and Gates (now chairman of the board and chief software architect) share the same vision for Microsoft: to dramatically boost the perceived value of the company's technology by developing seamlessly integrated software that connects all kinds of electronics, PCs, communication devices and the Internet through one system.[9] Getting employees psyched and motivated to rally around this vision has been a top priority for Ballmer. Working at Microsoft was always more of a quest than a job in the old days. When the dot-com bubble burst, IT hit hard times and the economy declined, morale at Microsoft suffered and some valued employees left the company. Ballmer infused empowered employees and managers with a new sense of purpose and instituted processes to ensure that they know what needs to be done and receive the information and feedback to make it happen. Ballmer's new mission for Microsoft was 'to enable people and businesses throughout the world to realise their full potential' (which replaces the former mission, penned in 1978, of 'a computer on every desk and in every home').[10] Corporate goals included integration with customers and safe, reliable computing; values included honesty, integrity, respect and open communication.[11]

Overview

Steve Ballmer exemplifies the many facets of effective leadership. Chapter 1 explained that one of the four primary tasks of managers is *leading*. It should thus come as no surprise that leadership is a key ingredient in effective management. When leaders are effective, the people who follow them are highly motivated, committed and high-performing. When leaders are ineffective, the chances are good that their subordinates do not perform up to their capabilities, are demotivated and may also be dissatisfied. CEO Ballmer is a leader at the very top of an organisation, but leadership is an important ingredient for managerial success at all levels of organisations: senior management, middle management and first-line management. Leadership is a key ingredient for managerial success in large and small organisations.

In this chapter, the concept of leadership will be defined and explained. The major theoretical models of leadership will be examined in order to emphasise the most important factors that contribute to a manager becoming an effective leader. Initially trait and behavioural perspectives will be discussed which focus on what leaders are like, and what they do. Second, contingency models, **Fiedler's contingency model**, **path-goal theory** and the leader substitute model will be examined – each of which takes into account the complexity surrounding leadership and how *context* can make a difference to leader effectiveness. This chapter will then consider how managers can use transformational leadership to dramatically affect their organisations. By the end of this chapter, students will have a better understanding of the key challenges that managers face in order to become effective leaders.

The Nature of Leadership

There are many ways of looking at leadership, and many different interpretations of it. In researching this complex area of management, researchers have often come up with different definitions of what leadership is. According to Crainer in 1995, there were over 400 definitions of leadership, and 'Leadership is a veritable minefield of misunderstanding and difference through which theorists and practitioners must tread warily'.[12]

Research suggests that everyone has a theory, but although we know a lot about management we don't know much about leadership.[13] Everyone has their own concept of leadership but generally it involves getting people to do things willingly and influencing others to follow you. It can be an attribute of position or based on a function of personality. Leadership can also be seen as a behavioural category.

Leadership can be defined as 'a process in which leader and follower interact in a way that enables the leader to influence the actions of the follower in a non-coercive way, towards the achievements of certain aims or objectives'.[14] Often definitions infer that leadership is a *one-way process*, over-simplifying the real meaning of a leader. However Rollinson *et al.*'s definition does include a number of factors that should be considered. Being 'non-coercive' means that members are willing to be influenced. The nature of leadership should always be goal-directed so that subordinates know what they are expected to achieve. Followers also have other *socio-emotive* needs; by consenting to being influenced by the leader, they are anticipating that these needs will be satisfied. However, followers only *believe* these needs will be met, so the relationship initially is based on a perception of *trust* (willingness to be influenced) in the hope that they achieve their desired outcome.

When leaders are effective, the influence they exert over others helps a group or organisation to achieve its performance goals. When leaders are ineffective, their influence does not contribute to, and often detracts from, goal attainment. Steve Ballmer is taking multiple steps to inspire and motivate Microsoft employees and influence their actions towards achieving Microsoft's goals.

Beyond facilitating the attainment of performance goals, effective leadership increases an organisation's ability to meet all the contemporary challenges discussed throughout this book, including the need to obtain a competitive advantage, the need to foster ethical behaviour and the need to manage a diverse workforce fairly and equitably. Leaders who are able to exert influence over organisational members to help meet these goals increase their organisations' chances of success.

In considering the nature of leadership, leadership styles will be discussed to see how they affect managerial tasks and what influences culture can have on different styles. There will then be a section on the role of power within a leadership role and the various sources that power can be drawn from. Finally, the contemporary dynamic of empowerment and how it relates to effective leadership will be considered

Personal Leadership Style and Managerial Tasks

A manager's *personal leadership style* – the specific ways in which a manager chooses to influence other people – shapes the way that manager approaches planning, organising and controlling (the other principal tasks of managing). Consider Steve Ballmer's personal leadership style: he is dynamic, passionate and enthusiastic. Yet he is also disciplined, analytical and driven to boost Microsoft's performance and promote innovation. He trusts and respects his employees and empowers them to make decisions, but he also looks out for their well-being by, for example, arranging for them to cash in on 'underwater' stock options. He has a vision for the future and is making changes to make that vision a reality while transforming Microsoft to effectively and efficiently function as a large, innovative company that really cares about its customers.[15]

Managers at all levels and in all kinds of organisations have their own personal leadership styles that determine not only how they lead their subordinates but also how they perform the other management tasks. Claire Owen, managing director of Stopgap, one of the UK's 'best companies to work for', takes a hands-on approach to leadership. Claire is the founder and sole authority of her own unique recruitment agency which she started in 1993. She maintains that the success of leadership is 'all about cultural fit'. She only employs people who are smart, passionate, hard working and fun, and that's what her business portrays. Her employees cannot speak more highly of her and say they have great faith in her. One employee commented: 'She is a leader who has built her reputation by building trust and respect for her staff. I have never know anyone quite like her and feel honoured to work for her.'

As discussed in Chapter 12, Gore are renowned for not only producing high performance but also for an unprecedented 'supportive ethos' allowing people to reach their actual potential. This means that at Gore leaders become leaders by leading, and then attract followers and others with similar talents and passions. Leaders are known in this organisation as 'talent magnets' and are elected through their own credibility of what they do and what they contribute to the company. Developing an effective personal leadership style often is a challenge for managers at all levels in an organisation. This challenge is often heightened when times are tough – due, for example, to an economic downturn or a decline in customer demand. The dot-com bust and the slowing economy in the early 2000s provided many leaders with just such a challenge.

While leading is one of the four principal tasks of managing, a distinction is often made between *managers* and *leaders*. Generally, one can say that managers are more likely to be given formal authority in terms of headship over their subordinates who allow them to direct their actions; this may be seen as a 'top-down' approach. However the leader–follower relationship is more fragile, as it is based on reciprocity and trust. Leaders have to earn their authority through influence, which is more of a 'bottom-up' approach. Research has acknowledged the interrelationship between leadership and management, and claimed that in order to be an effective manager one often has to have the ability to lead: management and leadership are inextricably linked.[16]

Others argue that not only is a manager required to lead but that leadership is in fact a subcategory of management, albeit distinguishable from other factors of management. Miller, Catt and Carlson distinguished between management and leadership by describing the job of a manager as utilising human equipment and information resources to achieve objectives. Leadership involves getting things done through others. In other words, you lead people, you manage things.[17]

The personal leadership style of a company's founders often has an enduring effect on an organisation, as indicated in Case 14.1.

Case 14.1: Developing A-team leadership skills

The personnel director for Tesco UK (Britain's top supermarket) Judith Nelson seems to have what it takes to be a great leader. In a review of leadership skills, Nelson was asked what the secret of her success was – her reply: 'by just being myself'.[18]

Judith Nelson oversees 75 employees who report to her and is in charge of the HR needs of 260,000 people at Tesco so she needs to lead from all directions – up, down, across and sometimes upside down! This is Nelson's *raison d'être* – by being herself people want to follow her, and believe she is genuine by the example she sets. People who are good leaders do not sit on the side-lines and are not afraid to 'get their hands dirty'. Of course, one needs to be a good communicator, empathiser and motivator of people, but the key to Nelson's success is that as well as these behaviours she believes that she is 'authentic'. She adapts her style of ▶

▶ leadership to suit the person, context and time that her skills are needed. She would tailor her body language, communication and interpersonal skills very differently if she were trying to achieve commitment from senior directors for funding a new project as opposed to attempting to persuade shop-floor workers to complete a job-satisfaction survey. Nelson advocates that if you treat every person as an individual – 'like they're the very first person you've met that day' – then you are more likely to come across as genuine. People who treat people as they expect to be treated themselves will command more respect and trust, and hence be perceived as better leaders.

A new text on leadership *Why Should Anyone be Led by You?*[19] confirms such sentiments. (Coincidentally, Nelson said in the interview that she had read this book.) The authors maintain that in order to be an 'authentic' leader one needs to have great self-knowledge. They need to know what they are like, how they differ from others and what their personal traits are. Authentic leaders learn to utilise those differences in such a way as to capitalise on the good and not allowing the not so good to 'get to them' but always adapt and change depending on what the goal is and who they're trying to lead. Good examples of such authentic leaders are Bill Gates, Richard Branson of Virgin and Michael Dell of Dell Computers. They all have the ability to adapt their style to suit the *social context*, which is their key to success.

Leadership Styles Across Cultures

Some evidence suggests that leadership styles vary not only among individuals but also among countries or cultures. Hofstede's research on *cross-cultural differences* in leadership styles can be traced back to basic differences in cultural programming.[20] Some research indicates that European managers tend to be more humanistic or people-oriented than both Japanese and American managers. According to Hofstede's global framework of cultures, those countries that are further along the *collectivistic continuum* (e.g. China, Denmark, Japan and Singapore) tend to be motivated towards working in groups rather than individually and tend to be less egocentric, so the importance of individuals' own personalities, needs and desires is minimised. Organisations in the US, and to some extent the UK, tend to be very profit-oriented and thus tend to downplay the importance of individual employees' needs and desires. Many countries in Europe have a more individualistic perspective than Japan and a more humanistic perspective than the US, and this may result in some European managers being more people-oriented than their Japanese or American counterparts. European managers, for example, tend to be reluctant to lay off employees, and when a layoff is absolutely necessary, they take careful steps to make it as painless as possible.[21]

Another cross-cultural difference occurs in *time horizons*. Managers in any one country often differ in their time horizons, but there are also cultural differences. For example, US organisations tend to have a short-term profit orientation, and so US managers' personal leadership styles emphasise short-term performance. Japanese organisations tend to have a long-term growth orientation, so Japanese managers' personal leadership styles emphasise long-term performance. Justus Mische, a personnel manager at the European organisation Hoechst, suggests that 'Europe, at least the big international firms in Europe, have a philosophy between the Japanese, long term, and the United States, short term'.[22] Research has measured performance individually or in groups of Asian and Caucasian students dependent upon cultural orientation against leadership style. Their results imply that style of leadership can be perceived differently by followers and can have very different effects on followers' performance and demotivation across collectivists and individualists. Such findings have implications for how leaders *manage diversity* and what tasks they ask different cultural groups to perform. Motivating and satisfying the social needs of collectivists may be achieved by allowing these employees simply to work together in groups. The fact that differences in leadership style can drastically affect follower performance depending on cultural differences also has implications for how organisations recruit and train leaders to more effectively influence and guide diverse teams.

Power: The Key to Leadership

No matter what one's leadership style, a key component of effective leadership can be found in the *power* the leader has to affect other people's behaviour and get them to act in certain ways.[23] There are several types of power: legitimate, reward, coercive, expert and referent power (Fig. 14.1).[24] Effective leaders should take steps to ensure that they have sufficient levels of each type, and that they use the power they have in beneficial ways.

Legitimate power

Legitimate power is the authority a manager has by virtue of his or her *position in an organisation's hierarchy*. Personal leadership style often influences how a manager exercises legitimate power. Take the case of Carol Loray, who is a first-line manager in a greeting card company and

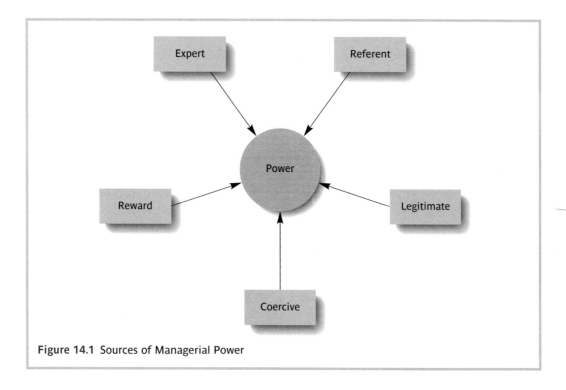

Figure 14.1 Sources of Managerial Power

leads a group of 15 artists and designers. Loray has the legitimate power to hire new employees, assign projects to the artists and designers, monitor their work and appraise their performance. She uses this power effectively. She always makes sure that her project assignments match the interests of her subordinates as much as possible so that they will enjoy their work. She monitors their work to make sure they are on track, but does not engage in close supervision, which can hamper creativity. She makes sure her performance appraisals are developmental, providing concrete advice for areas where improvements could be made. Recently, Loray negotiated with her manager to increase her legitimate power so that now she can initiate and develop proposals for new card lines.

Reward power

Reward power is the ability of a manager to give or withhold *tangible rewards* (pay rises, bonuses, choice job assignments) and *intangible* rewards (verbal praise, a pat on the back, respect). As discussed in Chapter 13, members of an organisation are motivated to perform at a high level by a variety of rewards. Being able to give or withhold rewards based on perform-ance is a major source of power that allows managers to have a highly motivated workforce. Managers of salespeople in particular department stores, in car dealerships like DaimlerChrysler and Ford and in travel agencies, often use their reward power to motivate their subordinates. Subordinates in organisations such as these often receive *commissions* on whatever they sell and rewards for the quality of their customer service, which motivate them to do the best they can.

Effective managers use their reward power in such a way that subordinates feel that their reward signals that they are doing a good job and their efforts are appreciated. Ineffective managers use rewards in a more controlling manner (wielding the 'stick' instead of offering the 'carrot') that signals to subordinates that the manager has the upper hand. Managers also can take steps to increase their reward power. Carol Loray had the legitimate power to appraise her subordinates' performance, but she lacked the reward power to distribute rises and end-of-year bonuses until she discussed with her own manager why this would be a valuable motivational tool for her to use. Loray now receives a pool of money each year for salary increases and bonuses, and has the reward power to distribute them as she sees fit.

Coercive power

Coercive power is the ability of a manager to punish others. Punishment can range from verbal reprimands to reductions in pay or working hours to actual dismissal. In Chapter 13, we discussed how punishment can have negative side-effects such as resentment and retaliation, and should be used only when absolutely necessary (for example, to curtail a dangerous behaviour). Man-agers who rely heavily on coercive power tend to be ineffective as leaders and sometimes even get fired themselves. One example of an inefficient use of coercive power is William J. Fife. He was appointed CEO to a manufacturer of factory equipment. In meetings, Fife often verbally criticised, attacked and embarrassed senior managers. Realising how destructive Fife's use of punish-ment was for them and the company, these managers complained to the board of directors, who, after a careful consideration of the issues, asked Fife to resign.[25] A different example is TV chef Gordon Ramsey, who continually fuels discussion about his leadership style. Most people would accuse the chef of inappropriately using his power to manage and lead his kitchen staff. However, recently an HR consultant from the Hay Group has argued that the use of coercive management techniques is not all bad, if it is used in conjunction with other leadership and management techniques, such as Ramsey's continuing attempts to build team spirit and his openness to answer questions. Excessive use of coercive power seldom produces high performance and is questionable ethically, but may at times be useful.

Sometimes coercive power can amount to a form of mental abuse, robbing workers of their dignity and causing excessive levels of stress. Over-use of coercive power can even result in dangerous working conditions. Better results – and, importantly, an ethical workplace that respects employees' dignity – can be obtained by using reward power.

Expert power

Expert power is based on the special knowledge, skills and expertise that a leader possesses. The nature of expert power varies, depending on the leader's level in the hierarchy. First-level and middle managers often have technical expertise relevant to the tasks that their subordinates perform. Their expert power gives them considerable influence over subordinates. Carol Loray has expert power: She is an artist herself and has drawn and designed some of her company's top-selling greeting cards.

Some senior managers derive expert power from their technical expertise. Craig Barret, CEO of Intel, has a PhD in materials science from Stanford University and is very knowledgeable about the ins and outs of Intel's business – producing semiconductors and microprocessors.[26] Similarly, Bill Gates, chairman of Microsoft, and CEO Steve Ballmer have expertise in software design; Tachi Yamada, executive director and chairman of R&D at GlaxoSmithKline (see Chapter 7), has a degree in medicine and was an active researcher and chairman of the Internal Medicine Department of the University of Michigan Medical School. Many senior-level managers, however, lack technical expertise and derive their expert power from their abilities as decision makers, planners and strategists. Jack Welch, well-known leader and the former CEO of General Electric, summed it up this way: 'The basic thing that we at the top of the company know is that we don't know the business. What we have, I hope, is the ability to allocate resources, people, and dollars.'[27]

Effective leaders take steps to ensure that they have an adequate amount of expert power to perform their leadership roles. They may obtain additional training or education in their fields, make sure they keep up to date with the latest developments and changes in technology, stay abreast of changes in their fields through involvement in professional associations and read widely to be aware of key changes in the organisation's task and general environments. Expert power tends to be best used in a guiding or coaching manner rather than in an arrogant, high-handed way.

Referent power

Referent power is more informal than the other kinds of power. Referent power is a function of the personal characteristics of a leader: it is the power that comes from subordinates' and co-workers' respect, admiration and loyalty. Leaders who are likable and whom subordinates wish to use as a role model are especially likely to possess referent power. Steve Walker, who is CEO of Tower Homes (this year's Number One small company to work for in the UK), is the role model behind the company's success. He explains: 'I'm evangelical about employee engagement', and this is rewarded by his employees' respect and the fact that 92 per cent of them would recommend Tower Homes as a company to work for.[28]

Reaction Time

1. Describe the steps managers can take to increase their power and ability to be effective leaders.

2. Think of specific situations in which it might be especially important for a manager to engage in consideration and in initiating structure.

3. For your current job or for a future job you expect to hold, describe what your supervisor could do to strongly motivate you to be a top performer.

4. Discuss why managers might want to change the behaviours they engage in, given their situation, their subordinates and the nature of the work being done. Do you think that managers are able readily to change their leadership behaviours? Why or why not?

Empowerment: An Ingredient in Modern Management

More and more managers today are incorporating into their personal leadership styles an aspect that at first glance seems to be the opposite of being a leader. Chapter 1 described how *empowerment* – the process of giving employees at all levels in the organisation the authority to make decisions, making them responsible for their outcomes, improving quality and cutting costs – is becoming increasingly popular in organisations. When leaders empower their subordinates, the subordinates typically take over some of the responsibilities, decisions and authority that used to reside with the leader or manager – such as the right to reject parts that do not meet quality standards, the right to check their own work and the right to schedule work activities.

Empowerment might seem to be the opposite of effective leadership because managers are allowing subordinates to take a more active role in leading. In actuality, however, empowerment can contribute to effective leadership, for three reasons:

■ Empowerment increases a manager's ability to get things done because the manager has the support and help of subordinates who may have special knowledge of work tasks.

■ Empowerment often increases workers' involvement, motivation and commitment, and this helps ensure that they are working toward organisational goals.

■ Empowerment gives managers more time to concentrate on their own pressing concerns because they spend less time on day-to-day supervisory activities.

Effective managers like Steve Ballmer realise the benefits of empowerment. The personal leadership style of managers who empower subordinates often entails developing their ability to make good decisions as well as being their guide, coach and source of inspiration. Empowerment is a popular trend in the UK at companies as diverse as Red Letter Days (a unique provider of unforgettable gifts) and Innocent (a producer of 'real fruit' smoothies). Empowerment is also significant around the world – for instance, companies in South Korea (such as Samsung, Hyundai and Daewoo), in which decision making was typically centralised with the founding families, are now empowering managers at lower levels to make decisions.[29]

Chief executive Rolf Eriksen of H&M (see Case 1.1) has managed to bring the company to record profitability through recruiting and empowering major designers to enter into collaborations with the company.[30]

Trait and Behaviour Models of Leadership

Leading is such an important process in all organisations – non-profit organisations, government agencies and schools, as well as for-profit corporations – that it has been extensively researched. Early approaches to leadership, called the *trait model* and the *behaviour model*, sought to determine what effective leaders were like as people and what they did that made them so effective.

The Trait Model

The trait model of leadership focused on identifying the *personal characteristics* that cause effective leadership. Researchers thought that effective leaders must have certain personal qualities that set them apart from ineffective leaders and from people who never become leaders at all. Decades of research (beginning in the 1930s) and hundreds of studies indicate that certain personal characteristics do appear to be associated with effective leadership (see Table 14.1 for a list of these).[31] Notice that although this model is called the 'trait' model, some of the personal characteristics that it identifies are not personality traits *per se* but are rather concerned with a leader's skills, abilities, knowledge and expertise. Steve Ballmer certainly appears to possess many of these characteristics – intelligence, knowledge and expertise, self-confidence, high energy and integrity and honesty. Leaders who do not possess these traits may be ineffective.

Traits alone are not the key to understanding leader effectiveness, however. Some effective leaders do not possess all of these traits, and some leaders who do possess them are not effective in their leadership roles. This lack of a consistent relationship between leader traits and leader effectiveness led researchers to shift their attention away from traits and to search for new explanations for effective leadership. Rather than focusing on what leaders are *like* (the traits they possess), researchers began looking at what effective leaders actually *do* – in other words, at the behaviours that allow effective leaders to influence their subordinates to achieve group and organisational goals.

Table 14.1 Traits and personal characteristics related to effective leadership

Trait	Description
Intelligence	Helps managers understand complex issues and solve problems
Knowledge and expertise	Helps managers make good decisions and discover ways to increase efficiency and effectiveness
Dominance	Helps managers influence their subordinates to achieve organisational goals
Self-confidence	Contributes to managers' effectively influencing subordinates and persisting when faced with obstacles or difficulties
High energy	Helps managers deal with the demands they face
Tolerance of stress	Helps managers deal with uncertainty and make difficult decisions
Integrity and honesty	Helps managers behave ethically and earn their subordinates' trust and confidence
Maturity	Helps managers avoid acting selfishly, control their feelings and admit when they have made a mistake

The Behaviour Model

After extensive study in the 1940s and 1950s, researchers at Ohio State University identified two basic kinds of leader behaviours in which many leaders in the US, Germany and other countries engaged to influence their subordinates: **consideration** and **initiating structure**.[32]

Consideration

Leaders engage in *consideration* when they show their subordinates that they trust, respect and care about them. Managers who truly look out for the well-being of their subordinates, and do what they can to help them feel good and enjoy their work, perform consideration behaviours. Steve Ballmer engaged in consideration when he arranged for employees to receive cash for their 'underwater' stock options.

Initiating structure

Leaders engage in *initiating structure* when they take steps to make sure that work gets done, subordinates perform their jobs acceptably and the organisation is efficient and effective. Assigning tasks to individuals or work groups, letting subordinates know what is expected of them, deciding how work should be done, making schedules, encouraging adherence to rules and regulations and motivating subordinates to do a good job are all examples of initiating structure. Steve Ballmer engaged in initiating structure when he divided Microsoft into divisions, instituted a formal performance appraisal system and revamped the compensation system.

Initiating structure and consideration are independent leader behaviours. Leaders can be high on both, low on both, or high on one and low on the other. As indicated in Case 14.2, many effective leaders like Fujio Cho of Toyota engage in both of these behaviours.

Case 14.2: Toyota is on a roll

Toyota President Fujio Cho is driven by speed and flexibility; cost-efficient and flexible production lines that can switch between multiple car models to meet changes in customer demand are his mantra. Toyota is close to becoming the third-largest automobile manufacturer in the US (Daimler-Chrysler currently has the Number Three spot), has sales of over £78 billion and has better profit margins than GM, Ford and Daimler-Chrysler.[33] Cho is leading a major transformation of Toyota to develop a global, flexible manufacturing system for making cars at record speed, with minimal defects and in a cost-effective manner. Toyota has £17 billion in cash and securities to weather any unforeseen problems: as Cho puts it, 'This is a company that does not fear failure.'[34] On all counts, Cho is effectively leading Toyota on a path to dominate the global car industry.[35]

Cho emphasises consideration in his modest, cheerful approach to being on top of every problem and issue that Toyota faces. He is down to earth and genial. When he led the opening of Toyota's biggest factory he often worked alongside employees on the factory floor and expressed appreciation for the work that they were doing. He also became involved in the local community and was a speaker at Rotary Club meetings. His concern for people shows through in his smile and affable manner of dealing with employees and letting them know he respects and cares about them.[36]

Cho has been engaging in initiating structure as he leads Toyota toward the goal of having 15 per cent of total global automobile sales by 2010. He spearheaded a programme with suppliers to dramatically reduce the number of steps in making car parts and cars, and reduced Toyota's costs (without layoffs or plant shutdowns) by over £1.4 billion. The flexible, global manufacturing system he is developing will enable Toyota factories around the world to both customise cars for their local markets and make cars for other markets where customer demand exceeds supply, all in a speedy, cost-efficient manner. Cho instituted Toyota's Construction of Cost Competitiveness for the 21st Century (CCC21) programme with the goal of reducing prices of components for new car models by 30 per cent. *Kaisen*, Toyota's renowned system of continuous improvement, is being taken to another level by Cho, who is striving to make each and every Toyota plant capable of producing high-quality vehicles at low costs. Cho's consideration and initiating structure are helping transform Toyota into a car maker to be reckoned with.[37]

Leadership researchers have identified leader behaviours similar to consideration and initiating structure. Researchers at the University of Michigan, for example, identified two categories of leadership behaviours, *employee-centred* behaviours and *job-oriented* behaviours that roughly correspond, respectively, to consideration and initiating structure.[38] Models of leadership popular with consultants also tend to zero in on these two kinds of behaviours. Robert Blake and Jane Mouton's Managerial Grid focuses on *concern for people* (similar to consideration) and *concern for production* (similar to initiating structure). Blake and Mouton advise that effective leadership often requires both a high level of concern for people and a high level of concern for production.[39] Paul Hersey and Kenneth Blanchard's model focuses on *supportive behaviours* (similar to consideration) and *task-oriented behaviours* (similar to initiating structure). According to Hersey and Blanchard, leaders need to consider the nature of their subordinates when trying to determine the extent to which they should perform these two behaviours.[40]

You might expect that effective leaders and managers would perform both kinds of behaviours, but research has found that this is not necessarily the case. The relationship between performance of consideration and initiating-structure behaviours and leader effectiveness is not clear-cut. Some leaders are effective even when they do not perform consideration or initiating-structure behaviours, and some leaders are ineffective even when they do perform both. Like the trait model of leadership, the behaviour model alone cannot explain leader effectiveness. Realising this, researchers began building more complicated models of leadership, focused not only on the leader and what he or she does, but also on the *situation* or *context* in which leadership occurs.

Contingency Models of Leadership

Simply possessing certain traits or performing certain behaviours does not ensure that a manager will be an effective leader in all situations calling for leadership. Some managers who seem to possess the 'right' traits and perform the 'right' behaviours turn out to be ineffective leaders. Managers lead in a wide variety of situations and organisations and have various kinds of subordinates performing diverse tasks in a multiplicity of environmental contexts. Given the wide variety of situations in which leadership occurs, what makes a manager an effective leader in one situation (such as certain traits or certain behaviours) is not necessarily what that manager needs to be equally effective in a different one. An effective army general might not be an effective university president; an effective manager of a restaurant might not be an effective manager of a clothing store; an effective coach of a football team might not be an effective manager of a fitness centre; an effective first-line manager in a manufacturing company might not be an effective middle manager. The traits or behaviours that may contribute to a manager's being an effective leader in one situation may actually result in the same manager being an ineffective leader in another one.

Contingency models of leadership take into account the situation or context within which leadership occurs. According to contingency models, whether or not a manager is an effective leader is the result of the interplay between what the manager is *like*, what he or she *does* and the *situation* in which leadership takes place. Contingency models propose that whether a leader who possesses certain traits or performs certain behaviours is effective depends on, or is *contingent* on, the situation or context. In this section, we discuss three prominent contingency models developed to shed light on what makes managers effective leaders: Fred E. Fiedler's contingency model, Robert House's path–goal theory and the leader substitutes model. As you will see, these leadership models are complementary; each focuses on a somewhat different aspect of effective leadership in organisations.

Fiedler's Contingency Model

Fred E. Fiedler was among the first leadership researchers to acknowledge that effective leadership is contingent on, or depends on, the characteristics of the leader *and* of the situation. Fiedler's contingency model helps explain why a manager may be an effective leader in one situation and ineffective in another; it also suggests which kinds of managers are likely to be most effective in which situations.[41]

Leader style

As with the trait approach, Fiedler hypothesised that personal characteristic can influence leader effectiveness. He used the term *leader style* to refer to a manager's characteristic approach to leadership and identified two basic leader styles: relationship-oriented and task-oriented. All managers can be described as having one style or the other.

Relationship-oriented leaders are primarily concerned with developing good relationships with their subordinates and being liked by them. Relationship-oriented managers focus on having *high-quality interpersonal relationships* with subordinates. This does not mean, however, that the job does not get done when relationship-oriented leaders are at the helm. But it does mean that the quality of interpersonal relationships with subordinates is a prime concern.

Task-oriented leaders are primarily concerned with ensuring that subordinates perform at a high level. Task-oriented managers focus on *task accomplishment* and making sure the job gets done.

In his research, Fiedler measured leader style by asking leaders to rate the co-worker with whom they have had the most difficulty working (called the *least-preferred co-worker* or *LPC*) on a number of dimensions, such as whether the person is boring or interesting, gloomy or cheerful, enthusiastic or unenthusiastic, co-operative or uncooperative. Relationship-oriented leaders tend to describe the LPC in relatively positive terms; their concern for good relationships leads them to think about others in positive terms. Task-oriented leaders tend to describe the LPC in negative terms; their concern for task accomplishment causes them to think badly about others who make getting the job done difficult. Relationship-oriented and task-oriented leaders are sometimes referred to as high-LPC and low-LPC leaders, respectively.

Situational characteristics

According to Fiedler, leadership style is an enduring characteristic: managers cannot change their style, nor can they adopt different styles in different kinds of situations. With this in mind, he identified three situational characteristics that are important determinants of how favourable a situation is for leading: **leader–member relations**, **task structure** and **position power**. When a situation is favourable for leading, it is relatively easy for a manager to influence subordinates so that they perform at a high level and contribute to organisational efficiency and effectiveness. In a situation unfavourable for leading, it is much more difficult for a manager to exert influence.

Leader–member relations

The first situational characteristic that Fiedler described, leader–member relations, is the extent to which followers like, trust and are loyal to their leader. Situations are more favourable for leading when leader–member relations are good.

Task structure

The second situational characteristic that Fiedler described, task structure, is the extent to which the work to be performed is clear-cut so that a leader's subordinates know what needs to be accomplished, and how to go about doing it. When task structure is high, the situation is favourable for leading. When task structure is low, goals may be vague, subordinates may be unsure of what they should be doing or how they should do it and the situation is unfavourable for leading.

Task structure was low for Geraldine Laybourne when she was a senior manager at Nickelodeon, the children's television network. It was never precisely clear what would appeal to her young viewers, whose tastes can change dramatically, or how to motivate her subordinates to come up with creative and novel ideas.[42] In contrast, Herman Mashaba, founder and owner of Black Like Me, a hair care products company based in South Africa, seems to have relatively high task structure in his leadership situation. His company's goals are to produce and sell inexpensive hair care products to native Africans, and managers accomplish these goals by using simple yet appealing packaging and distributing the products through neighbourhood beauty salons.[43]

Position power

The third situational characteristic that Fiedler described, *position power*, is the amount of legitimate, reward and coercive power a leader has by virtue of his or her position in an organisation. Leadership situations are more favourable for leading when position power is strong.

Combining leader style and the situation

By taking all possible combinations of good and poor leader–member relations, high and low task structure and strong and weak position power, Fiedler identified eight leadership situations, which vary in their favourability for leading (Fig. 14.2). After extensive research, he determined that relationship-oriented leaders were most effective in moderately favourable situations (situations IV, V, VI and VII in Fig. 14.2) and task-oriented leaders are most effective in very favourable (situations I, II and III) or very unfavourable situations (situation VIII).

Putting the contingency model into practice

Recall that, according to Fiedler, leader style is an enduring characteristic that managers cannot change. This suggests that, to be effective, either managers need to be placed in leadership situations that fit their style or situations need to be changed to suit the managers. Situations can be

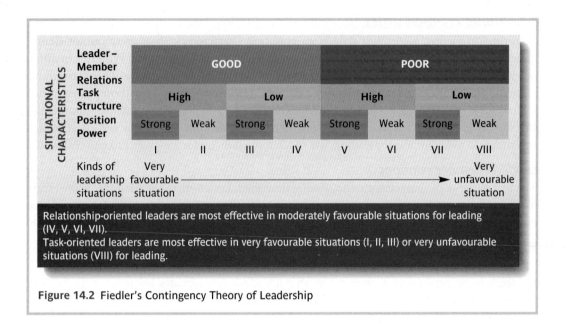

Figure 14.2 Fiedler's Contingency Theory of Leadership

changed, for example, by giving a manager more position power or taking steps to increase task structure, such as by clarifying goals.

Take the case of Mark Compton, a relationship-oriented leader employed by a small construction company, who was in a very unfavourable situation and having a difficult time leading his construction crew. His subordinates did not trust him to look out for their well-being (poor leader–member relations); the construction jobs he supervised tended to be novel and complex (low task structure); and he had no control over the rewards and disciplinary actions his subordinates received (weak position power). Recognising the need to improve matters, Compton's supervisor gave him the power to reward crew members with bonuses and overtime work as he saw fit and to discipline crew members for poor-quality work and unsafe on-the-job behaviour. As his leadership situation improved to moderately favourable, so too did Compton's effectiveness as a leader and the performance of his crew.

Research studies tend to support some aspects of Fiedler's model but also suggest that, like most theories, it needs some modifications.[44] Some researchers have questioned what the LPC scale really measures. Others find fault with the model's premise that leaders cannot alter their styles. It is likely that at least some leaders can diagnose the situation they are in and, when their style is inappropriate for the situation, modify their style so that it is more in line with what the leadership situation calls for.

House's Path–goal Theory

In what he called *path–goal theory*, leadership researcher Robert House focused on what leaders can do to motivate their subordinates to achieve group and organisational goals.[45] The premise of path–goal theory is that effective leaders motivate subordinates to achieve goals by (1) clearly identifying the *outcomes* that subordinates are trying to obtain from the workplace, (2) *rewarding* subordinates with these outcomes for high performance and the attainment of work goals and (3) clarifying for subordinates the *paths* leading to the attainment of work *goals*. Path–goal theory is a contingency model because it proposes that the steps managers should take to motivate subordinates depend on both the nature of the subordinates and the type of work they do.

Based on the expectancy theory of motivation (Chapter 13), path–goal theory provides managers with three guidelines to follow to be effective leaders:

1. *Find out what outcomes your subordinates are trying to obtain from their jobs and the organisation* These outcomes can range from satisfactory pay and job security to reasonable working hours and interesting and challenging job assignments. After identifying these outcomes, the manager should have the *reward power* needed to distribute or withhold the outcomes. Mark Crane, for example, is the deputy head teacher of a large elementary school. Crane determined that the teachers he leads are trying to obtain the following outcomes from their jobs: pay rises, autonomy in the classroom and the choice of which grades they teach. Crane had reward power for the latter two outcomes, but the school's head teacher determined how the pool of money for rises was to be distributed each year. Because Crane was the first-line manager who led the teachers and was most familiar with their performance, he asked the head teacher (his boss) to give him some say in determining pay rises. Realising that this made a lot of sense, his head teacher gave Crane full power to distribute rises and requested only that Crane review his decisions with him prior to informing the teachers about them.

2. *Reward subordinates for high performance and goal attainment with the outcomes they desire* The teachers and administrators at Crane's school considered several dimensions of teacher performance to be critical to achieving their goal of providing high-quality education: excellent in-class instruction, special programmes to enhance student interest and learning (such as science and computer projects) and availability for meetings with parents to discuss their children's progress and special needs. Crane distributed pay rises to the teachers based on the extent to which they performed highly on each of these dimensions. The top-performing teachers were given first choice of grade assignments and also had practically complete autonomy in their classrooms.

3. *Clarify the paths to goal attainment for subordinates, remove any obstacles to high performance and express confidence in subordinates' capabilities* This does not mean that a manager needs to tell subordinates what to do. Rather, it means that a manager needs to make sure that subordinates are clear about what they should be trying to accomplish and have the capabilities, resources and confidence levels needed to be successful. Crane made sure that all the teachers understood the importance of the three targeted goals and asked them whether, to reach them, they needed any special resources or supplies for their classes. Crane also gave additional coaching and guidance to teachers who seemed to be struggling. For example, Patrick Conolly, in his first year of teaching after graduate school, was unsure about how to use special projects in a third-grade class and how to react to parents who were critical. Conolly's actual teaching was excellent, but he felt insecure about how he was doing on this dimension. To help build Conolly's confidence, Crane told him that he truly thought he could be one of the school's top teachers (which was true). He gave Conolly some ideas about special projects that worked particularly well with the third grade, such as a writing project. Crane also role-played teacher–parent interactions with Conolly. Conolly played the role of a particularly dissatisfied or troubled parent, while Crane played the role of a teacher trying to solve the underlying problem while making the parent feel that his or her child's needs were being met. Crane's efforts to clarify the paths to goal attainment for Conolly paid off: within two years the local parent, teacher and student organisation (PTS) had voted him teacher of the year.

Path–goal theory identifies four kinds of leadership behaviours that can motivate subordinates:

- *Directive behaviours* are similar to initiating structure and include setting goals, assigning tasks, showing subordinates how to complete tasks and taking concrete steps to improve performance.

- *Supportive behaviours* are similar to consideration and include expressing concern for subordinates and looking out for their best interests.

- *Participative behaviours* give subordinates a say in matters and decisions that affect them.

- *Achievement-oriented behaviours* motivate subordinates to perform at the highest level possible – by, for example, setting very challenging goals, expecting that they be met and believing in subordinates' capabilities.

Which of these behaviours should managers use to lead effectively? The answer to this question depends, or is contingent on, the nature of the subordinates and the kind of work they do.

Directive behaviours may be beneficial when subordinates are having difficulty completing assigned tasks, but they may be detrimental when subordinates are independent thinkers who work best when left alone. *Supportive* behaviours are often advisable when subordinates are experiencing high levels of stress. *Participative* behaviours can be particularly effective when subordinates' support for a decision is required. *Achievement-oriented* behaviours may increase motivation levels of highly capable subordinates who are bored from having too few challenges, but they might backfire if used with subordinates who are already pushed to their limit.

Effective managers seem to have a knack for determining what kinds of leadership behaviours are likely to work in different situations and result in increased effectiveness (Case 14.3).

Case 14.3: **Supporting creativity**

What do playing in an orchestra and designing high-status automobiles have in common? Both activities require creativity from artistic individuals. Effectively leading workers who are engaged in creative activities can be a challenge – too much initiating structure can inhibit their creativity. Always outspoken and inventive, the London Symphony Orchestra (LSO) has led the way in orchestral development and initiative. Valery Gergiev is to take over as principal conductor of the LSO in 2007, succeeding the great Sir Colin Davis. Gergiev made his London debut in 1988 and is truly inspirational as a leader; alongside his unbelievable energy, passion for music and great qualities of friendship and idealism, this has forged him a unique place in the world of music. Gergiev realises that, rather than trying to control his musicians, he has to learn to work with them and this emphasises a positive style of leadership.[46]

This approach to leading creative workers is applied in other countries as well. Chris Bangle, who heads BMW's global design effort in Munich, Germany, takes great pains to shield the creative designers of BMW interiors and exteriors from critical comments or negative feedback from others in the organisation, such as market analysts and engineers. Rather than receiving critiques, designers above all else need support from leadership and the freedom to explore different designs, as well as encouraging direction to reach closure in a reasonably timely fashion.[47] Bangle sees this kind of supportive leadership as key to BMW's competitive advantage in designing cars like 'moving works of art that express the driver's love of quality'.[48]

The Leader Substitutes Model

The *leader substitutes model* suggests that leadership is sometimes unnecessary because substitutes for leadership are present. A **leadership substitute** is something that acts in place of the influence of a leader and makes leadership unnecessary. This model suggests that under certain conditions managers do not have to play a leadership role – that members of an organisation can sometimes perform highly without a manager exerting influence over them. The leader substitutes model is a contingency model because it suggests that in some situations leadership is unnecessary.

Take the case of David Cotsonas, who teaches English at a foreign-language school in Cyprus, an island in the Mediterranean Sea. Cotsonas is fluent in Greek, English and French, is an excellent teacher and is highly motivated. Many of his students are businesspeople who have some rudimentary English skills and wish to increase their fluency to be able to conduct more of their business in English. He enjoys not only teaching them English but also learning about the work they do, and he often keeps in touch with his students after they finish his classes. Cotsonas meets with the director of the school twice a year to discuss semi-annual class schedules and enrolments.

With practically no influence from a leader, Cotsonas is a highly motivated top performer at the school. In his situation, leadership is unnecessary because substitutes for leadership are present. Cotsonas's teaching expertise, his motivation and his enjoyment of his work all are substitutes for the influence of a leader – in this case, the school's director. If the school's director were to try to exert influence over the way Cotsonas goes about performing his job, Cotsonas would probably resent this infringement on his autonomy and it is unlikely that his performance would improve because he is already one of the school's best teachers.

As in Cotsonas' case, *characteristics of subordinates* – such as their skills, abilities, experience, knowledge and motivation – can be substitutes for leadership.[49] *Characteristics of the situation or context* – such as the extent to which the work is interesting and enjoyable – also can be substitutes. When work is interesting and enjoyable, as it is for Cotsonas, jobholders do not need to be coaxed into performing because performing is rewarding in its own right. Similarly, when managers *empower* their subordinates or use *self-managed work teams* (discussed in detail in Chapter 15), the need for leadership influence from a manager is decreased because team members manage themselves.

Substitutes for leadership can increase organisational efficiency and effectiveness because they free up some of managers' valuable time and allow them to focus their efforts on discovering new ways to improve organisational effectiveness. The director of the language school, for example, was able to spend much of his time making arrangements to open a second school in Rhodes, an island in the Aegean Sea, because of the presence of leadership substitutes, not only Cotsonas but most of the other teachers at the school as well.

Bringing it All Together

Effective leadership in organisations occurs when managers take steps to lead in a way that is appropriate for the situation or context in which leadership occurs and for the subordinates who are being led. The three contingency models of leadership discussed above help managers home in on the necessary ingredients for effective leadership. They are complementary in that each one looks at the leadership question from a different angle. Fiedler's contingency model explores

Table 14.2 Contingency models of leadership

Model	Focus	Key contingencies
Fiedler's contingency model	Describes two leader styles, relationship-oriented and task-oriented, and the kinds of situations in which each kind of leader will be most effective	Whether or not a relationship-oriented or a task-oriented leader is effective is contingent on the situation
House's path-goal theory	Describes how effective leaders motivate their followers	The behaviours that managers should engage in to be effective leaders are contingent on the nature of the subordinates and the work they do
Leader substitutes model	Describes when leadership is unnecessary	Whether or not leadership is necessary for subordinates to perform highly is contingent on the characteristics of the subordinates and the situation

how a manager's leadership style needs to be matched to that person's leadership situation for maximum effectiveness. House's path–goal theory focuses on how managers should motivate subordinates and describes the specific kinds of behaviours that managers can engage in to have a highly motivated workforce. The leadership substitutes model alerts managers to the fact that sometimes they do not need to exert influence over subordinates and thus can free up their time for other important activities. Table 14.2 recaps these three contingency models.

Transformational Leadership

Time and time again, throughout business history, certain leaders seem to literally transform their organisations, making sweeping changes to revitalise and renew operations. For example, in the 1990s, the chief executive of the German electronics company Siemens, Heinrich von Pierer, as we have seen, dramatically transformed his company. When von Pierer took over in 1992, Siemens had a rigid hierarchy in place, was suffering from increased global competition and was saddled with a conservative, perfectionist culture that stifled creativity and innovation and slowed decision making. Von Pierer's changes at Siemens were nothing short of revolutionary.[50] At the new Siemens, subordinates critique their managers, who receive training in how to be more democratic and participative and spur creativity. Employees are no longer afraid to speak their minds, and the quest for innovation is a driving force throughout the company.

Von Pierer has literally transformed Siemens and its thousands of employees into being more innovative and taking the steps needed to gain a competitive advantage. When managers have such dramatic effects on their subordinates and on an organisation as a whole, they are engaging in **transformational leadership**. Transformational leadership occurs when managers change (or transform) their subordinates in three important ways:[51]

1. *Transformational managers make subordinates aware of how important their jobs are for the organisation and how necessary it is for them to perform those jobs as best they can so that the*

organisation can attain its goals   Von Pierer sent the message throughout Siemens not only that innovating, cost-cutting and increasing customer service and satisfaction were everyone's responsibilities but also that improvements could be, and needed to be, made in these areas. When von Pierer realised that managers in charge of microprocessor sales were not aware of the importance of their jobs and of performing them in a top-notch fashion, he had managers from Siemens's top microprocessor customers give the Siemens' microprocessor managers feedback about their poor service and unreliable delivery schedules. The microprocessor managers quickly realised how important it was for them to take steps to improve customer service.

2. *Transformational managers make their subordinates aware of the subordinates' own needs for personal growth, development and accomplishment*   Von Pierer made Siemens' employees aware of their own needs in this regard through numerous workshops and training sessions, through empowering employees throughout the company, through the development of fast-track career programmes and through increased reliance on self-managed work teams.[52]

3. *Transformational managers motivate their subordinates to work for the good of the organisation as a whole, not just for their own personal gain or benefit*   Von Pierer's message to Siemens' employees was clear: dramatic changes in the way they perform their jobs were crucial for the future viability and success of Siemens. As von Pierer puts it: 'We have to keep asking ourselves: Are we flexible enough? Are we changing enough?'[53] One way von Pierer tried to get all employees thinking in these terms was by inserting self-addressed postcards in the company magazine distributed to all employees, urging them to send in their ideas for making improvements directly to him.

When a manager transforms subordinates in these three ways, subordinates trust the manager, are highly motivated and help the organisation achieve its goals. As a result of von Pierer's transformational leadership, for example, a team of Siemens' engineers working in blue jeans in a rented house developed a tool control system in one-third the time and at one-third the cost of other similar systems developed at Siemens.[54] How do managers like von Pierer transform subordinates and produce dramatic effects in their organisations? There are at least three ways in which managers and other transformational leaders can influence their followers: by being a **charismatic leader**, by giving subordinates **intellectual stimulation** and by engaging in **developmental consideration** (Table 14.3).

Table 14.3 Transformational leadership

Transformational managers

- Are charismatic
- Intellectually stimulate subordinates
- Engage in developmental consideration

Subordinates of transformational managers

- Have increased awareness of the importance of their jobs and high performance
- Are aware of their own needs for growth, development and accomplishment
- Work for the good of the organisation and not just their own personal benefit.

Being a Charismatic Leader

Transformational managers are *charismatic leaders*. They have a vision of how good things could be in their work groups and organisations that is in contrast with the status quo. Their vision usually entails dramatic improvements in group and organisational performance as a result of changes in the organisation's structure, culture, strategy, decision making and other critical processes and factors. This vision paves the way for gaining a competitive advantage. It is clear that part of Steve Ballmer's vision for Microsoft is boosting the perceived value of the company's technology through seamlessly integrated software, developing innovative software to meet the needs of corporate customers and consumers and having an empowered workforce that effectively and efficiently develops creative integrative software that sets new standards.

Charismatic leaders are excited and enthusiastic about their vision and clearly communicate it to their subordinates, as does Steve Ballmer. The excitement, enthusiasm and self-confidence of a charismatic leader contribute to their being able to inspire followers to enthusiastically support their vision.[55] People often think of charismatic leaders or managers as being 'larger than life': Steve Ballmer is often described this way. The essence of charisma, however, is having a vision and enthusiastically communicating it to others. Thus, managers who appear to be quiet and earnest can also be charismatic.

Stimulating Subordinates Intellectually

Transformational managers openly share information with their subordinates so that they are aware of both problems and the need for change. The manager causes subordinates to view problems in their groups and throughout the organisation from a different perspective, consistent with the manager's vision. Whereas in the past subordinates might not have been aware of some problems, may have viewed problems as a 'management issue' beyond their concern, or may have viewed problems as insurmountable, the transformational manager's *intellectual stimulation* leads subordinates to view problems as challenges that they can and will meet and conquer. The manager engages and empowers subordinates to take personal responsibility for helping solve problems.[56]

Engaging in Developmental Consideration

When managers engage in *developmental consideration*, they not only perform the consideration behaviours described earlier, such as demonstrating genuine concern for the well-being of subordinates, but go one step further. The manager goes out of their way to support and encourage subordinates, giving them opportunities to enhance their skills and capabilities and to grow and excel on the job.[57] Heinrich von Pierer engages in developmental consideration in numerous ways, such as providing counselling sessions with a psychologist for managers who are having a hard time adapting to the changes at Siemens and sponsoring hiking trips to stimulate employees to think and work in new ways.[58]

All organisations, no matter how large or small, successful or unsuccessful, can benefit when their managers engage in transformational leadership. Moreover, while the benefits of transformational leadership are often most apparent when an organisation is in trouble, transformational leadership can be an enduring approach to leadership, leading to long-run organisational effectiveness.

The Distinction Between Transformational and Transactional Leadership

Transformational leadership is often contrasted with **transactional leadership**. In transactional leadership, managers use their reward and coercive powers to encourage high performance. When managers reward high performers, reprimand or otherwise punish low performers and motivate subordinates by reinforcing desired behaviours and extinguishing or punishing undesired ones, they are engaging in transactional leadership. Managers who effectively influence their subordinates to achieve goals yet do not seem to be making the kind of dramatic changes that are part of transformational leadership are engaging in transactional leadership.

Many transformational leaders engage in transactional leadership. They reward subordinates for a job well done and notice and respond to substandard performance. But they also have their eyes on the bigger picture of how much better things could be in their organisations, how much more their subordinates are capable of achieving and how important it is to treat their subordinates with respect and to help them reach their full potential.

Research has found that when leaders engage in transformational leadership, their subordinates tend to have higher levels of job satisfaction and performance.[59] Subordinates of transformational leaders may be more likely to trust their leaders and their organisations and feel that they are being fairly treated and this, in turn, may positively influence their work motivation (Chapter 13).[60]

Gender and Leadership

The increasing number of women entering the ranks of management, as well as the problems some women face in their efforts to be hired as managers or promoted into management positions, has prompted researchers to explore the relationship between gender and leadership. Although there are more women in management positions today than there were 10 years ago, there are still relatively few women in senior management – and, in some organisations, even in middle management.

When women do advance to senior management positions, special attention often is focused on them and the fact that they are women. Women CEOs of large companies are still very rare; those who make it to the very top post, such as Meg Whitman of eBay, Anita Roddick of The Body Shop, Carly Fiorina of Hewlett-Packard and Andrea Jung of Avon, are very salient. As business writer Linda Tischler puts it: 'In a workplace where women CEOs of major companies are so scarce . . . they can be identified, like rock stars, by first name only – Meg, Anita, Carly and Andrea.'[61] While women have certainly made inroads into leadership positions in organisations, they continue to be very under-represented in top leadership posts (Chapter 5). Research into women in directorships of top UK boards reveals some interesting results. The lack of female representation on UK FTSE 100 company boards in 1999 and 2000 was compared and an actual fall from 64 per cent to 58 per cent of companies employing women as board-level directors was found. This was paralleled with US figures.[62] Even fewer females make it to executive directors and by 2000 only one woman had made it to CEO in the FTSE 100 list. This was Marjorie Scardino who was made CEO of Pearsons (the media/publishing company).

A widespread stereotype of women is that they are nurturing, supportive and concerned with interpersonal relations. Men are stereotypically viewed as being directive and focused on task accomplishment. Such stereotypes suggest that women tend to be more relationship-oriented as managers and engage in more consideration behaviours, whereas men are more task-oriented and engage in more initiating-structure behaviours. Does the behaviour of actual male and female managers bear out these stereotypes? Do women managers lead in different ways than men? Are male or female managers more effective as leaders?

Research suggests that male and female managers who have leadership positions in organisations behave in similar ways.[63] Women do not engage in more consideration than men, and men do not engage in more initiating structure than women. Research does suggest, however, that leadership style may vary between women and men. Women tend to be somewhat more participative as leaders than men, involving subordinates in decision making and seeking their input.[64] Male managers tend to be less participative than female managers, making more decisions on their own and wanting to do things their own way. Research suggests that men tend to be harsher when they punish their subordinates than women.[65] There are at least two reasons why female managers may be more participative as leaders than male managers. First, subordinates may try to resist the influence of female managers more than they do the influence of male managers. Some subordinates may never have reported to a woman before; some may incorrectly see a management role as being more appropriate for a man than for a woman; and some may just resist being led by a woman. To overcome this resistance and encourage subordinates' trust and respect, women managers may adopt a participative approach.

A second reason why female managers may be more participative is that they sometimes have better interpersonal skills than male managers.[66] A participative approach to leadership requires high levels of interaction and involvement between a manager and his or her subordinates, sensitivity to subordinates' feelings and the ability to make decisions that may be unpopular with subordinates but necessary for goal attainment. Good interpersonal skills may help female managers have the effective interactions with their subordinates that are crucial to a participative approach.[67] To the extent that male managers have more difficulty managing interpersonal relationships, they may shy away from the high levels of interaction with subordinates necessary for true participation.

The key finding from research on leader behaviours, however, is that male and female managers do *not* differ significantly in their propensities to perform different leader behaviours. Even though they may be more participative, female managers do not engage in more consideration or less initiating structure than male managers.

Perhaps an even more important question than whether male and female managers differ in the leadership behaviours they perform is whether they differ in *effectiveness*. Consistent with the findings for leader behaviours, research suggests that across different kinds of organisational settings, male and female managers tend to be *equally effective* as leaders.[68] There is thus no logical basis for stereotypes favouring male managers and leaders or for the existence of the 'glass ceiling' (Chapters 4 and 5). Because women and men are equally effective as leaders, the increasing number of women in the workforce should result in a larger pool of highly qualified candidates for management positions in organisations, ultimately enhancing organisational effectiveness.[69]

An important factor for women's advancement to top leadership positions is obtaining a variety of work experiences.[70] Varied work experiences have proved very beneficial for Anne E. Belec, CEO and President of Volvo Cars North America, as profiled in Case 14.4.

Case 14.4: **Anne E. Belec: At the forefront of the automotive industry**

Volvo is one of the best-known car brands in the world; synonymous with safety, good design and quality. While Volvo is now Ford-owned, it is not accountable to the Ford Motor Company, but to Volvo in Sweden and Ford Europe,[71] so Volvo retained its unique European heritage. Volvo North America, one of the strongest markets for Volvo, is led by an extraordinary woman, Anne E. Belec, President and CEO Volvo Cars North America. There are not many women in similar positions; in fact, Mrs Belec is the only woman heading a car division in the US.

Mrs Belec has an excellent reputation as being an outstanding leader, which was confirmed by her nomination to the '100 Leading Women in the North American Automotive Industry in 2005'.[72] Having fallen into the automotive industry by chance, she has held a number of high-profile positions on both sides of the Atlantic, including portfolio brand manager for Ford and general marketing manager for Lincoln Mercury; prior to her current role she was Vice President of sales for Volvo, based in Sweden.[73] Mrs Belec started her career in the car industry by meeting alumni from her university who persuaded her to join after her successful completion of a marketing degree. It was quickly realised that she had huge potential, which she developed in her various roles.

She is described as 'creative, efficient and effective',[74] and colleagues who have worked with her have described her as a 'good executive and leader'.[75]

Mrs Belec admits that being a female executive in the automotive industry sometimes feels lonely. But she remains positive and acknowledges the progress that has been made to attract women into the industry. Considering the demographic changes across the world, one can assume that the role of women in the car industry can only increase. Mrs Belec supports such 'star-gazing' and is confident that women are growing into the motor business at every level.

Volvo is showing this commitment to leading the market by launching a concept car entirely designed by women, but not just for women but for 'modern people'.[76] While some of its features are contested, the idea arose from the notion that women have a better eye for detail. In the UK women are a key part of the motoring market, with 43 per cent of all driving licences held by women.[77] In the US, 54 per cent of all Volvo buyers are women and in Europe this number is growing, slowly but steadily.[78]

Reaction Time

1. Discuss how substitutes for leadership can contribute to organisational effectiveness.

2. Describe what transformational leadership is, and explain how managers can engage in it.

3. Discuss why some people still think that men make better managers than women even though research indicates that men and women are equally effective as managers and leaders.

4. Imagine that you are working in an organisation in an entry-level position after graduation and have come up with what you think is a great idea for improving a critical process in the organisation that relates to your job. In what ways might your supervisor encourage you to actually implement your idea? How might your supervisor discourage you from even sharing your idea with others?

Emotional Intelligence and Leadership

Do the moods and emotions leaders experience on the job influence their behaviour and effectiveness as leaders? Preliminary research suggests that this is likely to be the case. One study found that when store managers experienced positive moods at work, salespeople in their stores provided high-quality customer service and were less likely to quit.[79]

A leader's level of *emotional intelligence* (Chapter 3) may play a particularly important role in leadership effectiveness.[80] Emotional intelligence may help leaders develop a vision for their organisations, motivate their subordinates to commit to this vision and energise them to enthusiastically work to achieve it. Emotional intelligence may also enable leaders to develop a significant identity for their organisation and instil high levels of trust and co-operation throughout while maintaining the flexibility needed to respond to changing conditions.[81]

Emotional intelligence also plays a crucial role in how leaders relate to and deal with their followers, particularly when it comes to encouraging them to be creative.[82] Creativity in organisations is an emotion-laden process, as it often entails challenging the status quo, being willing to take risks and accept and learn from failures and doing much hard work to bring creative ideas to fruition in terms of new products, services or procedures and processes when uncertainty is bound to be high.[83] Leaders who are high on emotional intelligence are more likely to understand all the emotions surrounding creative endeavours, to be able to awaken and support the creative pursuits of their followers and to provide the kind of support that enables creativity to flourish in organisations.[84]

TIPS FOR PRACTICE

1. Be aware that you should always assess if your leadership style is appropriate for the situation in which you find yourself.

2. Your role as a leader is to encourage your team. Help people around you – and yourself – to achieve their potential.

3. Leading is about enthusiasm – communicate visions of change or improvements as something exciting and challenging to convince colleagues and team members to follow.

4. Leadership is not about doing everything yourself: involve team members and colleagues in problem solving.

Summary and Review

The nature of leadership Leadership is the process by which a person exerts influence over other people and inspires, motivates and directs their activities to help achieve group or organisational goals. Leaders are able to influence others because they possess power. The five types of power available to managers are legitimate power, reward power, coercive power, expert power and referent power. Many managers use empowerment as a tool to increase their effectiveness as leaders.

Trait and behaviour models of leadership The trait model of leadership describes personal characteristics or traits that contribute to effective leadership. However, some managers who possess these traits are not effective leaders, and some managers who do not possess all these traits are nevertheless effective leaders. The behaviour model of leadership describes two kinds of behaviour that most leaders engage in: consideration and initiating structure.

Contingency models of leadership Contingency models take into account the complexity surrounding leadership and the role of the situation in determining whether a manager is an effective or ineffective leader. Fiedler's contingency model explains why managers may be effective leaders in one situation and ineffective in another. According to Fiedler's model, relationship-oriented leaders are most effective in situations that are moderately favourable for leading, and task-oriented leaders are most effective in situations that are very favourable or very unfavourable for leading. House's path–goal theory describes how effective managers can motivate their subordinates by determining what outcomes their subordinates want, rewarding them with these outcomes when they achieve their goals and perform at a high level, and clarifying the paths to goal attainment. Managers can engage in four different kinds of behaviours to motivate subordinates: directive behaviours, supportive behaviours, participative behaviours, or achievement-oriented behaviours. The leader substitutes model suggests that managers sometimes do not have to play a leadership role because their subordinates perform highly without the manager having to exert influence over them.

Transformational leadership Transformational leadership occurs when managers have dramatic effects on their subordinates and on the organisation as a whole and inspire and energise subordinates to solve problems and improve performance. These effects include making subordinates aware of the importance of their own jobs and high performance, making subordinates aware of their own needs for personal growth, development and accomplishment, and motivating subordinates to work for the good of the organisation and not just their own personal gain. Managers can engage in transformational leadership by being charismatic leaders, by intellectually stimulating subordinates and by engaging in developmental consideration. Transformational managers also often engage in transactional leadership by using their reward and coercive powers to encourage high performance.

Gender and leadership Female and male managers do not differ in the leadership behaviours that they perform, contrary to stereotypes suggesting that women are more relationship-oriented and men more task-oriented. However, female managers sometimes are more participative than male managers. Research has found that women and men are equally effective as managers and leaders.

Emotional intelligence and leadership The moods and emotions that leaders experience on the job, and their ability to effectively manage these feelings, can influence their effectiveness as leaders. Emotional intelligence has the potential to contribute to leadership effectiveness in multiple ways, including encouraging and supporting creativity among followers.

Topic for Action

- Interview a manager to find out how the three situational characteristics that Fiedler identified are affecting his or her ability to provide leadership.

- Find a company that has dramatically turned around its fortunes and improved its performance. Determine whether a transformational manager was behind the turnaround and, if one was, what this manager did.

Applied Independent Learning

Building Management Skills

Analysing Failures of Leadership

Think about a situation you are familiar with in which a leader was very ineffective. Then answer the following questions:

1. What sources of power did this leader have? Did the leader have enough power to influence his or her followers?

2. What kinds of behaviours did this leader engage in? Were they appropriate for the situation? Why or why not?

3. From what you know, do you think this leader was a task-oriented leader or a relationship-oriented leader? How favourable was this leader's situation for leading?

4. What steps did this leader take to motivate his or her followers? Were these steps appropriate or inappropriate? Why?

5. What signs, if any, did this leader show of being a transformational leader?

Managing Ethically

Managers who verbally criticise their subordinates, put them down in front of their co-workers, or use the threat of job loss to influence behaviour are exercising coercive power. Some employees subject to coercive power believe that using it is unethical.

Questions

1. Either alone or in a group, think about the ethical implications of the use of coercive power.

2. To what extent do managers and organisations have an ethical obligation to put limits on the amount of coercive power that is exercised?

Small Group Breakout Exercise

Improving Leadership Effectiveness

Form groups of three to five people, and appoint one member as the spokesperson who will communicate your findings and conclusions to the whole class when called on by the instructor. Then discuss the following scenario.

You are a team of HR consultants who have been hired by Carla Caruso, an entrepreneur who has started her own interior decorating business. A highly competent and creative interior decorator, Caruso established a working relationship with most of the major home builders in her community. At first, she worked on her own as an independent contractor. Then because of a dramatic increase in the number of new homes being built, she became swamped with requests for her services and decided to start her own company.

She hired a secretary-bookkeeper and four interior decorators, all of whom are highly competent. Caruso still does decorating jobs herself and has adopted a hands-off approach to leading the four decorators who report to her because she feels that interior design is a very personal, creative endeavour. Rather than pay the decorators on some kind of commission basis (such as a percentage of their customers' total billings), she pays them a premium salary, higher than average, so that they are motivated to do what's best for a customer's needs and not what will result in higher billings and commissions.

Caruso thought that everything was going smoothly until customer complaints started coming in. The complaints ranged from the decorators being hard to get hold of, promising unrealistic delivery times and being late for or failing to keep appointments to their being impatient and rude when customers had trouble making up their minds. Caruso knows that her decorators are very competent and is concerned that she is not effectively leading and managing them. She wonders, in particular, if her hands-off approach is to blame and if she should change the manner in which she rewards or pays her decorators. She has asked for your advice.

1. Analyse the sources of power that Caruso has available to her to influence the decorators. What advice can you give her to either increase her power base or use her existing power more effectively?

2. Given what you have learned in this chapter (for example, from the behaviour model and path–goal theory), does Caruso seem to be performing appropriate leader behaviours in this situation? What advice can you give her about the kinds of behaviours she should perform?

3. What steps would you advise Caruso to take to increase the decorators' motivation to deliver high-quality customer service?

4. Would you advise Caruso to try to engage in transformational leadership in this situation? If not, why not? If so, what steps would you advise her to take?

Exploring the World Wide Web

Go to the website of the Centre for Creative Leadership (www.ccl.org). Spend some time browsing through the site to learn more about this organisation, which specialises in leadership. Then click on 'Coaching' and read about the different coaching programmes and options the centre provides. How do you think leaders might benefit from coaching? What kinds of leaders/managers may find coaching especially beneficial? Do you think that coaching services such as those provided by the Centre for Creative Leadership can help leaders become more effective? Why or why not?

Application in Today's Business World

Reinventing Motorola

It takes Motorola, Inc. employees about 30 seconds after they meet Edward J. Sander to realise how different their new boss is from their last one. Where Sander's predecessor, Christopher B. Galvin, was reserved, polite and genteel, Sander is a brash Brooklynite, incessantly pumping hands and flashing his trademark mile-wide smile.

But in March 2004, three months after taking over the CEO post, Sander showed that he also was going to be much more demanding. He gathered his top 20 executives in the company's downtown Chicago offices, some 30 miles from the Schaumburg, IL, headquarters, for a two-day brainstorming session on how to improve Motorola's lacklustre performance. His message: employees will be held accountable for customer satisfaction, product quality and even collaboration among business units. 'If you don't co-operate and work together, I will kill you,' he said. Today, Sander laughs: 'That's surviving-and-growing-up-in-Brooklyn talk. It was my way of saying, "We're going to fix this thing".'

Sander is about as affable as CEOs come, but he's deadly serious about restoring Motorola to the top of the communications world. The tech veteran, who spent 15 years at computer giant Sun Microsystems, Inc. and eventually became its President, is trying to reinvent Motorola as a nimble, unified technology company. His most dramatic effort to date is a plan to dismantle Motorola's debilitating bureaucracy and end a culture of internecine rivalries so intense that Motorola's own employees have referred to its business units as 'warring tribes'. And he's not leaving it to chance: he has made co-operation a key factor in determining rises and bonuses. 'It's a damn different place,' says Patrick J. Canavan, a 24-year veteran and Motorola's director for global governance. 'Everyone is looking out for everyone else.'

The changes are just beginning. *BusinessWeek* has learned that Sander has been exploring a major reorganisation and the first steps of the restructuring were unveiled at an investor conference in Chicago on 27 July 2004. By October, Sander hoped to abandon Motorola's stovepipe divisions, which are focused on products like mobile phones and broadband gear, and reorganise operations around customer markets – one for the digital home, for example, and another for corporate buyers.

The reorganisation will help Sander deliver on several new initiatives. Perhaps the most important is what the chief executive calls 'seamless mobility'. The idea is that Motorola should make it easy for consumers to transport any digital information – music, video, email, phone calls – from the house to the car to the workplace. Mastering that technology would do more than boost cellphone sales. It also could make Motorola a key player in the digital home, helping it sell flat-panel TVs and broadband modems, home wireless networks and gateways to manage digital content. *BusinessWeek* has also learned that Motorola is planning a major push to sell more services to corporations. While Motorola sells communications gear to corporate customers now, Sander sees an important growth opportunity in managing networks for those companies. 'We have to get more focused on that,' he said in an interview with *BusinessWeek*. . . .

Honing a Concept

Sander is planning to trim costs in coming months by shedding employees, according to insiders and analysts. He's also plotting management changes that will bring in more hand-picked people to help execute his plans. On 20 July 2004 Motorola said that the head of its mobile-phone division, Tom Lynch, would leave the company at the end of the summer. Sander declined to discuss any details of cost-cutting or executive changes.

But investors that want Sander to jettison poorly performing businesses may be disappointed. The CEO proceeded with the spin-off of Motorola's semiconductor unit that had been put in motion before he arrived – the deal took place on 16 July 2004, despite the upheaval in the chips market. Still, insiders say he's impressed with the remaining portfolio of businesses, including the $4.4 billion wireless infrastructure business that some analysts have suggested that Motorola dump. . . .

'You're Sandbagging'

The Motorola vision starts with users sitting at home watching, say, the New York Yankees battling the Chicago White Sox. To leave home, they pause the video, transfer it to their phone, walk into the garage and transfer the video to the car as they drive away. The car would switch to audio so as not to distract the driver and then switch back to video if the driver stops at a traffic light. Motorola has the technology portfolio to pursue the entire scenario. Besides phones and cable set-top boxes, it has a $2.3 billion automotive-electronics business that develops technologies for cars to communicate with outside networks.

The key will be beating rivals to market with innovative solutions. That's why Sander's top priority has been improving execution. The main driver is a new incentive plan. In the past, workers were compensated based on the revenue, profit and cash generated in their particular sector. If one sector did well, its employees pulled in huge bonuses. A unit that didn't perform got little or nothing.

Sander has been relentless in trying to get the most out of his staff. A new bonus plan bases 25 per cent on three key areas: customer satisfaction, product reliability and the cost of poor quality. When the heads of each business unit first laid out their targets, Sander's no-nonsense roots showed; 'You're sandbagging', he barked. Before long, the targets were more difficult. 'We're driving for improvement year over year,' says Michael J. Fenger, a veteran Sander picked to improve corporate quality.

If Sander can maintain Motorola's momentum, the years ahead look promising. It's gaining share on the world's mobile-phone leader, Nokia, and the elements of Sander's master plan have yet to take root. 'It's a big ship,' Sander concedes – so it will take time to change direction. But it takes no time at all to see that Sander is committed to the challenge.

Questions

1. In what ways does Edward Sander differ from his predecessor, Christopher Galvin?
2. How is Edward Sander empowering Motorola employees?
3. What is Sander's vision for Motorola?
4. Do you think Sander will be able to successfully transform Motorola? Why or why not?

Source: R. O. Crockett, 'Reinventing Motorola', adapted and reprinted from *BusinessWeek*, August 2, 2004 by special permission. Copyright © 2004 by the McGraw-Hill Companies, Inc.

Notes and References

1   Philip Coggan, 'World's Most Respected Company', *Financial Times*, November 18, 2005.
2   B. Schlender, 'Ballmer Unbound: How Do You Impose Order on a Giant, Runaway Mensa Meeting? Just Watch Microsoft's CEO', *Fortune*, January 26, 2004, 117–24.

3   *Ibid.*

4   *Ibid.*

5   'Steve Ballmer', AskMen.com, July 24, 2004.

6   B. Schlender, 'Ballmer Unbound'.

7   J. Evers, 'Gates Pitches "Seamless Computing" to Developers', *InfoWorld*, July 24, 2004 www.infoworld.com; 'Bill Gates Talks Seamless Computing, Security, and Linux', *InformationWeek*, December 1, 2003; B. Gates, 'Seamless Computing: Hardware Advances for a New Generation of Software', Windows Hardware Engineering Conference (WinHEC), Washington State Convention and Trade Center, Seattle, May 4, 2004.

8   B. Schlender, 'Ballmer Unbound'.

9   Evers, 'Gates Pitches', 'Bill Gates Talks Seamless Computing'; Gates, 'Seamless Computing'.

10 B. Schlender, 'Ballmer Unbound'.

11 *Ibid.*

12 S. Crainer, 'Have the Corporate Superheroes had their Day?', *Professional Manager* (March 1995), 8–12.

13 P. Taffinder, *The New Leaders: Achieving Corporate Transformation through Dynamic Leadership* (London: Kogan Page, 1995).

14 D. Rollinson, A. Broadfield and D. Edwards, *Organizational Analysis and Behaviour: An Integrated Approach* (Harlow: Addison-Wesley, 1998).

15 Schlender, 'Ballmer Unbound'.

16 D. Dearlove, 'Reinventing Leadership', in S. Crainer and D. Dearlove, eds., *Financial Times Handbook of Management*, 2nd edn. (Englewood Cliffs, NJ: Financial Times/Prentice Hall, 2001), 538.

17 D. S. Miller, S. E. Catt and J. R. Carlson, *Fundamentals of Management: A Framework for Excellence* (West Publishing, 1996), 249.

18 www.timesonline.co.uk.

19 R. Goffee and J. Jones, *Why Should Anyone be Led by You?* (Cambridge, MA: Harvard Business School Publishing, 2006).

20 D. Jung and B. Avolio, 'Effects of Leadership Style and Followers' Cultural Orientation on Performance in Group and Individual Task Conditions', *Academy of Management Journal*, 42 (2) (1999), 208–20.

21 R. Calori and B. Dufour, 'Management European Style', *Academy of Management Executive* 9 (3) (1995), 61–70.

22 *Ibid.*

23 H. Mintzberg, *Power in and Around Organizations* (Englewood Cliffs, NJ: Prentice Hall, 1983); J. Pfeffer, *Power in Organizations* (Marshfield, MA: Pitman, 1981).

24 R. P. French, Jr. and B. Raven, 'The Bases of Social Power', in D. Cartwright and A. F. Zander, eds., *Group Dynamics* (Evanston, IL: Row, Peterson, 1960), 607–23.

25 R. L. Rose, 'After Turning Around Giddings and Lewis, Fife Is Turned Out Himself', *The Wall Street Journal*, June 22, 1993, A1.

26 A. Grove, 'How Intel Makes Spending Pay Off', *Fortune*, February 22, 1993, 56–61; 'Craig R. Barrett, Chief Executive Officer: Intel Corporation', *Intel*, July 28, 2004.

27 M. Loeb, 'Jack Welch Lets Fly on Budgets, Bonuses, and Buddy Boards', *Fortune*, May 29, 1995, 146.

28 http://business.timesonline.co.uk/.

29 C. Hymowitz, 'Home Depot's CEO Led a Revolution, but Left Some Behind', *The Wall Street Journal*, March 16, 2004, B1.

30 http://www.fashionunited.co.uk/news/hnm.htm.

31 Hymowitz, 'Home Depot's CEO Led a Revolution'.

32 *Ibid.*

33 http://www.microsoft.com/presspass/press/2001/aug01/08-27msntoyotapr.mspx.

34 B. Bremner and C. Dawson, 'Can Anything Stop Toyota?', *BusinessWeek*, November 17, 2003, 114–22.

35 T. M. Burton, 'Visionary's Reward: Combine "Simple Ideas" and Some Failures; Result: Sweet Revenge', *The Wall Street Journal*, February 3, 1995, A1, A5.

36 *Ibid.*

37 Toyota's Alabama Plant Featured in Company's Latest Corporate Ad, 'Toyota Announces Best-Ever June Sales: Sets Second-Quarter and First-Half Sales Records', www.toyota.com/about/news/corporate/2004/070/01-1-sales.html, 2 August 2004.

38 R. Likert, *New Patterns of Management* (New York: McGraw-Hill, 1961); N. C. Morse and E. Reimer, 'The Experimental Change of a Major Organizational Variable', *Journal of Abnormal and Social Psychology* 52 (1956), 120–29.

39 R. R. Blake and J. S. Mouton, *The New Managerial Grid* (Houston: Gulf, 1978).

40 P. Hersey and K. Blanchard, *Management of Organizational Behavior: Utilizing Human Resources* (Englewood Cliffs, NJ: Prentice Hall, 1982).

41 F. E. Fiedler, *A Theory of Leadership Effectiveness* (New York: McGraw-Hill, 1967); F. E. Fiedler, 'The Contingency Model and the Dynamics of the Leadership Process', in L. Berkowitz, ed., *Advances in Experimental Social Psychology* (New York: Academic Press, 1978).

42 J. Fierman, 'Winning Ideas from Maverick Managers', *Fortune*, 78 February 6 (1995), 66–80.

43 *Ibid.*

44 House and Baetz, 'Leadership'; L. H. Peters, D. D. Hartke and J. T. Pohlmann, 'Fiedler's Contingency Theory of Leadership: An Application of the Meta-Analysis Procedures of Schmidt and Hunter', *Psychological Bulletin* 97 (1985), 274–85; C. A. Schriesheim, B. J. Tepper and L. A. Tetrault, 'Least Preferred Co-Worker Score, Situational Control, and Leadership Effectiveness: A Meta-Analysis of Contingency Model Performance Predictions', *Journal of Applied Psychology* 79 (1994), 561–73.

45 M. G. Evans, 'The Effects of Supervisory Behavior on the Path–Goal Relationship', *Organizational Behavior and Human Performance* 5 (1970), 277–98; R. J. House, 'A Path–Goal Theory of Leader Effectiveness', *Administrative Science Quarterly* 16 (1971), 321–38; J. C. Wofford and L. Z. Liska, 'Path–Goal Theories of Leadership: A Meta-Analysis', *Journal of Management* 19 (1993), 857–76.

46 http://www.lso.co.uk/presskit/pressreleases/index.asp?id=246.

47 C. Bangle, 'The Ultimate Creativity Machine: How BMW Turns Art into Profit', *Harvard Business Review* (January 2001), 47–55.

48 *Ibid.*, 48; www.bmw.com.

49 S. Kerr and J. M. Jermier, 'Substitutes for Leadership: Their Meaning and Measurement', *Organizational Behavior and Human Performance* 22 (1978), 375–403; P. M. Podsakoff, B. P. Niehoff, S. B. MacKenzie and M. L. Williams, 'Do Substitutes for Leadership Really Substitute for Leadership? An Empirical Examination of Kerr and Jermier's Situational Leadership Model', *Organizational Behavior and Human Decision Processes* 54 (1993), 1–44.

50 K. Miller, 'Siemens Shapes Up', *BusinessWeek*, May 1, 1995, 52–53.

51 B. M. Bass, *Leadership and Performance Beyond Expectations* (New York: Free Press, 1985); B. M. Bass, *Bass and Stogdill's Handbook of Leadership: Theory, Research and Managerial Applications* (New York: Free Press, 0000); G. A. Yukl and D. D. Van Fleet, 'Theory and Research on Leadership, in Organizations', in M. D. Dunnette and L. M. Hough, eds. *Handbook of Industrial and Organizational Psychology*, 3, 2nd edn (Palo Alto, CA: Consulting Psychologists Press, Inc., 1992), 147–97.

52 G. E. Schares, J. B. Levine and P. Coy, 'The New Generation at Siemens', *BusinessWeek*, March 9, 1992, 46–48.

53 Miller, 'Siemens Shapes Up'.

54 *Ibid.*

55 J. A. Conger and R. N. Kanungo, 'Behavioral Dimensions of Charismatic Leadership', in J. A. Conger, R. N. Kanungo and Associates, *Charismatic Leadership* (San Francisco: Jossey-Bass, 1988).

56 Bass, *Leadership and Performance Beyond Expectations*; Bass, *Bass and Stogdill's Handbook of Leadership*; Yukl and Van Fleet, 'Theory and Research on Leadership'.

57 Yukl and Van Fleet, 'Theory and Research on Leadership'.

58 Miller, 'Siemens Shapes Up'.

59 Bass, *Bass and Stogdill's Handbook of Leadership*; B. M. Bass and B. J. Avolio, 'Transformational Leadership: A Response to Critiques', in M. M. Chemers and R. Ayman, eds., *Leadership Theory and Research: Perspectives and Directions* (San Diego: Academic Press, 1993), 49–80; B. M. Bass, B. J. Avolio and L. Goodheim, 'Biography and the Assessment of Transformational Leadership at the World Class Level', *Journal of Management* 13 (1987), 7–20; J. J. Hater and B. M. Bass, 'Supervisors' Evaluations and Subordinates' Perceptions of Transformational and Transactional Leadership', *Journal of Applied Psychology* 73, (1988), 695–702; R. Pillai, 'Crisis and Emergence of Charismatic Leadership in Groups: An Experimental Investigation', *Journal of Applied Psychology* 26 (1996), 543–62; J. Seltzer and B. M. Bass, 'Transformational Leadership: Beyond Initiation and Consideration', *Journal of Management* 16 (1990), 693–703; D. A. Waldman, B. M. Bass and W. O. Einstein, 'Effort, Performance, Transformational Leadership in Industrial and Military Service', *Journal of Occupation Psychology* 60 (1987), 1–10.

60 R. Pillai, C. A. Schriesheim and E. S. Williams, 'Fairness Perceptions and Trust as Mediators of Transformational and Transactional Leadership: A Two-Sample Study', *Journal of Management* 25 (1999), 897–933.

61 L. Tischler, 'Where Are the Women?', *Fast Company*, February, 2004, 52–60.

62 V. Singh, S. Vinnicombe and P. Johnson, 'Women Directors on Top UK Boards', *Corporate Governance*, 9 (3).

63 A. H. Eagly and B. T. Johnson, 'Gender and Leadership Style: A Meta-Analysis', *Psychological Bulletin* 108 (1990), 233–56.

64 *Ibid.*

65 'Workers Resent Scoldings from Female Bosses', *Houston Chronicle*, August 19, 2000, 1C.

66 *Ibid.*

67 *Ibid.*

68 A. H. Eagly, S. J. Karau and M. G. Makhijani, 'Gender and the Effectiveness of Leaders: A Meta-Analysis', *Psychological Bulletin* 117 (1995), 125–45.

69 *Ibid.*

70 Tischler, 'Where Are the Women?'

71 Marty Bernstein, 'One on One with Volvo's President, Anne E. Belec', *BusinessWeek*, April 20, 2006.

72 www.autonews.com.

73 www.autonews.com/leadingwomen.

74 www.volvocars-PR.com.

75 Marty Bernstein, 'One on One with Volvo's President'.

76 www.volvocars-PR.com.

77 C. Smith, 'The car designed by women, for women', *The Scotsman*, 15 May 2004.

78 www.volvocars-PR.com.

79 J. M. George and K. Bettenhausen, 'Understanding Prosocial Behavior, Sales Performance, and Turnover: A Group-Level Analysis in a Service Context', *Journal of Applied Psychology*, 75 (1990), 698–709.

80 J. M. George, 'Emotions and Leadership: The Role of Emotional Intelligence', *Human Relations* 53 (2000), 1027–55.

81 *Ibid.*

82 J. Zhou and J. M. George, 'Awakening Employee Creativity: The Role of Leader Emotional Intelligence', *The Leadership Quarterly* 14 (4–5), 545–68.

83 *Ibid.*

84 *Ibid.*

Chapter 15

Effective Groups and Teams

LEARNING OBJECTIVES

After studying this chapter, you should be able to:

☑ Explain why groups and teams are key contributors to organisational effectiveness.

☑ Identify the different types of groups and teams that help managers and organisations achieve their goals.

☑ Explain how different elements of group dynamics influence the functioning and effectiveness of groups and teams.

☑ Explain why it is important for groups and teams to have a balance of conformity and deviance and a moderate level of cohesiveness.

☑ Describe how managers can motivate group members to achieve organisational goals and reduce social loafing in groups and teams.

A Manager's Challenge

Teams Excel at Louis Vuitton and Nucor Corporation

How can managers use teams in different kinds of organisations and work environments to gain a competitive advantage?

Groups and teams are relied on in all kinds of organisations, from those specialising in heavy industrial manufacturing to those in high-tech fields ranging from computer software development to biotechnology. Relying on groups and teams to accomplish work tasks is one thing; managing groups and teams in ways that enable them to truly excel and help an organisation gain and maintain a competitive advantage is another, much more challenging endeavour. Managers at Louis Vuitton, the most profitable luxury brand in the world, and managers at Nucor Corporation, the largest producer of steel and biggest recycler in the US, have succeeded in effectively using teams to produce their goods. Teams at both companies are truly effective and excel, having helped to make the companies leaders in their respective industries.[1]

The LVHM group, which includes Louis Vuitton, had £9.7 billion in revenues in 2005, which was 11 per cent more than in 2004.[2] Louis Vuitton has an operating margin of 45 per cent and is the largest and most profitable producer of high-end luxury accessories.[3] Impeccable quality and high standards are an imperative for Louis Vuitton; when customers purchase a handbag such as the Boulogne Multicolour, which appeared in stores for the first time in March 2004 with a £850 price tag, they expect only the best. Teams at Louis Vuitton are so effective at making handbags and other accessories that not only are customers never disappointed but Vuitton's profit margins are much higher than those of its competitors such as Prada and Gucci.[4]

Teams with between 20 and 30 members make Vuitton handbags and accessories. The teams work on only one particular product at a time. A team with 24 members might produce about 120 handbags per day. Team members are empowered to take ownership for the goods they produce, are encouraged to suggest improvements and are kept up to date on key facts such as products' selling prices and popularity. As Thierry Nogues, a team leader at a Vuitton factory in Ducey, France, puts it: 'Our goal is to make everyone as multi-skilled and autonomous as possible.'[5]

In the case of the Boulogne Multicolour, a team found out that some of the studs on the handbag were interfering with the smooth operation of the zipper. The team's discovery led to a small design change that completely eliminated the problem. By being involved in all aspects of the goods they produce, and having the skills and autonomy to ensure that all products live up to the Vuitton brand name, employees take pride in their work and are highly motivated.

Similar success can also be seen across the Atlantic. Headquartered in Charlotte, NC, Nucor has operations in 14 states manufacturing all kinds of steel products ranging from steel joists, bars and beams to steel decks and metal building systems.[6] Nucor has over 9,900 employees and over £3.6 billion in annual sales.[7]

Production workers at Nucor are organised into teams ranging in size from 8 to 40 members, depending on the kind of work the team is responsible for, such as rolling steel or operating a furnace. Team members have considerable autonomy to make decisions and creatively respond to problems and opportunities. The organisational structure has relatively few layers and supports the empowerment of teams.[8] Teams develop their own informal rules of behaviour and make their own decisions. As long as team members follow organisational rules and policies (e.g. for safety) and meet quality standards, they are free to govern themselves. Managers act as coaches or advisers rather than supervisors, helping teams when they need some additional outside assistance.[9]

To ensure that production teams are motivated to help Nucor achieve its goals, team members are eligible for weekly bonuses based on the team's performance. Essentially, these production workers receive a base pay that does not vary and are eligible to receive weekly bonus pay that can average from 80 to 150 per cent of their regular pay.[10] The bonus rate is predetermined by the work a team performs and the capabilities of the machinery they use. Given the immediacy of the bonus and its potential magnitude, team members are highly motivated to perform at a high level, develop informal rules that support high performance and strive to help Nucor reach its goals. Moreover, because all members of a team receive the same amount of weekly bonus money, they are motivated to do their best for the team, co-operate and help one another out.

Crafting a luxury handbag and making steel joists couldn't be more different from each other in certain ways and work ethics and national culture distinguish the two examples. Yet the highly effective teams at Louis Vuitton and Nucor share certain fundamental qualities.

These teams take ownership of their work and are highly motivated to perform effectively. Team members have the skills and knowledge they need to be effective, they are empowered to make decisions about their work and they know that their teams are making vital contributions to their organisations.[11]

Overview

Louis Vuitton and Nucor are not alone in using groups and teams to produce goods and services that best meet customers' needs. Not only do managers in large companies rely on teams, but the positive effects of successful team work can also be observed in small companies.[12] This chapter looks in detail at how groups and teams can contribute to organisational effectiveness and the types of groups and teams used in organisations. It will discuss how different elements of group dynamics can influence the functioning and effectiveness of groups, and describe how managers can motivate group members to achieve organisational goals and reduce slack performance in groups and teams. By the end of this chapter, you will appreciate why the effective management of groups and teams is a key ingredient for organisational performance and a source of competitive advantage.

Groups, Teams and Organisational Effectiveness

A **group** may be defined as two or more people who interact with each other to accomplish certain goals or meet certain needs.[13] A **team** is a group whose members work intensely with one another to achieve a specific common goal or objective. As these definitions imply, all teams are groups but not all groups are teams. The two characteristics that distinguish teams from groups are the *intensity* with which team members work together and the presence of a *specific, overriding team goal or objective*.

Members of production teams in Louis Vuitton work intensely together to achieve their goals – crafting high-quality handbags. In contrast, accountants who work in a small firm are a group: they may interact with one another to achieve goals such as keeping up to date on the latest changes in accounting rules and regulations, maintaining a smoothly functioning office, satisfying clients and attracting new clients. But they are not a team because they do not work intensely with one another. Each accountant concentrates on serving the needs of his or her own clients.

Because all teams are also groups, whenever we use the term *group* in this chapter, it refers to both groups *and* teams. Because members of teams work intensely together, teams can sometimes be difficult to form and it may take time for members to learn how to effectively work together. Groups and teams can help an organisation gain a competitive advantage because they can (1) enhance its performance, (2) increase its responsiveness to customers, (3) increase innovation and (4) increase employees' motivation and satisfaction (Fig. 15.1). In this section, we shall look at each of these contributions in turn.

Groups and Teams as Performance Enhancers

One of the main advantages of using groups is the opportunity to obtain a type of *synergy*: people working in a group are potentially able to produce more or higher-quality outputs compared to

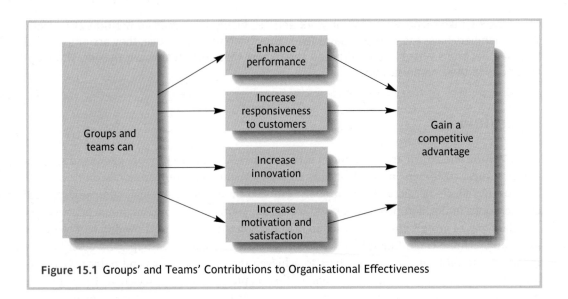

Figure 15.1 Groups' and Teams' Contributions to Organisational Effectiveness

individual outputs that are combined at a later stage. The essence of synergy is captured in the saying 'The whole is more than the sum of its parts', that has its origins in systems theory, discussed in Chapter 2. Factors that can contribute to synergy in groups include the ability of group members to bounce ideas off one another, to correct one another's mistakes, to solve problems immediately as they arise, to bring a diverse knowledge base to bear on a problem or goal and to accomplish work that is too big for any one individual to achieve on his or her own. At Louis Vuitton, the kinds of work the production teams are responsible for could not be performed by an individual acting alone; it is only through the *combined efforts* of team members that luxury accessories and products can be produced efficiently and effectively.

To take advantage of the potential for synergy in groups, managers need to make sure that groups are composed of members who have complementary skills and knowledge relevant to the group's work. At Hallmark Cards, synergies are created by bringing together all the different functions needed to create and produce a greeting card in a *cross-functional team* (a team composed of members from different departments or functions, see Chapter 10). Artists, writers, designers and marketing experts all work together as members of a team to develop new cards.[14]

At Hallmark, the skills and expertise of the artists complement the contributions of the writers and vice versa. Managers also need to give groups enough *autonomy* so that the groups, rather than the manager, are solving problems and determining how to achieve goals and objectives, as is true in the cross-functional teams at Hallmark and the production teams at Louis Vuitton. Every process needs to be owned by the team, not just individuals in the team. To promote synergy, managers need to empower their subordinates and be coaches, guides and resource providers for groups while refraining from playing a more directive or supervisory role, as is true at Louis Vuitton. The potential for synergy in groups may be the reason why more and more managers are incorporating empowerment into their personal leadership styles (see Chapter 14).

When tasks are complex and involve highly sophisticated and rapidly changing technologies, achieving synergies in teams often hinges on having the appropriate mix of backgrounds and areas of expertise represented on the team. In large organisations with operations in many countries it is often difficult for managers to determine which employees may have the expertise needed on a particular team or for a certain project, or create appropriate connections between dispersed team members. One way of creating those relationships among globally dispersed groups is to create *databases of expertise*. IBM has successfully implemented such a system in its consulting business: by entering employees onto the system, IBM was able to match consulting projects with the appropriate individuals and teams. As IBM says, it has already saved the company around £280 million.[15]

A different way to connect teams with appropriate expertise is to map the *interaction* of individuals and teams. MWH Global, an engineering and environmental consulting company operating in more than 36 countries,[16] has created such a map for its IT manager, who was relocated from Cheshire, UK, to New Zealand to manage the global network and systems of MWH Global. The map was created to understand who teams or individuals turn to for expertise. A computer program mapped the information and helped the IT manager to understand where expertise was located globally. This idea has also been adopted by the German pharmaceutical company Merck.[17]

Other practices to foster collaboration are the use of new and evolving IT. Some companies use wikis or blogs to form communities that are physically dispersed across the globe. The often very successful aim is to connect individuals and create 'virtual teams'.[18]

Groups, Teams and Responsiveness to Customers

Being responsive to customers is not always easy. In manufacturing organisations, for example, customers' needs and desires for new and improved products have to be balanced against engineering constraints, production costs and feasibilities, government safety regulations and marketing challenges. In service organisations such as health providers, being responsive to patients' needs and desires for prompt, high-quality medical care and treatment has to be balanced against meeting physicians' needs and desires and keeping health care costs under control – especially at a time when the NHS is in extreme financial difficulties. The same, however, applies to private health care providers, who have to see their business as a profit-making organisation. Being responsive to customers often requires the wide variety of skills and expertise found in different departments and at different levels in an organisation's hierarchy. Sometimes, for example, employees at lower levels in an organisation's hierarchy, such as sales representatives for a computer company, are closest to its customers and most attuned to their needs. However, salespeople often lack the technical expertise needed to come up with new product ideas; such expertise is found in the R&D department. Bringing salespeople, R&D experts and members of other departments together in a group or cross-functional team can enhance responsiveness to customers. When managers form a team, they need to make sure that the diversity of expertise and knowledge needed to be responsive to customers exists within the team; this is why cross-functional teams are so popular.

In a cross-functional team, the expertise and knowledge in different organisational departments is brought together in the skills and knowledge of the team members. Managers of high-performing organisations are careful to determine which types of expertise and knowledge are required for teams to be responsive to customers, and they use this information in forming teams.

Teams and Innovation

Innovation, the creative development of new products, new technologies, new services, or even new organisational structures, is a topic that is examined in more detail in Chapter 18. Often, an individual working alone does not possess the extensive and diverse set of skills, knowledge and expertise required for successful innovation. Managers can better encourage innovation by creating teams of diverse individuals who together have the knowledge relevant to a particular type of innovation rather than by relying on individuals working alone.

Using teams to innovate has other advantages. First, team members can often uncover one another's errors or false assumptions; an individual acting alone would not be able to do this. Second, team members can critique one another's approaches when needed. Using devil's advocacy and dialectical inquiry (discussed in Chapter 7) may help the team to use each other's strengths while compensating for any weaknesses.

Teams should also be empowered and feel fully responsible and accountable for the innovation process. The manager's role is to provide guidance, assistance, coaching and the resources for team members and not to closely direct or supervise their activities. Teams should be formed so that each member brings some unique resource to the team – such as engineering prowess, knowledge of production, marketing expertise or financial savvy. Successful innovation sometimes requires that teams comprise members from different countries and cultures.

Amazon uses teams to spur innovation, and many of the unique features on its website that enable it to be responsive to customers and meet their needs have been developed by teams, as indicated in Case 15.1.

Case 15.1: **Pizza teams at Amazon**

Jeff Bezos, founder and CEO of Amazon, is a firm believer in the power of teams to spur innovation. At Amazon, teams have considerable autonomy to develop their ideas and experiment without interference from managers or other groups. Teams are kept deliberately small: according to Bezos, no team should need more than two pizzas to feed its members. If more than two pizzas are needed to nourish a team, the team is too large. Teams at Amazon typically have no more than about five to seven members.[19]

'Pizza teams' have come up with unique and popular innovations that individuals working alone might never have thought of. A team developed the 'Bottom of the Page Deals' – low-priced offers ranging from electronics to CDs. The sign-up required 'Search Inside the Book', a massive undertaking that allows customers to search and read content from over 100,000 books, had its origins in a team.[20]

While Bezos gives teams autonomy to develop and run with their ideas, he also believes in the careful analysis and testing of ideas. A great advocate of the power of facts, data and analysis, Bezos feels that whenever an idea can be tested through analysis, analysis should rule. When an undertaking is just too large or too uncertain, or when data are lacking and hard to come by, Bezos and other experienced senior managers make the final call. But in order to make such judgment calls about implementing new ideas (either by data analysis or expert judgment), what really is needed are truly creative ideas. To date, teams have played a very important role in generating the ideas that have helped Amazon be responsive to its customers, have a widely known Internet brand name, survive through the dot-com bust and be the highly successful and innovative company it is today.[21]

Groups and Teams as Motivators

Managers often decide to form groups and teams to accomplish organisational goals and then find that using them brings additional benefits. Members of groups, and especially members of teams (because of the higher intensity of interaction), are likely to be more satisfied than they would have been if they had been working on their own. The experience of working alongside other highly charged and motivated people can be very stimulating. Working on a team can also be very motivating: team members more readily see how their efforts and expertise directly contribute to the achievement of team and organisational goals, and they feel personally responsible for the outcomes or results of their work. This has been the case at Louis Vuitton, Nucor and Hallmark Cards.

The increased motivation and satisfaction that can accompany the use of teams can also lead to other outcomes, such as lower turnover. This has been the experience of Pegasus Security Group, a privately owned guarding company located in London. To provide high-quality customer service, the core values of Pegasus Security Group include teamwork as a vital component, emphasising that mutual respect and understanding are vital to deliver excellence. Motivation and satisfaction levels seem to be higher than in other security firms, and turnover is believed to be the lowest in the contractual industry.[22]

Working in a group or team can also satisfy organisational members' needs for engaging in *social interaction*. For workers who perform highly stressful jobs, such as hospital emergency and operating room staff, group membership can be an important source of social support and motivation. Family members or friends may not be able to fully understand or appreciate the work stress that these group members experience first-hand. Group members may cope better with work stress when they are able to share it with other members of their group. Groups often devise techniques to relieve stress, such as the telling of jokes among hospital operating room staff.

Why do all kinds of organisations rely so heavily on groups and teams? Effectively managed groups and teams can help managers in their quest for high performance, responsiveness to customers and employee motivation. Before explaining how managers can effectively manage groups, however, we shall describe the types of groups that are formed in organisations.

Types of Groups and Teams

To achieve their goals of high performance, responsiveness to customers, innovation and employee motivation, organisations can use various types of groups and teams (Fig. 15.2). **Formal groups** are those that are established to achieve organisational goals. The formal work groups are *cross-functional* teams composed of members from different departments, such as those at Hallmark Cards, and *cross-cultural* teams composed of members from different cultures or countries, such as the teams at global car makers.

Organisational members, managers or non-managers, sometimes form groups because they feel that they will help them achieve their own goals or meet their own needs (for example, the need for social interaction). Groups formed in this way are **informal groups**. Four nurses who work in a hospital and have lunch together twice a week constitute an informal group.

The Senior Management Team

A central concern of the CEO or managing director of a company is to form a *senior management team* to help the organisation achieve its mission and goals. Such teams are responsible for

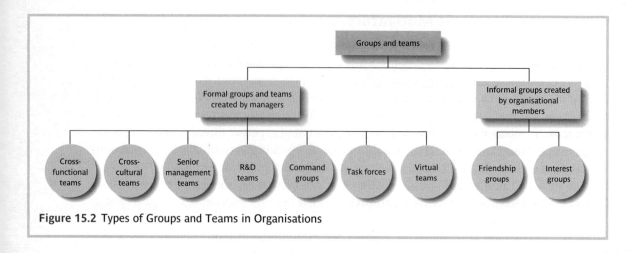

Figure 15.2 Types of Groups and Teams in Organisations

developing the strategies that result in an organisation's competitive advantage; most have between five and seven members. In forming their teams, CEOs are well advised to stress diversity – in expertise, skills, knowledge and experience. Many senior management teams are thus also cross-functional teams: they are composed of members from different departments, such as finance, marketing, production and engineering. Diversity helps ensure that the team will have all the background and resources it needs to make good decisions. Diversity also helps guard against *groupthink*, faulty group decision making that results when group members strive for agreement at the expense of an accurate assessment of the situation (see Chapter 7).

Research and Development Teams

Managers in pharmaceuticals, computers, electronics, electronic imaging and other high-tech industries often create **research and development (R&D) teams** to develop new products. The German pharmaceutical company Merck, the oldest pharmaceutical company in the world, assigns much of its success to its dynamic R&D agenda and to the way it has an employee-focused team structure.[23] Managers select R&D team members on the basis of their expertise and experience in a certain area. R&D teams are sometimes cross-functional teams with members from departments such as engineering, marketing and production in addition to members from the R&D department itself.

Command Groups

Subordinates who report to the same supervisor compose a **command group**. When senior managers design an organisation's structure and establish reporting relationships and a chain of command, they are essentially creating command groups. Such groups, often called *departments* or *units*, perform a significant amount of the work in many organisations. In order to have command groups that help an organisation gain a competitive advantage, managers not only need to motivate group members to perform at a high level but also need to be effective leaders. Examples of command groups include the sales assistants in a large John Lewis department store who report to the same department or floor supervisor, the employees of a small business who report to a general manager, or the workers on an automobile assembly line who report to the same first-line manager.

Task Forces

Task forces are formed to accomplish specific goals or solve problems in a certain time period; task forces are sometimes also called *ad hoc committees*. When an incident occurs in a company's or government's operations – such as the drug trial in 2006 in which six men ended up in hospital[24] – task forces may be formed to assess how it could have happened. Task forces may be given a set amount of time to achieve a specific goal; once the task force completes its report and reaches a conclusion, it is likely to be disbanded. Task forces can be a valuable tool for busy managers in the private or public sector who do not have the time to personally explore an important issue in depth.

Sometimes managers need to form task forces whose work is *never done*. The task force may be addressing a long-term or enduring problem or issue facing an organisation, such as how to most usefully contribute to the local community or how to make sure that the organisation provides opportunities for potential employees with disabilities. Task forces that are relatively permanent are often referred to as *standing committees*. Membership in standing committees changes over time – members may have a two- or three-year term, and memberships expire at varying times so that there are always some members with experience on the committee. Managers often form and maintain standing committees to make sure that important issues continue to be addressed.

Self-managed Work Teams

Self-managed work teams are teams in which team members are empowered and have the responsibility and autonomy to complete identifiable pieces of work. On a day-to-day basis, team members decide what the team will do, how it will do it and which team members will perform which specific tasks.[25] Managers provide self-managed work teams with their overall goals (such as assembling defect-free computer keyboards) but let team members decide how to meet them. Self-managed work teams are usually used to improve quality, increase motivation and satisfaction and lower costs. By creating self-managed work teams, tasks that individuals working separately used to perform are combined, so the team is responsible for a whole set of tasks that yields an identifiable output or end product.

In response to increasing competition, Johnson Wax (maker of well-known household products including Pledge furniture polish and Glade air freshener) formed self-managed work teams to find ways to cut costs. Traditionally, Johnson Wax used assembly-line production, in which workers were not encouraged or required to do much real thinking on the job, let alone determine how to cut costs. Things could not be more different at Johnson Wax now. A nine-member self-managed work team is responsible for moulding plastic containers. Team members choose their own leader, train new members, have their own budget to manage and are responsible for figuring out how to cut the costs of moulding plastic containers. Kim Litrenta, a 17-year veteran in one of the plants, sums up the effects of the change from assembly-line production to self-managed work teams this way: 'In the past you'd have no idea how much things cost because you weren't involved in decisions. Now it's amazing how many different ways people try to save money.'[26]

Managers can take a number of steps to ensure that self-managed work teams are effective and help an organisation gain a competitive advantage:[27]

- Give teams enough responsibility and autonomy to be truly *self-managing*. Refrain from telling team members what to do or solving problems for them even if you (as a manager) know what should be done.

- Make sure that a team's work is sufficiently complex so that it entails a number of different steps or procedures that must be performed and results in some kind of *finished end product*.

- Carefully *select* members of self-managed work teams. Team members should have the diversity of skills needed to complete the team's work, have the ability to work with others and want to be part of a team.

- As a manager, realise that your role *vis-à-vis* self-managed work teams calls for guidance, coaching and supporting, *not supervising*. You should be a resource for teams to turn to when needed.

- Analyse what type of training team members need and provide it. Working in a self-managed work team often requires employees to have extensive technical and interpersonal skills.

Managers in a wide variety of organisations have found that self-managed work teams help the organisation achieve its goals, as is certainly true at Louis Vuitton.[28] However, self-managed work teams can also run into trouble. Members are often reluctant to discipline one another by withholding bonuses from members who are not performing as well as others, or by firing members.[29]

An insurance company experimented with having members of self-managed teams evaluate one another's performance and determine pay levels. Team members did not feel comfortable assuming this role, however, and managers ended up evaluating performance and determining rewards.[30] One reason for team members' discomfort may be the close personal relationships they sometimes develop with one another. Members of self-managed work teams may also actually take longer to accomplish tasks, particularly when team members have difficulties co-ordinating their efforts.

Virtual Teams

Virtual teams are teams whose members rarely or never meet face-to-face but interact by using various forms of IT such as email, computer networks, telephone, fax and videoconferences; technology is constantly being developed, such as wikis and blogs, or podcasting, which are additional ways to communicate. As organisations become increasingly global, with operations in far-flung regions of the world, and as the need for specialised knowledge increases through advances in technology, managers can create virtual teams to solve problems or explore opportunities without being limited by the fact that team members need to be working in the same geographic location.[31]

Take the case of an organisation that has manufacturing facilities in Germany, the Czech Republic and Mexico and is encountering a quality problem in a complex manufacturing process. Each of its manufacturing facilities has a *quality control team* headed by a quality control manager. The Vice President for production does not try to solve the problem by forming and leading a team at one of the four manufacturing facilities; instead, a virtual team is formed, composed of the quality control managers of the four plants and the plants' general managers. When these team members communicate via email and videoconferencing, a wide array of knowledge and experience is brought to bear to solve the problem.

The principal advantage of virtual teams is that they enable managers to disregard geographic distance and form teams whose members have the knowledge, expertise and experience to tackle a particular problem or take advantage of a specific opportunity.[32] Virtual teams can also include members who are not actually employees of the organisation itself; a virtual team might include members of a company that is used for outsourcing. More and more companies, including Compaq-Hewlett-Packard, Motorola,[33] BP, Kodak, Whirlpool and VeriFone, are either using or exploring the use of virtual teams.[34]

Virtual teams rely on two forms of IT – *synchronous technologies* and *asynchronous technologies*.[35] Synchronous technologies enable virtual team members to communicate and interact with one another in real time simultaneously and include videoconferencing, teleconferencing and electronic meetings. Asynchronous technologies delay communication and include email, electronic bulletin boards and Internet websites. Many virtual teams use both kinds of technology, depending on the projects they are working on.

Increasing globalisation is likely to result in more organisations relying on virtual teams.[36] One of the major challenges members of virtual teams face is building a sense of camaraderie and trust among team members who rarely, if ever, meet face-to-face. To address this challenge, some organisations schedule recreational activities, such as ski trips, so that virtual team members can get together. Other organisations make sure that virtual team members have a chance to meet in person soon after the team is formed and then schedule periodic face-to-face meetings to promote trust, understanding and co-operation in the teams.[37] The need for such meetings is underscored by research that suggests that while some virtual teams can be as effective as teams that meet face to face, virtual team members may be less satisfied with teamwork efforts and have fewer feelings of camaraderie or cohesion. (Group cohesiveness is discussed in more detail later in the chapter.)[38]

Research also suggests that it is important for managers to keep track of virtual teams and intervene when necessary by, for example, encouraging members of teams who do not communicate often enough to monitor their team's progress and make sure that team members actually have the time, and are recognised for, their virtual teamwork.[39] When virtual teams are experiencing downtime or rough spots, managers may try to schedule face-to-face team time to bring team members together and help them focus on their goals.[40]

Friendship Groups

The groups described so far are *formal groups*, usually created by managers. **Friendship groups** are *informal groups* composed of employees who enjoy one another's company and socialise with one another. Members of friendship groups may have lunch together, take breaks together, or meet after work for meals, sports or other activities. Friendship groups help satisfy employees' needs for interpersonal interaction, can provide needed social support in times of stress and can contribute to people feeling good at work and being satisfied with their jobs. The informal relationships that are built in friendship groups can often help them solve work-related problems because members of these groups typically discuss work-related matters and offer advice.

Interest Groups

Employees form informal **interest groups** when they seek to achieve a common goal related to their membership in an organisation. Employees may form interest groups, for example, to encourage managers to consider instituting flexible working hours, providing on-site child care, improving working conditions, or more proactively supporting environmental protection. Interest groups can provide managers with valuable insights into the issues and concerns that are foremost in employees' minds. They also can signal the need for change. However, interest groups can also be external. An engineer in a small company, for example, may not have many colleagues whom he or she could approach to ask questions or exchange ideas with; so this engineer may join an interest group that specifically focuses on the type of area in which the engineer is interested. Virtual interest groups are now common and are likely to become an even more important source for expertise in the future.

Group Dynamics

The ways in which groups function – and, ultimately, their effectiveness – depend on group characteristics and processes known collectively as *group dynamics*. In this section, we discuss five key elements of group dynamics: group size, tasks and roles; group leadership; group development; group norms; and group cohesiveness.

Group Size, Tasks and Roles

Group size, group tasks and group roles all need to be taken into account if they are to create and maintain high-performing groups and teams.

Group size

The number of members in a group can be an important determinant of members' motivation, commitment and performance. There are several advantages to keeping a group relatively small – between two and nine members. Compared with members of large groups, members of small groups tend to (1) interact more with each other and find it easier to co-ordinate their efforts, (2) be more motivated, satisfied and committed, (3) find it easier to share information and (4) be better able to see the importance of their personal contributions for group success. A disadvantage of small rather than large groups, however, is that members of small groups have fewer resources available to accomplish their goals.

Large groups – with 10 or more members – also offer some advantages. They have more resources at their disposal to achieve group goals than small groups do – including the knowledge, experience, skills and abilities of group members as well as their actual time and effort. Large groups also enable managers to obtain the advantages stemming from the *division of labour* – splitting the work to be performed into particular tasks and assigning tasks to individual workers. Workers who specialise in particular tasks are likely to become skilled at performing them and contribute significantly to high group performance.

The disadvantages of large groups include the problems of communication and co-ordination and the lower levels of motivation, satisfaction and commitment that members sometimes experience. It is clearly more difficult to share information with, and co-ordinate the activities of, 16 people rather than 8 people. Members of large groups may also not think that their efforts are really needed, and sometimes may not even feel a part of the group.

In deciding on the appropriate size for any group, managers attempt to gain the advantages of small-group size and, at the same time, form groups with sufficient resources to accomplish their goals and have a well-developed division of labour, as is true at Louis Vuitton and Nucor. As a general rule of thumb, groups should have no more members than necessary to achieve a division of labour and provide the resources needed to achieve group goals. In R&D teams, for example, group size is too large when (1) members spend more time communicating what they know to others than applying what they know to solving problems and creating new products, (2) individual productivity decreases and (3) group performance suffers.[41]

Group tasks

The appropriate size of a high-performing group is affected by the kind of tasks the group is to perform. An important characteristic of group tasks that affects performance is **task interdependence**, the degree to which the work performed by one member of a group influences the work performed by others.[42] As task interdependence increases, group members need to interact more frequently and intensely with one another, and their efforts have to be more closely co-ordinated if they are to perform at a high level. Management expert James D. Thompson identified three types of task interdependence: pooled, sequential, and reciprocal (Fig. 15.3).[43]

Pooled task interdependence

Pooled task interdependence exists when group members make separate and independent contributions to group performance; overall group performance is the sum of the performance of

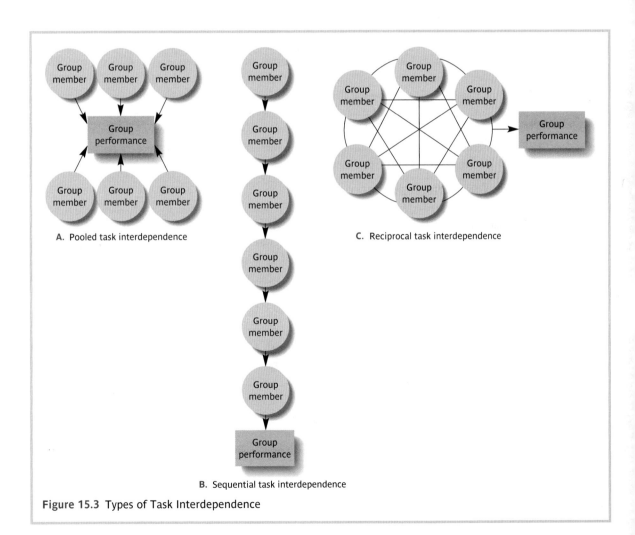

A. Pooled task interdependence

C. Reciprocal task interdependence

B. Sequential task interdependence

Figure 15.3 Types of Task Interdependence

the individual members (Fig. 15.3A). Examples of groups that have pooled task interdependence include a group of teachers in a primary school, a group of sales assistants in a department store, or a group of secretaries in an office. In these examples, group performance – whether it is the number of children who are taught and the quality of their education, the value of sales or the amount of secretarial work completed – is determined by *summing the individual contributions* of group members.

For groups with pooled interdependence, managers should determine the appropriate group size primarily from the amount of work to be accomplished. Large groups can be effective because group members work independently and do not have to interact frequently with one another. Motivation in groups with pooled interdependence will be highest when managers reward group members based on individual performance.

Sequential task interdependence

Sequential task interdependence exists when group members must perform specific tasks in a predetermined order: certain tasks have to be performed before others. The performance of one worker affects the work of others (Fig. 15.3B). Assembly lines and mass-production processes are characterised by sequential task interdependence.

When group members are sequentially interdependent, group size is usually dictated by the needs of the production process – for example, the number of steps needed in an assembly line to efficiently produce a CD player. With sequential interdependence, it is difficult to identify individual performance because one group member's performance depends on how well others perform their tasks. A slow worker at the start of an assembly line, for example, causes all workers further down to work slowly. Managers are often advised to reward group members for group performance: group members will be motivated to perform highly because if the group performs well, each member will benefit. In addition, group members may put pressure on poor performers to improve so that group performance and rewards do not suffer.

Reciprocal task interdependence

Reciprocal task interdependence exists when the work performed by each group member is fully dependent on the work performed by other group members: group members have to share information, intensely interact with one another, and co-ordinate their efforts in order for the group to achieve its goals (Fig. 15.3C). In general, reciprocal task interdependence characterises the operation of teams, rather than other kinds of groups. The task interdependence of R&D teams, senior management teams and many self-managed work teams is reciprocal.

When group members are reciprocally interdependent, managers are advised to keep group size relatively small because of the necessity of co-ordinating team members' activities. Communication difficulties can arise in teams with reciprocally interdependent tasks because team members need to interact frequently with one another and be available when needed. As group size increases, communication difficulties increase and can impair team performance.

When a group's members are reciprocally interdependent, managers also are advised to reward group members on the basis of group performance. Individual levels of performance are often difficult for managers to identify, and group-based rewards help ensure that group members will be motivated to perform at a high level and make valuable contributions to the group. Of course, if a manager can identify instances of individual performance in such groups, they too can be rewarded to maintain high levels of motivation. Microsoft and many other companies reward group members for their individual performance as well as for the performance of their group.

Group roles

A **group role** is a set of behaviours and tasks that a member of a group is expected to perform because of his or her position in the group. Members of cross-functional teams, for example, are expected to perform roles relevant to their special areas of expertise. At Hallmark Cards, it is the role of writers on the teams to create verses for new cards, the role of artists to draw illustrations and the role of designers to put verse and artwork together in an attractive and appealing card design. The roles of members of senior management teams are shaped primarily by their areas of expertise – production, marketing, finance, R&D – but members of such teams also typically draw on their broad-based expertise as planners and strategists.

In forming groups and teams, managers need to clearly communicate to group members the expectations for their roles in the group, what is required of them and how the different roles in the group fit together to accomplish group goals. Managers also need to realise that group roles often *change and evolve* as a group's tasks and goals change and as group members gain experience and knowledge. To get the performance gains that come from experience or 'learning by doing', managers should encourage group members to take the initiative to assume additional responsibilities as they see fit and modify their assigned roles. This process, called **role making**, can enhance individual and group performance.

In self-managed work teams and some other groups, group members themselves are responsible for creating and assigning roles. Many self-managed work teams also pick their own team leaders. When group members create their own roles, managers should be available to group members in an advisory capacity, helping them effectively settle conflicts and disagreements.

Team Roles

Various researchers (such as R. M. Belbin)[44] have tried to identify the *informal roles* people play in groups. These focus on the relationship of each member to other members and to the group task. Belbin's roles are categorised as Team leaders, Creative thinkers, Negotiators or Company workers:[45]

- *Team leaders*: Co-ordinators and shapers
- *Creative thinkers*: Monitor/evaluators, plant and specialists
- *Negotiators*: Implementers and completer/finishers
- *Company workers*: Resource/investigators and team workers.

Each role has both strengths and allowable weaknesses:

- *Co-ordinators* – usually respected leaders who help everyone focus on their task; at times can be seen as excessively controlling
- *Shapers* – tend to have lots of energy and action, challenge others to move forwards but can be insensitive
- *Monitor/evaluators* – see the big picture; think carefully and accurately about things, but may lack energy or ability to inspire others
- *Plants* – solve difficult problems with original and creative ideas; can be poor communicators and may ignore the details
- *Specialists* – have expert knowledge/skills in key areas and will solve many problems but can often be disinterested in all other areas

- *Implementers* – well-organised and predictable; take basic ideas and make them work in practice; can be slow and indecisive at times
- *Completer/finishers* – Reliably see things through to the end, ironing out the wrinkles and ensuring everything works well; can worry too much and not trust others
- *Resource investigators* – explore new ideas and possibilities with energy and with others; good networkers but can often be too optimistic and lose energy after the initial surge of motivation
- *Team workers* – care about people and how the team is getting on together, good listeners and work to resolve social problems; can have problems making difficult decisions.

Belbin's work is used extensively in organisations to identify team roles today, although there is still ambiguity among researchers as to whether these roles are valid. In trying to relate such roles to the division of labour within teams, Belbin does not maintain that these roles are 'types', as in personality traits, but that each role is related to identifiable *behaviours and competencies* that people can bring to the team, together with highlighting the allowable weaknesses of those roles. People can hold more than one role in a team but in degrees (one member may show 70 per cent Shaper (leader/coordination skills), 20 per cent Plant competencies and 10 per cent Completer/finisher skills, for example).

These roles should therefore be used as guidelines, not thought of as stable characteristics; team roles may differ according to the type of task that is performed and the team of which one is currently a part.

Group Leadership

All groups and teams need leadership. Indeed, as discussed in detail in Chapter 14, effective leadership is a key ingredient for high-performing groups, teams and organisations. Sometimes managers assume the leadership role in groups and teams, as is the case in many command groups and senior management teams. Or a manager may appoint a member of a group who is not a manager to be group leader or chairperson, as is the case in a task force or standing committee. In other cases, group or team members may choose their own leaders, or a leader may emerge naturally as members of a group work together to achieve shared goals. When managers empower members of self-managed work teams, they often let group members choose their own leaders. Some self-managed work teams find it effective to rotate the leadership role among their members. Whether leaders of groups and teams are managers or not, and whether they are appointed by managers or emerge naturally in a group, they play an important role in ensuring that groups and teams perform up to their potential. Leadership in R&D teams has been highlighted as a significant issue in driving forward effective and successful innovation.[46]

Group Development over Time

As many facilitators of self-managed teams have learned, it can take a self-managed work team two or three years to perform up to its true capabilities.[47] What a group is capable of achieving depends in part on its stage of development. Knowing that it takes considerable time for self-managed work teams to get up and running has helped managers have realistic expectations for new teams and know that they need to provide new team members with considerable training and guidance.

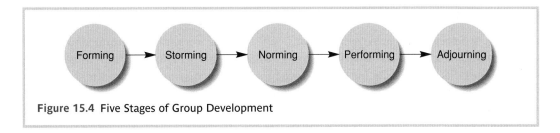

Figure 15.4 Five Stages of Group Development

Although every group's development over time is unique, researchers have identified five stages of group development that many groups seem to pass through (Fig. 15.4).[48]

Forming

In the first stage, *forming*, members try to get to know each other and reach a common understanding of what the group is trying to accomplish and how group members should behave. During this stage, managers should strive to make each member feel that he or she is a valued part of the group.

Storming

In the second stage, *storming*, group members experience conflict and disagreements because some members do not wish to submit to the demands of other group members. Disputes may arise over who should lead the group. Self-managed work teams can be particularly vulnerable during the storming stage. Managers need to keep an eye on groups at this stage to make sure that conflict does not get out of hand.

Norming

During the third stage, *norming*, close ties between group members develop, and feelings of friendship and camaraderie emerge. Group members arrive at a consensus about what goals they should be seeking to achieve, and how group members should behave toward one another.

Performing

In the fourth stage, *performing*, the real work of the group gets accomplished. Depending on the type of group in question, managers need to take different steps at this stage to help ensure that groups are effective. Managers of command groups need to make sure that group members are motivated and that they are effectively leading group members. Coaches overseeing self-managed work teams have to empower team members and make sure that teams are given enough responsibility and autonomy.

Adjourning

The last stage, *adjourning*, applies only to groups that are eventually broken up, such as task forces. During adjourning, a group is dispersed. Adjourning often takes place when a group completes a finished product, such as when a task force evaluating the pros and cons of providing on-site child care produces a report and recommendations.

Managers should have a flexible approach to group development and should keep attuned to the different needs and requirements of groups at various stages.[49] Above all else, and regardless of the stage of development, managers need to think of themselves as *resources* for groups. Managers always should be striving to find ways to help groups and teams function more effectively.

Group Norms

All groups, whether senior management teams, self-managed work teams or command groups, need to control their members' behaviours to ensure that the group performs effectively and efficiently and meets its goals. Assigning roles to each group member is one way to control behaviour in groups. Another important way in which groups influence members' behaviour is through the development and enforcement of **group norms**.[50] Group norms are shared guidelines or rules for behaviour that most group members follow. Groups develop norms concerning a wide variety of behaviours, including working hours, the sharing of information among group members, how certain group tasks should be performed and even how members of a group should dress. In the UK, such norms are often visible, as staff in banks or department stores wear uniforms.

Managers should encourage members of a group to develop norms that contribute to group performance and the attainment of group goals. Group norms that dictate that each member of a cross-functional team should always be available for the rest of the team when his or her input is needed, return phone calls as soon as possible, inform other team members of travel plans and give team members a phone number at which he or she can be reached when travelling on business help to ensure that the team is efficient, performs highly and achieves its goals. A norm in a command group of secretaries that secretaries who have a light workload in any given week should help out secretaries with heavier workloads helps to ensure that the group completes all assignments in a timely and efficient manner. A norm in a senior management team that dictates that team members should always consult with one another before making major decisions helps to ensure that good decisions are made with a minimum of errors and a maximum of consent.

Conformity and deviance

Group members conform to norms for three reasons: (1) they want to *obtain rewards* and *avoid punishments*, (2) they want to *imitate* group members whom they like and admire, (3) they have *internalised* the norm and believe it is the right and proper way to behave.[51] Consider the case of Robert King, who conformed to his department's norm of attending a charity event for raising money to provide food for homeless people. King's conformity could be due to (1) his desire to be a member of the group in good standing and to have friendly relationships with other group members (rewards), (2) his copying the behaviour of other members of the department whom he respects and who always attend the charity event (imitating other group members), or (3) his belief in the merits of supporting the activities of the charity (believing that is the right and proper way to behave).

Failure to conform, or *deviance*, occurs when a member of a group violates a group norm. Deviance signals that a group is not in control of one of its member's behaviours or that the deviant member is unsatisfied with one or more of the group's norms. Groups generally respond to members who behave defiantly in one of three ways:[52]

1. The group might try to get the member to change his or her deviant ways and conform to the norm. Group members might try to convince the member of the need to conform, or they might ignore or even punish the deviant. For example, in a food production plant Liz Senkbiel, a member of a self-managed work team responsible for weighing sausages, failed to conform to a group norm dictating that group members should periodically clean up an untidy room used to interview prospective employees. Because Senkbiel refused to take part in the team's cleanup efforts, team members reduced her monthly bonus for a two-month period.[53] Senkbiel clearly learned the costs of deviant behaviour in her team.

2. The group might expel the member.

3. The group might change the norm to be consistent with the member's behaviour.

That last alternative suggests that some deviant behaviour can be functional for groups. Deviance is functional for a group when it causes group members to evaluate norms that may be dysfunctional but are taken for granted by the group. Often, group members, like any individual, do not think about why they behave in a certain way or why they follow certain norms. Deviance can cause group members to reflect on their norms and change them when appropriate.

Take the case of a group of receptionists in a beauty salon who followed the norm that all appointments would be handwritten in an appointment book and at the end of each day the receptionist on duty would enter the appointments into the salon's computer system, which would print out the hairdressers' daily schedules. One day, a receptionist decided to enter appointments directly into the computer system at the time they were being made, bypassing the appointment book. This deviant behaviour caused the other receptionists to think about why they were using the appointment book in the first place, since all appointments could be entered into the computer directly. After consulting with the owner of the salon, the group changed its norm. Now appointments are entered directly into the computer, which saves time and cuts down on scheduling errors.

Encouraging a balance of conformity and deviance

To effectively help an organisation gain a competitive advantage, groups and teams need to have the right balance of conformity and deviance (Fig. 15.5). A group needs a certain level of conformity to ensure that it can control members' behaviour and channel it in the direction of high performance and group goal accomplishment. A group also needs a certain level of deviance to ensure that dysfunctional norms are discarded and replaced with functional ones. Balancing conformity and deviance is a pressing concern for all groups, whether they are senior management teams, R&D teams, command groups or self-managed work teams.

The extent of conformity and reactions to deviance within groups are determined by group members themselves. The three bases for conformity described above are powerful forces that more often than not result in group members conforming to norms. Sometimes these forces are so strong that deviance rarely occurs and, when it does, it is stamped out.

Managers can take several steps to ensure that there is enough tolerance of deviance in groups so that group members are willing to deviate from dysfunctional norms and, when deviance occurs in their group, reflect on the appropriateness of the violated norm and change it if necessary. First, managers or coaches can be *role models* for the groups and teams they oversee. When managers encourage and accept employees' suggestions for changes in procedures, do not rigidly insist that tasks be accomplished in a certain way and admit when a norm that they once supported is no longer functional, they signal to group members that conformity should not come at the expense of necessary changes and improvements. Second, managers should let employees know that there are always ways to improve group processes and performance levels and thus opportunities to *replace* existing norms with norms that will better enable a group to achieve its goals and perform at a high level. Third, managers should encourage members of groups and teams to periodically assess the *appropriateness* of their existing norms.

Managers in the innovative design firm Ideo, which has its UK office in London (Ideo's culture is described in Chapter 3) have excelled at ensuring that design teams have the right mix of conformity and deviance, resulting in Ideo's designing products in fields ranging from medicine to

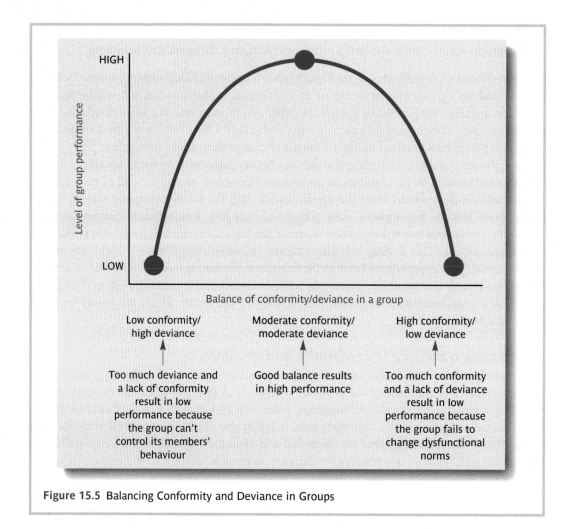

Figure 15.5 Balancing Conformity and Deviance in Groups

space travel to computing and personal hygiene, as indicated in Case 15.2. Its products are already labelled as antiques of the future; one of their design innovations that will be remembered is the BBC's interactive radio service.

Reaction Time

1. Why do all organisations need to rely on groups and teams to achieve their goals and gain a competitive advantage?

2. What kinds of employees would prefer to work in a virtual team? What kinds of employees would prefer to work in a team that meets face to face?

3. Think about a group that you are a member of, and describe that group's current stage of development. Does the development of this group seem to be following the forming, storming, norming, performing and adjourning stages?

Case 15.2: **Diversity of thought and respect for ideas**

Ideo designed many products we now take for granted – the first Apple mouse, the Palm handheld organiser, stand-up toothpaste containers, parts of the Oral-B toothbrush, flexible shelving for offices, self-sealing drink bottles for sports, blood analysers and even equipment used in space travel.[54] Managers and designers at Ideo pride themselves on being experts at the process of innovation in general, rather than in any particular domain. Of course, the company has technical design experts, such as mechanical and electrical engineers, who work on products requiring specialised knowledge, but on the same teams with the engineers might be an anthropologist, a biologist and a social scientist.[55]

Essentially, a guiding principle at Ideo is that innovation comes in many shapes and sizes and it is only through diversity in thought that people can recognise opportunities for innovation. To promote such diversity in thought, new product development at Ideo is a team effort.[56] Moreover, both conformity and deviance are encouraged in Ideo teams.

Deviance, thinking differently, and not conforming to expected ways of doing things and mind-sets are encouraged at Ideo. Innovative ideas often flow when designers try to see things as they really are and are not blinded by thoughts of what is appropriate, what is possible or how things should be. Often, constraints on new product design are created by designers themselves conforming to a certain mind-set about the nature of a product or what a product can or should do and look like. Ideo designers in their design teams are encouraged to actively break down these constraints.[57]

Managers at Ideo realise the need for a certain amount of conformity so that members of design teams can work effectively together and achieve their goals. Conformity to a few very central norms is emphasised in Ideo teams. These norms include understanding what the team is working on (e.g. the product, market or client need), observing real people in their natural environments, visualising how new products might work and be used, evaluating and refining product prototypes, encouraging wild ideas and never rejecting an idea simply because it sounds too crazy.[58] As long as these norms are followed, diversity of thought and even deviance serve to promote innovation. Another norm at Ideo is to study 'rule breakers' – people who don't follow instructions for products, for example, or who try to put products to different uses – as these individuals may help designers identify problems with existing products and consumer needs that are not satisfied.[59] Ideo's focus on encouraging both deviance and conformity in design teams has benefited all of us as we use Ideo-designed products that seem so familiar we take them for granted. We forget these products weren't in existence until a design team at Ideo was called on by a client to develop a new product or improve an existing one.[60]

Group Cohesiveness

Another important element of group dynamics that affects group performance and effectiveness is **group cohesiveness** – the degree to which members are attracted to or loyal to their group or team.[61] When group cohesiveness is high, individuals strongly value their group membership, find the group very appealing and have strong desires to remain a part of the group. When group cohesiveness is low, group members do not find their group particularly appealing and have little desire to retain their membership. Research suggests that managers should strive to have a moderate level of cohesiveness in the groups and teams they manage because that is most likely to contribute to an organisation's competitive advantage.

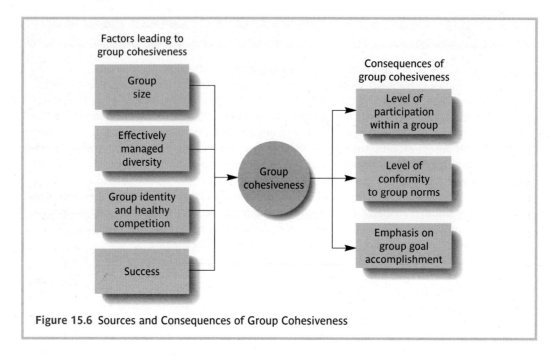

Figure 15.6 Sources and Consequences of Group Cohesiveness

Consequences of group cohesiveness

There are three major consequences of group cohesiveness: *level of participation* within a group, *level of conformity* to group norms and emphasis on group *goal accomplishment* (Fig. 15.6).[62]

Level of participation within a group

As group cohesiveness increases, the extent of group members' participation within the group increases. Participation contributes to group effectiveness because group members are actively involved in the group, ensure that group tasks get accomplished, readily share information with each other and have frequent and open communication (the important topic of communication is discussed in Chapter 16).

A moderate level of group cohesiveness helps to ensure that group members actively participate in the group and communicate effectively with one another. The reason why managers may not want to encourage high levels of cohesiveness is illustrated by the example of two cross-functional teams responsible for developing new toys. Members of the highly cohesive Team Alpha often have lengthy meetings that usually start with non-work-related conversations and jokes, meet more often than most of the other cross-functional teams in the company and spend a good portion of their time communicating the ins and outs of their department's contribution to toy development to other team members. Members of the moderately cohesive Team Beta generally have efficient meetings in which ideas are communicated and discussed as needed, do not meet more often than necessary and share the ins and outs of their expertise with one another only to the extent needed for the development process. Teams Alpha and Beta have both developed some top-selling toys. However, it generally takes Team Alpha 30 per cent longer to do so than Team Beta. This is why too much cohesiveness can be too much of a good thing.

Level of conformity to group norms

Increasing levels of group cohesiveness result in increasing levels of conformity to group norms, and when cohesiveness becomes high there may be so little deviance in groups that group members conform to norms even when they are dysfunctional. In contrast, low cohesiveness can result in too much deviance and undermine the ability of a group to influence its members' behaviours to get things done.

Teams Alpha and Beta both had the same norm for toy development. It directed that members of each team would discuss potential ideas for new toys, decide on a line of toys to pursue and then have the team member from R&D design a prototype. Recently, a new animated movie featuring a family of rabbits produced by a small film company was an unexpected hit, and major toy companies were scrambling to reach licensing agreements to produce toy lines featuring the rabbits. The senior management team in the toy company assigned Teams Alpha and Beta to develop the new toy lines and to do so quickly to beat the competition.

Members of Team Alpha followed their usual toy development norm even though the marketing expert on the team believed that the process could have been streamlined to save time. The marketing expert on Team Beta urged the team to deviate from its toy development norm. She suggested that the team not ask R&D to develop prototypes but, instead, modify top-selling toys the company already made to feature rabbits and then reach a licensing agreement with the film company based on the high sales potential (given the company's prior success). Once the licensing agreement was signed, the company could take the time needed to develop innovative and unique rabbit toys with more input from R&D.

As a result of the willingness of the marketing expert on Team Beta to deviate from the norm for toy development, the toy company obtained an exclusive licensing agreement with the film company and had its first rabbit toys on the shelves of stores in a record three months. Groups need a balance of conformity and deviance, so a moderate level of cohesiveness often yields the best outcome, as it did in the case of Team Beta.

Emphasis on group goal accomplishment

As group cohesiveness increases within a group, the emphasis placed on group goal accomplishment also increases. A very strong emphasis on group goal accomplishment, however, does not always lead to organisational effectiveness. For an organisation to be effective and gain a competitive advantage, the different groups and teams in the organisation must co-operate with one another and be motivated to achieve *organisational goals*, even if doing so sometimes comes at the expense of the achievement of group goals. A moderate level of cohesiveness motivates group members to accomplish both group and organisational goals. High levels of cohesiveness can cause group members to be so focused on group goal accomplishment that they may strive to achieve group goals no matter what – even when doing so is not in line with organisational performance.

At the toy company, the major goal of the cross-functional teams was to develop new toy lines that were truly innovative, utilised the latest in technology and were in some way fundamentally distinct from other toys on the market. When it came to the rabbit project, Team Alpha's high level of cohesiveness contributed to its continued emphasis of its group goal of developing an innovative line of toys; thus, the team stuck with its usual design process. Team Beta, in contrast, realised that developing the new line of toys quickly was an important organisational goal that should take precedence over the group's goal of developing groundbreaking new toys, at least in the short run. Team Beta's moderate level of cohesiveness contributed to team members doing what was best for the toy company in this case.

Factors leading to group cohesiveness

Four factors contribute to the level of group cohesiveness (Fig. 15.6).[63] By influencing these *determinants of group cohesiveness*, managers can raise or lower the level of cohesiveness to promote moderate levels in groups and teams.

Group size

As we mentioned earlier, members of small groups tend to be more motivated and committed than members of large groups. To promote cohesiveness in groups, when feasible, managers should form groups that are small-to-medium in size (about 2–15 members). If a group is low in cohesiveness and large in size, one way could be to divide the group in two and assign different tasks and goals to the two newly formed groups.

Effectively managed diversity

In general, people tend to like and get along with others who are similar to themselves. It is easier to communicate with someone, for example, who shares your values, has a similar background and has had similar experiences. However, as discussed in Chapter 5, diversity in groups, teams and organisations can help an organisation gain a competitive advantage. Diverse groups often come up with more innovative and creative ideas. One reason why cross-functional teams are so popular in organisations like Hallmark Cards is that the diversity in expertise represented in the teams results in higher levels of team performance.

In forming groups and teams, managers need to make sure that the diversity in knowledge, experience, expertise and other characteristics necessary for group goal accomplishment is represented in the new groups. Managers then have to make sure that this diversity in group membership is effectively managed so that groups will be cohesive.

Group identity and healthy competition

When group cohesiveness is low, managers can often increase it by encouraging groups to develop their own identities or personalities and to engage in healthy competition. Self-managed teams may be encouraged to perform better if they are publicly compared to one another – for example, by displaying their results in a common room.

If groups are too cohesive, managers can try to decrease cohesiveness by promoting organisational (rather than group) identity and making the organisation as a whole the focus of the group's efforts. Organisational identity can be promoted by making group members feel that they are valued members of the organisation as a whole and by stressing co-operation across groups to promote the achievement of organisational goals. Excessive levels of cohesiveness also can be reduced by limiting or eliminating competition among groups and rewarding co-operation.

Success

When it comes to promoting group cohesiveness, there is more than a grain of truth in the saying 'Nothing succeeds like success'. As groups become more successful, they become increasingly attractive to their members and their cohesiveness tends to increase (see Case 15.3). When cohesiveness is low, managers can increase it by making sure that a group can achieve some noticeable and visible successes.

Take the case of a group of sales assistants in the homeware department of a medium-sized department store. The homeware department was recently moved to a corner of the store's basement. Its remote location resulted in low sales because of infrequent customer traffic in that part of the store. The sales assistants, who were generally evaluated favourably by their supervisors and were valued members of the store, tried various initiatives to boost sales, but to no avail. As a result of this lack of success and the poor performance of their department, their cohesiveness started to plummet. To increase and preserve the cohesiveness of the group, the store manager implemented a group-based incentive across the store. In any month, members of the group with the best attendance and punctuality records would have their names and pictures posted on a bulletin board in the cafeteria and would each receive a gift certificate. The homeware group frequently had the best records, and their success on this dimension helped to build and maintain their cohesiveness. Moreover, this initiative boosted attendance and discouraged lateness throughout the store. The cohesiveness of teams at Louis Vuitton is enhanced by their success at producing high-quality accessories.

Case 15.3: Cohesiveness and success with Innocent and Virgin

Innocent Drinks have made a name for themselves by providing healthy and fun-looking fruit drinks. The company is also known for having one of the most innovative and successful business concepts. Part of the success is the way that the founders of Innocent treat their staff.

People and teams are greatly appreciated at Innocent, the company prides itself on providing an informal and enjoyable working environment. The founders aim to treat their staff well and believe that providing ample space for relaxation and doing things as a group make perfect business sense. Three-quarters of the offices of Innocent are *social spaces* – even table football is provided.

But it is not just social space during work time that encourages people to be together. Every year, all the staff are treated to a snowboarding holiday. Innocent also encourages the feeling of a family by providing ample support for a new parent, giving £2,000 for the birth of each child.

Cohesiveness and success is also formed by being content that what is given to the company is somehow returned. Innocent encourages staff to think outside the box, and be different. In order to keep staff motivated, Innocent offers scholarships of £1,000 to every staff member so people can do something different, something they have always wanted to do – such as recording a CD or taking flying lessons.

The continued success of Innocent speaks for itself. Innocent has taken its people and team issue seriously and has managed to encourage a family feel.[64]

Another company that has successfully been able to create cohesive teams that bring forward the business is Virgin Atlantic. The fun-loving, down-to-earth, friendly atmosphere associated with the brand has been adopted in its Cargo business. The business is divided into various parts, but all are organised around a team structure. Virgin's cargo service has won several awards that suggest that it got it right in encouraging teams.[65] Virgin Group's enthusiastic chairman, Richard Branson, summarises this by saying: 'The people who make up Virgin Atlantic make Virgin Atlantic.'

Managing Groups and Teams for High Performance

Now that you have a good understanding of why groups and teams are so important for organisations, the types of groups that managers create and group dynamics, we can consider some additional steps that managers can take to make sure that groups and teams perform highly and contribute to organisational effectiveness. Managers striving to have top-performing groups and teams need to (1) motivate group members to work toward the achievement of organisational goals, (2) reduce **social loafing**, and (3) help groups to manage conflict effectively.

Motivating Group Members to Achieve Organisational Goals

When work is difficult, tedious or requires a high level of commitment and energy, managers cannot assume that group members will always be motivated to work toward the achievement of organisational goals. Consider the case of a group of house painters who paint the interiors and exteriors of new homes for a construction company and are paid on an hourly basis. Why should they strive to complete painting jobs quickly and efficiently if doing so will just make them feel more tired at the end of the day and they will not receive any tangible benefits? It makes more sense for the painters to adopt a more relaxed approach, to take frequent breaks and to work at a leisurely pace. This relaxed approach, however, impairs the construction company's ability to gain a competitive advantage because it raises costs and increases the time needed to complete a new home.

Managers can motivate members of groups and teams to achieve organisational goals and create a competitive advantage by making sure that the members themselves benefit when the group or team performs highly, as is true at Luis Vuitton, Amazon or Innocent Drinks. If members of a self-managed work team know that they will receive a weekly bonus based on team performance, they will be highly motivated to perform at a high level. However, as described in earlier chapters, individuals are not motivated only by *extrinsic rewards* that promise financial bonuses in order to perform well within teams. Companies such as Innocent offer some financial rewards to achieve organisational goals, but also offer more *intrinsic rewards*.

Managers often rely on some combination of individual and group-based incentives to motivate members of groups and teams to work toward the achievement of organisational goals and a competitive advantage. When individual performance within a group can be assessed, pay is often determined by individual performance or by both individual and group performance. When individual performance within a group cannot be accurately assessed then group performance should be the key determinant of pay levels. Approximately 75 per cent of companies that use self-managed work teams base team members' pay in part on team performance.[66] A major challenge within self-managed teams is to develop a fair and equitable pay system that will lead to both high individual motivation and high group or team performance.

Other benefits that managers can make available to high-performance group members – in addition to monetary rewards – include extra resources such as equipment and computer software, awards and other forms of recognition and choice of future work assignments. Members of self-managed work teams that develop new software at companies like Microsoft often value working on interesting and important projects; members of teams that have performed highly are rewarded by being assigned to interesting and important new projects.

At Ideo, managers motivate team members by making them feel important: 'When people feel special, they'll perform beyond your wildest dreams.'[67] To make Ideo team members feel special, Ideo managers plan unique and fun year-end parties, give teams the opportunity to take time off if they feel they need or want to, encourage teams to take field trips and see pranks as a way to incorporate fun into the workplace.[68]

Reducing Social Loafing in Groups

We have focused on the steps that managers can take to encourage high levels of performance in groups. Managers, however, need to be aware of an important downside to group and team work: the potential for *social loafing*, which reduces group performance. Social loafing is the tendency of individuals to put forth less effort when they work in groups than when they work

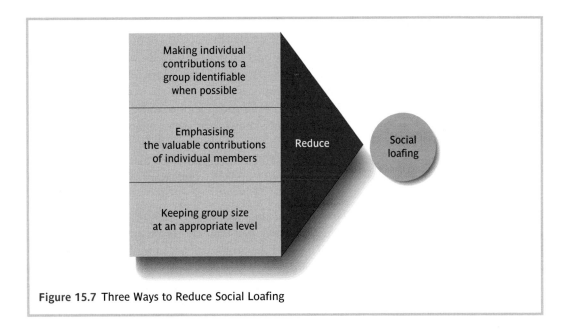

Figure 15.7 Three Ways to Reduce Social Loafing

alone.[69] Have you ever worked on a group project in which one or two group members never seemed to be pulling their weight? Have you ever worked in a student society or committee in which some members always seemed to be missing meetings and never volunteer for activities? Have you ever had a job in which one or two of your co-workers seemed to be doing less because they knew that you or other members of your work group would make up for their low levels of effort? If you have, you have witnessed social loafing in action.

Social loafing can occur in all kinds of groups and teams and in all kinds of organisations. It can result in lower group performance and may even prevent a group from attaining its goals. Fortunately, there are steps managers can take to reduce social loafing and sometimes completely eliminate it; we shall look at three (Fig. 15.7).

1. *Make individual contributions to a group identifiable*   Some people may engage in social loafing when they work in groups because they think that they can hide in the crowd – that no one will notice if they put forth less effort than they should. Other people may think that if they put forth high levels of effort and make substantial contributions to the group, their contributions will not be noticed and they will receive no rewards for their work – so why bother?[70]

   One way in which managers can effectively eliminate social loafing is by making individual contributions to a group *identifiable* so that group members perceive that low and high levels of effort will be noticed and individual contributions evaluated.[71] Managers can accomplish this by assigning specific tasks to group members and holding them *accountable* for their completion. Take the case of a group of eight employees responsible for reshelving returned books in a large public library. The head librarian was concerned that there was always a backlog of seven or eight carts of books to be reshelved, even though the employees never seemed to be particularly busy and some even found time to sit down in the current-periodicals section to read newspapers and magazines. The librarian decided to try to eliminate the apparent social loafing by assigning each employee sole responsibility for reshelving a particular section of the library. Because the library's front-desk employees sorted the books by section on the carts as they were returned, holding the shelvers responsible for particular sections was easily accomplished. Once the shelvers knew that the librarian could identify their effort or lack of effort, there were rarely any backlogs of books.

Sometimes the members of a group can co-operate to eliminate social loafing by making individual contributions identifiable. Members of a self-managed work team in a small security company who assemble control boxes for home alarm systems start each day by deciding who will perform which tasks, and how much work each member and the group as a whole should strive to accomplish. Each team member knows that, at the end of the day, the other team members will know exactly how much he or she has accomplished. With this system in place, social loafing never occurs in the team. Remember, however, that in some teams – as in teams whose members are reciprocally interdependent – individual contributions cannot be made identifiable.

2. *Emphasise the valuable contributions of individual members*   Another reason why social loafing may occur is that people sometimes think that their efforts are unnecessary or unimportant when they work in a group. They feel the group will accomplish its goals and perform at an acceptable level whether or not they personally perform at a high level. To counteract this belief, when managers form groups they should assign individuals to groups on the basis of the valuable contribution that *each* person can make to the group as a whole. Clearly communicating to group members why each person's contribution is valuable to the group is an effective means by which managers, and group members themselves, can reduce or eliminate social loafing.[72] This is most clearly illustrated in cross-functional teams where each member's valuable contribution to the team derives from a personal area of expertise. By emphasising why each member's skills are important, managers can reduce social loafing.

3. *Keep group size at an appropriate level*   Group size is related to the causes of social loafing we have just described. As size increases, identifying individual contributions becomes increasingly difficult and members are more likely to think that their individual contributions are not very important. To overcome this, managers should form groups with no more members than are needed to accomplish group goals and perform highly.[73]

Helping Groups to Manage Conflict Effectively

At some point, practically all groups experience conflict either within the group (*intra-group* conflict) or with other groups (*inter-group* conflict). In Chapter 17 an in-depth discussion and exploration of conflict, and ways to manage it effectively, is presented. You will learn that managers can take several steps to help groups manage conflict and disagreements.

TIPS FOR PRACTICE

1. Try to ensure that the benefits of team work and group work benefit individuals' needs.
2. Think about being able to control the size of teams or groups – make the size relevant for the task at hand.
3. Try to understand your own role in a team and the roles of others. Help others to clarify each individual's role and how different roles can help in achieving a goal.
4. Challenge group norms if you feel that they are inappropriate. Assessing group and team norms frequently is vital for a healthy team or group.

Reaction Time

1. Think about a group of employees who works in a fast food restaurant. What type of task interdependence characterises this group? What potential problems in the group should the restaurant manager be aware of, and take steps to avoid?

2. Discuss the reasons why too much conformity can hurt groups and their organisations.

3. Why do some groups have very low levels of cohesiveness?

Summary and Review

Groups, teams and organisational effectiveness A group is two or more people who interact with each other to accomplish certain goals or meet certain needs. A team is a group whose members work intensely with one another to achieve a specific common goal or objective. Groups and teams can contribute to organisational effectiveness by enhancing performance, increasing responsiveness to customers, increasing innovation and being a source of motivation for their members.

Types of groups and teams Formal groups are groups that managers establish to achieve organisational goals; they include cross-functional teams, cross-cultural teams, senior management teams, R&D teams, command groups, task forces, self-managed work teams and virtual teams. Informal groups are groups that employees form because they believe that they will help them achieve their own goals or meet their needs; they include friendship groups and interest groups.

Group dynamics Key elements of group dynamics are group size, tasks and roles; group leadership; group development; group norms; and group cohesiveness. The advantages and disadvantages of large and small groups suggest that managers should form groups with no more members than are needed to provide the group with the HR it needs to achieve its goals and use a division of labour. The type of task interdependence that characterises a group's work gives managers a clue about the appropriate size of the group. A group role is a set of behaviours and tasks that a member of a group is expected to perform because of his or her position in the group. All groups and teams need leadership.

Five stages of development that many groups pass through are forming, storming, norming, performing and adjourning. Group norms are shared rules for behaviour that most group members follow. To be effective, groups need a balance of conformity and deviance. Conformity allows a group to control its members' behaviour to achieve group goals; deviance provides the impetus for needed change.

Group cohesiveness is the attractiveness of a group or team to its members. As group cohesiveness increases, so, too, does the level of participation and communication within a group, the level of conformity to group norms and the emphasis on group goal accomplishment. Managers should strive to achieve a moderate level of group cohesiveness in the groups and teams they manage.

▶

▶ **Managing groups and teams for high performance** To make sure that groups and teams perform highly, managers need to motivate group members to work toward the achievement of organisational goals, reduce social loafing and help groups to effectively manage conflict. Managers can motivate members of groups and teams to work toward the achievement of organisational goals by making sure that members personally benefit when the group or team performs highly.

Topic for Action

■ Interview one or more managers in an organisation in your local community to identify the types of groups and teams that the organisation uses to achieve its goals. What challenges do these groups and teams face?

Applied Independent Learning

Building Management Skills

Diagnosing Group Failures

Think about the last dissatisfying or discouraging experience you had as a member of a group or team. Perhaps the group did not accomplish its goals, perhaps group members could agree about nothing, or perhaps there was too much social loafing. Now answer the following questions:

1. What type of group was this?
2. Were group members motivated to achieve group goals? Why or why not?
3. How large was the group, what type of task interdependence existed in the group and what group roles did members play?
4. What were the group's norms? How much conformity and deviance existed in the group?
5. How cohesive was the group? Why do you think the group's cohesiveness was at this level? What consequences did this level of group cohesiveness have for the group and its members?
6. Was social loafing a problem in this group? Why or why not?
7. What could the group's leader or manager have done differently to increase group effectiveness?
8. What could group members have done differently to increase group effectiveness?

Managing Ethically

Some self-managed teams encounter a vexing problem: One or more members engage in social loafing, and other members are reluctant to try to rectify the situation. Social loafing can be especially troubling if team members' pay is based on team performance and social loafing reduces the team's performance and thus the pay of all members (even the highest performers). Even if managers are aware of the problem, they may be reluctant to take action because the team is supposedly self-managing.

Questions

1. Either individually or in a group, think about the ethical implications of social loafing in a self-managed team.

2. Do managers have an ethical obligation to step in when they are aware of social loafing in a self-managed team? Why or why not? Do other team members have an obligation to try to curtail the social loafing? Why or why not?

Small Group Breakout Exercise

Creating a Cross-Functional Team

Form groups of three or four people, and appoint one member as the spokesperson who will communicate your findings to the whole class when called on by the instructor. Then discuss the following scenario.

You are a group of managers in charge of food services for a large state university in the Midwest. Recently a survey of students, faculty and staff was conducted to evaluate customer satisfaction with the food services provided by the university's eight cafeterias. The results were disappointing, to put it mildly. Complaints ranged from dissatisfaction with the type and range of meals and snacks provided, operating hours and food temperature to frustration about unresponsiveness to current concerns about low-carbohydrate diets and the needs of vegetarians. You have decided to form a cross-functional team that will further evaluate reactions to the food services and will develop a proposal for changes to be made to increase customer satisfaction.

1. Indicate who should be on this important cross-functional team, and explain why.

2. Describe the goals the team should be striving to achieve.

3. Describe the different roles that will need to be performed in this team.

4. Describe the steps you will take to help ensure that the team has a good balance between conformity and deviance, and has a moderate level of cohesiveness.

Exploring the World Wide Web

Many consultants and organisations provide team-building services to organisations. While some managers and teams have found these services to be helpful, others have found them to be a waste of time and money – another consulting fad that provides no real performance benefits. Search online for team-building services, and look at the websites of a few consultants/companies in depth. Based on what you have read, what might be some of the advantages and disadvantages of team-building services? For what kinds of problems/issues might these services be beneficial, and when might they have little benefit or perhaps even do more harm than good?

Application in Today's Business World

This Volvo Is Not a Guy Thing

Burning rubber, roaring engines. Grease and gas. Cars are a guy thing, right? The industry sure seems to think so. Auto ads tend to emphasise big, fast models, usually driven by a man – with a woman at his side, if at all – over user-friendly touches such as ergonomic seats. It's no surprise the crowd that designs, develops, builds and sells autos remains a boys' club.

Yet on the other side of the sales desk, women sway a disproportionate share of car sales. According to industry studies, women purchase about two-thirds of vehicles and influence 80 per cent of all sales. It's this gender gap that Volvo was trying to bridge with a concept car unveiled at the Geneva Auto Show on 2 March 2004. Shaped by all-female focus groups drawn from Volvo's workforce, the two-door hatchback was created by an all-woman management team. Dubbed Your Concept Car, or YCC, the resulting show car cost some $3 million to design and build and was packed with thoughtful design twists that attracted a big, spirited crowd in Geneva. 'We found that by meeting women's expectations, we exceeded those of most men,' said Hans-Olov Olsson, president and CEO of Volvo Cars, a unit of Ford Motor Co.

There's no guarantee the YCC will ever make it to a showroom. The auto industry uses concept cars as test beds for designs and technical innovations, and to gauge the public's reactions. Packed as it is with the latest gizmos, the YCC would be expensive: Volvo estimates a road version would cost about $65,000 and compete with luxury coupés built by the likes of Audi and Mercedes.

More James Bond than Soccer Mom, the YCC may just create enough buzz to hit the roads. Its gull-wing doors – which resemble the line of a bird's extended wings – are there as much for convenience and accessibility as for design chic. A button on the key fob stirs the YCC to life, raising the whole chassis a few inches to meet the driver, just as the upper door lifts hydraulically and the sill – the lower part of the door – slides under the car. The oversize opening makes stepping in and out a breeze, says Maria Widell Christiansen, the YCC's design manager. And because they're motor-driven, 'the driver doesn't even need to touch the car to get in', she adds.

This hands-off approach is deliberate and consistent. Rather than a dirty, tough-to-unscrew gas cap, the YCC borrows a technology from race cars: when the gas button is pressed in the cockpit, a ball valve on the outside of the car rotates, exposing an opening for the fuel pump. Ditto for windshield-wiper fluid. Body panels are low-maintenance, too. Clad in a non-stick paint, they repel dirt.

Smart Parking

Much of the advanced technology in the YCC is hidden from view. Women in Volvo's focus group weren't willing to give up power but wanted cleaner, more efficient performance. Hence the 215-horsepower, five-cylinder, near-zero emissions gas engine, which shuts off when not in motion and then fires up instantly with the help of an electric motor. This delivers a 10 per cent boost in mileage, says Olsson. There's also a nifty parallel parking aid. When the car is aligned in front of an empty spot, sensors can confirm that, yes, it's big enough. Then, while the driver controls the gas and brake, the system self-steers the car into the spot.

In the cockpit, the design team focused on ergonomics and styling. 'Access for women, in particular, can be difficult,' says Jennifer Stockburger, an automotive-test engineer at *Consumer Reports*, who has been testing vehicle ergonomics into her ninth month of pregnancy. For small women, especially, 'reaching out to shut a heavy door, or adjusting pedals, can be tough'.

To tailor the cockpit to drivers, the YCC team developed and applied for a patent on the Ergovision system. At a dealership, the driver's body is laser-scanned in a booth. Volvo then calculates optimal positions for the seat belt, pedals, headrest, steering wheel and seat, all of which is saved in the key fob. Each driver is 'automatically custom-fitted' when they get in the car, says Camilla Palmertz, YCC's project manager.

Whether or not the YCC is eventually built, some of its design innovations are likely to show up in future Volvo models, says Olsson. The concept car made its US debut on 7 April 2004 at the New York International Auto Show. And no doubt plenty of gearhead guys were there to admire its feminine wiles.

Questions

1. Why do men design most cars even though women are very influential in terms of actual car sales?

2. Why did Volvo rely on focus groups and a management team composed of women to design the Volvo YCC?

3. Designed by women, does the YCC appeal to men? Why or why not?

4. What lessons can other auto makers learn from Volvo's experience with the design of the YCC?

Source: A. Aston and G. Edmondson, 'This Volvo Is Not a Guy Thing', adapted and reprinted from *BusinessWeek*, March 15, 2004 by special permission. Copyright © 2004 by the McGraw-Hill Companies, Inc.

Notes and References

1 C. Matlack, R. Tiplady, D. Brady, R. Berner and H. Tashiro, 'The Vuitton Machine', *BusinessWeek*, March 22, 2004, 98–102; 'America's Most Admired Companies', *Fortune.com*, August 18, 2004, www.fortune.com/fortune/mostadmired/snapshot/0,15020,383,00.html; 'Art Samberg's Ode to Steel', *Big Money Weekly*, June 29, 2004, trading.sina/com/trading/rightside/bigmoney_weekly_040629.b5.shtml; 'Nucor Reports Record Results for First Quarter of 2004', www.nucor.com/financials.asp?finpage=newsreleases, August 18, 2004; 'Nucor Reports Results for First Half and Second Quarter of 2004', www.nucor.com/financials.asp?finpage=newsreleases; J. C. Cooper, 'The Price of Efficiency', *BusinessWeek Online*, March 22, 2004, www.businessweek.com/magazine/content/04_12/b3875603.htm.

2 http://webbolt.ecnext.com/coms2/news_58767_RET.

3 Matlack *et al.*, 'The Vuitton Machine'.

4 *Ibid.*

5 *Ibid.*

6 www.nucor.com.

7 'About Nucor', www.nucor.com/aboutus.htm, August 18, 2004.

8 M. Arndt, 'Out of the Forge and into the Fire', *BusinessWeek*, June 18, 2001.

9 S. Baker, 'The Minimill That Acts Like a Biggie', *BusinessWeek*, September 30, 1996, 101–04; S. Baker, 'Nucor', *BusinessWeek*, February 13, 1995, 70; S. Overman, 'No-Frills at Nucor', *HR Magazine*, July 1994, 56–60.

10 www.nucor.com.

11 Matlack *et al.*, 'The Vuitton Machine'; 'About Nucor'; 'America's Most Admired Companies'; 'Art Samberg's Ode to Steel'; 'Nucor Reports Record Results for First Quarter of 2004'; 'Nucor Reports Results for First Half and Second Quarter of 2004'.

12 W. R. Coradetti, 'Teamwork Takes Time and a Lot of Energy', *HR Magazine*, June 1994, 74–77; D. Fenn, 'Service Teams That Work', *Inc.*, August 1995, 99; 'Team Selling Catches On, but Is Sales Really a Team Sport?' *The Wall Street Journal*, March 29, 1994, A1.

13 T. M. Mills, *The Sociology of Small Groups* (Englewood Cliffs, NJ: Prentice Hall, 1967); M. E. Shaw, *Group Dynamics* (New York: McGraw-Hill, 1981).

14 R. S. Buday, 'Reengineering One Firm's Product Development and Another's Service Delivery', *Planning Review* (March–April 1993), 14–19; J. M. Burcke, 'Hallmark's Quest for Quality Is a Job Never Done', *Business Insurance*, April 26, 1993, 122; M. Hammer and J. Champy, *Reengineering the Corporation* (New York: HarperBusiness, 1993); T. A. Stewart, 'The Search for the Organization of Tomorrow', *Fortune*, May 18, 1992, 92–98.

15 *BusinessWeek Online Extra*, 'Six Best Web-Smart Practices', November 21 2005.

16 www.mwhglobal.com.

17 *BusinessWeek*, 'The Office Chart that Really Counts', January 26 2006.

18 *BusinessWeek Online Extra*, 'Six Best Web-Smart Practices'.

19 A. Deutschman, 'Inside the Mind of Jeff Bezos', *Fast Company*, August 2004, 50–58.

20 *Ibid.*

21 'Online Extra: Jeff Bezos on Word-of-Mouth Power', *BusinessWeek Online*, August 2, 2004, www. businessweek.com; R. D. Hof, 'Reprogramming Amazon', *BusinessWeek Online*, December 22, 2003, www.businessweek.com.

22 http://www.pegasus-security.co.uk/_pages/personnel.htm.

23 http://www.merck-pharmaceuticals.co.uk/files/Merck%20CIV(7.2).pdf.

24 www.bbc.co.uk/news March 15 2006.

25 J. A. Pearce II and E. C. Ravlin, 'The Design and Activation of Self-Regulating Work Groups', *Human Relations* 11 (1987), 751–82.

26 R. Henkoff, 'When to Take on the Giants', *Fortune*, May 30, 1994, 111, 114.

27 B. Dumaine, 'Who Needs a Boss?' *Fortune*, May 7, 1990, 52–60; Pearce and Ravlin, 'The Design and Activation of Self-Regulating Work Groups'.

28 Dumaine, 'Who Needs a Boss?'; A. R. Montebello and V. R. Buzzotta, 'Work Teams That Work', *Training and Development*, March 1993, 59–64.

29 T. D. Wall, N. J. Kemp, P. R. Jackson and C. W. Clegg, 'Outcomes of Autonomous Work Groups: A Long-Term Field Experiment', *Academy of Management Journal* 29 (1986): 280–304.

30 J. S. Lublin, 'My Colleague, My Boss', *The Wall Street Journal*, April 12, 1995, R4, R12.

31 W. R. Pape, 'Group Insurance', *Inc.* (Inc. Technology Supplement), June 17, 1997, 29–31; A. M. Townsend, S. M. DeMarie and A. R. Hendrickson, 'Are You Ready for Virtual Teams?' *HR Magazine*, September 1996, 122–26; A. M. Townsend, S. M. DeMarie and A. M. Hendrickson, 'Virtual Teams: Technology and the Workplace of the Future', *Academy of Management Executive* 12(3) (1998) 17–29.

32 Townsend *et al.*, 'Virtual Teams'.

33 J. Lipnack and J. Stamps, *Virtual Teams: People Working Across Boundaries with Technology* (Chichester: John Wiley, 2000).

34 Pape, 'Group Insurance'; Townsend *et al.*, 'Are You Ready for Virtual Teams?'.

35 D. L. Duarte and N. T. Snyder, *Mastering Virtual Teams* (San Francisco: Jossey-Bass, 1999); K. A. Karl, 'Book Reviews: *Mastering Virtual Teams*', *Academy of Management Executive*, August 1999, 118–19.

36 B. Geber, 'Virtual Teams', *Training* 32(4), 36–40; T. Finholt and L. S. Sproull, 'Electronic Groups at Work', *Organization Science* 1 (1990), 41–64.

37 Geber, 'Virtual Teams'.

38 E. J. Hill, B. C. Miller, S. P. Weiner and J. Colihan, 'Influences of the Virtual Office on Aspects of Work and Work/Life Balance', *Personnel Psychology* 31 (1998), 667–83; S. G. Strauss, 'Technology,

Group Process, and Group Outcomes: Testing the Connections in Computer-Mediated and Face-to-Face Groups', *Human–Computer Interaction* 12 (1997), 227–66; M. E. Warkentin, L. Sayeed and R. Hightower, 'Virtual Teams Versus Face-to-Face Teams: An Exploratory Study of a Web-Based Conference System', *Decision Sciences* 28(4), 975–96.

39 S. A. Furst, M. Reeves, B. Rosen and R. S. Blackburn, 'Managing the Life Cycle of Virtual Teams', *Academy of Management Executive* 18(2), 6–20.

40 *Ibid.*

41 A. Deutschman, 'The Managing Wisdom of High-Tech Superstars', *Fortune*, October 17, 1994, 197–206.

42 J. D. Thompson, *Organizations in Action* (New York: McGraw-Hill, 1967).

43 *Ibid.*

44 R. M. Belbin, *Management Teams: Why They Succeed or Fail* (Oxford: Butterworth-Heinemann, 1996).

45 R. M. Belbin, *Team Roles at Work* (London: Butterworth-Heinemann, 1993).

46 J. K. Wang, M. J. Ashleigh and E. Meyer, 'Knowledge Sharing and Team Trustworthiness: It's all about Social Ties', *Knowledge Management Research & Practice*, forthcoming.

47 R. G. LeFauve and A. C. Hax, 'Managerial and Technological Innovations at Saturn Corporation', *MIT Management*, Spring 1992, 8–19.

48 B. W. Tuckman, 'Developmental Sequences in Small Groups', *Psychological Bulletin* 63 (1965), 384–99; B. W. Tuckman and M. C. Jensen, 'Stages of Small Group Development', *Group and Organizational Studies* 2 (1977), 419–27.

49 C. J. G. Gersick, 'Time and Transition in Work Teams: Toward a New Model of Group Development', *Academy of Management Journal* 31 (1988), 9–41; C. J. G. Gersick, 'Marking Time: Predictable Transitions in Task Groups', *Academy of Management Journal* 32 (1989), 274–309.

50 J. R. Hackman, 'Group Influences on Individuals in Organizations', in M. D. Dunnette and L. M. Hough, eds., *Handbook of Industrial and Organizational Psychology* 3, 2nd ed., (Palo Alto, CA: Consulting Psychologists Press, 1992), 199–267.

51 *Ibid.*

52 *Ibid.*

53 Lublin, 'My Colleague, My Boss'.

54 T. Kelley and J. Littman, *The Art of Innovation* (New York: Doubleday, 2001).

55 B. Nussbaum, 'The Power of Design', *BusinessWeek*, May 17, 2004, 86–94.

56 *Ibid.*

57 *Ibid.*

58 Kelley and Littman, *The Art of Innovation*.

59 *Ibid.*; www.ideo.com; '1999 Idea Winners', *BusinessWeek*, June 7, 1999.

60 Nussbaum, 'The Power of Design'.

61 L. Festinger, 'Informal Social Communication', *Psychological Review* 57 (1950), 271–82; Shaw, *Group Dynamics*.

62 Hackman, 'Group Influences on Individuals in Organizations'; Shaw, *Group Dynamics*.

63 D. Cartwright, 'The Nature of Group Cohesiveness', in D. Cartwright and A. Zander, eds., *Group Dynamics*, 3rd ed. (New York: Harper & Row, 1968); L. Festinger, S. Schacter and K. Black, *Social Pressures in Informal Groups* (New York: Harper & Row, 1950); Shaw, *Group Dynamics*.

64 www.mybusiness.co.uk; www.innocentdrinks.co.uk.

65 www.virgin-atlantic.com.

66 Lublin, 'My Colleague, My Boss'.

67 Kelley and Littman, 'The Art of Innovation', p. 93

68 Kelley and Littman, 'The Art of Innovation'.

69 P. C. Earley, 'Social Loafing and Collectivism: A Comparison of the United States and the People's Republic of China', *Administrative Science Quarterly* 34 (1989), 565–81; J. M. George, 'Extrinsic and Intrinsic Origins of Perceived Social Loafing in Organizations', *Academy of Management Journal* 35

(1992), 191–202; S. G. Harkins, B. Latane and K. Williams, 'Social Loafing: Allocating Effort or Taking It Easy', *Journal of Experimental Social Psychology* 16 (1980), 457–65; B. Latane, K. D. Williams and S. Harkins, 'Many Hands Make Light the Work: The Causes and Consequences of Social Loafing', *Journal of Personality and Social Psychology* 37 (1979), 822–32; J. A. Shepperd, 'Productivity Loss in Performance Groups: A Motivation Analysis', *Psychological Bulletin* 113 (1993), 67–81.

70 George, 'Extrinsic and Intrinsic Origins'; G. R. Jones, 'Task Visibility, Free Riding, and Shirking: Explaining the Effect of Structure and Technology on Employee Behaviour', *Academy of Management Review* 9 (1984), 684–95; K. Williams, S. Harkins and B. Latane, 'Identifiability as a Deterrent to Social Loafing: Two Cheering Experiments', *Journal of Personality and Social Psychology* 40 (1981), 303–11.

71 S. Harkins and J. Jackson, 'The Role of Evaluation in Eliminating Social Loafing', *Personality and Social Psychology Bulletin* 11 (1985), 457–65; N. L. Kerr and S. E. Bruun, 'Ringelman Revisited: Alternative Explanations for the Social Loafing Effect', *Personality and Social Psychology Bulletin* 7 (1981), 224–31; Williams *et al.*, 'Identifiability as a Deterrent to Social Loafing'; Harkins and Jackson, 'The Role of Evaluation in Eliminating Social Loafing'; Kerr and Bruun, 'Ringelman Revisited'.

72 M. A. Brickner, S. G. Harkins and T. M. Ostrom, 'Effects of Personal Involvement: Thought-Provoking Implications for Social Loafing', *Journal of Personality and Social Psychology* 51 (1986), 763–69; S. G. Harkins and R. E. Petty, 'The Effects of Task Difficulty and Task Uniqueness on Social Loafing', *Journal of Personality and Social Psychology* 43 (1982), 1214–29.

73 B. Latane, 'Responsibility and Effort in Organizations', in P. S. Goodman, ed., *Designing Effective Work Groups* (San Franciso: Jossey-Bass, 1986); Latane *et al.*, 'Many Hands Make Light the Work'; I. D. Steiner, *Group Process and Productivity* (New York: Academic Press, 1972).

Chapter 16

Communication

LEARNING OBJECTIVES

After studying this chapter, you should be able to:

☑ Explain why effective communication helps an organisation gain a competitive advantage.

☑ Describe the communication process and explain the role of perception in communication.

☑ Define information richness, and describe the information richness of communication media available to managers.

☑ Describe the communication networks that exist in groups and teams.

☑ Explain how advances in technology have given new options for managing communication.

☑ Describe important communication skills that are needed as senders and as receivers of messages.

A Manager's Challenge

Electronic *versus* Face-to-Face Communication: Lessons to be Learned

Many people in organisations dread going on holiday or returning to work after a two-day training course. Their expectation? Hundreds of emails! There is no doubt that many employees are spending a considerable amount of time answering emails these days without feeling a sense of achievement. Modern communication technology has developed at a pace that has started to intrude on people's life. Siemens commissioned research to look into communication overload. The University of Surrey, UK, found out that too much instant communication, such as email, phone calls or other instant communication that is mediated by technology, is actually angering, stressing and distracting employees. One of the quotes from the research spells out the problem: 'In the workplace email has increased stress levels.' This is also hindering effective communication and Siemens' realisation led to a number of recommendations, one of them stating that you should break out of the 'email jail' and start communication with your colleagues again.[1]

Jong-Yong Yun, the celebrated CEO and Vice Chairman of Samsung Electronics, is one manager who seems to have a good handle on communication. Leading a company that is at the forefront of IT,[2] Yun knows how powerful and efficient electronic communication can be. At the same time, as a leader, he knows that email, videoconferences and other forms of electronic communication cannot replace face-to-face contact when managers are dealing with real issues in today's dynamic workplace.[3] Since becoming CEO in 1996, Yun has transformed Samsung into the most profitable global consumer electronics company and biggest manufacturer of DRAM chips in the world.[4] Prior to Yun's leadership, Samsung was a complacent bureaucracy, pursuing growth and not too concerned about profits.[5] Yun believes that the heart of any business is in the field and that no matter how convenient electronic communication can be (of which he, of course, takes advantage), it is no replacement for face-to-face communication. Yun devotes a lot of his time to communicating with employees on-site and face to face – both in Korea (where Samsung is based) and in other countries – so that he can personally witness ongoing operations and talk to employees at all levels about the challenges they face and opportunities for improvements. As Yun explains:

> This gives me the opportunity to freely discuss matters with the person directly involved, from the senior management to the junior staff of that work site. While many people believe that developments in digital technology have brought convenience . . . I still believe that no innovation can replace the valuable information that is gathered through direct discussions.[6]

Yun visits plants, sales offices and even retailers to learn what is going on in the field, listens to employees regardless of their rank or position in the company and frequently asks questions of those closest to operations to learn first-hand of problems and opportunities.[7] Of course, he also takes advantage of IT (but not as a replacement for face-to-face contact). He instituted an electronic hotline whereby any employee could send him suggestions or complaints with confidentiality guaranteed. Employees in one R&D unit in a factory complained that they were having trouble getting an air conditioner that was needed to keep important equipment at the proper temperature; the air conditioner was in place the day after the complaint was received.[8] Yun has propelled Samsung into being a global force with annual profits of £2.6 billion on sales of over £28.5 billion.[9] It is not surprising that he has received numerous accolades in the business press, such as being ranked the fifth most powerful person in business in Asia by *Fortune* magazine in 2004 and one of the best managers of 2003 by *BusinessWeek* magazine.[10] While Yun excels as a leader and manager in numerous ways, clearly his commitment to good communication has contributed to his ongoing success at Samsung.[11]

Overview

Even with all the advances in IT that are available to managers, face-to-face **communication** continues to play a very important role in organisations. While one can certainly take advantage of IT to receive and respond quickly to employee concerns, it is also important to communicate with employees in person at their work sites. Ironically, the proliferation of email has its downside; managers are deliberately scheduling time-outs from email to take control of their workdays and engage in strategic thinking.[12] The experiences of some managers and employees underscore the fact that IT is a *tool to improve* human communication, not a *substitute for* human communication. Managers must never lose sight of the fact that people are at the centre stage of effective communication. Ineffective communication is detrimental for managers, employees and organisations; it can lead to poor performance, strained interpersonal relations, poor-quality service and dissatisfied customers. For an organisation to be effective and gain a competitive advantage, managers at all levels need to be *good communicators*.

In this chapter, the nature of communication and the communication process will be explained, as well as why all managers and their subordinates need to be effective communicators. It will be shown what communication media are available to managers and the factors they need to consider in selecting a communication medium for each message they send. A consideration of the communication networks that organisational members rely on is made, and how advances in IT have expanded the range of communication options. The chapter also describes the communication skills that help managers be effective senders and receivers of messages. By the end of this chapter, you will have a good appreciation of the nature of communication and the steps that managers can take to ensure that they are effective communicators.

Communication and Management

Communication is the sharing of information between two or more individuals or groups to reach a common understanding.[13] Samsung highlights some important aspects of this definition: no matter how electronically based it is, communication is a *human endeavour* and involves *individuals and groups*. Second, communication does not take place unless a common understanding is reached. When you call a business to speak to a person in customer service or other information services and are bounced back and forth between endless automated messages and menu options and eventually hang up in frustration, communication has not taken place.

The Importance of Good Communication

Chapter 1 described how an organisation can gain a competitive advantage when managers strive to increase efficiency, quality, responsiveness to customers and innovation. Good communication is essential for attaining each of these four goals and is thus a necessity for gaining a competitive advantage.

Efficiency can be increased by updating the production process to take advantage of new and more efficient technologies and by training workers to operate them and expand their skills. Good communication is necessary to learn about new technologies, implement them in organisations and train workers in how to use them. Similarly, *improving quality* hinges on effective communication. Managers need to communicate to all members of an organisation the meaning and importance of high quality and the routes to attaining it. Subordinates need to communicate quality problems and suggestions for increasing quality to their superiors, and members of self-managed work teams need to share their ideas on improving quality with one another.

Good communication can also help to increase *responsiveness to customers*. When the organisational members who are closest to customers, such as department store salespeople and bank clerks, are empowered to communicate customers' needs and desires to managers, managers are better able to respond. Managers, in turn, must communicate with other organisational members to determine how best to respond to changing customer preferences.

Innovation also requires effective communication. Members of a cross-functional team developing a new kind of CD player, for example, must effectively communicate with one another to develop a disc player that customers will want, that will be of high quality and that can be produced efficiently. Members of the team also must communicate with managers to secure the resources they need for developing the disc player and to keep managers informed of progress on the project. Innovation in organisations is increasingly taking place on a global level, making effective communication all the more important, as illustrated in Case 16.1.

Case 16.1: Global innovation hinges on global communication

GE Healthcare Technologies makes CT scanners.[14] In order to make the best scanners that meet the needs of doctors and patients around the world with next-generation technology, new product development and manufacture is truly a global endeavour. Take the case of the new LightSpeed VCT scanner (VCT stands for 'volume controlled tomography'), which debuted in 2004 and is among the quickest and highest-resolution scanners available in the world.[15] The LightSpeed can perform a full-body scan in under 10 seconds and yields a three-dimensional picture of patients' hearts within five heartbeats.[16]

The LightSpeed was developed through true global collaboration. Managers not only spoke with doctors (including cardiologists and radiologists) around the world to find out what their needs were and what kinds of tests they would perform with the LightSpeed but also gathered information about differences among patients in various countries. Engineers in Hino (Japan), Buc (France), and the US developed the electronics for the LightSpeed. Other parts, such as the automated table that patients lie on, are made in Beijing (China) and Hino. Software for the LightSpeed was written in Haifa (Israel), Bangalore (India), Buc and the US.[17]

Effective global communication was a challenge and a necessity to successfully develop the LightSpeed. As GE's general manager for global CT, puts it: 'If we sat around in this cornfield west of Milwaukee, we wouldn't come up with the same breadth of good ideas. But yet, getting six countries on the phone to make a decision can be a pain.'[18]

GE managers facilitated effective communication in a number of ways – participating in daily conference calls, making sure that teams in different countries depended on one another, developing a website devoted to the LightSpeed, encouraging teams to ask one another for help and holding face-to-face meetings in different locations. While much communication took place electronically, such as through conference calls, face-to-face meetings were also important. As Bob Armstrong, GE's general manager for engineering, indicates: 'You need to get your people together in one place if you want them to really appreciate how good everyone is, and how good you are as a team.'[19]

Effective communication is necessary for all members of an organisation to increase efficiency, quality, responsiveness to customers and innovation and thus gain a competitive advantage for the organisation. Managers must therefore have a good understanding of the *communication process* if they are to perform effectively and implement effective and workable communication infrastructures.

The Communication Process

The simplest concept of the communication process is *sender – message – receiver*. An individual (the sender) aims to convey information (the message). He or she can deliver the information, or the message, in various different ways and with any particular intention in mind. The sender

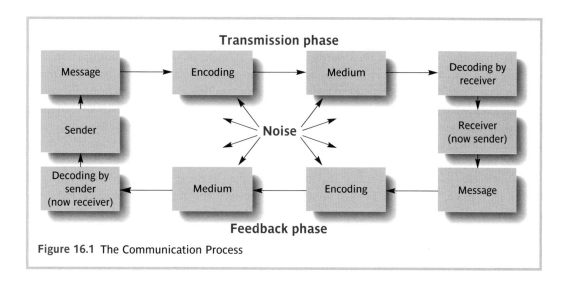

Figure 16.1 The Communication Process

codes the message – gives it a meaning. The role of the receiver of the message is then to *decode* the message and understand the intention and meaning of the sender. This can often lead to difficulties. In order to understand this process better, the following section will look at a more detailed model of communication that expands on the sender – message – receiver model.

In this model, the communication process consists of two phases. In the *transmission phase*, information is shared between two or more individuals or groups. In the *feedback phase*, a common understanding is ensured. In both phases, a number of distinct stages must occur for communication to take place (Fig. 16.1).[20]

Starting the transmission phase, the **sender** – the person or group wishing to share information with some other person or group – decides on the **message** – what information to communicate. Then the sender translates the message into symbols or language, a process called **encoding**; often messages are encoded into words. **Noise** is a general term that refers to anything that hampers any stage of the communication process – this could be culturally significant language that is misunderstood by the receiver who is from a different culture (i.e. noise during encoding); if a message is passed down through various channels noise could be created through the further interpretation of the message by the medium (i.e. noise induced by medium).

Once encoded, a message is transmitted through a medium to the **receiver**, the person or group for which the message is intended. A **medium** is simply the pathway, such as a phone call, a letter, a memo or face-to-face communication in a meeting, through which an encoded message is transmitted to a receiver. At the next stage, the receiver interprets and tries to make sense of the message, a process called **decoding**. This is a critical point in communication.

The feedback phase is initiated by the receiver (who becomes a sender). The receiver decides what message to send to the original sender (who becomes a receiver), encodes it and transmits it through a chosen medium (Fig. 16.1). The message may contain a confirmation that the original message was received and understood or a restatement of the original message to make sure that it has been correctly interpreted, or it may include a request for more information. The original sender decodes the message and makes sure that a common understanding has been reached. If the original sender determines that a common understanding has not been reached, sender and receiver cycle through the whole process as many times as needed to reach a common understanding. Feedback eliminates misunderstandings, ensures that messages are correctly interpreted and enables senders and receivers to reach a common understanding.

The encoding of messages into words, written or spoken, is **verbal communication**, but messages can also be encoded without using written or spoken language. *Non-verbal* **communication** shares information by means of facial expressions (smiling, raising an eyebrow, frowning, dropping one's jaw), body language (posture, gestures, nods and shrugs), and even style of dress (casual, formal, conservative, trendy). In manufacturing plants, managers would traditionally wear suits, distinguishing themselves from the 'blue-collar' (shopfloor) workers. These days, managers in many organisation wear less obvious distinguishers to communicate or signal that the old bureaucracy has been dismantled and that the company is decentralised and more informal than it used to be.[21] The trend toward increasing empowerment of the workforce has led some managers to dress informally to communicate that all employees of an organisation are *team members*, working together to create value for customers.

Non-verbal communication can be used to back up or reinforce verbal communication. Just as a warm and genuine smile can back up words of appreciation for a job well done, a concerned facial expression can back up words of sympathy for a personal problem. In such cases, the *congruence* between the verbal and the non-verbal communication helps to ensure that a common understanding is reached.

Sometimes when members of an organisation decide not to express a message verbally, they inadvertently do so non-verbally. People tend to have less control over non-verbal communication, and often a verbal message that is withheld gets expressed through body language or facial expressions. A manager who agrees to a proposal that she or he actually is not in favour of may unintentionally communicate her or his disfavour by grimacing, or by his or her posture.

Sometimes non-verbal communication can be used to send messages that cannot be sent through verbal channels. Many facilitators of groups, or therapists, use particular gestures or postures to convey a specific message. Non-verbal communication can also be very local, and differ within different cultures. Certain gestures, for example, may be considered rude or inappropriate in one culture, but are an acceptable sign in a different culture. Texas Longhorn fans use the Hook 'Em Horns'; if you use the same sign in Italy people will be very offended – something some American tourists in Italy noticed when they were arrested for disturbing public peace after celebrating a Texas Longhorns' win.[22]

The Role of Perception in Communication

Perception plays a central role in communication and affects both transmission and feedback. In Chapter 5, we defined perception as the process through which people select, organise and interpret sensory input to give meaning and order to the world around them. We saw that perception is inherently subjective and is influenced by people's personalities, values, attitudes and moods as well as by their experience and knowledge. When senders and receivers communicate with each other, they are doing so based on their own subjective perceptions. The encoding and decoding of messages, and even the choice of a medium, hinges on the perceptions of senders and receivers.

Perceptual biases can hamper effective communication. Chapter 5 showed that *biases* are systematic tendencies to use information about others in ways that result in inaccurate perceptions, and a number of biases that can result in the unfair treatment of diverse members of an organisation were described. The same biases also can lead to ineffective communication.

Stereotypes – simplified and often inaccurate beliefs about the characteristics of particular groups of people – can interfere with the encoding and decoding of messages, for example.

Suppose a manager stereotypes an older worker as being fearful of change. When this manager encodes a message to an older worker about an upcoming change in the organisation, he or she may downplay the extent of the change with the intention of not making the older worker feel stressed. The older worker, however, fears change no more than his or her younger colleagues and thus decodes the message to mean that only a minor change is going to be made. The older worker fails to adequately prepare for the change, and his performance subsequently suffers because of their lack of preparation. Clearly, the ineffective communication was in fact due to the manager's inaccurate assumptions about older workers. Instead of relying on stereotypes, effective managers should strive to perceive other people accurately by focusing on their actual behaviours, knowledge, skills and abilities. Accurate perceptions, in turn, contribute to effective communication.

The Dangers of Ineffective Communication

Because managers must communicate with others to perform their various roles and tasks, managers spend most of their time communicating, whether in meetings, in telephone conversations, through email or in face-to-face interactions. Some experts estimate that managers spend approximately 85 per cent of their time engaged in some form of communication.[23]

Effective communication is so important that managers cannot just be concerned that they themselves are effective communicators; they have also to help their subordinates to become effective communicators. When all members of an organisation are able to communicate effectively with one another, and with people outside the organisation, the organisation is much more likely to perform highly and gain a competitive advantage.

When managers and other members of an organisation are ineffective communicators, organisational performance often suffers and any competitive advantage the organisation might have may be lost. Poor communication can sometimes be downright dangerous, and even lead to tragic and unnecessary loss of life. Researchers have studied the causes of mistakes, such as a patient receiving the wrong medication, in two large hospitals. They discovered that some mistakes in hospitals occurred because of communication problems – physicians not having the information they needed to correctly order medication for their patients or nurses not having the information they needed to correctly administer medication. The researchers concluded that some of the responsibility for these mistakes lay with hospital management, which had not taken active steps to improve communication.[24]

Communication problems in the cockpit of airplanes and between flying crews and air traffic controllers can have deadly consequences. In the late 1970s, two jets collided in Tenerife (one of the Canary Islands) because of miscommunication between a pilot and the control tower, and 600 people were killed. The tower radioed to the pilot, 'Clipper 1736 report clear of runway'. The pilot mistakenly interpreted this message to mean that he was cleared for takeoff, whereas the tower actually meant the plane to delay take off.[25] Errors like this are not a thing of the past: a safety group at NASA tracked more than 6,000 unsafe flying incidents and found that communication difficulties had caused approximately 529 of them.[26] NASA has its own communication difficulties.[27] In 2004, it released a report detailing communication problems at the International Space Station jointly managed and staffed by NASA and the Russian space agency, including inadequate record keeping, missing information and failure to keep data up to date.[28]

Information Richness and Communication Media

To be effective communicators, members of an organisation need to select an appropriate communication medium for *each* message they send. Should a change in procedures be communicated to subordinates in a memo sent through email? Should a congratulatory message about a major accomplishment be communicated in a letter, in a phone call or over lunch? Should a layoff announcement be made in a memo or at a general assembly?

Should the members of a purchasing team fly to another country to cement a major agreement with a new supplier, or should they do so through faxes? Managers deal with these questions day in and day out.

There is no *one best communication medium* to rely on. In choosing a communication medium for any message, managers need to consider three factors. The first and most important is the level of **information richness** that is needed. Information richness is the amount of information a communication medium can carry, and the extent to which the medium enables the sender and receiver to reach a common understanding.[29] The communication media that managers use vary in their information richness (Fig. 16.2).[30] Media high in information richness are able to carry an extensive amount of information and generally enable receivers and senders to come to a common understanding.

The second factor that managers need to take into account in selecting a communication medium is the *time* needed for communication, because managers' and other organisational members' time is valuable. Managers at UPS, for example, dramatically reduced the amount of time they spent on communicating by using videoconferences instead of face-to-face communication which required that managers travel overseas.[31]

The third factor that affects the choice of a communication medium is the need for a *paper or electronic trail* or some kind of written documentation that a message was sent and received.

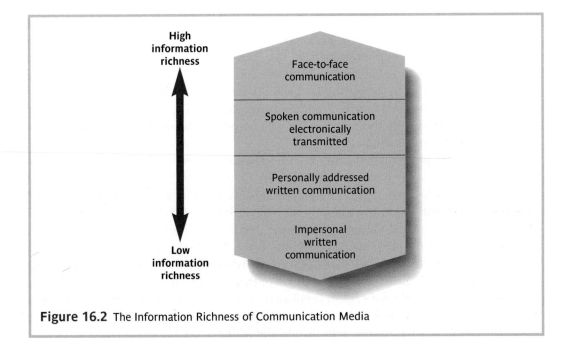

Figure 16.2 The Information Richness of Communication Media

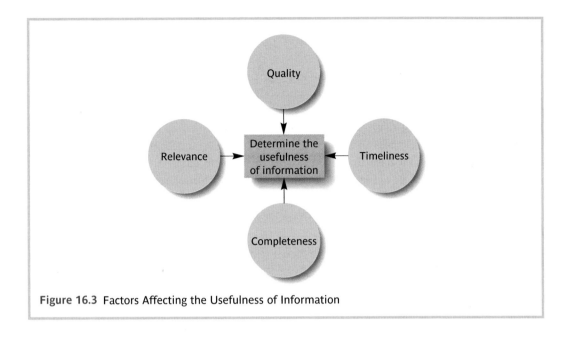

Figure 16.3 Factors Affecting the Usefulness of Information

A manager may wish to document in writing, for example, that a subordinate was given a formal warning about excessive lateness.

In the remainder of this section we examine four types of communication media that vary along these three dimensions (information richness, time and paper or electronic trail).[32]

Attributes of Useful Information

Four factors determine the usefulness of information to a manager: quality, timeliness, completeness and relevance (Fig. 16.3).

Quality
Accuracy and reliability determine the *quality* of information.[33] The greater the accuracy and reliability, the higher is the quality of information. For communication to be effective, the quality of information should be high in order for managers to feel confident about the decisions and arguments they put forward. Alternatively, if managers base decisions on low-quality information, poor and even disastrous decision making can result.

Timeliness
Information that is timely is available when it is needed for managerial action, not after the decision has been made. In today's rapidly changing world, the need for timely information often means that information must be available on a *real-time* basis.[34] **Real-time information** is information that reflects current conditions. In an industry that experiences rapid changes, real-time information may need to be updated frequently.

Airlines use real-time information on the number of flight bookings and competitors' prices to adjust their prices on an hour-to-hour basis to maximise their revenues. For example, the fare for flights from London to Stockholm might change from one hour to the next as fares are reduced to fill empty seats and raised when most seats have been sold. Airlines use real-time information on reservations to adjust fares at the last possible moment to fill planes and maximise revenues. Obviously, the managers who make such pricing decisions need real-time information about the current state of demand in the marketplace.

Completeness

Information that is complete gives managers all the information they need to exercise control, achieve co-ordination or make an effective decision. However, managers rarely have access to complete information and have to make do with incomplete data.[35] One of the functions of information systems may be to increase the completeness of the information that managers have at their disposal.

Relevance

Information that is relevant is useful and suits a manager's particular needs and circumstances. Irrelevant information is useless and may actually hurt the performance of a busy manager who has to spend valuable time determining whether information is relevant. Given the massive amounts of information to which employees, and people in general, are now exposed and humans' limited information-processing capabilities, information systems may aid in the process of *filtering* information. Most email providers have now 'spam' filters that automatically detect irrelevant emails and forward them to a different location to save people from having to read useless information, for instance.

Face-to-face Communication

Face-to-face communication is the medium that is highest in information richness. When managers communicate face-to-face, they not only can take advantage of verbal communication but can also interpret each other's non-verbal signals such as facial expressions and body language. A look of concern or puzzlement can sometimes say more than a thousand words, and managers can respond to such non-verbal signals on the spot. Face-to-face communication also enables managers to receive instant feedback. Points of confusion, ambiguity or misunderstanding can be resolved, and managers can cycle through the communication process as many times as needed to reach a common understanding.

Management by wandering around is a face-to-face communication technique that is effective for many managers at all levels in an organisation.[36] Rather than scheduling formal meetings with subordinates, managers walk around work areas and talk informally with employees about issues and concerns that both may have. These informal conversations provide managers and subordinates with important information and at the same time foster the development of positive relationships. William Hewlett and David Packard, founders and former senior managers of Hewlett-Packard, found management by wandering around to be a highly effective way of communicating with their employees.

Because face-to-face communication is highest in information richness, you may think that it should always be the medium of choice for managers. This is not the case, however, because of the amount of time it takes and the lack of a paper or electronic trail resulting from it. For messages that are important, personal or likely to be misunderstood, it is often well worth managers' time to use face-to-face communication – and, if need be, supplement it with some form of written communication documenting the message.

Advances in IT are providing managers with new communication media that are close substitutes for face-to-face communication. Many organisations are using *videoconferences* to capture some of the advantages of face-to-face communication (such as access to facial expressions) while saving time and money because managers in different locations do not have to travel to meet with one another. During a videoconference, managers in two or more locations communicate with each other over large TV or video screens; they can not only hear each other but also see each other throughout the meeting.

In addition to saving travel costs, videoconferences sometimes have other advantages. For example, when Deutsche Bank needed a system to allow them to communicate globally at a critical point in time to make decisions, it installed a system which felt like 'being in a real conference room'.[37] Managers at Hewlett-Packard found that videoconferences shortened new product development time by 30 per cent for similar reasons. Videoconferences also seem to lead to more efficient meetings. Some managers have found that their meetings are 20–30 per cent shorter when videoconferences instead of face-to-face meetings are used.

Taking videoconferences one step further, IBM and TelePort Corporation have joined forces to build virtual dining rooms in which senior managers can actually have 'power meals' with other managers in another location. Managers in one location are seated around a large, round table bisected by a huge video screen on which they are able to see (life-size) their dining partners in another location sitting around the same kind of table having the same kind of meal. Even though managers may be hundreds or thousands of miles apart, they can 'eat together' as they discuss pressing concerns. The cameras enabling the transmission of the video images are hidden in flower arrangements so as not to unnerve the diners.[38]

Spoken Communication Electronically Transmitted

After face-to-face communication, spoken communication electronically transmitted over phone lines is second highest in information richness (see Fig. 16.2). Although managers communicating over the telephone do not have access to body language and facial expressions, they do have access to the *tone of voice* in which a message is delivered, the parts of the message the sender emphasises and the general manner in which the message is spoken, in addition to the actual words themselves. Telephone conversations thus have the capacity to convey extensive amounts of information. Managers also can ensure that mutual understanding is reached, because they can get quick feedback over the phone and answer questions.

Voice mail systems and answering machines also allow managers to send and receive verbal electronic messages over telephone lines. Voice mail systems are companywide systems that enable senders to record messages for members of an organisation who are away from their desks and allow receivers to access their messages even when hundreds of miles away from the office. Such systems are obviously a necessity when managers are frequently out of the office, and managers on the road are well advised to periodically check their voice mail.

Personally Addressed Written Communication

Lower than electronically transmitted verbal communication in information richness is a personally addressed written communication (Fig. 16.2). One of the advantages of face-to-face communication and verbal communication electronically transmitted is that they both tend to demand attention, which helps ensure that receivers pay attention. Personally addressed written communications, such as memos and letters, also have this advantage. Because they are addressed to a particular person, the chances are good that the person will actually pay attention to (and read) them. Moreover, the sender can write the message in a way that the receiver is most likely to understand. Like voice mail, written communication does not enable a receiver to have his or her questions answered immediately, but when messages are clearly written and feedback is provided, a common understanding can still be reached.

Even if managers use face-to-face communication, sending a *follow-up* in writing is often necessary for messages that are important or complicated and need to be referred to later on. This is precisely what Karen Stracker, a hospital administrator, did when she needed to tell one of her subordinates about an important change in the way the hospital would be handling benefits claims. Stracker met with the subordinate and described the changes face-to-face. Once she was sure that the subordinate understood them, she handed her a sheet of instructions to follow, which essentially summarised the information they had discussed.

Email also fits into this category of communication media, because senders and receivers are communicating through personally addressed written words. The words, however, are appearing on their PC screens rather than on pieces of paper. Email is so widespread in the business world that some managers are finding that, as we have seen, they have to deliberately take time out from checking their email to get their work done, think about pressing concerns and come up with new and innovative ideas.[39] Email etiquette is a growing concern for managers whose inboxes are overloaded with ever more messages. Certain etiquette norms are obvious – don't send jokes or witty passages, and don't flag messages as important just to get someone's attention or make sure they are read. Other etiquette norms may be more subtle. For example, to save time, Andrew Giangola, a manager at a publishing house, used to type all his email messages in capital letters. He was surprised when a receiver of one of his messages responded: 'Why are you screaming at me?' Messages in capital letters are often perceived as being shouted or screamed, and thus Giangola's routine use of capital letters was bad email etiquette. Always punctuate messages; do not ramble on or say more than you need to; do not act as though you do not understand something when in fact you do understand it; and pay attention to spelling and format. To avoid embarrassments like Giangola's, managers at Simon & Schuster created a task force that developed guidelines for email etiquette.[40]

The growing popularity of email has also enabled many workers and managers to become *telecommuters*, people who are employed by organisations and work out of the office in their own homes. More than 18 per cent of the workforce in the Netherlands are telecommuters, with Denmark, Finland and Sweden also having a high proportion of their workforce working from home. Within the UK approximately 6 per cent of the workforce is engaged in telecommuting.[41] Many telecommuters indicate that the flexibility of working at home enables them to be more productive and, at the same time, be closer to their families and not waste time travelling to and from the office.[42] In one study, 75 per cent of the telecommuters surveyed said that their productivity had increased and 83 per cent said that their home life had improved once they started telecommuting.[43]

Unfortunately, the widespread use of email has been accompanied by growing abuse. There have been cases of employees sexually harassing co-workers, sending pornographic content and sending messages that disparage certain employees or groups.[44]

Managers need to develop a clear policy specifying what company email can and should be used for, and what is out of bounds. Managers also should clearly communicate this policy to all members of the organisation, as well as informing them of the procedures that will be used when email abuse is suspected and the consequences that will result when email abuse is confirmed.

While most organisations have a written policy about email usage, most do not have written guidelines for *instant messaging*.[45] Instant messaging allows people who are online and linked through a buddy or contact list to send instant messages back and forth through a small window on their computer screens without having to go through the steps of sending and receiving emails.[46]

What about surfing the Internet in company time? According to a study conducted by Websense, approximately half of the employees surveyed indicated that they surfed the Web at work, averaging about two hours per week.[47] Most visited news and travel sites, but about 22 per cent of the male respondents and 12 per cent of the female respondents indicated that they visited pornographic websites.[48] Of all those surveyed, 56 per cent said that they sent personal emails at work. The majority of those surveyed felt that sending personal emails and surfing the Web had no effect on their performance, and 27 per cent thought that doing so improved their productivity.[49] Other statistics suggest that while overall there is more Internet usage at home than at work, individuals who use the Internet at work spend more time on it and visit more sites than do those who use it at home.[50] As indicated in Case 16.2, personal emails and Internet surfing at work present managers with some challenging ethical dilemmas.

Case 16.2: **Monitoring Email and Internet Usage**

In 2004, statistics indicated that more than 50 per cent of Britain's SMEs were losing money because of staff using the Internet and email during work time. While it is widely acknowledged that the Internet and email are now a vital part of our working lives, its free availability offers distractions that are difficult to withstand.

However, companies need to be realistic; allowing employees to use the Internet during lunch time or for the odd search may even increase motivation and loyalty. But a balance needs to be struck. Defining what is acceptable behaviour is the best starting point from which to assess what type of use may be acceptable and what may harm the business. It is not only the time that individuals spent on surfing the Internet or replying to emails. It is the growing danger of viruses entering a system that organisations need to be concerned with.[51]

Many companies are now responding to this growing concern. IT solution companies and government agencies are now offer advice on Internet Usage Policy templates.[52] Organisations are also writing their own policies, many of which include statements on what is reasonable for staff to use company email and Internet resources for. Considering the growing number of illegal activities that are now conducted over the Internet, company policies on Internet and email use and on responsible use of technology also provide a legal framework in which staff can behave and which protects the organisation.[53]

Impersonal Written Communication

Impersonal written communication is lowest in information richness, but is well suited for messages that need to reach a large number of receivers. Because such messages are not addressed to particular receivers, feedback is unlikely, so managers must make sure that messages sent by this medium are written clearly in a language that all receivers will understand.

Managers often find *company newsletters* useful vehicles for reaching large numbers of employees. Many managers give their newsletters catchy names to spark employee interest and also to inject a bit of humour into the workplace. Managers at the pork-sausage maker Bob Evans Farms, Inc. called their newsletter 'The Squealer' for many years but recently changed the title to 'The Homesteader' to reflect the company's broadened line of products. The BBC interactive service has launched a website called 'Ouch!' that is aimed at disabled people, a name chosen to show its sensitivity to the cultural perception of disability and the taboos are associated with it. The site editor explains the name as a reflection of disability, 'from first becoming disabled right through to the looks you get on the street. Disability matter = ouch. People see disability as a minefield or a problem, but we know it's not – so there's a bit more Ouch for you.'[54]

Managers can use impersonal written communication for various messages, including announcements of rules, regulations, policies, newsworthy information, changes in procedures and the arrival of new organisational members. Impersonal written communication also can convey instructions about how to use machinery or how to process work orders or customer requests. For these kinds of messages, the paper or electronic trail left by this communication medium can be invaluable for employees.

Just as with personal written communication, impersonal written communication can be delivered and retrieved electronically, and this is increasingly the case in large and small companies. Unfortunately, the ease with which electronic messages can be spread has led to their proliferation. Many managers' and workers' electronic in-boxes are so backlogged that often they do not have time to read all the electronic work-related information available to them. The problem with such **information overload** is the potential for important information to be ignored or overlooked (even that which is personally addressed) while tangential information receives attention. Information overload can result in thousands of hours and millions of dollars in lost productivity: employees can get so overloaded with emails that it becomes increasingly difficult to read or respond to them all.

Communication Networks

Although various communication media are utilised, communication in organisations tends to flow in certain patterns. The *pathways* along which information flows in groups and teams and throughout an organisation are called **communication networks**. The type of communication network that exists in a group depends on the nature of the group's tasks and the extent to which group members need to communicate with one another in order to achieve group goals.

Communication Networks in Groups and Teams

As you learned in Chapter 15, groups and teams, whether they are cross-functional teams, senior management teams, command groups, self-managed work teams or task forces, are the building blocks of organisations. Four kinds of communication networks can develop in groups and teams: the *wheel*, the *chain*, the *circle* and the *all-channel* network (Fig. 16.4).

Wheel network
In a *wheel network*, information flows to and from one central member of the group. Other group members do not need to communicate with one another to perform highly, so the group

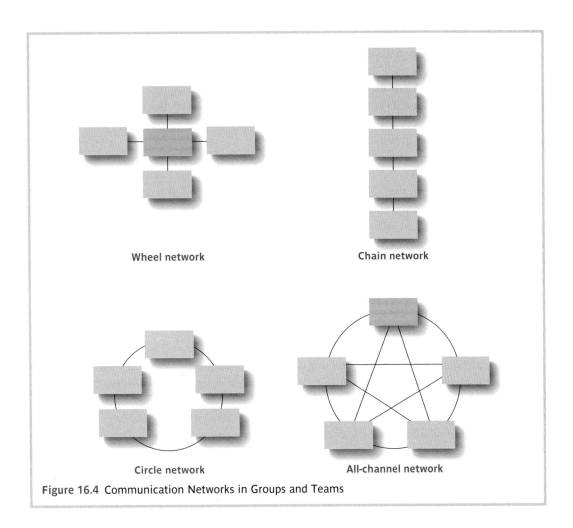

Figure 16.4 Communication Networks in Groups and Teams

can accomplish its goals by directing all communication to and from the central member. Wheel networks are often found in command groups with pooled task interdependence. Picture a group of taxi cab drivers which reports to the same dispatcher, who is also their supervisor. Each driver needs to communicate with the dispatcher, but the drivers do not need to communicate with one another. In groups such as this, the wheel network results in efficient communication, saving time without compromising performance. Although found in groups, wheel networks are not found in teams because they do not allow for the intense interactions characteristic of teamwork.

Chain network

In a *chain network*, members communicate with one another in a predetermined sequence. Chain networks are found in groups with sequential task interdependence, such as in assembly-line groups. When group work has to be performed in a predetermined order, the chain network is often found, because group members need to communicate with those whose work directly precedes and follows their own. Like wheel networks, chain networks tend not to exist in teams because of the limited amount of interaction among group members.

Circle network

In a *circle network*, group members communicate with others who are similar to them in experiences, beliefs, areas of expertise, background, office location or even where they sit when the group meets. Members of task forces and standing committees, for example, tend to communicate with others who have similar experiences or backgrounds. People also tend to communicate with people whose offices are next to their own. Like wheel and chain networks, circle networks are most often found in groups that are not teams.

All-channel network

An *all-channel network* is found in teams and is characterised by high levels of communication. Every team member communicates with every other team member. Senior management teams, cross-functional teams and self-managed work teams frequently have all-channel networks. The reciprocal task interdependence often found in such teams requires that information flows in all directions. Computer software specially designed for use by work groups can help maintain effective communication in teams with all-channel networks because it provides team members with an efficient way to share information with one another.

Organisational Communication Networks

An organisation chart may seem to be a good summary of an organisation's communication network, but often it is not. An organisation chart summarises the *formal* reporting relationships in an organisation and the formal pathways along which communication takes place. Often, however, communication is *informal* and flows around issues, goals, projects and ideas instead of moving up and down the organisational hierarchy in an orderly fashion. An organisation's communication network thus includes not only the formal communication pathways summarised in an organisation chart but also informal communication pathways along which a great deal of communication takes place (Fig. 16.5).

Communication can and should occur across departments and groups as well as within them and up and down and sideways in the corporate hierarchy. Communication up and down the corporate hierarchy is often called *vertical* communication. Communication among employees at the same level in the hierarchy, or sideways, is called *horizontal* communication. Managers obviously cannot determine in advance what an organisation's communication network will be, nor should they try to. Instead, to accomplish goals and perform at a high level, organisational members should be free to communicate with whomever they need to contact. Because organisational goals change over time, so too do organisational communication networks. Informal communication networks can contribute to an organisation's competitive advantage because they help ensure that organisational members have the information they need, when they need it, to accomplish their goals.

The **grapevine** is an informal organisational communication network along which unofficial information flows quickly, if not always accurately.[55] People in an organisation who seem to know everything about everyone are prominent in the grapevine. Information spread over the grapevine can be on issues of either a business nature (an impending takeover) or a personal nature (the sexual orientation of a co-worker, or the upcoming divorce of a colleague).

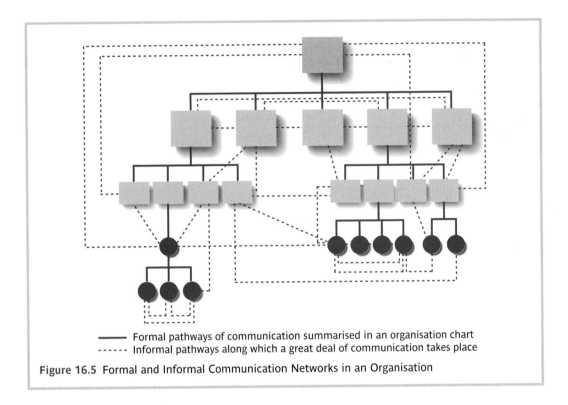

——— Formal pathways of communication summarised in an organisation chart
- - - - - Informal pathways along which a great deal of communication takes place

Figure 16.5 Formal and Informal Communication Networks in an Organisation

External Networks

In addition to participating in networks within an organisation, managers, professional employees and those with work-related ties outside their employing organisation often are part of external networks whose members span a variety of companies. Scientists working in universities and in corporations often communicate in networks formed around common underlying interests in a particular topic or subfield. Physicians working throughout the country belong to specialty professional associations that help them keep up to date on the latest advances in their fields. For some managers and professionals, participation in such interest-oriented networks is just as important, or even more important, than participation in internal company networks. Networks of contacts who are working in the same discipline or field or who have similar expertise and knowledge can be very helpful, for example, when an individual wants to change jobs or even find a job after a layoff. Unfortunately, as a result of discrimination and stereotypes, some of these networks are off-limits to certain individuals due to gender or race. For example, the term *old boys' network* alludes to the fact that networks of contacts for job leads, government contracts or venture capital (VC) funding have often been dominated by men and less welcoming of women.[56]

IT and Communication

Advances in IT have dramatically increased managers' abilities to communicate with others as well as to quickly access information to make decisions. Three advances that are having major impacts on managerial communication are the Internet, intranets and groupware. However,

Table 16.1 Top 15 countries in Internet usage, 2002

Country	Internet users
US	160,700,000
Japan	64,800,000
China	54,500,000
Germany	30,350,000
UK	27,150,000
South Korea	26,900,000
Italy	20,850,000
Canada	17,830,000
France	16,650,000
India	16,580,000
Brazil	15,840,000
Russia	13,500,000
Australia	10,450,000
Spain	10,390,000
Taiwan	9,510,000

Source: Computer Industry Almanac, Inc.; obtained from 'Top 15 Countries in Internet Usage, 2002', www.infoplease.com.

managers must not lose sight of the fact that communication is essentially a human endeavour, no matter how much it may be facilitated by IT: remember Yun and Samsung.

The Internet

The **Internet** is a global system of computer networks that is easy to join and is used by employees of organisations around the world to communicate inside and outside their companies. Over 27 million people in the UK alone use the Internet, and the use of broadband connections (in place of a dialup service) is dramatically increasing.[57] Table 16.1 lists the 15 countries with the most Internet users in 2002.[58]

On the Internet, the World Wide Web is the 'business district' with multimedia capabilities. Companies' home pages on the Web are like offices that potential customers can visit. In attractive graphic displays on home pages, managers communicate information about the goods and services they offer, why customers should want to purchase them, how to purchase them and where to purchase them. By surfing the Web, managers can see what their competitors are doing.[59] Each day, hundreds of new companies add themselves to the growing number of organisations on the World Wide Web.[60] According to a 2004 study, the six 'Web-savviest' nations (taking into account usage of broadband connections) in descending order are Denmark, Great Britain, Sweden, Norway, Finland and the US.[61]

Use of the Internet for communication is burgeoning. Nevertheless, some managers and organisations do not use it. Ironically, the very reason why the Internet was created and why it is so popular – it allows millions of senders and receivers of messages to share vast amounts of information with one another – has hampered its use for certain business transactions because of a lack of security. Just as managers do not want to freely distribute information about their accounts to the public, customers do not want to disclose their credit card numbers via the Internet. Experts suggest, however, that the Internet can be made reasonably secure so that accounts, credit cards, business documents and even monetary transactions should be relatively safe.

Gene Spafford, a professor who is working on Purdue University's computer-security research project called COAST, suggests that although perfect security can never be obtained with any form of communication, good security on the Internet is certainly possible.[62] When considering security on the Internet, managers also need to compare it to the security of alternative communication media. Scott McNealy, chairman and CEO of Sun Microsystems, says that his email is much more secure and harder for unwanted intruders to access than is his regular mail, which is just dropped into an unlocked box.[63]

Intranets

Growing numbers of managers are finding that the technology on which the World Wide Web and the Internet are based has enabled them to improve communication within their own companies. These managers are using the technology that allows information sharing over the Internet to share information within their own companies through company networks called **intranets**. Intranets are being used not just in high-tech companies such as Sun Microsystems and Digital Equipment but also in companies such as Levi Strauss, Pfizer, Motorola and Ford.[64]

Intranets allow employees to have many kinds of information at their fingertips (or keyboards). Directories, phone books, manuals, inventory figures, product specifications, information about customers, biographies of senior managers and the board of directors, global sales figures, minutes from meetings, annual reports, delivery schedules and up-to-the minute revenue, cost and profit figures are just a few examples of the information that can be shared through intranets. Intranets can be accessed with different kinds of computers so that all members of an organisation can be linked together. Intranets are protected from unwanted intrusions (by hackers or by competitors) by means of *firewall security systems* that ask users to provide passwords and other pieces of identification before they are allowed to access the intranet.[65]

The advantage of intranets lies in their versatility as a communication medium. They can be used for a number of different purposes by people who may have little expertise in computer software and programming. While some managers complain that the Internet is too crowded and the World Wide Web too glitzy, informed managers are realising that using the Internet's technology to create their own computer network may be one of its biggest contributions to organisational effectiveness.

Groupware and Collaboration Software

Groupware is computer software that enables members of groups and teams to share information with one another to improve their communication and performance. In some organisations, such as the Bank of Montreal, managers have had success in introducing groupware into the organisation; in others, such as the advertising agency Young & Rubicam, managers have encountered considerable resistance to groupware.[66] Even in companies where the introduction of groupware has been successful, some employees resist using it. Some clerical and secretarial workers at the Bank of Montreal, for example, were dismayed to find that their neat and accurate files were being consolidated into computer files that would be accessible to many of their co-workers.

Managers are most likely to be able to successfully use groupware in their organisations as a communication medium when certain conditions are met:[67]

1. The work is group- or team-based, and members are rewarded, at least in part, for group performance.

2. Groupware has the full support of senior management.

3. The culture of the organisation stresses flexibility and knowledge sharing, and the organisation does not have a rigid hierarchy of authority.

4. Groupware is being used for a specific purpose and is viewed as a tool that enables group or team members to work more effectively together, not as a personal source of power or advantage.

5. Employees receive adequate training in the use of computers and groupware.

Employees are likely to resist using groupware and managers are likely to have a difficult time implementing it when people are working primarily on their own and are rewarded for their own individual performances.[68] Under these circumstances, information is often viewed as a *source of power*, and people are reluctant to share information with others.

Take the case of three salespeople who sell insurance policies in the same geographic area; each is paid based on the number of policies he or she sells and on his or her retention of customers. Their supervisor invested in groupware and encouraged them to use it to share information about their sales, sales tactics, customers, insurance providers and claim histories. The supervisor told the salespeople that having all this information at their fingertips would allow them to be more efficient as well as sell more policies and provide better service to customers.

Even though they received extensive training in how to use the groupware, the salespeople never got around to using it. Why? They all were afraid that giving away their secrets to their co-workers might reduce their own commissions. The salespeople were essentially competing with one another and thus had no incentive to share information. Under such circumstances, a groupware system may not be a wise choice of communication medium. Had the salespeople been working as a team and had they received bonuses based on team performance, groupware might have been an effective communication medium.

For an organisation to gain a competitive advantage, managers need to keep up to date on advances in IT such as groupware. But managers should not adopt these or other advances without first considering carefully how the advance in question might improve communication and performance in their particular groups, teams or organisation. Moreover, as highlighted at Samsung, managers need to keep in mind that all of these advances in IT are tools for people to use to facilitate effective communication; they are not replacements for face-to-face communication.

Collaboration software is groupware that aims to promote collaborative, highly interdependent interactions among members of a team and provide the team with an electronic meeting site for communication.[69] For work that is truly team-based, entails a number of highly interdependent yet distinct components and involves team members with distinct areas of expertise who need to closely co-ordinate their efforts, collaboration software can be a powerful communication tool, as profiled in Case 16.3.

Reaction Time

1. Which medium (or media) do you think would be appropriate for each of the following kinds of messages that a subordinate could receive from his or her boss: (a) a rise, (b) not receiving a promotion, (c) an error in a report prepared by the subordinate, (d) additional job responsibilities, (e) the schedule for company holidays for the coming year? Explain your choices.

2. Discuss the pros and cons of using the Internet and World Wide Web for communication within and between organisations.

3. Why do some organisational members resist using groupware?

Case 16.3: **Collaboration software facilitates communication in teams**

Collaboration software provides members of a team with an online work site where they can post, share and save data, reports, sketches and other documents; keep calendars; have team-based online conferences; and send and receive messages. The software can also keep and update progress reports, survey team members about different issues, forward documents to managers and let users know which of their team members are also online and at the site.[70] Having an integrated online work area can help to organise and centralise the work of a team, help to ensure that information is readily available as needed and also help team members to make sure that important information is not overlooked. Collaboration software can be much more efficient than email or instant messaging for managing ongoing team collaboration and interaction that is not face-to-face. Moreover, when a team does meet face to face, all documents the team might need in the course of the meeting are just a click away.[71]

The New York–based public relations company Ketchum, Inc. uses collaboration software for some of its projects. Ketchum is managing public relations, marketing and advertising for a new charitable programme that the Fireman's Fund Insurance Co. has undertaken. By using the eRoom software provided by Documentum (a part of EMC Corporation), Ketchum employees working on the project at six different locations, employee representatives from Fireman's and a graphics company that is designing a website for the programme can share plans, documents, graphic designs and calendars at an online work site.[72] Members of the Ketchum–Fireman team get email alerts when something has been modified or added to the site. As Ketchum's chief information officer, Andy Roach, puts it: 'The fact that everyone has access to the same document means Ketchum isn't going to waste time on the logistics and can focus on the creative side.'[73]

Another company taking advantage of collaboration software is Honeywell International, who are represented at various sites in the UK. Managers at Honeywell decided to use the SharePoint collaboration software provided by Microsoft, in part because it can be integrated with other Microsoft software such as Outlook. If a team using SharePoint makes a change to the team's calendar, that change will be automatically made in team members' Outlook calendars.[74] Clearly, collaboration software has the potential to enhance communication efficiency and effectiveness in teams.

Communication Skills for Managers

Some of the barriers to effective communication in organisations have their origins in *senders*. When messages are unclear, incomplete or difficult to understand, when they are sent over an inappropriate medium, or when no provision for feedback is made, communication suffers. Other communication barriers have their origins in *receivers*. When receivers pay no attention to or do not listen to messages or when they make no effort to understand the meaning of a message, communication is likely to be ineffective. Sometimes advanced IT such as automated phone systems can hamper effective communication to the extent that the human element is missing.

To overcome these barriers and effectively communicate with others, managers (as well as other organisational members) must *possess* or *develop* certain communication skills. Some of these skills are particularly important when managers *send* messages; others are critical when managers *receive* them. These skills help ensure that managers will be able to share information, will have the information they need to make good decisions and take action and will be able to reach a common understanding with others.

Communication Skills for Managers as Senders

Organisational effectiveness depends on the ability of managers (as well as other organisational members) to effectively send messages to people both inside and outside the organisation. Table 16.2 summarises seven communication skills that help ensure that, when managers send messages, they are properly understood and the *transmission phase* of the communication process is effective. Let's see what each skill entails.

Send messages that are clear and complete

Managers need to learn how to send a message that is *clear and complete*. A message is clear when it is easy for the receiver to understand and interpret, and it is complete when it contains all the information that the sender and receiver need to reach a common understanding. In striving to send messages that are both clear and complete, managers must learn to anticipate how receivers will *interpret* messages and must adjust messages to eliminate *sources of misunderstanding or confusion*.

Encode messages in symbols that the receiver understands

Managers need to appreciate that when they encode messages, they should use symbols or language that the receiver understands. When sending messages in English to receivers whose

Table 16.2 Seven communication skills for managers as senders of messages

- Send messages that are clear and complete
- Encode messages in symbols that the receiver understands
- Select a medium that is appropriate for the message
- Select a medium that the receiver monitors
- Avoid filtering and information distortion
- Ensure that a feedback mechanism is built into messages
- Provide accurate information to ensure that misleading rumours are not spread

native language is not English, for example, it is important to use commonplace vocabulary and to avoid using clichés that, when translated, may make little sense and sometimes are either comical or insulting.

Jargon, specialised language that members of an occupation, group or organisation develop to facilitate communication among themselves, should never be used when communicating with people outside the occupation, group or organisation. In health professions, as in many other professions, abbreviations are common practice. In the UK, talking about WDDs (workforce development directorates) and SHAs (strategic health authorities), PCTs (primary care trusts) and HDUs (high dependency units) may mean something only to people who are part of this profession. Using this jargon among themselves results in effective communication because they know precisely what is being referred to. But if a health professional used this language to communicate with a builder, the receiver would have no idea what the message meant.

Select a medium that is appropriate for the message

As you have learned, managers can choose from a variety of communication media, including face-to-face communication in person, written letters, memos, newsletters, phone conversations, email, voice mail, faxes and videoconferences. When choosing among these media, managers need to take into account the level of information richness required, time constraints and the need for a paper or electronic trail. A primary concern in choosing an appropriate medium is the nature of the message. Is it personal, important, non-routine and likely to be misunderstood and in need of further clarification? If it is, face-to-face communication is likely to be in order.

Select a medium that the receiver monitors

Another factor that managers need to take into account when selecting a communication medium is whether the medium is one that the receiver monitors. Managers differ in the communication media they pay attention to. Many managers simply select the communication medium that they themselves use the most and are most comfortable with, but doing this can often lead to ineffective communication. Managers who dislike telephone conversations and too many face-to-face interactions may prefer to use email, send many email messages per day and check their own email every few hours. Managers who prefer to communicate with people in person or over the phone may have email addresses but rarely use email and forget to check for email messages. No matter how much a manager likes email, sending email to someone who does not check his or her email is futile. Learning which managers like things in writing and which prefer face-to-face interactions, and then using the appropriate medium, enhances the chance that receivers will actually receive and pay attention to messages.

A related consideration is whether receivers have disabilities that hamper their ability to decode certain messages. A blind receiver, for example, cannot read a written message. Managers should ensure that employees with disabilities have resources available to communicate effectively with others. Deaf employees can effectively communicate over the telephone by using text-typewriters that have a screen and a keyboard on which senders can type messages. The message travels along the phone lines to special operators called *communication assistants*, who translate the typed message into a text that the receiver can listen to. The receiver's spoken replies are translated into typewritten text by the communication assistants and appear on the sender's screen. The communication assistants relay messages back and forth to each sender and receiver.[75] Additionally, use of fax and email instead of phone conversations can aid employees with hearing impairments.

Avoid filtering and information distortion

Filtering occurs when senders withhold part of a message because they (mistakenly) think that the receiver does not need the information, or will not want to receive it. Filtering can occur at all levels in an organisation and in both vertical and horizontal communication. Rank-and-file workers may filter messages they send to first-line managers, first-line managers may filter messages to middle managers, and middle managers may filter messages to senior managers. Such filtering is most likely to take place when messages contain bad news or problems that subordinates are afraid they will be blamed for. Managers need to hear bad news and be aware of problems as soon as they occur, so that they can take swift steps to rectify the problem and limit the damage it may have caused.

Some filtering takes place because of *internal competition* in organisations or because organisational members fear that their power and influence will be diminished if others have access to some of their specialised knowledge. As indicated in Case 16.4, reducing filtering and improving communication are often key ingredients to the successful turnaround of a troubled organisation.

Case 16.4: Haruo Kawahara transforms Kenwood and improves communication

When Haruo Kawahara became CEO of Japanese Kenwood Corp., things couldn't be worse. Kenwood makes consumer electronics such as car audio and home audio systems, navigation systems and wireless radio. Kenwood had close to €80 million in debt and had been in the red for three consecutive years when Kawahara came on board.[76] As CEO, Kawahara proceeded quickly to make tough decisions (including reforms in financial, business, cost and management areas) to restructure Kenwood and help the company earn a €28.4 million profit in 2003.[77] Thus far, Kawahara's transformation of Kenwood has been praised in the business world.[78] As Prem Samtani, an analyst at hedge fund Sofear Global Research Ltd, indicates, 'Kawahara is an impressive leader'.[79]

Interestingly enough, working at General Electric (GE) and United Technologies in the late 1960s (Kawahara then went on to spend 41 years at Toshiba in Japan) made Kawahara realise the power of good communication. According to Kawahara, while Japanese employees excel at many things (such as product redesign, efficient manufacturing and continuous improvement) and are good communicators within their teams and work units, communication and transfer of knowledge and information throughout Japanese organisations is often lacking.[80]

In Kawahara's experience, outside some Japanese employees' teams or work units, much filtering of information takes place; secrecy rather than openness is the norm and complex projects that require collaboration across multiple units often run into trouble. This is partly due to the Japanese culture's tendency to use *oral communication* rather than documentation as in Germany or Sweden. Kawahara is changing this mindset at Kenwood and, by all counts, is succeeding.[81]

Information distortion occurs when the meaning of a message changes as the message passes through a series of senders and receivers. Some information distortion is accidental – due to faulty encoding and decoding or to a lack of feedback. Other information distortion is deliberate. Senders may alter a message to make themselves, or their groups, look good and to receive special treatment.

Managers themselves should avoid filtering and distorting information. But how can they eliminate these barriers to effective communication? They need to establish *trust* throughout the organisation. Subordinates who trust their managers believe that they will not be blamed for things beyond their control and will be treated fairly. Managers who trust their subordinates provide them with clear and complete information and do not hold things back.

Ensure that a feedback mechanism is built into messages

Because feedback is essential for effective communication, managers should build a *feedback mechanism* into the messages they send. They either should include a request for feedback or indicate when and how they will follow up on the message to make sure that it has been received and understood. When managers write letters and memos or send faxes, they can request that the receiver respond with comments and suggestions in a letter, memo or fax; schedule a meeting to discuss the issue; or follow up with a phone call. By building feedback mechanisms such as these into their messages, managers ensure that they get heard and are understood.

Provide accurate information to ensure that misleading rumours are not spread

Rumours are unofficial pieces of information of interest to organisational members, but with no identifiable source. Rumours spread quickly once they are started, and usually they concern topics that organisational members think are important, interesting or amusing. Rumours, however, can be misleading and can cause harm to individual employees and their organisations when they are false, malicious or unfounded. Managers can halt the spread of misleading rumours by providing organisational members with accurate information on matters that concern them.

Communication Skills for Managers as Receivers

Managers *receive* as many messages as they send. Managers must thus possess or develop communication skills that allow them to be effective receivers of messages. Table 16.3 summarises three of these important skills, examined here in greater detail.

Pay attention

Because of their multiple roles and tasks, managers often are overloaded and forced to think about several things at once. Pulled in many different directions, they sometimes do not pay sufficient attention to the messages they receive. To be effective, however, managers should always pay attention to messages they receive, no matter how busy they are. When discussing a project with a subordinate, an effective manager focuses on the project and not on an upcoming meeting with his or her own boss. Similarly, when managers are reading written communications, they

Table 16.3 Three communication skills for managers as receivers of messages

■ Pay attention
■ Be a good listener
■ Be empathetic

should focus their attention on understanding what they are reading; they should not be side-tracked into thinking about other issues.

Be a good listener

Managers (and all other members of an organisation) can do several things to be good listeners. First, managers should refrain from interrupting senders in the middle of a message so that senders do not lose their train of thought and managers do not jump to erroneous conclusions based on incomplete information. Second, managers should maintain good eye contact with senders so that senders feel that their listeners are paying attention; doing this also helps managers focus on what they are hearing. Third, after receiving a message, managers should ask questions to clarify points of ambiguity or confusion. Fourth, managers should *paraphrase*, or restate in their own words, points senders make that are important, complex or open to alternative interpretations; this is the *feedback component* so critical to successful communication.

Managers, like most people, often like to hear themselves talk rather than listen to others. Part of being a good communicator, however, is being a good listener, an essential communication skill for managers as receivers of messages transmitted face to face and over the telephone.

Be empathetic

Receivers are *empathetic* when they try to understand how the sender feels and try to interpret a message from the sender's perspective, rather than viewing the message only from their own point of view. Marcia Mazulo, an educational psychologist for a local authority (LA), learned this lesson after interacting with Karen Smith, a new psychologist on her staff. Smith was distraught after meeting with the parent of a child she had been working with extensively. The parent was difficult to talk to and argumentative and was not supportive of her own child. Smith told Mazulo how upset she was, and Mazulo responded by reminding Smith that she was a professional and that dealing with such a situation was part of her job. This feedback upset Smith further, and caused her to storm out of the room.

In hindsight, Mazulo realised that her response had been inappropriate. She had failed to empathise with Smith, who had spent so much time with the child and was deeply concerned about its well-being. Rather than dismissing Smith's concerns, Mazulo realised she should have tried to understand how Smith felt and given her some support and advice for dealing positively with the situation.

Understanding Linguistic Styles

Consider the following scenarios:

- Elizabeth compliments Bob on his presentation to upper management and asks Bob what he thought of her presentation. Bob launches into a lengthy critique of Elizabeth's presentation and describes how he would have handled it differently. This is hardly the response Elizabeth expected.

- Catherine shares with co-members of a self-managed work team a new way to cut costs. Michael, another team member, thinks her idea is a good one and encourages the rest of the team to support it. Catherine is quietly pleased by Michael's support. The group implements 'Michael's' suggestion and it is written up as such in the company newsletter.

- Robert was recently promoted and transferred from his company's English office to its headquarters in Italy. Robert is perplexed because he never seems to get a chance to talk in management meetings; someone else always seems to get the floor. Robert's new boss wonders whether Robert's new responsibilities are too much for him, although Robert's supervisor in England rated him highly and said he is a real 'go-getter'. Robert is timid in management meetings and rarely says a word.

What do these scenarios have in common? Essentially, they all describe situations in which a misunderstanding of linguistic styles leads to a *breakdown in communication*. The scenarios are based on the research of linguist Deborah Tannen, who describes **linguistic style** as a person's characteristic way of speaking. Elements of linguistic style include tone of voice, speed, volume, use of pauses, directness or indirectness, choice of words, credit taking and use of questions, jokes and other manners of speech.[82] When people's linguistic styles differ and these differences are not understood, ineffective communication will occur.

The last scenario just illustrated regional differences in linguistic style.[83] The Englishman expected the pauses that signal 'turn taking' in conversations to be longer than the pauses made by colleagues in Italy. This difference causes communication problems. The Englishman thought that his Italian colleagues never let him get a word in edgewise, and the Italians could not figure out why their colleague from England did not get more actively involved in conversations.

Differences in linguistic style can be a particularly insidious source of communication problems because linguistic style is often taken for granted. People rarely think about their own linguistic styles, and often are unaware of how styles can differ. Robert never realised that when dealing with his Italian colleagues, he could and should jump into conversations more quickly than he used to do in England, and his boss never realised that Robert felt that he was not being given a chance to speak.

This aspect of linguistic style – length of pauses – differs by region in Europe, and even within a country. Much more dramatic differences in linguistic style occur *cross-culturally*.

Cross-cultural differences

Managers from Japan tend to be more formal in their conversations and more deferential toward upper-level managers and people with high status than are managers from the western world. Japanese managers do not mind extensive pauses in conversations when they are thinking things through or when they think that further conversation might be detrimental. In contrast, western managers find very lengthy pauses disconcerting and feel obligated to talk to fill the silence.[84]

Another cross-cultural difference in linguistic style concerns the appropriate *physical distance* separating speakers and listeners in business-oriented conversations. The distance between speakers and listeners is greater in the UK, for example, than it is in Italy or Portugal. Citizens of different countries also vary in how *direct* or *indirect* they are in conversations and the extent to which they take individual credit for accomplishments. Southeast Asian culture, with its collectivist or group orientation, tends to encourage linguistic styles in which group rather than individual accomplishments are emphasised. The opposite tends to be true in western European countries.

These and other cross-cultural differences in linguistic style can, and often do, lead to misunderstandings. When a team of western managers presented a proposal for a joint venture (JV) to Japanese managers, the Japanese managers were silent as they thought about the implications of what they had just heard. Western managers took this silence as a sign that the Japanese managers wanted more information, so they went into more detail about the proposal. When they finished, the Japanese were silent again, not only frustrating the westerners but also making them wonder whether the Japanese were at all interested in the project. The western managers suggested that if the Japanese already had decided that they did not want to pursue the project, there was no reason for the meeting to continue. The Japanese were truly bewildered. They were trying to carefully think out the proposal, yet the Americans thought they were not interested!

Communication misunderstandings and problems like this can be overcome if managers make themselves familiar with cross-cultural differences in linguistic styles. If the western managers and the Japanese managers had realised that periods of silence are viewed differently in Japan and the US, their different linguistic styles might have been less troublesome barriers to communication. Before managers communicate with people from abroad they should try to find out as much as they can about the aspects of linguistic style that are specific to the country or culture in question. *Expatriate managers* who have lived in the country in question for an extended period of time can be good sources of information about linguistic styles, because they are likely to have experienced first-hand some of the differences that citizens of a country are not aware of. Finding out as much as possible about *cultural differences* also can help managers learn about differences in linguistic styles, because the two are often closely linked.

Gender differences

Referring again to the three scenarios that open this section, you may be wondering why Bob launched into a lengthy critique of Elizabeth's presentation after she paid him a routine compliment on his presentation, or you may be wondering why Michael got the credit for Catherine's idea in the self-managed work team. Research conducted by Tannen and other linguists has found that the linguistic styles of men and women differ in practically every culture or language.[85] Men and women take their own linguistic styles for granted and thus do not realise when they are talking with someone of a different gender that differences in their styles may lead to ineffective communication.

Women tend to downplay differences between people, are not overly concerned about receiving credit for their own accomplishments and want to make everyone feel more or less on an equal footing, so that even poor performers or low-status individuals feel valued. Men, in contrast, tend to emphasise their own superiority and are not reluctant to acknowledge differences in status. These differences in linguistic style led Elizabeth to routinely compliment Bob on his presentation even though she thought that he had not done a particularly good job. She asked him how her presentation was so that he could reciprocate and give her a routine compliment, putting them on an equal footing. Bob took Elizabeth's compliment and question about her own presentation as an opportunity to confirm his superiority, never realising that all she was expecting was a routine compliment. Similarly, Michael's enthusiastic support for Catherine's cost-cutting idea and her apparent surrender of ownership of the idea after she had described it led team members to assume incorrectly that the idea was Michael's.[86]

Do some women try to prove that they are better than everyone else, and are some men unconcerned about taking credit for ideas and accomplishments? Of course. The gender differences in linguistic style that Tannen and other linguists have uncovered are general tendencies evident in *many* women and men, not in *all* women and men.

Where do gender differences in linguistic style come from? Tannen suggests that they begin to develop in early childhood. Girls and boys tend to play with children of their own gender, and the ways in which girls and boys play are quite different. Girls play in small groups, engage in a lot of close conversation, emphasise how similar they are to one another and view boastfulness negatively. Boys play in large groups, emphasise status differences, expect leaders to emerge who boss others around and give one another challenges to try to meet. These differences in styles of play and interaction result in differences in linguistic styles when boys and girls grow up and communicate as adults. The ways in which men communicate emphasise status differences and play up relative strengths; the ways in which women communicate emphasise similarities and downplay individual strengths.

Interestingly, gender differences are also turning up in the ways that women and men use email and electronic forms of communication. Susan Herring, a researcher, has found that in public electronic forums such as message boards and chat rooms men tend to make stronger assertions, be more sarcastic and be more likely to use insults and profanity than women, while women are more likely to be supportive, agreeable and polite.[87] David Silver, a researcher at the University of Washington, has found that women are more expressive electronic communicators and encourage others to express their thoughts and feelings, while men are briefer and more to the point.[88] Interestingly enough, some men are finding email to be a welcome way to express their feelings to people they care about. Estate agent Mike Murname finds it easier to communicate with, and express his love for, his grown children via email, for example.[89]

Managing differences in linguistic styles

Managers should not expect to change people's linguistic styles, and should not try to. To be effective, managers need to understand differences in linguistic styles. Knowing, for example, that some women are reluctant to speak up in meetings, not because they have nothing to contribute but because of their linguistic style, should lead managers to ensure that these women have a chance to talk. And a manager who knows that certain people are reluctant to take credit for ideas can be extra careful to give credit where it is deserved. As Tannen points out: 'Talk is the lifeblood of managerial work, and understanding that different people have different ways of saying what they mean will make it possible to take advantage of the talents of people with a broad range of linguistic styles.'[90]

Reaction Time

1. Why do some managers find it difficult to be good listeners?
2. Explain why subordinates might filter and distort information about problems and performance shortfalls when communicating with their bosses. What steps can managers take to eliminate filtering and information distortion?
3. Explain why differences in linguistic style, when not understood by senders and receivers of messages, can lead to ineffective communication.

TIPS FOR PRACTICE

1. Consider which medium might be best used to convey the message you are intending to submit – whether it is spoken or written.
2. Be aware of what the policy is when using company resources such as Internet time and email.
3. Remind yourself that cultural differences exist in communication. Be aware of those differences and adapt your communication style, the symbols and signs you are using, and the medium.
4. Always allow for feedback from the receiver to ensure that your message has been understood.

Summary and Review

Communication and management Communication is the sharing of information between two or more individuals or groups to reach a common understanding. Good communication is necessary for an organisation to gain a competitive advantage. Communication occurs in a cyclical process that entails two phases – transmission and feedback.

Information richness and communication media Information richness is the amount of information a communication medium can carry and the extent to which the medium enables the sender and receiver to reach a common understanding. Four categories of communication media, in descending order of information richness, are face-to-face communication (including videoconferences), spoken communication electronically transmitted (including voice mail), personally addressed written communication (including email) and impersonal written communication.

Communication networks Communication networks are the pathways along which information flows in an organisation. Four communication networks found in groups and teams are the wheel, the chain, the circle and the all-channel network. An organisation chart summarises formal pathways of communication, but communication in organisations is often informal, as is true of communication through the grapevine.

IT and communication The Internet is a global system of computer networks that managers around the world use to communicate within and outside their companies. The World Wide Web is the multimedia business district on the Internet. Intranets are internal communication networks that managers can create to improve communication, performance and customer service. Intranets use the same technology on which the Internet and World Wide Web are based on. Groupware is computer software that enables members of groups and teams to share information with one another to improve their communication and performance.

Communication skills for managers There are various barriers to effective communication in organisations. To overcome these and communicate effectively with others, managers must possess or develop certain communication skills. As senders of messages, managers should send messages that are clear and complete, encode messages in symbols the receiver understands, choose a medium appropriate for the message and monitored by the receiver, avoid filtering and information distortion, include a feedback mechanism in the message and provide accurate information to ensure that misleading rumours are not spread. Communication skills for managers as receivers of messages include paying attention, being a good listener and being empathetic. Understanding linguistic styles is also an essential communication skill for managers. Linguistic styles can vary by geographic region, gender and country or culture. When these differences are not understood, ineffective communication can occur.

Topic for Action

- Interview a manager in an organisation in your community to determine with whom he or she communicates on a typical day, what communication media he or she uses and which typical communication problems he or she experiences.

Applied Independent Learning

Building Management Skills

Diagnosing Ineffective Communication

Think about the last time you experienced very ineffective communication with another person – someone you work with, a classmate, a friend or a member of your family. Describe the incident. Then answer the following questions:

1. Why was your communication ineffective in this incident?
2. What stages of the communication process were particularly problematic, and why?
3. Describe any filtering or information distortion that occurred.
4. Do you think that differences in linguistic styles adversely affected the communication that took place? Why or why not?
5. How could you have handled this situation differently so that communication would have been effective?

Managing Ethically

Many employees use their company's Internet connections and email systems to visit websites and send personal emails and instant messages.

Questions

1. Either individually or in a group, explore the ethics of using an organisation's Internet connection and email system for personal purposes at work and while away from the office. Should employees have some rights to use this resource? When does their behaviour become unethical?
2. Some companies keep track of the way their employees use the company's Internet connection and email system. Is it ethical for managers to read employees' personal emails or to record websites that employees visit? Why or why not?

Small Group Breakout Exercise

Reducing Resistance to Advances in IT

Form groups of three or four people, and appoint one member as the spokesperson who will communicate your findings to the whole class when called on by the instructor. Then discuss the following scenario.

▶ You are a team of managers in charge of information and communication in a large consumer products corporation. Your company has already implemented many advances in IT. Managers and workers have access to email, the Internet, your company's own intranet, groupware and collabouration software.

Many employees use the technology, but the resistance of some is causing communication problems. A case in point is the use of groupware and collaboration software. Many teams in your organisation have access to groupware and are encouraged to use it. While some teams welcome this communication tool and actually have made suggestions for improvements, others are highly resistant to sharing documents on their teams' online workspaces.

Although you do not want to force people to use the technology, you want them to at least try it and give it a chance. You are meeting today to develop strategies for reducing resistance to the new technologies.

1. One resistant group of employees is made up of senior managers. Some of them seem computer-phobic and are highly resistant to sharing information online, even with sophisticated security precautions in place. What steps will you take to get these managers to have more confidence in electronic communication?

2. A second group of resistant employees consists of middle managers. Some middle managers resist using your company's intranet. Although these managers do not resist the technology *per se* and do use electronic communication for multiple purposes, including communication, they seem to distrust the intranet as a viable way to communicate and get things done. What steps will you take to get these managers to take advantage of the intranet?

3. A third group of resistant employees is made up of members of groups and teams who do not want to use the groupware that has been provided for them. You think that the groupware could improve their communication and performance, but they seem to think otherwise. What steps will you take to get these members of groups and teams to start using groupware?

Exploring the World Wide Web

Atos Origin is a global IT company that provides IT services to major corporations to improve, facilitate, integrate and manage operations, information and communication across multiple locations. Based in France and the Netherlands, Atos Origin provided much of the IT for the 2004 Olympic Games in Athens, Greece. Visit Atos Origin's website (at www.atosorigin.com), and read about this company and the services it provides to improve communication. Then read the case studies on the website. How can companies like Atos Origin help managers improve communication effectiveness in their organisations? What kinds of organisations and groups are most likely to benefit from services provided by Atos Origin? Why is it beneficial for some organisations to contract with firms like Atos Origin for their IT and communication needs, rather than meet these needs internally with their own employees?

Application in Today's Business World

Fortress India?

A line of neatly dressed workers files into the Golden Millennium, a shimmering glass-and-steel building in central Bangalore. One by one, they swipe ID cards through a reader, then empty their pockets and bags and stuff cell phones, PDAs, and even pens and notebooks into lockers as a dour security guard watches. Staffers ending their shifts, meanwhile, are busy shredding notes of conversations with customers. At the reception desk, visitors sign a daunting four-page form promising not to divulge anything they see inside – and even then are only allowed to peer into the workspace through thick windows.

A top-secret military contractor? Hardly. This is one of four call centres run by ICICI Onesource, which employs 4,000 young Indians to process credit-card bills and make telemarketing calls for big US and European banks, insurers and retailers. And ICICI isn't the only outsourcing company worried about security. Call centre operators such as Mphasis BFL, Wipro Spectramind and 24/7 Customer, as well as back-office subsidiaries of companies such as General Electric (GE), are quickly adding state-of-the-art systems to monitor phone conversations, guard data and watch workers' every move.

Why the extreme caution? After rushing to shift telemarketing and back-office work to India in recent years to tap low wages, US and European companies are under growing pressure from regulators and legislators to guarantee the privacy of their customers' financial and health care data. India's $3.6 billion business-process services industry is eager to defuse the issue. When the backlash against offshore outsourcing erupted in 2003, opponents first focused on curbing government contracts and temporary US work visas for foreign tech workers. Now security and privacy fears have become the hot excuses 'for new barriers to trade in services and information technology', says Jerry Rao, chairman of the National Association of Service & Software Cos. (Nasscom), India's IT trade group.

Pending Legislation

Today 186 bills that aim to limit offshore outsourcing are pending in the US Congress and 40 state legislatures. Dozens of those involve restrictions on transmission of data. For example, the SAFE ID Act, sponsored by Senator Hillary Clinton (D–NY), and a similar House bill by Representative Edward J. Markey (D–MA), would require businesses to notify US consumers before sending personal information overseas – and would bar companies from denying service or charging a higher price if customers balk. Although no such bills have been enacted so far, '[in 2005] I think all of this legislation will be back and spike up again as a huge issue', especially if the US recovery stalls, says R. Bruce Josten, a US Chamber of Commerce Executive Vice-President who helped industry fight the legislation.

Identity theft and credit-card fraud are huge problems globally. There's little evidence, though, to suggest that consumer data are at any greater risk in India than in the US. Sure, India's privacy laws aren't as stringent as in the West. But most highly sensitive data belonging to US or European companies are stored on their own servers at home, with access from India tightly controlled. If an American is defrauded, the US company that farmed out the work is legally responsible. Indian call centres, meanwhile, sign their contracts in the US and can thus be sued there by their corporate customers. What's more, there is only one known case of fraud. In 2003 a programmer for India's Geometric Software Solutions Co. tried to sell a US client's intellectual property. He was arrested and is awaiting trial in India.

▶

▶   Still, given the charged emotions over outsourcing, India's IT industry knows that even a few incidents will generate devastating publicity. So call centres like Mphasis BFL Ltd, which employs 6,000 workers performing sensitive tasks such as processing personal tax returns and credit-card statements for US clients, are leaving little to chance. If the US company prefers, consumers' names, Social Security numbers and credit-card numbers can be masked. Computer terminals at Mphasis lack hard drives, email, CD-ROM drives or other ways to store, copy or forward data. Indian accountants view data from US servers only for specific tasks. Video cameras watch over the sea of cubicles. Every phone conversation is recorded and can be monitored on a system installed by Melville (NY)-based Verint Systems, Inc. And since data theft is often committed by disgruntled former employees, Mphasis can lock a staffer out and cut access to PCs and phones three minutes after a resignation. In 2003 that process took three days. 'Fears about identity theft can be aggravated when people learn their data are in a foreign country,' says Mphasis Vice-Chairman Jeroen Tas. 'So we feel it is better to address these concerns up front.'

Such precautions don't come cheap. It costs about $1,000 per worker to install the Verint system that records, stores and analyses voice conversations. Yet Verint has signed up 100 local and multinational centres in India. 'There has been a big push in the past year or so as the competition focuses more on quality', says Mariann McDonagh, Verint's vice-president for global marketing. Indian centres also pay up to $300 per worker for background checks, a big expense given their explosive growth, and high attrition rates. It's also cumbersome. Due to India's lack of online databases, verifying education and work experience can take weeks.

But while security practices in India now match or surpass those at most US call centres, the legal system still needs work. Indian law on computer hacking inside companies is fuzzy, and privacy enforcement is weak. India's IT industry is addressing those vulnerabilities; Nasscom is working with the government to bring India's data-privacy laws more in line with the US. And it intends to have the security practices of all its 860 members audited by international accounting firms. Nasscom has helped Bombay's police department set up a cybercrime unit, training officers to investigate data theft. Similar units are planned in nine other cities. India's goal, says Nasscom Vice-President Sunil Mehta, is 'to have the best data-security provisions and be a trusted sourcing destination'.

Given the ingenuity of today's cyberscammers, some embarrassing incident seems inevitable. But India's IT-services industry is determined to show that the world's financial and health secrets are as safe in Bangalore as they are anywhere.

Questions

1. What security and privacy concerns does outsourcing back-office work and telemarketing to India pose?

2. Do the same kinds of concerns apply to back-office work and telemarketing performed in countries like the US? Why or why not?

3. How do the precautions taken in India to protect security and privacy compare to those in the US?

4. What are the costs of these precautions, and do they have any unintended potential negative consequences?

Source: P. Engardio, J. Puliyenthuruthel and M. Kripalani, 'Fortress India?', adapted and reprinted from *BusinessWeek*, August 16, 2004 by special permission. Copyright © 2004 by the McGraw-Hill Companies, Inc.

Notes and References

1 'Communication Overload Makes Office Workers SAD' June 4, 2004 http://www.prnewswire.co.uk/.

2 Y. J. Yong, 'CEO Message', www.samsung.com, August 22, 2004; 'Yun Jong Yong: Biography', www.hwwilson.com, August 22, 2004.

3 C. Chandler, 'CEO Voices: Jong-Yong Yun', *Fortune*, July 26, 2004.

4 '2004 Most Powerful People in Business: Jong-Yong Yun', *Fortune*, August 22, 2004; 'Overhauling Samsung', *BusinessWeek Online*, January 10, 2000.

5 L. Kraar, 'Asia's Businessman of the Year', *Fortune*, January 24, 2000.

6 Chandler, 'CEO Voices'.

7 Kraar, 'Asia's Businessman of the Year'.

8 *Ibid.*

9 '2004 Most Powerful People in Business'.

10 'Yun Jong Yong', *BusinessWeek Online*, January 12, 2004, www.businessweek.com; 'Yun Jong Yong'; '2004 Most Powerful People in Business'; Kraar, 'Asia's Businessman of the Year'.

11 Chandler, 'CEO Voices'.

12 C. Hymowitz, 'Missing from Work: The Chance to Think, Even to Dream a Little', *The Wall Street Journal*, March 23, 2004, B1.

13 C. A. O'Reilly and L. R. Pondy, 'Organizational Communication', in S. Kerr, ed., *Organizational Behavior* (Columbus, OH: Grid, 1979).

14 'World's First Volume Computed Tomography (VCT) System, Developed by GE Healthcare, Scanning Patients at Froedtert', www.gehealthcare.com/company/pressroom/releases/pr_release_9722.html, June 18, 2004.

15 S. Kirsner, 'Time [Zone] Travelers', *Fast Company*, August, 2004, 60–66.

16 'New CT Scanner by GE Healthcare Advances Imaging Technology', *Wisconsin Technology Network*, June 21, 2004.

17 Kirsner, 'Time [Zone] Travelers'.

18 *Ibid.*

19 *Ibid.*

20 E. M. Rogers and R. Agarwala-Rogers, *Communication in Organizations* (New York: Free Press, 1976).

21 W. Nabers, 'The New Corporate Uniforms', *Fortune*, November 13, 1995, 132–56.

22 http://en.wikipedia.org/wiki/Gesture#Check.2C_please.

23 D. A. Adams, P. A. Todd and R. R. Nelson, 'A Comparative Evaluation of the Impact of Electronic and Voice Mail on Organizational Communication', *Information & Management* 24 (1993), 9–21.

24 R. Winslow, 'Hospitals' Weak Systems Hurt Patients, Study Says', *The Wall Street Journal*, July 5, 1995, B1, B6.

25 B. Newman, 'Global Chatter', *The Wall Street Journal*, March 22, 1995, A1, A15.

26 'Miscommunications Plague Pilots and Air-Traffic Controllers', *The Wall Street Journal*, August 22, 1995, A1.

27 P. Reinert, 'Miscommunication Seen as Threat to Space Station', *Houston Chronicle*, September 24, 2003, 6A.

28 W. E. Leary, 'NASA Report Says Problems Plague Space Station Program', *The New York Times*, February 28, 2004, A12.

29 R. L. Daft, R. H. Lengel and L. K. Trevino, 'Message Equivocality, Media Selection, and Manager Performance: Implications for Information Systems', *MIS Quarterly* 11 (1987), 355–66; R. L. Daft and R. H. Lengel, 'Information Richness: A New Approach to Managerial Behavior and Organization Design', in B. M. Staw and L. L. Cummings, eds., *Research in Organizational Behavior* (Greenwich, CT: JAI Press, 1984).

30 R. L. Daft, *Organization Theory and Design* (St Paul, MN: West, 1992).

31 'Lights, Camera, Meeting: Teleconferencing Becomes a Time-Saving Tool', *The Wall Street Journal*, February 21, 1995, A1.

32 Daft, *Organization Theory and Design*.

33 C. A. O'Reilly, 'Variations in Decision Makers' Use of Information: The Impact of Quality and Accessibility', *Academy of Management Journal* 25 (1982), 756–71.

34 G. Stalk and T. H. Hout, *Competing Against Time* (New York: Free Press, 1990).

35 R. Cyert and J. March, *Behavioral Theory of the Firm* (Englewood Cliffs, NJ: Prentice. Hall, 1963).

36 T. J. Peters and R. H. Waterman, Jr., *In Search of Excellence* (New York: Harper & Row, 1982); T. Peters and N. Austin, *A Passion for Excellence: The Leadership Difference* (New York: Random House, 1985).

37 http://www.genesys.com/asp/svc_ss_dtl.asp?country=4&language=1&id=5.

38 B. Ziegler, 'Virtual Power Lunches Will Make Passing the Salt an Impossibility', *The Wall Street Journal*, June 28, 1995, B1.

39 Hymowitz, 'Missing from Work'.

40 'Email Etiquette Starts to Take Shape for Business Messaging', *The Wall Street Journal*, October 12, 1995, A1.

41 http://eto.org.uk/faq/faq-numb.htm.

42 E. Baig, 'Taking Care of Business – Without Leaving the House', *BusinessWeek*, April 17, 1995, 106–07.

43 'Life Is Good for Telecommuters, but Some Problems Persist', *The Wall Street Journal*, August 3, 1995, A1.

44 'Email Abuse: Workers Discover High-Tech Ways to Cause Trouble in the Office', *The Wall Street Journal*, November 22, 1994, A1; 'Email Alert: Companies Lag in Devising Policies on How It Should Be Used', *The Wall Street Journal*, December 29, 1994, A1.

45 '2004 Workplace Email and Instant Messaging Survey Summary', American Management Association and the ePolicy Institute's Nancy Flynn, www.amanet.org, 2004.

46 J. Tyson, 'How Instant Messaging Works', computer.howstuffworks.com, August 23, 2004.

47 'Study: Workers Are Surfing on Company Time', www.medialifemagazine.com/news2004/may04/may03/3_wed/news8wednesday.html, May 5, 2004.

48 *Ibid*.

49 *Ibid*.

50 ClikZ Stats staff, 'US Web Usage and Traffic, July 2004', www.clickz.com/stats/big_picture/traffic_patterns/article.php/3395351, August 23, 2004.

51 http://www.star.net.uk/star/home/media_centre/library/articles/email_internet_usage.stml.

52 http://www.businesslink.gov.uk/bdotg/action/detail?type=RESOURCES&itemId=1074402879; www.venables.co.uk.

53 For an example see http://www.some.ox.ac.uk/docs/policy_on_staff_use_of_email_and_internet_Oct_02.pdf the Internet and email usage policy of Somerville College, Oxford.

54 http://www.bbc.co.uk/ouch/about/.

55 O. W. Baskin and C. E. Aronoff, *Interpersonal Communication in Organizations* (Santa Monica, CA: Goodyear, 1989).

56 T. Gutner, 'Move Over, Bohemian Grove', *BusinessWeek*, February 19, 2001, 102.

57 'We've All Got Mail', *Newsweek*, May 15, 2001, 73K; 'Diversity Deficit', *BusinessWeek Online*, May 14, 2001; 'Dial-Up Users Converting to Broadband in Droves', www.emarketer.com/Article.aspx?1003009, August 23, 2004.

58 'Top 15 Countries in Internet Usage, 2002', www.infoplease.com/ipa/A0908185.html, August 25, 2004.

59 J. Sandberg, 'Internet's Popularity in North America Appears to Be Soaring', *The Wall Street Journal*, October 30, 1995, B2.

60 'How to Research Companies', Oxford Knowledge Company, www.Oxford-Knowledge.co.uk, September 16, 2004.

61 'Survey: Denmark Is Web-Savviest Nation', *MSNBC.com*, April 19, 2004, www.msnbc.msn.com/id/4779944/1/displaymode/1098/; L. Grinsven, 'US Drops on Lists of Internet Savvy', *Houston Chronicle*, April 20, 2004, 6B.

62 J. W. Verity and R. Hof, 'Bullet-Proofing the Net', *BusinessWeek*, November 13, 1995, 98–99.

63 *Ibid.*

64 M. J. Cronin, 'Ford's Intranet Success', *Fortune*, March 30, 1998, 158; M. J. Cronin, 'Intranets Reach the Factory Floor', *Fortune*, June 10, 1997; A. L. Sprout, 'The Internet Inside Your Company', *Fortune*, November 27, 1995, 161–8; J. B. White, 'Chrysler's Intranet: Promise vs. Reality', *The Wall Street Journal*, May 13, 1997, B1, B6.

65 *Ibid.*

66 G. Rifkin, 'A Skeptic's Guide to Groupware', *Forbes ASAP*, 1995, 76–91.

67 *Ibid.*

68 'Groupware Requires a Group Effort', *BusinessWeek*, June 26, 1995, 154.

69 M. Totty, 'The Path to Better Teamwork', *The Wall Street Journal*, May 20, 2004, R4; 'Collaborative Software', *Wikipedia*, August 25, 2004, en.wikipedia.org/wiki/Collaborative_software; 'Collaborative Groupware Software', www.svpal.org/~grantbow/groupware.html, August 25, 2004.

70 Totty, 'The Path to Better Teamwork'; 'Collaborative Software'.

71 *Ibid.*

72 Totty, 'The Path to Better Teamwork'; 'Collaborative Software'.

73 *Ibid.*

74 *Ibid.*

75 A. Wakizaka, 'Faxes, Email, Help the Deaf Get Office Jobs', *The Wall Street Journal*, October 3, 1995, B1, B5.

76 I. M. Kunii, 'Tuning into a Turnaround', *BusinessWeek Online*, June 23, 2003.

77 D. Storey, 'Kenwood Chief Touts Turnaround', *Mobile Radio Technology*, February 1, 2003.

78 *Ibid.*

79 I. M. Kunii, 'Tuning into a Turnaround'.

80 'The American Way', *The Economist*, April 3, 2004, 88–90.

81 *Ibid.*

82 D. Tannen, 'The Power of Talk', *Harvard Business Review*, September–October 1995, 138–48; D. Tannen, *Talking from 9 to 5* (New York: Avon Books, 1995).

83 Tannen, 'The Power of Talk'; Tannen, *Talking from 9 to 5*.

84 Tannen, 'The Power of Talk'; Tannen, *Talking from 9 to 5*.

85 Tannen, 'The Power of Talk'.

86 *Ibid.*; Tannen, *Talking from 9 to 5*.

87 J. Cohen, 'He Writes, She Writes', *Houston Chronicle*, July 7, 2001, C1–C2.

88 *Ibid.*

89 *Ibid.*

90 Tannen, 'The Power of Talk', 148.

Chapter 17

Managing Organisational Conflict, Politics and Negotiation

LEARNING OBJECTIVES

After studying this chapter, you should be able to:

☑ Explain why conflict arises, and identify the types and sources of conflict in organisations.

☑ Describe the conflict management strategies that managers can use to resolve conflict effectively.

☑ Understand the nature of negotiation and why integrative bargaining is more effective than distributive negotiation.

☑ Describe the ways in which managers can promote integrative bargaining in organisations.

☑ Explain why managers need to be attuned to organisational politics, and describe the political strategies that managers can use to become politically skilled.

A Manager's Challenge

A Master at Managing Conflict

Sir Richard Branson is a master at effectively managing conflict and using power to help his Virgin Empire to achieve record levels of revenues and profits.

However he has not always had it easy and has suffered his own conflicts, particularly with various competitors along the way. Virgin is now a worldwide brand name; from its humble beginnings in the first Virgin record store in London in 1971, the Virgin group now boasts several holding companies and over 200 operating companies. In May 2005, the airline company Virgin Atlantic announced a pre-tax profit of £68 million based on a turnover of £1.630 billion. Virgin succeeded in producing the highest profit figure since 1999, a remarkable achievement considering the state of the airline industry since 9/11, with many leading players struggling to survive.

Virgin's success is primarily due to the attitude and behaviour of its founder, his deep understanding of this market and his ability to effectively manage conflict and bridge cultures and mind-sets. Branson maintains that failure and conflict are concepts that he sees as 'opportunities for learning'. He therefore always encourages all his employees to adopt the philosophy of *involvement* and gives them the authority to succeed. He is proud to have a low staff turnover and confirms that rather than losing his best people to start up their own company as a competitor he would rather make them a millionaire within Virgin – and he boasts quite a few![1]

Virgin's culture, values and norms have embraced the Japanese model of business (the *Keiretsu* system) 'where multiple companies have financial and management links and share a common identity'.[2] Unlike Japanese manufacturing industry, however, where managers tend to be risk-aversive, Branson, through his values of 'innocence, innovation and irreverence for authority', believes that without risk a business will die. In an interview where he was accused of attacking Britain's 'safety-first' culture, he commented that 'Britain's decision-makers were too conservative and would always go for the "more of the same" option rather than take a risk'.[3]

Similar to Toyota's ethos of efficiency, high-quality, lean production and continuous improvement, Virgin has created a structure where autonomy and ownership of many small companies is more preferable than one giant corporation. Branson sees his 200 companies bonded by a 'unity of the culture'. In a presentation to the Institute of Directors in 1993, he explained his business maxims as putting staff first, then customers, followed by shareholders. He maintained that businesses should be 'shaped around the people' and that one should 'build', not 'buy'; aim to be 'the best' and not necessarily 'the biggest'. This is borne out by his many JVs with other companies – for example the JV with Blockbuster to own and develop Mega stores in Europe, Australia and the US in 1992, and the JV with Bear Sterns to set up Lynx New Media, a £73 million (€105 million) Internet-focused venture capital (VC) fund in 2000. Branson is said to prefer to 'have a lot of exciting companies all making money, than one huge corporation with lots of divisions and departments that become slow growing and stagnant'.[4]

Branson is the driving force behind the individual successes of his employees and the success of Virgin Group as a whole. While Branson is known for his camaraderie, sense of fun, amazing entrepreneurial skills and for being a bit of a 'rebel', he also is someone with a sense of fairness and fair play. He has certainly experienced his share of conflict in his battles with giants such as British Airways (BA) and Coca-Cola. In the fight against BA's 'dirty tricks' campaign in the 1990s, Branson did not mirror BA's behaviour, nor did he use unethical practices when trying to compete for the franchise to win the National Lottery.

Overview

Successful leaders such as Richard Branson are able effectively to use their power to influence others and to manage conflict to achieve win–win solutions. In Chapter 14 it was shown how managers, as leaders, can exert influence over other people to achieve group and organisational goals and how managers' sources of power can enable them to exert such influence. This chapter will consider why managers need to develop the skills necessary to manage organisational conflict, politics and negotiation if they are going to be effective and achieve their goals.

Conflict, and the strategies that managers can use to resolve it effectively, are discussed and one major conflict resolution technique – negotiation – is discussed in detail, outlining the steps that managers can take to be good negotiators. The nature of organisational politics is also considered: the political strategies that managers can use to maintain and expand their power, and use it effectively. By the end of this chapter, students should appreciate why managers must develop the skills necessary to manage these important organisational processes if they are to be effective and achieve their organisational goals.

Organisational Conflict

Organisational conflict is the discord that can arise when the goals, interests or values of individuals, groups or organisations are incompatible and those individuals, groups or organisations block or thwart one another's attempts to achieve their objectives.[5] However, conflict is a *state of mind*: it cannot exist unless two or more parties perceive that one of them has either 'had a negative effect or is about to have a negative effect, on something that the other cares about'.[6]

Conflict can be explained differently, depending upon the frame of reference that one decides to have. For the purposes of this chapter, the four frames of reference identified by Alan Fox in the mid-1970s[7] will be used. Fox's four frames of reference are *Unitarist, Pluralist, Interactionist* and *Radical*.

Unitarist

From this perspective, conflict can be seen as unhealthy and 'bad' for the company, as this perspective takes the view that organisations should be seen as healthy and harmonious co-operative structures. Research has identified the nine key features of this perspective as:

1. An assumption of *common interests* across workers, managers and shareholders alike

2. The acceptance of the economic, political and social framework that management performs within, and unquestioningly adopts the *assumptions, goals and language* of management

3. Treating conflict and contradictions as peripheral to relationships between people, groups and social classes and *depoliticising* them

4. Seeing an observable act of conflict as *failure* in a co-ordinating function, or as an individual's psychological *deviant behaviour*

5. Applying a *humanistic approach* to conflict resolution which focuses on the individual

6. Believing that conflict resolution is the responsibility of *management* and that managers should be capable of changing employees' behaviour to move away from a conflict situation

7. Claiming that by the 1990s little non-sanctioned deviant behaviour could be observed by employees across organisations, due to changes in economic, technological and political developments

8. Focusing on *conflict resolution* techniques rather than examining the underlying cause for conflict in the workplace

9. Seeing *communication breakdown* as the predominant force behind workplace conflict and any external or third-party negotiators (e.g. unions) as agitators rather than negotiators in the relationship between employers and employees.[8]

The Unitarist framework rationalises conflict in four different ways:

- Conflict is *outside* the *control of the manager* and as such can change behaviours and eradicate trust and goodwill among workers.

- Conflict is the result of *poor communication structures* (e.g. not telling people early enough about the need for change).

- Conflict is the result of *power struggles between levels of management* – the solution is to appreciate each other's differences and problems and focus on the bigger picture.

- Conflict is the result of *interference of unions or other external agencies*, seen as disrupting the 'normal flow of harmony in working relationships'.[9]

Although such a perspective may seem a little far fetched in many European work environments in the twenty-first century, some companies may support such a philosophy. The UK Co-operative Bank states that its aim is: 'To develop a close affinity with organisations which promote fellowship between workers, customers, members and employers'. Similarly, BA's statement on Safety Culture states that: 'Safety is paramount. We all have a duty to take care of ourselves, colleagues and customers'. Such statements indicate that the company is striving for harmony and seems to consider conflict as a disturbance and something that ought to be avoided.

Pluralist

From a Pluralist frame of reference, conflict is seen as an *inevitable part of organisational life* because different parts of the organisation are likely to have different goals; it is therefore inevitable that different stakeholders such as managers and workers will see things differently as they each work towards pursuing their own interests and objectives. Organisational conflict also can exist between departments and divisions that are competing for resources, or even between managers who are competing for promotion to the next level in the organisational hierarchy. The Pluralist perspective believes that conflict therefore provides a *regulation mechanism* between these various groups and acts as a signal of potential breakdown in relationships, which is seen as problematic for everyone. So rather than differences preventing effective functionality, they are seen as signs for groups and departments to recognise that people need to *compromise and negotiate* in order to manage both functionality and dysfunctionality and maintain the status quo throughout the organisation. This perspective does not see conflict as harmful to organisations, but rather as being endemic: conflict from this point of view can also act as a *safety valve*, keeping people alert, making them aware that they need to check their own perceptions and stereotypes and also be flexible enough constantly to adapt to both internal and external changes in the workplace.

Interactionist

From the Interactionist frame of reference, conflict is seen as a very positive force which is necessary for organisations to perform effectively. It is considered a part of the Pluralist perspective, with the difference that an *optimum level of conflict* should exist in an organisation, which can be achieved through management interventions. This perspective believes that conflict, rather than being avoided or ignored, should be embraced and encouraged. Conflict prevents extreme cohesiveness within groups which can lead to the detrimental 'groupthink' syndrome (Chapter 7).[10] The Interactionist also argues that too little conflict can create apathy, reduce innovation, change and creativity and allow organisations to become stagnant. However this perspective emphasises that the type of conflict needs to be *appropriate*: functional conflict can support an organisation's objectives and enhance performance, dysfunctional conflict is detrimental to organisational performance.

It is important for managers to develop the skills necessary to manage conflict effectively, as the level of conflict present in an organisation has important implications for *organisational performance*. Figure 17.1 illustrates the relationship between organisational conflict and performance. At point A, there is little or no conflict and organisational performance suffers. Lack of conflict in an organisation often signals that managers emphasise conformity at the expense of new ideas, are resistant to change and strive for agreement rather than effective decision making. As the level of conflict increases from point A to point B, organisational effectiveness is likely to increase. When an organisation has an *optimum level of conflict* (point B), managers are likely to be open to, and encourage, a variety of perspectives, look for ways to improve organisational functioning and effectiveness and view debates and disagreements as a necessary ingredient for effective decision making. As the level of conflict increases from point B to point C, however, conflict escalates to the point where organisational performance suffers. When an organisation

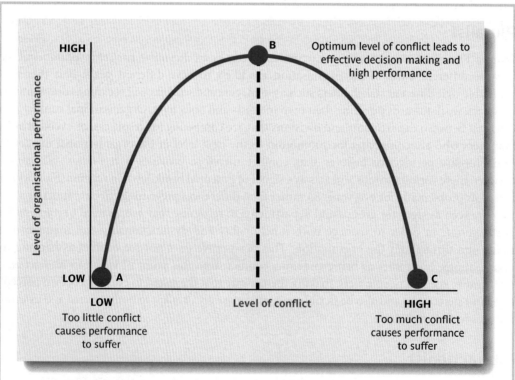

Figure 17.1 The Effect of Conflict on Organisational Performance from an Interactionist Perspective

has a dysfunctionally high level of conflict, managers are likely to waste organisational resources to achieve their own ends, to be more concerned about winning political battles than about doing what will lead to a competitive advantage for their organisation and to try to 'get even' with their opponents rather than make good decisions.

The benefits of promoting functional conflict were researched by Taffinder, who found that those organisations were most effective where *task conflict* was high while conflict surrounding *personal values* was eliminated.[11] Taffinder cited Levi Straus and Microsoft as two good examples of organisations that had sound cultural values that enabled them to be able to cope with change.

Radical

The Radical perspective originates in Marxism and Marx's critique of capitalism. This perspective sees conflict as an inevitable aspect of capitalism: it will be endemic in any organisation which is structured as a bureaucracy, and no amount of bargaining or negotiating will resolve it as it is a consequence of the exploitative nature of relationships within a capitalist economy. From this perspective, conflict is simply part of the relationship between managers and the workers. In Marxist terms, the owners of production are intent on driving down the cost of production and managers, who are the agents of the owners, simply exploit and control and dictate to the employees in order to keep the owners happy.[12]

Any behaviour such as racial harassment, sexual harassment and emotional or physical bullying are all examples of radical behaviour, and yet the other frames of reference have tended not to include them. Ackroyd and Thompson refer to 'organisational misbehaviour' and categorise such behaviours along dimensional factors – anything from time-wasting to sabotage. The authors refer to such behaviours as 'anything you do at work which you are not supposed to do'.[13]

Types of Conflict

There are four main types of conflict in organisations: *interpersonal, intra-group, inter-group* and *inter-organisational* (Fig. 17.2).[14] Understanding how these types differ can help managers to deal with conflict.

Figure 17.2 Types of Conflict in Organisations

Interpersonal conflict

Interpersonal conflict is conflict between *individual members of an organisation*, occurring because of differences in their *goals* or *values*. Two managers may experience interpersonal conflict when their values concerning protection of the environment differ. One may argue that the organisation should do only what is required by law. The other manager may counter that the organisation should invest in equipment to reduce emissions even though its current level of emissions is below the legal limit.

Intra-group conflict

Intra-group conflict is conflict that arises *within a group, team or department*. When members of the marketing department in a clothing company disagree about how they should spend budgeted advertising revenue for a new line of men's designer jeans, they are experiencing intra-group conflict. Some members want to spend all the money on advertisements in magazines, others to devote half of the money to billboards and ads in city buses and pedestrian areas.

Inter-group conflict

Inter-group conflict is conflict that occurs *between groups, teams or departments*. R&D depart-ments, for example, sometimes experience inter-group conflict with production departments. Members of the R&D department may develop a new product that they think production can make inexpensively by using existing manufacturing capabilities. Members of the produc-tion department, however, may disagree and believe that the costs of making the product will be much higher. Managers of departments usually play a key role in managing such inter-group conflicts.

Inter-organisational conflict

Inter-organisational conflict is conflict that arises *across organisations*. Sometimes it arises when managers in one organisation feel that another organisation is not behaving ethically and is threatening the well-being of certain stakeholder groups.

Sources of Conflict

Conflict in organisations emanates from a variety of sources. Those examined here are incom-patible goals and time horizons, overlapping authority, task interdependencies, incompatible evaluation or reward systems, scarce resources and status inconsistencies (Fig. 17.3).[15]

Incompatible goals and time horizons

Recall from Chapter 10 that an important managerial activity is organising people and tasks into *departments* and *divisions* to accomplish an organisation's goals. Almost inevitably, this grouping results in the creation of departments and divisions that have different goals and time horizons, and the result can be conflict. Production and production managers, for example, usually con-centrate on efficiency and cost-cutting; they have a relatively short time horizon, and focus on producing quality goods or services in a timely and efficient manner. In contrast, marketing and marketing managers focus on sales and responsiveness to customers. Their time horizon is longer than that of production because they are trying to be responsive not only to customers' needs today but also to their changing needs in the future in order to build long-term customer

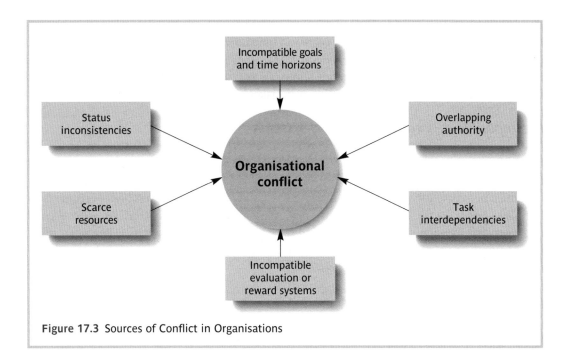

Figure 17.3 Sources of Conflict in Organisations

loyalty. These fundamental differences between marketing and production are often breeding grounds for conflict.

Overlapping authority

Role clarification is one way that can reduce ambiguities over who is responsible for what, and what authority they have. If people are not sure of who is responsible for performing which duties, or who has authority over who and who is in control of the current project, etc. then conflict can occur. This is particularly the case in young or growing companies where the management structure is still not in place, or people have two or three roles and tend to repeat tasks or get confused in what they should be doing. After mergers or acquisitions, people will often be unsure of what their roles and/or responsibilities are due to the radical change. An example of potential conflict resulting from overlapping authority is the preservation of the New Forest. The New Forest is a unique landscape in the south of England that has been named a National Park. National Parks are usually protected by a National Park Authority (NPA); however, in the case of the New Forest a large proportion of responsibility for the land is with the Verderers and the Forestry Commission and the locals are concerned that the establishment of an NPA will cause problems, as blurred lines of responsibility may prevent dynamic and flexible decision making to solve problems. The Department for Environment, Food and Rural Affairs (DEFRA), however, feels that the well-tested institution of an NPA will not interfere or hinder the preservation of the unique forest environment.[16]

Task interdependencies

Have you ever been assigned a group project for one of your classes and had one group member who consistently failed to get things done on time? This probably created some conflict in your group because other members were dependent on the late member's contributions to complete the project. Whenever individuals, groups, teams or departments are interdependent, the potential for such conflict exists.[17] With differing goals and time horizons, the managers of marketing and production come into conflict precisely because the departments are interdependent: marketing is dependent on production for the goods it markets and sells, and production is dependent on marketing for creating demand for the things it makes.

Incompatible evaluation or reward systems

The way in which interdependent groups, teams or departments are evaluated and rewarded can be another source of conflict.[18] Production managers, for example, are evaluated and rewarded for their success in staying within budget or lowering costs while maintaining quality. So they are reluctant to take any steps that will increase costs, such as paying workers high overtime rates to finish a late order for an important customer. Marketing managers, in contrast, are evaluated and rewarded for their success in generating sales and satisfying customers. They often think that overtime pay is a small price to pay for responsiveness to customers. Conflict between production and marketing is rarely unexpected.

Scarce resources

Management is the process of acquiring, developing, protecting and utilising the resources that make an organisation efficient and effective (Chapter 1). When resources are scarce, management is all the more difficult and conflict is likely.[19] Divisional managers may be in conflict over who has access to financial capital, and organisational members at all levels may be in conflict over who gets rises and promotions.

Status inconsistencies

The fact that some individuals, groups, teams or departments within an organisation are more highly regarded than others in the organisation can also create conflict. In some restaurants, for example, the chefs have relatively higher status than the people who wait on tables. Nevertheless, the chefs receive customers' orders from the waiters and the waiting staff can return to the chefs food that they or their customers think is not acceptable. This status inconsistency – high-status chefs taking orders from low-status waiting staff – can be the source of considerable conflict. For this reason some restaurants require that the waiting staff put orders on a spindle, thereby reducing the amount of direct order-giving.[20]

Status inconsistencies can also occur based on the perception of the *amount of power* that people hold. Power can be seen as someone's capacity to influence others who are in a dependent relationship with the power holder. A line manager, for example, can influence the tasks that are performed at any given time, as he has power through his role as the manager – also called *legitimate power*. Power is not always part of a formal organisational role, but can be exercised and obtained in different ways. *Expert power* and *referent power* are forms of power that are based on individual qualities of a person – for example, if you are the only person in your organisation, team or circle of friends who has expertise in developing software, you automatically have the power to influence others (expert power). However, you may be a worker who is well liked by others, which provides you with the ability to influence other people's thinking (referent power).

The concept of power underpins conflict, negotiations and organisational politics; power is a persuasive concept that is part of everyday organisational life.

Reaction Time

1. Discuss why too little conflict in an organisation can be just as detrimental as too much.
2. Think about the various examples that have been described as sources of conflict. Identify at least two more and discuss in what ways they could cause conflict between workers and managers.

Conflict Management Strategies

If an organisation is to achieve its goals, managers must be able to resolve conflicts in a functional manner. *Functional conflict resolution* means that the conflict is settled by *compromise* or by *collaboration* between the parties in conflict (later in the chapter we discuss other, typically less functional ways in which conflicts are sometimes resolved).[21] *Compromise* is possible when each party is concerned about not only its own goal accomplishment but also the goal accomplishment of the other party and is willing to engage in a give-and-take exchange and make concessions until a reasonable resolution of the conflict is reached. *Collaboration* is a way of handling conflict in which the parties to a conflict try to satisfy their goals without making any concessions and, instead, come up with a way to resolve their differences that leaves them both better off.[22]

In addition to compromise and collaboration, there are three other ways in which conflicts are sometimes handled: *accommodation, avoidance* and *competition.*[23] When *accommodation* takes place, one party to the conflict simply gives in to the demands of the other. Accommodation typically takes place when one party has more power than the other and is able to pursue its goal attainment at the expense of the weaker party. From an organisational perspective, accommodation is often ineffective, as the two parties are not co-operating with each other, they are unlikely to want to co-operate in the future and the weaker party who gives in or accommodates the more powerful party might look for ways to get back at the stronger party in the future.

When conflicts are handled by *avoidance*, the two parties to a conflict try to ignore the problem and do nothing to resolve the disagreement. Avoidance is often ineffective, since the real source of the disagreement has not been addressed, conflict is likely to continue and communication and co-operation are hindered.

Competition occurs when each party to a conflict tries to maximise its own gain and has little interest in understanding the other party's position and arriving at a solution that will allow both parties to achieve their goals. Competition can actually escalate levels of conflict as each party tries to outmanoeuvre the other. As a way of handling conflict, competition is ineffective, since the two sides are more concerned about 'winning' the battle than co-operating to arrive at a solution that is best for the organisation and acceptable to both sides. Handling conflicts through accommodation, avoidance or competition is ineffective because the two parties to a conflict do not co-operate with each other and work toward a mutually acceptable solution to their differences.

When the parties to a conflict are willing to co-operate with each other and through compromise or collaboration devise a solution that each finds acceptable, an organisation is more likely to achieve its goals.[24] Conflict management strategies that managers can use to ensure that conflicts are resolved in a functional manner focus on individuals and on the organisation as a whole. The following sections describe four strategies that focus on individuals: increasing awareness of the sources of conflict, increasing diversity awareness and skills, practising job rotation or temporary assignments and using permanent transfers, or dismissals, when necessary. Also two strategies are described that focus on the organisation as a whole: changing an organisation's *structure or culture*, and directly altering the *source* of conflict.

Strategies focused on individuals

Increasing awareness of the sources of conflict

Conflict can arise because of *communication problems* and *interpersonal misunderstandings*. For example, differences in linguistic styles (Chapter 16) may lead some men in work teams to talk more, and take more credit for ideas, than women in those teams. These communication differences can result in conflict when the men incorrectly assume that the women are uninterested or less capable because they participate less and the women incorrectly assume that the men are being bossy and are not interested in their ideas because they seem to do all the talking. By increasing people's awareness of this source of conflict, managers can help to resolve conflict functionally. Once men and women realise that the source of their conflict is differences in linguistic styles, they can take steps to interact with each other more effectively. The men can give the women more of a chance to provide input, and the women can be more proactive in providing it.

Personalities can clash in an organisation. In these situations, too, managers can help resolve conflicts functionally by increasing organisational members' awareness of the source of their difficulties. For example, some people who are not inclined to take risks may come into conflict with those who are prone to taking them. The non-risk takers may complain that those who welcome risk propose outlandish ideas without justification, while the risk takers may complain that their innovative ideas are always getting shot down. When both types of people are made aware that their conflicts are due to fundamental differences in their way of approaching problems, they will likely be better able to co-operate in coming up with innovative ideas that entail only moderate levels of risk.

Increasing diversity awareness and skills

Interpersonal conflicts also can arise because of diversity. Older workers may feel uncomfortable or resentful about reporting to a younger supervisor, an Asian may feel singled out in a group of white workers, or a female senior manager may feel that members of her predominantly male senior management team band together whenever one of them disagrees with one of her proposals. Whether these feelings are justified, they are likely to cause recurring conflicts. Many of the techniques described in Chapter 5 for increasing diversity awareness and skills can help managers effectively manage diversity and resolve conflicts that have their origins in differences between organisational members.

Today the workplace is becoming ever more 'virtual' as many companies, in order to manage resources and cut costs, are outsourcing some back-office and call-centre operations. This may be good for cost savings and increased profit in terms of cheaper HR, but for the UK employees who are in jeopardy of losing their jobs, it's a very different story, as is seen by Case 17.1.

Case 17.1: **Prudential causes concern**

The UK's second largest insurance company, Prudential, came into conflict with Amicus (the finance union) when the CEO announced that he was proposing to continue his cost-cutting strategy by closing three of Prudential's core sites; Belfast, Bristol and the headquarters in London. This will affect over 700 workers who are likely to lose their jobs or be forced to relocate in order to survive the reorganisation. Although Prudential had made an agreement in 2002 in which they had promised to not make anyone compulsorily redundant during the reorganisation process, this agreement expired in 2006. David Fleming, a representative of the Amicus union, commented in an interview in April that 'the Union is prepared to fight these proposals', and that they would do everything in their power to support employees in their endeavour to protect their jobs. Prudential has already cut 200 jobs across the UK and has plans to close another outlet in 2008. Fleming pointed out that Prudential has 'made no attempt to avoid compulsory redundancies', which is just another indication of how 'globalisation and weak employment protection is eating into the UK's economy'. It is unlikely, for instance, that employees in the Northern Ireland outlet would accept jobs elsewhere, as this would require relocation to England and a huge upheaval, not only physically but also culturally and psychologically. Such conflict highlights the deeper issues that often emerge from organisations making strategic decisions without communication to or consideration of its workforce. At a broader level, such organisational decisions are cause for increasing concern. Not only do such conflicts demotivate workers, but they drive people to leave the UK, decreasing the skill base even more. The unions are now calling on the government to strengthen employment rights before more UK jobs are lost to India and Asia.[25]

Practising job rotation or temporary assignments

Conflicts can arise because individual organisational members simply do not have a good understanding of the work activities and demands that others in an organisation face. A financial analyst, for example, may be required to submit monthly reports to a member of the accounting department. These reports have a low priority for the analyst, and he typically turns them in a couple of days late. On the due date, the accountant always calls up the financial analyst, and conflict ensues as the accountant describes in detail why she must have the reports on time and the financial analyst describes everything else he needs to do. In situations such as this, job rotation or temporary assignments, which expand organisational members' knowledge base and appreciation of other departments, can be a useful way of resolving the conflict. If the financial analyst spends some time working in the accounting department, he may appreciate the need for timely reports. A temporary assignment in the finance department may help the accountant realise the demands a financial analyst faces and the need to streamline unnecessary aspects of reporting.

Using permanent transfers, or dismissals, when necessary

When other conflict resolution strategies do not work, managers may need to take more drastic steps, including permanent transfers or dismissals.

Suppose two front-line managers who work in the same department are always at each other's throats; frequent bitter conflicts arise between them even though they both seem to get along well with the other employees. No matter what their supervisor does to increase their understanding of each other, these conflicts keep occurring. In this case, the supervisor may want to transfer one or both managers so that they do not have to interact as frequently.

When dysfunctionally high levels of conflict occur among employees who cannot resolve their differences and understand each other, it may be necessary for one of them to leave the company. One of the presenters of BBC News 24 resigned in early 2006, after working for the BBC for 37 years. The news anchor blamed a personality clash with his co-presenter of four months as the reason for resigning. Bill Hayton, who presented the 9 a.m.–1 p.m. Monday–Friday slot, asked for a change in co-presenter, but the senior management team did not accede to his request, leaving him no choice but to leave the channel. His main reason to leave was motivated by the fact that he had to present four hours of live television with someone he did not connect to on a personal level.[26]

Strategies focused on the whole organisation

Changing an organisation's structure or culture

Conflict can signal the need for changes in an organisation's structure or culture. Managers can sometimes effectively resolve conflict by changing the *organisational structure* they use to group people and tasks. As an organisation grows, for example, the *functional structure* (departments such as marketing, finance and production) that was effective when the organisation was small may cease to be effective, and a shift to a *product structure* might effectively resolve conflicts (Chapter 10).

Managers also can effectively resolve conflicts by increasing *levels of integration* in an organisation. Recall from Chapter 15 that Hallmark Cards increased integration by using cross-functional teams to produce new cards. The use of cross-functional teams speeded up new card development and helped to resolve conflicts between different departments. When a writer and an artist have a conflict over the appropriateness of the artist's illustrations, they do not pass criticisms back and forward from one department to another because they are on the same team and can directly resolve the issue on the spot.

Managers may sometimes need to take steps to change an *organisation's culture* to resolve conflict (Chapter 3). Norms and values in an organisational culture may inadvertently promote dysfunctionally high levels of conflict that are difficult to resolve. For instance, norms that stress respect for formal authority may create conflict that is difficult to resolve when an organisation creates self-managed work teams and managers' roles and the structure of authority in the organisation change. Values stressing individual competition may make it difficult to resolve conflicts when organisational members need to put others' interests ahead of their own. In circumstances such as these, taking steps to change norms and values can be an effective conflict resolution strategy.

Altering the source of conflict

When conflict is due to overlapping authority, different evaluation or reward systems and status inconsistencies, managers can sometimes effectively resolve the conflict by directly altering the *source of the conflict* – the overlapping authority, the evaluation or reward system, or the status inconsistency. Managers can, for example, clarify the chain of command and reassign tasks and responsibilities to resolve conflicts due to overlapping authority.

Negotiation

A particularly important conflict resolution technique for managers and other organisational members to use in situations where the parties to a conflict have approximately equal levels of power is **negotiation**. During negotiation, the parties to a conflict try to come up with an acceptable solution by considering various alternative ways to allocate resources.[27] Sometimes the two sides involved in a conflict negotiate directly with each other. At other times, a **third-party negotiator** is relied on. Third-party negotiators are impartial individuals who are not directly involved in the conflict and have special expertise in handling conflicts and negotiations;[28] they are relied on to help the two negotiating parties reach an acceptable resolution.[29] When a third-party negotiator acts as a *mediator*, his or her role in the negotiation process is to facilitate an effective negotiation between the two parties; mediators do not force either party to make concessions nor can they force an agreement to resolve a conflict. *Arbitrators*, on the other hand, are third-party negotiators who can impose what they believe is a fair solution to a dispute by which both parties are obligated to abide.[30]

Distributive Negotiation and Integrative Bargaining

There are two major types of negotiation – **distributive negotiation** and **integrative bargaining**.[31] In distributive negotiation, the two parties perceive that they have a 'fixed pie' of resources that they need to divide.[32] They take a competitive, adversarial stance. Each party realises that he or she must concede something but is out to get the lion's share of the resources.[33] The parties see no need to interact with each other in the future and do not care if their interpersonal relationship is damaged or destroyed by their competitive negotiation.[34] Conflicts are handled by *competition*.

In integrative bargaining, the parties perceive that they may be able to increase the 'resource pie' by trying to come up with a creative solution to the conflict. They do not view the conflict competitively, as a win-or-lose situation; instead, they view it co-operatively, as a win–win situation in which both parties can gain. Trust, information-sharing and the desire of both parties to achieve a good resolution of the conflict characterise integrative bargaining.[35] Conflicts are handled through *collaboration* and/or *compromise*.

Strategies to Encourage Integrative Bargaining

There are five strategies that managers in all kinds of organisations can rely on to facilitate integrative bargaining and avoid distributive negotiation: emphasising super-ordinate goals; focusing on the problem, not the people; focusing on interests, not demands; creating new options for joint gain; and focusing on what is fair (Table 17.1).[36]

Table 17.1 Negotiation strategies for integrative bargaining

■ Emphasise super-ordinate goals
■ Focus on the problem, not the people
■ Focus on interests, not demands
■ Create new options for joint gain
■ Focus on what is fair

Emphasising super-ordinate goals

Super-ordinate goals are goals that both parties agree to regardless of the source of their conflict. Increasing organisational effectiveness, increasing responsiveness to customers and gaining a competitive advantage are just a few of the many super-ordinate goals that members of an organisation can emphasise during integrative bargaining. Super-ordinate goals help parties in conflict to keep in mind the 'big picture' and the fact that they are working together for a larger purpose or goal despite their disagreements. Hofbeck and Steinberg emphasised three super-ordinate goals during their bargaining: ensuring that the restaurant continued to survive and prosper, allowing Hofbeck to retire and allowing Steinberg to remain an owner and manager as long as he wished.

As indicated in Case 17.2, a focus on super-ordinate goals helped promote integrative bargaining between the Chrysler Group and the United Autoworkers Union (UAW).

Case 17.2: Super-ordinate goals at DaimlerChrysler

Tom LaSorda, chief operating officer of the Chrysler Group, now part of the German-owned DaimlerChrysler, is the first child of union leaders to rise to a senior management position in any of the three largest auto companies.[37] LaSorda's parents were both active in trade unions, and his father, Frank LaSorda, was president of the Windsor, Ontario, local unit of the UAW from 1977 to 1982. Frank LaSorda was on a 12-member committee that negotiated with the loan guarantee board during Chrysler's bankruptcy bailout in the 1980s and made many concessions on the part of the union to keep Chrysler going. As Frank puts it, 'Tom wouldn't have that job, he wouldn't have any corporation to lead, if it weren't for the hard decisions. . . . We made three concessions in 13 months, and each was worse than the last.'[38]

The loan guarantee board, Chrysler management and the UAW were able to reach those historic agreements due to their super-ordinate goal of rescuing Chrysler. Today, relations between the UAW and US automakers, including Chrysler, are considered better than they have ever been, as both sides have the super-ordinate goal of surviving and thriving in the face of intense global competition from powerhouses such as Toyota.

Take the case of a recent and historic agreement made between the Chrysler Group, the UAW, and three auto suppliers.[39] The agreement involves a major investment in Chrysler's Toledo, Ohio, production facility that currently makes the Jeep Liberty and Wrangler SUVs.[40] Three suppliers, Durr Industries, Kuka Group and Hyundai Mobis, will build part of the Jeep Wrangler with their own employees in their own plants on the site, allowing Chrysler to spend less money on investing in plants and more on product development.[41] Suppliers, Tom LaSorda and other senior managers at Chrysler and the UAW see the agreement and overall £1.15 billion investment in the Toledo site as a way to help Chrysler remain competitive. This super-ordinate goal has allowed all parties to put aside their differences and work together.[42] As Lloyd Mahaffey, the regional director of the UAW for Toledo, puts it: 'This project keeps approximately 3,800 jobs right here in Toledo, it enables us to implement new ways to become competitive in a rapidly changing time for our industry.'[43] Volkswagen (VW) has undertaken a similar venture in one of its Brazilian plants. The modular consortium that VW created allowed the company to remain competitive in its lorry business, as it had only to carry the cost of marketing and quality checks.

Focusing on the problem, not the people

People who are in conflict may not be able to resist the temptation to focus on the other party's shortcomings and weaknesses, thereby personalising the conflict: instead of attacking the problem, the parties to the conflict attack each other. This approach is inconsistent with integrative bargaining and can easily lead both parties into a distributive negotiation mode. All parties to a conflict need to keep focused on the problem or on the source of the conflict and avoid the temptation to discredit one another.

Consider the example of Hofbeck and Steinberg, who have jointly owned a restaurant for many years, and have developed a friendship alongside their business partnership. Given their strong friendship, this was not much of an issue for Hofbeck and Steinberg, but they still had to be on their guard to avoid personalising the conflict. Steinberg recalls that when they were having a hard time coming up with a solution, he started thinking that Hofbeck, a healthy 57-year-old, was lazy to want to retire so young: 'If only he wasn't so lazy, we would never be in the mess we're in right now.' Steinberg never mentioned these thoughts to Hofbeck (who later admitted that he was sometimes annoyed with Steinberg for being such a workaholic), because he realised that doing so would hurt their chances for reaching an integrative solution.

Focusing on interests, not demands

Demands are *what* a person wants; interests are *why* the person wants them. When two people are in conflict, it is unlikely that the demands of both can be met. Their underlying interests, however, can be met, and meeting them is what integrative bargaining is all about.

Hofbeck's demand was that they sell the restaurant and split the proceeds. Steinberg's demand was that they keep the restaurant and maintain the status quo. Obviously, both demands could not be met, but perhaps their interests could be. Hofbeck wanted to be able to retire, invest his share of the money from the restaurant and live off the returns on the investment. Steinberg wanted to continue managing, owning and deriving income from the restaurant.

Creating new options for joint gain

Once two parties to a conflict focus on their interests, they are on the road to achieving creative solutions to the conflict that will benefit them both. This win–win scenario means that rather than having a fixed set of alternatives from which to choose, the two parties can come up with new alternatives that might even expand the 'resource pie'.

Hofbeck and Steinberg came up with three such alternatives. First, even though Steinberg did not have the capital, he could buy out Hofbeck's share of the restaurant. Hofbeck would provide the financing for the purchase and, in return, Steinberg would pay him a reasonable return on his investment (the same kind of return he could have obtained had he taken his money out of the restaurant and invested it). Second, the partners could seek to sell Hofbeck's share in the restaurant to a third party under the stipulation that Steinberg would continue to manage the restaurant and receive income for his services. Third, the partners could continue to jointly own the restaurant. Steinberg would manage it and receive a proportionally greater share of its profits than Hofbeck, who would be an absentee owner not involved in day-to-day operations but would still receive a return on his investment in the restaurant.

Focusing on what is fair

Focusing on what is fair is consistent with the principle of distributive justice, which emphasises the fair distribution of outcomes based on the meaningful contributions that people make to organisations (see Chapter 5). It is likely that two parties in conflict will disagree on certain points and prefer different alternatives that each party believes may better serve their own interests or maximise their own outcomes. Emphasising fairness and distributive justice will help the two parties come to a mutual agreement about what the best solution is to the problem.

Steinberg and Hofbeck agreed that Hofbeck should be able to cut his ties with the restaurant if he chose to do so. They thus decided to pursue the second alternative described above and seek a suitable buyer for Hofbeck's share. They were successful in finding an investor who was willing to buy out Hofbeck's share and let Steinberg continue managing the restaurant. And they remained good friends.

When managers pursue these five strategies and encourage other organisational members to do so, they are more likely to be able to effectively resolve their conflicts through integrative bargaining. In addition, throughout the negotiation process, managers and other organisational members need to be aware of, and on their guard against, the *biases* that can lead to faulty decision making (Chapter 7).[44]

As indicated in Case 17.3, when negotiations involve complex and multiple parameters, or negotiators lack the time to engage in the negotiation process themselves, *negotiation software* can sometimes be beneficial.

Case 17.3: **Computerised negotiations**

Some negotiations, especially those taking place between members of different organisations and involving multiple parameters, can be very time-consuming.

For negotiations that over-stretched employees simply do not have the time to deal with, negotiation software can be a blessing.[45] Physicians and insurance companies are often in the position of negotiating payment schedules; physicians want prompter payments for their services, while insurance companies prefer lengthier payment schedules. Using software provided by SplitTheDifference, the physicians and insurance companies can come to a mutually acceptable agreement.[46] Based on information from both parties, the software presents proposals to physicians (e.g. prompter payments for a discount on fees paid), who can accept the proposal or reject it and come back with a counter-offer. The negotiation proceeds until a deal has been struck; if after three rounds, no deal has been struck, both parties revert to the terms of the initial contract/claim between the physician and the insurance company.[47]

Other companies are developing software to deal with more complex kinds of negotiations. The Project A team at Fujitsu Laboratories is developing software that can tabulate millions of different scenarios involving negotiations where the two parties might initially have far more points of divergence than of agreement.[48] Computers can process information and find solutions more quickly than humans, so by using information on people's preferences, computers can come up with a vast array of potential solutions that can be cycled through. For example, the Project A team is working on software that can facilitate negotiations between a purchasing agent and a supplier by taking into account both parties' preferences and relative priorities for factors such as delivery times, quantities, reliability, quality, shipping costs and methods, size, colour and whatever else might be relevant for the negotiation at hand to come up with a solution that both parties find acceptable. Dave Marvit, who heads the Project A team, puts it this way: 'Good negotiators know you can do better if you add more business terms to the discussions . . . Not just price, but time and others. The computers can handle more parameters so more value can be squeezed out of the transaction. It's the opposite of a zero-sum game.'[49]

Organisational Politics

For an organisation to be effective, managers must develop the skills necessary to *manage organisational conflict*. Suppose, however, that senior managers are in conflict over the best strategy for an organisation to pursue or the best structure to adopt to utilise organisational resources efficiently. In such situations, resolving conflict is often difficult, and the parties to the conflict resort to *organisational politics* and **political strategies** to try to resolve the conflict in their favour.

Organisational politics are the activities that managers (and other members of an organisation) engage in to increase their power and use power effectively to achieve their goals and overcome resistance or opposition.[50] Managers often engage in organisational politics to *resolve conflicts in their favour*.

Political strategies are the *specific tactics* that managers (and other members of an organisation) use to increase their power and use power effectively to influence and gain the support of other people while overcoming resistance or opposition. Political strategies are especially important when managers are planning and implementing major changes in an organisation: managers need not only to gain support for their change initiatives and influence organisational members to behave in new ways but also to overcome often strong opposition from people who feel threatened by the change and prefer the status quo. By increasing their power, managers are better able to make the necessary changes. In addition to increasing their power, managers also must make sure that they use their power in a way that actually enables them to *influence others*.

The Importance of Organisational Politics

The term *politics* has a negative connotation for many people. Some may think that managers who are political have risen to the top not because of their own merit and capabilities but because of whom they know. Or people may think that political managers are self-interested and wield power to benefit themselves, not their organisation. There is a grain of truth in this negative connotation. Some managers do appear to misuse their power for personal benefit at the expense of their organisation's effectiveness.

Nevertheless, organisational politics are often a positive force. Managers striving to make necessary changes often encounter resistance from individuals and groups who feel threatened and wish to preserve the status quo. Effective managers engage in politics to gain support for and implement such changes. Managers often also face resistance from other managers who disagree with their goals for a group or for the organisation and with what they are trying to accomplish. Engaging in organisational politics can help managers overcome this resistance and achieve their goals.

Indeed, managers cannot afford to ignore organisational politics. Everyone engages in politics to a degree – other managers, co-workers and subordinates, as well as people outside an organisation, such as suppliers. Those who try to ignore politics might as well bury their heads in the sand because in all likelihood they will be unable to gain support for their initiatives and goals.

Political Strategies for Gaining and Maintaining Power

Managers who use political strategies to increase and maintain their power are better able to influence others to work toward the achievement of group and organisational goals. (Recall from Chapter 14 that legitimate, reward, coercive, expert and referent powers can help managers

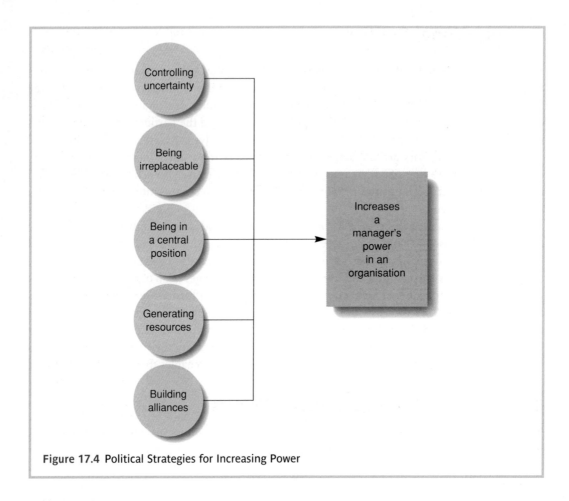

Figure 17.4 Political Strategies for Increasing Power

influence others as leaders.) By controlling uncertainty, being irreplaceable, being in a central position, generating resources and building alliances, managers can increase their power (Fig. 17.4).[51] We now look at each of these strategies.

Controlling uncertainty

Uncertainty is a threat for individuals, groups and whole organisations, and can interfere with effective performance and goal attainment. Uncertainty about job security is threatening for many workers and may cause top performers (who have the best chance of finding another job) to quit and take a more secure position with another organisation. When an R&D department faces uncertainty about customer preferences, its members may waste valuable resources on developing a product, such as smokeless cigarettes, that customers do not want. When senior managers face uncertainty about global demand, they may fail to export products to countries that want them and thus may lose a source of competitive advantage.

Managers who are able to control and reduce uncertainty for other managers, teams, departments and the organisation as a whole are likely to see their power increase.[52] Managers of trade unions gain power when they can eliminate uncertainty over job security. Marketing and sales managers gain power when they can eliminate uncertainty for other departments such as R&D by accurately forecasting customers' changing preferences. Senior managers gain power when they are knowledgeable about global demand for an organisation's products. Managers who are able to control uncertainty are likely to be in demand and be sought after by other organisations.

Being irreplaceable

Managers gain power when they have valuable knowledge and expertise that allows them to perform activities that no one else can handle. This is the essence of being irreplaceable.[53] The more central these activities are to organisational effectiveness, the more power managers gain from being irreplaceable. Richard Branson gains power from being irreplaceable: the combination of in-depth knowledge of what goes on within the Virgin group and the culture he has created by being unique, fun-loving and slightly quirky has made Branson the successful brand name it is today. His manner of collaboratively working through conflicts for win–win solutions is hard to find in other senior managers.[54]

Being in a central position

Managers in central positions are responsible for activities that are directly connected to an organisation's goals and sources of competitive advantage and are often located in key positions in important communication networks in an organisation.[55] Managers in central positions have control over crucial organisational activities and initiatives and have access to important information. Other organisational members are dependent on them for their knowledge, expertise, advice and support, and the success of the organisation as a whole is seen as riding on these managers. These consequences of being in a central position are likely to increase managers' power.

Managers who are outstanding performers, have a wide knowledge base and have made important and visible contributions to their organisations are likely to be offered central positions that will increase their power (think of Richard Branson).

Generating resources

Organisations need three kinds of resources to be effective: (1) *input* resources such as raw materials, skilled workers and financial capital; (2) *technical* resources such as machinery and computers; and (3) *knowledge* resources such as marketing or engineering expertise. To the extent that a manager is able to generate one or more of these kinds of resources for an organisation, that manager's power is likely to increase.[56] In universities, for example, professors who win large grants to fund their research (from associations such as Research Councils and the Wellcome Trust) gain power because of the financial resources they are generating for their departments and the university as a whole.

Building alliances

When managers build alliances, they develop mutually beneficial relationships with people both inside and outside the organisation. The two parties to an alliance support one another because doing so is in their best interests, and both parties benefit from the alliance. Alliances provide managers with power because they provide the managers with support for their initiatives. Partners to alliances provide support because they know that the managers will reciprocate when their partners need support. Alliances can help managers achieve their goals and implement necessary changes in organisations because they increase managers' levels of power.

Many powerful managers focus on building alliances not only inside their organisations but also with individuals, groups and organisations in the task and general environments on which their organisations are dependent for resources. These individuals, groups and organisations enter into alliances with managers because doing so is in their best interests and they know that they can count on the managers' support when they need it. When managers build alliances, they need to be on their guard to ensure that everything is above board, ethical and legal.

Political Strategies for Exercising Power

Politically skilled managers not only have a good understanding of, and ability to use, the five strategies to increase their power; they also have a good appreciation of *strategies* for exercising their power. These strategies generally focus on how managers can use their power unobtrusively.[57] When managers exercise power unobtrusively, other members of an organisation may not be aware that the managers are using their power to influence them. They may think that they support these managers for a variety of reasons: because they believe it is the rational or logical thing to do, because they believe that doing so is in their own best interests, or because they believe that the position or decision that the managers are advocating is legitimate or appropriate.

The unobtrusive use of power may sound devious, but managers typically use this strategy to bring about change and achieve organisational goals. Political strategies for exercising power to gain the support and concurrence of others include relying on objective information, bringing in an outside expert, controlling the agenda and making everyone a winner (Fig. 17.5).[58]

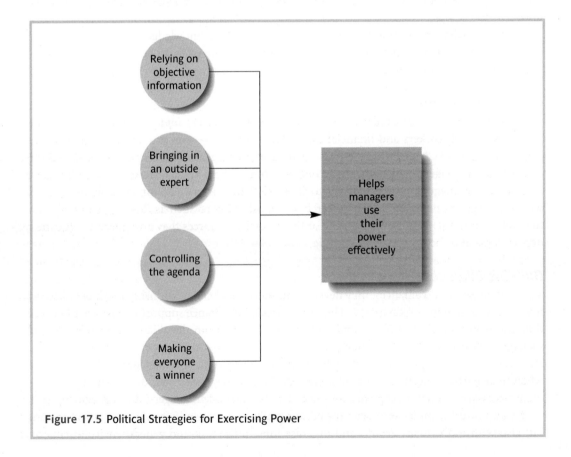

Figure 17.5 Political Strategies for Exercising Power

Relying on objective information

Managers require the support of others to achieve their goals, implement changes and overcome opposition. One way for a manager to gain this support and overcome opposition is to rely on objective information that supports the manager's initiatives. Reliance on objective information leads others to support the manager because of the facts; objective information causes others to believe that what the manager is proposing is the proper course of action. By relying on objective information, politically skilled managers unobtrusively exercise their power to influence others.

Take the case of Mary Callahan, a senior manager in a small carpentry company. Callahan is extremely influential in the company; practically every new initiative that she proposes to the President and owner of the company is implemented. Why is Callahan able to use her power in the company so effectively? Whenever she has an idea for a new initiative that she thinks the company might pursue, she and her subordinates begin by collecting objective information supporting the initiative. Recently, Callahan decided that the company should develop a line of high-priced kitchen cabinets. Before presenting her proposal, she compiled objective information showing that (1) there was strong unmet demand for these kinds of cabinets, (2) the company could manufacture them in its existing production facilities and (3) the new line had the potential to increase sales by 20 per cent while not detracting from sales of the company's other cabinets. Presented with this information, the President agreed to Callahan's proposal. Moreover, the President and other members of the company whose co-operation was needed to implement the proposal supported it because they thought it would help gain a competitive advantage. Using objective information to support her position enabled Callahan unobtrusively to exercise her power and influence others to support her proposal.

Bringing in an outside expert

Bringing in an outside expert to support a proposal or decision can, at times, provide managers with some of the same benefits that the use of objective information does. It lends credibility to a manager's initiatives and causes others to believe that what the manager is proposing is the appropriate or rational thing to do. Suppose Callahan had hired a consultant to evaluate whether her idea was a good one. The consultant reports back to the President that the new cabinets are likely to fulfil Callahan's promises and increase sales and profits. As with objective information, information provided by an objective expert can lend a sense of legitimacy to Callahan's proposal and allow her to unobtrusively exercise power to influence others.

Although you may think that consultants and other outside experts are neutral or objective, they sometimes are hired by managers who want them to support a certain position or decision in an organisation. For instance, when managers are facing strong opposition from others who fear that a decision will harm their or their departments' interests, the managers may bring in an outside expert. They hope this expert will be perceived as a *neutral observer* to lend credibility and 'objectivity' to their point of view. The support of an outside expert may cause others to believe that a decision is indeed the right one. Of course, consultants and other outside experts are often brought into organisations to be objective and provide managers with guidance on the appropriate course of action to take.

Controlling the agenda

Managers also can exercise power unobtrusively by controlling the agenda – influencing which alternatives are considered, or even whether a decision is made.[59] When managers influence the alternatives that are considered, they can make sure that each considered alternative is acceptable to them and that undesirable alternatives are not in the feasible set. In a hiring context, for example, managers can exert their power unobtrusively by ensuring that job candidates whom they do not find acceptable do not make their way onto the list of finalists for a vacant position. They do this by making sure that these candidates' drawbacks or deficiencies are communicated to everyone involved in making the hiring decision. When three finalists for a position are discussed and evaluated in a hiring meeting, a manager may seem to exert little power or influence and just go along with what the rest of the group wants. However, the manager may have exerted power in the hiring process unobtrusively, by controlling which candidates actually made it to the final stage.

Sometimes managers can prevent a decision from being made at all. A manager in charge of a community relations committee, for example, may not favour a proposal for the organisation to become more involved in local youth groups. The manager can exert influence in this situation by not including the proposal on the agenda for the committee's next meeting. Alternatively, the manager could place the proposal at the end of the agenda for the meeting and feel confident that the committee will run out of time and not get to the last item because that is what always happens. Either not including the proposal, or putting it at the end of the agenda, enables the manager to unobtrusively exercise power. Committee members do not perceive this manager as trying to influence them to turn down the proposal: the manager has made the proposal into a non-issue that is not even considered.

Making everyone a winner

Politically skilled managers are often able to exercise their power unobtrusively because they make sure that everyone whose support they need benefits personally from providing that support. By making everyone a winner, a manager is able to influence other organisational members because they see supporting the manager as being in their best interest.

When senior managers turn around troubled companies, while some organisational members and parts of the organisation are bound to suffer due to restructurings that often entail painful layoffs, the power of the turnaround CEO often accelerates as it becomes clear that the future of the company is on a surer footing and the organisation and its stakeholders are winners as a result of the change effort, as indicated in Case 17.4.

TIPS FOR PRACTICE

1. Be aware of the differences that people bring with them that may cause misunderstanding and result in conflict.

2. Try to see conflict as a multi-dimensional situation that has many components, such as organisational structure or dysfunctional culture.

3. When trying to solve a conflict, focus on the super-ordinate goals and the problem – not people or demands. Try to create alternatives.

4. Be aware of the political nature of your organisation – alliances with colleagues, resource bargaining, etc.

5. Always use solid information to advocate your plans and positions. It will help you to make a stronger argument and be more convincing and influential.

Case 17.4: Investors Save Luxury

Hand-crafted and beautifully designed furniture that speaks to the trendy and luxurious taste of the rich and famous has always come from Italy. No one has been able to maintain style, elegance, individuality and craftsmanship better than Italian companies. But since design has penetrated the mass market and production of many items, including furniture, has moved to China, Italian furniture design outlets have struggled. Many companies have been forced to close, as small businesses that rely on hand-crafted products cannot afford to compete with mass-produced furniture.

Take Poltrona Frau, a famous leather sofa producer, which was nearly forced out of business. With its long history in designing luxury sofas and armchairs it just about managed in 2000 to have revenues in the region of €473,000 a year. By 2005, the company had managed to increase its sales sevenfold. How was this possible?

The answer is a federation. Charme is a private-equity firm that has been able to amass a number of small furniture companies. Unlike a big corporation, this conglomerate is a loose grouping of individual production outlets – each of them still designing their own products, overseeing the production of their individual and unique goods and holding responsibility for distribution and marketing. It works because the number of outlets has now grown and other areas of economies of scale, such as purchasing of leathers or logistics and transport, can be exploited. This is all down to the power of a small number of savvy businessmen – people like the chairman of Ferrari and Fiat, or Diego Della Valle, who turned Italian icon Tod's shoes into a global brand. The influence and power of these people has been hugely important to turn individual small struggling luxury furniture makers into a conglomerate of small successful luxury furniture makers.[60]

Reaction Time

1. Why are compromise and collaboration more effective ways of handling conflict than accommodation, avoidance and competition?

2. Why should managers promote integrative bargaining rather than distributive negotiation?

3. How can managers promote integrative bargaining?

4. Why do organisational politics affect practically every organisation?

5. Why do effective managers need good political skills?

6. Think of a member of an organisation whom you know and who is particularly powerful. What political strategies does this person use to increase his or her power?

Summary and Review

Organisational conflict Organisational conflict is the discord that arises when the goals, interests or values of different individuals or groups are incompatible and those individuals or groups block or thwart each other's attempts to achieve their objectives. Four types of conflict arising in organisations are interpersonal conflict, intra-group conflict, ▶

▶ inter-group conflict and inter-organisational conflict. Sources of conflict in organisations include different goals and time horizons, overlapping authority, task interdependencies, different evaluation or reward systems, scarce resources and status inconsistencies. Conflict management strategies focused on individuals include increasing awareness of the sources of conflict, increasing diversity awareness and skills, practising job rotation or temporary assignments and using permanent transfers or dismissals when necessary. Strategies focused on the whole organisation include changing an organisation's structure or culture and altering the source of conflict.

Negotiation Negotiation is a conflict resolution technique used when parties to a conflict have approximately equal levels of power and try to come up with an acceptable way to allocate resources to each other. In distributive negotiation, the parties perceive that there is a fixed level of resources for them to allocate, and they compete to receive as much as possible at the expense of the other party, not caring about their relationship in the future. In integrative bargaining, both parties perceive that they may be able to increase the 'resource pie' by coming up with a creative solution to the conflict, trusting each other and co-operating with each other to achieve a win–win resolution. Five strategies that managers can use to facilitate integrative bargaining are to emphasise super-ordinate goals; focus on the problem, not the people; focus on interests, not demands; create new options for joint gain; and focus on what is fair.

Organisational politics Organisational politics are the activities that managers (and other members of an organisation) engage in to increase their power and to use power effectively to achieve their goals and overcome resistance or opposition. Effective managers realise that politics can be a positive force that enables them to make necessary changes in an organisation. Five important political strategies for gaining and maintaining power are controlling uncertainty, making oneself irreplaceable, being in a central position, generating resources and building alliances. Political strategies for effectively exercising power focus on how to use power unobtrusively and include relying on objective information, bringing in an outside expert, controlling the agenda and making everyone a winner.

Applied Independent Learning

Building Management Skills

Effective and Ineffective Conflict Resolution

Think about two recent conflicts that you had with other people, one conflict that you felt was effectively resolved (C1) and one that you felt was ineffectively resolved (C2). The other people involved could be co-workers, students, family members, friends or members of an organisation of which you are a member. Answer the following questions:

1. Briefly describe incidents C1 and C2. What type of conflict was involved in each of these incidents?

2. What was the source of the conflict in C1 and in C2?

3. What conflict management strategies were used in C1 and in C2?

4. What could you have done differently to more effectively manage conflict in C2?

5. How was conflict resolved in C1 and in C2?

Managing Ethically

One political strategy that managers can engage in is controlling the agenda by subtly influencing which alternatives are considered, or even whether a decision is up for discussion. Some employees believe that this can be unethical and prevent important issues from being raised and points of view from being expressed.

Questions

1. Either individually or in a group, think about the ethical implications of controlling the agenda as a political strategy.

2. What steps can managers and organisations take to ensure that this strategy does not result in important issues and differing points of view being suppressed in an organisation?

Small Group Breakout Exercise

Negotiating a Solution

Form groups of three or four people. One member of your group will play the role of Jane Rister, one member will play the role of Michael Schwarts, and one or two members will be observer(s) and spokesperson(s) for your group.

Jane Rister and Michael Schwarts are assistant managers in a large department store. They report directly to the store manager. Today they are meeting to discuss some important problems they need to solve but about which they disagree.

The first problem hinges on the fact that either Rister or Schwarts needs to be on duty whenever the store is open. For the last six months, Rister has taken most of the least desirable hours (nights and weekends). They are planning their schedules for the next six months. Rister thought Schwarts would take more of the undesirable times, but Schwarts has informed Rister that his wife has just got a nursing job which requires that she work weekends, so he needs to stay home weekends to take care of their infant daughter.

The second problem concerns a department manager who has had a hard time retaining salespeople in his department. The turnover rate in his department is twice that in the other store departments. Rister thinks the manager is ineffective and wants to fire him. Schwarts thinks the high turnover is just a fluke and that the manager is effective.

The last problem concerns Rister's and Schwarts' vacation schedules. Both managers want to take off the week of 4 July, but one of them needs to be in the store whenever it is open.

1. The group members playing Rister and Schwarts assume their roles and negotiate a solution to these three problems.

2. Observers take notes on how Rister and Schwarts negotiate solutions to their problems. ▶

▶ 3. Observers determine the extent to which Rister and Schwarts use distributive negotiation or integrative bargaining to resolve their conflicts.

4. When called on by the instructor, observers communicate to the rest of the class how Rister and Schwarts resolved their conflicts, whether they used distributive negotiation or integrative bargaining, and their actual solutions.

Exploring the World Wide Web

Think of a major conflict in the business world that you have read about in the newspaper in the past few weeks. Then search on the Web for magazine and newspaper articles presenting differing viewpoints and perspectives on the conflict. Based on what you have read, how are the parties to this conflict handling it? Is their approach functional or dysfunctional, and why?

Application in Today's Business World

Fiat's Last Chance

Ferrari Chief Executive Luca Cordero di Montesemolo has earned a hero's status in Italy for reviving the once-ailing auto icon and winning four Formula One championships in a row. He proved that Italy could rebuild a high-tech contender and come from behind just when all seemed lost. Now the 56-year-old manager has to do a command performance for Ferrari's $58 billion parent. On 30 May 2004, three days after the death of former Chairman Umberto Agnelli, Montesemolo was named chairman of troubled Fiat, Italy's largest industrial group.

Montesemolo's top priority is clinching a turnaround at the ailing, $24 billion Fiat Auto, which nearly pushed the group into bankruptcy in 2002. Over the past five years, Fiat Auto racked up $9.3 billion in net losses – and the bleeding hasn't stopped. Several new models finally seem to be reversing a dire decline in sales. But to secure a solid recovery, the Turin-based auto maker needs to keep hot models coming, boost factory flexibility and overhaul sales and marketing debilitated by years of under-investment and mismanagement.

Montesemolo, a skilled marketer with a deep appreciation for cutting-edge technology and production, might well be the steady hand that could help steer Fiat back to health. At Ferrari, Montesemolo restored lost brand lustre in part through ingenious marketing, including persuading the Museum of Modern Art in New York to do a splashy retrospective on Ferrari's design over the decades – a high-gloss exhibition that other major museums in Berlin and Tokyo have since restaged. Fiat, too, has a tarnished brand that needs refurbishing.

But fixing Fiat is not all Montesemolo has on his agenda. On 27 May he became President of the Italian employers' association, Confindustria, where Job One is reversing Italy's alarming industrial decline. The country's exports are eroding, investment is stymied and promised economic reforms are stalled: Fiat's woes writ large. This double role thrusts Montesemolo squarely into the void left by the death in March 2002 of former Fiat Chairman Giovanni Agnelli, who once ran Confindustria and who for a generation personified Italy, Inc.

For Montesemolo, who is known for his ability to coax opposing parties toward a common goal, the rescue of Fiat would be an object lesson in how Italy could reinvent itself.

A turnaround plan launched at Fiat in 2003 helped trim losses, while the sale of some $8.5 billion in group assets, including insurer Toro Assicurasioni, injected urgently needed capital for a new generation of cars. Vehicle sales at Fiat Auto were up 13 per cent in six months – and demand for Fiat's newly launched Panda supermini and Idea subcompact minivan was outstripping supply. 'The new products are wonderful. Fiat can finally join the race,' says Christoph Stürmer, senior market researcher at Global Insight in Frankfurt.

Problem-plagued

But the 105-year-old auto maker remains plagued by inflexible production lines that can produce only one model. To boot, intransigent labour unions have blocked plant closures, making it harder for Fiat to return to profitability. Its five factories in Italy plus those in Brazil and Poland can produce some 2.5 million cars a year, but in 2003 the company made only 1.8 million. Unable to trim its production overhead sharply, Fiat will need a strong rebound in sales to survive. 'Fiat's on its last chance,' says Jochen Gehrke, auto analyst at Kepler Equities in Frankfurt. 'If they produce flops, the game is over.' In the first quarter of 2004, the Fiat Group halved its losses to $192 million. But analysts noted a worrying rise in net debt to $5.4 billion and forecast that the group would run a negative free cash flow of $1 billion to $1.5 billion in 2004.

While Fiat raised $2.2 billion in a rights issue in 2003, its financial credibility will be on the line by June 2005, when a $3.6 billion convertible bond comes due. That's when a group of eight Italian banks has the option of turning the bonds into a controlling 24 per cent equity stake. Bankers and analysts say it is unlikely that Fiat will be able to repay the bond.

Even sooner, in January 2005, Fiat's put option with General Motors Corp. (GM) could trigger a crisis of confidence. The two are negotiating to eliminate the option which allows the Fiat Group to sell its share in its auto maker to GM. The Detroit company insists the put is no longer valid, but Fiat wants to be paid for the value it represents. Yet if Fiat fails to reach an agreement with GM by the year end and continues to post heavy losses, the put will be worthless, analysts say. 'That's the moment of truth,' says Albrecht Denninghoff, auto analyst at Hypo und Vereinsbank in Munich, noting that such an assessment would kill investors' appetite for another capital increase.

Adding to Fiat's woes, CEO Giuseppe Morchio resigned on 30 May 2004, following the appointment of Montesemolo. Morchio wanted the combined position of chairman and CEO. Fiat's board named board member Sergio Marchionne, 52, the CEO of Swiss testing and inspection company SGS, as successor on 2 June. Despite Marchionne's strong turnaround credentials, many worry about the discontinuity plaguing Fiat's senior management, which has seen five CEOs in three years.

Industry Boss

Those close to the company say Montesemolo will work closely with his team. The problem is that he may have taken on more than any manager could handle by agreeing to help oversee Fiat's recovery and turn around Italian industry at the same time. To be sure, the long-time friend of the Agnellis – he grew up playing with the Turin dynasty's children – has the complete trust of the family, including John P. Elkann, 28, the grandson of Gianni Agnelli, who was recently named Vice-Chairman of Fiat. Montesemolo also has able executives in Marchionne and Herbert Demel, the former Audi executive and first outsider brought in to run Fiat Auto. But Fiat's condition is fragile, and one more wrong turn might be its last.

▶

▶   Meanwhile, as industry boss, Montesemolo will seek to defuse tensions between Silvio Berlusconi's centre-right government, which has failed to deliver on economic reforms, and the unions, which have blocked them. Montesemolo will now sit in the hot seat on explosive issues such as pension reform, tax cuts and labour market reform. Also on the front burner is a vital overhaul of education, research and development and innovation policy. 'I don't ever tire of saying: It's innovation, innovation, innovation,' Montesemolo said during an inaugural speech as industry chief on 27 May. Exactly. If only Fiat – and Italy – had heard those words sooner.

Questions

1. What sources of power does Montesemolo possess?

2. How might he expand and maintain his power in the top job at Fiat?

3. Is conflict being effectively handled at Fiat?

4. What steps should Montesemolo take to effectively manage conflict at Fiat and turn around Fiat's fortunes?

Source: G. Edmondson, 'Fiat's Last Chance', adapted and reprinted from *BusinessWeek*, June 14, 2004 by special permission. Copyright © 2004 by the McGraw-Hill Companies, Inc.

Notes and References

1   www.blackwellpublishing.com/grant/docs/15virgin.pdf.

2   *Ibid.*

3   K. Ahmed, 'Branson attacks no-risk British culture, *The Observer*, 24 December 2000.

4   Robert Dick, 'Branson's Virgin: the coming of age of a counter-cultural enterprise', INSEAD, Fontainebleau, 1995.

5   J. A. Litterer, 'Conflict in Organizations: A Reexamination', *Academy of Management Journal* 9 (1966), 178–86; S. M. Schmidt and T. A. Kochan, 'Conflict: Towards Conceptual Clarity', *Administrative Science Quarterly* 13 (1972), 359–70; R. H. Miles, *Macro Organizational Behavior* (Santa Monica, CA: Goodyear, 1980).

6   Buchnan and Huczynski, *Organizational Behaviour: An Introductory Text*, 5th ed. (London: Prentice Hall, 2004), 792–6.

7   A. Fox., 'Industrial Relations: A Social Critique of Pluralist Ideology', in J. Child, ed., *Man and Organization* (London: Allen & Unwin, 1973), 185–233.

8   S. Ackroyd, and P. Thompson, *Organisational Misbehaviour* (London: Sage, 1999); R. Johnston, 'Hidden Capital', in J. Barry, J. Chandler, H. Clark, R. Johnston and De. Needle, eds., *Organization and Management; A Critical Text* (London: International Thomson Business Press, 2000), 16–35.

9   Buchnan and Huczynski, *Organizational Behaviour.*

10   I. L. Janis, *GroupThink: Psychological Studies of Policy Decisions and Disasters*, 2nd edn (Boston: Houghton Mifflin, 1982).

11   P. Taffinder, *Big Change: a route-map for corporate transformation* (Wiley, 1998).

12   R. Jonston, 'Hidden Capital'.

13   Ackroyd and Thompson, *Organisational Misbehaviour.*

14   L. L. Putnam and M. S. Poole, 'Conflict and Negotiation', in F. M. Jablin, L. L. Putnam, K. H. Roberts and L. W. Porter, eds., *Handbook of Organizational Communication: An Interdisciplinary Perspective* (Newbury Park, CA: Sage, 1987), 549–99.

15 L. R. Pondy, 'Organizational Conflict: Concepts and Models', *Administrative Science Quarterly* 2 (1967), 296–320; R. E. Walton and J. M. Dutton, 'The Management of Interdepartmental Conflict: A Model and Review', *Administrative Science Quarterly* 14 (1969), 62–73.

16 Explanatory Memorandum to the New Forest National Park Authority (Establishment) Order 2005, 2005, No. 421 http://www.opsi.gov.uk/si/em2005/uksiem_20050421_en.pdf.

17 J. A. Wall, Jr., 'Conflict and Its Management', *Journal of Management* 21 (1995), 515–58.

18 Walton and Dutton, 'The Management of Interdepartmental Conflict'.

19 Pondy, 'Organizational Conflict'.

20 W. F. White, *Human Relations in the Restaurant Industry* (New York: McGraw-Hill, 1948).

21 R. L. Pinkley and G. B. Northcraft, 'Conflict Frames of Reference: Implications for Dispute Processes and Outcomes', *Academy of Management Journal* 37 (February 1994), 193–206.

22 K. W. Thomas, 'Conflict and Negotiation Processes in Organizations', in M. D. Dunnette and L. M. Hough, eds., *Handbook of Industrial and Organizational Psychology*, 3, 2nd ed. (Palo Alto, CA: Consulting Psychologists Press, 1992), 651–717.

23 *Ibid*.

24 Pinkley and Northcraft, 'Conflict Frames of Reference'.

25 *Independent*, 27 April 2006, 46.

26 Adam Sherwin, 'Personality Clash drives Newsman from BBC', *The Times*, 27 September 2005.

27 R. J. Lewicki and J. R. Litterer, *Negotiation* (Homewood, IL: Irwin, 1985); G. B. Northcraft and M. A. Neale, *Organizational Behavior* (Fort Worth, TX: Dryden, 1994); J. Z. Rubin and B. R. Brown, *The Social Psychology of Bargaining and Negotiation* (New York: Academic Press, 1975).

28 C. Bendersky, 'Organizational Dispute Resolution Systems: A Complementarities Model', *Academy of Management Review* 28 (October 2003), 643–57.

29 R. E. Walton, 'Third Party Roles in Interdepartmental Conflicts', *Industrial Relations* 7 (1967), 29–43.

30 'Meaning of Arbitrator', *hyperdictionary*, September 4, 2004, www.hyperdictionary.com; 'Definitions of Arbitrator on the Web', www.google.com, September 4, 2004.

31 L. Thompson and R. Hastie, 'Social Perception in Negotiation', *Organizational Behavior and Human Decision Processes* 47 (1990), 98–123.

32 Thomas, 'Conflict and Negotiation Processes in Organizations'.

33 R. J. Lewicki, S. E. Weiss and D. Lewin, 'Models of Conflict, Negotiation and Third Party Intervention: A Review and Synthesis', *Journal of Organizational Behavior* 13 (1992), 209–52.

34 Northcraft and Neale, *Organizational Behavior*.

35 Lewicki *et al.*, 'Models of Conflict, Negotiation and Third Party Intervention'; Northcraft and Neale, *Organizational Behavior*; D. G. Pruitt, 'Integrative Agreements: Nature and Consequences', in M. H. Bazerman and R. J. Lewicki, eds., *Negotiating in Organizations* (Beverly Hills, CA: Sage, 1983).

36 R. Fischer and W. Ury, *Getting to Yes* (Boston: Houghton Mifflin, 1981); Northcraft and Neale, *Organizational Behavior*.

37 D. Hakim, 'A Union Label, Inside Out', *Sunday Business*, July 4, 2004.

38 Hakim, 'A Union Label, Inside Out'.

39 M. Phelan, 'DCX, UAW, Suppliers OK Historic Teamwork', *Detroit Free Press*, September 4, 2004.

40 'Chrysler Group's CEO Tom LaSorda Says "Fully Flexible Corporation Is Key to Weathering Rapidly Changing Market Conditions"', *Automotive.com*, August 4, 2004; D. Howes, 'Chrysler's LaSorda Faces His Biggest Challenge Yet', *The Detroit News Auto Insider*, February 17, 2004; 'Chrysler Group COO Tom LaSorda Frames "Moment of Opportunity for Young Leaders to Shape the Future of the Automotive Industry"', *Eyewitness News*, August 17, 2004; 'Supplier Co-location Concept', *PR Newswire*, August 3, 2004; D. Howes, 'Chrysler Hits Higher Gear, LaSorda Says', *The Detroit News Auto Insider*, February 20, 2004.

41 Phelan, 'DCX, UAW'.

42 'Chrysler Group's CEO Tom LaSorda'; Howes, 'Chrysler's LaSorda'; 'Chrysler Group COO'; 'Supplier Co-location Concept'; Howes, 'Chrysler Hits Higher Gear'.

43   'Chrysler Group Toledo Project Highlights Supplier Co-location Concept', www.daimlerchrysler.com, August 3, 2004.

44   P. J. Carnevale and D. G. Pruitt, 'Negotiation and Mediation', *Annual Review of Psychology* 43 (1992), 531–82.

45   K. Belson, 'Digital Dealmakers Meet in the Middle', *The New York Times*, September 11, 2003, E1, E4.

46   'About Us', www.splitthedifference.com/aboutUs/, September 5, 2004.

47   Belson, 'Digital Dealmakers Meet in the Middle'.

48   *Ibid.*; 'Fujitsu America, Inc.', www.fujitsu.com/us/about/OtherOps/FAI, September 5, 2004.

49   Belson, 'Digital Dealmakers Meet in the Middle'.

50   A. M. Pettigrew, *The Politics of Organizational Decision Making* (London: Tavistock, 1973); R. Miles, *Macro Organizational Behavior* (Santa Monica, CA: Goodyear, 1980).

51   D. J. Hickson, C. R. Hinings, C. A. Lee, R. E. Schneck and D. J. Pennings, 'A Strategic Contingencies Theory of Intraorganizational Power', *Administrative Science Quarterly* 16 (1971), 216–27; C. R. Hinings, D. J. Hickson, J. M. Pennings and R. E. Schneck, 'Structural Conditions of Interorganizational Power', *Administrative Science Quarterly* 19 (1974), 22–44; J. Pfeffer, *Power in Organizations* (Boston: Pitman, 1981).

52   Pfeffer, *Power in Organizations*.

53   *Ibid.*

54   www.blackwellpublishing.com/grant/docs/15virgin.pdf.

55   M. Crozier, 'Sources of Power of Lower Level Participants in Complex Organizations', *Administrative Science Quarterly* 7 (1962), 349–64; A. M. Pettigrew, 'Information Control as a Power Resource', *Sociology* 6 (1972), 187–204.

56   Pfeffer, *Power in Organizations*; G. R. Salancik and J. Pfeffer, 'The Bases and Uses of Power in Organizational Decision Making', *Administrative Science Quarterly* 19 (1974), 453–73; J. Pfeffer and G. R. Salancik, *The External Control of Organizations: A Resource Dependence View* (New York: Harper & Row, 1978).

57   Pfeffer, *Power in Organizations*.

58   *Ibid.*

59   *Ibid.*

60   Maureen Kline, 'Made in Italy: Keeps its Cachet', *BusinessWeek*, April 10, 2006.

18

Further Themes in Contemporary Management

LEARNING OBJECTIVES

After studying this chapter, you should be able to:

☑ Describe three reasons why managers must have access to information to perform their tasks and roles effectively.

☑ Describe the computer hardware and software innovations that have created the IT revolution.

☑ Differentiate among seven different kinds of management information systems.

☑ Explain how advances in IT can give an organisation a competitive advantage.

☑ Understand the product life cycle and the role of managers in this process.

☑ Describe how managers can encourage and promote entrepreneurship.

A Manager's Challenge

IBM's 'Business-on-Demand' IT

How can managers create competitive advantage through IT?
In the poor economic conditions of the early 2000s, the stock prices of most companies that make and sell IT plunged as their main customers – other business companies – slashed their IT budgets. Searching for ways to lower costs, the problem facing a company seeking to purchase new IT was deciding which components of computer hardware and software would result in the greatest gains in profitability. Convincing a company to spend millions or billions of pounds to buy new kinds of software and hardware is a daunting task.

One of the companies facing this challenge is IBM, which makes, sells and services a vast array of computer hardware and software. To maintain its leading position in the highly competitive IT industry, Sam Palmisano, who became IBM's CEO in 2002, announced a bold new business model for IBM called 'Business on Demand'. Over the long run, he claims, companies that adopt IBM's new IT will generate millions or billions of pounds in savings in operating costs.

To promote its new business model, IBM told its customers to think of information and computing power as being a fluid, like water, contained in the hundreds or thousands of computers that are the 'reservoirs' or 'lakes' of a large company's IT system. This water flows between computers in a company's computer network through the fibre-optic cables that connect them. Computing power, like water, can thus potentially be moved between computers both inside a company and between companies, as long as all the computers are linked seamlessly together. 'Seamless' means that computer hardware or software does not create information 'logjams', which disrupt the flow of information and computing power.

To allow the potential computing power of all a company's computers to be shared, IBM's software engineers developed new e-business software that enabled the computers to work seamlessly together. Among its other capabilities, this software allows computer operators to monitor hundreds of different computers at the same time and shift work from one machine to another to distribute a company's computing power to wherever it is most needed. This has several cost-saving advantages. First, companies can run their computers at a much higher level, close to capacity, thereby greatly improving IT productivity and reducing operating costs. Second, to ensure that its customers never experience a 'drought', IBM uses its own vast computer capacity as a kind of 'bank' or 'reservoir' that customers can tap into whenever their own systems become overloaded. For example, using IBM's e-business software, companies can shift any excess work to IBM's computers rather than investing tens of millions of pounds in extra computers – a huge cost saving. Third, when a company's computers are seamlessly networked together, they can function as a 'supercomputer', a computer with immense information processing power, which can easily cost upward of £27 million just to purchase and tens of millions more to maintain.

IBM decided to implement its new e-business IT in its own company to show customers the cost-saving potential of its new products. Previously, IBM had allowed its many different product divisions to choose whatever software they liked to manage their own purchasing and supply chain activities. In 2003, Palmisano appointed star manager Linda Stanford to overhaul IBM's whole supply chain, which amounts to £24 billion in yearly purchases. She is responsible for developing software to link them all into a single e-business system. IBM expects this will result in a 5 per cent productivity gain each year for the next 5–10 years, which translates into savings of £1.1 billion a year. IBM is telling its customers that they can expect to see similar savings if they purchase its software.

IBM's new e-business system has many other performance-enhancing benefits. Its thousands of consultants are experts in particular industries, such as the car, financial services or retail industries. They have a deep understanding of the particular problems facing companies in those industries, and how to solve them. Palmisano asked IBM's consultants to work closely with its software engineers to find ways to incorporate their knowledge into advanced software that can be implanted into a customer's IT system.

IBM has developed 17 industry-specific 'expert systems', which consist of problem-solving software that managers can use to make better business decisions and control a company's operations. One expert system is being developed for the pharmaceutical industry; using this new software, a pharmaceutical company's interlinked computers will be able to function as a supercomputer and simulate and model the potential success of new drugs under development. Currently, only 5–10 per cent of new drugs make it to the market; IBM believes that its new IT could raise that rate to over 50 per cent, which would lead to billions of pounds in cost savings.[1]

Overview

As the experience of IBM suggests, there are enormous opportunities for managers to find new ways to use advanced IT to increase the flow of knowledge and speed communication and decision making in an organisation. Previous chapters discussed the role of accurate, timely and relevant information for effective and efficient decision making and management. The adoption of new IT can help give an organisation a competitive advantage and lead to high performance.

This chapter begins by looking at the relationship between information and the manager's job and then examines the ongoing IT revolution. It then discusses several types of specific management information systems, each of which is based on a different sort of IT, which can help managers perform their jobs more efficiently and effectively.

Developing new products – services or goods – is a vital component of surviving in today's volatile business environment. The last part of this chapter discusses product development and the role of the manager in this process. The chapter will also discuss how individual efforts can enhance an organisation's knowledge base and how entrepreneurship can give an organisation a competitive advantage.

Information and the Manager's Job

Managers cannot plan, organise, lead and control effectively unless they have access to **information**. Information is the source of the knowledge and intelligence that they need to make the right decisions. Information, however, is not the same as **data**.[2] Data are raw, unsummarised and unanalysed facts such as volume of sales, level of costs or number of customers. Information is data that are organised in a meaningful fashion, such as in a graph showing the change in sales volume or costs over time. Data alone do not tell managers anything; information, in contrast, can communicate a great deal of useful knowledge to the person who receives it – such as a manager who sees sales falling or costs rising. The distinction between data and information is important because one of the purposes of IT is to help managers *transform data into information* in order to make better managerial decisions.

To further clarify the difference between data and information, consider the case of a manager in a supermarket who must decide how much shelf space to allocate to two breakfast cereal brands for children: Dentist's Delight and Sugar Supreme. Most supermarkets use checkout scanners to record individual sales and store the data on a computer. Accessing this computer, the manager might find that Dentist's Delight sells 50 boxes per day and Sugar Supreme sells 25 boxes per day. These raw data, however, are of little help in assisting the manager to decide how to allocate shelf space. The manager also needs to know how much shelf space each cereal currently occupies and how much profit each cereal generates for the supermarket.

Suppose the manager discovers that Dentist's Delight occupies 10 ft of shelf space and Sugar Supreme occupies 4 ft and that Dentist's Delight generates 20p profit a box while Sugar Supreme generates 40p profit a box. By putting these three bits of data together (number of boxes sold, amount of shelf space and profit per box), the manager gets some useful information on which to base a decision: Dentist's Delight generates £1 of profit per foot of shelf space per day [(50 boxes × £0.20)/10 feet], and Sugar Supreme generates £2.50 of profit per foot of shelf space per day [(25 boxes × £0.40)/4 feet]. Armed with this information, the manager might decide to allocate less shelf space to Dentist's Delight and more to Sugar Supreme.

What Is IT?

Throughout this book it has been highlighted how technology can aid managers and employees in the various processes that are part of everyday organisational life. One concept that was continuously referred to was *information technology*. Information technology is the set of methods or techniques for acquiring, organising, storing, manipulating and transmitting information.[3] A *management information system (MIS)* is a specific form of IT that managers select and utilise to generate the specific, detailed information they need to perform their roles effectively. MISs have existed for as long as there have been organisations; before the computer age, most systems were paper-based – administrators recorded important information on documents (often in duplicate or triplicate) in the form of words and numbers; sent a copy of the document to superiors, customers or suppliers; and stored other copies in files for future reference.

Rapid advances in the power of IT – specifically, through the development of more and more sophisticated computer hardware and software – are having a fundamental impact on managers, their organisations and their suppliers and customers, as suggested by the developments at IBM.[4] Organisations that have not adopted new IT, or have done so ineffectively, have become uncompetitive compared with those that have adopted it.[5] In the 2000s, advances in IT have underpinned the increasing productivity and efficiency of business.

In Chapters 7 and 16 we saw how decision making and communication were influenced by information and how the use of IT could aid those processes. In order to perform planning, organising, controlling and leading, managers need information.

The IT Revolution

Advances in IT have allowed managers to develop computer-based MISs that provide timely, complete, relevant and high-quality information. IT allows companies like IBM and the FinnGroup to improve their responsiveness to customers, minimise costs and thus improve their competitive position. We now examine several key aspects of advanced IT, to understand the revolution currently in progress (Case 18.1).

Case 18.1: Helsinki in front

The telecommunications environment is immensely competitive and nowhere more so than in Scandinavia. Helsinki Telephone is one of many operators that are part of FinnGroup, one of the three major telecommunication groups in Finland. Helsinki Telephone Telecommunication Group is Finland's largest privately owned provider of services to a local, national and international market. Originally founded in 1882, its current form has been operational since 1994. The group's services are classified as Mobile Services, Network Services and other operations.[6]

Helsinki Telephone's business is technology – on the one side to streamline their own performance and on the other to provide innovative new products and services to its customers.

The latter, for instance, was its exclusive contract with Nokia in 1997, in which Helsinki Telephone Telecommunication was the first company in the world to provide Internet technology integrated with the public telephone network. Now a reasonably common standard for mobile phones, at the time, Nokia and Helsinki Telephone were at the forefront of innovation.[7] Another example is Helsinki's involvement in creating an 'intelligent house' that is filled with technological innovations.[8]

But for Helsinki it is not just about developing and enhancing IT for its customers. For Helsinki to become the company with a market share of 90 per cent in Finland's capital, customer satisfaction is vital. The company's IT environment was heterogeneous and slowed some of the process down. Helsinki wanted to become more responsive to its customers by speeding up the process of changing their service provision to corporate and residential customers. At that time, all the different providers with which Helsinki was working were not well integrated into Helsinki's system. For customers to change their price plan, for instance, the current system was too prone to error to do it effectively. In order to be more responsive, Helsinki installed a new, Internet technology-based solution to access other information systems that would aid them in treating their customers both better and faster.[9]

The Tumbling Price of Information

The IT revolution began with the development of the first computers – the hardware of IT – in the 1950s. The language of computers is a *digital* language of zeros and ones. Words, numbers, images and sound can all be expressed in zeros and ones. Each letter in the alphabet has its own unique code of zeros and ones, as does each number, each colour and each sound – for example, the digital code for the number 20 is 10100. In the language of computers it takes a lot of zeros and ones to express even a simple sentence, to say nothing of complex colour graphics or moving video images. Nevertheless, modern computers can read, process and store millions of instructions per second (an *instruction* is a line of software code) and thus vast amounts of zeros and ones. It is this awesome power that forms the foundation of the current IT revolution.

The 'brains' of modern computers are *microprocessors* (like Intel's Pentium and Itanium chips). Between 1991 and 2001, the relative cost of computer processing fell so dramatically that Gordon Moore, a computer guru, noted: 'If the auto industry advanced as rapidly as the semiconductor industry, a Rolls Royce would get a half a million miles per gallon, and it would be cheaper to throw it away than to park it.'[10] As the costs of acquiring, organising, storing and transmitting information have tumbled, computers have become almost as common as wireless phones and microwaves.[11] Advances in microprocessor technology have also led to dramatic reductions in the cost of communication between computers, which has also contributed to the falling price of information and information systems.

Wireless Communications

Another trend of considerable significance for modern IT has been the rapid growth of wireless communication technologies, particularly digital communications. Wireless services were first offered in the early 1980s. Initially, growth was slow, and by the end of the 1980s less than 1 million subscribers were registered worldwide.[12] But since 1990 wireless service has spread rapidly, with more than 20 million registered users by 1990.[13] Nokia, the world's largest maker of mobile phones, said that it expected the number of global users to rise 33 per cent by 2007, to 2 billion up from 1.5 billion in 2004.[14]

Wireless communication is significant for the IT revolution because it facilitates the *linking together* of computers, which greatly increases their power and adaptability. It is already possible to purchase a battery-operated laptop computer that has a wireless modem built in to facilitate communication with other devices or the Internet. An engineer or salesperson working in the field can send information to, and receive information from, the home office by using the wireless capabilities built into computers. Because a computer no longer has to be plugged in to a hard-wired telephone line, accessing a company's centralised computer system is much easier than it used to be. The increase of Bluetooth has also aided in connecting different technological media.

Computer Networks

The tumbling price of computing power and information and the use of wireless communication channels have facilitated networking, the exchange of information through a group or network of interlinked computers. The most common arrangement now emerging is a four-tier network consisting of *personal digital assistants* (*PDAs*), *clients*, *servers* and a *mainframe* (Fig. 18.1). At the outer nodes of a typical four-tier system are the PDAs, such as wireless smart phones and electronic organisers like the Palm Pilot, which allow users to email co-workers and which provide access to files on their PCs and on the company's intranet. Next in the network are the personal computers (*PCs*) that sit on the desks of individual users. These PCs, referred to as 'clients', are linked to a local server, a high-powered mid-range computer that 'serves' the client PCs. Servers often store power-hungry software programmes that can be run more effectively on the server than on an individual's PC. Servers may also manage several printers that can be used by hundreds of clients, store data files and handle email communications between clients. The client computers linked directly to a server constitute a *local area network* (*LAN*). Within any organisation there may be several LANs – for example, one in every division and function.

At the hub of a four-tier system are *mainframe computers*. Mainframes are large and powerful computers that can be used to store and process vast amounts of information. The mainframe can also be used to handle electronic communications between PCs situated in different LANs. In addition, the mainframe may be connected to mainframes in other organisations and, through them, to LANs in other organisations. Increasingly, the Internet, a worldwide network of interlinked computers, is used as the conduit for connecting the computer systems of different organisations, but IBM can also perform this service.

A manager with a PDA or PC hooked into a four-tier system can access data and software stored in the local server, in the mainframe or through the Internet in computers based in another organisation. A manager can therefore communicate electronically with other individuals hooked into the system, whether they are in the manager's LAN, in another LAN within the manager's organisation, or in another organisation altogether. Moreover, with wireless communication an individual with the necessary IT can hook into the system from any location – at

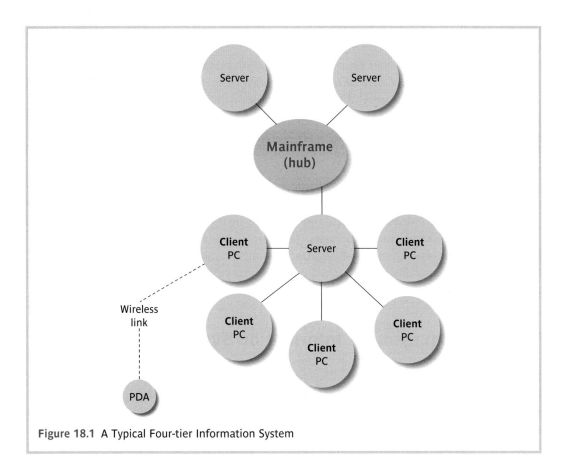

Figure 18.1 A Typical Four-tier Information System

home, on a boat, on the beach, in the air – anywhere a wireless communication link can be established.

Software Developments

If computer hardware has been developing rapidly, so has computer software. *Operating system software* tells the computer hardware how to run. **Applications software**, such as programmes for word processing, spreadsheets, graphics and database management, is software developed for a specific task or use. The increase in the power of computer hardware has allowed software developers to write increasingly powerful programmes that are, at the same time, increasingly user-friendly. By harnessing the rapidly growing power of microprocessors, applications software has vastly increased the ability of managers to acquire, organise, manipulate and transmit information. It also has increased the ability of managers to co-ordinate and control the activities of their organisation and to make decisions.

Artificial intelligence is another potentially fruitful software development. Artificial intelligence has been defined as behaviour by a machine that, if performed by a human being, would be called 'intelligent'.[15] Artificial intelligence has already made it possible to write programmes that can solve problems and perform simple tasks. For example, software programmes variously called *software agents*, *softbots* or *knowbots* can be used to perform simple managerial tasks such as sorting through reams of data or incoming email messages to look for important data and messages. The interesting feature of these programmes is that from 'watching' a manager sort through such data they can 'learn' what his or her preferences are. Having done this, they then can take over some of this work from the manager, freeing more time to work on other tasks. Most of these programmes are still in the development stage, but they may be commonplace within a decade.[16]

Another software development that is starting to have an impact on the manager's job is *speech recognition software*. Currently speech recognition software must be 'trained' to recognise and understand each individual's voice, and it requires that the speaker pause after each word. The increasing power of microprocessors, however, has enabled the development of faster speech recognition programmes that can handle more variables and much greater complexity. Now a manager driving down the road can communicate with a PC through a wireless link and give that computer complex voice instructions.[17]

Types of Management Information Systems

Six types of management information systems are particularly helpful in providing managers with the information they need to make decisions and to co-ordinate and control organisational resources: transaction-processing systems, operations information systems, decision support systems, expert systems, enterprise resource management systems and e-commerce systems (Fig. 18.2). These systems are arranged along a continuum according to the sophistication of the IT they are based on – IT that determines their ability to provide managers with the information they need to make non-programmed decisions. (Recall from Chapter 7 that non-programmed decision making occurs in response to unusual, unpredictable opportunities and threats.) We examine each of these systems after focusing on the MIS that preceded them all: the *organisational hierarchy*.

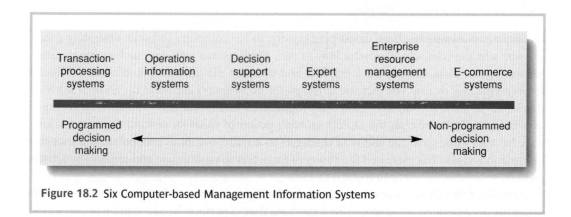

Figure 18.2 Six Computer-based Management Information Systems

The Organisational Hierarchy: The Traditional Information System

Traditionally, managers have used the organisational hierarchy as the main system for gathering the information necessary to make decisions and co-ordinate and control activities (see Chapter 10 for a detailed discussion of organisational structure and hierarchy). According to business historian Alfred Chandler, the use of the hierarchy as an information network was perfected by railroad companies during the 1850s.[18] By virtue of their size and geographic spread, they faced unique problems of co-ordination and control. In the 1850s, railroad companies started to solve these problems by designing hierarchical management structures that provided senior managers with the information they needed to achieve co-ordination and control and to make decisions about the running of the railroads.

Daniel McCallum, superintendent of the Erie Railroad in the 1850s, realised that the lines of authority and responsibility defining the Erie's management hierarchy also represented *channels of communication* along which information travelled. McCallum established what was perhaps the first modern MIS. Regular daily and monthly reports were sent up the management chain so that senior managers could make decisions about, for example, controlling costs and setting freight rates. Decisions were then relayed back down the hierarchy so they could be carried out. Imitating the railroads, most other organisations used their hierarchies as systems for collecting and channelling information. This practice began to change only when computer-based IT became more reasonably priced in the 1960s.

Although hierarchy is a useful information system, it has several drawbacks. First, when an organisation has many layers of managers it can take a long time for information and requests to travel up the hierarchy and for decisions and answers to travel back down. This slow pace can reduce the *timeliness* and usefulness of the information and prevent an organisation from responding quickly to changing market conditions.[19] Second, information can be *distorted* as it moves from one layer of management to another, and information distortion reduces the *quality* of information.[20] Third, because managers have only a limited span of control, as an organisation grows larger, its hierarchy lengthens and this 'tall' structure can make the hierarchy a very expensive information system. The popular idea that companies with tall management hierarchies are bureaucratic and unresponsive to the needs of their customers arises from the inability of tall hierarchies to effectively process data and provide managers with timely, complete, relevant and high-quality information. Until modern IT came along, however, the management hierarchy was the best information system available.

Transaction-processing Systems

A **transaction-processing system** is an MIS designed to handle large volumes of routine, recurring transactions (Fig. 18.2). Transaction-processing systems began to appear in the early 1960s with the advent of commercially available mainframe computers. They were the first type of computer-based IT adopted by many organisations, and today they are commonplace. Bank managers use a transaction-processing system to record deposits into, and payments out of, bank accounts. Supermarket managers use a transaction-processing system to record the sale of items and to track inventory levels. Most managers in large organisations use a transaction-processing system to handle tasks such as payroll preparation and payment, customer billing and payment of suppliers.

Operations Information Systems

Many types of MISs followed hard on the heels of transaction-processing systems in the 1960s as companies like IBM advanced their IT. An **operations information system** is an MIS that gathers comprehensive data, organises them and summarises them in a form that is of value to managers. Whereas a transaction-processing system processes *routine* transactions, an operations information system provides managers with information that they can use in their *non-routine* co-ordinating, controlling and decision-making tasks. Most operations information systems are coupled with a transaction-processing system. An operations information system typically accesses data gathered by a transaction-processing system, processes those data into useful information and organises that information into a form accessible to managers. Managers often use an operations information system to get sales, inventory, accounting and other performance-related information. DHL, for example, uses an operations information system to track the performance of its ground stations. Each ground station is evaluated according to four criteria: *delivery* (the goal is to deliver 95 per cent of all packages by noon the day after they are picked up), *productivity* (measured by the number of packages shipped per employee-hour), *controllable cost* and *station profitability*. Each ground station also has specific delivery, efficiency, cost and profitability targets that it must attain. Every month DHL's operations information system is used to gather information on these four criteria and summarise it for senior managers, who are then able to compare the performance of each station against its previously established targets. The system quickly alerts senior managers to any underperforming ground stations, so that they can intervene selectively to help solve any problems that may have given rise to the poor performance.[21]

Decision Support Systems

A **decision support system** provides computer-built models that help managers make better non-programmed decisions.[22] Recall from Chapter 7 that *non-programmed decisions* are decisions that are relatively unusual or novel, such as decisions to invest in new productive capacity, develop a new product, launch a new promotional campaign, enter a new market or expand internationally. Although an operations information system organises important information for managers, a decision support system gives managers a model building capability and so provides them with the ability to manipulate information in a variety of ways. Managers may use a decision support system to help them decide whether to cut prices for a product. The decision support system may contain models of how customers and competitors would respond to a price cut, and managers can run these models and use the results as an aid to decision making.

The emphasis on the word *aid* is important, for in the final analysis a decision support system is not meant to make decisions for managers. Rather, its function is to provide managers with valuable information that they can use to improve the *quality of their decisions*. A good example of a sophisticated decision support system was developed by Judy Lewent, CFO of the pharmaceutical company Merck, the oldest pharmaceutical–chemical business in the world (Case 18.2).[23]

Case 18.2: How Judy Lewent became one of the most powerful women in corporate America

With annual sales of over €58 billion in 2005,[24] Merck is one of the world's largest developers and marketers of advanced pharmaceuticals and chemicals.[25] In 2003, the company spent more than €2.4 billion on R&D to develop new drugs – an expensive and difficult process that is fraught with many risks. Most new drug ideas fail to make it through the development process: it takes an average of €235 million and 10 years to bring a new drug to market and 7 out of 10 new drugs fail to make a profit for the developing company.

Given the costs, risks and uncertainties involved in the new drug development process, Judy Lewent decided to develop a decision support system that could help managers make more effective R&D investment decisions. Her aim was to give Merck's senior managers the information they needed to evaluate proposed R&D projects on a case-by-case basis. The system that Lewent and her staff developed is referred to in Merck as the 'Research Planning Model'.[26] At the heart of this decision support system is a sophisticated model. The input variables to the model include data on R&D spending, manufacturing costs, selling costs and demand conditions. The relationships among the input variables are modelled by means of several equations that factor in the probability of a drug's making it through the development process and to market. The outputs of this modelling process are the revenues, cash flows and profits that a project might generate.

The Merck model does not use a single value for an input variable, nor does it compute a single value for each output. Rather, a *range* is specified for each input variable (such as high, medium and low R&D spending). The computer repeatedly samples at random from the range of values for each input variable and produces a probability distribution of values for each output. So, for example, instead of stating categorically that a proposed R&D project will yield a profit of €395 million, the decision support system produces a probability distribution. It might state that although €395 million is the most likely profit, there is a 25 per cent chance that the profit will be less than €395 million and a 25 per cent chance that it will be greater than €540 million.

Merck now uses Lewent's decision support system to evaluate all proposed R&D investment decisions. In addition, Lewent has developed other decision support system models that Merck's managers can use to help them decide, for example, whether to enter into JVs with other companies or how best to hedge foreign exchange risk. Lewent's reward was promotion to the position of CFO of Merck, and she became one of the most powerful women in corporate America.

Most decision support systems are geared toward aiding middle managers in the decision-making process. A loan manager at a bank, for example, might use a decision support system to evaluate the credit risk involved in lending money to a particular client. Only rarely does a senior manager use a decision support system, however. One reason for this may be that most electronic management information systems are not yet sophisticated enough to handle effectively the ambiguous types of problems facing senior managers. To improve this situation, information systems professionals have been developing a variant of the decision support system: an **executive support system**.

An executive support system is a sophisticated version of a decision support system that is designed to meet the needs of senior managers. Lewent's Research Planning Model is actually an executive support system. One of the defining characteristics of executive support systems is *user-friendliness*. Many of them include simple pull-down menus to take a manager through a decision analysis problem. Moreover, they may contain stunning graphics and other visual features to encourage senior managers to use them.[27] Increasingly, executive support systems are being used to link senior managers so that they can function as a *team*; this type of executive support system is called a **group decision support system**.

Expert Systems and Artificial Intelligence

Expert systems are the most advanced MISs available. An expert system is a system that employs human knowledge, embedded in computer software, to solve problems that ordinarily require human expertise.[28] Expert systems are a variant of artificial intelligence.[29] Mimicking human expertise (and intelligence) requires IT that can at a minimum (1) recognise, formulate and solve a problem; (2) explain the solution; and (3) learn from experience.

Recent developments in artificial intelligence that go by names such as 'fuzzy logic' and 'neural networks' have resulted in computer programmes that, in a primitive way, try to mimic human thought processes. Although artificial intelligence is still at a fairly early stage of development, an increasing number of business applications are beginning to emerge in the form of expert systems. General Electric (GE), for example, has developed an expert system to help troubleshoot problems in the diesel locomotive engines it manufactures. The expert system was originally based on knowledge collected from David Smith, GE's former top locomotive troubleshooter. A novice engineer or technician can use the system to uncover a fault by spending only a few minutes at a computer terminal. The system also can explain to the user the *logic* of its advice, thereby serving as a teacher as well as a problem solver. The system is based on a flexible, human-like thought process, and it can be updated to incorporate new knowledge as it becomes available. GE has installed the system in every railroad repair shop that it serves, thus eliminating delays and boosting maintenance productivity.[30]

Enterprise Resource Planning Systems

To achieve high performance, it is not sufficient just to develop an MIS inside each of a company's functions or divisions to provide better information and knowledge. It is also vital that managers in the different functions and divisions have access to information about the activities of managers in *other* functions and divisions. The greater the flow of information and knowledge among functions and divisions, the more learning can take place, and this builds a company stock of *knowledge and expertise*, the source of its competitive advantage and profitability.

In the last 25 years, a revolution has taken place in IT as software companies have worked to develop **enterprise resource planning (ERP) systems**, which essentially incorporate most aspects of the MISs just discussed, as well as much more. ERP systems are multi-module application software packages that allow a company to link and co-ordinate the entire set of functional activities and operations necessary to move products from the initial product design stage to the final customer stage. Essentially, ERP systems (1) help each individual function improve its functional-level skills and (2) improve integration among all functions so that they work together to build a competitive advantage for the company. Today, choosing and designing an ERP system to improve the way a company operates is the biggest challenge facing the IT function of a company. To understand why almost every large global company has installed an

ERP system in the last few decades, it is necessary to return to the concept of the *value chain*, introduced in Chapter 9.

Recall that a company's value chain is composed of the sequence of functional activities that are necessary to make and sell a product. The value-chain idea focuses attention on the fact that each function, in sequence, performs its activities to add or contribute value to a product. Once one function has made its contribution, it then hands the product over to the next function, which makes its own contribution and so on down the line.

The primary activity of marketing, for example, is to uncover new or changing customer needs or new groups of customers and then decide what kinds of products should be developed to appeal to them. It then shares or 'hands over' its information to product development, where engineers and scientists work to develop and design the new products. In turn, manufacturing and materials management then work to find ways to produce the new products as efficiently as possible. The sales department is then responsible for finding the best way to convince customers to buy these products.

The value chain is useful in demonstrating the sequence of activities necessary to bring products to the market successfully. In an IT context, however, it suggests the enormous amount of information and communication that needs to take place to link and co-ordinate the activities of all the various functions. Installing an ERP system for a large company can cost tens of millions of pounds. Case 18.3 discusses the ERP system designed and sold by the German IT company, SAP.

Case 18.3: **SAP's ERP system**

SAP is the world's leading supplier of ERP software; it introduced the world's first ERP system in 1973. So great was the demand for its software that it had to train thousands of consultants from companies like IBM, HP, Accenture and Cap Gemini to install and customise its software to meet the needs of companies in different industries throughout the world.

The popularity of SAP's ERP is that it manages all the stages of a company's value chain, both individually and as a collection. SAP's software has modules specifically devoted to each of a company's core functional activities. Each module contains a set of 'best practices', or the optimum way to perform specific activities, that SAP's IT experts have found results in the biggest increases in efficiency, quality, innovation and responsiveness to customers. SAP's ERP is therefore '*the* expert system of expert systems'. SAP claims that when a company reconfigures its IT system to make SAP's software work, it can achieve productivity gains of 30–50 per cent, which amounts to many billions of pounds of savings for large companies.[31]

For each function in the value chain, SAP has a software module that it installs on a function's LAN. Each function then inputs its data into that module in the way specified by SAP. For example, the sales function inputs all the information about customer needs required by SAP's sales module, and the materials management function inputs information about the product specifications it requires from suppliers into SAP's materials management module. These modules give functional managers real-time feedback on the status of their particular functional activities. Essentially, each SAP module functions as an expert system that can reason through the information functional managers put into it. It then provides them with recommendations as to how they can improve functional operations. However, the magic of ERP does not stop there.

▶

SAP's ERP software also connects *across functions*. Managers in all functions have access to the other functions' expert systems, and SAP's software is designed to alert managers when their functional activities will be affected by changes taking place in another function. Thus, SAP's ERP allows managers across the organisation to better co-ordinate their activities, and this can be a major source of competitive advantage. Moreover, SAP software on corporate mainframe computers takes the information from all the different functional and divisional expert systems and creates a companywide ERP system that provides senior managers with an overview of the operations of the whole company. In essence, SAP's ERP creates a sophisticated top-level expert system that can reason through the huge volume of information being provided by the company's functions. It can then recognise and diagnose common problems and issues in that information and develop and recommend organisationwide solutions. Senior managers armed with this information can then use it to improve the 'fit' between their strategies and the changing environment.

As an example of how an ERP system works, let us examine how SAP's software allows managers to better co-ordinate their activities to speed product development. Suppose marketing has discovered some new unmet customer need, suggested what kind of product needs to be developed and forecast that the demand for the product will be 40,000 units a year. With SAP's IT, engineers in product development use their expert system to work out how to design the new product in a way that builds in quality at the lowest possible cost. Manufacturing managers, watching product development's progress, are working *simultaneously* to find the best way to make the product, and thus use their expert system to find out how to keep operating costs at a minimum.

Remember that SAP's IT gives all the other functions access to this information; they can tap into what is going on between marketing and manufacturing in real time. So materials management managers watching manufacturing make its plans can simultaneously plan how to order supplies of inputs or components from global suppliers, or how and when to ship the final product to customers to keep costs at a minimum. At the same time, HRM is tied into the ERP system and uses its expert system to forecast the type and cost of labour that will be required to carry out the activities in the other functions – for example, the number of manufacturing employees who will be required to make the product, or the number of salespeople who will be needed to sell the product to achieve the 40,000 sales forecast.

How does this build competitive advantage and profitability? First, it speeds up the product development process; companies can bring products to market much more quickly, thereby generating higher sales revenues. Second, SAP's IT focuses on how to drive down operating costs while keeping quality high. Third, SAP's IT is oriented toward the final customer; its *customer relationship management* (CRM) module watches how customers respond to the new product and then feeds back this information quickly to the other functions.

To see what this means in practice, let's jump ahead three months and suppose that the CRM component of SAP's ERP software reports that actual sales are 20 per cent below target. Further, the software has reasoned that the problem is due to the fact that the product lacks one crucial feature that customers want. The product is a smart phone, for example, and customers must have a built-in digital camera. Sales decides this issue deserves major priority and alerts managers in all the other functions about the problem. Now managers can begin to make decisions about how to manage this unexpected situation.

Engineers in product development, for example, use their expert system to work out how much it would cost, and how long it would take, to modify the product so that it includes the missing feature, the digital camera, that customers require. Managers in other functions watch the engineers' progress through the ERP system and can make suggestions for improvement.

In the meantime, manufacturing managers know about the slow sales and have already cut back on production to avoid a build-up of the unsold product in the company's warehouse. They are also planning how to phase out this product and introduce the next version, with the digital camera, to keep costs as low as possible. Similarly, materials management managers are contacting digital-camera makers to find out how much such a camera will cost and when it can be supplied. In the meantime, marketing managers are researching how they came to miss this crucial product feature and are developing new sales forecasts to estimate demand for the modified product. They announce a revised sales forecast of 75,000 units of the modified product.

It takes the engineers one month to modify the product, but because SAP's IT has been providing information on the modified product to managers in manufacturing and materials management, the product hits the market only two months later. Within weeks, the sales function reports that early sales figures for the product have greatly exceeded even marketing's revised forecast. The company knows it has a winning product, and senior managers give the go-ahead for manufacturing to build a second production line to double production. All the other functions are expecting this decision; in fact, they have already been experimenting with their SAP modules to find out how long it will take them to respond to such a move. Each function provides the others with its latest information so that they can all adjust their functional activities accordingly.

All this quick and responsive action has been made possible because of the ERP system. Compare this situation to that of a company which relies only on a paper-based system, in which salespeople fill in paper sales reports. In such a company, it would take many times as long to find out about slow sales; it might take six months to a year for the company to find out that its sales projections were wrong. In the meantime, manufacturing, producing according to plan, will generate a huge stock of unsold products, which is a major source of operating costs. When the sales problem is finally uncovered, managers from the different functions will have to make frantic phone calls and hold face-to-face meetings to decide what to do. It might take another six months for the modified product to come into production, so more than one year of time, and huge potential profits, will have been lost.

In the ERP example, *efficiency* is promoted because a company has a better control of its manufacturing and materials management activities. *Quality* is increased because an increased flow of information between functions allows for a better-designed product. *Innovation* is speeded because a company can rapidly change its products to suit the changing needs of customers. Finally, *responsiveness to customers* improves because using its CRM software module, sales can better manage and react to customer's changing needs and provide better service and support to back up the sales of the product. This ability to promote competitive advantage is the reason why managers in so many companies, large and small, are moving to find the best ERP 'solution' for their particular companies.

E-Commerce Systems

E-commerce is trade that takes place between companies, and between companies and individual customers, using IT and the Internet. *Business-to-business (B2B) commerce* is trade that takes place between companies using IT and the Internet to link and co-ordinate the value chains

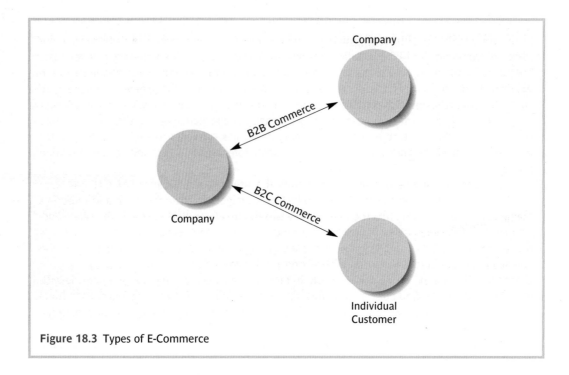

Figure 18.3 Types of E-Commerce

of *different* companies (Fig. 18.3). The goal of B2B commerce is to increase the profitability of making and selling goods and services. B2B commerce increases profitability because it allows companies to reduce their operating costs or because it may improve product quality. A principal B2B software application is the **B2B marketplace**, an Internet-based trading platform that has been set up in many industries to connect buyers and sellers. To participate in a B2B marketplace, companies adopt a *common software standard* that allows them to search for and share information with one another. Companies can then work together over time to find ways to reduce costs or improve quality.

Business-to-customer (B2C) commerce is trade that takes place between a company and *individual customers* using IT and the Internet. Using IT to connect directly to the customer means that companies can avoid having to use intermediaries, such as wholesalers and retailers, who capture a significant part of the profit being created in the value chain. The use of websites and online stores also allows companies to provide their customers with much more information about the value of their products. This often allows them to attract more customers and thus generate higher sales revenues.

Since 2000, computer software makers such as Microsoft, Oracle, SAP and IBM have rushed to make their products work seamlessly with the Internet to respond to global companies' growing demand for e-commerce software. Previously, their software had been configured to work only on a particular company's intranet; now, they had to develop software that would network the computer systems of companies to their suppliers and customers.

Today, the challenge facing managers is to select the e-commerce software that allows the seamless exchange of information between companies anywhere in the world. The stakes are high; we saw how IBM's new thrust is toward on-demand software. SAP has also updated its ERP modules to allow for transactions over the Internet. It calls its new B2B commerce software 'mySAP', and today every one of its modules is Internet-compatible. Microsoft is promoting its .Net Internet software, which is compatible with all its other Windows software and is vigorously competing with IBM and SAP to raise its share of this growing software market.

By using computer-based MISs, managers have more control over a company's activities and operations and can work to improve its competitive advantage and profitability. Today, the IT function is becoming increasingly important because IT managers select which kind of hardware and software a company will use and also train employees to use it.

Reaction Time

1. To be useful, information must be of high quality, be timely, be relevant and be as complete as possible. Why does a 'tall' management hierarchy, when used as an MIS, have negative effects on these desirable attributes?

2. What is the relationship between IT and competitive advantage?

3. Many companies have reported that it is difficult to implement advanced MISs such as ERP systems. Why do you think this is? How might the 'roadblocks' to implementation be removed?

Innovation, Technological Change and Competition

As discussed in Chapter 6, *technology* comprises the skills, know-how, experience, body of scientific knowledge, tools, machines, computers and equipment used in the design, production and distribution of goods and services. Technology is involved in all organisational activities, and its rapid development makes *technological change* a significant factor in almost every organisational innovation.[32]

The two main types of technological change are *quantum* and *incremental*. **Quantum technological change** is a *fundamental shift* in technology that results in the innovation of new kinds of goods and services. Two examples are the development of the Internet, which has revolutionised the computer industry, and the development of genetic engineering (biotechnology), which is promising to revolutionise the treatment of illness with the development of genetically engineered medicines. McDonald's development of the principles behind the provision of fast food also qualifies as a quantum technological change.

Incremental technological change is change that *refines existing technology* and leads to gradual improvements or refinements in products over time. Since 1971, for example, Intel has made a series of incremental improvements to its original 4004 microprocessor, leading to the introduction of its 8008, 8086, 286, 386 and 486; its first Pentium chip in 1993; the Pentium 4 in 2000; the Itanium in 2001; and the Pentium 4 with HT technology in 2004.[33] Similarly, Google's staffers have made thousands of incremental improvements to the company's search engine, such as those that have enhanced the Google directory and given the engine the ability to search via wireless devices. Staffers also led Google to think globally, and Google now has 10 language versions of its engine up and running for users who wish to search in their native tongues.

Products that result from quantum technological changes are called **quantum product innovations** and are relatively rare. Managers in most organisations spend most of their time managing products that result from incremental technological changes, called **incremental product**

innovations. Every time Dell or HP puts a new, faster Intel chip into a PC, or Google improves its search engine's capability, the company is making incremental product innovations. Every time engineers in an automobile company redesign a car model, and every time McDonald's managers try to improve the flavour and texture of burgers and fries, they are engaged in product development efforts designed to lead to incremental product innovations. The fact that incremental change is less dramatic than quantum change does not imply that incremental product innovations are unimportant. In fact, as discussed below, it is often managers' ability to successfully manage incremental product development that results in success or failure in an industry.

The Effects of Technological Change

The consequences of quantum and incremental technological change are all around us. Microprocessors, PCs, wireless smart phones, PDAs, word-processing software, computer networks, digital cameras and camcorders, DVD players, genetically engineered medicines, fast food, online information services, superstores and mass travel either did not exist a generation ago or were considered to be exotic and expensive. Now these products are commonplace, and they are being improved all the time. Many of the organisations whose managers helped develop and exploit new technologies have reaped enormous gains – Dell Computer (PCs), Microsoft (computer software), Intel (microprocessors), Nokia (microprocessors, wireless phones, pagers), Sony (camcorders, DVDs), Matsushita (videocassette recorders), Amgen (biotechnology), McDonald's (fast food), Tesco (superstores).

While some organisations have benefited from technological change, others have seen their markets threatened and their futures placed in doubt. Traditional telephone companies the world over have seen their market dominance threatened by new companies offering Internet, broadband and wireless telephone technology.

Technological change thus offers both an *opportunity* and a *threat*.[34] On the one hand, it helps create new product opportunities that managers and their organisations can exploit. On the other hand, new and improved products can harm or even destroy the demand for older, established products. Big supermarket chains have put thousands of small stores out of business, and McDonald's has caused thousands of small diners to close, in part because these organisations have been so innovative in their production systems that they can give customers lower-priced products. In the first five months of 2006 alone, 40 independent bookshops closed in the UK as a result of price cuts by online providers.[35]

Similarly, Intel's development of the microprocessor has helped create a host of new product opportunities for entrepreneurs, who have created thousands of companies that provide innovative computer software and hardware. At the same time, microprocessors have destroyed demand for older products and ruined organisations whose managers did not see the changes in time and act on them. Managers of typewriter companies, for example, might have noticed that the new technology would compete directly with their products and moved to acquire or merge with new computer companies. Most did not, however, and once-famous companies like Smith Corona are out of business. The nature of entrepreneurship is discussed in detail later in this chapter.

Product Life Cycles and Product Development

When technology is changing, organisational survival requires that managers quickly adopt and apply new technologies to innovate products. Managers who do not do so soon find that they

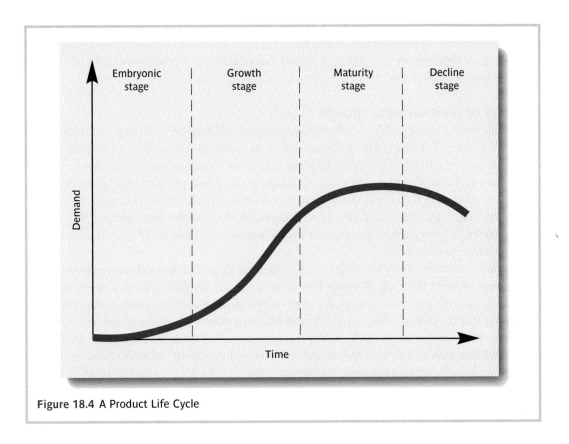

Figure 18.4 A Product Life Cycle

have no market for their products – and destroy their organisations. The rate of technological change in an industry – and particularly the length of the **product life cycle** – determines how important it is for managers to innovate.

The product life cycle reflects the changes in demand for a product that occur over time.[36] Demand for most successful products passes through four stages: the *embryonic* stage, *growth*, *maturity* and *decline* (Fig. 18.4). In the *embryonic* stage a product has yet to gain widespread acceptance; customers are unsure what the product has to offer, and demand for it is minimal. If a product does become accepted by customers (and many do not), demand takes off and the product enters its growth stage. In the *growth* stage many consumers are entering the market and buying the product for the first time; demand increases rapidly. This is the stage in which PDAs, such as smart phones, are currently.

The growth stage ends and the *mature* stage begins when market demand peaks because most customers have already bought the product (there are relatively few first-time buyers left). At this stage, demand is typically *replacement demand*. In the car market, for example, people already have a car and are either trading up or replacing an old model. Products such as wireless phones, PCs for home use and online information services are also currently in this stage. The *decline* stage follows the mature stage if and when demand for a product falls. Falling demand often occurs because a product has become technologically obsolescent and been superseded by a more advanced product. Demand for every generation of VCR, CD or DVD falls as the products are superseded by newer, technically advanced models with more features. In

2004, leading electronic companies such as Sony and Philips announced that they had adopted a new standard for DVD players known as the 'blue laser' standard because it uses a blue, rather than red, laser beam; the new technology means that new DVDs will be able to hold six times as much content as they did in 2004.

The rate of technological change

One of the main determinants of the length of a product's life cycle is the rate of technological change.[37] Figure 18.5 illustrates the relationship between the rate of technological change and the length of a product life cycle. In some industries – such as personal computers, semi-conductors and disk drives – technological change is rapid and product life cycles very short. Technological change is so rapid in the computer disk-drive industry, for example, that a disk-drive model becomes technologically obsolete about 12 months after introduction. The same is true in the PC industry, where product life cycles have shrunk from three years during the late 1980s to a few months today.

In other industries, the product life cycle is somewhat longer. In the car industry, for example, the average product life cycle is about five years. Even so, the life cycle of a car is relatively short because fairly rapid technological change is producing a continual stream of incremental innovations in car design – such as the introduction of door and overhead airbags, advanced electronic microcontrollers, plastic body parts and more fuel-efficient engines, as in Toyota's Prius, which is powered by gas and an electric motor. In contrast, in many basic industries, where the pace of technological change is slower, product life cycles tend to be much longer. In

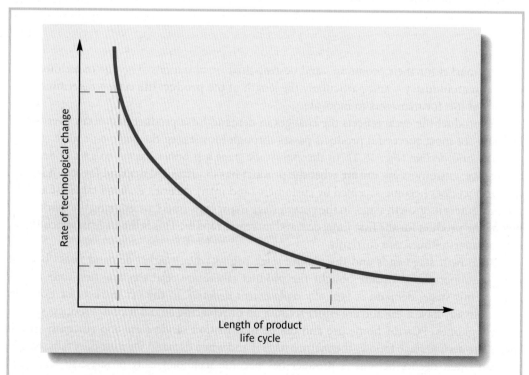

Figure 18.5 The Relationship Between Technological Change and Length of the Product Life Cycle

steel or electricity, for example, change in product technology is very limited, and products such as steel girders and electric cable can remain in the 'mature' stage indefinitely.

The role of fads and fashions

Fads and fashion are also important determinants of the length of product life cycles.[38] A five-year-old car design is likely to be technologically outmoded and look out of date and thus lose its attractiveness to customers. Such considerations are even more important in the high-fashion end of the clothing industry, where a season's clothing line is usually out of date by the next season and product life cycles may last no more than three months. Fads and fashions are thus another reason why product life cycles may be short.

Managerial implications

Whether short product life cycles are caused by rapid technological change, changing fads and fashions, or some combination of the two, the message for managers is clear: The shorter the length of a product's life cycle, the more important it is to innovate products quickly and continuously. In industries where product life cycles are very short, managers must continually develop new products – otherwise, their organisations may go out of business. The PC company that cannot develop a new and improved product line every three to six months will soon find itself in trouble. The fashion house that fails to develop a new line of clothing for every season cannot succeed, nor can the small restaurant, club or bar that is not alert to current fads and fashions. Car companies have a little more time, but even here it is vital that managers continually develop new and improved models every five years or so.

There is increasing evidence that in a wide range of industries product life cycles are becoming more compressed as managers focus their organisations' resources on innovation to increase responsiveness to customers. To attract new customers, managers are trying to outdo each other by being the first to market with a product that incorporates a new technology or that plays to a new fashion trend. In the automobile industry a typical five-year product life cycle is being reduced to three years as companies increasingly compete with one another to attract new customers and encourage existing customers to upgrade and buy their newest products.[39] The way in which shrinking product life cycles for microprocessors have affected competition is considered in Case 18.4.

Case 18.4: **Shrinking product life cycles hurt Intel and help AMD**

Intel's microprocessors are the brains of 85 per cent of the personal computers sold worldwide. Intel's dominance in this business can be traced back to IBM's 1980 decision to use Intel's 8086 microprocessor in its first PC. Since then, Intel has produced a series of ever-more-powerful microprocessors, including the 286, the 386, the 486 and the Pentium chips.

In 1965, Gordon Moore, one of Intel's founders, made a famous observation, now called 'Moore's law', in which he predicted that the number of transistors per integrated circuit would double every 18 months. Moore's law still holds true today thanks to the technology of companies like Intel, as indicated in Fig. 18.6, which shows how the power of Intel's chips has continued to increase.[40]

Intel has not had things all its own way, however. In the 1990s, several companies began making clones of Intel chips that could manipulate computer software in the same way. Once

▶

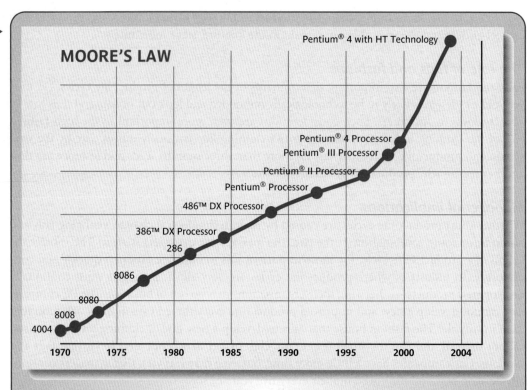

Figure 18.6 Moore's Law: Intel's Evolving Microprocessors

Source: www.intel.com/research/silicon/mooreslaw.htm. Reprinted by permission of Intel Corporation, copyright © Intel Corporation 2004.

a clone is introduced, chip prices fall and so do Intel's profit margins. One of these companies, AMD, has been having increasing success.

In the past, the source of Intel's competitive advantage over companies like AMD was that those companies could not start to design a clone of Intel's next microprocessor until they had actually obtained it. So, for each new microprocessor, Intel normally had months or even years of lead time before AMD could develop a clone. The time it takes AMD to clone an Intel microprocessor has been shrinking, however. It took AMD five years to come up with a compatible processor after Intel released its 386 chip in 1985. Matching Intel's next generation, the 486, took three years. Intel began volume production of the Pentium in early 1993; AMD introduced its clone, the P5, just two years later. To stay ahead of the competition, Intel responded by increasing the speed of its own product development process – effectively shrinking the length of its own product life cycles. Intel released its successor to the Pentium, the Pentium Pro, in 1995, developing it in half the time it had taken to replace the 486 with the Pentium, to keep the pressure on its rivals.

The unthinkable happened in 2000 when AMD announced that it was introducing a new chip, the Athlon, that was faster than Intel's then-fastest Pentium, the Pentium 4. AMD had the lead for several months. However, in August 2001 Intel announced that it had broken the key 2-gigahertz milestone, effectively doubling the speed of its computer processors in only 18 months, once again confirming Moore's law.[41] Since then, Intel has further upgraded its

Pentium 4 by adding 'HT' technology; however, by 2004 it had become clear that AMD had gained an important competitive advantage over Intel because Intel had made a major product development error when designing its Pentium chips.

Intel believed that computer speed was what customers wanted, so it designed its Pentium chip to be very fast; however, fast chips are power-hungry and produce a lot of heat. In fact, by 2003 what customers wanted was a chip that could handle the needs of multimedia computers, which demanded better video and sound quality. The new Pentium 4 produced too much heat to use in advanced multimedia PCs, as well as in notebook PCs and other wireless devices. The Pentium chip was not designed with this market in mind at all, and Intel was forced to scramble to design new chips that could be used in these applications. This process is extremely complicated and by 2004 Intel had fallen behind on its promise to provide a low-heat chip and announced that the chip would be delayed until 2005.[42] AMD, in the meantime, had no such problem and by 2004 had grabbed 50 per cent of the PC chip market. Moore's law seems to be in jeopardy because the way customers use PCs is changing and speed is no longer the most important quality of a leading microprocessor

Reaction Time

1. The microprocessor that Intel developed can be classified as a quantum product innovation. Identify two other quantum product innovations, and explore their implications for product development.

2. What do you think are the greatest impediments to successful product development within an organisation?

3. Why is it so important for managers to shorten the duration of product development? What steps can management take to reduce development time? What risks are associated with compressing development time?

Entrepreneurship

At the heart of innovation and product development are *entrepreneurs*, individuals who notice opportunities and take responsibility for mobilising the resources necessary to produce new and improved goods and services. Entrepreneurs start new business ventures and do all of the planning, organising, leading and controlling necessary to meet organisational goals. Most commonly, entrepreneurs assume all the risk and receive all the returns associated with the new business venture. These people are Bill Gates or John Lewis, the founder of the John Lewis partnership, the department stores and grocery chain that has all employees as its partners who make fortunes when their businesses succeed; or they are among the millions of people who start new business ventures only to lose their money when they fail. Despite the fact that an estimated 80 per cent of small businesses fail in the first three to five years, by some estimates 38 per cent of men and 50 per cent of women in today's workforce want to start their own companies.[43]

Some managers, scientists and researchers employed by existing companies engage in entrepreneurial activity. They are involved in the innovation and product development process described in this chapter. To distinguish these individuals from the entrepreneurs who found their own businesses, employees of existing organisations who notice opportunities for either quantum or incremental product improvements and are responsible for managing the product development process are known as **intrapreneurs**. In general, then, **entrepreneurship** is the mobilisation of resources to take advantage of an opportunity to provide customers with new or improved goods and services.

There is an interesting relationship between entrepreneurs and intrapreneurs. Many intrapreneurs become dissatisfied when their superiors decide neither to support nor to fund new product ideas and development efforts that the intrapreneurs think will succeed. What do intrapreneurs do who feel that they are getting nowhere? Very often, they decide to leave their employers and start their own organisations to take advantage of their new product ideas. In other words, intrapreneurs become entrepreneurs and found companies that may compete with the companies they left. Intrapreneurs can also be found in universities; many universities nowadays have *spin-out companies* that are based on the research and discoveries of its employees, but who are still earning revenue for the universities.

Frustrated intrapreneurs who became entrepreneurs have started many of the world's most successful organisations. William Hewlett and David Packard left Fairchild Semiconductor, an early industry leader, when managers of that company would not support their ideas; their company soon outperformed Fairchild. Compaq Computer was founded by Rod Canion and some of his colleagues, who left Texas Instruments (TI) when managers there would not support Canion's idea that TI should develop its own PC. To prevent the departure of talented people, organisations need to take steps to *promote internal entrepreneurship*. In the remainder of this section we consider the issues involved in promoting successful entrepreneurship in both new and existing organisations.

Entrepreneurship and New Ventures

The fact that a significant number of entrepreneurs are frustrated intrapreneurs provides a clue about the personal characteristics of people who are likely to start a new venture and bear all the uncertainty and risk associated with being an entrepreneur.

Characteristics of entrepreneurs

Entrepreneurs are likely to be high on the personality trait of *openness to experience*, meaning that they are predisposed to be original, to be open to a wide range of stimuli, to be daring and to take risks. Entrepreneurs also are likely to have an *internal locus of control* and believe that they are responsible for what happens to them and that their own actions determine important outcomes such as the success or failure of a new business. People with an external locus of control, in contrast, would be very unlikely to leave a secure job in an organisation and assume the risk associated with a new venture.

Entrepreneurs are likely to have a high level of *self-esteem* and feel competent and capable of handling most situations – including the stress and uncertainty surrounding a plunge into a risky new venture. Entrepreneurs are also likely to have a high *need for achievement* and have a strong desire to perform challenging tasks and meet high personal standards of excellence. A good example of an entrepreneur with these personal characteristics is the potter George Ohr, briefly discussed in Chapter 7 (see Case 7.4). He persevered over the years to produce pots and vases no one would buy, yet kept his confidence in his abilities, which shows the faith that entrepreneurs must have in themselves.

Entrepreneurship and management

Given that entrepreneurs are predisposed to activities that are somewhat adventurous and risky, how can people become involved in entrepreneurial ventures? One way is to start a business from scratch. Taking advantage of computer-based information systems, many people are starting solo ventures and going it alone.

When people who go it alone succeed, they frequently need to hire other people to help them run the business. Anita Roddick, for example, began selling her natural, home-made products in a small shop in Brighton, UK. The concept of *franchising* allowed The Body Shop to quickly expand so that it is now represented in 50 countries with over 1,900 outlets.[44]

Some entrepreneurs who found a new business often have difficulty managing the organisation as it grows; entrepreneurship is *not* the same as management. Management encompasses all the decisions involved in planning, organising, leading and controlling resources. Entrepreneurship is noticing an opportunity to satisfy a customer need and then mobilising resources to make a product that satisfies that need. When an entrepreneur has produced something that customers want, *entrepreneurship gives way to management*, as the pressing need becomes to provide the product both efficiently and effectively.

A founding entrepreneur frequently lacks the skills, patience and experience to engage in the difficult and challenging work of management. Some entrepreneurs find it very hard to delegate authority because they are afraid to risk their company by letting others manage it. As a result, they become overloaded, and the quality of their decision making declines. Other entrepreneurs lack the detailed knowledge necessary to establish state-of-the-art information systems and technology, or to create the operations management procedures that are vital to increase the efficiency of their organisations' production systems. To succeed, it is necessary to do more than create a new product: an entrepreneur must hire managers who can create an *operating system* that will let a new venture survive and prosper.

Developing a plan for a new business

One crucial factor that can help promote the success of a new venture is a clear *business plan*. The purpose of a business plan is to guide the development of the new business, just as the *stage-gate development funnel* guides the product development effort. The steps in the development of a business plan are listed in Table 18.1.

Planning for a new business begins when an entrepreneur notices an *opportunity* to develop a new or improved good or service for the whole market or for a specific market niche. An entrepreneur might notice an opportunity to sell beauty products that are free of chemicals and animal testing, for example: this was the niche Anita Roddick of The Body Shop discovered.

The next step is to test the *feasibility* of the new product idea. The entrepreneur conducts as thorough a strategic planning exercise as possible, using the SWOT analysis technique discussed in Chapter 8. First, the entrepreneur analyses opportunities and threats – a potential threat might be that other shopping outlets for beauty and grooming products also decide to stock products that are not animal tested. The entrepreneur should conduct a thorough analysis of the external environment (Chapter 6) to test the potential of a new product idea and must be willing to abandon an idea if it seems likely that the threats and risks may overwhelm the

Table 18.1 Developing a business plan

---

1. Notice a product opportunity, and develop a basic business idea
- Goods/services
- Customers/markets

---

2. Conduct a strategic (SWOT) analysis
- Identify opportunities
- Identify threats
- Identify strengths
- Identify weaknesses

---

3. Decide whether the business opportunity is feasible

---

4. Prepare a detailed business plan
- Statement of mission, goals and financial objectives
- Statement of strategic objectives
- List of necessary resources
- Organisational time line of events

---

opportunities and returns. Entrepreneurship is always a very risky process, and many entrepreneurs become so committed to their new ideas that they ignore or discount the potential threats and forge ahead – only to lose their shirts.

If the environmental analysis suggests that the product idea is feasible, the next step is to examine the *strengths* and *weaknesses* of the idea. At this stage, the main strength is the resources possessed by the entrepreneur. Does the entrepreneur have access to an adequate source of funds? Does the entrepreneur have any experience in the beauty product industry, such as having managed a shop? To identify weaknesses, the entrepreneur needs to assess how many and what kinds of resources will be necessary to establish a viable new venture – such as a chain of shops. Analysis might reveal that the new product idea will not generate an adequate return on investment (ROI). Or it might reveal that the entrepreneur needs to find partners to help provide the resources necessary to open a chain on a scale sufficient to generate a high enough return on investment.

After conducting a thorough SWOT analysis, if the entrepreneur decides that the new product idea is feasible, the hard work begins – developing the actual *business plan* that will be used to attract investors or funds from banks. Included in the business plan should be the same basic elements as in the **product development plan**: (1) a statement of the organisation's mission, goals and financial objectives; (2) a statement of the organisation's strategic objectives, including an analysis of the product's market potential, based on the SWOT analysis that has already been conducted; (3) a list of all the functional and organisational resources that will be required to successfully implement the new product idea, including a list of technological, financial and HR requirements; and (4) a time line that contains specific milestones for the entrepreneur and others to use to measure the progress of the venture, such as target dates for the final design and the opening of the first shop.

Many entrepreneurs do not have the luxury of having a team of cross-functional managers to help develop a detailed business plan. This is obviously true of solo ventures: one reason why *franchising* has become so popular is that an entrepreneur can purchase and draw on the business plan and experience of an already existing company, thereby reducing the risks associated with opening a new business. Entrepreneurs today can purchase the right to open an outlet of

The Body Shop. The founders of that chain, however, had to develop the initial business plan that made the franchise possible.

Entrepreneurs thus have a number of significant challenges to confront and conquer if they are to be successful. It is not uncommon for an entrepreneur to fail repeatedly before finding a venture that proves successful. It also is not uncommon for an entrepreneur who establishes a successful new company to sell it in order to move on to new ventures that promise new risks and returns. An example of such an entrepreneur is Sir Alan Sugar, who started his entrepreneurial life in 1963, selling car aerials and lighters out the back of a van. Five years later, in 1968,[45] Sir Alan registered his company Amstrad, with which he launched the low-priced computer called Viglen. Sir Alan is now estimated to be worth approximately £790 million and was placed 71st on the *Sunday Times Rich List* in 2006.[46]

Intrapreneurship and Organisational Learning

The intensity of competition today, particularly from agile, small companies, has made it increasingly important for large, established organisations to promote and encourage intrapreneurship to raise the level of innovation and organisational learning. A *learning organisation* (Chapter 7) encourages all its employees to identify opportunities and solve problems, thus enabling the organisation to continuously experiment, improve and increase its ability to provide customers with new and improved goods and services. The higher the level of intrapreneurship, the higher the levels of learning and innovation. How can organisations promote organisational learning and intrapreneurship?

Product champions

One way to promote intrapreneurship is to encourage individuals to assume the role of **product champion**; a product champion is a manager who takes 'ownership' of a project and provides the leadership and vision that can take a product from the idea stage to the final customer. 3M, the company behind the Post-it note, is well known for its attempts to promote intrapreneurship, and encourages all its managers to become product champions and identify new product ideas. A product champion becomes responsible for developing a business plan for the product. Armed with this business plan, the champion appears before 3M's product development committee, a team of senior 3M managers who probe the strengths and weaknesses of the plan to decide whether it should be funded. If the plan is accepted, the product champion assumes responsibility for product development.

Case 18.5 shows what enthusiasm and entrepreneurship can achieve.

Case 18.5: **The creation of an icon**

Lamborghini has long been associated with mad, fast, expensive, super-cars. But its origins are amongst the humble farm lands of Italy. Ferruccio Lamborghini was a wealthy entrepreneur who established himself as a manufacturer of tractors from Army surplus after the Second World War. After the successes in this business Ferruccio branched out into producing air-conditioning systems and oil burners. This was similarly successful and Ferruccio became the richest man in Italy. He could afford everything he wanted – one of the many pleasures was a Ferrari. However, this car of his had too many problems, and legend has it that this aggravated ▶

▶ Ferruccio so much that he went to see Enzo Ferrari, the founder of Ferrari. Ferrari, however, known for his arrogance, dismissed Ferruccio.

This was all the motivation Ferruccio needed. Money was no issue for Lamborghini and looking at the market for high-speed, well-finished cars it was obvious that it was less than competitive. The myth surrounding the creation of the first 350GTV has it that this particular branch of his business (Automobili Lamborghini SpA, established 1963) was set up in less than a year and the 350GTV was shown at the Auto Show in Turin in the same year.

But success involved not only the commitment of money and time to the project. In order to build a super-car, you need people. Ferruccio hired Giotto Bizzarrini, who had left Ferrari, to design and build the engine. Adding to his pool of staff, Ferruccio surrounded himself with an excellent team of engineers and Lamborghini was established as a name throughout the world. But Ferruccio was not only wise in spending time, money and effort on this project. The best move was to encourage entrepreneurship within the company. The reason Lamborghini is still legendary today, even after several failures and successes, is that Ferruccio allowed his engineers to design and built the Lamborghini Miura, the car that made Lamborghini's name.[47]

Skunkworks and new venture divisions

The idea behind the product champion role is that employees who feel ownership for a project are inclined to act like entrepreneurs and go to great lengths to make the project succeed. Using **skunkworks** and **new venture divisions** can also strengthen this feeling of ownership. A *skunkworks* is a group of intrapreneurs who are deliberately separated from the normal operation of an organisation – for example, from the normal chain of command – to encourage them to devote all their attention to developing new products. The idea is that if these people are isolated, they will become so intensely involved in a project that development time will be relatively brief and the quality of the final product will be enhanced.

Large organisations can become 'tall', inflexible and bureaucratic, and these conditions are not ideal for encouraging learning and experimentation. Recognising this problem, many organisations create new venture divisions, separate from the parent organisation and free from close scrutiny, to take charge of product development. A *new venture division* is an autonomous division that is given all the resources it needs to develop and market a new product. In essence, a new venture division functions in the same way that a new venture would; the division's managers become intrapreneurs in charge of product development. The hope is that this new setting will encourage a high level of organisational learning and entrepreneurship.

Rewards for innovation

To encourage managers to bear the uncertainty and risk associated with the hard work of entrepreneurship, it is necessary to link performance to rewards. Companies are increasingly rewarding intrapreneurs on the basis of the outcome of the product development process: intrapreneurs are granted large bonuses if their projects succeed, or they are granted stock options that can make them millionaires if the product sells well. In addition to receiving money, successful intrapreneurs can expect to receive promotion to the ranks of senior management. Most of 3M's senior managers, for example, reached the executive suite because they had a track record of successful entrepreneurship. Organisations must reward intrapreneurs equitably if they wish to prevent them from leaving and becoming outside entrepreneurs who may form a new venture that competes directly against them. Nevertheless, intrapreneurs frequently do so.

TIPS FOR PRACTICE

1. Think about taking risks and try to encourage colleagues and team members to be innovative. Analyse your organisation's structure and culture and assess if these are conducive to entrepreneurial activities and innovation.

2. Think about how an organisation can ensure an appropriate MIS – appropriate for its activities and for the people using it.

Summary and Review

Information and the manager's job Computer-based information systems are central to the operation of most organisations. By providing managers with high-quality, timely, relevant and relatively complete information, properly implemented information systems can improve managers' ability to co-ordinate and control the operations of an organisation and to make effective decisions. Information systems can also help the organisation to attain a competitive advantage through their beneficial impact on productivity, quality, innovation and responsiveness to customers. Modern information systems are an indispensable management tool.

The IT revolution Since the 1950s there have been rapid advances in the power, and rapid declines in the cost, of IT. Falling prices, wireless communication, computer networks and software developments have all radically improved the power and efficacy of computer-based information systems.

Types of management information systems Traditionally, managers used the organisational hierarchy as the main system for gathering the information they needed to co-ordinate and control the organisation, and to make effective decisions. Today, managers use six main types of computer-based information systems. Listed in ascending order of sophistication, they are transaction-processing systems, operations information systems, decision support systems, expert systems, enterprise resource planning systems and e-commerce systems.

Innovation, technological change and competition The high level of technological change in today's world creates new opportunities for managers to market new products, but can destroy the market for older products. Rapid technological change and changing fads and fashions can shorten product life cycles. The shorter a product life cycle is, the greater the importance of product development as a competitive weapon.

Entrepreneurship Entrepreneurship is the mobilisation of resources to take advantage of an opportunity to provide customers with new or improved goods and services. Entrepreneurs find new ventures of their own. Intrapreneurs work inside organisations and manage the product development process. Organisations need to encourage intrapreneurship because it leads to organisational learning and innovation.

Topic for Action

- Ask a manager to describe the main kinds of IT that he or she uses on a routine basis at work.
- Ask any manager you know what the policy for innovation is within their organisation.

Applied Independent Learning

Building Management Skills

Analysing Management Information Systems

Pick an organisation about which you have some direct knowledge. It may be an organisation that you worked for in the past or are in contact with now (such as the college or school that you attend). For this organisation, do the following:

1. Describe the MISs that are used to co-ordinate and control organisational activities and to help make decisions.

2. Do you think that the organisation's existing MISs provide managers with high-quality, timely, relevant and relatively complete information? Why or why not?

3. How might advanced IT be used to improve the competitive position of this organisation? In particular, try to identify the impact that a new MIS might have on the organisation's efficiency, quality, innovation and responsiveness to customers.

Managing Ethically

The use of MISs, such as ERPs, often gives employees access to confidential information from all functions and levels of an organisation. Employees have access to important information about the company's products that is of great value to competitors. As a result, many companies monitor employees' use of the intranet and Internet to prevent an employee from acting unethically – for example, by selling this information to competitors. On the other hand, with access to this information employees might discover that their company has been engaging in unethical or even illegal practices.

Questions

1. Ethically speaking, how far should a company go to protect its proprietary information, given that it needs to also protect the privacy of its employees? What steps can it take?

2. When is it ethical for employees to give information about a company's unethical or illegal practices to a third party such as a newspaper or government agency?

Small Group Breakout Exercise

Using New Management Information Systems

Form groups of three or four people, and appoint one member as the spokesperson who will communicate your findings to the whole class when called on by the instructor. Then discuss the following scenario.

You are a team of managing partners of a large management consultancy company. You are responsible for auditing your firm's MISs to determine whether they are appropriate and up to date. To your surprise, you find that although your organisation does have a wireless email system in place and consultants are connected into a powerful local area network (LAN) at all times, most of the consultants (including partners) are not using this technology. It seems that most important decision making still takes place through the organisational hierarchy.

Given this situation, you are concerned that your organisation is not exploiting the opportunities offered by new IT to obtain a competitive advantage. You have discussed this issue and are meeting to develop an action plan to get consultants to appreciate the need to learn and use the new IT.

1. What advantages can you tell consultants they will obtain when they use the new IT?
2. What problems do you think you may encounter in convincing consultants to use the new IT?
3. What kind of steps might you take to motivate consultants to learn to use the new technology?

Exploring the World Wide Web

Go to IBM's website (www.ibm.com), and under the 'services' tab click 'On Demand'. Read about the latest developments in IBM's on-demand business and look at the case studies. Then answer the following questions:

1. What are the main ways in which IBM's on-demand IT can help companies?
2. In what ways can IBM's IT help improve performance?

Application in Today's Business World

Exploiting Google for Entrepreneurial Success

In the US, ground zero of modern capitalism, it is almost an article of faith: Europeans have grown risk-averse and lack entrepreneurial zeal. But don't tell that to the thousands of folks who use eBay Inc. to do an end run around decades of state-imposed regulations and old ways of thinking. One of them is German businessman Norbert Otto, who recalls the exact moment he realised that selling ski gear over eBay had become far more than a hobby for him.

When Otto printed out his checking account statement at a local bank's automated teller machine (ATM), the statement had so many pages that the branch manager scolded Otto for

▶ tying up the ATM for so long. Soon after, Otto opened a commercial account for Sport Otto, his online business, which in 2005 sold $1.8 million worth of skates, skis, snowboards and other sporting goods exclusively over eBay.

Not bad for an operation that began in 2003 as a way for Otto's son to earn extra cash. Today, Sport Otto has 25 part-time employees, a large truck to haul merchandise from Dutch ports and operations that occupy much of Rabenkirchen, a hamlet of just 60 inhabitants two hours north of Hamburg. In this region close to Denmark, where old-timers speak a dialect incomprehensible to outsiders and unemployment is 12 per cent, Sport Otto is one of the few local employers creating new jobs. 'We're very thankful that this online platform exists,' says Otto, 58, a sports instructor by profession who manages the business with his 20-year-old son, Jan. 'In this region, it's the only chance we have.'

The Ottos' small but thriving operation provides a window into one of Europe's fastest-growing entrepreneurial sectors: the eBay store. According to a survey by ACNielsen International Research, the Ottos are among 64,000 Germans who earn at least 25 per cent of their income from eBay, selling all manner of collectibles, furniture, electronics and more. Germans snatched up $6 billion in merchandise on eBay in 2004, the most recent year for which such data are available.

Germany's eBay market is second only to the US. A decade of slow growth and stagnant wages have turned Europe's largest economy into a nation of bargain hunters, with 20 million registered eBay users. That's close to 25 per cent of the population, a greater share than in any other country in which eBay operates. With eBay gaining momentum, its success in Germany could portend a similar boom in France, Italy and elsewhere in Europe.

In red-tape-bound Germany, starting an eBay business is a relative snip for anyone with broadband and inventory and shipping software, which is readily available for a few thousand dollars. Logistics companies such as the German Post Office Deutsche Post offer services tailored to small e-commerce operations. Compare that with the difficulties of finding startup financing in a country where banks are reluctant to lend and relatively few people own houses that can serve as collateral. Even those who scrape together funds are constrained by myriad regulations: shops, for instance, must close on Sundays and by 8 p.m. on weekdays.

Giant Customer

Some experienced businesspeople see eBay as a growth opportunity in an otherwise slack economy. In 2003, Sven Asböck and Frank Hoffmann, who had worked for a mail-order company that went bankrupt, launched DTG Dynamic-Trade in Neumünster, an hour north of Hamburg. The business snatches up all sorts of surplus merchandise, then sells the stuff on eBay. Sales have doubled every year, to $6 million in 2005, and the company employs 22 full-time workers. 'We sell everything you can imagine,' says Asböck. No kidding: Current offerings include bedroom sets, toasters and telescopic rifle sights.

The business of supporting German e-merchants has also grown into a thriving industry. More package deliveries are generated by eBay for Deutsche Post and its DHL unit than the biggest catalogue retailers. One customer is Bielefeld-based SE.LL Marketing, which helps customers such as toy train maker Brio unload excess merchandise on eBay. SE.LL rarely even sees the goods it auctions off, having outsourced the warehousing, packing and shipping to DHL. 'We want to focus on services. Fulfilment is not our core business,' says SE.LL co-founder Christof Sander, 29, a former manager at German media company Bertelsmann.

In Rabenkirchen, eBay – combined with the easy availability of logistics services and software – has created a hotbed of e-commerce. For two decades Otto coached basketball, track and other sports at municipal sports clubs and ran a ski shop on the side. But then the financially strapped local government cut his hours in half and a recession devastated his shop's sales. In 2002, when son Jan, then 17, asked for money for driving lessons, Norbert told him he would have to earn it by selling off some of the ski shop's excess inventory. The skis sold quickly on eBay – at twice their wholesale price.

Soon Jan found himself behind the wheel of a battered blue cargo van, ferrying Chinese-made parkas and plastic sleds from the port of Rotterdam. Sport Otto began hiring staff, using part-timers to avoid paying health and pension contributions that can nearly equal an employee's take-home pay. The fledgling company also took over a cluster of small buildings in Rabenkirchen that had been vacant ever since the former tenant, a construction company, shut down.

Buying a Benz

At first glance, the Ottos don't appear to run an especially tight ship. Swim goggles, baseball bats and mosquito nets are arranged haphazardly on wooden shelves. Yet every item is bar-coded and scanned. From a desk equipped with two flat screens and littered with wholesale sporting goods catalogues, Jan knows when to redeploy snowboarding trousers from the barn to the packing shed. As customers bid, software tallies the average price and profit on each sale.

The business hasn't made the Ottos rich. Their one luxury is a Mercedes-Benz SUV. Jan lives in the same building used to pack orders, while Norbert occupies a modest apartment above Sport Otto's offices. Both start work at 7 a.m. and often don't finish until late in the evening. They dream of building a modern, computer-driven warehouse and buying products directly from Asian suppliers. For now, Norbert says, 'we're investing everything back into the business'. Spoken like a true entrepreneur.

Question

1. What are the benefits for budding entrepreneurs of trading via Ebay?

Source: Jack Ewing, 'e-Bay's Rhine Gold', adapted and reprinted from *BusinessWeek*, April 3, 2006 by special permission. Copyright © 2006 by the McGraw-Hill Companies, Inc.

Notes and References

1 www.ibm.com.

2 N. B. Macintosh, *The Social Software of Accounting Information Systems* (New York: Wiley, 1995).

3 E. Turban, *Decision Support and Expert Systems* (New York: Macmillan, 1988).

4 R. I. Benjamin and J. Blunt, 'Critical IT Issues: The Next Ten Years', *Sloan Management Review* (Summer 1992), 7–19; W. H. Davidow and M. S. Malone, *The Virtual Corporation* (New York: HarperBusiness, 1992).

5 Davidow and Malone, *The Virtual Corporation*; M. E. Porter, *Competitive Advantage* (New York: Free Press, 1984).

6 http://www.elisa.com/.

7 http://press.nokia.com/PR.

8 http://www.tekes.fi/eng/news/uutis_tiedot.asp?id=111.

9 www.opengroup.org.

10 www.intel.com.

11 J. J. Donovan, *Business Reengineering with IT* (Englewood Cliffs, NJ: Prentice Hall, 1994); C. W. L. Hill, 'The Computer Industry: The New Industry of Industries', in C. W. L. Hill and G. R. Jones, *Strategic Management: An Integrated Approach*, 3rd ed. (Boston: Houghton Mifflin, 1995).

12 http://www.galaxyphones.co.uk/mobile_phone_communications.asp.

13 *Ibid.*

14 www.nokia.com.

15 E. Rich, *Artificial Intelligence* (New York: McGraw-Hill, 1983).

16 R. Brandt, 'Agents and Artificial Life', *BusinessWeek: The Information Revolution*, special issue, 1994, 64–68.

17 www.ibm.com.

18 A. D. Chandler, *The Visible Hand* (Cambridge, MA: Harvard University Press, 1977).

19 C. W. L. Hill and J. F. Pickering, 'Divisionalization, Decentralization, and Performance of Large United Kingdom Companies', *Journal of Management Studies* 23 (1986), 26–50.

20 O. E. Williamson, *Markets and Hierarchies: Analysis and Antitrust Implications* (New York: Free Press, 1975).

21 C. W. L. Hill, 'Airborne Express', in C. W. L. Hill and G. R. Jones, *Strategic Management: An Integrated Approach*, 5th ed. (Boston: Houghton-Mifflin, 2004).

22 Turban, *Decision Support and Expert Systems.*

23 http://www.merck.de.

24 *Ibid.*

25 www.merck.com.

26 N. A. Nichols, 'Scientific Management at Merck: An Interview with CFO Judy Lewent', *Harvard Business Review* (January–February 1994), 88–91.

27 Turban, *Decision Support and Expert Systems.*

28 *Ibid.*

29 Rich, *Artificial Intelligence.*

30 P. P. Bonisson and H. E. Johnson, 'Expert Systems for Diesel Electric Locomotive Repair', *Human Systems Management* 4 (1985), 1–25.

31 G. R. Jones, 'SAP and the Enterprise Resource Planning Industry', in C. W. L. Hill and G. R. Jones, *Strategic Management: An Integrated Approach*, 6th ed. (Boston: Houghton Mifflin, 2003).

32 R. D'Aveni, *Hyper-Competition* (New York: Free Press, 1994); P. Anderson and M. L. Tushman, 'Technological Discontinuities and Dominant Design: A Cyclical Model of Technological Change', *Administrative Science Quarterly* 35 (1990), 604–33.

33 www.intel.com.

34 J. A. Schumpeter, *Capitalism, Socialism and Democracy* (New York: Harper, 1942).

35 David Smith 'Bookshops Fall Prey to Online Sale', *The Observer*, 7 May 2006.

36 V. P. Buell, *Marketing Management* (New York: McGraw-Hill, 1985).

37 M. M. J. Berry and J. H. Taggart, 'Managing Technology and Innovation: A Review', *R & D Management* 24 (1994), 341–53; K. B. Clark and S. C. Wheelwright, *Managing New Product and Process Development* (New York: Free Press, 1993).

38 E. Abrahamson, 'Managerial Fads and Fashions: The Diffusion and Rejection of Innovations', *Academy of Management Review* 16 (1991), 586–612.

39 Clark and Wheelwright, *Managing New Product and Process Development*. See also G. Stalk and T. M. Hout, *Competing Against Time* (New York: Free Press, 1990).

40 www.intel.com.

41 'Intel Chip Hits 2 Gigahertz Milestone', yahoo.com.

42 C. Edwards, 'This Is Not the Intel We All Know', *BusinessWeek Online*, August 6, 2004.

43   T. Lonier, 'Some Insights and Statistics on Working Solo', www.workingsolo.com.
44   http://www.thebodyshopinternational.com.
45   http://www.amstrad.com.
46   http://www.biogs.com.
47   http://www.lambostuff.com; http://www.lamborghini.com; www.lambocars.com.

360-degree performance appraisal A performance appraisal by peers, subordinates, superiors and sometimes clients who are in a position to evaluate a manager's performance.

A

accommodative approach Companies and their managers behave legally and ethically and try to balance the interests of different stakeholders as the need arises.

achievement orientation A worldview that values assertiveness, performance, success and competition.

adaptive culture Socially transmitted behaviour patterns, beliefs and artefacts that change or adapt according to the changing environment.

administrative decision-making model An approach to decision making that explains why it is inherently uncertain and risky, and why managers usually make satisfactory rather than optimum, decisions.

administrative management The study of how to create an organisational structure that leads to high efficiency and effectiveness.

agreeableness The tendency to get along well with other people.

Alderfer's ERG theory The theory that three universal needs – existence, relatedness and growth – constitute a hierarchy of needs and motivate behaviour. Alderfer proposed that needs at more than one level can be motivational at the same time.

ambiguous information Information that can be interpreted in multiple and often conflicting ways.

applications software Software designed for a specific task or use.

arbitrator A third-party negotiator who can impose what he or she thinks is a fair solution to a conflict by which both parties are obligated to abide.

artificial intelligence Behaviour performed by a machine that, if performed by a human being, would be called 'intelligent'.

attitude A collection of feelings and beliefs.

attraction–selection–attrition (ASA) framework A model that explains how personality may influence organisational culture.

authority The power to hold people accountable for their actions and to make decisions concerning the use of organisational resources.

B

B2B marketplace An Internet-based trading platform set up to connect buyers and sellers in an industry.

barriers to entry Factors that make it difficult and costly for an organisation to enter a particular task environment or industry.

behaviour control The perception of how behaviour is controlled by either internal or external forces (theory of planned behaviour, Ajzen 1991).

behavioural management The study of how managers should behave to motivate employees and encourage them to perform at high levels and be committed to the achievement of organisational goals. Mary Parker Follett, an early management thinker advocated that 'Authority should go with knowledge . . . whether it is up the line or down'.

benchmarking The process of comparing one company's performance on specific dimensions with the performance of other, high-performing organisations.

bias The systematic tendency to use information about others in ways that result in inaccurate perceptions.

'bottom-up change' A gradual or evolutionary approach to change in which managers at all levels work together to develop a detailed plan for change.

boundary spanning Interacting with individuals and groups outside the organisation to obtain valuable information from the environment.

boundaryless organisation An organisation whose members are linked by computers, faxes, computer-aided design (CAD) systems and video teleconferencing and who rarely, if ever, see one another face to face.

bounded rationality Cognitive limitations that constrain one's ability to interpret, process and act on information.

brainstorming A problem-solving technique that involves creating a list that includes a wide variety of related ideas.

brand loyalty Customers' preference for the products of organisations currently existing in the task environment.

bureaucracy A formal system of organisation and administration designed to ensure efficiency and effectiveness.

bureaucratic control Control of behaviour by means of a comprehensive system of rules and standard operating procedures.

business-level plan Divisional managers' decisions pertaining to divisions' long-term goals, overall strategy and structure.

business-level strategy A plan that indicates how a division intends to compete against its rivals in an industry.

business-to-business (B2B) commerce Trade that takes place between companies using IT and the Internet to link and co-ordinate the value chains of different companies.

business-to-business (B2B) network A group of organisations that join together and use IT to link themselves to potential global suppliers to increase efficiency and effectiveness.

business-to-customer (B2C) commerce Business transactions directly from a manufacturer or service provider to the customer via the use of the Internet.

C

cafeteria-style benefit plan A plan from which employees can choose the benefits that they want.

centralisation The concentration of authority at the senior of the managerial hierarchy.

CEO Chief executive officer.

CFO Chief financial officer.

charismatic leader An enthusiastic, self-confident leader who is able to clearly communicate his or her vision of how good things could be.

clan control The control exerted on individuals and groups in an organisation by shared values, norms, standards of behaviour and expectations.

classical decision-making model A prescriptive approach to decision making based on the assumption that the decision maker can identify and evaluate all possible alternatives and their consequences and rationally choose the most appropriate course of action.

closed system A system that is self-contained and thus not affected by changes occurring in its external environment.

coercive power The ability of a manager to punish others.

cognitive bias Preference or inclination towards thinking, reasoning and judging through knowledge.

collective bargaining Negotiations between labour unions and managers to resolve conflicts and disputes about issues such as working hours, wages, benefits, working conditions and job security.

collectivism A worldview that values subordination of the individual to the goals of the group and adherence to the principle that people should be judged by their contribution to the group.

command group A group composed of subordinates who report to the same supervisor; also called department or unit.

communication The sharing of information between two or more individuals or groups to reach a common understanding.

communication networks The pathways along which information flows in groups and teams and throughout the organisation.

community A group of people either living in the same locality and/or a collection of people sharing common interests.

competencies The specific set of skills, abilities and experiences that allows one manager to perform at a higher level than another in a particular setting.

competitive advantage The ability of one organisation to outperform other organisations because it produces desired goods or services more efficiently and effectively than they do.

competitors Organisations that produce goods and services that are similar to a particular organisation's goods and services.

conceptual skills The ability to analyse and diagnose a situation and to distinguish between cause and effect.

conceptual tools A structured, model-based way of proceeding to improve the problem-solving or decision-making process. In any given context, conceptual tools achieve this by providing thought structures, action steps and representation formats to facilitate convergent (analytical) or divergent (creative) thinking.

concurrent control Control that gives managers immediate feedback on how efficiently inputs are being transformed into outputs so that managers can correct problems as they arise.

concurrent engineering The simultaneous design of the product and of the process for manufacturing the product.

conscientiousness The tendency to be careful, scrupulous and persevering.

consideration Behaviour indicating that a manager

trusts, respects and cares about subordinates.

contingency theory The idea that the organisational structures and control systems managers choose depend on – are contingent on – characteristics of the external environment in which the organisation operates.

continuous-process technology Technology that is almost totally mechanised and is based on the use of automated machines working in sequence and controlled through computers from a central monitoring station.

contract book A written agreement that details product development factors such as responsibilities, resource commitments, budgets, time lines and development milestones.

control systems Formal target-setting, monitoring, evaluation and feedback systems that provide managers with information about how well the organisation's strategy and structure are working.

controlling Evaluating how well an organisation is achieving its goals and taking action to maintain or improve performance; one of the four principal functions of management.

COO Chief operations officer.

core members The members of a team who bear primary responsibility for the success of a project and who stay with a project from inception to completion.

corporate-level plan Senior management's decisions pertaining to the organisation's mission, overall strategy and structure.

corporate-level strategy A plan that indicates in which industries and national markets an organisation intends to compete.

corporate social responsibility An ethical position describing a company's obligation to be sensitive to the needs of everyone in its business operations and its environment.

cost–benefit analysis Weighing up what a new system will cost, i.e. time out, training, loss of production, for example, versus the ultimate benefits to production and the organisation, profits, people etc.

creativity A decision maker's ability to discover original and novel ideas that lead to feasible alternative courses of action.

cross-functional team A group of managers brought together from different departments to perform organisational tasks.

current ratio The arithmetic ratio of current assets to liabilities.

customers Individuals and groups that buy the goods and services that an organisation produces.

D

data Raw, unsummarized and unanalysed facts.

days sales outstanding (DSO) Keeping track of an organisation's outstanding money.

decision making The process by which managers respond to opportunities and threats by analysing options and making determinations about specific organisational goals and courses of action.

decision support system An interactive computer-based management information system that managers can use to make non-routine decisions.

decoding Interpreting and trying to make sense of a message.

defensive approach Companies and their managers behave ethically to the degree that they stay within the law and abide strictly with legal requirements.

Delphi technique A decision-making technique in which group members do not meet face-to-face but respond in writing to questions posed by the group leader.

demographic forces Outcomes of changes in, or changing attitudes toward, the characteristics of a population, such as age, gender, ethnic origin, race, sexual orientation and social class.

department A group of people who work together and possess similar skills or use the same knowledge, tools or techniques to perform their jobs.

development Building the knowledge and skills of organisational members so that they will be prepared to take on new responsibilities and challenges.

developmental consideration Behaviour a leader engages in to support and encourage followers and help them develop and grow on the job.

devil's advocacy Critical analysis of a preferred alternative, made in response to challenges raised by a group member who, playing the role of devil's advocate, defends unpopular or opposing alternatives for the sake of argument.

dialectical inquiry Critical analysis of two preferred alternatives in order to find an even better alternative for the organisation to adopt.

differentiation strategy Distinguishing an organisation's products from the products of competitors on dimensions such as product design, quality or after-sales service.

discipline Obedience, energy, application and other outward marks of respect for a superior's authority.

disseminator Someone who widely scatters or spreads ideas, beliefs, knowledge, etc.

distributive justice A moral principle calling for the distribution of pay rises, promotions and other organisational resources to be based on meaningful contributions that individuals have made and not on personal characteristics over which they have no control.

distributive negotiation Adversarial negotiation in which the parties in conflict compete to win the most resources while conceding as little as possible.

distributors Organisations that help other organisations sell their goods or services to customers.

disturbance handler Someone who is responsible for corrective action when the organisation faces unexpected threats or disturbances.

diversification Expanding operations into a new business or industry and producing new goods or services.

diversity Differences among people in age, gender, race, ethnicity, religion, sexual orientation, socio-economic background and capabilities/disabilities.

division A business unit that has its own set of managers and functions or departments and competes in a distinct industry.

division of labour Splitting the work to be performed into particular tasks and assigning tasks to individual workers.

divisional managers Managers who control the various divisions of an organisation.

divisional structure An organisational structure composed of separate business units within which are the functions that work together to produce a specific product for a specific customer.

DMAIC Define, measure, analyse, improve and control. Data-driven quality strategy to improve processes which is part of a Six Sigma approach to quality.

E

e-commerce Trade that takes place between companies, and between companies and individual customers, using IT and the Internet.

economic forces Interest rates, inflation, unemployment, economic growth and other factors that affect the general health and well-being of a nation or the regional economy of an organisation.

economies of scale Cost advantages associated with large operations.

effectiveness A measure of the appropriateness of the goals an organisation is pursuing, and of the degree to which the organisation achieves those goals.

efficiency A measure of how well or how productively resources are used to achieve a goal.

EFQM model A non-prescriptive, practical quality model aiming to improve all aspects of an organisation in order to achieve excellence.

emergent property Can appear when a number of simple entities or agents operate in an environment, forming more complex behaviours as a collective.

emotional intelligence The ability to understand and manage one's own moods and emotions, and the moods and emotions of other people.

emotions Intense, relatively short-lived feelings.

employee stock ownership plan (ESOP) A financial instrument that entitles the bearer to buy shares of an organisation's stock at a certain price during a certain period of time or under certain conditions.

empowerment The expansion of employees' knowledge, tasks and responsibilities.

encoding Translating a message into understandable symbols or language.

enterprise resource planning (ERP) systems Multi-module application software packages that co-ordinate the functional activities necessary to move products from the product design stage to the final customer stage.

entrepreneur An individual who notices opportunities and takes responsibility for mobilising the resources necessary to produce new and improved goods and services.

entrepreneurship The mobilisation of resources to take advantage of an opportunity to provide customers with new or improved goods and services.

entropy The tendency of a closed system to lose its ability to control itself, and thus to dissolve and disintegrate.

equal employment opportunity The equal right of all citizens to the opportunity to obtain employment regardless of their gender, age, race, country of origin, religion or disabilities.

equity The justice, impartiality and fairness to which all organisational members are entitled.

equity theory A theory of motivation that focuses

on people's perceptions of the fairness of their work outcomes relative to their work inputs.

escalating commitment A source of cognitive bias resulting from the tendency to commit additional resources to a project even if evidence shows that the project is failing.

esprit de corps Shared feelings of comradeship, enthusiasm or devotion to a common cause among members of a group.

ethical dilemma The quandary people find themselves in when they have to decide if they should act in a way that might help another person or group, even though doing so might go against their own self-interest.

ethics The inner-guiding moral principles, values and beliefs that people use to analyse or interpret a situation and then decide what is the 'right' or appropriate way to behave.

ethics ombudsman A manager responsible for communicating and teaching ethical standards to all employees and monitoring their conformity to those standards.

ethnicity The condition of belonging to a particular ethnic group.

EU-25 Refers to the number of member states of the European Union.

executive support system A sophisticated version of a decision support system that is designed to meet the needs of senior managers.

expectancy In expectancy theory, a perception about the extent to which effort results in a certain level of performance.

expectancy theory The theory that motivation will be high when workers believe that high levels of effort lead to high performance and high performance leads to the attainment of desired outcomes.

expert power Power that is based on the special knowledge, skills and expertise that a leader possesses.

expert system A management information system (MIS) that employs human knowledge, embedded in a computer, to solve problems that ordinarily require human expertise.

exporting Making products at home and selling them abroad.

external locus of control The tendency to locate responsibility for one's fate in outside forces and to believe that one's own behaviour has little impact on outcomes.

extinction Curtailing the performance of dysfunctional behaviours by eliminating whatever is reinforcing them.

extraversion The tendency to experience positive emotions and moods and to feel good about oneself and the rest of the world.

extrinsically motivated behaviour Behaviour that is performed to acquire material or social rewards or to avoid punishment.

F

facilities layout The process of designing the machine–worker interface to increase operating system efficiency.

feedback The return of information about the result of a process or activity; an evaluative response.

feedback control Control that gives managers information about customers' reactions to goods and services so that corrective action can be taken if necessary.

feedback mechanisms Ways of maintaining a steady state (homeostasis) in systems and people. A feedback mechanism occurs when the level of one substance influences the level of another substance or activity of another system.

feedforward control Control that allows managers to anticipate problems before they arise.

Fiedler's contingency model In this model, leadership is effective when the leader's style is appropriate to the situation, as determined by three principal factors: leader–membership relationship, task structure and position power.

figurehead A person who is given a position of nominal leadership but having no actual authority.

filtering Withholding part of a message because of the mistaken belief that the receiver does not need, or will not want, the information.

financial measures of performance Simple mechanisms of objectively explaining how a business or investment is doing. Often used because they are easily calculated and can be used to compare year-on-year results.

first-line manager A manager who is responsible for the daily supervision of nonmanagerial employees.

five forces model A strategic framework developed by Michael Porter (1979) to determine the attractiveness of a market or the competitive advantage of a company.

flexible manufacturing The set of techniques that attempts to reduce the costs associated with an operating system.

focused differentiation strategy Serving only one segment of the overall market and trying to be the most differentiated organisation serving that segment.

focused low-cost strategy Serving only one segment of the overall market and being the lowest-cost organisation serving that segment.

folkways The routine social conventions of everyday life.

Fordism The application of scientific management principles to workers' jobs; installation of bespoke machines to manufacture standardised parts; and the introduction of making cars through a mechanised assembly line (e.g. mass production).

formal appraisal An appraisal conducted at a set time during the year and based on performance dimensions and measures that were specified in advance.

formal group A group that managers establish to achieve organisational goals.

franchising Selling to a foreign organisation the rights to use a brand name and operating know-how in return for a lump-sum payment and a share of the profits.

free-trade doctrine The idea that if each country specialises in the production of the goods and services that it can produce most efficiently, this will make the best use of global resources.

friendship group An informal group composed of employees who enjoy one another's company and socialise with one another.

function A unit or department in which people have the same skills or use the same resources to perform their jobs.

functional-level plan Functional managers' decisions pertaining to the goals that they propose to pursue to help the division attain its business-level goals.

functional-level strategy A plan that indicates how a function intends to achieve its goals.

functional managers Managers who supervise the various functions, such as manufacturing, accounting and sales, within a division.

functional structure An organisational structure composed of all the departments that an organisation requires to produce its goods or services.

G

gatekeeping Deciding what information to allow into the organisation and what information to keep out.

gender schemas Preconceived beliefs or ideas about the nature of men and women, their traits, attitudes, behaviours and preferences.

general environment The wide-ranging economic, technological, socio-cultural, demographic, political and legal and global forces that affect an organisation and its task environment.

geographic structure An organisational structure in which each region of a country or area of the world is served by a self-contained division.

glass ceiling A metaphor alluding to the invisible barriers that prevent minorities and women from being promoted to top corporate positions.

global forces Outcomes of changes in international relationships, changes in nations' economic, political and legal systems and changes in technology, such as falling trade barriers, the growth of representative democracies and reliable and instantaneous communication.

global organisation An organisation that operates and competes in more than one country.

global outsourcing The purchase of inputs from foreign suppliers or the production of inputs abroad to lower production costs and improve product quality or design.

global strategy Selling the same standardised product and using the same basic marketing approach in each national market.

goal-setting theory A theory that focuses on identifying the types of goals that are most effective in producing high levels of motivation and performance, and explaining why goals have these effects.

grapevine An informal communication network along which unofficial information flows.

gross profit margin What remains from sales after a company pays out the cost of goods sold. To obtain gross profit margin, divide gross profit by sales. Gross profit margin is expressed as a percentage.

group Two or more people who interact with each other to accomplish certain goals or meet certain needs.

group cohesiveness The degree to which members are attracted to or loyal to their group.

group decision support system An executive support system that links senior managers so that they can function as a team.

group norms Shared guidelines or rules for behaviour that most group members follow.

group role A set of behaviours and tasks that a member of a group is expected to perform because of his or her position in the group.

groupthink A pattern of faulty and biased decision making that occurs in groups whose members strive for agreement among themselves at the expense of accurately assessing information relevant to a decision.

groupware Computer software that enables members of groups and teams to share information with one another.

H

Hawthorne effect The finding that a manager's behaviour or leadership approach can affect workers' level of performance.

Herzberg's motivator–hygiene theory A need theory that distinguishes between motivator needs (related to the nature of the work itself) and hygiene needs (related to the physical and psychological context in which the work is performed) and proposes that motivator needs must be met for motivation and job satisfaction to be high.

heuristics Rules of thumb that simplify decision making.

hierarchy of authority An organisation's chain of command, specifying the relative authority of each manager.

horizontal integration When a company expands its business into products that are similar to its current offerings.

hostile work environment sexual harassment Telling lewd jokes, displaying pornography, making sexually oriented remarks about someone's personal appearance and other sex-related actions that make the work environment unpleasant.

human relations movement Initiated by Carl Rogers and refers to those researchers of organizational development who study the behaviour of people in groups, in particular workplace groups. Examines the effects of social relations, motivation and employee satisfaction on factory productivity.

human resource (HR) planning Activities that managers engage in to forecast their current and future needs for human resources (HR).

human resources (HR) The field of personnel recruitment and selection within a company.

human resources management (HRM) Activities that managers engage in to attract and retain employees and to ensure that they perform at a high level and contribute to the accomplishment of organisational goals.

human skills The ability to understand, alter, lead and control the behaviour of other individuals and groups.

hybrid structure The structure of a large organisation that has many divisions and simultaneously uses many different organisational structures.

I

illusion of control A source of cognitive bias resulting from the tendency to over-estimate one's own ability to control activities and events.

importing Selling at home products that are made abroad.

incomplete information Lacking an essential element or piece of data/knowledge.

incremental product innovations Products that result from incremental technological changes.

incremental technological change Change that refines existing technology and leads to gradual improvements or refinements in products over time.

individual ethics Personal standards and values that determine how people view their responsibilities to others, and how they should act in situations when their own self-interest is at stake.

individualism A worldview that values individual freedom and self-expression and adherence to the principle that people should be judged by their individual achievements, rather than by their social background.

inequity Lack of fairness.

inert culture Behavioural patterns or beliefs that are static and do not change with the environment.

informal appraisal An unscheduled appraisal of ongoing progress and areas for improvement.

informal authority The degree of influence that managers may have that has no written formal definition.

informal group A group that managers or non-managerial employees form to help achieve their own goals or meet their own needs.

informal organisation The system of behavioural rules and norms that emerge in a group.

information Data that are organised in a meaningful fashion.

information distortion Changes in the meaning of a message as the message passes through a series of senders and receivers.

information overload The potential for important information to be ignored or overlooked while tangential information receives attention.

information richness The amount of information that a communication medium can carry and the extent to which the medium enables the sender and receiver to reach a common understanding.

information system function Organisational function dealing with all the IT requirements of an organisation, including hardware, software, knowledge management systems, etc.

information technology (IT) The set of methods or techniques for acquiring, organising, storing, manipulating and transmitting information.

initiating structure Behaviour that managers engage in to ensure that work gets done, subordinates perform their jobs acceptably and the organisation is efficient and effective.

initiative The ability to act on one's own, without direction from a superior.

input Anything a person contributes to his or her job or organisation.

instrumental value A mode of conduct that an individual seeks to follow.

instrumentality In expectancy theory, a perception about the extent to which performance results in the attainment of outcomes.

integrating mechanisms Organising tools that managers can use to increase communication and co-ordination among functions and divisions.

integrating role To bring together different qualities/abilities into one role or towards a common goal.

integrative bargaining Co-operative negotiation in which the parties in conflict work together to achieve a resolution that is good for them both.

intellectual stimulation Behaviour a leader engages in to make followers be aware of problems and view these problems in new ways, consistent with the leader's vision.

interest group An informal group composed of employees seeking to achieve a common goal related to their membership in an organisation.

internal locus of control The tendency to locate responsibility for one's fate within oneself.

Internet A global system of computer networks.

intranet A companywide system of computer networks.

intrapreneur A manager, scientist or researcher who works inside an existing organisation, notices opportunities for product improvements and is responsible for managing the product development process.

intrinsically motivated behaviour Behaviour that is performed for its own sake.

intuition Feelings, beliefs and hunches that come readily to mind, require little effort and information gathering and result in on-the-spot decisions.

inventory The stock of raw materials, inputs and component parts that an organisation has on hand at a particular time.

inventory turnover Equation that equals the cost of goods sold divided by the average inventory.

J

jargon Specialised language that members of an occupation, group or organisation develop to facilitate communication among themselves.

job analysis Identifying the tasks, duties and responsibilities that make up a job and the knowledge, skills and abilities needed to perform it.

job characteristics model Framework developed by Hackman and Oldham in the late 1970s for work redesign. The three stages are: core dimensions, psychological states and outcomes.

job design The process by which managers decide how to divide tasks into specific jobs.

job enlargement Increasing the number of different tasks in a given job by changing the division of labour.

job enrichment Increasing the degree of responsibility a worker has over his or her job.

job satisfaction The collection of feelings and beliefs that managers have about their current jobs.

job simplification The process of reducing the number of tasks that each worker performs.

job specialisation The process by which a division of labour occurs as different workers specialise in different tasks over time.

joint venture (JV) A strategic alliance among two or more companies that agree to jointly establish and share the ownership of a new business.

just-in-time (JIT) inventory system A system in which parts or supplies arrive at an organisation when they are needed, not before.

justice rule An ethical decision is a decision that distributes benefits and harms among people and groups in a fair, equitable, or impartial way.

K

knowledge management The sharing and integrating of expertise within and between functions and divisions through real-time, interconnected IT.

knowledge management system A company-specific virtual information system that allows workers to share their knowledge and expertise and find others to help solve ongoing problems.

L

labour relations The activities that managers engage in to ensure that they have effective working relationships with the labour unions that represent their employees' interests.

lateral move A job change that entails no major changes in responsibility or authority levels.

leader An individual who is able to exert influence over other people to help achieve group or organisational goals.

leader–member relations The extent to which followers like, trust and are loyal to their leader, a determinant of how favourable a situation is for leading.

leader substitutes model Where substitutes for a leader can come from characteristics of subordinates, the work context and/or worker empowerment, all of which reduce the need for a leader.

leadership The process by which an individual exerts influence over other people and inspires, motivates and directs their activities to help achieve group or organisational goals.

leadership substitute A characteristic of a subordinate or characteristic of a situation or context that acts in place of the influence of a leader and makes leadership unnecessary.

leading Articulating a clear vision and energising and enabling organisational members so that they understand the part they play in achieving organisational goals; one of the four principal functions of management.

lean manufacturing Elimination of any waste (time, materials, etc) during production process to reduce cost to a minimum.

learning A relatively permanent change in knowledge or behaviour that results from practice or experience.

learning organisation An organisation in which managers try to maximise the ability of individuals and groups to think

and behave creatively and thus maximise the potential for organisational learning to take place.

learning theories Theories that focus on increasing employee motivation and performance by linking the outcomes that employees receive to the performance of desired behaviours and the attainment of goals.

legitimate power The authority that a manager has by virtue of his or her position in an organisation's hierarchy.

leverage ratio Measures the extent to which an organisation is using long-term debt to assess its long-term solvency.

licensing Allowing a foreign organisation to take charge of manufacturing and distributing a product in its country or world region in return for a negotiated fee.

line manager Someone in the direct line or chain of command who has formal authority over people and resources lower down.

line of authority Usually represented by an organisation's hierarchy, indicating who has power and responsibilities over others.

linguistic style A person's characteristic way of speaking.

liquidity ratio Measures the extent to which a company can quickly liquidate assets to cover short-term liabilities.

long-term orientation A worldview that values thrift and persistence in achieving goals.

low-cost strategy Driving the organisation's costs down below those of its rivals.

M

management The planning, organising, leading and

controlling of human and other resources to achieve organisational goals efficiently and effectively.

management by objectives (MBO) A goal-setting process in which a manager and each of his or her subordinates negotiates specific goals and objectives for the subordinate to achieve and then periodically evaluates the extent to which the subordinate is achieving those goals.

management by wandering around A face-to-face communication technique in which a manager walks around a work area and talks informally with employees about issues and concerns.

management information system (MIS) A specific form of IT that managers utilise to generate the specific, detailed information they need to perform their roles effectively.

management science theory An approach to management that uses rigorous quantitative techniques to help managers make maximum use of organisational resources.

managerial role The set of specific tasks that a manager is expected to perform because of the position he or she holds in an organisation.

market structure An organisational structure in which each kind of customer is served by a self-contained division; also called customer structure.

marketing/sales function Function of an organisation responsible for assessing markets, advertising and selling products/services.

Maslow's hierarchy of needs An arrangement of five basic needs that, according to Maslow, motivate behaviour. Maslow proposed that the lowest level of unmet needs is the prime motivator and that only one level of needs is motivational at a time.

mass-production manufacturing Production of large amounts of standardised products at an assembly line. Originates from Fordism.

mass-production technology Technology that is based on the use of automated machines that are programmed to perform the same operations over and over again.

materials management function Function responsible for managing the inventory of the organisation.

matrix structure An organisational structure that simultaneously groups people and resources by function and by product.

mechanistic structure An organisational structure in which authority is centralised, tasks and rules are clearly specified and employees are closely supervised.

mediator A third-party negotiator who facilitates negotiations but has no authority to impose a solution.

medium The pathway through which an encoded message is transmitted to a receiver.

mentoring A process by which an experienced member of an organisation (the mentor) provides advice and guidance to a less experienced member (the protégé) and helps the less experienced member learn how to advance in the organisation and in his or her career.

merit pay plan A compensation plan that bases pay on performance.

message The information that a sender wants to share.

middle manager A manager who supervises first-line managers and is responsible for finding

the best way to use resources to achieve organisational goals.

minimum chain of command The number of managers within an organisation to perform all of its function.

mission statement A broad declaration of an organisation's purpose that identifies the organisation's products and customers and distinguishes it from its competitors.

monitor Process of continuously collecting information on performance.

mood A feeling or state of mind.

moral rights rule An ethical decision is one that best maintains and protects the fundamental or inalienable rights and privileges of the people affected by it.

mores Norms that are considered to be central to the functioning of society and to social life.

motivation Psychological forces that determine the direction of a person's behaviour in an organisation, a person's level of effort and a person's level of persistence.

multi-domestic strategy Customising products and marketing strategies to specific national conditions.

N

national culture The set of values that a society considers important and the norms of behaviour that are approved or sanctioned in that society.

need A requirement or necessity for survival and well-being.

need for achievement The extent to which an individual has a strong desire to perform challenging tasks well and to meet personal standards for excellence.

need for affiliation The extent to which an individual is concerned about establishing and maintaining good

interpersonal relations, being liked and having other people get along with each other.

need for power The extent to which an individual desires to control or influence others.

need theories Theories of motivation that focus on what needs people are trying to satisfy at work, and what outcomes will satisfy those needs.

needs assessment An assessment of which employees need training or development and what type of skills or knowledge they need to acquire.

negative affectivity The tendency to experience negative emotions and moods, to feel distressed and to be critical of oneself and others.

negative reinforcement Eliminating or removing undesired outcomes when people perform organisationally functional behaviours.

negotiation A method of conflict resolution in which the two parties in conflict consider various alternative ways to allocate resources to each other in order to come up with a solution acceptable to them both.

negotiator Person who assists the process where interested parties resolve disputes, agree upon courses of action, bargain for individual or collective advantage, and/or attempt to craft outcomes which serve their mutual interests.

network structure A series of strategic alliances that an organisation creates with suppliers, manufacturers and/or distributors to produce and market a product.

networking The exchange of information through a group or network of interlinked computers.

new venture division An autonomous division that is

given all the resources it needs to develop and market a new product.

noise Anything that hampers any stage of the communication process.

nominal group technique A decision-making technique in which group members write down ideas and solutions, read their suggestions to the whole group and discuss and then rank the alternatives.

non-programmed decision making Non-routine decision making that occurs in response to unusual, unpredictable opportunities and threats.

non-verbal communication The encoding of messages by means of facial expressions, body language and styles of dress.

norms Informal rules of conduct for behaviours considered important by most members of a group or organisation. Unwritten rules and codes of conduct that prescribe how people should act in particular situations.

nurturing orientation A worldview that values the quality of life, warm personal friendships and services and care for the weak.

O

objective appraisal An appraisal that is based on facts and is likely to be numerical.

obstructionist approach Companies and their managers choose not to behave in a socially responsible way and behave unethically and illegally.

occupational ethics Standards that govern how members of a profession, trade or craft should conduct themselves when performing work-related activities.

on-the-job training Training that takes place in the work setting as employees perform their job tasks.

open system A system that takes in resources from its external environment and converts them into goods and services that are then sent back to that environment for purchase by customers.

open systems theory Advocates that every system interacts with its environment.

openness to experience The tendency to be original, have broad interests, be open to a wide range of stimuli, be daring and take risks.

operant conditioning theory The theory that people learn to perform behaviours that lead to desired consequences and learn not to perform behaviours that lead to undesired consequences.

operating budget A budget that states how managers intend to use organisational resources to achieve organisational goals.

operating system The different functional activities an organisation combines and uses to acquire inputs, convert inputs into outputs and dispose of the outputs.

operating system software Software that tells computer hardware how to run.

operations information system A management information system (MIS) that gathers, organises and summarises comprehensive data in a form that managers can use in their non-routine co-ordinating, controlling and decision making tasks.

operations management Concerned with the production of goods and services and ensuring the effectiveness and efficiency of this process.

optimum decision The most appropriate decision in the light of what managers believe to be the most desirable future consequences for the organisation.

order The methodical arrangement of positions to provide the organisation with the greatest benefit and to provide employees with career opportunities.

organic structure An organisational structure in which authority is decentralised to middle and first-line managers and tasks and roles are left ambiguous to encourage employees to co-operate and respond quickly to the unexpected.

organisation change The movement of an organisation away from its present state and toward some desired future state to increase its efficiency and effectiveness.

organisational architecture The organisational structure, control systems, culture and human resource management (HRM) systems that together determine how efficiently and effectively organisational resources are used.

organisational behaviour The study of the factors that have an impact on how individuals and groups respond to and act in organisations.

organisational behaviour modification (OB MOD) The systematic application of operant conditioning techniques to promote the performance of organisationally functional behaviours and discourage the performance of dysfunctional behaviours.

organisational citizenship behaviours (OCBs) Behaviours that are not required of organisational members but that contribute to and are necessary for organisational efficiency, effectiveness and gaining a competitive advantage.

organisational commitment The collection of feelings and beliefs that managers have about their organisation as a whole.

organisational conflict The discord that arises when the goals, interests or values of different individuals or groups are incompatible and those individuals or groups block or thwart one another's attempts to achieve their objectives.

organisational culture The set of values, norms, standards of behaviour and common expectations that controls the ways in which individuals and groups in an organisation interact with one another and work to achieve organisational goals.

organisational design The process by which managers make specific organising choices that result in a particular kind of organisational structure.

organisational environment The set of forces and conditions that operate beyond an organisation's boundaries but affect a manager's ability to acquire and utilise resources.

organisational ethics The guiding practices and beliefs through which a particular company and its managers view their responsibility toward their stakeholders.

organisational goals The overall objectives and aims that an organisation tries to achieve.

organisational hierarchy The structure of an organisation and its chain of command.

organisational learning The process through which managers seek to improve

employees' desire and ability to understand and manage the organisation and its task environment.

organisational performance A measure of how efficiently and effectively a manager uses resources to satisfy customers and achieve organisational goals.

organisational politics Activities that managers engage in to increase their power and to use it effectively to achieve their goals and overcome resistance or opposition.

organisational socialisation The process by which newcomers learn an organisation's values and norms and acquire the work behaviours necessary to perform jobs effectively.

organisational structure A formal system of task and reporting relationships that co-ordinates and motivates organisational members so that they work together to achieve organisational goals.

organising Structuring working relationships in a way that allows organisational members to work together to achieve organisational goals; one of the four principal functions of management.

outcome Anything a person gets from a job or organisation.

outsource To use outside suppliers and manufacturers to produce goods and services.

outsourcing Contracting with another company, usually abroad, to have it perform an activity the organisation previously performed itself.

over-payment inequity The inequity that exists when a person perceives that his or her own outcome–input ratio is greater than the ratio of a referent.

overt discrimination Knowingly and willingly denying diverse individuals access to opportunities and outcomes in an organisation.

P

path–goal theory A contingency model of leadership proposing that leaders can motivate subordinates by identifying their desired outcomes, rewarding them for high performance and the attainment of work goals with these desired outcomes and clarifying for them the paths leading to the attainment of work goals.

pay differential Difference in levels of pay, depending on qualification, geography or area of work.

pay level The relative position of an organisation's pay incentives in comparison with those of other organisations in the same industry employing similar kinds of workers.

pay structure The arrangement of jobs into categories reflecting their relative importance to the organisation and its goals, level of skill required and other characteristics.

perception The process through which people select, organise and interpret what they see, hear, touch, smell and taste to give meaning and order to the world around them.

performance appraisal The evaluation of employees' job performance and contributions to their organisation.

performance feedback The process through which managers share performance appraisal information with subordinates, give subordinates an opportunity to reflect on their own performance and develop, with subordinates, plans for the future.

personality traits Enduring tendencies to feel, think and act in certain ways.

planning Identifying and selecting appropriate goals and courses of action; one of the four principal functions of management.

political and legal forces Outcomes of changes in laws and regulations, such as the deregulation of industries, the privatisation of organisations and the increased emphasis on environmental protection.

political strategies Tactics that managers use to increase their power and to use power effectively to influence and gain the support of other people while overcoming resistance or opposition.

pooled task interdependence The task interdependence that exists when group members make separate and independent contributions to group performance.

position power The amount of legitimate, reward and coercive power that a leader has by virtue of his or her position in an organisation; a determinant of how favorable a situation is for leading.

positive reinforcement Giving people outcomes they desire when they perform organisationally functional behaviours.

potential competitors Organisations that presently are not in a task environment but could enter if they so choose.

power distance The degree to which societies accept the idea that inequalities in the power and well-being of their citizens are due to differences in individuals' physical and intellectual capabilities and heritage.

practical rule An ethical decision is one that a manager has no reluctance about communicating to people outside the company because the typical person in a society would think it is acceptable.

prior-hypothesis bias A cognitive bias resulting from the tendency to base decisions on strong prior beliefs, even if evidence shows that those beliefs are wrong.

proactive approach Companies and their managers actively embrace socially responsible behaviour, going out of their way to learn about the needs of different stakeholder groups and utilising organisational resources to promote the interests of all stakeholders.

procedural justice A moral principle calling for the use of fair procedures to determine how to distribute outcomes to organisational members.

process re-engineering The fundamental rethinking and radical redesign of business processes to achieve dramatic improvement in critical measures of performance such as cost, quality, service and speed.

product champion A manager who takes 'ownership' of a project and provides the leadership and vision that take a product from the idea stage to the final customer.

product development plan A plan that specifies all of the relevant information that managers need in order to decide whether to proceed with a full-blown product development effort.

product life cycle Changes in demand for a product that occur from its introduction through its growth and maturity to its decline.

product structure An organisational structure in which each product line or business is handled by a self-contained division.

product team structure An organisational structure in which employees are permanently assigned to a cross-functional team and report only to the product team manager or to one of his or her direct subordinates.

production blocking A loss of productivity in brainstorming sessions due to the unstructured nature of brainstorming.

profit ratio Also referred to as profit margin. Net profit after all expenditures have been paid.

programmed decision making Routine, virtually automatic decision making that follows established rules or guidelines.

punishment Administering an undesired or negative consequence when dysfunctional behaviour occurs.

Q

quality circles (QCs) Groups of employees who meet regularly to discuss ways to increase quality.

quantitative techniques Managerial techniques that use predominantly financial measures to evaluate performance or enhance productivity.

quantum product innovations Products that result from quantum technological changes.

quantum technological change A fundamental shift in technology that results in the innovation of new kinds of goods and services.

quick ratio The ratio expressing an organisation's liquidity and ability to meet all its obligations.

quid pro quo sexual harassment Asking for or forcing an employee to perform sexual favours in exchange for some reward or to avoid negative consequences.

R

real-time information Frequently updated information that reflects current conditions.

realistic job preview An honest assessment of the advantages and disadvantages of a job and organisation.

reasoned judgement A decision that takes time and effort to make and results from careful information gathering, generation of alternatives and evaluation of alternatives.

receiver The person or group for which a message is intended.

reciprocal task interdependence The task interdependence that exists when the work performed by each group member is fully dependent on the work performed by other group members.

recruitment Activities that managers engage in to develop a pool of qualified candidates for open positions.

referent power Power that comes from subordinates' and co-workers' respect, admiration and loyalty.

related diversification Entering a new business or industry to create a competitive advantage in one or more of an organisation's existing divisions or businesses.

relationship-oriented leaders Leaders whose primary concern is to develop good relationships with their subordinates, and to be liked by them.

reliability The degree to which a tool or test measures the same thing each time it is used.

representativeness bias A cognitive bias resulting from the tendency to generalise inappropriately from a small sample or from a single vivid event or episode.

reputation The esteem or high repute that individuals or organisations gain when they behave ethically.

research and development (R&D) team A team whose members have the expertise and experience needed to develop new products.

resource allocator Person within an organisation whose role is to obtain and distribute necessary resources. Also a specific team role that refers to a person able to support a team's activity by locating and distributing resources.

restructuring Downsizing an organisation by eliminating the jobs of large numbers of top, middle and first-line managers and non-managerial employees.

reward power The ability of a manager to give or withhold tangible and intangible rewards.

reward systems Set of organisational procedures and policies outlining how staff are incentivised to increase performance.

risk The degree of probability that the possible outcomes of a particular course of action will occur.

ROI (return on investment) Evaluates an investment by calculating how much profit over time is needed to recuperate the cost of the investment.

role making Taking the initiative to modify an assigned role by assuming additional responsibilities.

rules Formal written instructions that specify actions to be taken under different circumstances to achieve specific goals.

rumours Unofficial pieces of information of interest to organisational members but with no identifiable source.

S

satisficing Searching for and choosing an acceptable, or satisfactory, response to problems and opportunities, rather than trying to make the best decision.

scenario planning The generation of multiple forecasts of future conditions followed by an analysis of how to respond effectively to each of those conditions; also called contingency planning.

schema An abstract knowledge structure that is stored in memory and makes possible the interpretation and organisation of information about a person, event or situation.

scientific management The systematic study of relationships between people and tasks for the purpose of redesigning the work process to increase efficiency.

selection The process that managers use to determine the relative qualifications of job applicants and their potential for performing well in a particular job.

self-efficacy A person's belief about his or her ability to perform a behaviour successfully.

self-esteem The degree to which individuals feel good about themselves and their capabilities.

self-managed team A group of employees who supervises their own activities and monitors the quality of the goods and services they provide.

self-reinforcer Any desired or attractive outcome or reward that a person gives to himself or herself for good performance.

sender The person or group wishing to share information.

senior manager A manager who establishes organisational goals, decides how departments should interact and monitors the performance of middle managers.

senior management team A group composed of the CEO, the president/COO and the heads of the most important departments.

sequential task interdependence The task interdependence that exists when group members must perform specific tasks in a predetermined order.

shareholders Individuals or organisation holding shares in stocks of an organisation and expecting dividends.

short-term orientation A worldview that values personal stability or happiness and living for the present.

Six Sigma Disciplined, data-driven approach for eliminating faults in any process. Methodology to measure quality that aims for near perfection in any process.

skunkworks A group of intrapreneurs who are deliberately separated from the normal operation of an organisation to encourage them to devote all their attention to developing new products.

small-batch production Production process focusing on small numbers of outputs, usually of specialised products.

small-batch technology Technology that is used to produce small quantities of customised, one-of-a-kind products and is based on the skills of people who work together in small groups.

social learning theory A theory that takes into account how learning and motivation are influenced by people's thoughts and beliefs and their observations of other people's behaviour.

social loafing The tendency of individuals to put forth less effort when they work in groups than when they work alone.

social responsibility The way a company's managers and employees view their duty or obligation to make decisions that protect, enhance and promote the welfare and well-being of stakeholders and society as a whole.

social structure The arrangement of relationships between individuals and groups in a society.

societal ethics Standards that govern how members of a society should deal with one another in matters involving issues such as fairness, justice, poverty and the rights of the individual.

socio-cultural forces Pressures emanating from the social structure of a country or society or from the national culture.

socio-economic background Factors such as income, education, ethnicity, culture, etc making up an individual's circumstances.

span of control The number of subordinates who report directly to a manager.

staff manager A manager responsible for managing a specialist function, such as finance or marketing.

stage-gate development funnel A planning model that forces managers to make choices among competing projects so that organisational resources are not spread thinly over too many projects.

stakeholders The people and groups that supply a company with its productive resources and so have a claim on and stake in the company.

standard operating procedures (SOPs) Specific sets of written instructions about how to perform a certain aspect of a task.

stereotype Simplistic and often inaccurate beliefs about the typical characteristics of particular groups of people.

strategic alliance An agreement in which managers pool or share their organisation's resources and know-how with a foreign company, and the two organisations share the rewards and risks of starting a new venture.

strategic human resource management (HRM) The process by which managers design the components of a human resource management (HRM) system to be consistent with each other, with other elements of organisational architecture and with the organisation's strategy and goals.

strategy A cluster of decisions about what goals to pursue, what actions to take and how to use resources to achieve goals.

strategy formulation Analysis of an organisation's current situation followed by the development of strategies to accomplish its mission and achieve its goals.

stretch goals Goals that are set to positively challenge employees in achieving the goals, i.e. stretch their abilities. Usually goals that are difficult but attainable.

subjective appraisal An appraisal that is based on perceptions of traits, behaviours or results.

suppliers Individuals and organisations that provide an organisation with the input resources that it needs to produce goods and services.

SWOT analysis A planning exercise in which managers identify organisational strengths (**S**), weaknesses (**W**), environmental opportunities (**O**) and threats (**T**).

synergy Performance gains that result when individuals and departments co-ordinate their actions.

systematic errors Errors that people make over and over again and that result in poor decision making.

T

tariff A tax that a government imposes on imported – or, occasionally, exported – goods.

task environment The set of forces and conditions that originates with suppliers, distributors, customers and competitors and affects an organisation's ability to obtain inputs and dispose of its outputs because they influence managers on a daily basis.

task force A committee of managers or non-managerial employees from various functions or divisions who meet to solve a specific, mutual problem; also called ad hoc committee.

task interdependence The degree to which the work performed by one member of a group influences the work performed by other members.

task-oriented leaders Leaders whose primary concern is to ensure that subordinates perform at a high level.

task structure The extent to which the work to be performed is clear-cut so that a leader's subordinates know what needs to be accomplished and how to go about doing it; a determinant of how favourable a situation is for leading.

team A group whose members work intensely with one another to achieve a specific common goal or objective.

technical skills The job-specific knowledge and techniques required to perform an organisational role.

technological forces Outcomes of changes in the technology that managers use to design,

produce, or distribute goods and services.

technology The combination of skills and equipment that managers use in the design, production and distribution of goods and services.

terminal value A lifelong goal or objective that an individual seeks to achieve.

Theory X A set of negative assumptions about workers that leads to the conclusion that a manager's task is to supervise workers closely and control their behaviour.

Theory Y A set of positive assumptions about workers that leads to the conclusion that a manager's task is to create a work setting that encourages commitment to organisational goals and provides opportunities for workers to be imaginative and to exercise initiative and self-direction.

third-party negotiator An impartial individual with expertise in handling conflicts and negotiations who helps parties in conflict reach an acceptable solution.

time horizon The intended duration of a plan.

times-covered ratio Measures the extent to which a company's gross profit covers its annual interest payments.

'top-down change' A fast, revolutionary approach to change in which senior managers identify what needs to be changed and then move quickly to implement the changes throughout the organisation.

total quality management (TQM) A management technique that focuses on improving the quality of an organisation's products and services.

training Teaching organisational members how to perform their current jobs and helping them

acquire the knowledge and skills they need to be effective performers.

transaction-processing system A management information system designed to handle large volumes of routine, recurring transactions.

transactional leadership Leadership that motivates subordinates by rewarding them for high performance and reprimanding them for low performance.

transformational leadership Leadership that makes subordinates aware of the importance of their jobs and performance to the organisation and aware of their own needs for personal growth and that motivates subordinates to work for the good of the organisation.

trust A person's confidence and faith in another person's goodwill.

U

uncertainty Unpredictability.

uncertainty avoidance The degree to which societies are willing to tolerate uncertainty and risk.

under-payment inequity The inequity that exists when a person perceives that his or her own outcome–input ratio is less than the ratio of a referent.

unity of command A reporting relationship in which an employee receives orders from, and reports to, only one superior.

unity of direction The singleness of purpose that makes possible the creation of one plan of action to guide managers and workers as they use organisational resources.

unrelated diversification Entering a new industry or buying a company in a new industry that is not related in any way to an organisation's current businesses or industries.

utilitarian rule An ethical decision, a decision that produces the greatest good for the greatest number of people.

V

valence In expectancy theory, how desirable each of the outcomes available from a job or organisation is to a person.

validity The degree to which a tool or test measures what it purports to measure.

value chain The idea that a company is a chain of functional activities that transforms inputs into an output of goods or services that customers value.

value-chain management The development of a set of functional-level strategies that increases the performance of the operating system a company uses to transform inputs into finished goods and services.

value system The terminal and instrumental values that are guiding principles in an individual's life.

values Ideas about what a society believes to be good, right, desirable or beautiful.

verbal communication The encoding of messages into words, either written or spoken.

vertical integration A strategy that allows an organisation to create value by producing its own inputs or distributing and selling its own outputs.

vicarious learning Learning that occurs when the learner becomes motivated to perform a behaviour by watching another person perform it and be reinforced for doing so; also called observational learning.

virtual team A team whose members rarely or never meet face to face but interact by using various forms of IT such as email, computer networks, telephone, fax and videoconferences.

W

wholly-owned foreign subsidiary Production operations established in a foreign country independent of any local direct involvement.

worker–task mix Identifies the best match of employee to any given task in order to make production as efficient as possible.

Z

zero-sum Describes a situation in which a participant's gain or loss is exactly balanced by the losses or gains of the other participant.

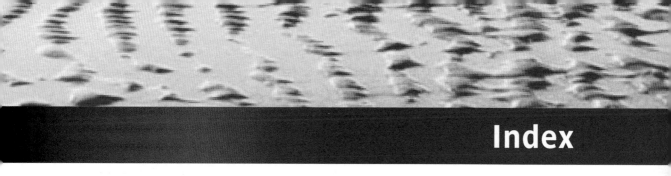

Index

Page numbers for figures have suffix **f**, those for tables have suffix **t**